Egypt

Andrew Humphreys
Siona Jenkins
Leanne Logan
Geert Cole
Damien Simonis

LONELY PLANET PUBLICATIONS
Melbourne • Oakland • London • Paris

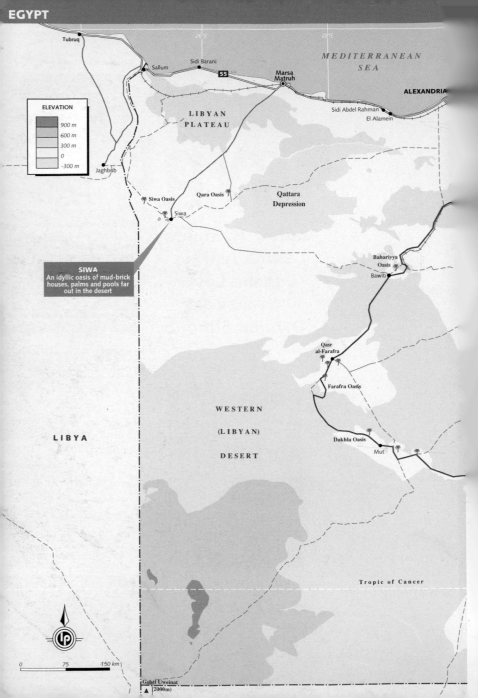

MEDITERRANEAN SEA

Tubruq

Sidi Barani

Sallum

55

Marsa Matruh

ALEXANDRIA

LIBYAN PLATEAU

Sidi Abdel Rahman

El Alamein

ELEVATION

900 m
600 m
300 m
0
-300 m

Jaghbub

Siwa Oasis

Qara Oasis

Qattara Depression

Siwa

SIWA
An idyllic oasis of mud-brick houses, palms and pools far out in the desert

Bahariyya Oasis

Bawiti

LIBYA

Qasr al-Farafra

Farafra Oasis

W E S T E R N

(L I B Y A N)

D E S E R T

Dakhla Oasis

Mut

Tropic of Cancer

0   75   150 km

Gebel Uweinat
▲ (2000m)

CAIRO
Chaotic and vibrant centre of Arab culture, plus the pyramids and splendours of the Egyptian Museum

Baltim

Damietta (Dumyat)

Port Said

Tel Aviv

Jerusalem

✪ AMMAN

Gaza

Al-Arish

Rafah

ISRAEL & PALESTINIAN TERRITORIES

hanhur

Mansura

Abu Kabir

Tanta

Zagazig

Benha

Ismailia

Suez Canal

Great Bitter Lake

JORDAN

Giza

CAIRO

Pyramids of Giza

Saqqara

Pyramids of Dahshur

Pyramid of Meidum

Port Tawfiq

Suez

Fayoum Oasis

Medinet

Pyramid of Hawara

Pyramid of Al-Lahun

Zafarana

SINAI PENINSULA

Taba

Eilat

Aqaba

Al-Fayoum

Beni Suef

Minya

Mallawi

Deir Mawas

Asyut

Sohag

Al-Balyana

Nag 'Hammadi Barrage

Qena

South Gala Plateau

Ras Gharib

RAS ABU GALLUM RESERVE

Nuweiba

Watia Pass

Dahab

El-Tor

Mt Sinai (2285m)

DAHAB RESERVE

NABQ RESERVE

Sharm el-Sheikh

TIRAN & SANAFIR ISLANDS RESERVE

RAS MOHAMED NATIONAL PARK

Hurghada

EASTERN (ARABIAN) DESERT

SAUDI ARABIA

SOUTH SINAI
Striking canyons and desert landscapes inland, plus stunning coral scenery and marine life just offshore

RED SEA
Dive sites teeming with abundant marine life and spectacular coral, plus the intriguing WWII wreck *The Thistlegorm*

Port Safaga

Brother Island

Al-Quseir

RED SEA MOUNTAINS

RED SEA

Qus

Valley of the Kings

Luxor

Esna

Edfu

Marsa Alam

LUXOR
Gateway to spectacular temples and painted tombs of Pharaonic Thebes

Al-Kharga

Kharga Oasis

Gebel Hamata (1977m)

Baris

Tombs of the Nobles

Aswan

Aswan Dam

Temple of Philae

ASWAN
Beautiful Nileside setting and a colourful souq, plus the culture and arts of the Nubian people

Limestone Plateau

Berenice

Mukawwa Island

Foul Bay

Lake Nasser

ABU SIMBEL
One of the most awesome monuments of Ancient Egypt

Temples of Abu Simbel

Abu Simbel

Administrative Boundary

Halaib

SUDAN

Political Boundary

GHARD ABU MUHARIQ

Gulf of Suez

Gulf of Aqaba

Nile River

Egypt
5th edition – September 1999
First published – February 1977

Published by
Lonely Planet Publications Pty Ltd A.C.N. 005 607 983
192 Burwood Rd, Hawthorn, Victoria 3122, Australia

Lonely Planet Offices
Australia PO Box 617, Hawthorn, Victoria 3122
USA 150 Linden St, Oakland, CA 94607
UK 10a Spring Place, London NW5 3BH
France 1 rue du Dahomey, 75011 Paris

Photographs
Many of the images in this guide are available for licensing from
Lonely Planet Images.
email: lpi@lonelyplanet.com.au

Front cover photograph
Feluccas gliding along the Nile River at Aswan. (Leanne Logan)

ISBN 0 86442 677 1

Contents – Text

THE AUTHORS 7

THIS BOOK 9

FOREWORD 10

INTRODUCTION 13

FACTS ABOUT EGYPT 14

History 14
Geography 28
Climate 28
Ecology & Environment 29
Flora & Fauna 31
Government & Politics 32
Economy 33
Population 33
People 34
Education 34
Arts 35
Society & Conduct 41
Religion 42
Language 45

PHARAONIC EGYPT 47

Tomb & Temple
Architecture 48
Early Buildings 48
Columns 50
Funerary Architecture 51
Temple Architecture 55
Gods & Goddesses 58

FACTS FOR THE VISITOR 63

Planning 63
Highlights & Suggested
Itineraries 65
Tourist Offices 64
Visas & Documents 64
Embassies & Consulates 68
Customs 70
Money 71
Post & Communications 74
Internet Resources 77
Books 77
Newspapers & Magazines 80
Radio & TV 80
Photography & Video 82
Time 83
Electricity 83
Weights & Measures 83
Laundry 83
Toilets 83
Health 83
Women Travellers 93
Gay & Lesbian Travellers 95
Disabled Travellers 95
Senior Travellers 95
Travel with Children 95
Dangers & Annoyances 96
Legal Matters 98
Business Hours 98
Public Holidays & Special
Events 98
Activities 101
Courses 101
Work 102
Accommodation 103
Food 106
Drinks 107
Entertainment 108
Spectator Sport 111
Shopping 111

GETTING THERE & AWAY 116

Air 116
Land 122
Sea 124
Organised Tours 125

GETTING AROUND 129

Air 129
Bus 129
Train 130
Taxi 130
Car & Motorcycle 131
Bicycle 132
Hitching 132
Boat 132
Local Transport 133

CAIRO 136

History 137
Orientation 140
Information 140
Central Cairo 145
Egyptian Museum.............149
Islamic Cairo 163

1

Old Cairo 180
Gezira & Zamalek 185
Mohandiseen, Agouza &
Doqqi 188
Giza 190

The Pyramids 191
Heliopolis 197
Activities 199
Organised Tours 200
Places to Stay 201

Places to Eat 20
Entertainment 21
Shopping 21
Getting There & Away 21
Getting Around 22

AROUND CAIRO   22

Memphis 224
Abu Sir 226
Saqqara 227

Dahshur 233
Al-Fayoum Oasis 234
Pyramid of Meidum 240

Birqash Camel Market 24
Wadi Natrun 242
The Nile Delta 243

NILE VALLEY – BENI SUEF TO QUS   247

Beni Suef 249
Gebel at-Teir & Frazer
Tombs 250
Minya 251
Beni Hasan 253
Mallawi 254

Hermopolis 255
Tuna al-Gebel 255
Tell al-Amarna 256
Dairut 258
Al-Qusiya 258
Asyut 259

Around Asyut 261
Sohag 261
Al-Balyana 263
Qena 266
Qift 269
Qus 269

NILE VALLEY – LUXOR   270

History 270
Orientation 271
Information 274
Luxor Museum 275
Mummification Museum 275
Luxor Temple 275
Temples of Karnak 277

Brooke Hospital for
Animals 282
West Bank 282
Activities 304
Organised Tours 305
Special Events 305
Places to Stay 306

Places to Eat 312
Entertainment 314
Shopping 315
Getting There & Away 316
Getting Around 317

NILE VALLEY – ESNA TO ABU SIMBEL   318

Esna 318
Al-Kab & Kom al-Ahmar 320
Edfu 321
Silsila 323
Kom Ombo 323
Daraw 325
Aswan 326
Information 327
The Town & East Bank 328

The River 331
The West Bank 332
Activities 334
Organised Tours 334
Places to Stay 334
Places to Eat 337
Entertainment 338
Shopping 339
Getting There & Away 339

Getting Around 342
Around Aswan 342
Aswan Dam 342
Sehel Island 342
Temple of Philae 342
High Dam 344
Lower Nubia & Lake
Nasser 345
Lake Nasser 349

WESTERN OASES   356

Kharga Oasis 357
South to Baris 364
Dakhla Oasis 365

Farafra Oasis 371
Bahariyya Oasis 373
Siwa Oasis 377

Siwan Crafts 384

ALEXANDRIA & THE MEDITERRANEAN COAST   387

Alexandria 387
History 387
Orientation 390
Information 391

Ancient Alexandria 395
Central Alexandria 399
Eastern Suburbs 402
Beaches 405

Places to Stay 405
Places to Eat 407
Entertainment 410
Shopping 411

etting There & Away 411
etting Around 413
round Alexandria 413
Abu Qir 413
Abu Mina 413

Rosetta (Rashid) 414
Mediterranean Coast 417
El Alamein 417
Sidi Abdel Rahman 419
Ras al-Hikma 419

Marsa Matruh 419
Sidi Barani 423
Sallum 423

SUEZ CANAL   425

Port Said 425
Qantara 431

Ismailia 432

Suez 436

RED SEA COAST   441

Ain Sukhna 441
Zafarana 442
Monasteries 442
Al-Gouna 444
Hurghada (Al-Ghardaka) 445

Around Hurghada 459
Port Safaga 460
Around Port Safaga 461
Al-Quseir 461
Around Al-Quseir 463

Marsa Alam 464
Berenice 465
Bir Shalatein 465

DIVING THE RED SEA   466

Marine Life 467
Reef Protection 468
Dive Sites 469

Dive Clubs 472
Tips for Safe Diving in the Red
Sea 475

Further Information 476

SINAI   477

Oyun Musa 481
Ras as-Sudr 481
Qalaat al-Gindi & Nakhl 482
Hammam Fara'un 482
Serabit al-Khadim 482
El-Tor 483
Ras Mohammed National
Park 483

Sharm el-Sheikh &
Na'ama Bay 483
Shark's Bay 492
Dahab 492
Nuweiba 499
Nuweiba to Taba 504
Taba 506
St Katherine's Monastery 506

Wadi Feiran 510
Al-Arish 510
Rafah 513

LANGUAGE   514

GLOSSARY   521

ACKNOWLEDGMENTS   524

INDEX   537

Text 537

Boxed Text.........................543

MAP LEGEND   back page

METRIC CONVERSION   inside back cover

Contents – Maps

CAIRO

Greater Cairo 138
Central Cairo 146
Egyptian Museum 150
Tutankhamun Galleries 156
Midan Ramses & Around ..163
Al-Azhar & Khan
al-Khalili 165
North of Khan al-Khalili 167

Al-Azhar to the Citadel 171
Museum of Islamic Art 174
The Citadel 175
The Citadel to Ibn Tulun 178
Northern Cemetery 179
Old Cairo 181
Mohandiseen, Agouza &
Zamalek 186

Doqqi, Giza & Gezira 18
The Giza Plateau 19
Heliopolis 19
Ramses Train Station 21
The Cairo Metro 22

AROUND CAIRO

Around Cairo 225
Abu Sir & Saqqara 226

North Saqqara 228

Medinat al-Fayoum 236

NILE VALLEY – BENI SUEF TO QUS

Nile Valley 248
Beni Suef 250
Minya 252
Hermopolis, Tuna al-Gebel
& Tell al-Amarna 255

Asyut 260
Sohag 262
Abydos 264
Qena 267
Dendara 268

NILE VALLEY – LUXOR

Around Luxor 271
Luxor (East Bank) 272
Luxor Temple 276
Karnak: Amun Temple
Enclosure 278
Luxor (West Bank) 283
Valley of the Kings 287
Tomb of Queen Tawsert/
Sethnakt 289

Tomb of Tuthmosis III 290
Tomb of Amenhotep II 291
Tomb of Tuthmosis IV 291
Tomb of Horemheb 292
Tomb of Tutankhamun 292
Tomb of Hatshepsut 294
Tomb of Khaemhet 298
Tomb of Ramose 298
The Ramesseum 299

Tomb of Nefertari 301
Tomb of
Amunherkhepshep 302
Medinat Habu 303

NILE VALLEY – ESNA TO ABU SIMBEL

Southern Upper Egypt 319
Esna 320
Edfu 321
Temple of Horus 322

Temple of Kom Ombo 324
Aswan 327
Central Aswan 329
Aswan Dams 342

Temple of Philae 343
Lower Nubia & Lake
Nasser 346
Temple of Abu Simbel 353

WESTERN OASES

Western Oases 357
Kharga Oasis 360
Al-Kharga 361
Dakhla Oasis 366

Mut 367
Farafra Oasis 371
Qasr al-Farafra 372
Bahariyya Oasis 374

Bawati 375
Siwa Oasis 378
Siwa 379

ALEXANDRIA & THE MEDITERRANEAN COAST

Mediterranean Coast 388
Alexandria 390
Central Alexandria 392

Midan Ramla & Around 394
Catacombs of Kom
ash-Shuqqafa 399

Rosetta (Rashid) 415
Marsa Matruh 420

4

SUEZ CANAL

Suez Canal 426	Ismailia 433	Suez & Port Tawfiq 437
Port Said 428		

RED SEA COAST

Red Sea Coast 442	Ad-Dahar, Hurghada 446	Al-Quseir 462
Hurghada Coast 445	Sigala, Hurghada 451	

DIVING THE RED SEA

Diving the Red Sea 467

SINAI

Sinai 478	Sharm el-Sheikh &	Nuweiba 500
Sharm el-Sheikh 484	Na'ama Bay 486	St Katherine's Monastery 507
Na'ama Bay 485	Dahab 493	Al-Arish 511

EGYPT REGIONAL MAPS

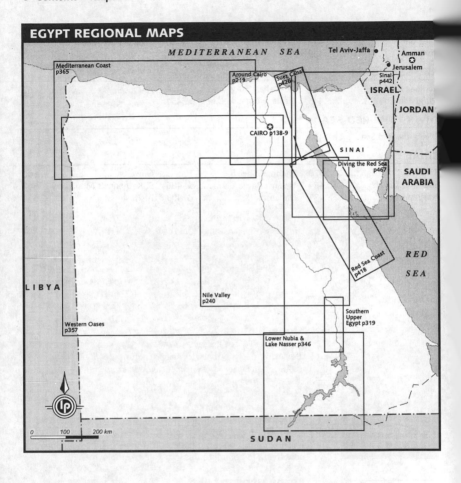

MEDITERRANEAN SEA

Tel Aviv-Jaffa

Amman

Jerusalem

Mediterranean Coast
p365

Around Cairo
p219

Suez Canal
p426

Sinai
p442

ISRAEL

JORDAN

CAIRO p138-9

SINAI

Diving the Red Sea
p467

SAUDI
ARABIA

RED

SEA

Red Sea Coast
p418

LIBYA

Nile Valley
p240

Western Oases
p357

Southern
Upper
Egypt p319

Lower Nubia &
Lake Nasser p346

0   100   200 km

SUDAN

The Authors

Andrew Humphreys & Gadi Farfour

Andrew has been living, travelling and working in the Middle East on and off since 1988 when he arrived in Cairo on holiday and took three years to leave. Originally trained in London as an architect, he slid over into writing through a growing fascination with Islamic buildings. Following a spell in mainstream journalism based for several years in the Baltic States, Andrew returned his attention to the Middle East and has since authored or co-authored Lonely Planet guides to *Central Asia,* the *Middle East, Israel & the Palestinian Territories, Jerusalem, Cairo* and *Syria*.

Born of Egyptian-Estonian parents, Gadi grew up spending summers in Tallinn and the rest of the year in Alexandria. A designer by profession, she has accompanied Andrew on his research trips, using her formidable language skills to reach the places he never could. Gadi produced most of this book's maps.

Andrew and Gadi are two of the co-founders of the *Cairo Times*, an Egypt-based, English-language newspaper. They currently live in London but wonder for how long.

Siona Jenkins

Born in the UK but brought up in Canada, Siona has been visiting the Middle East since her teens, when her parents began working and living in Saudi Arabia. She arrived in Egypt for six months of language study after completing a Masters degree in Middle East Studies; 10 years later she's still there, splitting her time between Cairo and a mud-brick house on Luxor's West Bank. She wrote for various aid organisations before slipping into journalism. Now she works as a freelancer for *The Irish Times*, among others. While working on this book Siona became a desert enthusiast and she's now trying to commute this into gainful employment.

Leanne Logan

Bitten by the travel bug before even reaching her teens, Leanne has long been lured by travel. From Brisbane, Australia, she explored her homeland while reporting for several newspapers and Australian Associated Press and then set off for Asia and the Middle East. In London, as deputy editor of a travel magazine, her wander lust was temporarily fed but never sated. Eventually she bought a one-way ticket to Africa. Leanne joined Lonely Planet in 1991 and, while conducting research into Belgium's 350-odd beers, she met a local connoisseur, Geert Cole. Together they have worked on many Lonely Planet travel guides.

Geert Cole

Born in Belgium, Geert swapped university and art studies in the 1970s to discover broader horizons. Each trip meant an extra diary being put on the shelf and another job experience being added to life's list. In recent times, when not running his stained-glass studio, Geert could be found sailing the Pacific, sorting Aussie sheep, and trekking through Alaska and diving tropical reefs.

Damien Simonis

Following a degree in languages and several years' reporting and sub-editing on several Australian newspapers (including *The Australian* and *The Age*), Sydney-born Damien left Australia in 1989. He has lived, worked and travelled extensively throughout Europe, the Middle East and North Africa.

FROM THE AUTHORS

Andrew Humphreys My contribution is dedicated to Neil Turner, whose infectious love of living and inability to sit still got me to Egypt in the first place.

Siona Jenkins Thanks to Terry Weston, Dr Adel Taher, Rafel al-Maary and Arman Gazeryan for diving tips and horror stories. Thanks also to Samira and Sherif Ebeid for their hospitality and enthusiasm about Dahab, to Angela Godfrey for Ras Shaitan and her commitment to reef conservation, and also to John Grainger and the National Parks Office for their help and their Herculean efforts to preserve Sinai. Because of Amr Shannon the Western Desert will forever remain a magical place and his efforts to educate others about the area's fragile environment might just help preserve it for future generations. Special mention must also be made to Lisa Truett. Thanks to Rene Gebhard for his determination to help stop the destruction of vulnerable desert archaeological sites.

In Siwa thanks to Abdallah Baghi for his navigation skills in the Great Sand Sea and for trying to save what's left of his community's heritage; and to Mounir Naematallah, whose determination is helping to keep the oasis special. Shukry Saad made Aswan special, and Lake Nasser would have been less intriguing without having hooked a Nile perch with Pascal Artieda or hearing Nubian oud from Fikry. In Luxor Dr Boutros was helpful, while Nick Warner was a wealth of information on Al-Quseir, as was amateur historian and Al-Quseir enthusiast Kamal El-Din Hussein, who sadly passed away at the end of 1998. Thanks too to Betsy.

Thanks to Max Rodenbeck and Karima Khalil, to Anthony Sattin and Sylvie Franquet and to Andrew and Gadi. And of course, many thanks to David for staying home and Leo for being more understanding than a five year old should have to be.

This Book

Scott Wayne researched and wrote the first two editions of *Egypt & the Sudan* and Damien Simonis researched the 3rd edition. Leanne Logan and Geert Cole researched the 4th edition of *Egypt* and this 5th edition was researched by Andrew Humphries, Gadi Farfour and Siona Jenkins.

From the Publisher

This edition of *Egypt* was edited in Lonely Planet's Melbourne office by Justin Flynn. He was ably assisted by Liz Filleul, Jocelyn Harewood, Susan Holtham, Sarah Mathers, Shelley Muir, Sally O'Brien and Julia Taylor. Trudi Canavan coordinated the design. Gadi Farfour drew the maps with assistance from Shahara Ahmed, Brett Moore and Katie Butterworth. Illustrations were expertly drawn by Trudi Canavan, Golo, Verity Campbell and Geoff Stringer. Special thanks to Quentin Frayne for putting together the Language chapter, Paul Piaia for the climate charts, Maria Vallianos for the front cover, Leonie Mugavin for checking the Getting There & Away chapter, Isabelle Young for casting her eagle eye over the Health section and Jeremy Smith for adding his own personal touch to the Pharaonic Egypt special section.

Ph. Village, Giza

Al Barahar Al Azam St.

9

Foreword

ABOUT LONELY PLANET GUIDEBOOKS

The story begins with a classic travel adventure: Tony and Maureen Wheeler's 1972 journey across Europe and Asia to Australia. Useful information about the overland trail did not exist at that time, so Tony and Maureen published the first Lonely Planet guidebook to meet a growing need.

From a kitchen table, then from a tiny office in Melbourne (Australia), Lonely Planet has become the largest independent travel publisher in the world, an international company with offices in Melbourne, Oakland (USA), London (UK) and Paris (France).

Today Lonely Planet guidebooks cover the globe. There is an ever-growing list of books and there's information in a variety of forms and media. Some things haven't changed. The main aim is still to help make it possible for adventurous travellers to get out there – to explore and better understand the world.

At Lonely Planet we believe travellers can make a positive contribution to the countries they visit – if they respect their host communities and spend their money wisely. Since 1986 a percentage of the income from each book has been donated to aid projects and human rights campaigns.

Updates Lonely Planet thoroughly updates each guidebook as often as possible. This usually means there are around two years between editions, although for more unusual or more stable destinations the gap can be longer. Check the imprint page (following the colour map at the beginning of the book) for publication dates.

Between editions up-to-date information is available in two free newsletters – the paper *Planet Talk* and email *Comet* (to subscribe, contact any Lonely Planet office) – and on our Web site at www.lonelyplanet.com. The *Upgrades* section of the Web site covers a number of important and volatile destinations and is regularly updated by Lonely Planet authors. *Scoop* covers news and current affairs relevant to travellers. And, lastly, the *Thorn Tree* bulletin board and *Postcards* section of the site carry unverified, but fascinating, reports from travellers.

Correspondence The process of creating new editions begins with the letters, postcards and emails received from travellers. This correspondence often includes suggestions, criticisms and comments about the current editions. Interesting excerpts are immediately passed on via newsletters and the Web site, and everything goes to our authors to be verified when they're researching on the road. We're keen to get more feedback from organisations or individuals who represent communities visited by travellers.

Lonely Planet gathers information for everyone who's curious about the planet – and especially for those who explore it first-hand. Through guidebooks, phrasebooks, activity guides, maps, literature, newsletters, image library, TV series and Web site we act as an information exchange for a worldwide community of travellers.

Research Authors aim to gather sufficient practical information to enable travellers to make informed choices and to make the mechanics of a journey run smoothly. They also research historical and cultural background to help enrich the travel experience and allow travellers to understand and respond appropriately to cultural and environmental issues.

Authors don't stay in every hotel because that would mean spending a couple of months in each medium-sized city and, no, they don't eat at every restaurant because that would mean stretching belts beyond capacity. They do visit hotels and restaurants to check standards and prices, but feedback based on readers' direct experiences can be very helpful.

Many of our authors work undercover, others aren't so secretive. None of them accept freebies in exchange for positive write-ups. And none of our guidebooks contain any advertising.

Production Authors submit their raw manuscripts and maps to offices in Australia, USA, UK or France. Editors and cartographers – all experienced travellers themselves – then begin the process of assembling the pieces. When the book finally hits the shops, some things are already out of date, we start getting feedback from readers and the process begins again ...

WARNING & REQUEST

Things change – prices go up, schedules change, good places go bad and bad places go bankrupt – nothing stays the same. So, if you find things better or worse, recently opened or long since closed, please tell us and help make the next edition even more accurate and useful. We genuinely value all the feedback we receive. Julie Young coordinates a well travelled team that reads and acknowledges every letter, postcard and email and ensures that every morsel of information finds its way to the appropriate authors, editors and cartographers for verification.

Everyone who writes to us will find their name in the next edition of the appropriate guidebook. They will also receive the latest issue of *Planet Talk*, our quarterly printed newsletter, or *Comet*, our monthly email newsletter. Subscriptions to both newsletters are free. The very best contributions will be rewarded with a free guidebook.

Excerpts from your correspondence may appear in new editions of Lonely Planet guidebooks, the Lonely Planet Web site, *Planet Talk* or *Comet*, so please let us know if you *don't* want your letter published or your name acknowledged.

Send all correspondence to the Lonely Planet office closest to you:

Australia: PO Box 617, Hawthorn, Victoria 3122
USA: 150 Linden St, Oakland, CA 94607
UK: 10A Spring Place, London NW5 3BH
France: 1 rue du Dahomey, 75011 Paris

Or email us at: talk2us@lonelyplanet.com.au

For news, views and updates see our Web site: www.lonelyplanet.com

HOW TO USE A LONELY PLANET GUIDEBOOK

The best way to use a Lonely Planet guidebook is any way you choose. At Lonely Planet we believe the most memorable travel experiences are often those that are unexpected, and the finest discoveries are those you make yourself. Guidebooks are not intended to be used as if they provide a detailed set of infallible instructions!

Contents All Lonely Planet guidebooks follow roughly the same format. The Facts about the Destination chapters or sections give background information ranging from history to weather. Facts for the Visitor gives practical information on issues like visas and health. Getting There & Away gives a brief starting point for re-searching travel to and from the destination. Getting Around gives an overview of the transport options when you arrive.

The peculiar demands of each destination determine how sub-sequent chapters are broken up, but some things remain constant. We always start with background, then proceed to sights, places to stay, places to eat, entertainment, getting there and away, and getting around information – in that order.

Heading Hierarchy Lonely Planet headings are used in a strict hierarchical structure that can be visualised as a set of Russian dolls. Each heading (and its following text) is encompassed by any preceding heading that is higher on the hierarchical ladder.

Entry Points We do not assume guidebooks will be read from beginning to end, but that people will dip into them. The tradi-tional entry points are the list of contents and the index. In addition, however, some books have a complete list of maps and an index map illustrating map coverage.

There may also be a colour map that shows highlights. These highlights are dealt with in greater detail in the Facts for the Visitor chapter, along with planning questions and suggested itin-eraries. Each chapter covering a geographical region usually begins with a locator map and another list of highlights. Once you find something of interest in a list of highlights, turn to the index.

Maps Maps play a crucial role in Lonely Planet guidebooks and include a huge amount of information. A legend is printed on the back page. We seek to have complete consistency between maps and text, and to have every important place in the text captured on a map. Map key numbers usually start in the top left corner.

> Although inclusion in a guidebook usually implies a recommen-dation we cannot list every good place. Exclusion does not necessarily imply criticism. In fact there are a number of reasons why we might exclude a place – sometimes it is simply inappropriate to encourage an influx of travellers.

Introduction

Ever since Herodotus, the ancient Greek historian and traveller, first described Egypt as 'the gift of the Nile', the country has been capturing the imagination of all who visit.

The awe-inspiring monuments, left by the pharaohs, Greeks and Romans as well as by early Christians and Muslims, attract thousands of visitors every year – but the pyramids, temples, tombs, monasteries and mosques are just part of this country's fascination.

Modern Egypt – where mud-brick villages stand beside pharaonic ruins surrounded by towering steel, stone and glass buildings – is at the cultural crossroads of east and west, ancient and modern. While TV antennae decorate rooftops everywhere, from the crowded apartment blocks of Cairo to the mud-brick homes of farming villages and the goatskin tents of the Bedouins, the *fellaheen* (farmers) throughout the Nile's fertile valley still tend their fields with the archaic tools of their ancestors.

In the gargantuan city of Cairo the sound of the *muezzin* summoning the faithful to prayer or the mesmerising voice of Umm Kolthum, the 'Mother of Egypt', compete with the pop music of ghetto blasters and the screech of car horns. And everywhere there are people: swathed in long flowing robes or western-style clothes, hanging from buses, weaving through an obstacle course of animals and exhaust-spewing traffic or spilling from hive-like buildings.

Spectacular edifices aside, the attraction of this country, which is officially known as the Arab Republic of Egypt, lies in its incredible natural beauty and in the overwhelming hospitality of the Egyptian people.

Through everything the Nile River flows serene and majestic, the lifeblood of Egypt as it has been since the beginning of history.

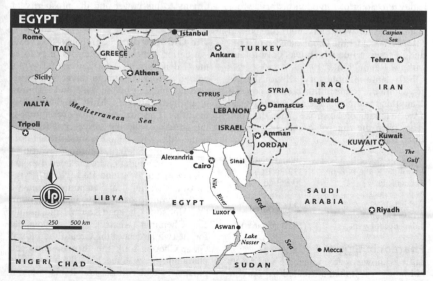

Facts about Egypt

HISTORY

The history of Egypt is inextricably linked to the Nile. Ever since the earliest known communities settled its valley, the river has inspired and controlled the religious, economic, social and political life of the Egyptians. For many centuries the narrow, elongated layout of the country's fertile lands hampered the fusion of those early settlements, which held fast to their local independence. But with the river as a common highway providing an avenue for commercial traffic and communication, those barriers were eventually broken. The small kingdoms developed into two important states, one comprising of the long thin valley, from its furthest navigable reaches at Aswan north to the Delta (an area known as Upper Egypt), the other consisting of the flat marshy Delta itself (Lower Egypt). The unification of these two states, by Menes in about 3000 BC, set the scene for the greatest era of ancient Egyptian civilisation. This is the zero point of Egyptian history. More than 30 dynasties, 50 rulers and 2700 years of almost exclusively indigenous rule passed before Alexander the Great ushered in a period of foreign rule which was only to end with the Revolution of 1952.

Fifty centuries of history! Obviously, it's not within the scope of this book to cover it in anything but the broadest of strokes. And if we're talking broad strokes, then the 5000 years from the time of Menes can be divided roughly into seven periods:

Pharaonic Egypt	(3000-341 BC)
Alexander & the Ptolemies	(332-30 BC)
Roman Rule	(30 BC-638 AD)
Arab Conquest	(640-1517)
Turkish Rule	(1517-1882)
British Occupation	(1882-1952)
Independent Egypt	(1952 onwards)

Pharaonic Egypt

Little is known of the immediate successors of Menes except that, attributed with divine ancestry, they promoted the development of a highly stratified society, patronised the arts and built many temples and public works. Their capital, founded by Menes, was Memphis, which lay 24km south of what is now modern Cairo, a site which at that time marked the meeting point of Upper and Lower Egypt. The city survived for 3½ millennia as the cradle of pharaonic civilisation, where writing and administration, art and architecture where nurtured and developed. Though nothing of the greatest ancient Egyptian city remains, we can get an idea of the size and importance of Memphis by the remarkable funerary complexes that were created for its kings. Foremost of these is the necropolis of Saqqara, which spread over 7km and which has as its centrepiece a stepped pyramid, the earliest of the many pyramids to follow.

Dating from around 2700 BC, the Step Pyramid, built for a king by the name of Zoser (Djoser), was not only a striking testimony to his power and the prosperity of the period but the start of a whole new trend.

The Old Kingdom For the next 500 years – a period which Egyptologists refer to as the Old Kingdom – the power of Egypt's pharaohs would seem to have greatly increased, judging by the scale and ambition of their monuments. Most of these drew their direct inspiration from Zoser's imposing structure, earning this period its other name, 'the Age of the Pyramids'.

First came Sneferu, the most prolific of the pyramid builders, who presided over the raising of the Bent and Red (North) Pyramids at Dahshur near Saqqara, and maybe of the Pyramid of Meidum in Al-Fayoum, too. His son, Cheops (Khufu), and grandson, Chephren (Khafre), were responsible for the two largest of the Great Pyramids at Giza. Cheops took the throne when the pharaonic era was reaching the apex of its prosperity and culture, and if his colossal pyramid is any indication he must have been one of the greatest of all the pharaohs. Its sheer size and mathematical precision is not only a monument to the extraordinary development of Egyptian architecture, it also suggests through the enormous labour and discipline involved, that the era of Cheops saw the emergence, for the first time in human history, of an organisational principle.

As the centuries passed and the 5th dynasty (about 2490 to 2330 BC) began, there were changes in the power and rule of the pharaohs. One of the first indications of this was the comparatively small pyramids built at Abu Sir, 12km south of Giza. The pharaohs had begun to share power with various high officials and nobles in the vast bureaucracies they had created, so unlike their predecessors they were no longer absolute monarchs and did not have the same resources for the construction of immense funerary monuments.

Control became even more diffuse during the 6th and 7th dynasties (about 2330 to 2170 BC), allowing the formation of a number of small local principalities, and a second capital was established at Heracleopolis, near present-day Beni Suef. The growing disunity eventually led to the complete collapse of the centralised state and power was seized by the governors of the provinces (or *nomes*). By this time, the grandeur of the earlier pharaonic dynasties had been dissipated by constant feudal struggles that also prevented any possibility of economic or artistic development.

Civil war at the beginning of the 11th dynasty finally put an end to the squabbling. An enterprising member of the Intef family rallied all the principalities of the south against the weakness of Heracleopolis, and established an independent kingdom with Thebes (present-day Luxor) as its capital. Under Mentuhotep II the north and south were again united under the leadership of a single pharaoh. The princes of Thebes became rulers of all Egypt, marking the beginning of what Egyptologists refer to as the Middle Kingdom period.

The Middle Kingdom The return to political order was marked by another spurt of tomb and temple building. The Middle Kingdom pharaohs Mentuhotep, Amenemhet and Sesostris built extensively throughout the land with lasting monuments (pyramids) at Lisht, Dahshur, Hawara and Lahun – all of which are near Al-Fayoum and Saqqara. At the same time, the boundaries of Egyptian rule were also pushed southwards into the land of Nubia, and Nubian tribesmen were pressed into the armies of the pharaohs. (There's a model of Nubian soldiers dating from this period on display at the Egyptian Museum in Cairo.) But the building frenzy diminished and the territorial expansion halted as the governors and nobles of the nomes once again took to squabbling among themselves. Royal power was undermined

The Narmer Palette (dating from around 3200 BC) is one of the earliest documents of ancient Egyptian history. It commemorates the victory of King Narmer, ruler of Upper Egypt, over Lower Egypt.

Chronology of the Pharaohs

This is not a complete listing but it does include all those rulers mentioned throughout this book.

Dynasty	Period (BC)	Important Monument
EARLY DYNASTIC PERIOD		
1st Dynasty	**2920-2770**	
including		
Menes		Memphis
2nd Dynasty	**2770-2649**	
3rd Dynasty	**2649-2575**	
including		
Zoser	2630-2611	Step Pyramid at Saqqara
Sekhemket	2611-2603	Pyramid at Saqqara
OLD KINGDOM		
4th Dynasty	**2575-2465**	
Sneferu	2575-2551	Pyramids at Dahshur
Cheops (Khufu)	2551-2528	Pyramid at Giza
Djedefre	2528-2520	
Chephren (Khafre)	2520-2494	Pyramid at Giza
Mycerinus (Menkaure)	2490-2472	Pyramid at Giza
Shepseskaf	2472-2467	
5th Dynasty	**2465-2323**	
including		
Userkef	2465-2458	Pyramid at Saqqara
Sahure	2458-2446	Pyramid at Abu Sir
Neferirkare	2446-2426	Pyramid at Abu Sir
Shepseskare	2426-2419	
Raneferef	2419-2416	
Nyuserre	2416-2388	Pyramid at Abu Sir
Unas	2356-2323	Pyramid at Saqqara
6th Dynasty	**2323-2150**	
including		
Teti	2323-2291	
Pepi I	2289-2255	
Pepi II	2246-2152	
7th/8th Dynasties	**2150-2134**	
FIRST INTERMEDIATE PERIOD		
9th/10th Dynasties	**2134-2040**	

Chronology of the Pharaohs

Dynasty	Period (BC)	Important Monument
MIDDLE KINGDOM		
11th Dynasty	**2040-1991**	
including		
Mentuhotep I	2061-2010	
Mentuhotep II	2010-1998	
Mentuhotep III	1998-1991	
12th Dynasty 1991-1783		
including		
Amenemhet I	1991-1962	
Sesostris I (Senwosret)	1971-1926	oldest parts of Karnak
13th/14th Dynasties	**1783-1640**	
SECOND INTERMEDIATE PERIOD		
15th-17th Dynasties	**1640-1532**	
New Kingdom		
18th Dynasty	**1550-1319**	
including		
Amenhotep I (Amenophis I)	1525-1504	Luxor Temple
Tuthmosis I	1504-1492	Valley of the Kings
Tuthmosis II	1492-1479	
Tuthmosis III	1479-1425	
Hatshepsut	1473-1458	Deir al-Bahri
Amenhotep II (Amenophis II)	1427-1401	
Tuthmosis IV	1401 1391	
Amenhotep III (Amenophis III)	1391-1353	Colossi of Memnon
Akhenaten	1353-1333	Tell al-Amarna
Tutankhamun	1333-1323	
19th Dynasty	**1319-1196**	
including		
Horemheb	1319-1307	
Ramses I	1307-1306	
Seti I	1306-1290	Abydos
Ramses II	1290-1224	Ramesseum, Abu Simbel
Seti II	1210-1204	
20th Dynasty	**1196-1070**	
including		
Ramses III	1194-1163	Medinat Habu
THIRD INTERMEDIATE PERIOD		
21st Dynasty	**1070-945**	
including		
Psusennes I	1040-992	

and the divided empire was ripe for conquest by an outside power.

The invaders came from the north-east, from what would later become Palestine, and occupied the Delta. The Egyptians called the leaders of these marauding tribes *hekaw-khasut*, 'rulers of foreign lands', a name that was later corrupted to Hyksos. They were the full stop to the 250 years of the Middle Kingdom. The Hyksos challenged for the rule of Egypt for just over a century, but they're remembered for little more than having introduced the horse-drawn chariot. By about 1550 BC the Egyptians had routed the invaders and ended their challenge. A new kingdom was initiated that would raise Egypt to unequalled greatness, with a lineage of power that would continue, more or less unbroken, for some 500 years.

The New Kingdom Beginning with Amosis (c 1550 BC), more than 30 monarchs from three successive dynasties ruled through what is commonly regarded as the golden age of the pharaohs. Most of the incredible monuments to be seen at Luxor date from the period of the New Kingdom. As Thebes it was the religious and political centre of the kingdom, while the age-old capital of Memphis took care of the practical affairs like administration. For a new age, a new god, and Amun-Ra became the Egyptians' principle divinity. He was a composite of a Theban god, Amun, and the old sun god of Memphis, Ra. Great temples were built in his honour, particularly at Karnak, which became an important symbolic power centre, swelling in size as the empire expanded. Each successive pharaoh of the 18th and 19th dynasties added a room, hall or pylon, replete with intricately carved hieroglyphic inscriptions. A lot of what is known about Egyptian life during this period comes from these carvings and reliefs.

Significant expansion of the empire began with the reign of Tuthmosis I – he grabbed Upper Nubia (now part of Sudan). On his death, he was also the first pharaoh to be entombed in the Valley of the Kings on the west bank across from Thebes. The Theban area had been in use as a necropolis since the time of the 11th dynasty and Mentuhotep I, first ruler of the Middle Kingdom, had already built an impressive mortuary temple at Deir al-Bahri, but the Valley of the Kings marked a new style of burrowed tomb building.

The daughter of Tuthmosis I, Hatshepsut, is well known as one of Egypt's few female rulers. She had a spectacular mortuary temple built for her at Deir al-Bahri, next to and dwarfing that of Mentuhotep. Tuthmosis III, Hatshepsut's nephew, was next in line; he became Egypt's greatest conqueror, expanding the empire beyond Syria and into western Asia. His son and successor, Amenophis II, shared his war-like nature but not so the subsequent pharaohs Tuthmosis IV and Amenophis III. Their reigns were marked by peace and a fantastic prosperity that supported ever more extravagant building, including, under the direction of Amenophis III, Luxor Temple and a massive mortuary complex, of which the only remains are the Colossi of Memnon.

While Amenophis III is regarded as the most splendid of the pharaohs, his son and successor Amenophis IV proved, in the way that these things happen, to be wayward to the extent that he irreversibly changed the course of Egyptian history. He quarrelled with the priesthood of Amun and within six years of taking the throne he'd changed his name to Akhenaten, 'he who is beneficial to the Aten' (Aten being the disc of the rising sun) and abandoned the traditional gods and their personnel. The heretic king and his wife, Nefertiti, also spurned Thebes and moved north to establish a new capital, called Akhetaten, devoted solely to the worship of the new god. Some historians believe that this worship represented the first organised form of monotheism. Today, the scant remains of Akhenaten's capital can be seen at Tell al-Amarna, near the town of Minya (see the Tell al-Amarna section in The Nile Valley – Beni Suef to Qus chapter for more on Akhenaten).

After Akhenaten's death, the revengeful priests of Thebes went on a rampage and destroyed all sign of his rule and his religion. The throne passed to his more pleasingly pliant adolescent son-in-law, Tutankhamun, who didn't reach manhood before his sudden (and unexplained) death removed him from the scene. The boy-king would have remained of only minor importance to pharaonic history were it not for the discovery of his treasure-filled tomb in 1922.

For the next few centuries, Egypt was ruled by generals: Ramses I, II and III, and Seti I. Like good pharaohs and military leaders they built massive monuments, such as the temples at Abydos and Abu Simbel, and waged war against the Libyans and Hittites. However, by the time Ramses III came to power (1198 BC) as the second king of the 20th dynasty, disunity had once more set in. The empire was shrinking and Egypt was subsequently subjected to attack from outsiders and eventually occupied piecemeal. The kings of Libya captured the Delta and ruled from Tanis, until replaced by the princes of Sais, while in the south, the Nubians took control of Thebes. In 671 BC the Assyrians invaded and then in 525 BC they, in turn, were swept aside by the Persians, who managed to hold power for almost 200 years until the whole game of dynastic musical chairs was brought to a stop by the arrival of Alexander (332 BC).

Alexander & the Ptolemies

During their rule over Egypt the Persians had shown scant respect for the local pharaonic deities and so Alexander was greeted as something of a liberator. After his legitimacy to the throne of Egypt had been confirmed by the priests in Memphis, the Macedonian general founded a new city on the north coast, named after himself (for more detail see the History section in the Alexandria & the Mediterranean Coast chapter). Through this new Mediterranean port, Alexander could secure a direct sea link with Greece, allowing for a free flow of communication, trade and immigration.

Although Alexander was killed soon after the first stones of his city had been laid, Alexandria very quickly eclipsed the faded cities of Memphis and Thebes in the role of capital. The right to succeed Alexander as ruler of Egypt had been contended and won by one of his generals, Ptolemy I, who founded a dynasty that held sway for the next 300 years.

From wholly Greek origins, the Ptolemies would come to assimilate much of Egypt's heritage, adopting pharaonic dress, reworking Egyptian gods into a new Graeco-Egyptian pantheon and, most visibly, adopting pharaonic building styles – the temples of Dendara, Edfu and Philae all date from the time of the Ptolemies.

Apart from its cultural and intellectual achievements (and, second only to Rome, Alexandria was regarded as the greatest centre of learning in the known world), the Ptolemies' rule was not without its share of murder, intrigue and threats from abroad. Rome felt threatened by the growing importance and power of Alexandria and so attempted to manipulate the Ptolemaic bickering and plotting to its own ends. The litany of events that eventually led to complete Roman rule over Egypt reads like a bloody soap opera.

Cleopatra VII (*the* Cleopatra, of asp, Elizabeth Taylor, and four hour boreathon film fame) and her younger brother Ptolemy XIII together ruled Egypt, under Roman protection. Rome's representative and watchdog at the Egyptian court was Pompey, but Ptolemy XIII had him killed. He also banished Cleopatra, which, in the event, proved by far the more foolhardy of the two acts. The queen approached Julius Caesar and the two briefly became lovers with the result that Ptolemy XIII was tossed into the Nile. Following the assassination of Caesar, Cleopatra found herself a new protector – and husband – in Marc Antony, a strong contender for the vacated role of emperor of Rome. But the union of the Egyptian queen and the Roman general was not popular in Rome, especially with Caesar's nephew Octavian, whose sister was already married to Antony. In the ensuing power struggle, the Egyptian fleet was defeated at Actium in 31 BC by the superior forces of Octavian (who later became the emperor Augustus). As the victorious Roman fleet sailed towards Egypt, Cleopatra, rather than face capture, reputedly put an asp to her breast and so ended the Ptolemaic dynasty.

Roman Rule

Under Octavian, the Romans established themselves in Alexandria. They did little to develop the country, which served largely as the granary of the Roman empire, but they established trading posts down the Red Sea coast and out across the Western Desert to link up with their territories in Cyrenaica (now Libya). They also established a fortress on the site of a pharaonic river crossing near Memphis, 10km to the east of the Pyramids. Controlling the access to the upper Nile, the fortress of Babylon-in-Egypt, as it became known, grew to become a busy port and major frontier stronghold.

To impose their rule on the native population, the Romans set about eradicating the old pharaonic religions. This led many Egyptians to turn to the growing, alternative cult of Christianity, which had arrived in the country via the preaching of St Mark around 40 AD. This proved no more palatable to the Romans who regarded the new religion as a potential political threat. Despite this, or, indeed, even because of it, Egyptian Christianity, known as Coptic Christianity, flourished. Over time, Christianity would flourish all around the Mediterranean and in 323 AD it was adopted as the official religion of the Holy Roman Empire. However, the Roman church deemed the Copts' monophysitic doctrine (the belief that Christ is divine, rather than both human and divine) heretical and the Egyptians were expelled from the main body of Christianity.

Within Egypt, the Roman overlords continued to persecute the local population. This oppressive state of affairs came to an end in 640 AD with the arrival of an army of mounted warriors riding out of the deserts of the Arabian peninsula.

The Arab Conquest

The Arab conquest brought Islam to Egypt. By 642 AD the new rulers had established a base immediately north of the walls of the Roman fortress of Babylon. This encampment, called Fustat, was the precursor of the city of Cairo. From this point on, the history of Egypt becomes synonymous with the history of Cairo.

From the arrival of Islam onwards, all Egypt's existing historical capitals – Memphis, Thebes, Akhetaten, Alexandria – were allowed to decline, and in a relatively short space of time all became thinly populated backwaters. Their monuments served as quarries for the stone needed for the walls, palaces and religious buildings of the new Islamic capital.

But like Christianity before it, though still in its infancy Islam was already subject to splinter factions and dynasties. In 658 AD the Umayyads, an Arab dynasty based in Damascus, snatched control of Egypt and held the country for just short of 100 years before losing out to the Abbassids of Baghdad. They lasted 200 years. Unlike the Umayyads, who failed to leave any mark on the country, Cairo has a splendid Abbassid legacy – the Ibn Tulun Mosque, built on the orders of the governor of the same name. Next in line were the Fatimids, a north African dynasty that claimed possession of Cairo and Egypt in 969 AD.

As Alexander and the first invading Arab army had done before them, the Fatimids chose not to base their authority in any existing city. Instead they marked out territory to the north of Fustat. The fortified walled city they built formed the core of Cairo until the mid-19th century (for more detail see the History section in the Cairo chapter). The Fatimids though, were not popular rulers. They held themselves aloof from the country's indigenous Egyptian citizens, who they kept outside the city walls. The division was made even greater by the fact that the Fatimids were Shi'ias, a brand of Islam at odds with the orthodox Sunnism of the locals (see the boxed text 'Shi'ia Head, Sunni Body' on page 166).

Around this time the Christians of western Europe took up arms against the heathen armies in occupation of the holy sites of the Bible. Their prime goal was to wrest Jerusalem from the Muslims, and this they achieved in 1099. By 1168, having bloodily rampaged through Palestine, the Crusaders were now advancing into Egypt. They only got as far as the Delta. They were driven off by the Seljuks of Damascus, a powerful warrior dynasty to whom the Fatimids had appealed for help. The Seljuks were Sunni Muslims and once in Al-Qahira they promptly deposed the Shi'ia dynasty they had come to aid and sent the Fatimids into exile.

The restorer of Sunni rule and the new overlord of Cairo was Salah ad-Din al-Ayyubi (known to the Crusaders, and later to the west, as Saladin), who established a new dynasty, the Ayyubids. A soldier foremost, Salah ad-Din made his mark on Cairo by looping it with a great defensive wall and by establishing the Citadel that still dominates the city's eastern skyline today.

The Ayyubid line ran to only four rulers before a vicious bout of scheming and betrayals resulted in the seizure of power by a group of former mercenaries, the Mamluks.

The Mamluks The Mamluks were a Turkish slave-soldier class whose military service had been rewarded by Salah ad-Din with gifts of land. They were organised in a quasi-feudal manner, with groups of Mamluks each attached to their own lord or emir. The groups were maintained by the purchase of new young slaves. There was no system of hereditary lineage, instead it was rule by the strongest. Rare was the sultan who died of old age.

Natural born soldiers, the military prowess of the Mamluks led to a succession of successful campaigns that gave Egypt control of all Palestine and Syria. At the same time, while renowned for their savagery, the Mamluks also endowed Cairo with the most exquisite architectural constructions, and during their 267 year reign the city was the intellectual and cultural centre of the Islamic world. The contradictions in the make-up of the Mamluks are typified in the figure of Qaitbey, who was bought as a slave-boy by one sultan and witnessed the brief reigns of nine more before he himself clawed his way to the throne. As sultan he rapaciously taxed all his subjects and dealt out vicious punishments with his own hands, once tearing out the eyes and tongue of a court chemist who had failed to transform lead into gold. Yet Qaitbey marked his ruthless sultanship with some of Cairo's most beautiful monuments, notably his mosque which stands in the Northern Cemetery.

The funding for the Mamluks' great buildings came from trade. A canal existed that connected the Red Sea with the Nile at Cairo, and thus the Mediterranean, forming a vital link in the busy commercial route between Europe and India and the Orient. In the 14th and 15th centuries, the Mamluks, in partnership with Venice, virtually controlled east-west trade and grew fabulously rich off it.

The end of these fabled days came in the closing years of the 15th century when Vasco da Gama discovered the sea route around the Cape of Good Hope, so freeing European merchants from the heavy taxes raked in by Cairo and Venice. At around the same time the Turks were emerging as a mighty new empire looking to unify the Muslim world, a goal that included the conquest of Egypt. In 1516, the Mamluks, under the command of their last sultan, Al-Ghouri, were obliged to meet the Turkish threat. The battle, which took place at Aleppo in Syria, resulted in complete defeat for the Mamluks. In January of the following year the Turkish sultan Selim I entered Cairo.

Turkish Rule

Egypt's days as a great imperial centre were at an end. Under the Ottomans the country was once again, as it had been under the Romans, reduced to the level of a far-flung province. What trading revenues there were went back to Constantinople, as did the

Chronology of the Islamic Period

This is not a complete listing but it does include all those rulers mentioned throughout this book.

Ruler	Period (AD)	Important Monument
EARLY ISLAM	640-61	
Amr ibn al-As	conqueror of Egypt	Mosque of Amr
UMAYYADS	661-750	
ABBASIDS	750-969	
including		
Ibn Tulun	868-905	Mosque of ibn Tulun
FATIMIDS	969-1171	
including		
Al-Muizz	969-75	founder of Al-Qahira
Abu Mansour al-Aziz	975-96	
Al-Hakim	996-1021	Mosque of al-Hakim
AYYUBIDS	1171-1250	
including		
Salah ad-Din (Saladin)	1169-93	Citadel, Cairo
Shagaret ad-Durr	1250	Mausoleum of as-Salih Ayyub
MAMLUKS	1250-1517	
including		
Qalaun	1279-90	Madrassa & Mausoleum of Qalaun
An-Nasir Mohammed	1293-1340	Mausoleum of an-Nasir Mohammed
Barquq	1382-98	Madrassa & Mausoleum of Barquq
Farag (ibn Barquq)	1398-1412	Khanqah-Mausoleum of ibn Barquq
Al-Mu'ayyad	1412-21	Mosque of al-Mu'ayyad
Al-Ashraf Barsbey	1422-38	Complex of Sultan Ashraf Barsbey
Qaitbey	1468-98	Mosque of Qaitbey
Al-Ghouri	1501-16	Al-Ghouri complex
Tumanbey	1516-17	
OTTOMAN TURKS		

Rule from Constantinople from 1517 to the invasion of the French in 1798.

taxes that were squeezed from the local population.

Although the Mamluk sultanate had been abolished, the Mamluks themselves lived on in the form of lords known as *beys* and maintained considerable power. Over time the Turkish hold on Egypt became weaker as its empire went into decline. In 1796 one of the Mamluk beys was confident enough to take on the Turkish garrison in Cairo, defeat them and dispatch the Ottoman governor back to Constantinople. But the Mamluks' re-emergence was short-lived. Within two years they were unseated again, though not by the

Turks but by a new force in Egypt – Europeans in the form of Napoleon and the French army.

Napoleon & Description d'Egypte

Napoleon and his musket-armed forces blew apart the sword-wielding Mamluk cavalry, supposedly as a show of support for the Ottoman sultan. In reality, Napoleon wanted to strike a blow at Britain's eastern trade by gaining control of the land and sea routes to India. He was also keen to 'civilise' Egypt.

The diminutive general established a French-style government, revamped the tax system, implemented public works projects and introduced new crops and a new system of weights and measures. Napoleon was also accompanied by a hundred or more savants and artists who were set to work making a complete study of Egypt's monuments, crafts, arts, flora and fauna, and of its society and people. The resulting work was published as the 24 volume *Description de l'Egypte*; it's still in print today, albeit in a radically slimmed-down, one volume edition.

Anthropological efforts aside, Napoleon's Egyptian adventure seemed doomed from the beginning. Less than a month after he arrived, the British navy under Admiral Nelson appeared off the coast of Alexandria and destroyed the French fleet. Then the Ottoman sultan sent an army which, though trounced by the French, put paid to any pretence that they were in Egypt with the complicity of Istanbul. Relations between the occupied and occupier deteriorated rapidly and uprisings in the capital could only be quashed by shelling which left 3000 Egyptians dead.

Sitting on a powder keg in Cairo with the British and Turks allying in Syria, the French forces readily agreed to an armistice and in 1801 departed the way they had come, via Alexandria.

Mohammed Ali Although brief, the French occupation had significantly weakened Egyptian political stability. Turkish rule was reinstated but it was tenuous and masked great internal strife. A lieutenant in an Albanian contingent of the Ottoman army named Mohammed Ali took advantage of the melee. Within five years of the departure of the French he had fought and intrigued his way to become the *pasha* of Egypt, nominally the vassal of Constantinople but in practice looking on the country as his own.

The sultan in Constantinople was too weak to challenge the usurpation and the only possible threat to Mohammed Ali's

Comprising more than 3000 illustrations, *Description de l'Egypte* introduced the world to a new science: Egyptology.

power could have come from the Mamluk beys. Any danger here was swiftly and viciously snuffed out by a very deadly dinner invitation – see the boxed text 'Massacre of the Mamluks' on page 176. Secure at home, Mohammed Ali sent his troops out to successful gains in Sudan, Greece, Syria and Arabia, and by 1839 he controlled most of the Ottoman empire.

Although Mohammed Ali's means of achieving his ends could be barbarous, his reign is pivotal in the history of Egypt, as under his uncompromising rule the country underwent a transition from medieval-style feudalism to something approaching industrialisation. Mohammed Ali is credited with introducing a public education system and with planting Egypt's fields with the valuable cash crop of cotton. He was said to have a mania for all things new and foreign; conversely, during his reign, a growing number of foreigners became ever more fascinated by Egypt and all things 'Oriental' – see the boxed text 'The Discovery of the Orient & its Subsequent Plunder' on the opposite page.

On his death, Mohammed Ali's preoccupations were taken up by his heirs who continued the work of implementing reforms and social projects, foremost of which were the establishment of the railway system, factories, and a telegraph and postal system that was one of the first in the world. (Now, 150 years on, it's about time it was given an overhaul.) Egypt's fledgling cotton industry boomed as production in America was disrupted by the civil war between the north and south, and revenues were directed into ever grander schemes. Grandest of all was the Suez Canal, which opened to great fanfare and an audience composed of most of the crowned heads of Europe in 1869.

Egypt was attracting ever-increasing numbers of foreign tourists. As early as 1860 Thomas Cook had begun leading organised tours down the Nile. Cairo had gained a large foreign population who were involved in running businesses and conducting trade and the place almost had the character of a gold rush town. The pickings were particularly rich for the European bankers who, with the connivance of their governments, bestowed lavish loans upon the Egyptian khedive Ismail for his grandiose schemes. They advanced the kind of money Egypt could never conceivably repay, at insatiable rates of interest, providing a convenient excuse for Britain to intervene in 1882 and announce that until such time as Egypt could repay its debts, it was taking control.

British Occupation

The British allowed the heirs of Mohammed Ali to remain on the throne but all real power was concentrated in the hands of the British Agent. It has been written that the British viewed their role in Egypt as a stern sort of paternalism, acting for a country that couldn't look after itself but, more honestly, at the heart of the matter was the desire to ensure the security of the Suez Canal for continued British use. And while the British introduced a form of Egyptian legislative assembly and many local landowners benefited from the improved administration, the bottom line was that this was occupation by might. In this were sown the seeds of a national movement toward independence.

The Egyptians' desire for self-determination was strengthened by the Allies' use of the country as a glorified barracks during WWI. Popular national sentiments were articulated by riots in 1919 and, more eloquently, by the likes of Saad Zaghloul, the most brilliant of an emerging breed of young Egyptian politicians, who said of the British, 'I have no quarrel with them personally ... but I want to see an independent Egypt'.

As a sop to the independence movement, the British allowed the formation of a nationalist political party, called the Wafd (Delegation), and granted Egypt its sovereignty. But this was very much an empty gesture; 'King' Fuad enjoyed little popularity among his people and the British kept tight hold of the reins. Moreover, they came in ever greater numbers with the outbreak of WWII. The war wasn't all bad news for

The Discovery of the Orient & its Subsequent Plunder

In the decades following Napoleon's doomed expedition, Egypt attracted attention like no place ever before. During the 1820s, 30s and 40s the country was visited by a stream of adventurers and intrepid early travellers, including Mark Twain, Gustave Flaubert, Florence Nightingale and Richard Burton, translator of *The Thousand and One Nights*. The resulting accounts and journals were eagerly devoured by western audiences enraptured by tales of temples in the sand, veiled harems and the bare-breasted women of the slave markets.

Artists too found Egypt a rich source of material and several made the journey to set up their easels in backstreets and before temples to record images little changed since the medieval days of the Mamluks. The most prolific was a Scot, David Roberts, who produced an immense body of work from Egypt and the Holy Lands that ensured him a fortune in his lifetime.

As a result of this import of fantastic images and texts, Europe and the 'civilised' world was swept by Egyptomania. Sphinxes and pharaonic motifs adorned architecture from Melbourne to Chicago, operas were written around ancient Egyptian themes, and a new vogue in painting was inspired. Known as Orientalism, this drew heavily on scenes of sensuous figures depicted against sumptuously ornate backgrounds, all usually a product of the artist's imagination aided by studio props and models, but lent an air of authenticity by the ultra-realist manner in which the canvases were painted. Now widely derided for its imperialistic and exploitative undertones, the Orientalist movement at the time attracted well known practitioners including the respected French painters Ingres and Renoir.

The appetite for all things Egyptian didn't halt with words and images. The imperial powers had to have antiquities. Some were presented as gifts and, intent on dragging his country into the industrial age, Mohammed Ali, ruler of Egypt, readily gave away the obelisks that now adorn the Place de la Concorde in Paris, London's Embankment and Central Park in New York.

But during the 19th century the core of the great collections of Egyptian antiquities at the British Museum in London, the Louvre in Paris, Germany's Berlin Museum and the Metropolitan Museum in New York was built up with pieces hauled back as booty by wealthy traveller-collectors and treasure hunters. The most famous, an Italian circus strongman named Giovanni Belzoni, supplied the British with the Memnon fragment, looted from the Ramesseum, which now rests in the British Museum, along with one of the institution's biggest draws, the famed Rosetta stone (see the boxed text 'The Rosetta Stone' on page 416). The stone was originally discovered by the French but the British claimed it as a spoil of war following the surrender of Napoleon's army in Egypt.

In recent years there have been requests from the Egyptian government for the return of key pieces including the Rosetta stone, a bust of Nefertiti held by the Berlin Museum and some statues of Hatshepsut held in New York. But although the western fascination with 'Oriental' Egypt has long since abated the chances of these treasures being returned is very slight.

the Egyptians, certainly not for the shopkeepers and businessmen who saw thousands of Allied soldiers pouring into the towns and cities with money to burn on 48 hour leave from the desert. There was also a vocal element that saw the Germans as potential liberators. Students held rallies in support of Rommel and in the Egyptian army a small cabal of officers, which included future presidents Nasser and Sadat, plotted to aid the German general's advance on their city.

Rommel pushed the Allied forces back almost to Alexandria, which had the British hurriedly burning documents in such quantity that the skies over Cairo turned dark with the ash, but the Germans did not break through. Instead, the British were to remain for almost 10 more years until a day of flames was to drive them out for good.

Independent Egypt

On Saturday, 26 January 1952, 'Black Saturday', Cairo was set on fire. After years of demonstrations, strikes and riots against foreign rule, the storming by the British of a rebellious Egyptian police station in the Suez Canal zone provided a spark that ignited the capital. Foreign-owned and foreigner-frequented shops and businesses were put to the torch by mobs and all the landmarks of 80 years of British rule were reduced to charred ruins within the space of a day.

The British must have realised that as far as they were concerned Egypt was ungovernable, so when just a few weeks later a group of young army officers seized power in a coup it was accepted as a *fait accompli*. On 26 July 1952, the Egyptian puppet-king Farouk, descendant of the Albanian Mohammed Ali, departed Alexandria harbour aboard the royal yacht, leaving Egypt to be ruled by Egyptians for the first time since the pharaohs.

Colonel Gamal Abdel Nasser, leader of the revolutionary Free Officers, ascended to power and was confirmed as president in elections held in 1956. With the aim of returning Egypt to the long put upon Egyptian peasantry, in an echo of the events of Russia in 1917, the country's landowners were dispossessed and their assets nationalised. This applied equally, if not more so, to foreigners, so while the country's huge foreign community was not forced to go, they nevertheless began to hurriedly sell up and stream out of the country.

The same year of his inauguration, the colonial legacy was finally and dramatically shaken off in full world view when Nasser successfully faced down Britain and France over the Suez Canal. To finance the building of a great dam that would control the flooding of the Nile, Nasser had announced his intention to nationalise the Suez Canal. The military attempt by the two former occupiers of Egypt to seize the waterway resulted in diplomatic embarrassment and undignified retreat, leaving Nasser the hero of the developing world, a sort of Robin Hood and Ramses rolled into one.

Egypt became a beacon for all those countries in Africa and Asia that had recently thrown off European colonial administrations, and in particular to those of the Arab world, from Algeria to Iraq and Yemen. Nasser became the lauded spokesman of pan-Arabism.

War & Peace with Israel Little more than 10 years later, the brave new Egypt came crashing down. On 5 June 1967, Israel wiped out Egypt's airforce in a surprise attack. With it went the confidence and credibility of Nasser and his nation.

Relations with Israel had been hostile ever since its founding in 1948. Egypt had sent soldiers to aid the Palestinians in fighting the newly proclaimed Jewish state and ended up on the losing side. Since that time, the Arabs had kept up a barrage of anti-Zionist rhetoric. Although privately Nasser acknowledged that the Arabs would probably lose another war against Israel, for public consumption he gave rabble-rousing speeches about liberating Palestine. But he was a skilled orator and by early 1967 the mood engendered throughout the Arab world by these speeches was beginning to catch up with him. Soon, other Arab leaders started to accuse him of cowardice and of hiding behind the UN troops stationed in Sinai since the Suez Crisis. Nasser responded by ordering the peacekeepers out and blockading the Straits of Tiran, effectively closing the southern Israeli port of Eilat. He gave Israel reassurances that he wasn't going to attack but meanwhile massed his forces east of Suez. So Israel struck first.

When the shooting stopped six days later Israel controlled all of the Sinai peninsula and had closed the Suez Canal. A humiliated Nasser offered to resign but in a spontaneous outpouring of support the Egyptian people wouldn't accept it and he remained in office. It was to be for only another three more years though, as abruptly in November 1970, the president dropped dead of a heart attack.

Little more than 30 years after his death, the Nasser years – pre 1967, that is – are already viewed by a great many Egyptians as a lost golden era, and one of the biggest cinema hits of recent years has been *Nasser '56*, a flattering bio-pic of the president's finest moment.

Local opinion regarding Sadat, Nasser's successor, is less adulatory. Egypt's second president initiated a complete about face; where Nasser looked to the USSR for his inspiration, Sadat looked to the US. Out went socialist principles, in came capitalist opportunism. After a decade and a half of keeping a low profile the wealthy resurfaced and were joined by a large, new moneyed middle class grown rich on the back of Sadat's much-touted *al-infitah* or 'open door policy'. Sadat also believed that to truly revitalise Egypt's economy he would have to deal with Israel. But first he needed bargaining power, a basis for negotiations.

On 6 October 1973, the Jewish holiday of Yom Kippur, Egypt launched a surprise attack across the Suez Canal. Its army beat back the much better armed Israelis and although these initial gains were later reversed, Egypt's national pride was restored. Sadat's negotiating strategy had succeeded.

In November 1977, Sadat travelled to Jerusalem to begin negotiating a peace with Israel, a process that ended two years later with the co-signing of the Camp David Agreement. Israel agreed to withdraw from Sinai while Egypt recognised Israel's right to exist. This was a complete abandonment of Nasser's pan-Arabist principles and Sadat's peace was viewed by the Arab world as no less than a betrayal. It cost Sadat his life: on 6 October 1981 as he observed a parade in commemoration of the 1973 War one of his soldiers broke from the marching ranks and sprayed the presidential stand with gunfire. Sadat was killed instantly.

Islamic Extremism Sadat's assassin was a member of the Muslim Brotherhood, an uncompromising political organisation that aimed to establish an Islamic state in Egypt. Mass round-ups of Islamists and suspected Islamists were immediately carried out on the orders of Sadat's successor Hosni Mubarak, a former air force general and vice-president.

Less flamboyant than Sadat and less charismatic than Nasser, Mubarak has often been criticised as being both unimaginative and indecisive. Nevertheless, he managed to carry out a balancing act on several fronts, abroad and at home. To the irritation of more hardline states like Syria and Libya, he was able to rehabilitate Egypt in the eyes of the Arab world, without abandoning the treaty with Israel. The Arab League headquarters, which was removed to Tunis in 1979 in protest at Sadat's recognition of the Jewish state, was returned to Cairo in 1990. And for almost a decade he managed to keep the lid on the Islamist extremists.

But in the early 1990s the lid blew off. Despite its use of religious symbolism the Islamist's is essentially a political movement that has grown out of harsh socio-economic conditions. In the 1980s discontent had been brewing among the poorer sections of society. Government promises had failed to keep up with the population explosion and a generation of youths were finding themselves without jobs and living in squalid, overcrowded housing with little or no hope for the future. With a repressive political system that allowed little chance to legitimately voice opposition, the only hope lay with the Islamic parties and their calls for change.

Denied recognition by the state as a legal political entity, the Islamists turned to force. There were frequent attempts on the life of the president and his ministers and frequent clashes with the security forces. Perhaps even more alarmingly, the matter escalated from a domestic issue to a matter of international concern when the Islamists began to target one of the state's most vulnerable sources of income: tourists.

Several groups of foreign tourists were shot at or bombed in the last months of 1992 and into 1993 resulting in a handful of deaths. The government responded with a heavy-handed lightning crackdown arresting thousands and introducing the death penalty for terrorism. Human rights groups were up in arms at the mass arrests and reports of confessions extracted by torture and other police brutalities but by the mid-1990s, the violence had receded from the capital, retreating to the religious heartland of middle Egypt. The Egyptian government proclaimed the Islamist extremists 'utterly crushed'.

Egypt Today

Egypt is on a slow but gradual climb. Over the last 10 years the country's public debt has fallen. Foreign currency reserves have climbed. The pound is stable. Inflation is under control. Population growth has been checked. The Egyptian president is a respected guarantor of peace and a vital ally of the west in the Middle East. On the home front, the government looks stable. But as anyone who wasn't on Mars in late 1997 knows, terrorist violence is far from being completely a thing of the past in Egypt. The sickening one-two of the fire bomb attack on a tour bus outside the Egyptian Museum in Cairo, followed a few weeks later by the massacre of 58 holiday-makers at the Temple of Hatshepsut in Luxor stunned the whole world. The world responded by staying away and tourism figures plummeted. Since that time Egypt has been frantically wooing back the holiday-makers with high profile events like opera at the Pyramids and shopping festivals and millions spent on tourist office advertising. It's a strategy that seems to have paid off and at the time of writing Egypt's international profile is all pharaohs and frolicking at the Red Sea. It's an attractive combination but one that's very much at odds with the Egypt experienced by the majority of the 60-plus million who actually live there. Until more is done to bridge this disparity the sunny outlook of the tourist posters is bound to remain tinged with the threat of dark clouds.

GEOGRAPHY

For most Egyptians the Nile Valley is home. Although the country covers roughly one million square kilometres, some 90% of the population lives in the narrow carpet of fertile land bordering the great river. To the south the river is hemmed in by mountains and the agricultural plain ranges from only 20km to 30km in width, but as it flows north, the land becomes flatter and the valley widens.

To the east of the valley is the Eastern (Arabian) Desert, a barren plateau bounded on its eastern edge by a high ridge of mountains that rises to more than 2000m and extends for about 800km. To the west is the Western (Libyan) Desert, a plateau punctuated by huge clumps of bizarre geological formations and a string of luxuriant oases.

North of Cairo, the Nile splits into several tributaries and the valley becomes a 200km-wide delta, a vast green fan of fertile countryside running into the Mediterranean Sea.

To the east, across the Suez Canal, is the triangular wedge of Sinai. A geological extension of the Eastern Desert, terrain here slopes from the high mountain ridges, which include Mt Sinai and Mt Katherine (or Gebel Katerina, the highest mountain in Egypt, at 2642m) in the south, to desert coastal plains and lagoons in the north.

CLIMATE

Egypt's climate is easy to summarise. Hot and dry. This holds for most of the country for most of the year, with the exception of the winter months of December, January and February, which can be quite cold in the north. Average temperatures range from 20°C (68°F) on the Mediterranean coast to 26°C (80°F) in Aswan. Maximum temperatures for the same places can get up to 31°C (88°F) and 50°C (122°F) respectively. At night in winter the temperature some-

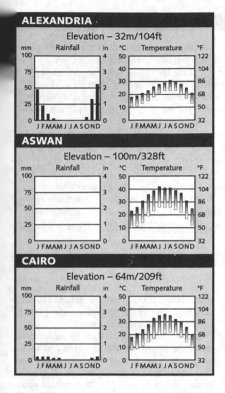

ECOLOGY & ENVIRONMENT

Caring about the environment is a luxury that traditionally few Egyptians have had time to indulge in, but this is starting to change. In recent years an Egyptian Environmental Affairs Agency has been established and a Minister of the Environment was appointed in 1997. While the post is sometimes criticised as being little more than a sop to critics, some action has been taken on industrial polluters in Cairo and plans are being drawn to deal with the waste that boat cruisers dump into the Nile.

Urban Issues

Cairo is the great upturned ashtray (a phrase coined by Tony Horwitz in his book *Baghdad Without a Map*) with an air so full of filth and ill health that breathing it is said to be equivalent to smoking a packet of cigarettes a day. More than one million vehicles, most old and badly maintained, jam the city's roads, belching out clouds of noxious fumes. There is next to no control on vehicle emissions, and unleaded fuel has yet to catch on. Add to that the factories on the edge of town that spew crap into the air and the net result is that Cairo may well be the world's second most-polluted urban centre after Mexico City. The level of lead in the air is three to 20 times higher than internationally permissible levels (depending on which agency you ask), while the density of suspended solid particles (the main cause of respiratory problems) is between five and 10 times the recommended international level.

The government is finally sufficiently alarmed to do something about all this: factories are now required to install filters (reportedly, few have so far done so); a pilot scheme has introduced compressed natural gas to power state-owned vehicles (so far limited to a small fleet of microbuses); and a US$200 million USAID sponsored air improvement project has been launched. But it's very little and for the time being residents of Cairo are forced to resign themselves to the incredibly nasty habit of passive smoking.

times plummets to as low as 8°C in Cairo and along the Mediterranean coast. In the desert it's even more extreme – often scorching during the day and bitterly cold at night.

Alexandria receives the most rain – approximately 19cm a year – while far to the south in Aswan the average is about 10mm in five years. Kharga in the Western Desert once went 17 years without any rain at all.

Between March and April the *khamseen* – a dry, hot and very dusty wind – blows in from the parched Western Desert at up to 150km/h. The sky becomes dark orange and choked with dust, and no matter that everyone closes tight all doors and windows, inside every house is covered with a patina of grit so that it resembles an undisturbed tomb.

Responsible Tourism

Tourism is vital to the Egyptian economy and the country would be in a mess without it but, at the same time, millions of visitors a year can't help but add to the ecological overload. As long as outsiders have been stumbling upon or searching for the wonders of ancient Egypt, they have also been crawling all over them, chipping bits off or leaving their own contributions engraved in the stones. This is not sustainable tourism. So visitors are now rightly forbidden to climb the pyramids at Giza. But people still do it, and local guides will make exceptions for people willing to pay a little baksheesh. Don't.

The same goes with adventuring off-road in protected areas such as Ras Mohammed. True, you're in the middle of nowhere and who's going to know anyway? But it's illegal to drive off the beaten tracks and the fragile desert environment needs you to enforce this law.

Few places in Egypt are likely to win a tidy-town award – inadequate waste disposal and little regard for the environmental issues that are popular in the west produces some ugly sights. But some of the refuse – plastic mineral water bottles for instance – is actually recycled, so don't be too quick to point an accusing finger at the Egyptians. More than one traveller has reported being disgusted by the garbage left behind by visitors climbing Mt Sinai. Try not to add to it.

The other big problem is overcrowding. Although the latest census results show that Egypt's population growth rate is falling, it still stands at 2.1%. And around 16 million people still inhabit Cairo. By the government's own admission, parts of the city continue to house the densest number of people per kilometre anywhere in the world. The strain placed on the city's decaying infrastructure is enormous and more than it can cope with. The result is one of the world's most lethal public transport systems with a regular roll-call of train wrecks and bus smashes; and cities of hastily thrown up buildings which all too frequently crash to the ground again, with horrific consequences.

Countrywide Issues

Ill-planned touristic development remains one of the biggest threats to the Red Sea coast and Sinai. The construction of a new airport halfway between Al-Quseir and Marsa Alam is expected to unleash a frenzy of development along this wild coastline. There are fewer than 15 places along here where people can enter the sea without stepping on coral. Environmentalists are worried that the 100-plus hotels planned for this area will simply dump sand on the coral to let their guests swim more easily.

In Sinai, the coast north of Nuweiba is already the site of a building boom and a wall of resorts is connecting the town to the border crossing of Taba. Whether or not the businessmen investing in the area will make good on their promises to protect the reefs around the area remains to be seen. Given their past record there is little reason to believe them. For more on reef protection see the Diving the Red Sea chapter.

So far, though, the solid waste generated by the thousands of visitors who come here remains one of the peninsula's biggest problems. In Dahab, for example, periodic cleanups of the beaches and reefs have been rendered useless by the municipality's refusal to allocate land for a dump (at the moment all the area's garbage is put at the end of a wadi prone to flooding; what is not blown away by the constant wind is periodically swept down into the sea with flash floods, choking coral and marine life).

Also troubling is that the Ministry of Tourism – not known for its attention to enironmental considerations – is now actively promoting the Western Desert and the oases as a tourist destination. There is already a boom in so-called adventure ourism in this remote place and it is leaving its mark on the landscape: garbage can sometimes be seen rolling over the dunes of the Great Sand Sea and visitors have made off with many of the fossil remains that lie throughout the area. And despite crackdowns on illegal desert hunting, parties of Gulf Arabs and others continue to arrive with high-tech weaponry and shoot the species that they have decimated in their own lands – sometimes with the Egyptian military acting as guide.

There have been some positive developments too. At the end of 1997 Nuweiba saw the establishment of a recycling program to deal with its solid waste problem. Moreover, there are now five protected areas in Sinai. A National Parks office has also been created in Hurghada and it is hoping to rein in some of the more grandiose development plans in the Marsa Alam area. Finally, the government is looking into environmentally friendly tourism as a marketing strategy and Egypt's first ecolodge has been built in Siwa oasis and is expected to be the prototype for more sensitive touristic development.

FLORA & FAUNA

Egypt is often described as being about 94% desert. Such a figure conjures up images of vast, barren wastelands where nothing can live. But that's not the case. While there are areas that are extremely arid and incapable of supporting life, there are also plenty of desert regions where fragile ecosystems have adapted over millennia to extremely hostile conditions. For more information on desert flora, see the boxed text 'Balancing Sinai's Ecosystem' on page 480. You could also pick up *Natural Selections: A Year of Egypt's Wildlife*, written and illustrated by Richard Hoath and published locally by the American University in Cairo Press – it's a passionate account of the birds, animals, insects and marine crea-

tures that make Egypt their home. Look out also for Hoath's *Field Guide to the Mammals of Egypt*, which should hit the bookshelves in 1999.

Flora

The lotus that symbolises ancient Egypt can be found, albeit rarely, in the Delta area, but the papyrus reed, depicted in ancient art as vast swamps where the pharaohs hunted hippos, has been lost. Except for one clump found in 1968 in Wadi Natrun, papyrus can only be found in botanical gardens.

More than 100 kinds of grasses thrive in areas where there is water, and the date palm is to be seen in virtually every cultivable area. Along with tamarisk and acacia, the imported jacaranda and poinciana (red and orange flowers) have come to mark Egyptian summers with their vivid colours. You'll also see a water hyacinth, known as the 'Nile rose', choking parts of the Nile and many canals.

In Ras Mohammed National Park in Sinai, there is a stand of mangroves which, according to environmentalists, is the second most northerly mangrove group in the world. These trees live in salt water and are extremely important to the area's ecosystem.

Fauna

Mammals Egypt is home to about 100 types of mammals. There are still a few exotic species about, however, the most common critters are house mice, black and brown rats, and bats. You'll be lucky to see anything other than camels, donkeys, and to a lesser extent domesticated horses and buffalo.

Egypt's deserts used to be sanctuaries for an amazing variety of larger mammals, such as leopard, cheetah, oryx, aardwolf (which feeds on termites), striped hyena and caracal (a desert lynx with long black ear tufts). All of these, however, have been brought to the brink of extinction through hunting. In fact, there's only one known family of cheetah still living in Egypt, and many years have passed since a leopard was sighted. Other creatures such as the sand cat (the soles of their feet are covered in fur to aid hunting), the Fennec fox (the world's smallest vulpine) and the Nubian ibex (the males of this species have long, backswept horns) are very occasionally sighted.

There are three types of gazelle in Egypt – the Arabian, Dorcas and white. The first species is thought to be extinct, and of the other two groups only individual sightings are made these days, despite the fact that herds of Dorcas gazelle were, up until 30 or so years ago, common features of the desert landscape.

The zorilla, a kind of weasel, lives in the Gebel Elba region, while in Sinai you may see rock hyrax – small creatures about the size of a large rabbit which, like elephants (whom they're most closely related to!), live in large groups and are extremely sociable.

Birds About 430 species have been sighted in Egypt, of which about one-third actually breed in Egypt, while most of the others are passage migrants or winter visitors. Each year, an estimated one to two million large birds migrate via certain routes from Europe to Africa through Egypt. Most large birds, including flamingo, stork, crane, heron, and all large birds of prey are protected under Egyptian law.

The most ubiquitous birds are the house sparrow and the hooded crow; one of the most distinctive is the hoopoe. This cinnamon-toned bird has a head shaped very much like a hammer and, when excited, it extends its crest. Hoopoes are often seen hunting for insects in gardens in central Cairo, though they're more commonly found in the countryside.

Birdwatchers should keep their eyes open in particular during autumn and spring. However, at any time of the year, Birket Qarun in the Al-Fayoum region is a good place for watching, with birds ranging from spoonbill to marsh sandpiper. The saltwater lagoons in the northern Delta and the Zaranik Reserve on Lake Bardawil in northern Sinai are home to such creatures as the greater flamingo, white pelican and spoonbill (all winter visitors). It's also possible to see huge flocks of pelicans around the small lakes near Abu Simbel in southern Egypt. On star-filled nights in the desert you may see, or hear, eagle owl. The Gebel Elba region is renowned for tropical birds such as the shining sunbird, the Nubian nightjar and the Sudanese golden sparrow.

Marine Life See the Diving the Red Sea chapter for details on Egypt's marine life.

Other Creatures Some 34 species of snakes live in Egypt. The best known is the cobra, which featured on the headdress of the ancient pharaohs. Another one to see is the horned viper, a thickset snake that has horns over its eyes to keep the sand out when it buries itself.

There are plenty of scorpions throughout the country and, although some are capable of a fatal sting, they're largely nocturnal and rarely seen. Be careful if lifting up stones as they like to burrow into cool spots.

Once plentiful up and down the length of the Nile, crocodiles have been extinct north of the Aswan Dam since 1891 when the last one was shot by a British officer. These days they are protected, and live only in Lake Nasser south of the High Dam near Aswan.

GOVERNMENT & POLITICS

The bulk of power is concentrated in the hands of the president (present incumbent, Mohammed Hosni Mubarak), who is nominated by the People's Assembly and elected by popular referendum for six years. This term can be renewed at least once, although, at the time of writing, Mubarak is close to completing a third term and has indicated he's going for a fourth. There is no question of him failing to secure further time in office. Mubarak himself admits democracy in Egypt is 'limited' and there are no serious opposition parties to the ruling National Democratic Party (NDP). In the last elections most seats were contested by rivals from within the NDP.

The president appoints vice presidents and ministers, as well as 10 members of the 454-member People's Assembly and 70 of

While Egypt is blessed with pharaonic treasures galore and the natural splendours of Sinai and the Red Sea, its greatest asset is its inhabitants who are some of the most hospitable and good-natured people imaginable.

GLENN BEANLAND

JULIET COOMBE / LA BELLE AURORE

LEANNE LOGAN

CHRIS MELLOR

Egypt offers interesting alternatives when it comes to getting around – drift down the Nile on an ancient felucca, take to the sky in a hot-air balloon at the Valley of the Kings, get to know the locals in 3rd class train travel or trek through the Sinai astride a 'ship of the sands'.

the 210-member Majlis ash-Shura (Advisory Council).

ECONOMY

Egypt remains a big exporter of cotton, the crop introduced to the country in the 19th century by its reformist-minded ruler Mohammed Ali. It continues to sell 1½ times what the USA sells overseas. The country is also a net exporter of oil, and more oil and gas finds in the Western Desert have boosted hopes of continuing export profits to be made from that sector. Despite the vicious blows dealt to it by recent terrorist attacks, tourism is also a major component in the backbone of the economy, not just because it puts US$1 billion a year into the government's coffers but also because so many small businesses and individual livelihoods depend on the continued coach-loads of foreign visitors. Above all, Egypt's largest single foreign currency earner is the Suez Canal – dues from commercial users now amount to more than US$2 billion per year.

These represent Egypt's traditional revenue earners, but since the mid-1990s the face of the country's economy has been undergoing a rapid change. In recent times the excited talk is of Egypt being one of the world's most attractive emerging markets, with great potential for fast growth. The change has been brought about by a seeming 'road to Damascus' type conversion at the highest levels. After decades of subsidising unproductive and over-staffed state-owned industries, the government has begun dismantling the Nasserist system of central planning, selling off businesses and introducing packages of liberalising reforms to encourage foreign investment.

The new policies paid immediate dividends and in 1996 more than US$500 million flowed into the Cairo stock exchange, while foreign investment increased by a factor of almost 150%. While the last 18 months have been a becalming of the bourse and the business community, despite the Luxor massacre, global crisis and falling oil prices, Egypt's economic stability has managed to hold firm.

New money is well in evidence: in recent times Rolls Royce has set up a showroom in Cairo, hot on the heels of Jaguar; a new Nile-side apartment block in Giza offers three-bedroom units at a starting price of US$1.3 million; and a rash of US-style shopping malls is springing up around town filled with designer clothes stores, Continental confectioners and sushi bars.

All this comes with its own problems. As part of its reform program the government is also committed to cutting subsidies on housing, food, electricity, and transport. The less well-off – and that's by far the greater part of Egyptian society – are soon going to be wondering why the cost of their daily bread is rising while they're seeing more and more luxury cars on the roads. This isn't yet Brazil, but with the present absence of any real wealth redistribution, Egypt is looking at a startling widening of the rich-poor divide.

POPULATION

Egypt is the most populous country in the Arab world and has the second highest population in Africa after Nigeria. Its population has, in a sense, become its greatest problem – see Urban Issues in the Ecology & Environment section earlier in this chapter. From about 6½ million people at the first census in 1882, the population was counted at 61½ million in 1997. It is predicted by some to reach 65 million by the year 2000. With annual growth of about 2.1% – or more than a million new bodies every year – it hardly seems to matter what Egypt does to improve its economic situation, the gains are always eaten up by the extra mouths to feed and people to house.

Something like 99% of the population occupies only 4% to 6% of the total surface area of the country, which corresponds to the cultivable area. About 16½ million people, or 27% of the population, live in the greater Cairo area (so there are more Cairenes than there are Austrians, Belgians or Greeks), with about a further five million in Alexandria and outlying zones.

One result of the rapid population growth is that half the population is now under 18 years, and the government hasn't been able to construct schools and train teachers quickly enough to keep up.

PEOPLE

Anthropologists divide the Egyptian people very roughly into three racial groups, of which the biggest is descended from the Hamito-Semitic race that has peopled the Nile (as well as many other parts of north Africa and neighbouring Arabia) for millennia. Included in this race are the Berbers, a minority group who settled around Siwa in the country's Western Desert. The second group, the truly Arab element, is made up of the Bedouin Arab nomads who migrated from Arabia and who also live in desert areas, particularly Sinai. The third group are the Nubians, in the Aswan area. Of course there has been much intermingling and many other peoples have come and gone, leaving their own contributions.

Berbers

A small number of Berbers who settled in the west of the country, particularly in and around Siwa, have retained much of their own identity. They are quite easily distinguished from other Egyptians by, for instance, the dress of the women – usually in *meliyyas*, head-to-toe garments with slits for the eyes. Although many speak Arabic, they have preserved their own language.

Bedouins

The nomadic lifestyle of the 500,000 Bedouins of Egypt is rapidly changing as the 20th century encroaches on the age-old customs of these desert people. Traditionally they lived in the harshest, most desolate parts of the Western and Eastern deserts and Sinai but the interests of the rest of the country are increasingly intruding into their previously isolated domains. The Western Desert oases have long been slated for massive agricultural development and resettlement to ease urban overcrowding, and there are also plans to increase tourism in this region. The same goes for Sinai, plans to begin resettlement programs are being drawn up, and as tourism and hotel projects continue to spring up along the Sinai coasts the Bedouins are gradually becoming more settled and less self-sufficient.

Most of their ancestors came from the Arabian peninsula, however, the Bedouins' laws, customs and religion (which blend Islamic and pagan beliefs), as well as their resilience and amazing hospitality, were born of their lifestyle in Sinai and the Libyan Desert – the isolation, the harsh, dry climate and the need to keep moving in search of water.

Nowadays, you may see the traditional Bedouin goatskin tents and camels in Sinai, but you'll see more pick-up trucks and settlements of crude cement huts, or palm-frond shacks, with corrugated roofs and TV antennae.

Nubians

Tall and with darker skin than the average Egyptian, the Nubians are the bridge between Egypt and Africa. They originate from Nubia, the region between Aswan in the south of Egypt and Khartoum in Sudan, a land that almost completely disappeared in the 1970s when the High Dam was created and the subsequent build-up of water behind it drowned their traditional lands. See the Lake Nasser & Lower Nubia section in The Nile Valley – Esna to Abu Simbel chapter.

EDUCATION

Although nine years of primary school education are supposedly compulsory in Egypt, and about 97% of children from six to 15 attend school, the adult illiteracy rate was estimated by UNESCO to be 50% in 1992. To westerners that may seem startlingly high, but 16 years earlier the level was 61.8%. Two-thirds of Egypt's illiterates are women.

Those who are literate have usually received inferior education because classes are often too large for individual attention.

Secondary education lasts for six years, beginning at 11 years of age. Education is free at all levels, which is perhaps why it is not uncommon to find lawyers, engineers and other professionals working for their brother's factory or driving taxis – there is often nothing for Egypt's educated to do. Many of its professionals (and a good number of its less educated people) are compelled to seek work in other Arab countries – more than two million are said to be abroad, the bulk of them in the Gulf States, Libya and, despite harassment, in Iraq.

Males have to do three years' military service; if they complete high school it's two; if they go through university it's dropped to one. Only-sons are exempt from service.

ARTS
Literature
Naguib Mahfouz is not just the most famous Egyptian writer of all time, he can also claim to have single-handedly shaped the nature of Arabic literature this century. Born in 1911 in Cairo's Islamic quarter (see the boxed text 'Mahfouz's Cairo' on page 168) Mahfouz began writing when he was 17. His first efforts were very much influenced by European models, but over the course of his 66-year writing career (brutally terminated by a would-be assassin – see the boxed text 'A Lesson to Salman Rushdie' on this page) he developed a voice that was uniquely of the Arab world and that drew its inspiration from the talk in the coffeehouses and the dialect and slang of Cairo's streets.

His masterpiece is usually considered to be *The Cairo Trilogy*, a generational saga of family life set in the districts of Mahfouz's youth, but also well worth reading are *Midaq Alley*, a soap operatic portrayal of life in a poor back-alley in Islamic Cairo, and *The Harafish*, perhaps the definitive Mahfouz book, written in an episodic, almost folkloric style that owes much to the tradition of *The Thousand and One Nights*.

On the strength of what's available in English it's all too easy to view Egyptian literature as beginning and ending with Mahfouz, but he's only the best known of a canon of respected writers that includes Taha Hussein, a blind author and intellectual who spent much of his life in trouble with whichever establishment happened to

A Lesson to Salman Rushdie

The Nobel Prize for Literature awarded to Naguib Mahfouz for his lifetime's body of work, also, ironically, precipitated the end of his writing career. The publicity attendant to the prize revived the long dormant issue of his novel *Children of the Alley*, which, upon its newspaper serialisation in 1959, had been condemned by religious authorities for its alleged allegorical depictions of Allah and his prophets. Four months after Mahfouz was thrust into the limelight by the Nobel committee, blind Sheikh Omar Abdel Rahman – currently imprisoned in the US for involvement in the World Trade Building bombing – was widely reported as saying that if Mahfouz had been punished when he wrote *Children of the Alley* then Salman Rushdie would never have dared write *The Satanic Verses*.

For a small extremist minority this was as good as a *fatwa* against Mahfouz. On one October afternoon in 1994, as the writer was climbing into a friend's car outside his home, he was approached by a young man who drew a knife and stabbed his victim twice in the neck. Mahfouz miraculously survived but the attack left his right arm and hand paralysed and he can now write little more than his own name.

Non-Arabic readers, however, still have the pleasure of more Mahfouz to come. Only half of his 40 or so novels and short story collections have so far been translated into English. Many of the rest are scheduled to appear over the next few years as part of an ambitious publishing program shared between the American University in Cairo Press and Anchor/Doubleday in the US.

be in power, and Yousef Idris, a writer of powerful short stories based on the experiences in his own life. Unfortunately, neither of these authors (both now dead) has gained anything like the international attention they deserve and they're only published in English-language editions by the AUC Press, a small Cairo-based academic publishing house.

Of Mahfouz's peers, only Gamal al-Ghitani has achieved anything in the way of widespread acclaim with *Zayni Barakat*, a tale of intrigue in Mamluk-era Cairo that was picked up in translation by major US and UK publishing houses.

Curiously, though under-represented at home, Egypt's women writers are arguably enjoying more international success than the men. After Mahfouz, the country's best known writer abroad is Nawal al-Saadawi, whose most popular fictional work *Woman At Point Zero* has been published, at last count, in 28 languages. An outspoken critic on behalf of women, she is very much marginalised at home – her nonfiction book *The Hidden Face of Eve*, which considers the role of women in the Arab world, is banned in Egypt.

Equally as forthright and uncompromising is Salwa Bakr, another writer who tackles taboo subjects like sexual prejudice and social inequality. Her sole novel available in English *The Golden Chariot* tells the stories of a group of women prison inmates driven to transgress the law through poverty and oppression. It's a surprisingly warm hearted and funny book, and definitely recommended.

One other writer worth mentioning here is Ahdaf Soueif. Though Egyptian she's something of an anomaly in that she writes in English and, so far, most of her work has yet to appear in Arabic. Her 790-page coming-of-age (and highly autobiographical) novel about a middle class Cairene girl *In the Eye of the Sun* and her two short-story collections *Aisha* and *Sandpiper* flit between grey, drizzly London, where she has lived for many years, and the close, muggy city of her birth. The predominant theme of much of her work is, unsurprisingly, the notion of foreignness.

Painting

While Egypt has produced one or two outstanding painters, contemporary art is very much in the doldrums. The problem stems from the Egyptian art school system, where a student's success largely depends on their ability to emulate the artistic styles favoured or practiced by their professors. Nepotism reigns over originality and as a result much of what finds its way into the galleries is of very dubious merit. Unsurprisingly, some of the most interesting work comes from artists with no formal training at all. Such artists are often shunned by the state-run galleries but there are several private exhibition spaces that are happy to show nonconformist work. Anyone seriously interested in contemporary art should visit the Mashrabia, Cairo-Berlin or Extra galleries in Cairo (see that chapter for addresses and opening times).

Things have not always been so stagnant and it is worth paying a visit to Cairo's Museum of Modern Art in the Opera House grounds in Gezira. In particular look out for the work of Abdel Hady al-Gazzar, a true one-off, who painted Egypt as a kind of colourful but slightly freakish circus. The rich, warm portraits of Alexandrian Mahmoud Said, several of which hang in the museum, are also quite beautiful.

For more information there's a good book by Lilliane Karnouk, *Modern Egyptian Art*, or pick up Fatma Ismail's *29 Artists in the Museum of Egyptian Modern Art*; both are available at the art museum and at the Mashrabia gallery. There's also a Web site (www.egyptart.org.eg) with a growing gallery of contemporary Egyptian art accompanied by brief biographies.

Music

Unlike literature and painting, which are take it or leave it affairs, there's no getting away from music in Egypt. Taking a taxi, shopping or just walking the streets; the routines of daily life are played out to a constant musical accompaniment blasted from wheezing, tinny cassette players. The music you hear can be broadly divided into two categories: classical and pop. Down in the south of the country you're also likely to come across some more regional music types – see the boxed texts 'Saidi Music' on page 315 and 'Nubian Music' on page 348.

Classical Classical Arabic music peaked in the 1940s and 50s. It fitted the age. These were the golden days of a rushing tide of nationalism and then, later, of Nasser's rule when Cairo was the virile heart of the Arab-speaking world. Its singers were icons and through the radio their impassioned words captured and inflamed the spirits of listeners from Algiers to Baghdad. Chief icon of all was Umm Kolthum, the most famous Arab singer of the 20th century. Her protracted love songs and *qasa'id* (long poems) were the very expression of the Arab world's collective identity. Egypt's love affair with Umm Kolthum was such that on the afternoon of the first Thursday of each month, streets would become deserted as the whole country sat beside a radio to listen to her regular live-broadcast performance.

She had her male counterparts in Abdel Halim Hafez and Farid al-Attrache but they never attracted anything like the devotion accorded to 'the Mother of Egypt'. She sang well into the mid-1970s, and when she died in 1975 her death caused havoc with millions of grieving Egyptians pouring out onto the streets of Cairo.

Her cassettes still sell as well now as any platinum pop and her presence is strongly felt in the media, including a radio station that broadcasts four hours of her music daily. Her appeal hasn't been purely confined to the Arab world either; former Led Zeppelin vocalist Robert Plant was reported as saying that one of his lifetime ambitions was to reform the Middle Eastern Orchestra, Umm Kolthum's group of backing musicians.

The kind of orchestra in question is a curious cross-fertilisation of east and west, with the instruments familiar to western ears augmented by the *oud* (a type of lute), *nai* (reed pipe), *qanun* (zither) and *tabla* (a small hand-held drum).

It's now fairly easy to find Umm Kolthum CDs in western music stores – look out in particular for *Inta Omri*, which is considered by many to be her finest performance.

Umm Kolthum's voice would regularly bring Cairo to a standstill until her death in 1975. She lives on in taxis everywhere.

Pop Although to this day the likes of Umm Kolthum and Abdel Halim Hafez are still eulogised and revered, as Egypt experienced a population boom and the mean age decreased, a gap in popular culture developed which the memory of the greats couldn't fill. Enter Ahmed Adawiyya, who did for Arabic music what punk did in the west. Throwing out traditional melodies and melodramas, his backstreet, streetwise and, to some, politically subversive songs captured the spirit of the time and dominated popular culture throughout the entire 1970s.

Adawiyya set the blueprint for a new kind of music known as *al-jeel* (the generation), characterised by a clattering, hand-clapping rhythm overlaid with synthesised twirling and a catchy, repetitive vocal. Adawiyya's legacy also spawned something called *shaabi* (from the word for popular), which is considered the real music of the working class; it's much cruder than al-jeel and its lyrics are often satirical or politically provocative. Shaabi artists rarely make it onto TV.

In recent years the biggest selling artists come from Iraq, Syria or Lebanon. Of the home-grown talent, the top names (the industry is solo vocal artist oriented, there are no pop groups) are Hakim, Amr Diab and Mohammed Fuad, but selling half a million albums in Cairo doesn't mean that their tapes are accessible to unattuned western ears. Despite constant exposure in taxis, shops and on the street, Egyptian pop is an acquired taste and one that few non-Arabs pick up.

Dance

Tomb paintings in Egypt prove that the tradition of formalised dancing goes back as far as the pharaohs. During medieval times dancing became institutionalised in the form of the *ghawazee*, a cast of dancers who travelled with storytellers and poets and performed publicly or for hire, rather like the troubadours of medieval Europe. Performances were often segregated, with women dancers either performing for other women or appearing before men veiled.

A Beginners Guide to Egyptian Pop

The list below is not based on best-sellers or the best cassettes, it is purely a sample of the vast array of sounds available.

Zahma, by Ahmed Adawiyya. From the 1970s when Adawiyya's irreverent backstreet sound was at the peak of its popularity. The title means 'crowded'.

Shababik or *Al-Malek*, by Mohammed Mounir. Dubbed the 'thinking person's pop star' Mounir, a Nubian, fuses traditional Arabic music with jazz to create a fairly sophisticated sound that's very accessible to western ears.

Nazra, by Hakim, one of the most popular shaabi singers of the moment. This is his first and best album.

Lo Laki, by Ali Hameida. Lo Laki (Without You) dominated Cairo for several years after its release in 1988. It was the song that crystallised the al-jeel formula – rasping synthesiser and catchy, nonsensical lyrics. Listen at your peril.

Alimouni Hawak, by Amr Diab. A huge hit in 1998 throughout the Middle East for the golden boy of Egyptian pop.

Omar Khayrat, primarily a composer of scores for films and TV, Khayrat's music mixes classical and Arabic motifs to create what some would call Egyptian lift music.

Yalla, compiled by David Lodge. A cassette/CD compilation of Egyptian street music of which half is al-jeel, half shaabi. It has excellent sleeve notes. Released by Mango Records (1990) a division of Island.

Songs From The City Victorious, a collaboration between Jaz Coleman (Killing Joke), Anne Dudley (Art of Noise) and a bunch of Egyptian musicians – the Egyptians like it so much that it's all over state TV. It's available on cheap cassette in Egypt under the name 'Masryat'.

Diaspora, by Natacha Atlas. Another east-west collaboration, this time between trance vocalist Atlas and her band and a bunch of Cairo musicians. It's successful only in parts.

The last three are not available in Cairo but major stores in the west such as Tower, HMV or Virgin should stock or at least be able to order them.

The arrival of 19th century European travellers irrevocably changed this tradition. Religious authorities, outraged that Muslim women were performing for 'infidel' men, pressured the government to impose heavy taxes on the dancers. When the high prices failed to stop the western thrill seekers, the dancers were banished from Cairo. Cut off from most of their clientele, many turned to prostitution to survive. For intrepid male travellers, this only increased their lure and they went out of their way to fulfil their erotic fantasies. One of the most famous was Gustave Flaubert, whose infamous account of his journey to Esna in pursuit of a well-known dancer/prostitute (see Books in the Facts for the Visitor chapter) titillated Victorian Europeans and helped cement the less-than-respectable reputation of Egyptian dance.

Belly-dancing as we see it today began to gain credibility and popularity in Egypt with the advent of cinema, when dancers were lifted out of nightclubs and put on the screen before mass audiences. The cinema imbued belly-dancing with glamour and made household names of a handful of dancers. It also borrowed liberally from Hollywood, adopting Tinseltown's fanciful costumes of hip-hugging bikini bottoms and swathes of diaphanous veils.

Also imported from the western movie industry was the modern phenomenon of the belly-dancer as a superstar capable of commanding Hollywood-style fees for an appearance. Such is the present-day earning power of the top dancers that in 1997 a series of court cases was able to haul in E£900 million in back taxes from 12 of the country's top artists.

Despite its long history and the wealth of some of its practitioners, belly-dancing is still not considered completely respectable and, according to many aficionados, is slowly dying out. In the early 1990s, Islamist conservatives patrolled weddings in poor areas of Cairo and forcibly prevented women from dancing or singing, cutting off a vital source of income for lower echelon performers. In an attempt to placate the religious right, the government joined in and declared that bare midriffs, cleavage and thighs were out. At the same time a number of high-profile entertainers donned the veil and retired, denouncing their former profession as sinful. Since then, bellies have once more been bared but the industry has not recovered. For information on where to see belly-dancing see the Entertainment section in the Cairo chapter.

Away from the glitz of the professional scene, dance in Egypt survives at a grassroots level where it is known as *raqs sharqi* (eastern dancing). Visit the humblest of weddings and you'll witness the unmarried girls moving to the tabla beat, hands clasped above their heads and pelvises gyrating – to attract a groom of their own? When the women are not around, men are often just as skilful at moving to the beat.

Also keeping the dance alive is its popularity abroad: belly-dancing is the one native Egyptian art form to have been successfully exported worldwide, reaching nightschools and community centres where Tutankhamun has yet to be heard of.

Belly-dancing and raqs sharqi are exclusively female pursuits but there is also a male dance performed with wooden staves. Called *tahtib*, it looks something like a stylised, slow motion martial art. It can be seen at moulids in Upper Egypt and is often part of the folkloric shows on the five star hotel circuit.

Sufi Dancing In its true form this isn't dancing but a form of worship. The Sufis are adherents of a Muslim mystic order who spin and whirl to attain a trance-like state of devotion. There's a Sufi troupe that performs regularly in Islamic Cairo – see Entertainment in the Cairo chapter for details.

Film

In the halcyon years of the 1940s and 50s Cairo's film studios would be turning out more than 100 movies annually, filling cinemas throughout the Arab world. These days, the average number of films made is around 20 a year. The chief reason for the decline, according to the producers, is excessive government taxation and restrictive censorship. Asked what sort of things they censor, one film industry figure replied, 'Sex, politics, religion … that's all'. However, at least one Cairo film critic has suggested that another reason for the demise of local film is that so much of what is made is trash. The ingredients of the typical Egyptian film are moronic slapstick humour, over-the-top acting and perhaps a little belly-dancing.

There are exceptions. Every year one or two films come out which do display artistic skill and quite often handle social themes of a controversial nature. The one director who consistently stands apart from the mainstream detritus is Yousef Chahine. Born in 1926, he's directed 37 films to date in a career that defies classification. Accorded messiah-like status by critics at home (though he's far from being a huge hit with the general public), he's been called Egypt's Fellini and he was honoured at Cannes in 1997 with a lifetime achievement award. Chahine's films are also some of the very few Egyptian productions that are ever subtitled into English or French, and they regularly do the rounds of international film festivals. His most recent works are 1997's *Al-Masir* (Destiny) and from three years earlier *Al-Muhagir* (The Emigrant), effectively banned in Egypt because of Islamist claims that it portrays scenes from the life of the Prophet. Others to look out for are *Al-Widaa Bonaparte* (Adieu Bonaparte), a historical drama about the French occupation, and *Iskandariyya Ley?* (Alexandria Why?), an autobiographical meditation on the Mediterranean city of Chahine's birth.

For anyone wondering what happened to Omar Sherif, star of *Dr Zhivago* and *Lawrence of Arabia*, he's living in Cairo making very poor films for the local market and appearing in TV ads pushing ceramic tiles.

Architecture

The rich heritage of pharaonic-era buildings is discussed at length throughout this book, as well as specifically in the Pharaonic Egypt section, but there is another side to monumental Egypt that often passes less noticed: Cairo is one of the greatest repositories in the world of medieval Islamic architecture.

Medieval Islamic Starting with the Mosque of Amr (827 AD), the earliest existent Islamic structure in Cairo, it's possible to trace the unbroken development of Muslim architecture through more than a thousand years and a succession of dynasties.

The earliest Islamic constructions inherited much from Christian and Graeco-Roman models. However, various styles soon developed that owed increasingly less to their architectural forebears. The Fatimids (969 to 1171), for example, were the first to introduce the use of the dome and the keel arch, the pointed arch that has come to typify Islamic architecture. They also introduced the use of heavy stone masonry, where previously mud-brick and stucco had been the main building materials. The Ayyubids (1171 to 1250) did little to advance on these techniques, though Salah ad-Din made good use of stone in constructing the walls of the Citadel.

From these beginnings, the vocabulary of Islamic architecture quickly became very sophisticated and expressive, reaching its apotheosis under the Mamluks (1250 to 1517). The Mamluks extended the types of buildings to include not only mosques, walls and gates but also *madrassas* (theological schools), *khanqahs* (Sufi monasteries) and mausoleum complexes. Their buildings are typically characterised by the banding of red and white stone (a technique known as *ablaq*) and by the elaborate stalactite carvings *(muqarnas)* and patterning around windows and in the recessed portals. The Mamluks were also responsible for the transformation of the minaret from a squat, stubby, often square tower, into the slender cylindrical thing that is the typical Cairo minaret, and they nurtured stone dome carving into a fine art (shown at its best in some of the monuments in Cairo's Northern Cemetery).

When the Ottoman Turks defeated the Mamluks and took control of Egypt, they brought their own architectural styles from Constantinople. But there were to be no grand mosques like that city's Haga Sophia or Blue Mosque. Egypt was a distant province and as such any new buildings were small in scale: practical structures like houses, merchants' hostels and public works like fountains and schools. Cairo's handful of Ottoman era mosques are modest, though instantly recognisable by their slim pencil-shaped minarets. This imported style fell out of favour toward the end of the 19th century as Egypt pulled free of Constantinople; since that time the Mamluk style has regained popularity as the model for the design of new mosques.

SOCIETY & CONDUCT

There's no simple definition of Egyptian society. On the one hand there's traditional conservatism, reinforced by poverty, in which the diet is one of *fuul, ta'amiyya* and vegetables; women wear the long black, all-concealing *abeyyas* and men *galabiyyas*; cousins marry; going to Alexandria constitutes the trip of a lifetime; and all is 'God's will'. On the other hand, there are sections of society who order out from McDonald's; whose daughters wear little black slinky numbers and flirt outrageously; who think nothing of regular trips to the USA; and who never set foot in a mosque until the day they're laid out in one.

While this latter group is definitely in the minority, due to their money and status they exert an influence on society vastly disproportionate to their numbers. Occasionally there is a backlash, as in 1997 when around 80 sons and daughters of the westernised elite were rounded up on charges of Satan worshipping. They were accused of drinking the blood of rats, digging up corpses and burning the Quran when in reality all they had done was listen to western music, dress like kids of the MTV generation, and enjoy access to satellite TV and the Internet. Within two weeks they were all released without charges.

The bulk of the Egyptian populace falls somewhere between these two extremes.

City Life

The make-up of Egypt's towns and cities is predominantly working class. The typical family lives in the hemmed-in side streets of an overcrowded suburb in a six floor breeze-block apartment building with cracking walls and dodgy plumbing. If they're lucky they may own a small Fiat or Lada which will be 10 or more years old. Otherwise the husband will take the Metro to work or, more likely, fight for a handhold on one of the city's sardine-can buses. He may well be a university graduate (about 40,000 people graduate each year), although that is no longer any guarantee of a job. He may well also be one of the million-plus paper-pushing civil servants, earning a pittance to while away each day in an undemanding job. This at least allows him to slip away early each afternoon to borrow his cousin's taxi for a few hours and bring in some much needed supplementary income. His wife remains at home each day cooking, looking after the three or more children, and swapping visits with his mother, her mother and various other family members.

The aspirations of this family are to move up the social scale. With no class system as such or aristocracy, movement upwards is completely dependent on money. In the 1970s, Sadat's free market policies resulted in a rapid influx of wealth, which laid the foundations for a 'middle class' that had never previously existed in Egyptian society.

At the other end of the scale are the masses of *fellaheen* (farmers), who traditionally have moved to the city to escape the poverty of working the land. They end up living in 'unplanned housing', make-shift shanty towns that fringe Egypt's bigger cities. If they're lucky they find employment as construction labourers or as *bawwabs*, doormen to middle-class apartment blocks.

Country Life

Just more than half of Egypt's population lives in rural areas, and the popular image of the countryside is of galabiyya-clad peasant farmers, the fellaheen, working the land much as they have since the time of their pharaonic forebears, holding onto their traditions in the face of Egypt's growing westernisation. Reality is less simple.

Life in rural Egypt at the end of the 20th century is undergoing an immense transformation. The population density on Egypt's agricultural land, on which most cities and villages are built, is one of the highest in the world. What little land remains is divided into small plots averaging just 1.5 acres, which does not support even a medium-sized family. As many as 50% of the rural population no longer make their living off the land. For those who do, the small size of their plots prevents the mechanisation needed to increase yields and they increasingly rely on animal husbandry or are forced to look for other ways of surviving. So the *fellah* you see working his field is probably spending his afternoons working as a labourer or selling cigarettes in a home-made kiosk in an effort to make ends meet. He knows there's no hope of finding work in the cities; the migration to urban areas that took place in the 1970s and 80s has all but stopped and the country's 5000 villages have swollen to an average population of 10,000.

Still, for all the changes, the countryside remains the repository of traditional culture and values. Large families are still the norm, particularly in Upper Egypt, where government family planning campaigns have had far less effect than in the rest of the country. Extended families still live together in the same house, building additions as sons get married and have children. The houses used to be made of mud-brick and shelter animals as well as people, but increasingly peasants are building in red brick and concrete with separate pens for animals.

Rural traditions are at their strongest when it comes to women. High rates of female illiteracy are the norm in much of the countryside and women dress conservatively, often with long black overdresses worn on top of long dresses. Heads are almost always covered, although among peasants the head-scarf is worn to protect hair and is often worn by Christians as well as Muslims.

Whether all this will change with the steady diet of urban Cairene values and western soap operas that is currently beamed into village cafes and farmhouses each night remains to be seen.

Dos & Don'ts

Dress Although this is dealt with under Women Travellers in the Facts for the Visitor chapter, dressing prudently is just as much a male issue. In places less used to tourists, the sight of a man in shorts is considered offensive, while in Cairo, you'll be looked at like someone who's forgotten to put his trousers on. Count the number of Egyptian men in shorts.

Drink While alcohol is *haram* (forbidden) in the eyes of many Muslims, it is tolerated by most, drunk by a fair few, and quite freely available throughout most of the country. That said, getting blasted is not a widespread national pastime. It is advisable not to go reeling around Egypt's streets otherwise you may end up cooling your heels in a police cell.

RELIGION

About 90% of Egypt's population are Muslims; most of the rest are Coptic Christians. Generally speaking the two communities enjoy a more or less easy coexistence. Though western newspapers from time to time run stories claiming that Copts are a persecuted minority, virtually all prominent Christians in Egypt insist they are neither persecuted nor a minority. Intermarrying between Christians and Muslims is forbidden.

Islam

Islam is the predominant religion of Egypt. It shares its roots with two of the world's other major religions – Judaism and Christianity. Adam, Abraham (Ibrahim), Noah, Moses and Jesus are all accepted as Muslim prophets, although Jesus is not recognised as the son of God. Muslim teachings correspond closely to the Torah (the first five chapters of the Old Testament and the foundation of the Jewish religion) and the Gospels. The essence of Islam is the Quran (or Koran) and the Prophet Mohammed who was the last and truest prophet to deliver messages from Allah to the people.

Islam was founded in the early 7th century by Mohammed, who was born around 570 AD in Mecca (now in Saudi Arabia). Mohammed received his first divine message at about the age of 40. The revelations continued for the rest of his life and they were transcribed to become the holy Quran. To this day not one dot of the Quran has been changed, making it, Muslims claim, the direct word of Allah.

Mohammed's teachings were not an immediate success. He started preaching in 613 AD, three years after the first revelation, but could only attract a few dozen followers. Having attacked the ways of Meccan life, especially the worship of a wealth of idols, he made many enemies. In 622 he and his followers retreated to Medina, an oasis town some 360km from Mecca. This *hejira*, or migration, marks the start of the Muslim calendar.

Mohammed died in 632 AD but the new religion continued its rapid spread, reaching all of Arabia by 634 AD and Egypt in 642 AD.

Islam means 'submission' and this principle is visible in the daily life of Muslims. The faith is expressed by observance of the five so-called pillars of Islam. Muslims must:

1. Publicly declare that 'there is no God but Allah and Mohammed is his Prophet'.
2. Pray five times a day: at sunrise, noon, mid-afternoon, sunset, and night.
3. Give *zakat*, alms, for the propagation of Islam and to help the needy.
4. Fast during daylight hours during the month of Ramadan.
5. Complete the *haj*, the pilgrimage to Mecca.

The first pillar is accomplished through prayer, which is the second pillar. Prayer is an essential part of the daily life of a believer. Five times a day the muezzins bellow out the call to prayer through speakers on top of the minarets. It is perfectly permissible to pray at home or elsewhere – only the noon prayer on Friday should be conducted in the mosque. It is preferred that women pray at home. (For information about Islamic holidays and festivals, see Public Holidays in the Facts for the Visitor chapter.)

The ultimate Islamic authority in Egypt is the Sheikh of Al-Azhar, a position currently held by Mohammed Sayyed Tantawi. It is the role of the supreme Sheikh to define the official Islamic line on any particular matter from organ donations to heavy-metal music.

Coptic Christianity

Before the arrival of Islam, Christianity was the predominant religion in Egypt. St Mark, companion of the apostles Paul and Peter, began preaching Christianity in Egypt around 35 AD and although it didn't become the official religion of the country until the 4th century, Egypt was one of the first countries to embrace the new faith.

Egyptian Christians split from the orthodox church of the Eastern (or Byzantine) Empire, of which Egypt was then a part, after the main body of the church described Christ as both human and divine. Dioscurus, the patriarch of Alexandria, refused to accept this description. He embraced the theory that Christ is totally absorbed by his divinity and that it is blasphemous to consider him human. Since that time, Egyptian Christians have been referred to as Coptic Christians. The term 'Copt' is derived from the Greek word *Aegyptios* (meaning Egyptian), which the Arabs transliterated and eventually shortened to Copt.

The Coptic Church is ruled by a patriarch (presently Pope Shenouda), other members of the religious hierarchy, and an ecclesiastical council of laypeople. It has a long history of monasticism and can justly claim that the first Christian monks, St Anthony and St Pachomius, were Copts. The Coptic language is still used in religious ceremonies, sometimes in conjunction with Arabic for the benefit of the congregation. It has its origins in several Egyptian hieroglyphs and Ancient Greek. Today, the Coptic

The Mosque & How it Functions

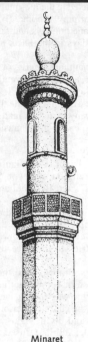

Embodying the Islamic faith, and representing its most predominant architectural feature is the mosque, or *masgid* or *gamaa*.

The house belonging to the Prophet Mohammed is said to have provided the prototype for the mosque. The original setting was an enclosed oblong courtyard with huts (housing Mohammed's wives) along one wall and a rough portico providing shade. This plan developed with the courtyard becoming the *sahn*, the portico the arcaded *riwaqs* and the houses the *haram* or prayer hall.

Typically divided into a series of aisles, the centre aisle in the prayer hall is wider than the rest and leads to a vaulted niche in the wall called the *mihrab*, which indicates the direction of Mecca, which Muslims must face when they pray.

Islam does not have priests as such. The closest equivalent is the mosque's *imam*, a man schooled in Islam and Islamic law. He often doubles as the *muezzin*, who calls the faithful to prayer from the tower of the minaret – except these days recorded cassettes and loud speakers do away with the need for him to climb up there. At the main Friday noon prayers, the imam gives

Minaret

Mihrab

language is based on the Greek alphabet with an additional seven characters taken from hieroglyphs.

The Copts have long provided something of an educated elite in Egypt, filling many important government and bureaucratic posts, and they've always been an economically powerful minority. Internationally, the most famous Copt today is the former United Nations secretary-general, Boutros Boutros Ghali.

Other Creeds

Other Christian denominations are represented in Egypt, each by a few thousand adherents, or sometimes fewer. In total, there are about one million members of other Christian groups. Among Catholics, apart from Roman Catholics of the Latin rite, the whole gamut of the fragmented Middle Eastern rites is represented, including the Armenian, Syrian, Chaldean, Maronite and Melkite rites. The Anglican communion comes under the Episcopal Church in Jerusalem. The Armenian Apostolic Church has 10,000 members, and the Greek Orthodox church is based in Alexandria.

Egypt was formerly home to a significant number of Jews but, from an all-time peak of 80,000, they now number no more than

The Mosque & How it Functions

Kursi

a *khutba* (sermon) from the *minbar*, a wooden pulpit that stands beside the mihrab. In older, grander mosques these minbars are often beautifully decorated.

Before entering the prayer hall and participating in the communal worship, Muslims must perform a ritual washing of hands, forearms and face. For this purpose mosques have traditionally had a large ablutions fountain at the centre of the courtyard, often carved from marble and worn by centuries of use. These days, modern mosques just have rows of taps.

The mosque also serves as a kind of community centre, and often you'll find groups of children or adults receiving lessons (usually in the Quran), people in quiet prayer and others simply dozing – mosques provide wonderfully tranquil havens from the chaos of the street.

Visiting Mosques

With just a couple of exceptions, non-Muslims are quite welcome to visit any mosques in Egypt at any time other than during Friday prayers. (Two of the mosques that can not be entered by non-Muslims are the mosques of Sayyida Zeinab and Al-Hussein in Cairo.) You must dress modestly. For men that means no shorts; for women that means no shorts, tight pants, shirts that aren't done up, or anything else that might be considered immodest. You must also either take off your shoes or use the shoe coverings that are available at most mosques for just a few piastres.

Minbar

---

200. Historical sources record that there were 7000 Jews living in Cairo back as far as 1168 and in Mamluk times there was a Jewish quarter, Haret al-Yahud, in the vicinity of the Al-Azhar mosque. The first four decades of this century constituted something of a golden age for Egyptian Jews as their numbers expanded and they came to play a bigger role in society and the affairs of state. Jews were responsible for the modernisation of the country's finances, including the founding of the national bank, the founding of most of Cairo's great department stores, plus major financial involvement in new urban developments.

The reversal began with the creation of Israel in 1948. Not long after, the exodus received further impetus with the nationalisation that followed Nasser's seizure of power. In the present climate of media-led anti-Israeli hysteria mention of the 'J' word in connection with Egypt is virtually taboo but the evidence is there in Cairo's Ben Ezra and Sharia Adly synagogues, and in synagogues in Alexandria and Minya.

LANGUAGE

Arabic is the official language of Egypt. However, the Arabic spoken on the streets differs greatly from the standard Classical

Arabic written in newspapers, spoken on the radio or recited in prayers at the mosque all throughout the Arab world. Egyptian Colloquial Arabic (ECA) is a dialect of Arabic, but so different in many respects to Classical Arabic as to be virtually another language. As with most dialects, it is the everyday language that differs the most from that of Egypt's other Arabic-speaking neighbours. More specialised or educated language tends to be pretty much the same across the Arab world, although pronunciation may vary considerably. An Arab from, say, Jordan or Iraq, will have no problem having a chat about politics or literature with an Egyptian, but might have trouble making himself understood in the bakery.

For further notes on Egyptian Colloquial Arabic, plus a vocabulary and pronunciation guide, see the Language chapter at the back of the book.

PHARAONIC
EGYPT

TOMB & TEMPLE ARCHITECTURE

Ask anyone what they'd like to see when they visit Egypt and nine times out of 10 they'll mention the Pyramids at Giza, the tombs in the Valley of the Kings or the ruined temples at Luxor and Karnak. It is hardly surprising that today we are fascinated by Egyptian architecture. For 5000 years, people have been gazing in awe and wonder at the temples and tombs of ancient Egypt. However, despite the extreme antiquity of these monuments, scholars believe that they can accurately trace the gradual development of architectural techniques and styles all the way back to the dawn of Egyptian civilisation.

Early Buildings

When people first settled beside the Nile, they built their homes from reeds, mud and palm trees. The appearance and qualities of these materials continued to exert an influence over all facets of Egyptian architecture. The origin of many of the characteristic features of Egypt's stone temples and tombs, including columns, cornices and friezes, can

BETHUNE CARMICHAEL

Box: The silhouette of a pyramid against the evening sky shows the perfect geometry involved in creating these monuments (photo by Tony Wheeler).

Title page: Osiride pillars at the Ramasseum. Each has been carved into a representation of the king in the form of Osiris, god of the underworld (see also page 50).

Left: The columns in the Hall of Khnum's Temple in Esna are carved and painted to represent the palm trunks or bound papyrus stems that supported the roofs of predynastic temples.

BETHUNE CARMICHAEL

Top: Zoser's Step Pyramid at Saqqara rises in six steps to create a structure that served as the prototype for ancient Egypt's most enduring architectural legacy.

JOHN BORTHWICK

Middle: The Pyramid of Meidum represents the architectural transition from the stepped pyramid to the true pyramid. It rises in eight stepped stages which were once encased in a sloping outer face. That outer facing has long since collapsed to reveal the inner stepped tower.

GADI FARFOUR

Bottom: The pyramids of Cheops, Chephren (pictured) and Mycerinus at Giza represent the apex of pyramid building. Pyramids continued to be built after the reign of these pharaohs but their construction became ever more modest in scale as the strength and influence of the pharaohs diminished.

TIM FLOWER

GLENN BEANLAND

JULIET COOMBE / LA BELLE AURORE

Top: Sphinxes line the processional route to the Amun Temple at Karnak.

Middle: The massive pylons of the Temple of Horus at Edfu are carved with huge figures of the gods and the king.

Bottom: Fourteen large columns (to the right of the picture) support the Colonnade of Amenophis III at Luxor Temple. Rising from the centre of the temple are the minarets of the Mosque of Abu al-Haggag.

all be traced back to the way in which the Predynastic wattle-and-daub houses were constructed.

These simple mud houses were made from bundles of rushes and reeds plastered over with mud. The plant stalks that protruded from the wall tops were tied into bundles that later inspired the design of the *kheker* frieze and cavetto cornice, which were often used to decorate the walls of stone buildings. Columns made from palm trunks, or bundles of tall papyrus stems, were often used to support the flat roofs. Their splaying tops were bound with cords and ropes to prevent them splitting. Later stonemasons faithfully imitated the appearance of these columns, first naturalistically but gradually in more stylised forms.

By the Early Dynastic period, larger and more complicated buildings made of mud brick had begun to appear. Due to its strength, versatility and ease of manufacture sun-dried mud brick architecture dominated until the 3rd dynasty. Eventually, mud brick was replaced by stone as the prefered material for the construction of temples and tombs – buildings that could 'endure forever'. However, domestic architecture, royal palaces, fortresses and the walls of temple precincts continued to be built of mud brick.

One of the most enduring decorative forms that developed from the Early Dynastic mud-brick architecture was the palace-facade niche design which consisted of a succession of square towers projecting either side of a false entrance portal. The great plaza and token palace in front of the Step Pyramid complex at Saqqara is one of the best examples of this design translated into stone.

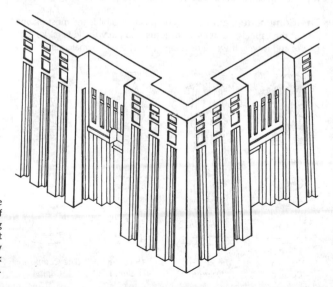

Right: The palace-facade niche design is one of the most enduring decorative forms that developed from the Early Dynastic mud-brick architecture.

Columns

The first stonemasons imitated the forms of early organic columns, even reproducing their swelling bases and rope-bindings, and splaying fronds and lotus and papyrus buds in the capitals. By the Middle Kingdom, other types of columns were being developed that often incorporated depictions of deities.

The Palm Column One of the earliest types of column, the palm column represents eight palm fronds that are gathered and bound, curving to a slender capital. It was commonly used in the Old Kingdom and the later Ptolemaic period.

The Papyrus Column The papyrus column tapers from a thickened base decorated with leaves and stem sheaths that represent the primeval marsh. It was usually seen in colonnaded temple courts and hypostyle halls. A variation of this style, known as the open papyrus column, had a bell-shaped capital and was used during the New Kingdom.

The Lotus Column The Lotus Column is distinguished by a straight shaft crowned by a capital in the shape of a lotus bud or flower. It was commonly used in domestic constructions.

The Osiride Pillar The Osiride pillar was carved with a statue of the king in the form of Osiris. The Osiride pillar maintained its square shape with the addition of the carved mummiform statue decorating one face.

The Composite Capital The composite capital is the most elaborate of the capitals, comprising of lotus and papyrus flowers, wheat, grapes and leaves. It was a development of the Ptolemaic period.

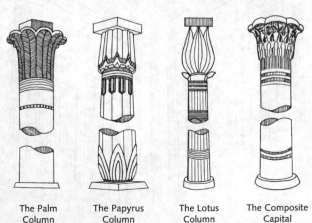

| The Palm Column | The Papyrus Column | The Lotus Column | The Composite Capital |

Funerary Architecture

The earliest Egyptian burials were very different from their well known dynastic descendants, being little more than shallow pits in the desert sometimes containing a few grave goods. Over time, with the desire to create a more protected dwelling for the dead, the graves became deeper and were covered with a mound of rocks and sand. For the majority of the population this continued to be the standard type of burial until modern times. However, with the rise of the belief that the tomb was the 'house of eternity' for the spirit of the deceased, the graves of the wealthy slowly became more and more elaborate.

In order to protect the body and burial goods from grave robbers, the graves of the wealthy were eventually constructed as deep shafts lined with matting, mud brick or wood. Other chambers were added to house growing collections of grave goods. The simple above ground covering mound also increased in size and became a low rectangular mud brick slab-like structure known as a mastaba, meaning 'bench' in Arabic.

Mastabas The building of mastabas was well established by the beginning of the 1st dynasty. By this time, the tomb's covering mud brick superstructure regularly rose to a height of 6m. Inside it was a subterranean labyrinth of storage rooms for grave goods and burial chambers. A stone or wood stele was placed against one of the faces of the early mastabas, acting both as a tombstone and as the focus of the funerary cult. Priests and relatives could come here on certain days and leave offerings on a small altar near the stele.

With the rise to power of the 3rd dynasty and the introduction of stone as a building material at the Step Pyramid complex at Saqqara, more extensive changes to mastaba design developed. Stone replaced the mastaba's mud brick outer-casing and the external offering niche

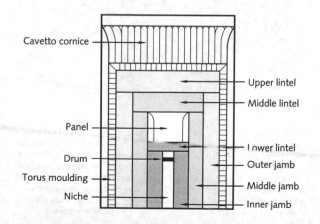

Right: Evolving from the 'tombstone' stelae of early mastabas, the false door stele, it was believed, allowed the ka to pass between the burial chamber and the world of the living.

Cavetto cornice

Upper lintel

Middle lintel

Panel

Lower lintel

Drum

Outer jamb

Torus moulding

Middle jamb

Niche

Inner jamb

was moved to become the focus of a shrine built inside the mastaba superstructure. The contents of the stelae, depicting the deceased sitting at a table laden with offerings of food and beer were transferred to a panel above the false door. Sometimes a ka-statue which represented the deceased stood in front of the false door. Both it and the increasingly detailed reliefs decorating the tombs were meant to ensure that the deceased enjoyed a comfortable existence in the afterworld.

Artwork in tombs represented more than just a decorative record of each individuals' life. Carvings, paintings and statues were meant to guarantee that everything depicted in the tomb would come to life in the afterworld. If the mummy was destroyed it was believed that the ka would continue to survive through the likenesses of the deceased as represented in stone and wood.

Over time, the walls of mastaba tombs were elaborately decorated with painted bas-reliefs. The floor plan also became more complex, expanding to include burial shafts, shrines and storage rooms for other family members. One particular mastaba at Saqqara belonging to Mereruka, a vizier of the first king of the 6th dynasty, had 31 rooms – 21 for his own funerary purposes and the rest for his wife and son.

Pyramids Architecturally, the pyramid exemplified the culmination of the mortuary structures developed from the Early Dynastic period. Egypt's first pyramid, in Pharaoh Zoser's mortuary complex at Saqqara, was a 62m-high marvel of masonry completed in the 27th century BC. In this early model, a series of stone mastabas were placed on top of one another in a graduated design, and sheathed in fine limestone. This was the first time stone had been used to such an extent and with such artistry and precision. It became known as the Step Pyramid. (For further details, see Saqqara in the Around Cairo chapter.) Other step

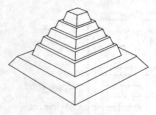

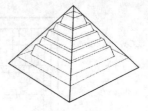

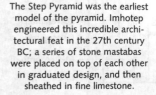

The Step Pyramid was the earliest model of the pyramid. Imhotep engineered this incredible architectural feat in the 27th century BC; a series of stone mastabas were placed on top of each other in graduated design, and then sheathed in fine limestone.

The early models of the true pyramid can be found at Meidum and Dahshur; however, it was at Giza that the style attained its highest form. The true pyramid was built as a Step Pyramid which was then encased in polished stone.

pyramids were built shortly after Zoser's reign, and have been found at Zawiyet el-Mayitin, Sheila, el-Kula, Edfu and on Elephantine Island.

The first true pyramid was built at Meidum at the end of the 3rd dynasty. The style attained its most triumphant form in the great pyramids at Giza. (For further information on the pyramids at Giza, see the Cairo chapter.)

Different theories exist concerning the construction of the pyramids. Some pyramids, like Zoser's Step Pyramid, were solid stone; others had exterior walls supported by masonry and filled with rubble, mud and sand. It is thought that ramps were used to build each level, and were extended as the pyramid rose in height. Another possibility is that great mounds were piled up against the sides of the pyramid and removed after completion. Stones were apparently moved with levers and rollers, and pulleys were used to lift the stone blocks which sealed the entrance and passageways.

A total of about 70 pyramids stretch the length of the Nile as far south as Sudan. Although the age of the pyramids lasted only a few hundred years, for four and a half millennia these ancient structures have inspired, awed and baffled.

Rock-Cut Tombs By the end of the Old Kingdom, an alternate type of tomb architecture was developing in Middle and Upper Egypt. Since the narrow band of the Nile valley left little room to build pyramids or mastabas, the people living in these regions cut their tombs into the rock of the cliffs overlooking the Nile. Originally, most of these tombs were very simple single chambers. However, as was the case with mastabas, the Egyptians gradually developed a more elaborate plan. The design of rock-cut tombs evolved to consist of an open courtyard and entrance facade, which was carved out of the cliff wall, enclosing

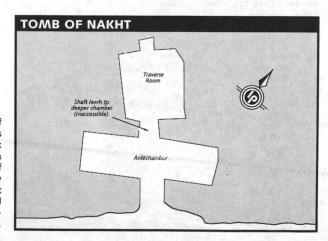

TOMB OF NAKHT

Traverse Room

Shaft leads to deeper chamber (inaccessible)

Antechamber

Right: Nakht was one of Amun's astronomers. His tomb, on the west bank of Luxor, represents a very basic plan typical of the smaller New Kingdom rock-cut tombs. It is noted particularly for its detailed artwork.

an offering shrine. An undecorated burial chamber was excavated at the bottom of a shaft connected to the court or chapel.

The basic plan of New Kingdom rock-cut royal tombs differed little from their predecessors except that they were more elaborate in both their decoration and floor plan. Often comprising a labyrinth of corridors and chambers tunnelling deep into the cliff, they were decorated with images and religious texts meant to smooth the king's passage into the underworld and symbolise his deification. The Tomb of Seti I, 2nd king of the 19th dynasty, is one of the most striking examples, extending 100m into the hillside and containing an impressively decorated barrel-vaulted burial chamber, intended to represent the vault of heaven.

One of the most original developments of the New Kingdom was the decision of the kings of the 18th and 19th dynasties to bury their dead in a remote valley near Thebes, now known as the Valley of the Kings. It seems that the original motive behind the construction of the Valley of the Kings necropolis was tomb security. Unlike earlier funerary monuments, the tombs in the valley were designed to be concealed and never visited by relatives. Funeral cult rituals were carried out instead at a separate mortuary temple which supplanted the tomb's role as a memorial monument – a radical departure from tradition. However, when it became evident that any efforts to maintain the secrecy of tomb locations were fruitless, the pharaohs of the 20th dynasty again marked their tombs with impressive facades.

Tombs of this type continued to be constructed until the middle of the 1st millennium BC, when production slowly ceased. Instead existing rock-cut tombs were reused, becoming the repository for mass burials, initially by descendants of the tomb's original owner, but later by just anyone. By the Graeco-Roman period, it was not unusual for one small tomb to contain 50 bodies.

BETHUNE CARMICHAEL

Left: The eroded hills of the Valley of the Queens are riddled with tunnels and tombs.

Temple Architecture

It is generally accepted, based on hieroglyphic depictions, that the earliest shrines differed little in their outward form from the early houses. Rectangular in plan with their eaves and corners embellished with a concave cornice of tied plant stem bundles, these early temples were distinguished by coloured pennants hanging from wooden flagpoles at their entrances. The tendency of the ancient Egyptians to build later temples at the sites occupied by these early shrines, as well as the habit of each pharaoh of adding his own 'personal touch' to existing structures, has meant that little of the temple architecture that survives today actually predates the New Kingdom. The enormous Temple of Amun at Karnak reflects the culmination of at least 2000 years of architectural reconstruction, from the 12th dynasty onwards. However, the tendency of the ancient Egyptians to archaise means that even the more recent Graeco-Roman temples can be considered stylistic imitations of earlier structures.

Two distinct types of temple developed in ancient Egypt: **cult temples**, the house of the principal god of the region; and **mortuary temples**, dedicated to the worship of the dead king. Originally a simple structure connected to the king's pyramid, mortuary temples developed into huge elaborate complexes during the New Kingdom when they were built away from the pharaoh's tomb. The design of individual mortuary temples was often influenced by the preferences of particular monarchs so these temples do not show the same conformity to a plan as the cult temples do. One of the most original and beautiful mortuary temples is that of Queen Hatshepsut at Deir al-Bahri, near Luxor.

Below: Cult temples were constructed so that rooms became smaller, darker and more mysterious as the sanctuary was approached. Floor heights were raised, ceilings lowered and doorways narrowed to achieve this effect.

Cult Temples Cult temples served as the god's house on earth. Like tombs, they were constructed of stone so that they would last for eternity. A massive mud-brick enclosure wall separated the temple

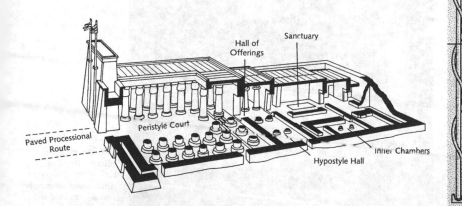

Hall of Offerings

Sanctuary

Peristyle Court

Paved Processional Route

Hypostyle Hall

Inner Chambers

precincts from its surroundings, protecting the consecrated ground from human and supernatural intrusion. Inside this wall lay the temple itself, the priests' residences, the temple workshops and storehouses and the sacred lake, used for ritual ablutions. In the Graeco-Roman period, a *mammisi* or birth house, originally located on the temple roof and dedicated to Osirian rituals of rebirth, was also moved into the grounds.

Art was an integral feature of temple architecture and, as in tomb architecture, was functional as well as decorative. The reliefs and paintings acted both as magical protection against evil influences and also as a guarantee that temple rituals were continually enacted. The various rooms of the temple were decorated in a style that reflected the room's function and ritual significance. For example, the scenes in the brightly lit outer precincts tend to show the king performing public acts and duties, but in the inner regions the scenes change and emphasise the intimate relationship between the king and the god.

Access to the temple and its different sectors was based on an individual's status. Whilse the priests and a few privileged lay people could gather in the temple forecourt, only the king and members of the priesthood were allowed to progress into the temple's darker heart – the domain of the god.

To enter the temple, worshippers would travel along a paved **processional route** – sometimes lined with sphinxes as at the Temple of Amun at Karnak – that led up to the massive pylons guarding the main gateway. Carved with gigantic reliefs of the king smiting Egypt's foes, this huge entrance, the largest part of the temple, served both as a focal point for public processions and as a powerful tool to reinforce the power of the king and his link with the gods. As at the earlier shrines, tall wooden flagpoles sporting brightly coloured pennants symbolising guardian deities were placed in niches in front of the pylons.

TM FLOWER

Left: The massive columns that line the halls of the Temple of Amun form an imposing pathway toward the inner sanctuary.

The majority of Egyptian religious rituals were processional in nature. This is clear from the single axis upon which temples were built. On festival days, worshippers could congregate in the paved courtyard in front of the pylons or, for the privileged few, pass through the pylons to assemble in the peristyle court.

The **peristyle court** consisted of an open courtyard surrounded on three of its sides by a covered colonnade. As a semi-public area, the decoration of this court often featured coronation scenes.

The priestly procession would then move through the three other main temple areas: the hypostyle hall, the inner chambers and the sanctuary or *naos*. Architecturally, the design of the temple changed noticeably as one moved from the bright peristyle court into the succeeding rooms. The temple was planned so that the rooms became smaller, darker and more mysterious as the sanctuary was approached. This effect was achieved by gradually raising the height of the floor, lowering the ceiling and narrowing the doorways.

Separated from the peristyle hall by either a screen wall or raised portico was one of the most imposing parts of the temple, the **hypostyle hall**. This hall, with its massive, towering plant columns lit only by slashes of clerestory lighting, was designed to resemble the primitive ancient forest and marsh surrounding the primeval mound. The number and size of such halls varied – most New Kingdom temples only had one, but by the Graeco-Roman period a second such hall was included in the plan. The columns of hypostyle halls were cleverly positioned so that, when viewed from certain angles, there seems to be no space between them. This hall symbolised the primeval marsh of creation and its decoration was meant to be representative of the whole world: the column capitals and bases displayed aquatic plants; the architraves and ceiling were covered in reliefs of winged discs, stars or astronomical calendars, representing the sky; and the activities of the world, scenes of people bringing gifts and the king making offerings and performing rituals to the god, were depicted on its walls.

From the hypostyle hall a door led into the temple's dimly lit **inner chambers**. On the main axis, often directly behind the hypostyle hall was the small, often columned, **hall of offerings**. Here the daily offerings were prepared before they were offered to the god. The decoration on the walls of different offerings reflects this. Side doors from this hall led, via corridors, into subsidiary chapels, a maze of rooms used for storage and stairways leading to the roof and the crypts.

Representing both the god's home and the primeval mound, the **sanctuary** stood at the highest and most remote part of the temple. This unlit, free-standing shrine, was only accessible to the king or high priest. Inside was the stone naos which supported the god's statue as well as a pedestal for the sacred barque – a boat-shaped shrine in which the god was carried in processions. Its walls were covered with reliefs depicting the king performing every stage of the offering ceremonies, that occurred twice each day.

GODS & GODDESSES

Ancient Egypt produced a wealth of gods and goddesses, animal deities and magical practices that have captured the modern imagination. Describing the gods, goddesses and belief systems of Ancient Egypt is a tricky business. First is the sheer amount of time – their history spanned some 3000 years. Next is the proliferation of local deities and the tendency over time for some of these to assume the characteristics of others. Then there are the deities' various manifestations; one god could take many forms. At least four cosmogonies provide slightly different explanations of how the world began. In addition, there are a number of myths (for example, the struggle between the brothers Horus and Seth for control of the world) which may well echo an even more distant past and the struggle between Upper and Lower Egypt for supremacy. Following are brief descriptions of just a few of the major gods and goddesses that you're likely to encounter while visiting Egypt's museums and monuments.

Aker An earth-god who watched over the western and eastern gates of the duat (underworld). Shown with a lion's head or with two human heads facing opposite directions.

Amun (Amen) The hidden one. Amun is portrayed as a man with blue-coloured flesh. He is sometimes depicted with ram's horns (the ram being one of his sacred animals, along with the goose) but more often he is shown wearing a crown topped with two tall plumes and holding a crook and a flail (symbols of sovereignty). Amun was initially a minor deity in Thebes, but during the Middle Kingdom began to eclipse and assimilate other gods, such as the Theban god of war, Montu, and the fertility-god Min. In the New Kingdom, Amun became associated with the sun-god Ra. As Amun-Ra he was regarded as King of the Gods and father of the Pharaoh.

Anubis God of cemeteries and of embalming, and patron of embalmers. Anubis is depicted as a man with a canine head, or as a reclining dog, often thought to be a jackal. His coat is black, and it is suggested this represents the discolouration of the corpse after it has been treated with natron and other substances during mummification. It could also be symbolic of renewed life, a reference to the rich, dark Nile silt vital for crops. In the Book of the Dead Anubis, in the presence of 42 assessor gods, weighs the deceased's heart (regarded as the centre of the intellect and emotions) against the feather of truth (the symbol of Maat, goddess of truth, justice and cosmic order).

Box: Thoth, god of writing and counting, graces a wall at the Temple of Hathor in Dendara (photo by Bethune Carmichael).

Amun

Anubis

Bastet

Bes

Hathor

Apophis The snake god. Embodiment of darkness, symbolic of chaos and enemy of the sun-god Ra. As Ra enters and leaves the underworld in his solar boat, he is attacked by Apophis, who is in turn beheaded (some versions of the legend say by Bastet, others, Seth). His blood stains the morning and evening skies as the struggle is endlessly repeated.

Aten (Aton) An aspect of the sun-god Ra. The sun at noon. Aten is depicted as a disc from which rays extend ending in outstretched hands. Those pointing towards the king or queen clutch ankhs (the hieroglyph for life). At the base of the disc is the uraeus (a symbol of sovereignty).

Atum Creator god of Heliopolis and identified from earliest times with the sun-god Ra (generally an aged aspect of the sun; the setting sun). Atum embodies the notion of completeness and is generally depicted as a man wearing the crowns of both Upper and Lower Egypt. Atum was said to have arisen from Nun (chaos or primordial ocean) and to have formed from himself both men and gods. According to the Heliopolitan cosmology (which eventually became the most widely accepted), Atum created the sky deities Shu (air) and Tefnut (moisture). They in turn produced Geb (earth-god) and Nut (sky-goddess). From them came Osiris, Seth, Isis and Nephthys. The entire 'family' is often referred to as the divine ennead (nine).

Bastet Cat goddess and daughter of sun-god Ra. Her cult centred on Bubastis in the north-east Delta. Bastet could be ferocious, associated as she was with the sun's vengeance, but she was more usually regarded as a friendly deity and associated with joy.

Bes Despite his grotesque appearance, dwarfish, bandy-legged Bes was a benign character fond of music and dancing. He protected women in childbirth by frightening away evil spirits (see Taweret later) and watched over newborns.

Geb Earth-god Geb was married to his sister, the sky-goddess Nut. He is usually depicted as a reclining man. According to legend, Geb divided Egypt in two, giving one son, Horus, the lower half and another son, Seth, the upper.

Hapy Hapy symbolised the Nile's annual flood. He appears as a man and, as he embodies fertility and abundance, often possesses female breasts and a rounded abdomen, and wears aquatic plants on his head.

Hathor Hathor, daughter of the sun-god Ra, was goddess of joy and love. She also protected women and travellers, although one myth depicts her as very violent, wishing to destroy humankind. She is often represented as a cow, or as a woman with cow's ears or horns between which sits a sun disc.

Horus Sky god and Lower Egyptian counterpart of Seth. Horus came to be acknowledged as the son of Osiris and Isis. He sometimes appears as a hawk, but is more often depicted in the form of a man with a hawk's head.

Isis Isis, sister/wife of Osiris, mother goddess and (as mother of Horus) symbolic mother of the king, possessed great magical powers. Isis is depicted as a woman wearing either a throne on her head or a sun disc flanked with cow's horns. Sometimes she appears (along with her sister Nephthys) as a kite, mourning the dead. She used her magical powers to restore Osiris to life and to protect the young Horus. Those seeking protection or healing for children therefore appealed to her for assistance.

Horus

Khepri The rising sun. Khepri was regarded as self-created and depicted as a scarab beetle, whose habit of rolling balls of dirt over the ground could be viewed as analogous to the divine task of pushing the sun disc up from the underworld to begin its journey across the sky. Hence the symbol of daily resurrection when incorporated into funerary jewellery. Small stone or faience scarabs were made in their thousands as amulets and stamp seals.

Khons Moon-god Khons (wanderer or traveller) is depicted as a man (sometimes with a hawk's head), wearing a crown topped with a crescent moon cradling a full moon. As the son of Amun and Mut, he also appears wearing the lock of youth.

Isis

Maat Personification of cosmic order (truth, justice, harmony). Maat is depicted as a woman wearing an ostrich feather on her head, although sometimes she is symbolised solely by the feather (she is represented as such during the weighing of the heart ceremony).

Meretseger Cobra goddess. Her name means 'she who loves silence'. She is represented as a coiled cobra or with a snake's body and a woman's head.

Khepri

Khons

Maat

Montu Falcon-headed Theban god of war. He is depicted wearing a sun disc on his head with two tall plumes.

Mut A symbolic mother of the king, Amun's consort and Thebes' principal goddess. She appears as a slender woman wearing a vulture-shaped headdress. Sometimes she appears with the head of a lion.

Nekhbet Vulture goddess of Nekheb (Al-Kab). Nekhbet appears as a vulture clutching the symbol for eternity in her talons. She is often included in the pharaoh's crown, and represents Upper Egypt.

Nut Sky goddess and both sister and wife of the earth-god Geb. Mother of Osiris, Isis, Seth and Nephthys. She usually appears as a woman, but sometimes as a cow, and is often depicted stretched across the ceilings of tombs, swallowing the sun and creating the night.

Montu

Mut

Geb, Nut & Shu are often depicted together. The sky goddess, Nut, is supported by Shu, god of air and light, who separates her from the reclining earth god Geb.

Osiris God of the underworld and of fertility. He generally appears in mummy wrappings holding the crook and flail (representing kingship) and wearing a conical headdress that includes a pair of ram's horns and a tall plume. He is the brother of Isis and father of Horus. See the boxed text 'The Cult of Osiris' on page 265.

Ptah Anthropomorphic creator god of Memphis. Ptah was also regarded as a skilled artisan and leader of craftsmen. He appears wearing a tight cap on his shaven head and he carries a was (sceptre) on which are the emblems of power, life and stability. Ptah is sometimes linked with the solar-god Sokar.

Ptah

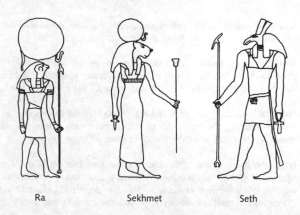

Ra   Sekhmet   Seth

Ra Sun god and creator god of Heliopolis. Ra takes many forms (for example, as Khepri, Aten), and other deities also merge with him, enhancing their own powers (for example, Amun-Ra). He is generally shown as a man with a falcon's head upon which rests a sun disc. The ancient Egyptians believed that Ra traversed the sky in a solar boat, rising from the underworld in the east and re-entering it in the land of the dead in the west.

Sekhmet Lion goddess and daughter of sun-god Ra. Sekhmet's name means 'powerful' and she represents the burning heat of the sun. According to legend, the sun-god Ra sent Sekhmet (his 'eye') to punish an irreverent humankind.

Seth Worshipped from very early times. Upper Egyptian counterpart to Horus. Seth is often seen as synonymous with evil. His birth was indeed violent – he wrenched himself apart from Nut, his mother. God of chaotic forces (and associated with wind, rain, storms and thunder), Seth has some redeeming features. For example, sitting in the prow of Ra's solar boat, he spears the evil snake Apophis as the boat begins its entry from the western horizon into the underworld.

Taweret Like Bes, Taweret protected women in childbirth, her eccentric appearance (hippo head, lion legs and arms, crocodile tail and pendulous breasts) supposedly scaring off evil forces. There's a wonderful statue of her in room 24 on the ground floor of the Egyptian Museum in Cairo.

Thoth God of writing and counting, and patron of scribes. Thoth was worshipped in the form of a baboon or an ibis. He is usually depicted during the weighing of the heart ceremony as poised to record the results before the assessor gods.

Thoth

Facts for the Visitor

PLANNING
When to Go
The best time to go to Egypt depends on where you want to go. June to August is unbearable in Upper Egypt with daytime temperatures soaring up to 40°C. Summer in Cairo is almost as hot, and the combination of heat, dust, pollution, noise and crush makes walking the city streets a real test of endurance. But then a scorching sun might be exactly what's wanted for a week or two of slow roasting on the beaches of southern Sinai.

For visiting Upper Egypt, winter is easily the most comfortable time – though hotel rates are at a premium. However, in Cairo from December to February skies are often overcast and evenings can be chilly, while up on the Mediterranean coast, Alexandria is subject to frequent downpours resulting in flooded, muddy streets.

The happiest compromise for an all-Egypt trip is to visit in spring (March to May) or autumn (October, November).

Religious Holidays & Festivals Most of Egypt's religious and state holidays (for dates see Public Holidays & Special Events later in this chapter) last only one or two days at most and should not seriously disrupt any travel plans. The exception is Ramadan, the Muslim month of fasting. During daylight hours many cafes and restaurants are closed, while bars cease business completely for the duration. Offices also operate reduced and very erratic hours.

Maps
Lonely Planet's *Egypt Travel Atlas* is designed to complement this guide; it covers the country in 40 pages of detailed maps (scales 1:900,000 and 1:1,800,000) and it's fully indexed and light to carry.

Kümmerly & Frey has a map covering all of Egypt on a scale of 1:950,000, which sells for about US$9. It also produces a separate map of Sinai and a pictorial (but fairly useless) map of the Nile for about US$7.50.

The Freytag & Berndt map includes a plan of the Great Pyramids of Giza and covers all of Egypt except the western quarter at a scale of 1:1,000,000. It includes small insets of Cairo and central Alexandria.

Nelles Verlag has one of the most complete, though dated, general maps of Egypt (scale 1:2,500,000) including, on the reverse side, a map of the Nile Valley (scale 1:750,000) and a good enlargement of central Cairo.

The Macmillan Publisher's *Map of Egypt* (scale 1:1,000,000) has a map of the Nile Valley and a small map of the whole of Egypt, plus good maps of Cairo and Alexandria, and a variety of enlargements, temple plans and the like for around US$7.

Clyde Surveys, of England, has an excellent map of eastern Egypt. It covers the Nile region from the coast to Aswan, and has detailed maps of Cairo, Alexandria, Luxor and Thebes, and the Great Pyramids of Giza, with notes in English, French and German. It is entitled *Clyde Leisure Map No 6: Egypt & Cairo*.

The Bartholomew *World Travel Map of Egypt* (scale 1:1,000,000) is a tad simplistic and it's missing a large part of the Western Desert. On the same scale is the French IGN map which concentrates on the Nile Valley. Michelin map No 954 (scale 1:4,000,000) covers north-east Africa as well as other parts of the Middle East.

Falk produces a detailed map of Cairo (scale 1:13,000) with a small Alexandria addition and a booklet packed with details about the two cities. But you have to appreciate Falk's style of unravelling map. It costs about US$8.50, or E£33 in Cairo bookshops.

Maps Available in Egypt Many of these maps are available in Egypt, as is an ever increasing range of local products. There are several Cairo maps, the best of which is the *City Map of Cairo* (1:25,000) which, despite the small scale, is clear and it has larger scale inserts of Downtown and Heliopolis. It's conveniently pocket-sized and cheap at E£5. If you're spending a long time in Cairo you may find the *Cairo A-Z* (E£40) helpful, although at 150 pages it is bulky and quite heavy. There's a slimmer (32 pages), handier booklet, *Cairo Maps* (E£20), produced by the AUC Press.

In addition, once in Egypt you'll be able to pick up good maps of Saqqara, Aswan and Luxor, Alexandria, the Western Desert and Sinai.

What to Bring

There is very little that you might need that you won't be able to find in Egypt, but the choice might be more limited than at home. So bring: sunglasses, a flashlight (torch), a water bottle/canteen, sunscreen (anything above factor eight is hard to find anywhere in Egypt), a hat, a flat drain stopper (not a plug), a pocket knife, a sleeping sheet, a small sewing kit and a money belt or pouch.

If you are visiting during winter then a sweater is useful in the evenings, especially in desert areas.

Although most toiletries can be found in city pharmacies and supermarkets (and at major hotels), certain items can be difficult to get, and expensive, so you may want to bring your own contact lens solution, tampons (Tampax are about the only kind available) and contraceptives (Tops condoms are available – to men – but apparently have a distressingly high failure rate). Women living in Egypt suggest it is better to bring your own sanitary pads and panty liners, although they are available.

TOURIST OFFICES

The Egyptian government has tourist information offices throughout Egypt (addresses are given in the regional chapters), some of which are better than others. The usefulness of the offices depends largely on the staff – while they are usually pleasant and well-meaning, they're not always that knowledgeable. Also, government-produced reference

material, such as maps and brochures, tends to be out of date and too general. However, there are exceptions – the Aswan, Dakhla and Siwa offices are staffed by people who have wide-ranging local knowledge and will go out of their way to help you.

Egyptian tourist offices abroad tend to be well stocked with brochures, free maps and booklets and have fairly helpful staff.

Following is a selected list of tourist offices outside Egypt:

Australia
(☎ 02-6273 4260, fax 6273 4629)
Press & Information Bureau of the Arab Republic of Egypt, 1 Darwin Ave, Yarralumla, Canberra 2600
Canada
(☎ 514-851 4606, fax 861 8071)
Egyptian Tourist Authority, Suite 250, 1253 McGill College Ave, Montreal, Quebec H3B 2Y5
France
(☎ 01 45 62 94 42, fax 01 42 89 34 81)
Bureau de Tourisme, Ambassade de la RAE, 90 Ave des Champs Élysées, Paris
Germany
(☎ 69-252319, fax 239876)
Aegyptisches Fremdenverkehrsamt, 64A Kaiserstrasse, 60329, Frankfurt-am-Main
UK
(☎ 0171-493 5282, fax 408 0295, from 22 April 2000 ☎ 020-7493 5282, fax 020-7408 0295)
Egyptian Tourist Authority, 3rd Floor West, Egyptian House, 170 Piccadilly, London W1V 9DD
USA
(☎ 212-332 2570, fax 956 6439)
Egyptian Tourist Authority, Suite 1706, 630 5th Ave, New York, NY 10111
(☎ 213-781 7676, fax 653 8961)
Egyptian Tourist Authority, Suite 215, 83 Wilshire Boulevard, Wilshire San Vincente Plaza, Beverly Hills, CA 90211
(☎ 312-280 4666, fax 280 4788)
Egyptian Tourist Authority, Suite 829, 645 North Michigan Ave, Chicago, IL 60611

VISAS & DOCUMENTS
Passport

Make sure that your passport remains valid well beyond the period of your intended stay. If it's just about to expire, Egyptian

Highlights & Suggested Itineraries

The hundreds of letters about Egypt sent to Lonely Planet show that travellers rave most about:

1. Karnak and the monuments at Luxor
2. The Pyramids
3. The Egyptian Museum, Cairo
4. Abu Simbel
5. Dahab and the Red Sea
6. Siwa

To this list we've added our own highlights, placed in boxes at the start of each regional chapter.

Suggested Itineraries

Egypt is a big country and, unless you have the money to fly, getting around takes time. If you hit the ground running you can cover a lot, though if you're short on time then it's better to limit yourself to one or two places and save the rest for next time.

The following itineraries assume that you're not taking internal flights.

One Week You'll need two days in Cairo to take in the Pyramids and the Egyptian Museum, after which you could take the overnight train to Luxor and spend the next couple of days visiting the ancient necropolis of Thebes and the east bank temples. Jump on a morning bus to Aswan (five hours) and you'll be able to spend the afternoon sailing on a felucca on the Nile. At a push, the next day you could fit in a trip to Abu Simbel before hightailing it by train or bus back to Cairo.

Two Weeks A fortnight is an ideal amount of time. Take three days in Cairo, using the third day to explore the medieval quarters of Islamic Cairo. Follow two days in Luxor with two in Aswan, taking in Abu Simbel and the Temple of Philae, before moving into relaxation mode with two nights on a felucca sailing up to Edfu. Head back to Luxor for the bus across the Eastern Desert to Hurghada on the Red Sea. Ferry across to Sharm el-Sheikh in southern Sinai where you can delight in the underwater world before climbing to the peak of Mt Sinai.

Alternatively, if you're not interested in beaches and snorkelling, or diving, head west from Luxor on a circuit of the oases of Bahariyya, Farafra, Dakhla and Kharga, finishing up in Cairo. Or return directly to Cairo from Luxor and head west via Alexandria to Siwa.

One Month In a month you could cover most of Egypt's main sites, but you'd still have to travel at a steady pace. Spend four or five days in and around Cairo before hightailing it west to Siwa. After two days in this tranquil haven, backtrack along the Mediterranean coast to Alexandria, which is well worth an overnight stay. Take an early morning train to Cairo and you'll be in time to get the bus on to Bahariyya or Farafra, where you can arrange an overnight trip in the White Desert. From the oases you can bus it to the Nile Valley, and then split a week between Luxor, Aswan and the neighbouring sites. Head east to Hurghada on the coast for the ferry across the Red Sea. You'll then have another six or so days to explore Sinai.

immigration may not let you into the country. Also, make sure it has sufficient space for any new visa stamps that you're liable to pick up – with the visa and all the associated stamps you'll need two full pages for Egypt alone.

Visas

All foreigners entering Egypt, except nationals of Malta, South Africa, Zimbabwe and Arab countries, must obtain visas from Egyptian consulates overseas or at the airport or port upon arrival. As a general rule, it is cheaper to get a visa at Cairo airport, where the whole process takes only a few minutes; the required stamps are bought from Thomas Cook or one of the other 24 hour exchange booths just before passport control and no photo is required. The cost is US$15/UK£10.

Elsewhere, processing of visa applications varies. In the USA and the UK, processing takes about 24 to 48 hours if you drop your application off in person, or anything from 10 days to six weeks if you mail it.

A single-entry visa is valid for three months and entitles the holder to stay in Egypt for one month. Multiple-entry visas (for three visits) are also available but although good for presentation for six months, they still only entitle the bearer to a total of one month in the country.

Costs at embassies and consulates vary depending on your nationality and the country where you apply. As an example, a single-entry tourist visa costs most western applicants the equivalent of UK£15 (about US$22) in the UK.

Getting Your Visa in the Middle East

It is possible to get your visa while on the road in the Middle East. Neighbouring countries Israel, Jordan, Sudan and Libya all have Egyptian representations. In Jordan there's an embassy in Amman and a consulate in Aqaba – see Embassies & Consulates later for addresses. At the former, drop your passport off in the morning and collect the visa that same afternoon; at the latter, visas are issued on the spot. The cost is JD17 and you need one photo.

You can also get a visa in Nuweiba upon arrival (by ferry) but the Egyptian officials make a bit of a song and dance about it, and will want payment in US dollars.

If you are coming from Israel, you *cannot* get a visa on the Israeli-Egyptian border. Instead, you have to get the visa beforehand at either the embassy in Tel Aviv or the consulate in Eilat. At both places the visa is issued the same day and costs 60NIS (US$18).

Sinai Permits It is not necessary to get a full visa if your visit is confined to the area of Sinai between Sharm el-Sheikh and Taba (on the Israeli border), including St Katherine's Monastery. Instead you are issued with an entry stamp, free of charge, allowing you a 14 day stay. Points of entry where such visa-free stamps are issued are Taba, Nuweiba (port) and Sharm el-Sheikh (airport or port).

Visa Extensions & Re-Entry Visas Visa extensions beyond the first month can easily be obtained for anything up to 12 months and cost E£8.20. You need one photograph and a modicum of patience. For details of passport offices where visas can be extended see the Information sections under Cairo and other cities.

If you do not have a multiple-entry visa, it is also possible to get a re-entry visa, valid to the expiry date of your visa and any extensions, at most passport offices. A single/multiple re-entry visa costs E£10/14.

There is a two week grace period beyond the expiry date of your visa. In other words, a one month stay is to all intents and purposes six weeks. If you stay beyond that, a fine of E£60 is imposed on exit, and there are also the costs and hassles of getting an extension. If you are caught at the airport in this situation, you could well have to kiss your flight goodbye.

Photocopies

It's a good idea to make photocopies of all vital documents – such as the data pages of your passport, your birth certificate, credit cards, airline tickets, the serial numbers of your travellers cheques and other travel documents – and keep them separate from your real documents. Add to this an emergency stash of about US$50. Also leave copies of all these things with someone at home.

Travel Permits

Travel permits *used to be* required for travel westward past Marsa Matruh or to Siwa Oasis but as a result of a warmer relations between Egypt and Libya since 1989, this is no longer the case. That said, continued good neighbourliness can never be taken for granted and the need for permits could quickly be reimposed if the two countries again find themselves at loggerheads.

Military permits issued by the Ministry of the Interior in Cairo *are* required for travel south beyond Marsa Alam on the Red Sea coast. They are very hard to come by, particularly as long as Egypt and Sudan continue to squabble about the Halaib region. For further details see the Red Sea Coast chapter.

Travel Insurance

However you're travelling, it's worth taking out travel insurance. Consult your travel agent for the most appropriate policy. You may not want to insure that grotty old army surplus backpack but everyone should be covered for the worst possible case: an accident, for example, that will require hospital treatment and a flight home. Check out the details. In most cases you need to pay extra to cover you for 'dangerous sports' such as diving. Also, you often need to pay a surcharge for expensive camera equipment and the like.

It's a good idea to make a copy of your policy, in case the original is lost. If you are planning to travel for a long time, the insurance may seem very expensive but if you can't afford it, you won't be able to afford to deal with a medical emergency overseas.

Driving Licence & Permits

If you plan to drive in Egypt you should obtain an international driving permit from your local automobile association before you leave home – you'll need a passport photo and a valid licence. For information about driving in Egypt, see the Getting Around chapter.

Hostel Card

Some Egyptian hostels don't require that you be a hostelling member, but often charge a pound or two less if you have a card. Occasionally they'll issue a membership card on the spot, otherwise they're available at the Hostelling International (HI) office in Cairo (see the Accommodation section later in this chapter for details).

Student Cards

For years, it has been notoriously easy to get a legitimate International Student Identification Card (ISIC) in Cairo. That situation has now changed. Proof of student status is now required before an ISIC card will be issued. That proof must be an ID card or letter from your own college or university. If you have such a document then you can go along to the Medical Scientific Centre (MSC) (☎ 363 8815) at 103 Mathaf al-Manial on Rhoda Island in Cairo – there's no number on the building but it stands immediately to the right of the blue Co-op petrol station. The MSC office is on the ground floor, through an unmarked door on the left-hand side of the foyer. Cards are issued in minutes and cost E£25; you'll also require a passport photo (preferably colour). The office is open from 9 am to 9 pm daily.

Most of Cairo's backpacker hotels and budget travel agencies can also get the cards but you still require proof of student status. In Luxor, if you're under 30 years old (or have proof of student status) you can get an ISIC card from an office next to the Venus Hotel (☎ 372 625). You need a photo, your passport and E£40, and the process can take as little as 15 minutes. The office is open from 8.30 am to 11 pm.

It is well worth having a student card as it entitles you to a 50% discount on admission to almost all of the antiquities and museums, as well as significant reductions on train travel.

Travellers have reported using a wide range of other cards to get student discounts for museum entry and transport, from HI cards to Eurail cards.

International Health Card

You'll need this yellow booklet proving that you have been vaccinated for yellow fever and/or cholera only if you are coming from an infected area (such as most of sub-Saharan Africa and South America). Yellow fever is not endemic in Egypt.

See the Health section later in this chapter for further information.

EMBASSIES & CONSULATES
Egyptian Embassies & Consulates

Following are the addresses and telephone numbers of Egyptian embassies and consulates in major cities around the world:

Australia
  Embassy:
  (☎ 06-273 4437/8)
  1 Darwin Ave, Yarralumla, Canberra, ACT 2600
  Consulate:
  (☎ 03-9654 8869/8634)
  9th floor, 124 Exhibition St, Melbourne, Vic 3000
  Consulate:
  (☎ 02-9362 3483)
  335 New South Head Rd, Double Bay, Sydney NSW 2028
Canada
  Embassy:
  (☎ 613-234 4931/35/58)
  454 Laurier Ave East, Ottawa, Ontario K1N 6R3
  Consulate:
  (☎ 514-866 8455)
  1 Place Sainte Marie, 2617 Montreal, Quebec H3B 4S3
France
  Embassy:
  (☎ 01 47 23 06 43, 01 53 67 88 30)
  56 Ave d'Iena, 75116 Paris
  Consulate:
  (☎ 01 45 00 49 52, 01 45 00 77 10)
  58 Ave Foch, 75116 Paris
  Consulate:
  (☎ 91 25 04 04)
  166 Ave d'Hambourg, 13008 Marseilles

Germany
  Embassy:
  (☎ 228-956 8311/2/3)
  Kronprinzenstrasse 2, Bad Godesberg, 53173 Bonn
  Embassy branch:
  (☎ 30-477 1048)
  Waldstrasse 15, 13156 Berlin
  Consulate:
  (☎ 69-590557/8)
  Eysseneckstrasse 34, 60322 Frankfurt-am-Main
Ireland
  (☎ 1-660 6566, 660 6718)
  12 Clyde Rd, Dublin 4
Israel
  Embassy:
  (☎ 03-546 4151/2)
  54 Rehov Basel, Tel Aviv
  Consulate:
  (☎ 07-597 6115)
  68 Afraty St, Bna Betkha, Eilat
Jordan
  Embassy:
  (☎ 6-605202, fax 604082)
  Karbata Ben El-Dawar St, 4th floor, Amman or PO Box 35178
  Consulate:
  (☎ 3-316171/81)
  Al-Wahdat al-Jarbiyya, al-Istiqlal St, Aqaba
Libya
  (☎ 61-92488, fax 96291)
  Omar Khayyam Hotel, 5th floor, Benghazi
Netherlands
  (☎ 70-354 2000)
  Badhuisweg 92, 2587 CL, The Hague
Sudan
  Embassy:
  (☎/fax 11-778741)
  Sharia al-Gama'a, al-Mogran, Khartoum
  Consulate:
  (☎ 11-772191)
  Sharia al-Gomhurriya, Khartoum
UK
  Embassy:
  (☎ 0171-499 2401, from 22 April 2000
  ☎ 020-7499 2401)
  26 South St, Mayfair, London W1
  Consulate:
  (☎ 0171-235 9777/9719, from 22 April 2000
  ☎ 020-7235 9777/9719)
  2 Lowndes St, London SW1
USA
  Embassy:
  (☎ 202-895 5400)
  3521 International Court NW, Washington DC 20008

Consulate:
(☎ 212-759 7120/1/2)
1110 2nd Ave, New York, NY 10022
Consulate:
(☎ 415-346 9700/2)
3001 Pacific Ave, San Francisco, CA 94115
Consulate:
(☎ 713-961 4915/6)
Suite 2180, 1990 Post Oak Blvd, Houston,
TX 77056
Consulate:
(☎ 312-828 9162/64/67)
Suite 1900, 500 N Michigan Ave, Chicago,
IL 60611

Embassies & Consulates in Egypt

Most embassies and consulates are open from around 8 am to 3 pm from Sunday to Thursday. The addresses of some of the foreign embassies and consulates in Egypt are as follows:

Australia
    (☎ 575 0444, fax 578 1638)
    World Trade Centre, 11th floor, 1191
    Corniche el-Nil, Cairo
Canada
    (☎ 354 3110, fax 356 3548)
    5 Al-Saraya al-Kubra, Garden City, Cairo
Denmark
    (☎ 340 2503, fax 341 1780)
    12 Hassan Sabry, Zamalek, Cairo
Eritrea
    (☎ 303 0517)
    13 Mohammed Shafik, Mohandiseen, Cairo
    Visas valid for one month are issued within 24 hours. You need a letter of recommendation from your embassy and two photos. You may be asked to show a return or onward air ticket. Visas cost E£135.
Ethiopia
    (☎ 335 3696, fax 335 3699)
    6 Abdel Rahman Hussein, Doqqi, Cairo
    You need a letter of recommendation from your embassy and two photos, and you must be able to show a return air ticket. If you fulfil these requirements the visa is issued the next day and costs US$63. Hours are from 8.30 am to noon daily except Friday.
France
    Embassy:
    (☎ 570 3916, fax 571 0276)
    29 Sharia al-Giza, Giza
    Consulate:
    (☎ 393 4645)

5 Sharia Fadl (off Talaat Harb), Cairo
    Consulate:
    (☎ 482 7950)
    2 Midan Orabi, Mansheya, Alexandria
Germany
    Embassy:
    (☎ 341 0015, fax 341 0530)
    8 Hassan Sabry, Zamalek, Cairo
    Consulate:
    (☎ 545 7025)
    5 Sharia Mena, Rushdy, Alexandria
Ireland
    Embassy:
    (☎ 340 8264, fax 341 2863)
    7th floor, 3 Abu al-Feda, Zamalek, Cairo
    Consulate:
    (☎ 546 4686)
    Honorary Consul, Hisham Helmy, 36 Sharia
    Kafr Abdu, Rushdy, Alexandria
Israel
    Embassy:
    (☎ 361 0528, fax 361 0414)
    18th floor, 6 Ibn al-Malek, Giza
    Consulate:
    (☎ 586 0492)
    207 Sharia Abdel Salem Aref, Alexandria
Jordan
    (☎ 348 5566, fax 360 1027)
    6 Al-Shaheed Basem al-Khatib (previously
    Gohainy), Doqqi, Cairo
    Visas cost from nothing for Australians to E£63 for UK citizens, E£77 for Americans and E£91 for Canadians. Apply in the morning and collect the visa at 2 pm. You need one photo. Hours are from 9 am to 3 pm, Sunday to Thursday.
Kenya
    (☎ 345 3907, fax 344 3400)
    7 Sharia al-Mohandis Galal, Doqqi, Cairo
    Visas valid for three months and good for travel for one month cost E£26 for most western nationalities. You need one photo. The embassy is open from 8 am to 2 pm, but is closed on Saturday and Sunday.
Lebanon
    (☎ 361 0623, fax 361 0463)
    5 Ahmed Nessim, Giza, Cairo
Libya
    (☎ 340 1864, fax 340 0072)
    7 Sharia Salah ad-Din, Zamalek, Cairo
    Do not count on getting a Libyan visa in Cairo. The embassy has to contact Tripoli and there is little likelihood of permission being given.
Netherlands
    Embassy:
    (☎ 340 1936, fax 341 5249)
    18 Hassan Sabry, Zamalek, Cairo

Consulate:
(☎ 482 9044)
3rd floor, 18 Tariq al-Horeyya, Alexandria

New Zealand
New Zealand's affairs are handled by the UK embassy.

Saudi Arabia
Embassy:
(☎ 349 0757, fax 349 3495)
2 Ahmed Nessim, Giza
The place to get your Saudi visa is a consular building in Garden City near the Canadian embassy, which will issue transit visas for those with passengers on a boat from Suez to Eritrea via Jeddah. Phone the embassy for the address. The consulate in Suez also supposedly issues transit visas.
Consulate:
(☎ 482 9911)
9 Sharia Batalsa, Alexandria
(☎ 222 461)
Port Tawfiq (around the corner from the tourist office), Suez

Sudan
Embassy:
(☎ 354 5043, fax 354 2693)
4 Sharia al-Ibrahimy, Garden City, Cairo
Consulate:
(☎ 354 9661)
1 Mohammed Fahmy as-Said, Garden City
Obtaining a visa for Sudan in Cairo would seem to be governed by cloud formations, coffee grinds, or the Nikkei index. The consul himself said it would take at least a month to commune with Khartoum on the question of a visa, but a German girl, along with an American friend, got their visas in less than a week. To make the application you need four passport-size photos and a letter of recommendation from your embassy. They do not take your passport while processing your application. If successful you pay US$64 cash (no other currency accepted) on receipt of the visa, valid for use within a month and for a month's stay.

Syria
(☎ 337 7020, fax 335 8232)
18 Abdel Rahim Sabry, Doqqi, Cairo
Visas are issued the same or next day depending on how early in the morning you get your application in. You need two photos. For Australians the visa is free, US citizens pay E£116, UK citizens pay E£210 and most other nationalities pay E£185. Hours are Saturday to Thursday.

UK
Embassy:
(☎ 354 0850, fax 354 0959)
7 Ahmed Ragheb, Garden City, Cairo

Consulate:
(☎ 546 7001)
3 Sharia Mena, Rushdy, Alexandria

USA
Embassy:
(☎ 355 7371, fax 357 3200)
5 Sharia Latin America, Garden City, Cairo
Consulate:
(☎ 472 1009)
3 Sharia al-Faraana, Alexandria

CUSTOMS

The duty-free limit on arrival is 1L of alcohol, 1L of perfume, 200 cigarettes and 25 cigars. On top of that, you can buy another 3L of alcohol (4L in Alexandria) plus a wide range of other duty-free articles within the next 30 days.

A grand total of E£1000 can be imported into or exported out of the country. There are no restrictions on the import of foreign currencies, although you are supposed to declare all you have when you enter, and you aren't supposed to take out more than you have brought in and declared. This is all highly theoretical and we've never heard of anyone being asked to declare any currency.

Sometimes the Customs Declaration Form D is given to arriving tourists to list all cameras, jewellery, cash, travellers cheques and electronics (personal stereos, computers, radios, VCRs etc). No-one seems to be asked for this form on departure, and few tourists are given it on arrival. Travellers are, however, regularly asked to declare their video cameras and some have reported being slapped with a hefty 'import tax'.

There are prohibited and restricted articles including books, printed matter, motion pictures, phonographs and materials which the government considers 'subversive or constituting a national risk or incompatible with the public interest'. Articles for espionage or 'intelligence activities', and explosives are banned.

Duty-Free Shops

There are quite a few branches of the Egypt Free Shops Company scattered around the country. They stock imported spirits, wine, beer, cigarettes, plus a range of electrical goods and other items. Wine costs from US$8 to US$20, whisky, gin and vodka from US$12 upwards and a crate of 24 cans of Heineken beer is US$16. Take your passport. Branches can be found at:

Alexandria
  (☎ 586 8546) 513 Tariq al-Horreyya
  (☎ 483 3429) 16 Sharia Salah Salem
Cairo
  (☎ 348 9059) Cairo Sheraton, Doqqi
  (☎ 349 7094) 106 Sharia Gamiat ad-Dowal al-Arabiyya, Mohandiseen
  (☎ 393 1985) 19 Sharia Talaat Harb, Central Cairo. Alcohol and cigarettes are not sold at this branch.
  (☎ 391 5134) 17 Sharia al-Gomhuriyya, Central Cairo
Luxor
  Just off Sharia al-Karnak, one block north of the Emilio Hotel
Port Said
  (☎ 325 151) Sharia al-Gomhuriyya

It is also possible to purchase duty free in Aswan (on the Corniche), Hurghada (opposite Banque Masr on the resort strip), Na'ama Bay (at the Aquamarine Hotel) and in Nuweiba (port area).

MONEY
Currency
The official currency is the Egyptian pound (E£) – in Arabic, a *guinay*. One pound consists of 100 piastres (pt). There are notes in denominations of 10, 25 and 50pt and E£1, E£5, E£10, E£20, E£50, E£100 and E£200 (the latter is new and rarely seen). Coins in circulation are for denominations of 10, 20 and 25pt.

Prices can be written with or without a decimal point. For example, E£3.35 can also be written as 335pt.

There is a severe shortage of small change in Egypt. The 25pt, 50pt and E£1 notes, which are useful for tipping, local transport (taxis especially) and avoiding the painfully repetitious incidence of not being given the correct change, are not always easy to come by – they should be hoarded.

Exchange Rates
The Egyptian pound was partly floated in 1987, so that it fluctuates in value according to economic conditions and, much to the surprise of many, it has remained fairly steady since late 1990.

Exchange rates for a range of foreign currencies were as follows when this book went to print:

country	unit		Egyptian pound
Australia	A$1	=	E£2.27
Canada	C$1	=	E£2.35
Euro	€1	=	E£3.62
France	10FF	=	E£5.52
Germany	DM1	=	E£1.85
Israel	NIS1	=	E£0.83
Japan	¥100	=	E£2.86
Jordan	JD1	=	E£4.82
New Zealand	NZ$1	=	E£1.92
UK	UK£1	=	E£5.51
USA	US$1	=	E£3.42

Exchanging Money
Money can be officially changed at American Express (Amex) and Thomas Cook offices, commercial banks, foreign exchange (forex) bureaus and some hotels. Rates don't tend to vary much especially on the US dollar but if you're keen to squeeze out the last piastre then the forex bureaus generally offer marginally better rates than the banks and they usually don't charge commission.

Most hard currencies can be changed in Egypt although in smaller places US dollars, UK pounds and deutschmarks are easiest.

Look at the money you're given when exchanging and don't accept any badly defaced, shabby or torn notes (there are plenty of them around) as you'll have great difficulty offloading them. The same goes for transactions in shops and taxis etc.

Egyptian pounds can be changed back into hard currency at the end of your stay, or during if you wish, at some banks, forex bureaus and Thomas Cook and Amex offices.

See Business Hours later in this chapter for opening hours of banks and other institutions.

Travellers Cheques While there is no problem cashing well known brands of travellers cheques at major banks, like

Banque Masr or the National Bank of Egypt, many forex bureaus don't take them. Cheques issued on post office accounts (common in Europe) or cards linked to such accounts cannot be used in Egypt.

Banks sometimes have a small handling charge on travellers cheques, usually about 50pt per cheque, plus E£2 to E£3 for stamps. Always ask about commission as it can vary. Those forex bureaus that do take cheques tend not to charge any commission.

Amex and Thomas Cook travellers cheques can be cashed at one of their offices (addresses are given in the individual city sections). There's a small handling charge. Some souvenir shops and hotels will also accept payment with travellers cheques, but check with them beforehand.

Black Market The black market for hard currency is negligible and few travellers can be bothered hunting it out for the fraction of the difference it makes.

ATMs

Although it's only a couple of years since they first appeared in Egypt, ATMs have spread rapidly throughout the country; as well as in Cairo you'll find them in Alexandria, Luxor and Aswan, Hurghada and Sharm el-Sheikh – see the relevant city sections for locations. There are two sorts: those belonging to Banque Masr and those belonging to the Egyptian British Bank (EBB). If you have your PIN number then Banque Masr machines will dispense cash on Visa and MasterCard and any Cirrus or Plus compatible bits of plastic. EBB machines respond to Visa, Midland Bank and Plus.

Recently Banque Masr machines have had a scary habit of telling you that 'your card has been retained' in the middle of a transaction – don't panic if this happens, after an agonising wait it carries on as normal.

Credit Cards

Amex, Visa and MasterCard are becoming ever more useful in Egypt and are now accepted quite widely in shops and restaurants – though away from touristic establish-

ments they are far less common and in remote areas they remain useless.

Make sure you retain any receipts to check later against your statements as there have been cases of shop owners adding extra noughts – it's a dumb, easily detected crime, but the swindlers are playing on the fact that they will only be found out once the victim has returned home and is thousands of miles from Egypt.

Visa and MasterCard can be used for cash advances at Banque Masr and the National Bank of Egypt, as well as at Thomas Cook offices (see individual city sections for addresses). Banque Masr does not generally charge commission for cash advances, but does set a limit of E£1500.

In case of lost cards in Egypt phone: Amex (☎ 570 3411); MasterCard and Visa (☎ 357 1148/9); Diners Club (☎ 579 8813).

International Transfers

Western Union, the international money transfer specialist, operates jointly in Egypt with Masr America International Bank and IBA business centres.

Alexandria
  (☎ 420 1148) 281 Tariq al-Horreyya. Receive only.
  (☎ 492 0900) 73 Tariq al-Horreyya. Send and receive.
Cairo
  (☎ 393 4906) 19 Qasr el-Nil, Downtown. Send and receive money.
  (☎ 357 1385) 1079 Corniche el-Nil, Garden City. Receive only.
  (☎ 355 7071) 8 Ibrahim Naguib, Garden City. Send and receive.
  (☎ 331 3500) 24 Sharia Syria, Mohandiseen. Receive only.
  (☎ 249 0607) 67 Sharia Hegaz, Heliopolis. Receive only.
  (☎ 258 8646) 6 Sharia Boutros Ghali, Heliopolis. Send and receive.
Dahab
  (☎ 640 320) Nesima Hotel and Diving Centre. Receive only.
Hurghada
  (☎ 442 772) Redcon Mall, unit 19, Sheraton road. Receive only.
Luxor
  (☎ 372 292) Mina Palace Hotel, Corniche el-Nil. Receive only.

Port Said

  (☎ 326 404) Sonesta shopping centre, unit 621. Receive only.

Sharm el-Sheikh

  (☎ 602 222) Rossetta Hotel, Na'ama Bay. Receive only.

The opening hours for these offices are the same as those of the banks. For details call the Western Union hotline on ☎ 355 5023.

It is also possible to have money wired from home through Amex. This service operates through most of its branches, and can be used by anyone, regardless of whether you have one of their cards or not. The charge for this service is about US$80 per US$1000, payable in the country from which the money is sent.

Costs

By international standards Egypt is still fairly cheap. It is possible to get by on US$15 a day or maybe less if you are willing to stick to the cheapest hotels (you can get a bed for as little as E£7 – US$2), eat the staple snacks of *fuul* or *ta'amiyya*, and limit yourself to one historic site per day. At the other end of the scale, Cairo has plenty of accommodation where you can pay US$100 for a room, and some of the better restaurants will set you back US$20 per person or more.

However, if you stay in a modest hotel and have a room with a fan and private bathroom, eat in regular restaurants, with the occasional splurge, and aim to see a couple of sites each day, you'll be looking at between US$20 and US$30 a day.

To give some indication of daily costs, a fuul or ta'amiyya sandwich costs about 35pt (around US$0.10), while a Big Mac goes for E£5.95 (US$1.75). A meal in a cheap restaurant will set you back around E£10 (US$3) but if you prefer to go a little up-market you can eat very well for E£20 to E£30 (US$7 to US$10). A cup of coffee is anything between 50pt and E£2 (US$0.17 to US$0.66), a beer retails for around E£6

Backhand Economy – The Art Of Baksheesh

Tipping in Egypt is called *baksheesh*, although it is more than just a reward for services rendered. Salaries and wages in Egypt are much lower than in western countries, so baksheesh is an often essential means of supplementing income. To a cleaner in a one or two star hotel who might earn only about E£150 per month, the daily tips can be the mainstay of his or her salary.

For travellers who are not used to continual tipping, demands for baksheesh for doing anything from opening doors to pointing out the obvious in museums can be quite irritating. But it is the accepted way in Egypt. Don't be intimidated into paying baksheesh when you don't think the service warrants it, but remember that more things warrant baksheesh here than anywhere in the west.

In hotels and restaurants, a 12% service charge is included at the bottom of the bill, but the money goes into the till; it's necessary therefore to leave an additional tip for the waiter. Services such as opening a door or carrying your bags warrant 25pt or 50pt. A guard who shows you something off the beaten track at an ancient site should receive about E£1. Baksheesh is not necessary when asking for directions.

Baksheesh, by the way, is not a custom exclusively reserved for foreigners. Egyptians have to constantly dole out the baksheesh too – to park their cars, receive their mail, ensure they get fresh produce at the grocers and to be shown to their seat at the cinema.

One tip: carry lots of small change with you but keep it separate from bigger bills; flashing your cash will lead to demands for greater baksheesh.

(US$2), and a bottle of mineral water is E£1.50 (US$0.50).

Getting around the country is cheap: the 10-hour train ride between Cairo and Luxor can cost as little as E£31 (just under US$10) in 2nd class.

The major expense is going to be the entry fees to tourist sites. Foreigners are seen as dollars on legs so places where they flock tend to be pricey. A complete visit to the Pyramids will cost E£80 (US$27) in admission charges, and if you want to see the mummies at the Egyptian Museum, the combined fee is E£60 (US$20).

A service charge of 12% is applied in restaurants and hotels to which a 5% to 7% sales tax is added. In other words, the price you are quoted at a hotel or read on a menu could be almost 20% higher when it comes to paying the bill.

Bargaining

Bargaining is part of everyday life in Egypt and almost everything is open to haggling, from hotel rooms to the price of a packet of imported Marlboros. Even in shops when prices are clearly marked, many Egyptians will still try to shave something off the bill. Of course, when buying in the souqs like Khan al-Khalili, bargaining is unavoidable unless you are willing to pay well over the odds. See the Shopping section later in this chapter for a few hints on how to go about it.

POST & COMMUNICATIONS
Post

Postcards and letters up to 15g cost 80pt to most countries and take four or five days to get to Europe and a week to 10 days to the USA and Australia. Stamps are available at post offices, and some souvenir kiosks, shops, newsstands and the reception desks of major hotels. Stamps bought outside the post office generally cost a little more than their face value. Sending mail from the post boxes at major hotels instead of from post offices seems to be quicker. If you use the post boxes, blue is international air mail, red is internal mail and green internal express mail.

Post offices are generally open from 8.30 am to 3 pm daily except Friday.

Receiving Mail Letters usually take a week to arrive from Europe, and a week to 10 days from the USA or Australia. The poste restante (addresses are given in the individual city sections) in Egypt functions remarkably well and is generally free (though in Alexandria there's a small fee to collect letters). If you plan to pick up mail there, ensure that the clerk checks under Mr, Ms or Mrs in addition to your first and last names.

Another option is to have your mail sent to an Amex office. You don't need to have an Amex card or travellers cheques to use the mail pick-up service. For Amex office addresses see the individual city sections. Take your passport when you go to pick it up.

If you receive a package, you'll get a card (written in Arabic) directing you to some far-flung corner of the city to collect it. Take your passport, money and patience.

Packages Packages going by normal sea mail or air mail are sent from the GPO, although in Cairo they can only go from the huge post traffic centre at Midan Ramses. As an indication of fees, a parcel to Australia costs E£32.50 per kilogram for air mail; E£16 to the UK. Sea mail to both is E£8.35 (and arrival times impossible to guess). Parcels of more than 20kg for Western Europe and Africa, and 30kg to the USA, will not be accepted. Nor should they be bigger than 1m long and deep, and 50cm wide.

There is usually a long and complicated process of customs inspection and form filling – don't close the parcel until the procedures are over. You may have to get export licences or have goods inspected, depending on what they are. Printed matter and audio and visual material will be checked and foodstuffs (except dried food) and medicines also need clearance.

The easiest way to send a package is to pay someone else a small fee and have them do it for you. Some shopkeepers will provide this service, especially if you've bought the article in their bazaar. It should nclude obtaining an export licence, packaging and mailing.

Express Mail Service It is possible to send a letter of up to 100g by Express Mail Service (EMS). There are several branches of this service around the main cities. An express letter to the UK costs E£37 and arrival is 'guaranteed' within two days. Parcels of up to 10kg to Australia cost E£259 and take at least three days to arrive. To the UK, parcels of 500g cost E£34 while parcels weighing 1kg/10kg cost E£45/243; they supposedly take only two days to arrive.

In addition to EMS, Egypt has DHL, Federal Express, TNT Skypack and various other courier services. Their addresses are listed under Post in the Information sections of individual city sections.

Telephone

Egypt's phone system is currently being given a badly needed shake up. The private sector has been allowed in to the previously state-only telecommunications, and there are two or three rival companies setting up

card phone networks. It's early days and the card phones have so far appeared in Cairo only and in small numbers, but it's a sign that things are improving.

In Cairo, the central telephone and telegraph offices, known as *centrales*, at Sharia Adly, Midan Tahrir and Sharia Alfy are open 24 hours a day, seven days a week. Other telephone offices, such as the one on Sharia Ramses in Cairo, are generally open from 8 am to 10 pm. Offices elsewhere around the country set their own opening hours.

For general enquiries	☎ 140
For police	☎ 122
For tourist police	☎ 126
For an ambulance	☎ 123
For fire service	☎ 125

Local Calls Local telephone calls from pay phones cost 10pt for anywhere between 30 seconds and three minutes, depending on the mood of the phone. Public phones (which come in a variety of colours) are usually found in front of telephone offices or, in Cairo, in metro stations. Most phones

Dialling Codes

The country code for Egypt is 20, while the international access code (to call abroad from Egypt) is 00. Area codes for some cities and towns within Egypt are:

Al-Arish	068	Farafra	019+1405	Ras al-Bar	057
Al-Fayoum	084	Hurghada	065	Ras as-Sudr	062
Al-Quseir	088	Ismailia	064	Sharm el-Sheikh	062
Alexandria	03	Kharga	092	Sidi Abdel	03
Aswan	097	Kom Ombo	097	Rahman	
Asyut	088	Luxor	095	Siwa	046
Bahariyya	018	Marsa Matruh	03	Sohag	093
Beni Suef	082	Minya	086	Suez	062
Cairo	02	Na'ama Bay	062	Taba	062
Dahab	062	Nuweiba	062	Tanta	040
Dakhla	092	Port Safaga	065		
Damietta	057	Port Said	066		
El Alamein	03	Qena	096		

are out of order for much of the time so there's always queuing at the few that work. Alternatively, many kiosks and small shops have telephones for public use, for 50pt per local call. Hotels usually charge E£1.

National & International Calls To make a national or international call use one of the bright orange card phones in the centrales. Phone cards for these are bought from the desk and cost E£15 or E£30. Alternatively, you can book a call at the desk which must be paid for in advance (there is a three minute minimum). The operator directs you to a booth when a connection is made. Note that Egyptian minutes seem to be shorter than the norm. There are different rates for day (8 am to 8 pm) and night (8 pm to 8 am) calls. As an example, a three minute call to the USA costs E£19.60/12.40 at the day/night rates; to Australia E£26.40/23.50; to the UK and Europe E£19.60/13.80.

Otherwise, many hotels, though not the very cheap ones, have direct international lines but they charge anything up to double the centrale rates. There's now also the option of making international calls from the new, privately-operated card phones, though these work out slightly more expensive than calls made at the centrale.

If you're heading to Sinai, buy your phone cards in Cairo before you leave, otherwise you'll pay a lot more for a card.

Collect Calls Collect calls can be made from Egypt, but only to those countries – such as Canada, Italy, South Korea, the UK and the USA – which have set up Home Country Direct phones. With this service, you can get through to an operator in one of the above mentioned countries and then reverse the charges or, depending on the service, charge the call to a credit card. At the time of writing, this service was offered by only a few places – all in Cairo – such as the Marriott or Semiramis InterContinental hotels, the telephone office in the departure hall at the new airport terminal, or at British Airways (calls to the UK only).

Phonophobia

It is tough to get phone numbers in Egypt. According to a report in a local paper, in one year the phone numbers in part of the city were changed three times. Even more astounding is that the subscribers weren't always informed that they had new numbers.

There is also a random element in making connections – just because you've dialled the right number it does not mean you're going to end up on the right line.

If you are sure that the number we have listed is inaccurate then you could try dialling 140 for directory inquiries, but if you can get through – the lines aren't busy and they decide to pick up – there's still no guarantee that you'll be given the correct number.

International Calling Cards These cards can be accessed through these Cairo numbers: AT&T ☎ 510 0200; MCI ☎ 355 5770; Sprint ☎ 356 4777; Global One ☎ 356 4777.

Fax & Telegraph
Fax machines are available for sending and receiving documents at the main centrales in the big cities, at EMS offices, at most three to five-star hotels and at some of the smaller hotels as well. You can receive a fax for free at Amex offices but it's not possible to send faxes from there.

From a telephone office, a one page fax to the UK or USA costs about E£14, and E£20 to Australia. Hotel rates are quite a bit more. The minimum from the Nile Hilton to the UK is E£38.50, and E£51.25 to Australia. Receiving a fax message costs E£6 at a telephone office, or E£5.50 at an EMS office.

Telegrams in English or French can be sent from the telephone and telegraph offices in central Cairo. The rates to the UK, USA and Europe are 67pt per word and to Australia 84pt per word. Each word in an address is also counted. Major hotels also offer this service but rates vary.

Email & Internet Access

Egypt has taken up the Internet in a big way and there are cybercafes throughout the country including in Cairo, Alexandria, Sharm el-Sheikh, Dahab, Hurghada, Luxor and Aswan – for addresses see the relevant regional chapters. Unfortunately Internet connection can be infuriatingly slow, a result of too much demand on insufficient international bandwidth. There are also problems with plugging your laptop into the wall in hotel rooms – there is a variety of phone sockets and in many cases the phone cable is wired straight into the wall.

Service Providers There are more than 30 Internet service providers (ISP) in Egypt. Of these, companies that we've heard are good include InternetEgypt (☎ 356 2882, Web site www.ie-eg.com), Soficom (☎ 342 1954, Web site www.soficom.com.eg) and Gega Net (☎ 414 9700, Web site www.gega.net). ISP rates in Egypt are much higher than the international average, starting at about E£100 per month plus anything between E£50 and E£100 as a start-up fee.

INTERNET RESOURCES

Entering the word 'Egypt' into one of the many Net search engines will result in several thousand links, offering everything from current prayer times to current theories on who built the Pyramids. Narrowing the field down a little, these are some of our recommendations:

http://www.lonelyplanet.com
This is the Lonely Planet site home page. Follow the links to the Traveller's Reports for the latest updates on Egypt.

http://pharos.bu.edu/Egypt/Home.html
This is the Egypt World Wide Web index with hundreds of links broken down into categories including Egyptology, travel, media and cooking. This is *the* place to start surfing.

http://pharos.bu.edu/Egypt/Cairo/home
Billing itself as The Cairo Guide, this contains a lot of information similar to that contained in this book. If the site is updated regularly it may be useful.

http://interoz.com/Egypt
The official site of the Egyptian Ministry of Tourism. Pretty standard stuff like travel tips and travel news updates but also has more interesting features such as the virtual dive centre with plenty of graphics and descriptions of wreck dive sites.

http://www.cairocafe.com.eg
A good, lively site devoted to what's on in Cairo. It includes new openings, restaurant reviews and an events calendar, and is particularly good on nightlife. It's updated regularly.

http://watt.seas.Virginia.EDU/~aoa5v
Exodus Egypt, an online magazine and database including some interesting photo features and daily updated news from Cairo translated from the local press.

http://www.mt.net/~watcher/pyramid.html
Just one of the many, many sites devoted to pyramidology. One of the more wacky and technically adept examples, this is run by the Watcher Ministries who believe that angels built the Pyramids and Sphinx – and a parallel city on Mars.

For the Web site addresses of online editions of some of Egypt's English-language periodicals, see the Newspapers & Magazines section later in this chapter.

BOOKS

The following is a very short, personal list of recommended reading. Most of these titles can be found at bookshops in Egypt, particularly at the excellent American University in Cairo bookstore. Outside Egypt you may have to order them.

Lonely Planet

As well as this book, Lonely Planet also publishes a separate 224 page city guide to Cairo, complete with colour street maps. *Israel & the Palestinian Territories* and *Jordan & Syria* are guides dedicated to two of Egypt's neighbours, while Sudan can be found in the mammoth *Africa* (along with chapters on every other country on the continent), and Libya is included in *Middle East* (which also takes in Jordan, Syria, Lebanon, Israel & the Palestinian Territories, Turkey, Iran, Iraq, the Gulf States and Yemen).

Guidebooks

There are numerous locally produced guide books available in Egypt devoted to every square inch of the country, from the oasis of Siwa in the west to the dive sites of the Red Sea in the east.

We highlight a few guidebooks in relevant places in the text but a few others to look out for include:

Cairo: A Practical Guide, by Claire E Francy. Published by the American University in Cairo Press, this is aimed at people setting up home in the city and focuses on matters such as finding a flat and a school for the kids, but it also contains a wealth of information of use to the visitor, such as a very comprehensive shopping section.

Islands of the Blest, by Cassandra Vivien. Despite some problems with place names and distances (and the author's irresponsible recommendation to add grafitti to rocks and antiquities) this remains the most comprehensive guide to the Western Desert. A new and hopefully improved edition went to the printer in late 1999.

A Guide to the Nubian Monuments on Lake Nasser, by Jocelyn Gohary. The most comprehensive guide to the temples and tombs of the Lake Nasser area, newly published and with a comprehensive history of the area and temple diagrams.

Mount Sinai, by Joseph J Hobbs. A wide-ranging and eclectic view of Mt Sinai, examining its history, religious significance, ecology and the threats posed to it by tourism.

Siwa Oasis, by Ahmed Fakhry. This exhaustive look at the history and archeology of Egypt's most beautiful oasis is still the best, despite being written in 1973.

Travel

In Search of the 40 Days Road, by Mike Asher. Recounts his search for the trail which Sudanese camel traders follow when taking their camels north to Egypt.

From the Holy Mountain, by William Dalrymple. Not strictly about Egypt, this is a ramble through eastern Christendom revisiting, 1500 years on, places described in the 6th century record left by a wandering monk. The potentially heavy subject matter is handled with a light touch and the book is filled with some truly memorable characters, both past and present.

Letters from Egypt, by Lucy Duff Gordon. Letters written by a famous 19th century consumptive who lived inside Luxor temple before it was cleared for the admiration of tourists. There she was able to get to know her neighbours and portrayed them far more sympathetically than most other travellers of the time.

A Thousand Miles Up the Nile, by Amelia Edwards. A thousand miles was a long way on a *dahabiyya* and Amelia Edwards evidently had a lot of time on her hands – her famous book runs to more than 1000 pages, or a page per mile. Still, it gives a good idea of travel in Egypt before air-con buses and aeroplanes turned it into a five-day jaunt from Europe.

Flaubert in Egypt, by Gustave Flaubert. Reprints extracts from diaries Flaubert kept when he visited the country for a few months in 1849. The Pyramids receive short shrift as Flaubert prefers to focus on his exploits in the bathhouses and bordellos.

In An Antique Land, by Amitav Ghosh. Almost an anthropological work, except it's too warm and funny, this is a wonderfully observed account of the author's stay in a Delta village. It's one of the few travel books which is not patronising towards its subject.

From Giza to Galipolli, by Garrie Hutchinson. An Aussie's account of a pilgrimage to WWI and WWII battlefields throughout the Middle East, which kicks off in Egypt. It's very much a first-impressions book but the research is solid and it's an entertaining read.

Beyond the Pyramids, by Douglas Kennedy. Some parts are noticeably weaker than others and it is very dated but this is one of the very few travelogues written about Egypt in recent years.

Eothen, by Alexander Kinglake. An account of a journey undertaken in 1830 from Constantinople to Egypt; at the time Kinglake visited Cairo, the city was suffering from one of its periodic plagues.

The Nile – A Traveller's Anthology, Deborah Manley (ed). A collection of literary titbits from some of Egypt's more illustrious visitors such as Lawrence Durrell, EM Forster, Mark Twain and Agatha Christie.

Egypt – A Traveller's Anthology, Christopher Pick (ed). As above.

Pharaonic Egypt

The Mysterious Fayoum Portraits: Faces from Ancient Egypt, by Euphrosyne Doxiadis. Beautifully produced study of the incredibly lifelike Graeco-Roman funerary portraits. An expensive coffee-table book but worth the money.

The Rape of the Nile: Tomb Robbers, Tourists and Archeologists in Egypt, by Brian M Fagan. The title says it all – a lively account of the damage done to Egypt's heritage, particularly in the last 200 years.

The Mummy in Ancient Egypt: Equipping the Dead for Eternity, by Aidan Dodson & Salima Ikram. The most comprehensive book yet on mummies, mummification and our morbid fascination with the subject by two of the world's foremost experts.

The Complete Pyramids, by Mark Lehner. Everything you ever wanted to know about pyramids – a coffee table book with more than just pictures – by a respected American scholar.

The Penguin Guide to Ancient Egypt, by William J Murnane. One of the best overall books on the life and monuments of ancient Egypt. There are plenty of illustrations and descriptions of almost every major monument in the country.

The British Museum Book of Ancient Egypt, Stephen Quirke & Jeffrey Spencer (eds). Gives an authoritative overview of ancient Egypt, but is surprisingly short on plans and diagrams of monuments.

The Complete Valley of the Kings, by Nicholas Reeves & Richard H Wilkinson. Lively compendium of information accompanied by many photos and specially drawn illustrations. Companion volume to *The Complete Pyramids* – both are highly recommended.

General History

Alexandria Rediscovered, by Jean-Yves Empreur. An exploration of Graeco-Roman Alexandria including sections on the Pharos lighthouse and the search for Alexander's tomb, written by the archaeologist currently leading the underwater excavations in the city's harbour. A beautiful, sumptuously illustrated book.

A Short History of Modern Egypt, by Afaf Lutfi al-Sayyid Marsot. A concise, if dry, history of Egypt from 639 AD onwards written by one of Egypt's foremost historians.

Cairo: The City Victorious, by Max Rodenbeck. Only very recently published, this is an entertaining and prodigiously researched anecdotal meander through 5000 years of history, written by the long-standing Egypt correspondent for *The Economist*.

A History of Egypt, by PJ Vatiokis. The single best introduction to the history of Egypt, though the emphasis is firmly on the 19th and 20th centuries and the new social order that evolved since the 1952 Revolution.

Zarafa, by Michael Allin. The charming story of a giraffe (Zarafa) sent as gift from the ruler of Egypt to the king of France overlies a fascinating study of the meeting between Age of Enlightenment Europe and an Egypt barely out of the Middle Ages. Very readable and a surprising best-seller on its publication in 1998.

Culture & Society

Veiled Sentiments: Honour and Poetry in a Bedouin Society, by Lila Abu Lughod. A study of the Awlad Ali tribe in the Western Desert and how they speak their mind through poetry. A great insight into a Bedouin society.

Khul-Khaal: Five Egyptian Women Tell their Stories, Nayra Atiya (ed). Five women from different backgrounds tell their stories. Often harrowing but revealing portrait of women's lives in Egypt. Could use an update in light of the effect of Islamism on Egyptian society.

Egypt: Moulids, Saints and Sufis, by Nicholas Biegman. One of the best nonacademic books on the subject, written by a former Dutch ambassador to Cairo. Biegman has also produced a coffee table book, *Egypt's Sideshows* with photos of moulids, weddings and other traditional occasions.

Shahhat: An Egyptian, by Richard Critchfield. This book has become an anthropology classic, even though much of its content was recently debunked as a copy of a 1930s ethnographic study. So long as you keep this in mind it's still a good read if you're spending time on Luxor's West Bank.

An Account of the Manners & Customs of the Modern Egyptians, by Edward Lane. A wonderful classic, first published in 1839, which continues to offer insight into the traditional Arab culture of Egypt.

The Hidden Face of Eve, by Nawal Al-Saadawi. Considers the role of women in the Arab world and is banned in Egypt. For more on Al-Saadawi see the Arts section in the Facts about Egypt chapter.

Literature

With a vivid history stretching back some 5000 years encompassing pyramid builders (human or otherwise), Hammer horror caliphs, the enchantment of *The Thousand and One Nights*, colonial hi-jinks and romance, and the modern day tinderbox that is the Middle East, little wonder that Egypt has provided a perfect backdrop for the imaginings of writers.

In addition to the following list, for books to do with Alexandria see the boxed text 'Literary Alexandria' in the Alexandria &

the Mediterranean Coast chapter, while for literature by Egyptian writers see the Arts section in the Facts about Egypt chapter.

A Woman of Cairo, by Noel Barber. One of those historical novels of breathtaking sweep in which dynasties crash and fall about star-crossed lovers. In this, British and Egyptian neighbours are in the run up to the revolution; King Farouk, Nasser and Sadat all get walk on parts.

Death on the Nile, by Agatha Christie. Draws on Christie's experiences of a winter in Upper Egypt. She writes in the introduction, 'When I read it now I feel myself back on the steamer from Aswan to Wadi Halfa'.

The Name of the Beast, by Daniel Easterman. For a flight of fantasy – the leader of a bunch of Islamists turns out to be the anti-Christ and the Pyramids are dismantled to build a wall around the borders of Egypt. It's great fun but it would have worked far better as a Nintendo game.

City of the Horizon, City of Dreams, City of the Dead, by Anton Gill. Highly readable mystery trilogy set in the turmoil of post-Akhenaten Egypt.

Ramses: The Son of Light, by Christian Jacq. First of a five volume trashy and immensely popular hagiography of the famous pharaoh. Prose is simplistic, with long descriptions of rippling muscles and Nefertari's diaphanous robes, but Jacq is an Egyptologist so it must be true.

Leo the African, by Amin Maalouf. The eponymous hero of the book visits a superbly evoked Ottoman-era Cairo where he gets caught up in the tumultuous events of the day. The result is an historical fiction that reads like a thriller.

The Levant Trilogy, by Olivia Manning. Cairo during the war serves as the setting for the trials and traumas of the dislikable bunch of expats. It was filmed by the BBC as *Fortunes of War* starring Kenneth Branagh and Emma Thompson.

The English Patient, by Michael Ondaatjie. Although it has little to do with the film of the same name and has a highly impressionistic sense of history, this story of love and destiny in WWII remains a beautifully written, poetic novel. And a bit of it is set in Egypt.

The Snake-Catcher's Daughter, by Michael Pearce. One of a series of lightweight mystery novels featuring the Mamur Zapt, a police inspector in 19th century Cairo. It reads a bit like Tintin but without the pictures.

NEWSPAPERS & MAGAZINES

The *Egyptian Gazette* is Egypt's awful daily English-language newspaper. It serves largely as a press puff for the office of the president, although it does offer great entertainment for lovers of typos and seriously screwed-up headlines. The Saturday issue is called the *Egyptian Mail*. The French-language equivalents are the daily *Le Progrès Égyptien* and Sunday's *Progrès Dimanche*.

Al-Ahram Weekly (Web site www.ahram .org.eg/weekly) and *Middle East Times* both appear every Thursday and do a much better job of keeping English-readers informed of what's going on. Of the two, the *Middle East Times* is the more readable but the overly academic *Weekly* does benefit from good comprehensive listings covering cinema, theatre, classical music, the arts and lectures. *Al-Ahram* also puts out a weekly French edition, *Hebdo*.

Cairo Times is a fortnightly glossy with great writing. It contains mainly hard news and analysis but there are good cultural features and a lively 'around town' section.

Egypt Today (Web site www.egyptto day.com) is an ad-saturated, general interest glossy with excellent listings but its monthly schedule means that in this most unpredictable of countries, much of the information has a hypothetical quality. *Egypt Today* also has two monthly sister publications: *Sports & Fitness* and *Business Today*.

An extremely broad range of western newspapers and magazines are sold at hotel bookshops and street side newsstands. Papers are just a day old and monthly magazines usually make it within a week of their home publication dates, but expect to pay up to twice the cover price.

Of the local Arab-language press, the venerable state-owned *Al-Ahram* remains the best known of the national dailies, though the journalism is very stilted and conservative in comparison to some of the newer publications such as the progressive business-focused *Al-Alam al-Yom* and the Egyptian edition of the Arab world daily *Al-Hayat*.

RADIO & TV

Despite a firm state stranglehold, Egyptian TV is booming. In the last few years the traditional three channels have been supple-

Egypt at the Cinema

The meticulously painted backdrops of 1998's animated *Prince of Egypt* aside, it's quite some time since Egypt has been seen at the cinema. True, a large part of the Oscar-sweeping *The English Patient* was set in the Western Desert and Cairo but this was silver screen trickery, achieved with scenic doubles. The Egyptian locations were actually Tunisia and, in the case of some interiors, Venice.

It's not that Egypt is unphotogenic – quite the opposite. Its deserts, temples and colourful bazaars appear beguilingly seductive on a wide screen. So much so, that the country experienced a surge in tourism in the wake of *The English Patient*, despite the best attempts of the Tunisian tourist authority to set the record straight. But extortionate taxes levied on foreign film companies keep the cameras away. So it was that in *The Raiders of the Lost Ark*, a long chase scene through the streets of Cairo wasn't Cairo at all but, again, Tunisia.

The last Hollywood production to brave the bureaucracy was *Ruby Cairo* (1993), a limp tale of a wife who tracks down her missing-presumed-dead husband to a hideaway in Egypt. Though headlined by Andie MacDowell and Liam Neeson, the real star of the film is Cairo, where no cliché is left unshown, including camels, Pyramids, moulids and feluccas. The previous year Cairo had a brief supporting role in Spike Lee's *Malcolm X* (1992); newly converted to Islam, Malcolm embraces the Arab world and prays at the Mosque of Mohammed Ali.

There was a time when the romance of Egypt was a very bankable asset for a big budget production. The Pyramids, Islamic Cairo and Karnak were glamorous backdrops for the antics of James Bond in 1977's *The Spy Who Loved Me*. Just a year later many of the same locations were back on screen for the all-star dramatics of *Death On The Nile* (1978). The real mystery here is not a whodunit but how the steamer manages to sail from Aswan down to Karnak and back up to Abu Simbel all in the same day. And we'll leave logic aside completely for 1981's *Sphinx*, shot entirely in Cairo and Luxor, but from which no one emerges with any credit except the location scout.

Egypt's rich history has also provided a wealth of great stories that have inspired many great (and some not so great) films. Before Walt Disney and the *Prince of Egypt* there was Cecil B de Mille and *The Ten Commandments*, which he made twice, while the story of Cleopatra and Marc Anthony has been filmed numerous times, most memorably in 1963 as *Cleopatra* starring Elizabeth Taylor and Richard Burton in a fabulously expensive production which involved several months shooting in the Egyptian desert. *Gallipoli* (1981) shows Egypt as a base for Aussie soldiers during WWI, training for the fateful battle of the title; and *Ice Cold in Alex* (1958) is a classic drama of a British ambulance officer and crew fleeing Rommel's forces across the Western Desert and dreaming of an ice cold beer in a little bar in Alexandria.

mented by half a dozen or more, as throughout the country every governorate gets in on the act with their own station. Nile TV, which is based in Cairo, broadcasts news and current affairs exclusively in English and French from 7 am each day until past midnight. Otherwise, there's little for non-Arabic speakers, apart from the occasional old American movie (the Saturday night Cine Club on Channel One sometimes screens the odd good one) and a nightly English-language news bulletin on Channel Two at 8 pm.

Satellite has made a big splash (check the number of dishes on the city skylines), and cable to a lesser extent. Many hotels have satellite TV, even some of the budget places. MTV seems to be a staple at fast-food joints country wide.

Radio-wise, FM95 broadcasts news in English on 557 kHz at 7.30 am and 2.30 and 8 pm daily. This is the European-language station and, in addition to English-language programs, it has programs in French, German, Italian, and Greek. BBC and Voice of America (VOA) broadcasts can be picked up on medium wave at various times of the morning and evening. The BBC can be heard on both 639 kHz and 1320 kHz, and VOA on 1290 kHz.

Check the *Egyptian Gazette* for the day's TV (both local and satellite) and radio program information. There are also a couple of special monthly program-listing magazines for satellite and cable.

PHOTOGRAPHY & VIDEO

Egypt is full of opportunities for great photography. Early morning and late afternoon are the best times as during the rest of the day, the sunlight can be too bright and the sky too hazy, resulting in washed out photos. There are a few remedies for this: a polarisation filter will cut glare and reflection off sand and water; a lens hood will cut some of the glare; Kodachrome film with an ASA of 64 or 25 and Fujichrome 50 and 100 are good slide films to use when the sun is bright.

Cameras and lenses collect dust quickly in Egypt. Lens paper and cleaner are difficult to find, so bring your own. A dust brush is also useful.

Photography is allowed at all ancient sites, however, flash photography is banned in some of the tombs to help preserve the paintings. You can take photos of the interior of mosques and temples, although at an increasing number of sites the government now charges E£5 to E£15 for the privilege.

Outrageous fees have also been introduced for using a video camera at many ancient sites. In most cases it's around E£25, but fees of E£100 or even E£150 are becoming more common.

Film & Equipment

Film generally costs as much as, if not more than, it does in the west; for example, Ko-

dacolor 100/200 (36 exposures) costs about E£22, while for Kodachrome 100 slide film you'll pay E£24 (36 exposures). If you do buy film in Egypt always check the expiry date and don't buy from anywhere that keeps its stock in direct sunlight.

Colour print processing costs from E£2 to E£5 depending on whether it's a one hour or overnight service, plus from 50 to 135pt per print depending on print size. B&W processing is not recommended, but colour processing is usually adequate for nonprofessional purposes. Developing a roll of slide film costs between E£10 and E£13. There are quite a few labs and one hour processing places in the big cities and tourist centres, and many of these outlets also do passport photos.

Restrictions

Be careful when taking photos of anything other than tourist sites. It is forbidden to photograph bridges, train stations, anything military, airports and any other public works; a photographer had her film confiscated for shooting pictures of public telephones, while another spent a day at a police station for inadvertently snapping a factory. If anyone kicks up a fuss at where you point your camera apologise and get the message across that you're just a 'dumb tourist' who doesn't know any better.

Egyptians are also sensitive about the negative aspects of their country. It is not uncommon for someone to yell at you when you're trying to take photos of things like a crowded bus, a dilapidated building or a donkey cart full of garbage. Exercise discretion.

Photographing People

It can sometimes be tricky taking photos of people, so it's always better to ask first. Children will almost always say yes, but their parents or other adults might say no. Some Muslims believe that by taking photos of children you might be casting an 'evil eye' upon them. Similar attitudes sometimes apply to taking photos of women, especially in the countryside.

TIME

Egypt is two hours ahead of GMT/UTC and daylight saving time is observed (it begins on May and ends on 30 September). So, without allowing for variations due to daylight saving, when it's noon in Cairo it is: 2 am in Los Angeles; 5 am in New York and Montreal; 10 am in London; 1 pm in Moscow; and 7 pm in Melbourne and Sydney.

ELECTRICITY

Electric current is 220 volts AC, 50 Hz. Wall sockets are the round, two pin European type (though for some strange reason the socket holes are often too narrow to accept European plugs). Adaptor plugs are easily found in city stores but bring a transformer if you need one as these are difficult to obtain in Egypt.

WEIGHTS & MEASURES

Egypt is on the metric system. Basic conversion charts are given on the inside of the back cover of this book.

LAUNDRY

There are a few self-service laundries around Cairo but virtually none elsewhere. Another option is to take your clothes to one of Egypt's many 'hole-in-the-wall' laundries where they wash and iron your clothes by hand. The process is fascinating to watch. The *mukwagee* (ironing man) takes an ancient iron which opens at the top, places hot coals inside and then fills his mouth with water from a bottle on the table. The water is sprayed from his mouth over the clothes as he vigorously irons. Most hotels can organise to have your washing done.

In a few of the places where travellers hang out, like Luxor and Dahab, some of the cheaper hotels lure guests with advertisements about 'washing machines'. Don't be fooled into thinking they've got a Zanussi stashed away in a back room; the reality is a humble machine that lethargically twists your clothes around and leaves you to do the rinsing and wringing out. These machines are almost as laborious as

your last – and most common – option, which is to do your own washing by hand.

TOILETS

Public toilets, when they can be found, are bad news: fly-infested, dirty and smelly. Some toilets are still of the 'squat over a hole in a little room' variety. Only in mid-range and top-end hotels will toilet paper be provided; most toilets simply come equipped with a water squirter for washing yourself when you're finished. It's a good idea to adopt this practice if you can as toilets in Egypt are not capable of swallowing much toilet paper and it's not uncommon to find toilets in hotels frequented by westerners absolutely choked with the stuff. If you do use toilet paper, put it in the bucket that's usually provided.

In cities it's a good idea to make a mental note of all western-style fast food joints, like McDonald's and KFC, and of the five-star hotels, as these are the places where you'll find the most sanitary facilities.

While on the subject of ablutions, when trekking in the desert, climbing Mt Sinai or camping out on a beach somewhere do not leave used toilet paper lying around. Burying it is no good either; sand is blown away in strong winds. So either take a plastic bag with you and put it in there, to be thrown in a bin later, or take some matches and burn it.

HEALTH

Travel health depends on your predeparture preparations, your daily health care while travelling and how you handle any medical problem that does develop. While the potential dangers can seem quite frightening, in reality few travellers to Egypt ever experience anything more than upset stomachs.

Predeparture Planning

Before travelling, it's a good idea to ensure that your tetanus, diphtheria and polio vaccinations are up to date. Discuss your requirements with your doctor. Other diseases you should consider having vaccinations for are typhoid and hepatitis A, which are food-borne diseases, and hepatitis B, which is transmitted through sexual activity and blood (for more details about the diseases themselves, see the individual entries later).

Immunisations Plan ahead for getting your vaccinations: some of them require more than one injection, while some should not be given together. Note that some vaccinations should not be given during pregnancy or to people with allergies – discuss with your doctor.

It is recommended you seek medical advice at least six weeks before travel. Be aware that there is often a greater risk of disease with children and during pregnancy.

It's a good idea to carry proof of your vaccinations. If you are coming into Egypt from most of sub-Saharan Africa and parts of South America you'll need a certificate but there is no risk of yellow fever in Egypt.

Diphtheria & Tetanus Vaccinations for these two diseases are usually combined and are recommended for everyone. After an initial course of three injections (usually given in childhood), boosters are necessary every 10 years.

Polio Everyone should keep up to date with this vaccination, normally given in childhood. A booster every 10 years maintains immunity.

Hepatitis A Hepatitis A vaccine (eg Avaxim, Havrix 1440 or VAQTA) provides long-term immunity (possibly more than 10 years) after an initial injection and a booster at six to 12 months. Alternatively, an injection of gamma globulin can provide short-term protection against hepatitis A – two to six months, depending on the dose given. It is not a vaccine, but is a ready-made antibody collected from blood donations. It is reasonably effective and, unlike the vaccine, it is protective immediately, but because it is a blood product, there are current concerns about its long-term safety. Hepatitis A vaccine is also available in a combined form, Twinrix, with hepatitis B vaccine. Three injections over a six-month period are required, the first two providing substantial protection against hepatitis A.

Typhoid Vaccination against typhoid may be required if you are travelling for more than a couple of weeks in most parts of Asia, Africa, Central and South America and Central and Eastern Europe. It is now available either as an injection or as capsules to be taken orally.

Cholera The current injectable vaccine against cholera is poorly protective and has many side effects, so it is not generally recommended. However, in some situations it may be necessary to have a certificate as travellers are very occasionally asked by immigration officials to present one, even though all countries and the WHO have dropped cholera immunisation as a health requirement for entry.

Hepatitis B Travellers who should consider vaccination against hepatitis B include those on a long trip, as well as those visiting countries where there are high levels of hepatitis B infection, where blood transfusions may not be adequately screened or where sexual contact or needle sharing is a possibility. Vaccination involves three injections, with a booster at 12 months. More rapid courses are available if necessary.

Rabies Vaccination should be considered by those who will spend a month or longer in Egypt, especially if they are cycling, handling animals, caving or travelling to remote areas, and for children (who may not report a bite). Pretravel rabies vaccination involves having three injections over 21 to 28 days. If someone who has been vaccinated is bitten or scratched by an animal, they will require two booster injections of vaccine; those not vaccinated require more.

Malaria Medication There is a risk of malaria in the Al-Fayoum area only, with the highest risks from June to October.

Antimalarial drugs do not prevent you from being infected but kill the malaria parasites during a stage in their development and significantly reduce the risk of becoming very ill or dying. Expert advice on medication should be sought, as there are many factors to consider, including the area to be visited, the risk of exposure to malaria-carrying mosquitoes, the side effects of medication, your medical history and whether you are a child or an adult or pregnant. Travellers going to isolated areas in high-risk countries may like to carry a treatment dose of medication for use if symptoms occur.

Health Insurance Make sure that you have adequate health insurance. See Travel Insurance under Visas & Documents earlier in this chapter for details.

Medical Kit Check List

Following is a list of items you should consider including in your medical kit – consult
your pharmacist for brands available in
your country.

- ☐ **Aspirin** or **paracetamol** (acetamin-
ophen in the US) – for pain or fever.
- ☐ **Antihistamine** – for allergies, eg hay
fever; to ease the itch from insect bites
or stings; and to prevent motion sickness.
- ☐ **Antibiotics** – consider including these
if you're travelling well off the beaten
track; see your doctor, as they must be
prescribed, and carry the prescription
with you.
- ☐ **Loperamide** or **diphenoxylate** –
'blockers' for diarrhoea; **prochlorper-
azine** or **metaclopramide** for nausea
and vomiting.
- ☐ **Rehydration mixture** – to prevent dehydration, eg due to severe diarrhoea;
particularly important when travelling
with children.
- ☐ **Insect repellent, sunscreen, lip balm**
and **eye drops**.
- ☐ **Calamine lotion, sting relief spray** or
aloe vera – to ease irritation from sunburn and insect bites or stings.
- ☐ **Antifungal cream** or **powder** – for
fungal skin infections and thrush.
- ☐ **Antiseptic** (such as povidone-iodine)
– for cuts and grazes.
- ☐ **Bandages, Band-Aids (plasters)** and
other wound dressings.
- ☐ **Water purification tablets** or **iodine**.
- ☐ **Scissors, tweezers** and a **thermometer**
(note that mercury thermometers are
prohibited by airlines).
- ☐ **Syringes** and **needles** – in case you
need injections in a country with medical hygine problems. Ask your doctor
for a note explaining why you have
them.
- ☐ **Cold** and **flu tablets, throat lozenges**
and **nasal decongestant**.
- ☐ **Multivitamins** – consider for long
trips, when dietary vitamin intake may
be inadequate.

Travel Health Guides If you are planning
to be away or travelling in remote areas for
a long period of time, you may like to consider taking a more detailed health guide
with you.

CDC's Complete Guide to Healthy Travel, Open
Road Publishing, 1997. The US Centers for
Disease Control & Prevention recommendations for international travel.
*Staying Healthy in Asia, Africa & Latin Amer-
ica*, by Dirk Schroeder, Moon Publications,
1994. Probably the best all-round guide to
carry; it's detailed and well organised.
Travellers' Health, Dr Richard Dawood, Oxford
University Press, 1995. Comprehensive, easy
to read, authoritative and highly recommended, although it's rather large to lug
around.
Where There Is No Doctor, David Werner,
Macmillan, 1994. A very detailed guide intended for someone, such as a Peace Corps
worker, going to work in an underdeveloped
country.
Travel with Children, Maureen Wheeler, Lonely
Planet Publications, 1995. Includes advice on
travel health for younger children.

There are also a number of excellent travel
health sites on the Internet. From the
Lonely Planet home page there are links at
www.lonelyplanet.com/health/health.htm/h
links.htm to the World Health Organization
and the US Centers for Disease Control &
Prevention.

Other Preparations If you require a particular medication take an adequate supply,
as it may not be available locally. Take part
of the packaging showing the generic name
rather than the brand, which will make getting replacements easier. It's a good idea to
have a legible prescription or letter from
your doctor to show that you legally use the
medication to avoid any problems.

Basic Rules
The main concern in Egypt for most of the
year is the heat. Drink plenty of fluids to
prevent dehydration. Avoid sunburn by
using sunscreen and wearing a hat, and protect your eyes with good quality sunglasses.

For further details on how to recognise and combat heat-related sickness see Heat Exhaustion later.

Food There is an old colonial adage which says: 'If you can cook it, boil it or peel it you can eat it … otherwise forget it'. Vegetables and fruit should be washed with purified water or peeled where possible. Beware of ice cream which is sold in the street or anywhere it might have been melted and refrozen; if there's any doubt (eg a power cut in the last day or two), steer well clear. Shellfish such as mussels, oysters and clams should be avoided as well as undercooked meat, particularly in the form of mince. Steaming does not make shellfish safe for eating.

If a place looks clean and well run and the vendor also looks clean and healthy, then the food is probably safe to eat. In general, places that are packed with travellers or locals will be fine, while empty restaurants are always questionable. The food in busy restaurants is cooked and eaten quickly with little time to stand around and is probably not reheated.

Water US embassy tests on local tap water have confirmed it to be safe – the funny taste is due to its high chlorine content, which makes it a great antiseptic for washing fruit and vegetables.

However, if you are in Egypt on a short-term stay, doctors recommend sticking to mineral water as it takes a while for digestive systems to adapt to even minor changes in water content. There are several good local brands widely available such as 'Baraka' or 'Siwa'. When you buy, check that the seal on the bottle is not broken – it's not unknown for shopkeepers to refill mineral water bottles with tap water.

Take care with fruit juice, particularly if water may have been added. Milk should be treated with suspicion as it is often unpasteurised, though boiled milk is fine if it is kept hygienically. Tea or coffee should also be OK, since the water should have been boiled.

Nutrition

If your diet is poor or limited in variety, if you're travelling hard and fast and therefore missing meals or if you simply lose your appetite, you can soon start to lose weight and place your health at risk.

Make sure your diet is well balanced. Cooked eggs, tofu, beans, lentils (dhal in India) and nuts are all safe ways to get protein. Fruit you can peel (bananas, oranges or mandarins for example) is usually safe (melons can harbour bacteria in their flesh and are best avoided) and a good source of vitamins. Try to eat plenty of grains (including rice) and bread. Remember that although food is generally safer if it is cooked well, overcooked food loses much of its nutritional value. If your diet isn't well balanced or if your food intake is insufficient, it's a good idea to take vitamin and iron pills.

In hot climates make sure you drink enough – don't rely on feeling thirsty to indicate when you should drink. Not needing to urinate or small amounts of very dark yellow urine is a danger sign. Always carry a water bottle with you on long trips. Excessive sweating can lead to loss of salt and therefore muscle cramping. Salt tablets are not a good idea as a preventative, but in places where salt is not used much, adding salt to food can help.

Medical Problems & Treatment

Self-diagnosis and treatment can be risky, so you should always seek medical help. An embassy, consulate or five-star hotel can usually recommend a local doctor or clinic. Although we do give drug dosages in this section, they are for emergency use only. Correct diagnosis is vital. In this section we have used the generic names for medications – check with a pharmacist for brands available locally.

Note that antibiotics should ideally be administered only under medical supervision.

Take only the recommended dose at the prescribed intervals and use the whole course, even if the illness seems to be cured earlier. Stop immediately if there are any serious reactions and don't use the antibiotic at all if you are unsure that you have the correct one. Some people are allergic to commonly prescribed antibiotics such as penicillin; carry this information (eg on a bracelet) when travelling.

Doctors, Dentists & Hospitals

It's best to inquire at your embassy for the latest list of recommended doctors and dentists. The UK and US embassies also have health units that can direct people with special problems, or who need immediate care, to suitable physicians. Doctors and hospitals usually expect immediate cash payment for their services.

It may also be worth contacting SOS Assistance, especially if you are considering a long stay in Egypt. This organisation can be contacted care of Cairoscan (☎ 360 0965), 35 Suleiman Abaza, Mohandiseen. Its policy offers full medical cover in case of emergency, including a flight out to the country of your choice under the SOS MEDEVAC scheme. Contact SOS Assistance for more information.

Addresses of hospitals and medical centres are provided in individual city sections throughout this book.

Pharmacies Pharmacies in Egypt (at least those in the bigger cities) are surprisingly good and almost anything can be obtained without a prescription. In addition to western products there are homegrown medications some of which are extremely good. For example, Smecta is a good locally produced compound to ease stomach complaints. Unlike Imodium it doesn't trap the parasites and is a much safer drug to use and quite suitable for children.

Addresses of pharmacies are given in individual city sections of this book, or you can also refer to the listings in the back of *Business Today* magazine and in the *Al-Ahram Weekly* newspaper.

Environmental Hazards

Heat Exhaustion Dehydration and salt deficiency can cause heat exhaustion. Take time to acclimatise to high temperatures, drink sufficient liquids and do not do anything too physically demanding.

Salt deficiency is characterised by fatigue, lethargy, headaches, giddiness and muscle cramps; salt tablets may help, but adding extra salt to your food is better.

Anhidrotic heat exhaustion is a rare form of heat exhaustion that is caused by an inability to sweat. It tends to affect people who have been in a hot climate for some time, rather than newcomers. It can progress to heatstroke. Treatment involves going to a cooler climate.

Heatstroke This serious, occasionally fatal, condition can occur if the body's heat-regulating mechanism breaks down and the body temperature rises to dangerous levels. Long, continuous periods of exposure to high temperatures and insufficient fluids can leave you vulnerable to heatstroke.

The symptoms are feeling unwell, not sweating very much (or at all) and a high body temperature (39°C to 41°C or 102°F to 106°F). Where sweating has ceased, the skin becomes flushed and red. Severe, throbbing headaches and lack of coordination will also occur, and the sufferer may be confused or aggressive. Eventually the victim will become delirious or convulse. Hospitalisation is essential, but in the interim get victims out of the sun, remove their clothing, cover them with a wet sheet or towel and then fan continually. Give fluids if they are conscious.

Prickly Heat Prickly heat is an itchy rash caused by excessive perspiration trapped under the skin. It usually strikes people who have just arrived in a hot climate. Keeping cool, bathing often, drying the skin and using a mild talcum or prickly heat powder or resorting to air-conditioning may help.

Sunburn In Egypt you can get sunburnt surprisingly quickly, even through cloud.

Use a sunscreen, a hat, and a barrier cream for your nose and lips. Calamine lotion or Stingose are good for mild sunburn. Wear good quality sunglasses, particularly if you will be near water, sand or snow.

Infectious Diseases

Diarrhoea Simple things like a change of water, food or climate can all cause a mild bout of diarrhoea, but a few rushed toilet trips with no other symptoms is not indicative of a major problem.

Dehydration is the main danger with any diarrhoea, particularly in children or the elderly as it can occur quite quickly. Under all circumstances *fluid replacement* (at least equal to the volume being lost) is the most important thing. Weak black tea with a little sugar, soda water, or soft drinks allowed to go flat and diluted 50% with clean water are all good. With severe diarrhoea a rehydrating solution is preferable to replace minerals and salts lost. Commercially available oral rehydration salts (ORS) are very useful; add them to boiled or bottled water. In Egypt they are available in boxes of six sachets for a little more than E£1. Just ask for Rehydran. Add one sachet to about 250ml of water. In an emergency you can make up a solution of six teaspoons of sugar and a half teaspoon of salt to 1L of boiled or bottled water. You need to drink at least the same volume of fluid that you are losing in bowel movements and vomiting. Urine is the best guide to the adequacy of replacement – if you have small amounts of concentrated urine, you need to drink more.

Gut-paralysing drugs such as diphenoxylate or loperamide can be used to bring relief from the symptoms, although they do not cure the problem. Only use these drugs if you do not have access to toilets, eg if you *must* travel. Note that they are not recommended for children under 12 years. Do not use these drugs if the person has a high fever or is severely dehydrated.

In certain situations antibiotics may be required: diarrhoea with blood or mucus (dysentery), any diarrhoea with fever, profuse watery diarrhoea, persistent diarrhoea

Bilharzia

Schistosomiasis, more commonly known as bilharzia, is a frighteningly debilitating disease carried in fresh water by minute worms. The worm enters through the skin and attaches itself to your intestines or bladder. The first symptom may be a general feeling of being unwell, or a tingling and sometimes a light rash around the area where it entered. Weeks later a high fever may develop. Once the disease is established, abdominal pain and blood in the urine are other signs. The infection often causes no symptoms until the disease is well established (several months to years after exposure) and damage to internal organs is irreversible.

It's prevalent in the Nile Delta area and in the Nile Valley. To be on the safe side, do not drink, wash, paddle or even stand in water except swimming pools, the ocean or the oases pools out in the Western Desert. Above all, do not swim in the Nile.

Seek medical attention if you think you may have been exposed to the disease. A blood test is the most reliable way to diagnose the disease, but the test will not show positive until a number of weeks after exposure.

not improving after 48 hours and severe diarrhoea. These suggest a more serious cause and gut-paralysing drugs should be avoided.

In these situations, a stool test may be necessary to diagnose what bug is causing your diarrhoea, so you should seek medical help urgently. Where this is not possible the recommended drugs for bacterial diarrhoea (the most likely cause of severe diarrhoea in travellers) are norfloxacin 400mg twice daily for three days or ciprofloxacin 500mg twice daily for five days. These are not recommended for children or pregnant women. The drug of choice for children would be co-trimoxazole with dosage dependent on weight. A five day course is given. Ampicillin or amoxycillin may be given in pregnancy, but medical care is necessary.

Two causes of persistent diarrhoea in travellers are giardiasis and amoebic dysentery. **Giardiasis** is caused by a common parasite, *Giardia lamblia*. Symptoms include stomach cramps, nausea, a bloated stomach, watery, foul-smelling diarrhoea and frequent gas. Giardiasis can appear several weeks after you have been exposed to the parasite. The symptoms may disappear for a few days and then return; this can go on for several weeks.

Amoebic dysentery, caused by the protozoan *Entamoeba histolytica*, is characterised by a gradual onset of low-grade diarrhoea, often with blood and mucus. Cramping abdominal pain and vomiting are less likely than in other types of diarrhoea, and fever may not be present. It will persist until treated and can recur and cause other problems.

You should seek medical advice if you think you have giardiasis or amoebic dysentery, but where this is not possible, tinidazole or metronidazole are the recommended drugs. Treatment is a 2g single dose of tinidazole or 250mg of metronidazole three times daily for five to 10 days.

Fungal Infections Fungal infections occur more commonly in hot weather and are usually found on the scalp, between the toes (athlete's foot) or fingers, in the groin and on the body (ringworm). You get ringworm (which is a fungal infection, not a worm) from infected animals or other people. Moisture encourages these infections.

To prevent fungal infections wear loose, comfortable clothes, avoid artificial fibres, wash frequently and dry yourself carefully. If you do get an infection, wash the infected area at least daily with a disinfectant or medicated soap and water, and rinse and dry well. Apply an antifungal cream or powder like tolnaftate (Tinaderm). Try to expose the infected area to air or sunlight as much as possible and wash all towels and underwear in hot water, change them often and let them dry in the sun.

Hepatitis Hepatitis is a general term for inflammation of the liver. It is a common disease worldwide. There are several different viruses that cause hepatitis, and they differ in the way that they are transmitted. The symptoms are similar in all forms of the illness, and include fever, chills, headache, fatigue, feelings of weakness and aches and pains, followed by loss of appetite, nausea, vomiting, abdominal pain, dark urine, lightcoloured faeces, jaundiced (yellow) skin and yellowing of the whites of the eyes. People who have had hepatitis should avoid alcohol for some time after the illness, as the liver needs time to recover.

Hepatitis A is transmitted by contaminated food and drinking water. You should seek medical advice, but there is not much you can do apart from resting, drinking lots of fluids, eating lightly and avoiding fatty foods. Hepatitis E is transmitted in the same way as hepatitis A; it can be particularly serious in pregnant women.

There are almost 300 million chronic carriers of **hepatitis B** in the world. It is spread through contact with infected blood, blood products or body fluids, for example through sexual contact, unsterilised needles and blood transfusions, or contact with blood via small breaks in the skin. Other risk situations include having a shave, tattoo or body piercing with contaminated equipment. The symptoms of hepatitis B may be more severe than type A and the disease can lead to long term problems such as chronic liver damage, liver cancer or a long term carrier state. Hepatitis C and D are spread in the same way as hepatitis B and can also lead to long term complications.

There are vaccines against hepatitis A and B, but there are currently no vaccines against the other types of hepatitis. Following the basic rules about food and water (hepatitis A and E) and avoiding risk situations (hepatitis B, C and D) are important preventative measures.

HIV & AIDS Infection with the human immunodeficiency virus (HIV) may lead to acquired immune deficiency syndrome (AIDS), which is a fatal disease. Any exposure to blood, blood products or body fluids may put the individual at risk. The disease is often transmitted through sexual contact or dirty needles – vaccinations, acupuncture, tattooing and body piercing can be potentially as dangerous as intravenous drug use. HIV/AIDS can also be spread through infected blood transfusions; some countries, including Egypt, cannot afford to screen blood used for transfusions.

If you do need an injection, ask to see the syringe unwrapped in front of you, or take a needle and syringe pack with you.

Fear of HIV infection should never preclude treatment for serious medical conditions.

Intestinal Worms These parasites are most common in rural, tropical areas. The different worms have different ways of infecting people. Some may be ingested on food such as undercooked meat (eg tapeworms) and some enter through your skin (eg hookworms). Infestations may not show up for some time, and although they are generally not serious, if left untreated some can cause severe health problems later. Consider having a stool test when you return home to check for these and determine the appropriate treatment.

Typhoid Typhoid fever is a dangerous gut infection caused by contaminated water and food. Medical help must be sought.

In its early stages sufferers may feel they have a bad cold or flu on the way, as early symptoms are a headache, body aches and a fever which rises a little each day until it is around 40°C (104°F) or more. The victim's pulse is often slow relative to the degree of fever present – unlike a normal fever where the pulse increases. There may also be vomiting, abdominal pain, diarrhoea or constipation.

In the second week the high fever and slow pulse continue and a few pink spots may appear on the body; trembling, delirium, weakness, weight loss and dehydration may occur. Complications such as pneumonia, perforated bowel or meningitis may occur.

Everyday Health

Normal body temperature is up to 37°C (98.6°F); more than 2°C (4°F) higher indicates a high fever. The normal adult pulse rate is 60 to 100 per minute (children 80 to 100, babies 100 to 140). As a general rule the pulse increases about 20 beats per minute for each 1°C (2°F) rise in fever.

Respiration (breathing) rate is also an indicator of illness. Count the number of breaths per minute: between 12 and 20 is normal for adults and older children (up to 30 for younger children, 40 for babies). People with a high fever or serious respiratory illness breathe more quickly than normal. More than 40 shallow breaths a minute may indicate pneumonia.

Insect-Borne Diseases

Dengue fever, leishmaniasis and typhus are insect-borne diseases, but they do not pose a great risk to travellers. For more information on them see Less Common Diseases at the end of this health section.

Malaria This serious and potentially fatal disease is spread by mosquito bites. If you are travelling to the El-Fayoum area it is extremely important to avoid mosquito bites and perhaps to take tablets to prevent this disease (discuss this with your doctor before you leave). Symptoms range from fever, chills and sweating, headache, diarrhoea and abdominal pains to a vague feeling of ill-health. Seek medical help immediately if malaria is suspected. Without treatment malaria can rapidly become more serious and can be fatal.

If medical care is not available, malaria tablets can be used for treatment. You need to use a malaria tablet which is different from the one you were taking when you contracted malaria. The standard treatment dose of mefloquine is two 250mg tablets and a further two six hours later. For Fansidar, it's a single dose of three tablets. If you vere previously taking mefloquine and cannot obtain Fansidar, then other alternatives are Malarone (atovaquone-proguanil; four tablets once daily for three days), halofantrine (three doses of two 250mg tablets every six hours) or quinine sulphate (600mg every six hours). There is a greater risk of side effects with these dosages than in normal use if used with mefloquine, so medical advice is preferable. Be aware also that halofantrine is no longer recommended by the WHO as emergency standby treatment, because of side effects, and should only be used if no other drugs are available.

Travellers are advised to prevent mosquito bites at all times. The main messages are:

- wear light-coloured clothing;
- wear long trousers and long-sleeved shirts;
- use mosquito repellents containing the compound DEET on exposed areas (prolonged overuse of DEET may be harmful, especially to children, but its use is considered preferable to being bitten by disease-transmitting mosquitoes);
- avoid perfumes or aftershave;
- use a mosquito net impregnated with mosquito repellent (permethrin) – it may be worth taking your own;
- impregnating clothes with permethrin effectively deters mosquitoes and other insects.

Cuts, Bites & Stings

See Less Common Diseases for details of rabies, which is passed through animal bites.

Cuts & Scratches Wash well and treat any cut with an antiseptic such as povidone-iodine. Where possible avoid bandages and Band-Aids, which can keep wounds wet. Coral cuts are notoriously slow to heal and if they are not adequately cleaned, small pieces of coral can become embedded in the wound.

Bedbugs & Lice Bedbugs live in various places, but particularly in dirty mattresses and bedding, evidenced by spots of blood on bedclothes or on the wall. Bedbugs leave itchy bites in neat rows. Calamine lotion or antihistamine cream may help.

All lice cause itching and discomfort. They make themselves at home in your hair (head lice), your clothing (body lice) or in your pubic hair (crabs). You catch lice through direct contact with infected people or by sharing combs, clothing and the like. Powder or shampoo treatment will kill the lice and infected clothing should then be washed in very hot, soapy water and left in the sun to dry.

Bites & Stings Bee and wasp stings are usually painful rather than dangerous. However, in people who are allergic to them severe breathing difficulties may occur and require urgent medical care. Calamine lotion or antihistamine cream will give relief and ice packs will reduce the pain and swelling. There are some spiders with dangerous bites but antivenins are usually available. Scorpion stings are notoriously painful and in some parts of the Middle East can actually be fatal. Scorpions often shelter in shoes or clothing.

Less Common Diseases

The following diseases pose a small risk to travellers, and so are only mentioned in passing. Seek medical advice if you think you may have any of these diseases.

Cholera This is the worst of the watery diarrhoeas and medical help should be sought. Outbreaks of cholera are generally widely reported, so you can avoid such problem areas. *Fluid replacement is the most vital treatment* – the risk of dehydration is severe as you may lose up to 20L a day. If there is a delay in getting to hospital, then begin taking tetracycline. The adult dose is 250mg four times daily. It is not recommended for children under nine years nor for pregnant women. Tetracycline may help shorten the illness, but adequate fluids are required to save lives.

Dengue Fever There is no prophylactic available for this mosquito-spread disease; the main preventative measure is to avoid mosquito bites. A sudden onset of fever, headaches and severe joint and muscle pains are the first signs before a rash starts on the trunk of the body and spreads to the limbs and face. After a further few days, the fever will subside and recovery will begin. Serious complications are not common but full recovery can take up to a month or more.

Leishmaniasis This is a group of parasitic diseases transmitted by sandflies, which are found in Egypt, as well as many parts of the Middle East, Africa, India, Central and South America and the Mediterranean. Cutaneous leishmaniasis affects the skin tissue causing ulceration and disfigurement, and visceral leishmaniasis affects the internal organs. Seek medical advice, as laboratory testing is required for diagnosis and correct treatment. Avoiding sandfly bites is the best precaution. Bites are usually painless, itchy and yet another reason to cover up and apply repellent.

Rabies This fatal viral infection is found in many countries including Egypt. Many animals can be infected (such as dogs, cats, bats and monkeys) and it is their saliva which is infectious. Any bite, scratch or even lick from an animal should be cleaned immediately and thoroughly. Scrub with soap and running water, and then apply alcohol or iodine solution. Medical help should be sought promptly to receive a course of injections to prevent the onset of symptoms and death.

Tetanus This disease is caused by a germ which lives in soil and in the faeces of horses and other animals. It enters the body via breaks in the skin. The first symptom may be discomfort in swallowing, or stiffening of the jaw and neck; this is followed by painful convulsions of the jaw and whole body. The disease can be fatal. It can be prevented by vaccination.

Tuberculosis (TB) TB is a bacterial infection usually transmitted from person to person by coughing but which may be transmitted through consumption of unpasteurised milk. Milk that has been boiled i safe to drink, and the souring of milk to make yoghurt or cheese also kills the bacilli. Travellers are not often at risk as close household contact with the infected person is usually required before the disease is passed on. You may need to have a TB test before you travel as this can help diagnose the disease later if you become ill.

Typhus This disease is spread by ticks, mites or lice. It begins with fever, chills, headache and muscle pains followed by a few days later by a body rash. There is often a large painful sore at the site of the bite and nearby lymph nodes are swollen and painful. Typhus can be treated under medical supervision. Seek local advice on areas where ticks pose a danger and always check your skin carefully for ticks after walking in a danger area such as a tropical forest. An insect repellent can help, and walkers in tick-infested areas should consider having their boots and trousers impregnated with benzyl benzoate and dibutylphthalate.

Women's Health

Gynaecological Problems Antibiotic use, synthetic underwear, sweating and contraceptive pills can lead to fungal vaginal infections, especially when travelling in hot climates. Fungal infections are characterised by a rash, itch and discharge and can be treated with a vinegar or lemon-juice douche, or with yoghurt. Nystatin, miconazole or clotrimazole pessaries or vaginal cream are the usual treatment. Maintaining good personal hygiene and wearing loose-fitting clothes and cotton underwear may help prevent these infections.

Sexually transmitted diseases are a major cause of vaginal problems. Symptoms include a smelly discharge, painful intercourse and sometimes a burning sensation when urinating. Medical attention should be sought and male sexual partners must also be treated. Remember that in addition to these diseases HIV or hepatitis B may also be acquired during exposure. Besides abstiıence, the best thing is to practise safe sex ɪsing condoms.

Pregnancy It is not advisable to travel to some places while pregnant as some vaccinations normally used to prevent serious diseases are not advisable during pregnancy (eg yellow fever). In addition, some diseases are much more serious for the mother (and may increase the risk of a stillborn child) in pregnancy (eg malaria).

Most miscarriages occur during the first three months of pregnancy. They are not uncommon and can occasionally lead to severe bleeding. The last three months should also be spent within reasonable distance of good medical care. A baby born as early as 24 weeks stands a chance of survival, but only in a good modern hospital. Pregnant women should avoid all unnecessary medication, but vaccinations and malarial prophylactics should still be taken where needed. Additional care should be taken to prevent illness and particular attention should be paid to diet and nutrition. Alcohol and nicotine, for example, should be avoided.

WOMEN TRAVELLERS

Egyptians are conservative, especially about matters concerning sex and women; Egyptian women that is, not foreign women.

An entire book could be written from the comments and stories of women travellers about their adventures and misadventures in Egypt. Most of the incidents are nonthreatening nuisances, like a fly buzzing in your ear: you can swat it away and keep it at a distance, but it's always out there buzzing around.

Attitudes to Women

Some of the biggest misunderstandings between Egyptians and westerners occur over the issue of women. Half-truths and stereotypes exist on both sides: many westerners assume all Egyptian women are veiled, repressed victims, while a large number of Egyptians see western women as sex-obsessed and immoral.

For many Egyptians, both men and women, the role of a woman is specifically defined: she is mother and matron of the household. The man is the provider. However, as with any society, generalisations can be misleading and the reality is far more nuanced. There are thousands of middle and upper-middle class professional women in Egypt who, like their counterparts in the west, juggle work and family responsibilities. Among the working classes, where adherence to tradition is strongest, the ideal may be for women to concentrate on home and family, but economic reality means that millions of women are forced to work (but are still responsible for all domestic chores).

The discomfiture of many Egyptians at this mixing of roles has been exploited by Islamists, who have politicised the issue of women and the family in their constant battle to undermine the government. Interspersed with the politics is a general wave of conservatism that has swept the country in recent years. The most visible sign of this return to 'traditional values' has been the huge number of women adopting more conservative dress and wearing the *higab* or headscarf. But again, the issue is more complex than first meets the eye. For every woman who adopts the *higab* for religious reasons, there are many others who wear it because it allows them to walk around freely – not many men would dare hassle a *muhaggaba*! Or because it means they don't have to worry about fashion, or, paradoxically, because it *is* the fashion (check out the different ways to wear a headscarf). It is also a socio-economic phenomenon: only a fraction of wealthy upper-middle or middle-class women have their heads covered

Away from dress, the issue of sex is where the differences between western and Egyptian women are most apparent. Premarital sex (or, indeed, any sex outside marriage) is taboo in Egypt, although, as with anything forbidden, it still happens. Nevertheless, it is the exception rather than the rule – and that goes for men as well as women. However, for women the issue is potentially far more serious. With the

Safety Tips for Women Travellers

- Wear a wedding band. Generally, Egyptian men seem to have more respect for a married woman (this seems not always to work; sometimes Egyptians assume you are not really married).
- If you are travelling with a man, it is better to say you're married rather than 'just friends'.
- Avoid direct eye contact with an Egyptian man unless you know him well; dark sunglasses could help.
- Try not to respond to an obnoxious comment from a man – act as if you didn't hear it.
- Be careful in crowds and other situations where you are crammed between people as it is not unusual for crude things to happen behind you.
- On public transport, sit next to a woman if possible. This is not difficult on the Cairo Metro where the first compartment is reserved for women only.
- If you're in the countryside (off the beaten track) be extra conservative in what you wear.
- Be very careful about behaving in a flirtatious or suggestive manner – it could create more problems than you ever imagined.
- If you need help for any reason (directions etc), ask a woman first. Egyptian women are very friendly and will not threaten or follow you.
- Be wary when horse or camel riding, especially at touristy places. It's not unknown for a guy to ride close to you and grab your horse, among other things. Riding in front of a man on a camel is simply asking for trouble.
- Egypt is not the place for acquiring a full suntan. Only on private beaches in the top-end resorts along the Red Sea and in southern Sinai are you likely to feel comfortable stripping down to a bikini. Along the Mediterranean coast and in oases pools, you'll have to swim in shorts and a T-shirt, at the very minimum, and even then you'll attract a flock of male onlookers. Egyptian women rarely go swimming on public beaches; when they do, they swim fully clothed, scarf and all.
- You may find it handy to learn the Arabic for 'don't touch me' *(aa tilmasni)*. You may find it handy to learn the following Arabic phrases: *'ihtirim nafsak'* (literally 'behave yourself') or *'haasib eedak'* (literally 'watch your hand'). Stronger language will only make it worse.
- Being befriended by an Egyptian woman is a great way to learn more about life in Egypt and, at the same time, have someone totally nonthreatening to guide you around. Getting to know an Egyptian woman is, however, easier said than done. You won't find them in cafes or teahouses and, while many do speak at least some English, fewer women speak English than men.

possible exception of the upper classes, women are expected to be virgins when they get married and a family's reputation can rest upon this point. In such a context, the restrictions placed on a young girl – no matter how onerous they may seem to a westerner – are to protect her and her reputation from the potentially disastrous attentions of men.

The presence of foreign women presents, in the eyes of some Egyptian men, a chance to get around these norms with ease and without consequences. This possibility is reinforced by distorted impressions gained from western TV and, it has to be said, by the behaviour of some foreign women – as one young man in Luxor remarked when asked why he harassed every western woman he saw, 'For every ten that say no, there's one that says yes'. So, as a woman traveller you can expect some verbal harassment at the very least. Sometimes it will go as far as pinching bottoms or brushing breasts but flashing and masturbating in front of the victim are much less common. Serious physical harassment and rape are not significant threats.

What to Wear

Away from the Sinai and Red Sea beaches, Egyptians are quite conservative about dress. Wearing shorts and a tight T-shirt on the street is, in some people's eyes, confirmation of the worst views held of western women. Generally, if you're alone or with other women, the amount of harassment you get will be directly related to how you dress: the more skin exposed, the more harassment. You'll have fewer hassles if you don't dress for hot weather in the same way you might at home. Baggy T-shirts and loose cotton trousers or long skirts won't make you sweat as much as you think and will protect your skin from the sun as well as from unwanted comments. As with anywhere, take your cues from those around you: if you're in a rural area and all the women are in long, concealing dresses, you should be conservatively dressed. If you're going out to a hip Cairo night spot, you're likely to see middle and upper-class Egyptian girls in the briefest designer gear and can dress accordingly – just don't walk there.

Unfortunately, although dressing conservatively should reduce the incidence of any such harassment, it by no means guarantees you'll be left alone.

GAY & LESBIAN TRAVELLERS

Homosexuality in Egypt is no more or less prevalent than elsewhere in the world. It is, however, relatively clandestine. Certainly no Egyptian man would openly attest to being homosexual as gay men are popularly perceived to be weak and feminine.

There is no mention in the law of sexual behaviour between consenting adults of the same sex being a criminal offence, however, discretion is advisable.

There are no national support groups or gay information lines but there are a few

places that are recognised gay hang-outs. Chief of these is Casanova's disco at the Burg Hotel on Gezira (closed at the time of writing but it may reopen again). The Taverne du Champs de Mars and Jackie's Disco, both in the Nile Hilton Hotel, are also popular with gays.

DISABLED TRAVELLERS

Egypt is not well equipped for travellers with a mobility problem; ramps are few, public facilities don't necessarily have lifts, and gaining entrance to some of the ancient sites – such as the Pyramids of Giza or the tombs on the west bank near Luxor – is all but impossible due to their narrow entrances and steep stairs. Temples tend to be more accessible as they're generally built on level ground, and some museums have ramps or lifts.

If you have a physical disability, you should get in touch with your national support organisation (preferably the 'travel officer' if there is one) before you leave.

SENIOR TRAVELLERS

Unlike in many western countries, there are no discounts on public transport, museum admission fees and the like for senior travellers in Egypt.

If you plan to stay in cheap hotels, you'll need to be fit enough to cope with numerous flights of stairs. Many tombs are also accessed by stairs, some of which are steep. The corridors inside tombs are sometimes very low, forcing you to bend over double; some people find this, coupled with the heat and dim lights, quite claustrophobic.

TRAVEL WITH CHILDREN

Egypt is a very child-friendly place and having kids along with you can be a great icebreaker with locals. And with a little creativity, easily bored young people can also have fun visiting temples and antiquities. Seeking out gruesome temple reliefs (of which there are many) or searching for Tutankhamun's toys in the Egyptian Museum are both good ways to pique a child's interest. Although pricey, Dr Ragab's Pharaonic

Village, a theme park with boat rides is usually a big hit with kids of all ages and it gives them an idea of what the pharaohs were about. It's in Giza in Cairo (you'll have to take a taxi to get there), open from 9 am to 5 pm daily and entry is E£40.

Bookshops at most five-star hotels in Cairo and the major tourist centres stock a wide variety of Egyptology-related children's books that will help kids relate to what they're seeing. Locally-produced history books, such as Salima Ikram's *The Pharaohs* are excellent and reasonably priced. (Hoopoe Books is a local children's publisher with a great list of titles that make good souvenirs or presents, too. Visit their Web site at www.hoopoebooks.com.) For something set in modern Egypt, look for *The Day of Ahmed's Secret*, a wonderful story of a day in the life of a small boy who delivers gas canisters in one of Cairo's poor neighbourhoods.

Away from antiquities there are the ever-popular camel or donkey rides. The stables around the Pyramids also have plenty of docile horses suitable for young people. Also for animal fans, Cairo Zoo is good in that it's one of the few zoos where children get to feed the animals – the keepers sell the appropriate foodstuffs.

Swimming is a good way of getting rid of excess energy in the heat. Most four and five-star hotels will let nonresidents pay to use their swimming pools (see Activities in the Cairo chapter) and many let children in for free. If you're in Cairo you might want to check out one of the water parks on the outskirts of the city. Crazy Water has half a dozen or more water slides, a wave pool, a kiddies pool, and a playground area with sand, slides and tunnels. Admission is E£15, or E£12 for small fry. It's open daily from 10 am to 10 pm. To get there, drive 15km from the intersection of the Giza road and Cairo-Alexandria road, then turn left on the route to 6th of October City.

If you're looking for somewhere children-friendly to dine out in Cairo away from the ubiquitous McDonald's and Pizza Hut, then Andrea's and Al-Dar, both open-air chicken restaurants out near the Pyramids, are great. The kids can roam around the gardens, and there are big climbing frames, swings and donkey rides. Children also enjoy the local chain Felfela – most branches have caged birds and aquariums and the Maadi Felfela, which is on the Corniche, has trampolines and bumper cars.

There are a couple of things to keep in mind while you're out and about with kids in Egypt. One is that child-safety awareness is minimal. Seatbelts are nonexistent in the back seats of most cars and taxis, and if you're renting a car remember to specify that you want them. Also, don't expect felucca or other boat operators to have children's lifejackets. If you can't do without them, bring your own. Likewise with helmets for horse riding.

Another potential worry is the high incidence of diarrhoea and stomach problems that hit travellers in Egypt. If your children get sick, keep in mind that they dehydrate far more quickly than adults and given the dry climate it is crucial to keep giving them liquids even if they just throw them up again. It's worth having some rehydration salts on hand just in case (they do double duty as effective hangover cures). These are available at all pharmacies (ask for 'rehydran') and cost about 90pt for a box of six sachets. They can prevent a bad case of the runs from turning into something more serious. Just stir a packet into 200ml of water (the size of a small coke bottle) and keep giving it until the diarrhoea has passed.

DANGERS & ANNOYANCES

The amount of violent crime in Egypt is negligible compared with most western countries. (Crimes of passion are another thing. The *Egyptian Gazette* carries a column called 'Red Handed' which most days is filled with tales of murderous wives, revengeful jilted lovers, and assorted cases of fratricide, patricide and matricide. It makes fascinating reading.) Most visitors and residents would agree that Egyptian towns and cities are some of the world's safest, places in which pedestrians can walk abroad, any-

Scams & Hustles

Egyptians, like the bulk of Arabs, take hospitality to strangers seriously. You'll receive a steady stream of salaams and the odd *'ahlan w'sahlan'* inviting you to sit and have tea. Which makes it difficult to spot the occasional hook.

In certain parts of the country – notably Downtown Cairo and Luxor – you are a magnet attracting instant friends who coincidentally have a papyrus 'factory' they'd like to show you. As an English-speaker you may also be asked to spare a moment to check the spelling of a letter to a relative in America, and while you're at it how about some special perfume for the lady …

It's all pretty harmless stuff but it can become very wearing. Everyone works out their own strategy to reduce this to a minimum. A colleague kept interest at bay by saying 'Ya Russki' – the hustlers would be defeated by the language and besides, every one knew that the Russians had no money. But now that Egypt is a popular holiday destination for newly rich Muscovites, the street shark entrepreneurs are just as fluent in Slavic sales patter as they are in English, German, French, Dutch and Japanese.

About the only way to deal with unwanted attention is to be polite but firm and when you're in for a pitch cut it short with 'Sorry, no thanks'.

Aside from the hustling, there are a few irritating scams. The most common one involves touts who lie and misinform to get newly arrived travellers into hotels for which they get a commission – see the Cairo chapter for more information. Hustlers in Downtown Cairo might loiter outside a central branch of EgyptAir to intercept foreigners and redirect them across the road to an independent travel agent which they falsely claim is the only place non-Egyptians could buy EgyptAir tickets. There are well-dressed guys who cruise Midan Tahrir offering their friendship as a smokescreen for whatever they can get out of it. One reader's letter confesses being taken in by a 'schoolteacher' named Omar who helped arrange a camel ride around the Pyramids for E£110 (fair price: E£10).

If you do get stung, or feel one more, 'Excuse me, where are you from?' will make you crack, bear in mind that acting brusquely will offend the majority of locals who would never dream of hassling a foreigner.

where, at any hour of the day or night. Unfortunately, the hassle factor often means that this isn't quite the case for an unaccompanied foreign woman – see Women Travellers earlier in this chapter.

Neither is petty theft a major problem – Lonely Planet has received very few stories of outright stealing and the few letters we have on this matter point to fellow travellers as the culprits. However, there are certain areas where pickpockets reportedly operate, notably the Metro in Cairo and the packed, local buses running from Midan Tahrir to the Pyramids. Tourists aren't the specific targets but be careful how you carry your money in crowded places.

Most unwary visitors are parted from their money through scams and these are something that you really do have to watch out for – see the boxed text 'Scams & Hustles'.

For further potential dangers and annoyances see the boxed texts 'Warning – Land Mines' on page 479 and 'Drugs & Dahab' on page 494.

Terrorism

Given that an end to the conflict between Islamic extremists and Egypt's secular government seems unlikely any time soon, terrorism must remain a factor to consider. In the wake of the November 1997 slaughter of 58 foreign tourists in Luxor – only two months after the murder of 10 tourists aboard a bus outside Cairo's Egyptian Museum – security remains at an all-time high. But while the phalanxes of heavily armed soldiers around hotels and tourist sights are there to keep the extremists at bay, they can't help but give visitors the jitters.

LEGAL MATTERS

Foreign travellers are subject to Egyptian laws and get no special consideration. If arrested, you have the right to immediately telephone your embassy. For information on driving laws, see Road Rules in the Getting Around chapter.

BUSINESS HOURS

Banking hours are from 8 or 8.30 am to 2 pm from Sunday to Thursday. Many banks in Cairo and other cities open again from 5 or 6 pm for two or three hours, largely for foreign exchange transactions. Some of them also open on Friday and Saturday for the same purposes. (In the Cairo chapter you'll also find listings for a couple of banks that are open 24 hours seven days a week.) During Ramadan, banks are open between 10 am and 1.30 pm. Foreign exchange offices, or forex bureaus, are generally open throughout the day.

Most government offices operate from about 8 am to 2 pm, Sunday to Thursday, but tourist offices are exceptions (for details see city sections).

Shops generally have different hours at different times of the year. In summer most shops are open from 9 am to 1 pm and from 5 to 10 pm or even later. Winter hours are from 10 am to 6 pm. Hours during Ramadan are from 9.30 am to 3.30 pm and 8 to 10 pm. There are no real hard and fast rules however, and even on Fridays, shops are sometimes open for most of the day.

PUBLIC HOLIDAYS & SPECIAL EVENTS

Egypt's holidays and festivals are primarily Islamic or Coptic religious celebrations, although all holidays are celebrated equally by the entire population regardless of creed.

Because the Islamic, or Hjira (meaning 'flight', as in the flight of Mohammed from Mecca to Medina in 622 AD), calendar is 11 days shorter than the Gregorian (western) calendar, Islamic holidays fall 11 days earlier each year. The 11 day rule is not entirely strict – the holidays can fall from 10 to 12 days earlier. The precise dates are known only shortly before they fall as they're dependent upon the sighting of the moon. See the Islamic Holidays table for the approximate dates for the next few years.

Like the Gregorian, the Hjira calendar has 12 lunar months, which are:

1st	Moharrem	30 days
2nd	Safar	29 days
3rd	Rabei al-Awal	30 days
4th	Rabei at-Tani	29 days
5th	Gamada al-Awal	30 days
6th	Gamada at-Taniyya	29 days
7th	Ragab	30 days
8th	Sha'aban	29 days
9th	Ramadan	30 days
10th	Shawal	29 days
11th	Zuu'l Qeda	30 days
12th	Zuu'l Hagga	29 days, 30 in leap years

These also shift forward by approximately 11 days per year. The Islamic Holidays table gives the dates for Ramadan from which you should be able to fix the other months.

The following are public holidays in Egypt:

New Year's Day
  1 January
  Official national holiday but many businesses stay open.
Christmas
  7 January
  Coptic Christmas is a fairly low key affair and only Coptic businesses are closed for the day.
Eid al-Adha
  See Islamic Holidays table.
  Also known as Eid al-Kebir, the 'great feast', this marks the time of the haj, the pilgrimage to Mecca. Those who can afford it buy a sheep to slaughter on the day of the feast, which lasts for three days (although many businesses re-open on the second day). Many families also head out of town, so if you intend travelling at this time secure your tickets well in advance.

The Moulid

A cross between a funfair and a religious festival, a moulid celebrates the birthday of a local saint or holy person. They are often a colourful riot of celebrations with hundreds of thousands of people. Those from out of town set up camp in the streets close to the saints' tomb, where children's rides, sideshows and food stalls are erected. In the midst of the chaos, barbers perform mass circumcisions; snake charmers induce cobras out of baskets; children are presented at the shrine to be blessed and the sick to be cured. *Tartours* (cone-shaped hats) and *fanous* (lanterns) are made and sold to passers-by and in the evenings local Sufis usually hold hypnotic *zikrs* in colourful tents.

A zikr (literally 'remembrance') is where the Sufis chant the name of Allah to achieve a trance-like state that brings them closer to god. The *mugzzabin* (the 'drawn-in') stand in straight lines and sway from side to side to rhythmic clapping that gradually increases in intensity. As the clapping gains momentum, the zikr reaches its peak and the mugzzabin, having attained oneness with Allah, awake sweating and blinking. Other zikrs are formidable endurance tests where troupes of musicians perform for hours in the company of ecstatic dancers.

Most moulids last for about a week, and climax with the *leila kebira* (the big night). Much of the infrastructure is provided by 'professional' moulid people *(mawladiyya)* who spend their lives going from one moulid to another.

For visitors, the hardest part about attending a moulid is ascertaining dates. Events are tied to either the Islamic or Gregorian calendars, and dates can be different each year. Also, you'll need to be prepared for immense crowds (hold onto your valuables or, better still, leave them behind) and women should be escorted by a male.

The country's biggest moulid, the Moulid of al-Badawi, is held in Tanta in October, while Cairo hosts three major moulids dedicated to Sayyida Zeinab, Al-Hussein and Imam ash-Shafi (held during the Islamic months of Ragab, Rabei al-Tani and Sha'aban, respectively). You'll need to ask a local for the exact dates in any particular year.

See also the boxed text 'Moulids Around Luxor' on page 305.

Ras as-Sana
  See Islamic Holidays table.
  Islamic New Year's Day. The entire country has the day off but celebrations are low key.
Easter
  March/April
  The most important date on the Coptic calendar.
Sham an-Nessim
  A Coptic holiday with pharaonic origins, it literally means 'the smell of the breeze'. It falls on the first Monday after the Coptic Easter and is celebrated by all Egyptians with family picnics and outings.
Sinai Liberation Day
  25 April
  Official national holiday. Celebrates Israel's return of the Sinai in 1982.
May Day
  1 May
  Official national holiday.

Moulid an-Nabi
  See Islamic Holidays table.
  Birthday of the Prophet Mohammed. One of the major holidays of the year – the streets are a feast of lights and food.
Revolution Day
  23 July
  Official national holiday. Commemorates the date of the 1952 coup when the Free Officers seized power from the puppet monarchy.
National Day
  6 October
  Official national holiday. Celebrates Egyptian successes during the 1973 War with Israel. The day is marked by military parades and air displays and a long speech by the president.
Ramadan
  See Islamic Holidays table.
  Ramadan is the ninth month of the Muslim calendar, when all believers fast during the

Islamic Holidays

Hjira Year	New Year	Prophet's Birthday	Ramadan Begins	Eid al-Fitr	Eid al-Adha
1420	17.04.99	25.06.99	08.12.99	07.01.00	17.03.00
1421	06.04.00	14.06.00	27.11.00	27.12.00	06.03.01
1422	26.03.01	03.06.01	16.11.01	16.12.01	23.02.02
1423	15.03.02	23.05.02	05.11.02	05.12.02	12.02.03

day. Pious Muslims do not allow *anything* to pass their lips in daylight hours. Although many Muslims do not follow the injunctions to the letter, most conform to some extent. However, the impact of the fasting is often lessened by a shift in waking hours – many only get up in the afternoon when there are just a few hours of fasting left to observe. They then feast through the night until sunrise. The combination of abstinence and lack of sleep means that tempers are often short during Ramadan. Although there are no public holidays until Eid al-Fitr (see later), it is difficult to get anything done because of erratic hours. Almost everything closes in the afternoon or has shorter daytime hours; this does not apply to businesses that cater mostly to foreign tourists, but some restaurants and hotels may be closed for the entire month. Although non-Muslims are not expected to fast it is considered impolite to eat or drink in public during fasting hours. The evening meal during Ramadan, called *iftar* (breaking the fast), is always a celebration. In some parts of town tables are laid out in the street as charitable acts by the wealthy to provide food for the less fortunate. Evenings are imbued with a party atmosphere and there's plenty of street entertainment which often goes throughout the night until sunrise.

Eid al-Fitr
See Islamic Holidays table.
A three day feast that marks the end of Ramadan fasting – see the comments for Eid al-Adha.

Special Events
Arabic Music Festival Held in early November, this is a 10 day festival of classical, traditional and orchestral Arabic music held at the Cairo Opera House. Programs are usually in Arabic only but the tourist office should have details.

Book Fair Held every January at the Cairo Exhibition Grounds, this is one of the major events on the city's cultural calendar. It draws in massive crowds, most of whom are there for a day out rather than because of any literary leanings. Far more burgers, soft drinks and balloons are sold than books.

Cairo International Film Festival Held in early December every year, this 14 day festival gives Cairenes the chance to watch a vast range of recent films from all over the world. The main attraction however, is that the films are all supposedly uncensored. Anything that sounds like it might contain scenes of exposed flesh sells out immediately, despite the fact that ticket prices cost twice as much as at other times of the year. The local press carries details of the screenings.

Experimental Theatre Festival Held each September over 10 days, this theatre festival brings to Egypt a vast selection (40 at the last outing) of international theatre troupes. Directors have complained in the past that government censorship effectively prevents any 'experimentation' but nevertheless the festival represents almost the only time each year that it's worth turning out for the theatre in Cairo.

Pharaohs' Rally Held each October, this is a 4WD race through the desert beginning and ending at the Pyramids. It attracts competitors from all over the world.

ACTIVITIES

The heat and predominantly desert landscape greatly limit the types of activities available in Egypt but following is a brief index of some of the possibilities.

Birdwatching Egypt is an ornithologists delight with several excellent birdwatching areas; see Flora & Fauna in the Facts about Egypt chapter for details.

Cycling High temperatures, a limited road network and some fairly dull landscape mean that Egypt is not the ideal place for cycle touring, but see the Getting Around chapter for making the best of what there is.

Desert Safaris The desert safari is only just taking off. Unless you have your own 4WD it's an expensive business but those who've done it say it's an incredible experience well worth your while. The options include the Western Desert with its fantastic sand landscapes, weirdly eroded rocks and Roman ruins, and the more rugged, rocky surrounds of Sinai. Western Desert trips can be arranged in the oases or in Cairo; Sinai safaris are organised at one of the south Sinai resorts like Nuweiba or Dahab or, alternatively, you can book a complete holiday with a specialised Sinai outfit like Wind, Sand & Stars (see Organised Tours in the Getting There & Away chapter).

Diving Many visitors to Egypt rarely have their heads above water. No wonder, as some of the best diving in the world is to be found along the Red Sea coast. The pick of the crop is along the southern stretch towards the border with Sudan and along the southern coast of the Sinai peninsula. Away from the expensive resort atmosphere, there are possibilities further north, such as in Dahab or you can cross the Gulf of Suez to Hurghada. See the Diving the Red Sea chapter.

Fishing See the Fishing Safaris section in the Lake Nasser part of the Nile Valley – Esna to Abu Simbel chapter.

Horse Riding There are two main options: horse trekking in Sinai or renting a horse by the hour from one of the stables near the Pyramids in Cairo.

Snorkelling It isn't necessary to dive to enjoy the marine life of the Red Sea, you can see plenty with just a snorkel, mask and flippers. Along the Sinai coast the reefs are only 15m out and in some places you don't even need to swim out of your depth to be amongst shoals of brightly coloured fish. The best places are Basata, Nuweiba and Dahab, all of which have equipment for hire for around E£10 a day.

Windsurfing Moon Beach in Sinai is reckoned to be one of the world's best windsurfing centres – see Water Sports and Ras as-Sudr in the Sinai chapter.

COURSES

Learning Arabic

Several institutions in Cairo offer Arabic courses. The full-blown option is to sign up at the Arabic Language Institute (☎ 354 2964, fax 355 7665, email alu@auc.acs .eun.eg), a department of the American University in Cairo (AUC; PO Box 2511, Cairo 11511). It offers intensive instruction in Arabic language at elementary, intermediate and advanced levels. The courses incorporate both Egyptian colloquial Arabic and classical Arabic – in other words, as well as learning to speak, you learn how to read and write. The intensive, full-time course costs US$10,485 for a full year's tuition, or US$5285 per semester (20 hours per week over 14 weeks). The institute also offers intensive summer programs (20 hours per week for six weeks) for US$2620.

The Arabic Department (☎ 303 1514, fax 344 3076) at the British Council (192 Sharia el-Nil, Agouza, Cairo, Web site www.brit coun.org) also does colloquial and classical courses – the former eight hours a week (afternoons) over six weeks for E£835; the latter 12 hours a week (mornings) over six weeks for E£1275. There are also colloquial evening classes, two hours twice a week for 12 weeks for E£835.

The third and cheapest option is to study at one of the two International Language Institutes (ILI) – in Mohandiseen (☎ 346 3087, fax 303 5624, email ili@starnet .com.eg) at 3 Sharia Mahmoud Azmy, Sahafayeen; or in Heliopolis (☎ 291 9295, fax 418 7273) at 2 Sharia Mohammed Bayoumi. They both charge E£350/390 for a 60 hour program of colloquial/classical. They also offer residential summer courses (running from late June to late July) ranging from E£275 for 40 hours of tuition to E£500 for 100 hours.

Studying at the American University in Cairo

The AUC is one of the premier universities in the Middle East. Some 4300 students, the bulk of whom are Egyptian, study at its campus on Midan Tahrir in the heart of Cairo. The curriculum, and a third of the full-time faculty of 275, are American and accredited in the USA.

The AUC offers degree, nondegree and summer-school programs. Any of the regular courses offered can be taken. Popular subjects include Arabic Language and Literature, Arab History & Culture, Egyptology, Islamic Art and Architecture, Middle East Studies and Social Science courses on the Arab world. Up to 15 unit hours can be taken per semester at the undergraduate level.

Summer programs offer similar courses. The term lasts from mid-June to the end of July. Two three unit courses can be taken and several well-guided field trips throughout Egypt are usually included.

Applications for programs with the Arabic Language Institute (previously detailed) and undergraduate and graduate studies at the university are separate. Specify which you want when requesting an application form. A catalogue and program information can be obtained from: The Office of Admissions, The American University in Cairo, 866 United Nations Plaza, New York, NY 10017 (☎ 212-421 6320, fax 688 5341); or you can write to PO Box 2511,

Cairo 11511 (☎ 354 2964 ext 5011/2/3, fax 355 7565).

Egyptian Universities

It is also possible to study at Egyptian universities such as Al-Azhar, Alexandria, 'Ain Shams and Cairo. Courses offered to foreign students include Arabic Language, Islamic History, Islamic Religion, and Egyptology. For information on courses, tuition fees and applications contact The Cultural Counsellor, The Egyptian Educational Bureau (☎ 202-296 3888), 2200 Kalorama Rd NW, Washington DC 20008. In London, contact the Cultural Affairs Office (☎ 0171-491 7720, from 22 April 2000 ☎ 020-7491 7720).

Dive Courses

For information on the various dive courses offered in Egypt see the Diving the Red Sea chapter.

WORK

More than 40,000 foreigners live and work in Egypt. That figure alone should give you some idea of the immense presence foreign companies have in the country. It is possible to find work with one of these companies, especially if you begin your research before you leave home. *Cairo: A Practical Guide*, published by The American University in Cairo Press, has lists of all foreign companies operating in Egypt. Once you have an employer, securing a work permit through an Egyptian consulate or, in Egypt, from the Ministry of the Interior, should not be difficult.

If you are looking for casual work to extend your stay in Cairo then teaching English at a cowboy school (see Teaching English later) is the probably easiest way. It's also sometimes possible to find other types of work in the resorts. Dahab in particular has a relatively large number of travellers who find short term work as bartenders or administrators in the many hotels and dive centres that dot the beach. There are also a few enterprising travellers who've financed their stay by setting up shop as masseurs, acupuncturists and herbalists. Windsurfing outfits occasionally need staff, although there are not enough of them for much turnover.

Away from the beaches, some of the larger hotels in Luxor and Aswan occasionally take on foreigners as entertainment directors, but many of the large chains have their own staff sent in from abroad.

Teaching English
The most easily available work for native or fluent English speakers is teaching the language to the locals. The best places to do this are reputable schools like the British Council, the ILI in Heliopolis and the Centre for Adult & Continuing Education (☎ 354 2964) at the American University in Cairo – see Learning Arabic earlier for contact details. However, you need to be qualified. The RSA Teaching English as a Foreign Language to Adults (TEFLA) Certificate is the minimum requirement. Full-time teachers (100 hours per month) at the ILI earn E£2450. The British Council pays higher rates but only UK citizens can get full-year contract packages there, though other nationals often work part time.

If you have no qualifications or experience, you could try one of the 'cowboy schools' such as the International Living Language Institute (ILLI) at 34 Talaat Harb in central Cairo. These are fly-by-night places (that said, the ILLI has been around for at least 12 years) that take on unqualified staff and work them hard for little financial return. But they do pay enough to allow you stay on and maybe earn enough to take the TEFLA and gravitate to better paid employment. The ILI in Heliopolis runs several one-month intensive TEFLA courses each year.

Journalism
Another possible source of work for English speakers with a good sense of grammar is in copy-editing for one of Cairo's many English-language publications. *The Egyptian Gazette* and *Al-Ahram Weekly* are probably the best two places to inquire, although new

English-language magazines are springing up all the time. The pay is nothing terrific but it could be enough to scrape by on.

Film & TV Extras
Europeans are often in demand to appear as background decoration in local TV commercials, dramas or even films. The work is far from glamorous and involves hanging around all day when often you're only required for five minutes of shooting. Still, it pays about E£40 to E£50 per session. Notices for persons wanted are sometimes posted at the hostels in the Tawfiqiyya souq in Cairo or, more commonly, middlemen will tell you. They haunt Ash-Shams coffeehouse (see Entertainment in the Cairo chapter) at the top end of Talaat Harb.

Dive Instructors
If you are a divemaster or diving instructor you can find work in Egypt's diving resorts fairly easily. As many divers fund their travels through such work the turnover is high and you're likely to find an opening if you can hang around for a couple of weeks. Owners say that apart from the basic diving qualifications, they look for languages and an ability to get along with people. If you're interested in a job, a dive centre will usually take you along on a few dive trips to assess your diving skills and to see how you interact with others before offering you work.

ACCOMMODATION
Egypt offers visitors the full spectrum of accommodation, from the big international five-star chains to flea-ridden dives. There are hotels, flotels (Nile cruisers), pensions, youth hostels, a few camping grounds and even the odd eco-friendly resort.

As a general rule there is a review of prices each year in October and, on average, prices rise by about 15%.

Residents in Egypt are often entitled to something closer to the local rate for rooms in the bigger hotels. Yes, there is one rate for foreigners and another for locals. If you are a resident, ask about resident rates, as they mean a considerable saving.

Bed, Board & Legends

Egypt was one of tourism's pioneer destinations. Thomas Cook was already running trips up the Nile by the 1860s, and a glance at a Baedecker guide published in 1902 reveals that Cairo had no less than 12 large hotels, catering for intrepid tourists and east-west travellers. Most splendid was the famed Shepheard's Hotel, base camp not just for Egypt but for the Middle East and Africa too. Early guests included General Gordon before setting forth on his ill-fated mission to Khartoum, Stanley bound for Africa and his historic meeting with Livingstone, Sir Richard Burton on his return from Mecca, and Rudyard Kipling en route between England and India. With a fabulous Moorish Hall lit by a dome of coloured glass and a ballroom with lotus-topped pillars modelled on those at Karnak, Shepheard's was the embodiment of imperial hoteliery. Sadly, the place was destroyed in the Black Saturday rioting of 1952.

However, Egypt still has several other exceptional establishments with the magic of a bygone era – along with air-con and other modern creature comforts.

On the official opening in January 1900 of Aswan's Cataract Hotel (now renamed the Old Cataract), *The Daily Telegraph* of London reported that its dining room was 'unmatched even in Europe'. Exactly 99 years later, *The Times*, in its travel pages, still ranks the Cataract among its 100 world's top hotels and regards its terrace to have 'possibly the greatest view in the world'. That view provided inspiration for Agatha Christie, who wrote part of *Death on the Nile* here.

One thing that's available to everyone is bargaining. Just because a hotel has its rates displayed in a glass frame on the wall, it doesn't mean they are untouchable. In off-peak seasons haggling will often get you significant discounts, even in mid-range places.

Camping

Officially, camping is allowed at only a few places around Egypt such as at Harraniyya near Giza in Cairo, Luxor, Aswan, Farafra and Ras Mohammed National Park. At official sites, facilities tend to be rudimentary. A few private hotels around the country also allow campers to set up in their backyard, such as at Abu Simbel, Kharga, Nuweiba, Basata, Qena and Abydos. Facilities in most of these places are also basic.

Hostels

Egypt has 15 hostels recognised by Hostelling International (HI), located in Cairo, Alexandria, Al-Fayoum, Aswan, Asyut, Damanhur, Hurghada, Ismailia, Luxor, Marsa Matruh, Port Said, Sharm el-Sheikh, Sohag, Suez and Tanta. They generally range in price from about E£3 to E£10. The one in Ismailia has beds as expensive as E£16 – it's virtually a hotel. In some cases the price includes breakfast. Having an HI card is not absolutely necessary as nonmembers are admitted but a card will save you between E£2 and E£4, depending on the hostel. The youth hostels tend to be noisy, crowded and often a bit grimy. In some there are rooms for mixed couples or families, but on the whole the sexes are segregated. Reservations are not usually needed.

The offices of the Egyptian Youth Hostels Association (☎ 354 0527, fax 355 0329) at 1 Ibrahimy, Garden City, Cairo, can give you the latest information.

Hotels

Budget The two, one and no-star hotels form the budget group. Often the ratings mean nothing at all, as a hotel without a star can be as good as a two star hotel, only cheaper. You can spend as little as E£10 a

Bed, Board & Legends

The Winter Palace in Luxor predates the Cataract by some 14 years. At first it was reserved exclusively for the use of Egypt's royalty and nobility. Later opened to the public, it served as the gateway to the tombs and temples of the Theban necropolis, visible across the river on the west bank of the Nile. Howard Carter's first announcement of his discovery of the tomb of Tutankhamun was a posting on the guests' bulletin board at the Winter Palace.

With the passing of the Shepheard's, the mantel of top-notch hotel in Cairo passed to the Mena House. Built in the shadow of the Great Pyramids in the 1860s as a hunting lodge for Egypt's ruler, the khedive Ismail, it passed into private hands in the 1890s and was converted into a hotel. At first it could only be reached from Cairo by horse and carriage but when Cairo gained its electric streetcars in the early 20th century a line ran out here. 'At tea hour', according to a pre-WWI description, 'the terraces are crowded with a gay and brilliant throng'. The hotel's isolation from the city was seen as a distinct security advantage when in 1943 Roosevelt and Churchill met there to hammer out plans for the D-Day invasions.

They've all been renovated and remodelled to varying degrees and some have passed into the hands of international chains (Oberoi run the Mena House, the Marriott group has the former royal Gezira Palace in Cairo, and Sofitel runs Alexandria's classic Cecil). However, Egypt's historic hotels still charm. Even if you can't afford to stay, they are worth visiting for a reminder of when hotels were as individual and famed as the celebrities that signed their guest books.

night for a clean single room with hot water or E£40 or more for a dirty double room without a shower. Generally the prices quoted include any charges and quite often breakfast – but don't harbour any great expectations about breakfast as it is usually a couple of pieces of bread, a chunk of frozen butter, a dollop of jam, and tea or coffee.

Most hotels will tell you they have hot water when they don't. They may not even have warm water. Before paying, turn the tap on and check for yourself or keep an eye out for an electric water heater when viewing the bathroom. If there's no plug in your bathroom sink and you forgot to bring your own, then try using the lid of a Baraka mineral water bottle – according to one ingenious traveller, they fit 90% of the time.

Also, many budget establishments economise on sheets, putting only one, or sometimes none, between you and blankets that may never have seen the inside of a washing machine. If you aren't carrying your own sleeping sheet, then just ask for clean sheets – most hotels will oblige.

Mid-Range Mid-range hotels are generally clean, comfortable and relatively good value at E£50 to E£100 per night. However, beware the extras. Breakfast is often compulsory and sometimes you are charged extra for the fridge and TV in your room. You can take an ordinary double room, add E£4 each for two breakfasts, E£2 for the fridge you never used and E£2 for the TV you never turned on, whack 10% service on the whole lot and then 5% sales tax and possibly a government tax on top of that, and your E£50 room is suddenly costing you more than E£70.

Top End At the five star end of the price range are hotels representing most of the world's major chains. But while their prices (typically starting at about US$100 per night, not including a series of taxes and service charges of between 19% and 23%) and amenities are usually up to international standards, service hardly ever is.

Although all five star and many much cheaper hotels still quote prices in US dollars, it is usually no problem paying in Egyptian pounds. Hotels quoting prices in dollars will accept most credit cards, particularly Visa, MasterCard and Amex. Even many smaller places will accept credit cards.

FOOD

While there are many wonderful things about Egypt, food is not one of them. Egyptian cuisine is crude: salads are boring, vinegary and often far from fresh; vegetables have the flavour boiled out of them; typical main dishes of potato, rice and meat are heavy and oily. In fact, Egypt introduced the world to one of the most revolting dishes of all time – *molokhiyya*. Made by stewing the molokhiyya leaf in chicken stock, the resulting soup looks like green algae and has the consistency of mucus. The 11th century caliph Al-Hakim found the stuff so repulsive he had the dish banned.

That said, it is possible to eat well (not to mention cheaply) in Egypt, if you can accept the lack of variety and pack your taste buds off on holiday.

Incidentally, the old cliche of eating at a local home to experience the best of a country's food, does not hold up in Egypt.

Vegetarians

Vegetarians should have no trouble eating in Egypt, even though the concept of vegetarianism is not understood at all. A friend ordered vegetable casserole at a Cairo restaurant and was served up a hunk of lamb in broth. When he complained about his order the waiter replied, 'But there are vegetables in there'.

Misconceptions aside, avoiding meat is easy as salads, dips, pulse-based dishes and stuffed vegetables feature heavily on most restaurant menus. The basic staples of the Egyptian diet are wholly vegetarian too: fuul, ta'amiyya and *kushari*. If you can find it on menus, *musaga* is a great dish; it's a mixture of eggplant, tomatoes, garlic, oil and spices baked in the oven.

Egyptian Staples

Fuul & Ta'amiyya Fuul is mashed fava beans, usually ladled into a piece of *shammy* bread (like pitta) and sells for 35pt to 50pt; ta'amiyya is mashed chickpeas and spices fried in a patty (it's known elsewhere as felafel) and stuffed into a piece of shammy with salad and tahina. A ta'amiyya sandwich costs about 50pt and two make a substantial snack. Bright pink pickled vegetables, known as *torshi*, are usually served complimentary. Sit-down restaurants offer variations on the fuul and ta'amiyya theme serving them up with egg, garlic, butter, mincemeat or *basturma*, a smoked meat which resembles pastrami.

Kushari Next in national affections after fuul and ta'amiyya is *kushari*, a mix of noodles, rice, black lentils, fried onions and tomato sauce. The ingredients are served up together in a bowl (small, *sughayyer*; medium, *metawasit*; or large, *kebir)* for sitdown meals, or spooned into a polythene bag for takeaway. It's very good and has some taste to it. A medium serve, containing more than most people can eat, costs from E£1 to E£1.50. You can recognise kushari joints by the great tureens of noodles and rice in their windows.

Shwarma This is the Egyptian equivalent of the Greek *gyros* sandwich or the Turkish *doner kebab*. Strips of lamb or chicken are sliced from a spit, sizzled on a hot plate with chopped tomatoes and garnish, and then stuffed in a pocket of shammy. Unfortunately, the meat is often unappetisingly fatty and it's difficult to find decent shwarma.

Starters

Although the practice of dining on mezze isn't as ingrained as say with Lebanese cuisine, there are plenty of popular Egyptian side dishes. *Mashi* is various vegetables, such as vine leaves (in summer), cabbage (in winter), peppers, or white and black aubergines, stuffed with minced meat, rice, onions, parsley and herbs and then baked. It's good when just cooked and hot but less so when cold. *Baba ghanoug* is a thick paste made of mashed eggplant with garlic, similar in appearance to *houmos* (cooked chickpeas ground into a paste and mixed with garlic and lemon) and *tahina* (a thinner paste made from sesame seeds).

Egyptians are keen on offal. *Kebda firekh* (chicken livers) are often excellent – if done right they should be beautifully soft with an almost patê-like consistency. Less appealing is *mokh*, or brains. This is served crumbed and deep fried or whole, garnished with salad. Lambs testicles are another delicacy, although these are rarely served alone and are usually included within a mixed grill.

Main Meals

Kofta and *kebab* are two of the most popular dishes in Egypt. Kofta is ground meat peppered with spices, skewered and grilled. Kebab is skewered and flame-grilled chunks of meat, usually lamb (the chicken equivalent is called *shish tawouk*). The meat usually comes on a bed of *badounis* (parsley) and may be served in upmarket restaurants with grilled tomatoes and onions. Otherwise you eat it with bread, salad and tahina. Kofta and kebab are always ordered by weight; 250g ('roba kilo') is usually sufficient for one person and it typically costs from E£9 to E£12.

Firekh (chicken) is common, roasted on a spit and, in restaurants, ordered by the half. Takeaway spit-roasted whole chickens are available from many small restaurants for about E£8 to E£12 depending on the weight. *Hamam* (pigeon) is also extremely popular and usually served stuffed with rice and spices. It's also served as a stew cooked in a deep clay pot, known as a *tagen*, with onions, tomatoes, and rice or cracked wheat. In Alexandria, you'll also get quail.

Alexandria is great for fish – it's easily the best place in the country for eating seafood. Although there's not much variety and the cooking methods are not wildly inventive (baked or grilled), the quality of the catch is good. Open-air fish dining in Alexandria is one of the best dining experiences Egypt has to offer.

Fiteer

Fiteer is a kind of pizza made with a flaky pastry base. The filling can be served as a topping or stuffed inside, and can be sweet or savoury. The place that serves fiteer is called a *fatatri*. Part of the attraction of eating fiteer is watching the dough being pounded, stretched and whirled around the cook's head like a lasso. At most fatatris all the toppings are arrayed in dishes around the cook and you can point to what you want; the typical mix is egg, cheese and chopped tomato. Avoid the meat as it's usually terrible.

Bread & Cheese

For those who find themselves on long train or bus rides, it is also essential to know about bread and cheese – the easily transportable staples of the traveller. Bread, including pita, is called *a'aish* (the word a'aish also means 'life'). Most of the a'aish which you'll see and eat is *a'aish baladi*, a round flat, plate-sized bread which is very coarse and spongy. The other main type is called *a'aish fransawi*, or French bread, which are rolls in the European style.

There are also two main types of cheese: *gibna beida*, or white cheese, which tastes like Greek feta; and *gibna rumi*, or Roman cheese, which is a hard, sharp, yellow-white cheese.

DRINKS
Nonalcoholic Drinks

Tea & Coffee *Shai* and *ahwa* – tea and coffee – are both served strong and sugary.

Tea is served in glasses at traditional Egyptian coffeehouses and in teacups at western-style restaurants. At coffeehouses, the tea leaves are boiled with the water making a very black, tannin-loaded drink; the alternative is to ask for 'shai libton', Lipton being the generic term for teabag. Specify how much sugar you want on ordering, otherwise it'll be assumed that you want four or five spoonfuls. 'Sukar shwaiyya' is 'with a little sugar', 'mingheer sukar' is 'without'. If you want milk ask for 'b'laban', although it's much more refreshing taken with fresh mint ('b'naanaa').

If you ask for coffee, you will probably get *ahwa turki* (Turkish coffee), which comes in a small, two-sip cup. It is gritty and *very* strong. Let the grains settle before drinking. As with tea, specify how much sugar: 'ahwa mazboot' is medium sweet; 'ahwa saada' is no sugar. Coffee is often flavoured with cardamom. If you want western-style coffee ask for 'neskaf'.

Fruit Juices On practically every street in every town throughout Egypt, there is a juice stand where you can get a drink squeezed out of just about any fruit or vegetable in season. Standard *asiir* (juices) include: *moz* (banana); *guafa* (guava); *limoon* (lemon); *manga* (mango); *bortuaan* (orange); *rumman* (pomegranate); *farawla* (strawberry); and *asab* (sugar cane).

Depending on the type of fruit, a glass costs from 50pt to E£1.50. You can also take along an empty mineral water bottle and get that filled up.

Alcoholic Drinks

For notes on Egyptian attitudes to beer and alcohol see Society & Conduct in the Facts about Egypt chapter.

Beer For beer in Egypt say 'Stella'. It's been brewed and bottled in Cairo now for more than 100 years, and for at least the last 40 of those it's been almost the only beer available. It's a yeasty lager, the taste of which varies enormously by batch. Since 1998, the standard Stella (sold in 75cL dark green bottles at E£4 in shops and anywhere from E£5.25 to E£10 in bars) has been supplemented by sister brews including Stella Meister (a light lager) and Stella Premium (which tastes like a particularly rough home brew). Most locals just stick to the unfussy basic brew – it's the cheapest and if served cold it's not bad.

Some bars in five-star hotels do serve imported beers but prices are always outrageous. The duty-free shops (see Customs earlier in this chapter) also often have crates of imported beer.

Wine & Liquor The good news is that there is Egyptian wine; the bad news is that it's undrinkable. From vineyards in the Delta region, Egypt produces red, rosé and white wines and gives them names like Gianaclis Chateaux, Rubis d'Egypte and Cru des Ptolemies. It's all revolting and at E£30 a bottle it isn't cheap either. Unfortunately, outrageous import taxes mean that imported wine, when available, sells for a minimum of E£125 a bottle.

Worse than the local wine is the local liquor, which isn't just bad, it's potentially lethal. Egypt produces its own gin, whisky, vodka and brandy. They all taste roughly the same, which is to say dreadful. Amusingly, the spirits are marketed to resemble foreign imports – the whiskies include Johnny Wadie and Robert Horse, while bottles of Garden's Gin used to carry a bold claim to the effect that 'The Queen drinks this'. What's less funny is that some is truly poisonous. Tales have long circulated among Cairo folk of deaths caused by drinking local spirits. The stories were always apocryphal until the Canadian embassy issued a circular, warning that two deaths had proven to be as a result of drinking local whisky. Leave this stuff well alone.

ENTERTAINMENT

For locals, entertainment depends on gender and age. The great social activity for older males is hanging out at the *ahwa* (coffeehouse). For younger males it's the club and the cinema, while for women of all ages, it's the club and visiting family.

The Ahwa

The coffeehouse or *ahwa* (in Arabic the word means both coffee and the place in which it's drunk) is one of the great Egyptian social institutions. Typically just a collection of cheap tin plate-topped tables and wooden chairs in a sawdust strewn room open to the street, the ahwa is a relaxed and unfussy place where the average Ahmed hangs out for part of each day reading the papers, meeting friends, sipping tea and whiling away the time. The hubbub of conversation is usually accompanied by the incessant clacking of *domina* (dominoes) and

Sheesha smoking at the local ahwa is the great national pastime, but it's mostly an all-male affair.

towla (backgammon) pieces, and the burbling of smokers drawing heavily on their *sheeshas*, the cumbersome waterpipes.

Ahwa-going is an all-male preserve. With few exceptions Egyptian women do not frequent ahwas. That said, there is absolutely no reason why a foreign women shouldn't do so – although if you are unaccompanied by a male choose a large busy ahwa in which you aren't going to stand out too much.

In the hot summer months many ahwa-goers forgo the tea and coffee for cooler drinks like iced *karkadey*, a beautiful drink made from boiled hibiscus leaves, *limoon* (homemade lemon squash), or *zabaady* (yoghurt). In winter many prefer *sahleb*, a warm drink made with semolina powder, milk and chopped nuts, or *yunsoon* a medicinal-tasting aniseed drink.

With the sheesha there's usually a choice of two types of tobacco: the standard *m'aasil*, which is soaked in molasses, or *tofah*, which is soaked in apple juice and has a sweet aroma but a slightly sickly taste.

Filtered by the water in the glass bowl, the smoke is mild but the effort required to draw it can leave you light headed. A good sheesha can last 15 to 20 minutes. When the tobacco is burnt out or the coals have cooled the *raiyis* (waiter) will change the little clay pot of tobacco (the *hagar* or 'stone') for a fresh one. Each hagar costs 50pt to E£1. Most Egyptians smoke two or three at a sitting.

When it comes time to pay catch the eye of the raiyis and shout *Filoos!* (Money!)

There are ahwas on almost every street in every city, town and village in Egypt and throughout this book we point out some of the more interesting ones.

The Club

The *al-nadi* (club) is the other great keystone of Egyptian social life. Unfortunately, this is not so easy for the casual visitor to penetrate. Any local who can afford to do so and has the right connections is a member of a club, which gains them access to a private swathe of the city's precious greenery, along with whatever sporting facilities are on offer. Some of the clubs do allow day memberships and these are worth taking advantage of if you fancy swimming or jogging or simply spending a day away from traffic and crowds surrounded by greenery.

Nightlife

Certain towns and cities like Cairo, the southern Sinai resorts and to a certain extent Alexandria, have a great nightlife scene. Cairo, for instance, only comes to life with the setting of the sun. During the summer months, families don't head out to shop until 8 or 9 pm when the heat of the day is less intense, and the smarter set never make dinner reservations before 10 pm. Bars get busy towards midnight and the witching hour is long past before any discos start to fill. It's after 1 am before the bands kick in and the belly-dancers take to their five-star stages, and 3 or 4 am when the last ones bow out. For those still unwilling to call it a night, Cairo has places that just don't close at all.

Bars Not just in Cairo, but throughout Egypt you'll find plenty of local spit-and-sawdust bars. These places are euphemistically known as 'cafeterias', though the only food present is usually a small plate of *termis* (small yellow beans that you nip with your teeth and squeeze out through their skin), used to salt up the palate and quicken the down flow of beer. Such places are fairly discreet and don't advertise themselves, but if you know what you are looking for they're pretty easy to spot – saloon-type doors leading to a dark interior. A beer typically costs E£5 to E£6 and opening hours are usually from around 11 am to anywhere between 1 and 4 am.

Cairo also has an ever-increasing number of chi-chi bars catering for the city's young moneyed crowd.

You should be aware that all bars except those in hotels are closed for the duration of Ramadan (see Public Holidays & Special Events earlier).

Discos You'll find discos only in Cairo and the southern Sinai resorts, usually attached to upmarket hotels. They almost always have a ridiculously high door charge and many have fairly strict dress codes. They're no great shakes and really not worth the admission with the exception of Cairo's African discos which are a riot – see that chapter for details.

Live Music Live music stops at cabaret artists in hotel lounges backed by a perma-grin keyboardist in an ultra-brite suit. There are a few exceptions. In Aswan and the surrounding villages it's possible to see Nubian artists but it's on a fairly ad hoc basis – see the Aswan section for information. In Cairo, there's live jazz at the Cairo Jazz Club. But that's about it.

Nightclubs & Belly-Dancing Nightclub in the Egyptian sense means a place to sit down and eat, or possibly just drink, and watch a floor show. The floor show can feature folkloric dancing or a star singer, but the ones that really pull in the crowds concentrate on belly-dancing.

The best dancers perform at Cairo's five-star hotels but at the other end of the scale, it is possible to watch belly-dancing for just a few pounds. There are several places Downtown plus plenty more along Pyramids Rd (generally expensive rip-off joints) that cater mainly to Egyptians. These places are fairly seedy and most of the dancers have the appearance and grace of amateur wrestlers, but it can be fun especially when the inebriated patrons join in as they invariably do.

Casinos Some five-star hotels throughout the country have casinos, open to non-Egyptians only (take your passport). All games are conducted in US dollars or other major foreign currencies, with a minimum stake of US$1. Smart casual attire is required.

These casinos are not to be confused with local *casinos*, the name given for certain restaurants popular with families.

The Cultural Scene

Cinema Cinema-going in Egypt is booming. Old movie houses are being refurbished while, in Cairo and Alexandria at least, new multiplexes have either recently opened or are being built. Screens are split between local output and the latest Hollywood releases. Films are subtitled rather than dubbed. Being able to read what's going on allows patrons to carry on their own conversations. Egyptian cinema-goers are also big on participation – great fun if it's a no-brain adventure flick, but the whooping, cheering and applause can be a bit distracting if you're trying to settle into something a bit more subtle.

Films are subject to censorship. How heavy-handed this is depends on the mood of the moment but even seemingly innocuous movies often arrive on screen with tell-tale hiccups indicating the cut of the scissors.

Beware – Egypt's anti-terrorism laws mean that no one, no matter how bad the film is, can leave a cinema before the screening ends.

Screenings are usually at 1.30, 3.30, 6.30 and 9.30 pm. A few cinemas have midnight shows on Friday and Saturday. Tickets range from E£8 to E£18 depending on the venue.

Theatre, Music & Dance Cairo Opera House (☎ 342 0598) on Gezira is the city's premier performing arts venue. Well-known international troupes sometimes perform here; the Bolshoi Ballet visits almost annually and recitals by local companies, such as the Cairo Opera Ballet Company and the Cairo Orchestra, are worth catching too. In addition to a main hall and small hall, the Opera House has an open-air theatre and summer amphitheatre. Check *Egypt Today* and *Al-Ahram Weekly* for what's on, or pass by and pick up a program. Jacket and tie are required by males for main hall performances, but less well-dressed travellers have been known to borrow them from staff.

There are often music recitals and plays of varying quality at Ewart Hall and Wallace Theatre, both part of the American University in Cairo campus. In Islamic Cairo, theatre performances and music evenings are held at the House of Zeinab Khatoun and the Al-Ghouri complex, especially during Ramadan. It's worth attending something at each of these places at least once, if only for the setting. Also worth checking, especially if you have children, is the Cairo Puppet Theatre in the Ezbekiyya Gardens, just north of Ataba. Performances are usually held late in the morning from Sunday to Thursday from October to May. Again, check the two publications mentioned earlier in this section for notices of events.

Weddings

Visitors often find themselves invited by locals to weddings, which are always raucous affairs with troupes of drummers and ululating women. But you don't necessarily need an invitation. Just head along to almost any five star hotel on a Thursday night. These are the prized venues for brides and grooms to flaunt their good fortunes, and usually involves a procession up the staircase with relatives and guests showering the couple with confetti or rose petals. The entire process can last a good half hour. Later in the evening the newly married couples head out for the photographs which, in the case of Cairo, are often taken on the 6th of October bridge.

SPECTATOR SPORT

Football is king in Egypt. Of the Arab nations, Egypt is the one country with players of international capacity (Hazem Emam, formerly of Cairo club Zamalek now currently plays for Udinese of Italy). In conversation with any Egyptian male, premier teams Zamalek and Al-Ahly arouse greater passions than almost any other subject. Demand for tickets makes them hard to get, especially for derbies. The season begins in September and continues until May. The big matches are held in the Cairo Stadium in Medinat Nasr.

SHOPPING

Egypt is both a budget souvenir and a kitsch-shoppers' paradise. Tourists with shelf space to fill back home can indulge in an orgy of alabaster pyramids, onyx Pharaonic cats, sawdust stuffed camels, and the ubiquitous painted papyrus. Hieroglyphic drawings of Pharaohs, gods and goddesses embellish and blemish everything from leather wallets to engraved brass tables. Every town and village in Egypt has a small market (or souq, as they're known in Arabic) but there's no doubt that the greatest is Cairo's great Khan al-Khalili bazaar – although you will have to be prepared to bargain hard (see the boxed text 'The Art of Bargaining' on the next page).

Antiques

There are few real antique bargains around. Dealers here know what they're about and study the latest Sotheby's catalogues. It is also illegal to export anything of antique value out of Egypt without a licence from the Department of Antiquities. But if you're interested then the places to browse are: Alexandria's Attarine district, a maze of narrow, antique shop-lined alleys; and the emporiums along Sharia Hoda Shaarawi in Downtown, Cairo. For the true connoisseur, Osiris (☎ 392 6609) at 15 Sharia Sherif, opposite the Banque Masr, Downtown, is

The Art of Bargaining

All prices are negotiable in the souq and bargaining is expected. Prices of souvenirs are always inflated to allow for it. For those not used to it, bargaining can be a hassle, but keep your cool and remember it's a game not a fight.

The first rule is never to show too much interest in the item you want to buy. Second, don't buy the first item that takes your fancy. Wander around and price things up, but don't make it obvious otherwise when you return to the first shop the vendor knows it's because he or she is the cheapest.

Decide how much you would be happy paying and then express a casual interest in buying. The vendor will state their price and you state a figure somewhat less than that you have fixed in your mind. So the bargaining begins. The shopkeeper will inevitably huff about how absurd that is and then tell you the 'lowest' price. If it is still not low enough, then be insistent and keep smiling. Tea or coffee might be served as part of the bargaining ritual; accepting it doesn't place you under any obligation to buy. If you still can't get your price, walk away. This often has the effect of closing the sale in your favour. If not, there are thousands more shops in the bazaar.

If you do get your price or lower, never feel guilty – no vendor, no matter what they may tell you, ever sells below cost.

Cairo's best auction house and a place where the occasional genuine bargain can be had. Auctions are held every few weeks, preceded by three days of viewing.

Backgammon Boards & Sheeshas

Backgammon boards and sheeshas make for great conversation pieces back home, and they're practical too. Well, maybe not. A plain backgammon box with plastic counters, like those used in many Egyptian coffeehouses, goes for as little as E£20. As the boards get more fancy the price goes up – a board inlaid with bone will set you back more than E£100.

Sheeshas start around E£30 but if you might actually use it and not just stick flowers in the top you need to buy a supply of the little clay tobacco holders and some tobacco. The entire package is bulky and heavy. Khan al-Khalili is probably the best place to buy them.

Brass & Copperware

Plates, coffeepots and a variety of other objects make good gifts, and are often fairly cheap. Engraved trays and plates start around E£15, depending on their intricacy and age. Watch for the quality of any engraving work and be wary of claims that an object is 100 years old – more often than not it rolled off the production line a couple of weeks ago. The best place for this sort of thing is Khan al-Khalili, particularly around Sharia an-Nahassin (Street of the Coppersmiths).

Carpets & Rugs

You can find carpets and rugs all over the place, but if you have time and happen to be in the area of the Pyramids, visit some of the carpet and tapestry schools along Saqqara Rd. The Wissa Wassef Art Centre is particularly interesting (see under Giza in the Cairo chapter for details).

Other good rug places include the weekly market at Al-Arish in northern Sinai and at Dahab, where there's a plethora of shops selling cheap, colourful cotton rugs made by the Bedouins.

Crafts

Appliqué The place to go for appliqué is the Street of the Tentmakers (Sharia al-Khayamiyya), south of Bab Zuweila in Islamic Cairo, where a dozen or more workshops are clustered in a medieval, covered market. The colours are bright and the patterns range from arabesques and calligraphy to more figurative dervish dancers or pharaonic motifs. The price depends on the intricacy of the pattern (arabesques and calligraphy cost the most), the quality of the

That Special Something

Belly-Dancing Outfits Sequined spangled and bright, these flimsy little numbers have little to do with what belly-dancers really wear but are a great gift to anyone who likes to shake their midriff. Available in every tourist bazaar at wildly fluctuating prices (expect to pay at least E£45).

Golden Pyramid Paperweight A clear resin pyramid with a golden sphinx inside. When you shake it golden 'snow' rains down. Available at the airport, at hotel bookshops and just about anywhere tourists congregate. Costs about E£20.

Nefertiti Head Lamp Haven't you always wanted Nefertiti to light up your life? Now she can be yours in onyx/alabaster with a little light bulb inside for only E£50. Pyramid lovers can have one in the shape of a pyramid.

King Tut Galabiyya Perfect for lounging around the house, a short-sleeved, brightly coloured robe that is usually too short and festooned with a giant iron-on reproduction of the famous funerary mask. It costs E£35 and more, depending on the size and brightness of Tut's face. Nefertiti is widely available too. Often modelled by groups of middle aged package tourists. ·

Gold Cartouche For the pharaoh in everyone: write your name and a goldsmith will translate it into hieroglyphics and fashion you a pharoanic-style cartouche. About E£200 and more, depending on the weight of the gold.

Hieroglyphic Sun Hat White cotton sun hat available at all outdoor antiquities sites and covered in a mishmash of blue hieroglyphics and the word 'Egypt' just in case you don't get it. About E£10 to E£15, depending on your bargaining skills.

King Tut Hologram Lamp White plaster bust of the famous boy-king that appears to float like a hologram when plugged in. Available in some museum shops and in Khan al-Khalili for a mere E£150.

Cairo Taxi Cab Ornament Turn your car into a Cairo taxi: a red plastic heart with 'I love you' written across the middle and small lights that blink in time to your *al-jeel* cassette. To get one, ask a Cairo cab driver or go to a car accessories shop in Muski. Should cost around E£15.

Pop-Up Postcards Open up the card and out pops the Qaaba at Mecca – for the less religious minded an elaborate Abu Simbel Temple model is also available. Get them at the stalls near the central post office in Midan Ataba for about E£1.

Light-Up Shrines Jesus, Mary or your favourite saint, encased in plastic, set against a mirrored backdrop, surrounded by plastic flowers and lit with a single red Christmas tree light. Available in different sizes to fit different budgets – and you'll be giving a donation to the church at the same time. Available at the Hanging Church in Coptic Cairo. Prices start at about E£15.

work and the size. As a guide a small cushion cover costs E£20; a larger one E£40. Wall hangings of about 1.5 square metres range from E£80 to almost E£200.

Inlaid Boxes & Chess Boards Second only in popularity to papyrus as souvenir items are the inlaid boxes piled high in most of the shops at Cairo's Khan al-Khalili. They are very inexpensive, a small one selling for as little as E£6. For that price you'll get poor quality (it will not be inlaid with mother-of-pearl, as the shopkeeper may tell you, but plastic) but for a higher price you can buy something beautifully crafted like a mirror frame or jewellery casket. A mother-of-pearl chess board together with camel bone pieces would sell for E£240 to E£300. You may be offered ivory – see the boxed text 'Responsible Shopping'.

Leather Leather is another popular buy. However, you will generally be offered items in the soft leather of gazelle hide and these creatures are protected and are becoming rare in Egypt.

Mashrabiyya Virtually nobody these days still makes complete mashrabiyya screens. What you get are things that look like magazine racks (actually Quran holders) or table bases. It is still possible to find large screens in some of the antique stores, but they'll be prohibitively expensive. The one exception is NADIM (the National Art Development Institute for Mashrabiyya (☎ 348 1075), a craftshop dedicated to keeping the art of mashrabiyya alive. It has all manner of mashrabiyya products, screens included (from E£2000 to E£3000), and visitors are welcome to watch the artisans at work with no obligation to buy. It's in Cairo on Sharia al-Mazaniyya, off Sharia Sudan behind the Coca Cola factory.

Clothing

Since cotton is one of Egypt's major crops it is no surprise that cotton clothing is popular. Cotton shirts, pants and *galabiyyas* (the loose gowns worn by many Egyptians) can be made

Responsible Shopping

In line with international treaties Egypt no longer imports ivory. However, large quantities still continue to be smuggled in. Most of it comes from Sudan and Kenya, where the elephant populations were decimated in the 1970s and 80s to meet demands for ivory jewellery and trinkets. Many countries – Australia, the UK and the US included – prohibit the import of ivory in any form or quantity, including souvenirs.

Other animals which have fallen victim to illegal trading are birds and desert creatures. You'll see plenty of these stuffed and sold at Kerdassa, a village near the Pyramids in Cairo, as well as in Khan al-Khalili.

to your specifications. Many Cairene tailors can work from photographs of the clothing. The area between Al-Azhar and Bab Zuweila in Cairo is teeming with shops selling galabiyyas, ready and tailor-made. You can also try at the village of Kerdassa, near the Pyramids. T-shirts abound all over the country.

A lot of travellers have suits and other clothes tailor-made in Egypt, at prices that are ridiculously low by western standards.

In Dahab, in Sinai, cotton trousers and printed shirts are popular. A pair of light, simple trousers will cost around E£8. The Bedouins also make traditional clothing for sale. Canvas bags are cheap and popular, at around E£5 depending on size and quality.

Jewellery

Gold and silver jewellery can be made to specification for not much more than the cost of the metal. A cartouche with the name of a friend spelt in hieroglyphs makes a good gift.

Although gold shops are concentrated in the centre of the Khan al-Khalili, gold can be bought all over Islamic Cairo. It is generally sold by weight. Buying gold and jewellery is always a little fraught. The Assay Office in Birmingham, UK, says that hallmarking for gold of at least 12 carats and silver of 600 parts per thousand or more is compulsory in Egypt – verifying this is another matter. The hallmark contains a standard mark showing where a piece was assayed and a date mark in Arabic. Foreign goods cannot be resold, in the UK at least, unless they are first assayed there. Storekeepers have an irritating habit of weighing the gold out of sight. Insist that they put the scales on the counter and let you see what's happening. This doesn't eliminate the chances of cheating, but does reduce them. Another precaution may be to check the day's gold prices in the *Egyptian Gazette*.

Much the same cautionary rules apply to silver and other jewellery. An endless assortment of rings, bracelets, necklaces and the like can be found all over Islamic Cairo. Hunt around, and beware of the 'antiques' made to look so.

Music Cassettes

Locally produced cassettes sell for E£8 or E£9. Quality, needless to say, is bad. As well as Egyptian and other Arab artists (see Arts in the Facts about Egypt chapter for some recommended listening) most places have a limited selection of pirate copies of western artists. The biggest choice is at the shops along Sharia Shawarby in Cairo or, for Nubian music, see the Aswan chapter.

Imported western CDs and a growing number of CD recordings by Egyptian artists are available in Cairo (try Maestro and Juke Box both at the World Trade Centre on the Corniche el-Nil, Bulaq) but they're expensive at E£80 to E£90.

Musical Instruments

Traditional musical instruments such as an *oud* (lute), *kamaan* (violin), *nay* (flute), *tabla* (drum) and various others are made and sold in about a dozen shops in Cairo on Sharia Muhammad Ali, which runs southeast from Midan Ataba to the Museum of Islamic Art. Gamil Georges at No 170 sells ouds, for example, with prices ranging from E£150 to E£300.

Papyrus

You can pick up cheap, poor quality papyrus all over Egypt for virtually nothing. Equally, you can pay large sums of money for exactly the same thing. Look long and hard at what you are getting. If you are considering buying an expensive piece it should be hand-painted not machine printed. And is it papyrus, which will not be damaged by rolling, or is it in fact banana leaf which will crack?

The name Dr Ragab has long been associated with papyrus, and he has several 'institutes' throughout Egypt. His stuff is good quality but it's also expensive. A good alternative is Said Delta Papyrus Centre in Islamic Cairo. The posted prices seem to be negotiable. The shop is on Sharia al-Muizz li-Din Allah, north of Bab Zuweyla. It's on the 3rd floor above a shoe shop; look for a yellow sign at 1st floor level.

Perfumes

Egypt is a big producer of many of the essences that make up French perfume, hence it's no surprise that part of Cairo's Khan al-Khalili is devoted to a perfume bazaar. Here you can buy pure essence (anywhere from E£8 to E£20 an ounce) as well as cheaper substances diluted with alcohol or oil. Some of the perfume traders have price tags on their goods, but that doesn't mean you can't haggle.

Intricate perfume bottles are also popular. Again, there are expensive and cheap varieties. Small glass bottles start at about E£3; the heavier and more durable pyrex bottles cost from E£10.

Spices

Every conceivable herb and spice, and many you will never have heard of or seen, can be bought in most markets throughout the country. Generally they are fresher and better quality than any of the packaged stuff you'll find in the west, and four to five times cheaper. Exactly how much cheaper will, of course, depend on your bargaining skills.

Getting There & Away

If you're heading to Egypt from Europe, you have the choice of either flying direct or, if you've plenty of time on your hands, going overland. If you're coming from any other continent, it can sometimes be cheaper to fly first to Europe, and then make your way to Egypt. There are also the overland combinations of bus, taxi and ferry from other countries in Africa, and from Jordan, Kuwait, Saudi Arabia, Israel and Libya.

Whichever route you take there is always the inescapable search for the cheapest ticket and the certainty that no matter how great a deal you find, there's always someone out there with a better one.

AIR
Airports & Airlines

Egypt's international and national carrier is EgyptAir. It's not a particularly good airline – in our experience the food is usually poor and the flight attendants are often surly. Fares are not cheap and you can usually get a seat on a much better carrier for the same price if not less.

Egypt has a handful of airports but only six are international ports of entry: Cairo, Alexandria and, increasingly gaining status, the 'international' airports at Luxor, Aswan, Hurghada and Sharm el-Sheikh. Most air travellers enter Egypt through Cairo. The other airports tend to be used by charter and package-deal flights, except for Alexandria which handles the scheduled services of British Mediterranean, Lufthansa and Olympic.

EgyptAir and Air Sinai have internal flights linking nine destinations within Egypt. See the Getting Around chapter for details.

Cairo The airport is 25km north-east of central Cairo. There are two terminals about 3km apart; Terminal II, the 'new terminal', services most international airlines, while Terminal I, the 'old terminal', is mainly used by EgyptAir (domestic and international flights).

Neighbouring Countries

- **Israel & the Palestinian Territories**
  There are two land routes (see page 123), from Cairo direct (10 hours; E£120) and via Sinai, both by bus, or you can fly (see page 122) for E£629 one way.

- **Jordan** The options from Cairo are a bus to Nuweiba (seven hours; E£50) and then one of two ferries (see page 125) across the Red Sea (US$32 for the slow boat, US$42 for the catamaran), or by air (see page 122) for E£833 one way.

- **Libya** As we go to press it's been announced that international sanctions against Libya are to be lifted. This should mean that flights between Cairo and Tripoli will resume. Until then, the only option is still to take a bus from Cairo or Alexandria (see page 124).

- **Sudan** At the time of writing it was not possible to go from Egypt to Sudan overland, so the options are to fly (see page 122) for E£1342 one way or take the Wadi Halfa ferry (see page 124) from Aswan (12 to 17 hours; E£88.50 or E£142 depending on the class of travel).

Arriving at Terminal II, you'll pass a couple of duty-free shops, exchange offices, several banks and a Thomas Cook office before arriving at customs control. The exchange offices are next to each other and their rates are about the same. They can also issue stamps for a visa (see the Visas & Documents section in the Facts for the Visitor chapter for details). Similar banking facilities are available at Terminal I. There's also a (quite useless) tourist information office at Terminal II.

The departure lounge at Terminal II has a handful of duty-free shops (Egyptian pounds are not accepted) and a post and telephone office. Card phones and a Home Country Direct telephone are available, as are telex and telegraphic services.

Between the arrival and departure lounges is a left-luggage room that is open 24 hours. It charges E£3 for items less than 25kg, and E£6 for those weighing more.

Most major car rental companies have booths in the arrivals hall. Outside Terminal I is a lost-and-found booth.

For details on getting between the airport and central Cairo, see the Getting Around section in the Cairo chapter.

Warning Many travellers arriving at Cairo airport are met by the infamous 'tourist officials'. For more on the tactics of these touts, see the boxed text 'The Great Cairo Hotel Scam' in the Cairo chapter.

Buying Tickets

The plane ticket will probably be the single most expensive item in your budget, and buying it can be an intimidating business. There is likely to be a multitude of airlines and travel agents hoping to separate you from your money, and it is always worth putting aside a few hours to research the current state of the market. Start early: some of the cheapest tickets have to be bought months in advance, and some popular flights sell out early. Talk to other recent travellers – they may save you from making a mistake. Look at the ads in newspapers and magazines (not forgetting the press of the ethnic group whose country you plan to visit), and watch for special offers. Then phone round travel agents for bargains. Airlines can supply information on routes and timetables; however, except at times of inter-airline war they do not supply the cheapest tickets. Find out the fare, the route, the duration of the journey and flexibility of the ticket. (See Restrictions in the Air Travel Glossary.) Then sit back and decide which is best for you.

You may discover that those impossibly cheap flights are 'fully booked, but we have another one that costs a bit more ...' Or the flight is on an airline notorious for its poor safety standards and will leave you in the world's least favourite airport for 14 hours. Or the agent claims to have the last two seats available for that country in the whole of July, which can be held for you for a maximum of two hours. Don't panic – keep ringing around.

Use the fares quoted in this book as a guide only. They are approximate and based on the rates advertised by travel agents at the time of going to press. Quoted airfares do not necessarily constitute a recommendation for the carrier.

If you are travelling from the UK or the USA, you will probably find that the cheapest flights are being advertised by obscure bucket shops whose names haven't yet reached the telephone directory. Many such firms are honest and solvent, but there are a few rogues who will take your money and disappear, to reopen elsewhere a month or two later under a new name. If you feel suspicious about a firm, don't give them all the money at once – leave a deposit of 20% or so and pay the balance when you get the ticket. If they insist on cash in advance, go somewhere else. And once you have the ticket, ring the airline to confirm that you are actually booked onto the flight.

You may decide to pay more than the rock-bottom fare by opting for the safety of a better-known travel agent. Firms such as STA, who have offices worldwide, Council Travel in the USA or Travel CUTS in Canada are not going to disappear overnight, leaving you clutching a receipt for a nonexistent ticket, but they do offer good prices to most destinations.

Once you have your ticket, write its number down, together with the flight number and other details, and keep the information somewhere separate. If the ticket is lost or stolen, this will help you get a replacement.

It's sensible to purchase travel insurance as early as you possibly can. If you buy it the week before you fly, you may find, for example, that you are not covered for delays to your flight that are caused by industrial action.

Air Travel Glossary

Baggage Allowance This will be written on your ticket and usually includes one 20kg item to go in the hold, plus one item of hand luggage.

Bucket Shops These are unbonded travel agencies specialising in discounted airline tickets.

Bumped Just because you have a confirmed seat doesn't mean you're going to get on the plane (see Overbooking).

Cancellation Penalties If you have to cancel or change a discounted ticket, there are often heavy penalties involved; insurance can sometimes be taken out against these penalties. Some airlines impose penalties on regular tickets as well, particularly against 'no-show' passengers.

Check-In Airlines ask you to check in a certain time ahead of the flight departure (usually one to two hours on international flights). If you fail to check in on time and the flight is overbooked, the airline can cancel your booking and give your seat to somebody else.

Confirmation Having a ticket written out with the flight and date you want doesn't mean you have a seat until the agent has checked with the airline that your status is 'OK' or confirmed. Meanwhile you could just be 'on request'.

Courier Fares Businesses often need to send urgent documents or freight securely and quickly. Courier companies hire people to accompany the package through customs and, in return, offer a discount ticket which is sometimes a phenomenal bargain. In effect, what the companies do is ship their freight as your luggage on regular commercial flights. This is a legitimate operation, but there are two shortcomings – the short turnaround time of the ticket (usually not longer than a month) and the limitation on your luggage allowance. You may have to surrender all your allowance and take only carry-on luggage.

Full Fares Airlines traditionally offer 1st class (coded F), business class (coded J) and economy class (coded Y) tickets. These days there are so many promotional and discounted fares available that few passengers pay full economy fare.

ITX An ITX, or 'independent inclusive tour excursion', is often available on tickets to popular holiday destinations. Officially it's a package deal combined with hotel accommodation, but many agents will sell you one of these for the flight only and give you phoney hotel vouchers in the unlikely event that you're challenged at the airport.

Lost Tickets If you lose your airline ticket an airline will usually treat it like a travellers cheque and, after inquiries, issue you with another one. Legally, however, an airline is entitled to treat it like cash and if you lose it then it's gone forever. Take good care of your tickets.

MCO An MCO, or 'miscellaneous charge order', is a voucher that looks like an airline ticket but carries no destination or date. It can be exchanged through any International Association of Travel Agents (IATA) airline for a ticket on a specific flight. It's a useful alternative to an onward ticket in those countries that demand one, and is more flexible than an ordinary ticket if you're unsure of your route.

No-Shows No-shows are passengers who fail to show up for their flight. Full-fare passengers who fail to turn up are sometimes entitled to travel on a later flight. The rest are penalised (see Cancellation Penalties).

On Request This is an unconfirmed booking for a flight.

Air Travel Glossary

Onward Tickets An entry requirement for many countries is that you have a ticket out of the country. If you're unsure of your next move, the easiest solution is to buy the cheapest onward ticket to a neighbouring country or a ticket from a reliable airline which can later be refunded if you do not use it.

Open Jaw Tickets These are return tickets where you fly out to one place but return from another. If available, this can save you backtracking to your arrival point.

Overbooking Airlines hate to fly empty seats and since every flight has some passengers who fail to show up, airlines often book more passengers than they have seats. Usually excess passengers make up for the no-shows, but occasionally somebody gets bumped. Guess who it is most likely to be? The passengers who check in late.

Point-to-Point Tickets These are discount tickets that can be bought on some routes in return for passengers waiving their rights to a stopover.

Promotional Fares These are officially discounted fares, available from travel agencies or direct from the airline.

Reconfirmation At least 72 hours prior to departure time of an onward or return flight, you must contact the airline and 'reconfirm' that you intend to be on the flight. If you don't do this the airline can delete your name from the passenger list and you could lose your seat.

Restrictions Discounted tickets often have various restrictions on them – such as needing to be paid for in advance and incurring a penalty to be altered. Others are restrictions on the minimum and maximum period you must be away, such as a minimum of 14 days or a maximum of one year.

Round-the-World Tickets RTW tickets give you a limited period (usually a year) in which to circumnavigate the globe. You can go anywhere the carrying airlines go, as long as you don't backtrack. The number of stopovers or total number of separate flights is decided before you set off and they usually cost a bit more than a basic return flight.

Stand-by This is a discounted ticket where you only fly if there is a seat free at the last moment. Stand-by fares are usually available only on domestic routes.

Transferred Tickets Airline tickets cannot be transferred from one person to another. Travellers sometimes try to sell the return half of their ticket, but officials can ask you to prove that you are the person named on the ticket. This is less likely to happen on domestic flights, but on an international flight tickets are compared with passports.

Travel Agencies Travel agencies vary widely and you should choose one that suits your needs. Some simply handle tours, while full-services agencies handle everything from tours and tickets to car rental and hotel bookings. If all you want is a ticket at the lowest possible price, then go to an agency specialising in discounted tickets.

Travel Periods Ticket prices vary with the time of year. There is a low (off-peak) season and a high (peak) season, and often a low-shoulder season and a high-shoulder season as well. Usually the fare depends on your outward flight – if you depart in the high season and return in the low season, you pay the high-season fare.

Air Travellers with Special Needs

If you have special needs of any sort – you've broken a leg, you're vegetarian, travelling in a wheelchair, taking the baby, terrified of flying – you should let the airline know as soon as possible so that they can make arrangements accordingly. You should remind them when you reconfirm your booking (at least 72 hours before departure) and again when you check in at the airport. It may also be worth ringing round the airlines before you make your booking to find out how they can handle your particular needs.

Airports and airlines can be surprisingly helpful, but they do need advance warning. Most international airports will provide escorts from the check-in desk to the plane where needed, and there should be ramps, lifts, accessible toilets and reachable phones. Aircraft toilets, on the other hand, are likely to present a problem; travellers should discuss this with the airline at an early stage and, if necessary, with their doctor.

Guide dogs for the blind will often have to travel in a specially pressurised baggage compartment with other animals, away from their owner; though smaller guide dogs may be admitted to the cabin. All guide dogs will be subject to the same quarantine laws (six months in isolation etc) as any other animal when entering or returning to countries currently free of rabies such as Britain or Australia.

Deaf travellers can ask for airport and inflight announcements to be written down.

Children under two travel for 10% of the standard fare (or free, on some airlines), as long as they don't occupy a seat. They don't get a baggage allowance either. 'Skycots' should be provided by the airline if requested in advance; these will take a child weighing up to about 10kg. Children between two and 12 can usually occupy a seat for half to two-thirds of the full fare, and do get a baggage allowance. Pushchairs can often be taken as hand luggage.

The USA & Canada

The *New York Times*, the *Los Angeles Times*, the *Chicago Tribune* and the *San Francisco Examiner* all produce weekly travel sections in which you will find a number of travel agency ads.

Falcon Wings Travel INC. (☎ 310-417 3589, 9841 Airport BLVD Suite 822, Los Angeles, CA 90045) has been recommended for cheap fares to Egypt. Council Travel, America's largest student travel organisation, has around 60 offices in the USA; its head office (☎ 800-226 8624) is at 205 E 42 St, New York, NY 10017. Call it for the office nearest you or visit its Web site at www.ciee.org. STA Travel (☎ 800-777 0112, 411 Santa Monica Blvd, Santa Monica, CA 90401) also has offices in Boston, Chicago, Miami, New York, Philadelphia, San Francisco and other major cities. Call the toll-free 800 number for office locations or visit its Web site at www.statravel.com.

In Canada, the *Globe & Mail*, *Toronto Star*, *Montreal Gazette* and *Vancouver Sun* carry travel agents' ads and are a good place to look for cheap fares.

Travel CUTS (☎ 800-663 6000, 171 College St, Toronto, ON M5T 1P7) is Canada's national student travel agency and has offices in all major cities. Its Web site is www.travelcuts.com. STA Travel (☎ 416-977 5228, 187 College St, Toronto, ON M5T 1P7) also has offices in Montreal, Calgary, Edmonton and Vancouver. Visit its Web site at www.statravel.com.

The cheapest way from the USA and Canada to the Middle East and Africa is usually a return flight to London and a cheap fare from there. A Round-the-World (RTW) ticket including a stopover in Cairo is also a possibility.

EgyptAir flies from New York and Los Angeles to Cairo. The cheapest advance tickets are for a minimum stay of seven days and a maximum stay of two months. Regular fares from New York/Los Angeles are approximately low season US$1300/1800 high season US$1900/2200.

Lufthansa has connections to Cairo via Frankfurt from many cities in the USA. Advance fairs are available. From Los Angeles, the return fare is US$2200 and entails a minimum stay of seven days and a maximum of two months. A one-way ticket is US$1750.

From New York, the same two tickets in high season are US$1600/1155 respectively.

The UK

London is one of the best centres in the world for discounted air tickets. If you start looking early and are prepared to phone around then you shouldn't have to pay more than about UK£250 for a return ticket, London-Cairo-London. At the time of writing, the cheapest deal was a 12 month open return with Olympic Airways for approximately UK£240. Best bets for this are Trailfinders (☎ 0171-938 3366, from 22 April 2000 ☎ 020-7938 3366) and STA Travel (☎ 0171-937 9962, from 22 April 2000 ☎ 020-7937 9962). Both have several branches in the UK.

It's also well worth trying Suleiman Travel (☎ 0171-244 6855, from 22 April 2000 ☎ 020-7244 6855) at 113 Earls Court Rd, London, which is a long-established Egypt specialist. Its prices are usually very competitive and they can sometimes come up with cheaper alternatives to scheduled Cairo flights such as charters into Luxor or Sharm el-Sheikh.

Check the listings in magazines such as *Time Out* and *TNT* and the ads in the Sunday papers and *Exchange & Mart* for alternatives. Also look out for the free magazines widely available in London – start by looking outside the main train stations.

Most British travel agents are registered with ABTA (Association of British Travel Agents). If you have paid for your flight to an ABTA-registered agent who then goes out of business, ABTA will guarantee a refund or an alternative. Unregistered bucket shops are riskier but also sometimes cheaper.

For shorter trips, it's worth looking into packages or combined air fare and hotel deals offered by many of the high street travel agents. For instance, at the time of writing you could get seven nights halfboard at a four star Hurghada hotel for UK£399, flights included.

Australia & New Zealand

Quite a few travel offices specialise in discount air tickets. Some travel agents, particularly smaller ones, advertise cheap air fares in the travel sections of weekend newspapers, such as *The Age* in Melbourne and the *Sydney Morning Herald*.

Two well known agents for cheap fares are STA Travel and Flight Centre. STA Travel (☎ 03-9349 2411) has its main office at 224 Faraday St, Carlton, VIC 3053, and offices in all major cities and on many university campuses. Call 131 776 Australiawide for the location of your nearest branch or visit its Web site at www.statravel .com.au. Flight Centre (☎ 131 600 Australiawide) has a central office at 82 Elizabeth St, Sydney, and there are dozens of offices throughout Australia. Its Web site address is www.flightcentre.com.au.

From Australia, low season return fares to Cairo range from A$1359 with Alitalia to A$1759 with Lauda Airlines. RTW fares with a stopover in Cairo are offered by Singapore Airlines, KLM, Qantas and British Airways. In the low season, expect to pay around A$2400.

The *New Zealand Herald* has a travel section in which travel agents advertise fares. Flight Centre (☎ 09-309 6171) has a large central office in Auckland at National Bank Towers (corner Queen and Darby Sts) and many branches throughout the country. STA Travel (☎ 09-309 0458) has its main office at 10 High St, Auckland, and has other offices in Auckland as well as in Hamilton, Palmerston North, Wellington, Christchurch and Dunedin. The Web site address is www.sta.travel.com.au.

Air New Zealand flies to Cairo via Singapore or London. Fares start at around NZ$2480 in the low season.

Continental Europe

Lufthansa and its charter subsidiary Condor offer some of the most frequent connections with flights to and from Egypt. There are direct scheduled flights from Frankfurt to Cairo and Alexandria. During the high season (October to April), there are several flights weekly to Sharm el-Sheikh and Luxor.

In Munich, a great source of travel information and gear is Travel Overland (☎ 89-2727 6300) at Bourerstrasse 73, 80799, Munich. Aside from producing a comprehensive travel equipment catalogue, it also runs an 'Expedition Service' with current flight information available.

In Berlin, Kilroy Travel (☎ 30-3100 0433), at Hardenbergstrasse 9, near Berlin Zoo (with five branches around the city), is a popular travel agency.

Amsterdam is a popular departure point. Some of the best fares are offered by the student travel agency NBBS Reizen (☎ 020-624 0989) in Amsterdam at Rokin 66 and there are other agencies throughout the city.

Paris is not a bad place to organise a trip to Egypt. It abounds with Egypt and desert specialists. Try Voyageurs en Egypte et au Proche Orient (☎ 01 42 86 17 90) at 55, rue Sainte-Anne, 75002 Paris.

Explorator (☎ 01 42 66 66 24), 16, Place de la Madeleine, 75008 Paris is also worth looking at, particularly if you want something more organised on the ground or a desert expedition.

Middle East

If you have the time travelling overland between Egypt and Israel, Jordan or Syria is much cheaper and relatively simple. The only drawback is the time factor.

For the addresses of the following airlines see Getting There & Away in the Cairo chapter.

Israel Air Sinai and El Al regularly fly between Cairo and Tel Aviv with five flights a week each. Fares are E£629 one way or E£895 return (valid for one month).

Jordan There are daily flights with Royal Jordanian Airlines and EgyptAir between Cairo and Amman, but there is no discounting. The fare from Egypt is E£833 one way and E£1084 return with EgyptAir, or about E£80 cheaper with Royal Jordanian. There are no student reductions.

Syria Syrian Air flies five times a week to Damascus for a one-way fare of E£720.

Africa

Despite the proximity, there is nothing cheap about travelling from Egypt into Africa. In fact, for most African capitals a ticket bought in London will be cheaper than one bought in Cairo. The best bet is to buy your African ticket with a stopover in Egypt.

For the addresses of the following airlines see Getting There & Away in the Cairo chapter.

Ethiopia There are flights from Egypt to Addis Ababa twice a week (currently in the early hours of Saturday and Thursday mornings) with a one-way fare of US$584, or US$811 return. However, one-way tickets can only be purchased if you can show a credit card or travellers cheques to cover the cost of a return ticket.

Kenya Kenya Airlines flies to Nairobi three times a week for a one-way fare of E£2116. From Nairobi there are onward connections to Rwanda (Kigali), Tanzania (Dar es Salaam), Democratic Republic of Congo (Zaïre) (Kinshasa) and Zimbabwe (Harare).

Libya At the time of writing, international flights to and from Libya were still suspended as a result of the UN air embargo imposed on Libya over the Lockerbie affair.

Sudan Sudan Airways and EgyptAir both have two flights a week between Cairo and Khartoum. The 2½ hour flight costs E£1342 one way or E£1633 return (valid for one month). However, one-way tickets will not be sold unless you can show a ticket from Sudan to your home country, and no ticket will be issued until you've got your Sudanese visa.

LAND
Your Own Transport

Drivers of cars and riders of motorcycles will need the vehicle's registration papers, liability insurance and an international drivers' permit in addition to their domestic licence. Beware: there are two kinds of international permits; one is needed mostly for former British colonies. You will also need a *carnet de passage en douane*, which is effectively a passport for the vehicle, and acts as a temporary waiver of import duty. The carnet may also need to list any expensive spares that you're planning to carry with you, such as a gearbox. Contact your local automobile association for details about all documentation.

At the Egyptian border, you will be issued with a licence valid for three months (less if your visa is valid for less time). You can renew the licence every three months for a maximum of two years but you'll have to pay a varying fee each time. A recent readers' letter gave the fees for bringing in a car as E£142 for entry tax and E£291 for customs and insurance.

The Egyptians themselves give conflicting advice on whether or not diesel-powered vehicles may enter the country. People wishing to bring in 4WDs should check at an Egyptian embassy first, as the rules governing these vehicles are contentious. For further information try contacting the Automobile and Touring Club of Egypt (☎ 574 3355) at 10 Qasr el-Nil in Cairo, which is open daily except Friday from 9 am to 1.30 pm.

If you plan to take your own vehicle, check in advance what spares and petrol are likely to be available. In Egypt, lead-free was introduced in 1995 but is available only in Cairo and Alexandria. You are also likely to have trouble finding some parts for your car.

Israel & Palestinian Territories

There are two ways to do this: if you want to go directly to Tel Aviv or Jerusalem you go via Rafah; but if you want to spend time in Sinai and are happy to enter Israel at Eilat, from where you make your own onward travel arrangements, then you can also go via Taba.

Most nationalities do not need a visa to enter Israel but if you are returning to Egypt then you must have a re-entry or multi-entry

visa – see Visas & Documents in the Facts for the Visitor chapter.

Rafah There is a bus every Sunday, Monday, Wednesday and Thursday from central Cairo to Tel Aviv and Jerusalem operated by Travco (☎ 340 4493) of 13 Mahmoud Azmy, Zamalek. Tickets are E£136 one way. They can also be bought from the Masr Travel offices at 7 Talaat Harb and on the 1st floor of the Cairo Sheraton hotel. The many travel agencies around Midan Tahrir can sell you tickets, too, but we really don't recommend that you deal with these companies. The bus departs from the Cairo Sheraton at 5.30 am and takes 10 hours – roughly five hours to Rafah, a couple of hours crossing (involving E£10 for a shuttle between the Egyptian and Israeli immigration halls), then a further three hours onward in a bus run by the Israeli company Mazada Tours. There's a E£17 departure tax to be paid at the border.

Alternatively, you can catch a local bus to Rafah from Midan Ulali in Cairo (see Getting There and Away in the Cairo chapter) but it's risky as there's only one bus a day on the Israeli side for Jerusalem and Tel Aviv and it departs at 3 pm – theoretically, the Cairo bus should get you to the border for 1.30 pm giving you an hour and a half to clear formalities but it doesn't always pan out and there's every chance you won't make the connection. That leaves you having to catch a service taxi up through the Gaza Strip to Gaza City where you can pick up another service for Jerusalem, which is a long drawn out and expensive way of doing things.

Taba Another possible route is to catch a bus to Taba in Sinai. There are two buses daily from Cairo, one at 8 am (E£50) and one at 11 pm (E£70), both departing from the Sinai bus terminal. The journey takes anywhere between seven and nine hours. If you're already at one of the south Sinai resorts, like Dahab or Sharm el-Sheikh, then there are plenty of buses heading up the coast or you can jump in a service taxi.

Once at Taba you can walk across the border (which is open 24 hours) into Israel and take a taxi to Eilat from where there are frequent buses onward to Jerusalem and Tel Aviv (but not on Friday evenings or before sundown Saturday, the Jewish holy day of Shabbat). From capital to capital this route is more expensive and more time-consuming than the Rafah bus, but if you were planning on visiting Sinai or Eilat anyway, then it's a good way to go.

Libya

There are direct buses running between Cairo, Benghazi and Tripoli (Tarabulus). You can also get buses to the same destinations from Alexandria. Fares from here tend to be slightly cheaper. For more details see Getting There & Away in the Cairo and Alexandria chapters. A more laborious, but cheaper alternative would be to get local transport to Sallum in the far north-west of Egypt (there are buses from Alexandria – see Getting There & Away in that chapter) and a service taxi to the border. From there you can get Libyan transport heading west. See under Sallum in the Alexandria & the Mediterranean Coast chapter for details.

SEA
Europe

MenaTours acts as the agent for the limited passenger-ship services that operate between Port Said and various Mediterranean destinations, including Beirut (Lebanon) and Antalya (Turkey). There are no passenger boats operating between Egyptian ports and any ports in Europe at present. The last services between Alexandria and Athens ceased in 1997 and boats between Port Said and Lebanon halted the same year.

Sudan

Via Wadi Halfa After a six year hiatus, boat services along Lake Nasser to Wadi Halfa in Sudan resumed in 1998. The long gap in services has made for some improvements – the boats are new and now make the trip in 12 to 17 hours (the old ones could take as long as 24 hours).

You can go 1st or 2nd class, at a cost of E£142/88.50. First class means bunks in small cabins; 2nd class means seats, if you can find one. The fare includes a meal – *fuu* in 2nd class or meat and rice in 1st. If you've gone 2nd class, you can still buy a 1st class meal for E£3. Tea and soft drinks are also available on board. Bring some food yourself, too.

Tickets are bought at the Nile Valley Navigation Company in Aswan (☎ 303 348), next to the tourist office, one street in from the Corniche. The office is open from 8 am to 2.30 pm every day except Friday. Note that the office will not sell you a ticket unless you've got a Sudanese visa stamp in your passport.

The boat leaves Aswan every Monday at around 3 pm, arriving in Wadi Halfa about 8 am Tuesday morning. You should be at the port at the High Dam by noon. As a foreigner, you should be ushered through the various customs and passport hurdles. Some of the Sudanese immigration formalities are carried out on the boat – they will ask for a yellow fever certificate. The boat returns from Wadi Halfa every Wednesday afternoon and arrives in Aswan on Thursday morning.

If you want to take a vehicle into Sudan, the Nile Valley Navigation Company also has a cargo ferry that will carry up to five or six cars. However, there are no fixed departures and you have to pay for the entire boat, a whopping E£8000. There are no facilities on the boat (you are expected to bring your own food and sleep in your car) and the trip takes about two days. For more information call the Nile Valley Navigation Company.

If you have any bureaucracy troubles in Aswan related to attempts to get to Sudan, you could try contacting Mohammed Amin – see under Getting There & Away in the Aswan section of the Nile Valley – Esna to Abu Simbel chapter.

Via the Red Sea At present there are no scheduled ships heading from Egypt to Port Sudan. You can get a boat from Jeddah but your transit visa will only be issued if you ensure that it leaves the same day that you arrive from Suez. For more information call the MenaTours office in Suez (☎ 062-228 821) and see the Suez Getting There & Away section in The Suez Canal chapter. You can also try to find a private yacht heading south, but there are very few and they may not be willing to take on passengers. Mohammed Moseilhy at Damanhur Shipping Agency in Suez can sometimes help find willing yacht owners; call him on ☎ 062-330 418.

Jordan

There's a sea link between Egypt and Jordan via the Red Sea port of Nuweiba in Sinai. A ferry and a catamaran both shuttle over from Aqaba and back, making one round trip a day. The ferry leaves Nuweiba at 3 pm and takes three hours. Tickets cost US$32 one way, or US$20 for children between five and 12 years of age. You must be at the port at least three hours before departure. The catamaran also leaves at 3 pm but it only takes one hour to reach Aqaba. A ticket costs US$42 one way, US$26 for three to 10 year olds; $US16 under three years old. You must be at the harbour two hours before departure.

Tickets must be paid for in dollars and you must have a Jordanian visa before boarding.

For details of buses to Nuweiba see the Getting There & Away section of whichever city you're travelling from. You can book a ferry and bus combination ticket from Cairo or Alexandria through to Aqaba, or even on to Amman if you wish. From Cairo's Sinai terminal the trip to Amman is US$32 plus E£63.

Saudi Arabia & Kuwait

There are regular ferries between Jeddah and Suez (about 36 hours). Several lines compete on the route and fares can vary from one agent to another but, generally, tickets start at around E£145 for deck class to E£300 for 1st class. Most of the ferries on the route also carry cars, at a significant

cost. Getting a berth during the haj is virtually impossible. You can get information at Masr Travel agencies, or buy a ticket directly from their office in Port Tawfiq, Suez – for more details see Getting There & Away in the Suez and Port Safaga sections in The Suez Canal and Red Sea Coast chapters respectively.

There are also regular services between Hurghada and Port Safaga, both on the Red Sea coast, and Dubai in Saudi Arabia. See the Hurghada and Port Safaga Getting There & Away sections for more details or call MenaTours in Cairo (☎ 348 2230) or the Telestar Line office in Port Safaga (☎ 452 315).

In the same way that a passage can be booked straight through to Aqaba and Amman, you can purchase tickets through to many destinations in the Gulf, either at Cairo's Sinai terminal or Turgoman garage or in Alexandria. From Cairo to Riyadh (daily departures at 1 pm) the fare is E£250 to E£275, and to Kuwait E£380.

ORGANISED TOURS

There are any number of tour possibilities to Egypt, and a plethora of agents dealing with everything from Nile cruises to overland safaris or diving trips – depending on what kind of tour you want, or the area of Egypt you want to cover. The programs on such trips are usually fairly tight, leaving little room for roaming around on your own, but they take away much of the hassle. It pays to shop around. Check itinerary details, accommodation, who does the ticketing, visa and other documentation footwork, insurance and tour conditions carefully.

Following is a list of specialist operators who do Egypt packages tailored for independently minded travellers looking for a bit more than just two weeks in the sun:

Australia

Australia Adventure World
    (☎ 1800-133 322, fax 9956 7707)
    73 Walker St, North Sydney, NSW 2060
    Agents for the UK's Explore Worldwide and
    Exodus. Also in Adelaide, Brisbane, Melbourne and Perth.

Gateway Tours
(☎ 02-9745 3333, fax 9745 3237, email gatrav@ magna.com.au)
48 The Boulevarde, Strathfield, NSW 2135
Stopover Cairo packages, Cairo to Aswan tours (by train or air) and Nile cruises.

Insight International
(☎ 02-9512 0767, fax 9438 5209)
Suite 201, 39-41 Chandos St, St Leonards NSW2065
Sinai tours and Nile cruises, among other things.

Peregrine
(☎ 03-663 8611, fax 663 8618)
258 Lonsdale St, Melbourne, VIC 3000
Agents for the UK's Dragoman and The Imaginative Traveller. Also in Adelaide, Brisbane, Perth and Sydney.

Ya'lla
(☎ 03-9510 2844, fax 9510 8425, email yal lamel@yallatours.com.au)
West Tower, 608 St Kilda Rd, Melbourne, VIC 3000
Wide variety of pick 'n' mix package tours, private arrangement tours and Nile cruises.

UK

Bales Tours
(☎ 01306-885 991, fax 740 048)
Bales House, Junction Rd, Dorking, Surrey RH4 3HL
Pricey upmarket tours utilising five star accommodation.

Encounter Overland
(☎ 0171-370 6845, fax 244 9737, from 22 April 2000 ☎ 020-7370 6845, fax 020-7244 9737, email adventure@encounter.co.uk)
267 Old Brompton Rd, London SW5 9JA
Mainly extensive overland tours which take in Egypt as part of a larger Asia or Africa tour but it also does a round-Egypt 21 day excursion.

Exodus
(☎ 0181-673 0859, fax 673 0779, from 22 April 2000 ☎ 020-8673 0859, fax 020-8673 0779, Web site www.exodustravels.co.uk)
9 Weir Rd, London SW12 OLT
Does three reasonably priced Egypt packages, one of which takes in the Western oases.

Explore Worldwide
(☎ 01252-760 000, fax 760 001, Web site www.explore.co.uk)
1 Fredrick St, Aldershot, Hampshire GU11 1LQ
Offers three short tours: a 'Nile Felucca Sailtrek'; a Nile cruise; and a Sinai Insight tour. In addition there are longer itineraries departing throughout the year. Most trips average about UK£550 including flights and accommodation.

Hayes and Jarvis
(☎ 0181-222 7800, fax 741 0299, from 22 April 2000 ☎ 020-8222 7800, fax 020-8741 0299, email res@hayes-jarvis.com)
Hayes House, 152 King St, London W6 OQU
Respected Egypt specialists with a large variety of mainstream holiday packages including cruises.

The Imaginative Traveller
(☎ 0181-742 3049, fax 742 3045, from 22 April 2000 ☎ 020-8742 3049, fax 020-8742 3045, Web site www.imaginative-traveller.com)
14 Barley Mow Passage, Chiswick, London W4 4PH
Small group tours with at least 20 different Egypt itineraries from felucca trips and cruises to a Red Sea Diving for Beginners trip based in Hurghada.

Top Deck
(☎ 0171-244 8641, fax 373 6201, from 22 April 2000 ☎ 020-7244 8641, fax 020-7373 6201, email topdeck@dial.pipex.com)
131-135 Earls Court Rd, London SW5 9RH
Does Egypt on its own or as part of a Jordan and Israel package.

Travelbag Adventures
(☎ 01420-541 007, Web site www.travelbag adventures.co.uk)
15 Turk St, Alton, Hants GU34 1AG
Small group tours with structured itineraries.

Voyages Jules Vernes
(☎ 0171-723 5066, fax 723 8629, from 22 April 2000 ☎ 020-7723 5066, fax 020-7723 8629, email sales@vjv.co.uk)
21 Dorset Sq, London NW1 6QG
Top class (and top price) tour operator offering seductively packaged itineraries including St Katherines and the Pyramids (seven nights for UK£695).

USA & Canada

Abercrombie & Kent
(☎ 1800-323 7308, fax 630-954 3324, Web site www.abercrombiekent.com)
1520 Kensington Rd, suite 212, Oak Brook IL 60523-2141
Classy packages using top-end hotels, domestic flights and their own custom-built Nile cruisers.

Adventure Center
(☎ 1800-227 8747, fax 510-654 4200, email tripinfo@adventure-center.com)
1311 63rd St, suite 200, Emeryville, CA 94608
Agents for the UK's Dragoman, Encounter Overland and Explore Worldwide.

Bestway Tours & Safaris
(☎ 604-264 7378, fax 264 7774, email bestway@ bestway.com, Web site www.bestway.com)

103-3540 West 41st Ave, Vancouver, BC
V6N 3E6
Small group tours.
Overseas Adventure Travel
(☎ 1800-955 1925)
625 Mt Auburn St, Cambridge MA 02138
Specialises in small group tours for mature
travellers. The Egypt trip is 15 days including
a three day Nile cruise and round-trip flights
from New York for US$3290.

Nile Cruises

Since militant activity in middle Egypt has
been preventing cruise ships from sailing
between Cairo and Luxor, many overseas
companies have dropped their Nile cruise
packages, and one or two companies that
specialised in just Nile cruises have gone
bust. However, it is still possible – and safe
– to sail a three or four day stretch of the
river south from Luxor (see the Nile Cruises
section under Boat in the Getting Around
chapter). Abercrombie & Kent and Hayes
and Jarvis (details earlier) both do good
cruise packages, and you should also have
no problem booking something through a
high street travel agent. Take a look at the
option of a Lake Nasser cruise, too, a trip
we can't recommend too highly (see the
Cruising Lake Nasser in the Nile Valley –
Esna to Abu Simbel chapter).

Adventure & Overland Safaris

A popular mode of travelling through
Africa and Asia is by overland truck. This
is not everyone's cup of tea, as you spend a
lot of time with the same group of people,
travelling, camping and cooking. Organisers of these tours do take much of the hassle out of the bureaucratic footwork,
helping out with visas and dodging a lot of
the cross-border hassles. Egypt features as
a leg on trips run by the following outfits
(which all happen to be UK based):

African Trails
(☎ 0181-742 7724, fax 960 1414, from 22
April 2000 ☎ 020-8742 7724, fax 020-8960
1414)
3 Flanders Rd, Chiswick, London W4 1NQ
Egypt to Turkey in six weeks for UK£600.

Dragoman
(☎ 01728-861 133, fax 861 127, Web site
www.dragoman.co.uk)
99 Camp Green, Debenham, Suffolk IP14 6LA
Overland specialists with numerous itineraries
through North Africa and the Middle East.
Economic Expeditions
(☎ 0181-995 7707, fax 742 7707, from 22
April 2000 ☎ 020-8995 7707, fax 020-8742
7707, email ecoexped@mcmail.com)
29 Cunnington St, Chiswick, London W4 5ER
Istanbul to Cairo (five weeks) for UK£380.
Exodus
(☎ 0181- 673 0859, fax 673 0779, from 22 April
2000 ☎ 020-8673 0859, fax 020-8673 0779,
Web site www.exodustravels.co.uk)
9 Weir Rd, London SW12 OLT
Offers Cairo to Nairobi (nine weeks) and Cairo
to Cape Town (18 weeks).
Hinterland Travel
(☎ 01883-743 584 or 743 861, fax 743 912)
2 Ivy Mill Lane, Godstone, Surrey RH9 8NH
Kumuka
(☎ 0171-937 8855, fax 937 6664, from 22
April 2000 ☎ 020-7937 8855, fax 020-7937
6664, email sales@kumuka.co.uk)
40 Earls Court Rd, London W8 6EJ
Istanbul to Cairo over four or six weeks for
UK£695/990.
Oasis Overland
(☎ 0181-759 5597, fax 897 2713, from 22 April
2000 ☎ 020-8759 5597, fax 020-8897 2713)
33 Travellers Way, Hounslow, London TW4 7QB
Five week Turkey-Syria-Jordan-Egypt trip for
UK£590.

Other adventure travel companies worth a
look for their Egypt activities include:

High Places
(☎ 0114-275 7500, fax 275 3870, Web site
www.highplaces.co.uk)
Globe Works, Penistone Rd, Sheffield S6 3AE
It does an eight day camel trek around Sinai.
Wind Sand & Stars
(☎ 0171-433 3684, fax 431 3247, from 22 April
2000 ☎ 020-7433 3684, fax 020-7431 3247)
2 Arkwright Rd, London NW3 6AD
Sinai specialists who organise trips involving
climbing and walking, desert camping, birdwatching and snorkelling.

Diving Tours

While it's quite possible to just book yourself a basic package to Sinai or Hurghada

and sort out your own diving arrangements with a local company when you get there (see the Diving the Red Sea chapter), there are numerous agencies who specialise in Red Sea diving holidays. The following are just a few that we know of:

Crusader Travel
(☎ 0181-744 0474, fax 744 0574, from 22 April 2000 ☎ 020-8744 0474, fax 020-8744 0574, email crusader@divers.co.uk, Web site www.divers.co.uk)
57 Church St, Twickenham TW1 3NR
Primarily does diving packages in the Red Sea out of Eilat, Nuweiba and Taba. Also does special diving for the disabled.

Destination Red Sea
(☎ 0181-440 9900, fax 440 9905, from 22 April 2000 ☎ 020-8440 9900, fax 020-8440 9905, email sales@redsea.co.uk, Web site www.redsea.co.uk)
125 East Barnet Rd, New Barnet, Herts EN4 8RF
Diving tours out of Sharm el-Sheikh, Hurghada and Port Safaga. Also liveaboard trips.

The Imaginative Traveller
(☎ 0181-742 3049, fax 742 3045, from 22 April 2000 ☎ 020-8742 3049, fax 020-8742 3045, Web site www.imaginative-traveller.com)
14 Barley Mow Passage, Chiswick, London W4 4PH
It does a Red Sea Diving for Beginners trip based in Hurghada including a PADI open water course.

Oonasdivers
(☎ 01323-648 924, fax 738 356, email info@oonasdivers.com, Web site www.oonas divers.com)
23 Enys Rd, Eastbourne BN21 2DG
Diving tours based out of the Oonas dive club at Na'ama Bay. Also Red Sea diving safaris from the Marsa Alam region and liveaboard

Warning

The information in this chapter is particularly vulnerable to change: prices for international travel are volatile, routes are introduced and cancelled, schedules change, special deals come and go, and rules and visa requirements are amended. Airlines and governments seem to take a perverse pleasure in making price structures and regulations as complicated as possible. You should check directly with the airline or a travel agent to make sure you understand how a fare (and ticket you may buy) works. In addition, the travel industry is highly competitive and there are many lurks and perks.

The upshot of this is that you should get opinions, quotes and advice from as many airlines and travel agents as possible before you part with your hard-earned cash. The details given in this chapter should be regarded as pointers and are not a substitute for your own careful, up-to-date research.

trips. Prices seem very reasonable, eg eight days liveaboard, unlimited diving plus return flights from UK for UK£830.

Regal Holidays
(☎ 01353-778 096, fax 777 897)
22 High St, Sutton, Ely, Cambridgeshire CB6 2RB
Diving tours out of Sharm el-Sheikh and Hurghada, also some liveaboards. Fairly up-market accommodation but prices still seem reasonable.

Getting Around

Egypt has a very extensive public and private transport system. If you don't suffer from claustrophobia, and have plenty of patience and a tough stomach, you can travel just about anywhere in Egypt for relatively little money.

AIR

EgyptAir is the main domestic carrier. Air Sinai, which to all intents and purposes is EgyptAir by another name, is virtually the only other operator. Fares are expensive and probably out of the range of most budget travellers. In general, it is only worth flying if your time is very limited.

During the high season (October to April), many flights are full so it's wise to book as far in advance as you can.

from	to	one way	return
Aswan	Abu Simbel		E£290
Cairo	Abu Simbel	E£818	E£1631
	Alexandria	E£248	E£490
	Aswan	E£576	E£1146
	Hurghada	E£453	E£900
	Luxor	E£419	E£832
	Sharm el-Sheikh	E£477	E£948
Luxor	Aswan	E£190	E£380
	Hurghada	E£190	E£380

For the contact details of EgyptAir see the Getting There & Away sections under individual cities and towns.

BUS

Buses service just about every city, town and village in Egypt. Ticket prices are generally comparable with the cost of 2nd class train tickets. Intercity buses, especially on shorter runs and in Upper Egypt, tend to become quite crowded, and even if you are lucky enough to get a seat in the first place, you'll probably end up with something or somebody on your lap.

Deluxe buses travel between some of the main towns. For instance, the Superjet and West Delta Bus companies run luxury buses between Cairo and Alexandria daily. Similar services are offered to other parts of the country, and air-con, comfortable buses run between Cairo, Ismailia, Port Said, Suez, St Katherine's Monastery, Sharm el-Sheikh, Hurghada and Luxor. Tickets cost a bit more than on standard buses but they're still cheap. The bulk of buses running south of Cairo along the Nile tend to be more basic.

Often the prices of tickets for buses on the same route will vary according to whether or not they have air-con and video, how old the bus is and how long it takes to make the journey – the more you pay, the more comfort you travel in and the quicker you get there. However, there are a few serious drawbacks to luxury bus travel, foremost of which is the video. This goes on as soon as the bus is out of the station and plays throughout the journey at a ridiculous volume that totally precludes any reading or any chance of sleep. You might find a sweater handy on overnight buses as the air-con brings the temperature down to a level where, according to one traveller, 'polar bears would feel at home'. Also, *beware*, snacks are not included in the price of the ticket so, unless you want to pay E£10 or more for a cup of tea and a biscuit, decline the on-board service.

One other problem associated with all bus travel in Egypt is smoking. Egyptian men are prolific smokers and nonsmokers may find long journeys to be a hazy nightmare of endless smog, despite the fact that many buses actually sport 'no smoking' signs. Protesting may make the guy next to you stop, but it's unlikely to change the habits of the rest of those on board.

Tickets can be bought at the bus stations or often on the bus. Hang on to your ticket until you get off, as inspectors almost always board the bus to check fares. It is advisable to book tickets, at least on very popular routes (such as from Cairo to Sinai) and those with few buses running (out to the Western Oases from Cairo), a day or two in advance. There are no student discounts on bus fares. Where you are allowed to buy tickets on the bus, you generally end up standing if you don't have an assigned seat with a booked ticket. On short runs there are no bookings and it's a case of first on, best seated.

TRAIN

Although trains travel along more than 5000km of track to almost every major city and town in Egypt, the system is badly in need of modernisation and most of the services are grimy and battered and a poor second option to the deluxe bus. The exceptions are some of the trains to Alexandria and the tourist trains down to Luxor and Aswan – on these routes the train is preferable to the bus.

If you have an International Student Identification Card (ISIC) discounts of about 33% are granted on all fares except those for wagons-lit (cars with deluxe sleeper compartments). Some travellers report getting a discount with International Youth Hostel Federation cards and Youth International Educational Exchange cards. It is possible to travel from Cairo to Aswan for only a few pounds if you have an ISIC and are willing to suffer in the 3rd class cars.

One advantage (for a change) of being a woman here is that you go straight to the head of the queue for train tickets.

Classes

Services range from relatively cheap (compared to the USA and Europe) 1st class wagons-lit through 1st class sitting, 2nd class air-con and 2nd class ordinary to the ridiculously cheap 3rd class cars.

Wagons-Lit Trains with wagons-lit are the most comfortable and among the fastest in Egypt. The cars are the same as those used by trains in Europe and only sleeper compartments are available. Two wagons-lit trains used to travel between Cairo, Luxor

and Aswan every day, but the number dropped to one a couple of years ago.

Wagons-lit trains are 1st class only, have air-con, are carpeted, and each compartment has towels, coat hangers, hot and cold water and Venetian blinds. There are lounge cars, and dinner and breakfast are served in the compartments.

Other Classes Regular night trains with and without sleeper compartments and meals included leave for Luxor and Aswan every day and cost much less than the wagons-lit. Reservations must be made in advance at Ramses station in Cairo. Unless you specify otherwise, you'll be issued with a ticket that includes meals on board. For this you'll pay, for example, an extra E£10 on the trip from Cairo to Luxor. Many travellers have said the food is tasteless and, for what you get, a waste of money so you may want to flout the rules and bring your own. Both 1st and 2nd class compartments have air-con and they can get chilly at night; have something warm to put on.

Non-air-con trains are next down the scale. Classes here are divided into ordinary 2nd class, which generally has padded seats, and 3rd class, where seating is of the wooden bench variety. These trains tend to spend a lot of time at a lot of stations and can be subject to interminable delays.

TAXI
Service Taxi

Travelling by 'ser-vees' is one of the fastest ways to go from city to city. Service taxis are generally big Peugeot 504 cars that run intercity routes. Drivers congregate near bus and train stations and tout for passengers by shouting their destination. When the car's full, it's off. A driver won't leave before his car is full unless you and/or the other passengers want to pay more money. Fares are usually cheaper than either the buses or trains and there are no set departure times, you just turn up and find a car. The drawbacks are that with six or seven squeezed in, journeys tend to be a bit uncomfortable and there's no room for baggage. Service taxi rides can also be a little hairy at times – the drivers tend to be over-confident and often tired from long shifts on the road. Accidents involving service taxis are all too common and for this reason we don't recommend using them unless as a last resort.

Microbus

A slightly bigger version of the service taxi is the 'meecrobus', a Toyota van that would normally take about 12 people but in Egypt takes as many as 22. These run on the same principle as service taxis and cost about the same but operate on fewer routes.

Pick-Ups

Toyota and Chevrolet pick-up trucks cover a lot of the routes between smaller towns and villages off the main roads. The general rule is to get 12 inside the covered rear of the truck, often with an assortment of goods squeezed in around feet on the floor. After that, it's a matter of how many can and want to scramble on to the roof or hang off at the rear.

CAR & MOTORCYCLE

Driving in Cairo is a crazy affair, so think seriously before you decide to rent a car there. However, driving in other parts of the country, at least in daylight, isn't so bad. Having a car – or better still a 4WD – opens up whole areas of the country where public transport is nonexistent.

Motorcycle would be an ideal way to travel around Egypt. The only snag is that you have to bring your own and the red tape involved is extensive. Ask your country's automobile association and Egyptian embassy about regulations.

Petrol is readily available. Normal, or *tamaneen*, costs 90pt a litre but is tough on the engine. Better is the higher-octane super, or *tisa'een* at E£1 a litre. Lead-free was introduced in 1995 but, with only a handful of pumps in Cairo (mainly in Mohandiseen, Zamalek and Ma'adi) and Alexandria, there might be a queue. When travelling out of Cairo, remember that petrol stations are not always that plentiful; when you see one, fill up. Although the fast increase in car ownership over the past five years has improved petrol distribution in the country, many provincial stations still run out of the high octane tisa'een, so if you're worried about your engine bring an extra can along with you.

Road Rules

Driving is on the right-hand side. The official speed limit outside towns is 90km/h (though it is often less in some areas) and 100km/h on four-lane highways such as the one between Cairo and Alexandria. If you're caught speeding the police confiscate your licence and you have to go to the traffic headquarters in the area to get it back – a lengthy and laborious process. A few roads, such as the Cairo-Alexandria Desert Highway, the Cairo-Fayoum road and the road through the Ahmed Hamdi Tunnel (which goes under the Suez Canal near Suez) are subject to tolls of about E£1.25.

Many roads have checkpoints where police often ask for identity papers, so make sure you've got your passport and driving licence on hand or you may be liable for a US$100 on-the-spot fine.

Although city driving may seem chaotic, there is one cardinal rule: whoever is in front has the right of way – even if a car is only 1cm ahead of you and then cuts across your path suddenly, you will be liable if you hit it. As long as you do not assume that anybody looks in his or her rearview mirror and you use your horn to announce your presence, you'll be fine.

When driving through the countryside, keep in mind that children and adults are liable to wander into your path, even on main roads. Drive very carefully and use your horn liberally – hitting someone, even if it was their own fault, can sometimes result in the driver being attacked by angry villagers. If you do have an accident, get to the nearest police station as quickly as possible and report what happened.

For more information on road rules, suggested routes and other advice, it might be worth picking up a copy of *On the Road in*

Egypt: A Motorist's Guide by Mary Dungan Megalli. It was printed in 1989, so it's starting to become outdated, but it's still available at Lehnert & Landrock bookshop in Cairo.

Rental

Several car rental agencies have offices in Egypt, including Avis, Hertz and Budget (for contact details see the Getting Around section in the Cairo chapter). Their rates match international charges and finding a cheap deal with local dealers is virtually impossible. No matter who you go with, make sure you read the fine print.

An international driving permit is required and you can be liable to a heavy fine if you're caught renting a car without one. Drivers should be over the age of 25.

As an indication of prices, for a small car like a Suzuki Swift you'll be looking at about US$33 to US$40 per day, plus up to US$0.20 for each extra kilometre. A Toyota Corolla is about US$56 to US$60 per day, plus around US$0.25 per kilometre. These prices generally include insurance and the first 100km, but check this before signing. For unlimited kilometres, you'll be looking at about US$47/70 per day respectively for the above cars. Some companies set a minimum of seven days for unlimited-kilometre rentals, in which case you'll be looking at about US$240 to US$275 per week for a Toyota Starlet. Remember there will be a 10% to 17% tax added to your bill. It's usually possible to pay with travellers cheques or by credit card.

Some companies, such as Europcar, offer the option of one-way rentals from, for example, Cairo to Sharm el-Sheikh. It's also possible to hire a car plus a driver for those who don't feel like tackling the Egyptian roads.

BICYCLE

Bicycles are a practical way of getting around a town and its surrounding sites. In most places, particularly Luxor, you can rent a bicycle quite cheaply; prices start at around E£4 per day. Bicycles are, however, somewhat impractical for covering long distances or for getting around in big cities. The biggest problem is the possibility of getting flattened by one of Egypt's crazy drivers, who are not the slightest bit accustomed to cyclists on the roads.

HITCHING

Hitching is never entirely safe in any country in the world, and we don't recommend it. Travellers who decide to hitch should understand that they are taking a small but potentially serious risk. Hitching is certainly not recommended for women travellers. Should you decide to hitch, you'll find many drivers expect to be paid for giving you a ride and therefore you probably won't save very much money by hitching anyway.

BOAT
Nile Cruises

For centuries taking a boat was the only way to travel in Egypt. The pharaohs would view their realm from the river, people would visit one another via the waterway, barges with precious cargo would traverse the length of the country. In death, ancient Egyptians would even take boats to the underworld. Travellers too have historically gazed out over the country from the deck of a boat. From the 5th century BC, when that most famous of travel writers, Herodotus, was wandering through Egypt, up to modern times, a trip to Egypt meant sailing up the Nile.

Thomas Cook changed all that at the end of the 1860s, when he launched steamboats on the Nile, in the process inaugurating package tourism in Egypt. Rudyard Kipling's hilarious account of his cruise in 1913 does not differ vastly from the experience many tourists have today:

For three weeks we sat on copiously chaired and carpeted decks, carefully isolated from everything that had anything to do with Egypt, under chaperonage of a properly orientalised dragoman. Twice or thrice daily, our steamer drew up at a mud-bank covered with donkeys. Saddles were hauled out of a hatch in our bows; the donkeys were dressed, dealt round like cards: we rode off through crops or desert, as the case might be, were introduced in ringing tones to a temple, and were then duly returned to our bridge and our Baedekers.

Unfortunately, the threat of terrorist attacks in middle Egypt has meant that since the early 1990s there have been no cruise ships sailing the length of the Nile from Cairo to Aswan, or vice versa. However, there are currently more than 250 cruise boats plying the waters between Luxor and Aswan that still make for a relaxing, timeless way to take in the monuments in this part of the country. Most cruises involve a three or four day sail between the two towns, stopping at the temple sites along the way.

Most of the boats are rated as either four or five-star hotels, although there are some three stars available. Cruises on a top level boat, with all meals and sightseeing for four days (three nights) start at around US$200 to US$300 per person, but if it's low season, you can get them for much less. The cheapest deals come from booking in advance in your home country but you can also, space permitting, book yourself onto a cruise once in Egypt.

The most reputable boats are managed by international hotel chains, such as Mövenpick or Sheraton. Cairo-based travel agencies such as Abercrombie & Kent (☎ 394 7735) and Thomas Cook (☎ 574 3955) also have their own boats complete with excellent reputations.

Other operators include Masr Travel Co & Hilton International (☎ 383 3444), Presidential Nile Cruises (☎ 340 0517), Travcotels (☎ 340 0959) and Seti First Travel (☎ 341 9820).

Felucca

The ancient sailboats of the Nile are still a fairly common means of transport up and down the river. As far as getting around, many people use them for a trip between Aswan and Esna, Edfu or Kom Ombo – it's not the most rapid way of travelling but that's not the point. For more information on how to arrange a trip see under The

River in the Aswan section of the Nile Valley – Esna to Abu Simbel chapter.

Yacht

It is possible to take a yacht into Egyptian waters and ports. There are 12 designated ports of entry, including Alexandria, Port Said, Sharm el-Sheikh, Dahab, Nuweiba, Hurghada, Suez and Ismailia. A security permit is required to enter the Nile River, and transit fees of US$10 per person and US$20 per yacht need to be paid to negotiate the Suez Canal. These and other fees are liable to change.

You will need all the usual documentation for the yacht, plus six copies of the crew list. You will also need valid visas and a raft of other bits of paper, including a health certificate, a customs list of the yacht's equipment and an insurance policy (for the Suez Canal). You can get visas on arrival in your first port.

It is also possible to shelter in other 'nonentry' ports, but you cannot go ashore.

Fuel is available in all ports of entry, and navigational charts are available in Alexandria, Port Said and Suez (ask for 'Marinkart'). There are nine yacht clubs in Egypt. For more details, contact your own yacht club before heading for Egypt.

Before leaving Egypt, a departure permit has to be obtained from the Coast Guard and you are supposed to leave within 24 hours of obtaining it.

If you want to get a lift on a yacht heading down to the Red Sea or elsewhere, it's best to try in Suez or Port Said.

LOCAL TRANSPORT

As well as the local transport options described here, some cities and towns have their own – most are variations on the pony and trap theme.

Bus & Minibus

Cairo and Alexandria are the only cities in Egypt with their own bus systems and taking a bus in either place is an experience far beyond the simple notion of getting from A to B. First, there's getting on. Egyptians stampede buses, charging the entrance before the thing has even slowed down. Hand-to-hand combat ensues as they run alongside trying to leap aboard. If you wait for the bus to stop, the pushing and shoving to get on is even worse. Often several passengers don't quite manage to get on and they make their journey hanging off the back doorway, clinging perilously to the frame or to someone with a firmer hold.

The scene inside the bus in this case usually resembles a Guinness World Record attempt on the greatest number of people in a fixed space. There are times when, crammed up the back with exhaust fumes billowing around you and ever more people squeezing on, asphyxiation seems perilously close. At some point during the trip, a man will somehow manage to squeeze his way through to sell you your ticket, which is usually 25pt.

Just as the buses only ever slow to pick up passengers, so they rarely completely stop to let you off. You stand in the doorway, wait for the opportune moment and launch yourself onto the road.

Taking a minibus is an easier option. Passengers are not allowed to stand (although this rule is frequently overlooked), and each minibus leaves as soon as every seat is taken. It costs 25pt to 50pt (depending on your destination) for a seat.

Travelling Salesmen

Buses and trams idling at terminals are the perfect pitch for street vendors. Men and young boys wander up and down the aisle with sweets, hair brushes, toiletries, lottery tickets, cards with Quranic verses ... the usual sales method is to drop one of whatever it is into the lap of each passenger. If this happens to you, don't bother protesting or trying to give it back – just before the bus or tram departs, the vendor returns along the aisle collecting up all his goods and the money from anyone who is buying.

Microbus

Privately owned and usually unmarked microbuses shuttle around all the larger cities. For the average traveller, they can be difficult to use, as it is quite unclear where most of them go, however, quite often there's a small boy hanging out of the doorway yelling the destination. In Cairo, you might have occasion to use a microbus to get out to the Pyramids, while in Alex they shuttle the length of Tariq al-Horreyya and the Corniche to Montazah. Most of the smaller cities and towns have similar microbuses doing set runs around town.

Metro

Cairo is the only city in Egypt (indeed in Africa) with a metro system (for more details see the Getting Around section in that chapter).

Tram

Cairo and Alexandria are also the only two cities in the country with tram systems. While Alexandria still has a fairly extensive and efficient network, Cairo now only has a handful of lines. See the Getting Around sections in the two city chapters for more details.

Taxi

There are taxis in most cities in Egypt; in Cairo they're all black and white, while in Alex they're black and orange. Almost every second car is a taxi and they are by far the most convenient way of getting about. Stand at the side of the road, stick your hand out and shout your destination at any cab passing in the right direction. It doesn't matter if there is already someone inside, as taxis are shared. When a taxi stops, restate where you want to go and if the driver's amenable, hop in.

Do not ask 'how much?' The etiquette is that you get in knowing what to pay and when you arrive, you get out and hand the money through the window. Make sure that you have the correct money (hoard E£1 bills) because getting change out of drivers is like having your teeth pulled. If a driver

Taxi!

Taxis are at once a blessing and a curse. They're a remarkably convenient and easily affordable way of getting around the city but they can also be a frequent source of unpleasantness when it comes to paying the fare. The problem comes with the un-metered system of payment, which almost guarantees discontent. Passengers frequently feel they're been taken advantage of (which they often are), while drivers are occasionally genuinely aggrieved by what they see as underpayment. So why don't  the drivers use the meter? Because they were all calibrated at a time when petrol was ludicrously cheap. That time has long passed and any driver relying on his meter would now be out of pocket every time he came to fill up.

Taxi driving is far from being a lucrative profession. Of the 60,000 plus taxis on the road in Cairo it would be a safe bet to assume none of the drivers are yet millionaires. Average earnings after fuel has been paid for are about E£8 per hour. Consider too, that many drivers don't even own their car and have to hand over part of their earnings as 'rent'.

Which isn't to say that next time you flag a taxi for a short hop across town and he hisses 'Ten bounds' that you should smile and say 'OK', but maybe you can see that from a certain point of view, it was worth his while trying.

suspects that you don't know what the correct fare is then you're fair game for fleecing. If once you get in the taxi the driver starts talking money then just state a fair price (we give examples of correct fares throughout this book) and if it's not accepted, get out and find another car.

Often when you come to paying, a driver will demand more money, sometimes yelling. Don't be intimidated and don't be drawn into an argument. As long as you know you are not underpaying (and the fares we give in this book are generous), just walk away. It's all bluster and the driver is playing on the fact that you are a *khawaga* (foreigner) and don't know any better.

The big Peugeot 504 service taxis, sometimes marked 'special', charge more than other taxis. The advantage of these taxis is that you can get a group together and commandeer one for a long trip.

Pick-Ups As well as servicing routes between smaller towns, covered pick-up trucks are sometimes used within towns as local taxis. This is especially so in some of the oases towns and smaller places along the Nile. Should you end up in one of these, there are a couple of ways you can indicate to the driver when you want to get out: if you happen to be lucky enough to have a seat, pound on the floor with your foot; alternatively ask one of the front passengers to hammer on the window behind the driver; or, lastly, use the buzzer that you'll occasionally find rigged up.

Cairo

Few other countries can be so dominated by their capital: Cairo *is* Egypt. Both of them are known by the same name, *Masr*, and for Egyptians, to speak of one is to speak of the other at the same time. The city's stature spreads beyond borders – to millions of Arabic speakers, Cairo is the semi-mythical capital of the Arab world. One tale in *The Thousand and One Nights* begins with a circle of men in a mosque in Mosul talking of foreign lands and the marvels of cities. 'Baghdad is Paradise', says one, to which the eldest sagely counters, 'He who has not seen Cairo has not seen the world. Its dust is gold; its Nile is a wonder; its women are like the black-eyed virgins of paradise: and how could it not be otherwise, when she is the Mother of the World'.

These days, she is mother to around 16 million Egyptians, Arabs, Africans and sundry international hangers-on. She's overburdened with one of the world's highest densities of people per square kilometre, which makes for a seething compress of people, buildings and traffic and all the attendant cacophony and jostling for space that that brings.

Cairo's lack of room to develop or expand constantly throws up startling juxtapositions. In one central Nileside district, less than 500m from a new computer superstore, there are mud-brick houses where goats wander through living rooms and water has to be obtained from spigots in the street. Across town, a recently completed funfair/restaurant complex has gone up on the fringes of a 1000-year-old cemetery, which itself, is still in use with the dead vying for space with the living.

Cairenes see nothing strange in this. They aren't driven by the western obsession to update and upgrade; possibly as a result of living in such close proximity to 4½ millennia of history (the Pyramids are visible from the upper storeys of buildings all over the city). The resulting pervasive sense of

HIGHLIGHTS

- **The Pyramids at dawn** With hawkers and camel owners in your face its hard to be duly awed by the world's greatest ancient wonders but at dawn, it's a different story – you have them to yourself.

- **2 am at Fishawi's** Any time of the day is fine at Cairo's oldest coffeehouse but after midnight the visitors are gone and the place returns to the locals.

- **Sunset felucca rides** Drift on the Nile and watch the sun sink behind the Cairo skyline.

- **Tutankhamun at the Egyptian Museum** Badly displayed but still some of the most magnificent objects held by any museum anywhere in the world.

- **Up the minarets at Bab Zuweila** Lots of Cairo's minarets are climbable but for peering into the heart of the medieval city the best view is from either of the two towers atop Bab Zuweila.

- **Early morning at the Hanging Church** One of the most serene and understated attractive sites in Cairo, best visited early before the coach parties arrive.

- **Evening drinks at the Oberoi Mena House** You don't have to be staying at Cairo's most famous hotel to sit beside the pool, sip something cool and gaze on the floodlit Pyramids rising beyond the palm trees.

timelessness is one of the city's great charms. In the space of a few hours it's possible to move from the medieval backstreets of Islamic Cairo to the pharaonic monumentalism of the Pyramids, take time out in a coffeehouse that looks every bit identical to those portrayed in 19th century prints and then drink in a bar locked in time in pre-Revolutionary days. And what is really wonderful is that none of these places feels 'historical', they all just feel like Cairo. That's to say, they're chaotic, noisy, totally unpredictable and seething with humanity. It's an exhilarating place for those with the patience to appreciate it.

HISTORY

Cairo is not a pharaonic city, though the presence of the Pyramids leads many to believe otherwise. At the time the Pyramids were built the capital of ancient Egypt was Memphis, 22km south of the Giza Plateau.

The core foundations of the city of Cairo were laid in 969 AD by the Fatimid dynasty. There had been earlier settlements, notably the Roman fortress of Babylon and the early Islamic city of Fustat, established by Amr ibn al-As, the general who conquered Egypt for Islam in 642 AD. Fustat became one of the richest cities of the new Muslim world order, its wealth based on Egypt's excessively rich soil and the taxes imposed on the heavy Nile traffic. Descriptions left by 10th century travellers tell of a cosmopolitan metropolis with public gardens, street lighting and buildings up to 14 storeys high. Yet when the Fatimids marched in out of North Africa they spurned Fustat and instead set about building a new city.

The area for the new city, so the story goes, was pegged out, and labourers were waiting for a signal from the astrologers to begin digging. The signal was to be the ringing of bells attached to the ropes marking off the construction area, but a raven landed on the rope and set off the bells prematurely. As the planet Mars (Al-Qahir, 'the Victorious') was in the ascendant, the Fatimid caliph decided to call the city Al-Qahira, from which Europeans would later derive the word Cairo.

Much of the city the Fatimids built remains today: the great Fatimid mosque and

university of Al-Azhar is still Egypt's main centre of Islamic study, while the three great gates of Bab an-Nasr, Bab al-Futuh and Bab Zuweila still straddle two of Islamic Cairo's main thoroughfares. Although the Fatimids were not to remain long in power (see the History section in the Facts about Egypt chapter for more details) their city grew under subsequent dynasties to become a capital of great wealth, filled with merchants from distant lands, laden with bazaars of exotic wares, ruled by cruel and fickle sultans. This was the city that inspired many of the tales that make up *The Thousand and One Nights*.

Cairo swelled and burst its walls, spreading north, spawning a port area, Bulaq, to the west, extending south onto the island of Rhoda, and filling the desert to the east with a series of grand funerary monuments. But at its heart it remained a medieval city for 900 years. It wasn't until the reign of Ismail, grandson of Mohammed Ali, in the mid-19th century that Cairo started to change in any significant way. In his 16-year reign Ismail (1830-95) did more than anyone since the Fatimids to alter the city's appearance.

Before the 1860s Cairo extended west only as far as what is today Midan Opera. The future site of modern central Cairo was then a swampy plain subject to the annual flooding of the Nile. In 1863, when the French-educated Ismail came to power, he was determined to upgrade the image of his capital, which he believed could only be done by dismissing what had gone before and starting afresh. For 10 years the former marsh became one vast building site as Ismail invited architects from Belgium, France and Italy to design and build a new European-style Cairo beside the old Islamic city.

Since the Revolution, Cairo has grown spectacularly in population and urban planners have struggled to keep pace. In the 1960s and 1970s the previously sparsely populated west bank of the Nile was concreted over with new suburbs like Medinat Mohandiseen (Engineers' City) and Medinat

GREATER CAIRO

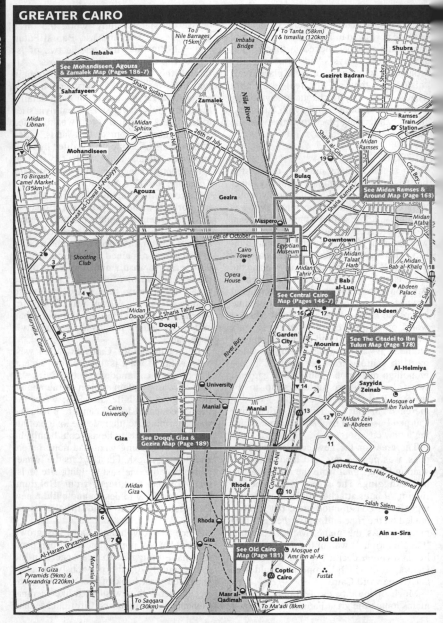

To Nile Barrages (15km)

To Tanta (58km) & Ismailia (120km)

Imbaba Bridge

Imbaba

Shubra

See Mohandiseen, Agouza & Zamalek Map (Pages 186-7)

Geziret Badran

Sahafayeen

Zamalek

Sharia Sudan

Midan Sphinx

Midan Libnan

Ramses Train Station

Midan Ramses

Mohandiseen

26th of July

Sharia el-Nil

Sharia al-Gisr

Nile River

To Birqash Camel Market (35km)

Agouza

Camel al-Dowal al-Arabyya

Gezira

Bulaq

See Midan Ramses & Around Map (Page 163)

Midan Ataba

Maspero

Sharia Ramses

Shooting Club

6th of October

Cairo Tower

Egyptian Museum

Downtown

Midan Bab al-Khalq

Opera House

Midan Tahrir

Midan Talaat Harb

Maryuta Canal

Midan Doqqi

Sharia Tahrir

Doqqi

Bab al-Luq

Abdeen Palace

See Central Cairo Map (Pages 146-7)

Abdeen

Port Said (Bur Said)

River Bus

Garden City

Mounira

See The Citadel to Ibn Tulun Map (Page 178)

Cairo University

University

Sharia al-Giza

Manial

Manial

Al-Helmiya

Sayyida Zeinab

Mosque of Ibn Tulun

Giza

Corniche el-Nil

Midan Zein al-Abdeen

See Doqqi, Giza & Gezira Map (Page 189)

Aqueduct of an-Nasr Mohammed

Midan Giza

Rhoda

Salah Salem

Rhoda

Ain as-Sira

Giza

Old Cairo

Al-Haram (Pyramids Rd)

Coptic Cairo

Fustat

To Giza Pyramids (9km) & Alexandria (220km)

Maryuta Canal

See Old Cairo Map (Page 181)

Mosque of Amr ibn al-As

Masr al-Qadimah

To Saqqara (30km)

To Ma'adi (8km)

GREATER CAIRO

Midan Abbassiyya
Ain Shams
Al-Uruba (Airport Road)
To Heliopolis (1km) & Airport (12km)
Abbassiyya
Sharia Ramses
Al-Wahli
Ghamra
Midan Sakakini
Salah Salem
To Suez (125km)
Port Said (Bur Said)
See North of Khan al-Khalili Map (Page 157)
Mosque of al-Hakim
Islamic Cairo
Al-Gebel al-Ahmar
Medinat Nasr
Muski
Khan al-Khalili
See Northern Cemetery Map (Page 179)
Northern Cemetery
Al-Azhar Mosque
See Al-Azhar to the Citadel Map (Page 171)
Darb al-Ahmar
See The Citadel Map (Page 175)
The Citadel
Muqattam City
Southern Cemetery
To Ma'adi (8km)

0   0.5   1 km

PLACES TO EAT
1 Maroosh Lebanese Restaurant
3 Tia Maria, El Gato Negro
4 Tabasco
11 Abu Ramy's
12 Ouf
14 Abu Shaqra

OTHER
2 Egypt Free Shop
5 National Art Development
   Institute for Mashrabiyya
6 Buses & Services to Al-Fayoum
7 Giza Train Station
8 Mar Girgis Metro Station
9 Cairo Land
10 Al-Malek as-Saleh Metro Station
13 Sayyida Zeinab Metro Station
15 French Cultural Centre
16 Sudanese Consulate
17 Egyptian Parliament Building
18 Museum of Islamic Art
19 Turgoman Garage (Bus Station)
20 Ghamra Metro Station
21 Coptic Patriarchate
22 Sinai Bus Terminal
23 Cairo Exhibition Grounds
24 October War Panorama
25 Cairo Stadium
26 Sadat's Tomb
27 Western Oases Bus Station
28 Mosque of Sayyida Aisha
29 Mausoleum of Imam ash-Shafi
30 Haush al-Basha
31 Animal & Bric-a-Brac Market

Sahafayeen (Journalists' City), while expansion continued north, most notably in the hideous form of Medinat Nasr (Victory City).

More recently, population pressure has meant that the rocky Muqattam Hills – which had traditionally halted the city's eastward spread – have been leap-frogged, and the once-barren desert is now a vast and messy construction site for a series of overspill-soaking satellite cities.

ORIENTATION

Finding your way about the vast sprawl of Cairo is not as difficult as it may first seem. Midan Tahrir is the centre. North-east of Tahrir is Downtown. Centred on Midan Talaat Harb, Downtown is a noisy, busy commercial district and it's where you'll find most of the cheap eating places and budget accommodation. Midan Ramses, location of the city's main train station, marks the northernmost extent of Downtown. Beyond are teeming working-class suburbs like Shubra (the true soul of modern-day Cairo) and Abbassiyya (site of the Sinai bus terminal). Abbassiyya leads on to Heliopolis, a one-time desert suburb with wonderfully fanciful architecture that has now been swallowed up by the creeping metropolis. Cairo's airport lies on the north-eastern fringes of Heliopolis, some 22km from Downtown.

Back in the city centre and heading east, Downtown ends at Midan Ataba and Islamic Cairo takes over. This is the old medieval heart of the city, still very much alive today. At its centre is the great bazaar of Khan al-Khalili. Eastwards, beyond Islamic Cairo, are the Northern and Southern cemeteries, vast necropolises inhabited by both the living and the dead.

South of Midan Tahrir are the curving tree-lined streets of Garden City – prime embassy territory. Once past Garden City you are out of central Cairo and into a succession of ramshackle neighbourhoods loosely termed Old Cairo. Buried in here is the small, walled enclave of Coptic Cairo, a feature on many tourist agendas. Some 8km

further south along the riverside Corniche is Ma'adi, a very green, very suburban neighbourhood much loved by American expats.

West of all the above is the Nile which is obstructed by two sizeable islands. The more central of these, connected directly to Downtown by three bridges, is Gezira, home to the Cairo Tower and the Opera House complex. The northern half of Gezira is an affluent, leafy suburb called Zamalek, historically favoured by the city's European residents and home to many embassies. The southern island is known as Rhoda but its northern part goes by the name of Manial.

The west bank of the Nile is less historical and much more residential than areas along the east bank. The primary districts, north to south are Mohandiseen, Agouza, Doqqi and Giza, all of which are heavy on concrete and light on charm. Giza covers by far the largest area of the four, stretching some 20km west either side of one long, straight road that ends at the foot of the Pyramids.

INFORMATION
Visas

All visa business is carried out at the Mogamma, the 14 storey monolithic white building on Midan Tahrir. Not so long ago, to venture into this place was to see days of your life pass interminably waiting for counter clerks to give you their attention, waiting at desks for signatures, waiting at more counters to be told to go back and get yet more signatures. That's all changed: processes have been simplified and streamlined and if the place is not yet exactly user-friendly, you can at least usually now get in and out within the hour.

Foreigners go up to the 1st floor, pass through the door on the right then circle around to the left and straight down the corridor ahead. Go to window No 42 and ask for an extension or re-entry form. Visa extensions up to six months cost E£12.10, you'll need one photograph. Hand in the completed form at window Nos 27 or 28. Re-entry forms are handed in at window

Nos 16 or 17, again, you'll need one photograph. Single/multiple re-entry visas cost E£10/14.

The Mogamma is open daily (except Friday) from 8 am to 2 pm.

Tourist Offices

Cairo's main tourist office (☎ 391 3454) is at 5 Sharia Adly, close to Midan Opera. The staff are helpful, if not particularly well clued-up. The office is open daily from 8.30 am to 8 pm (9 am to 5 pm during Ramadan).

There are tourist offices at both Cairo international airport's Terminal I (☎ 667 475) and Terminal II (☎ 291 4255). The office at Terminal II should be open 24 hours, but don't bank on it.

There's also a tourist office (☎ 385 0259) at the Pyramids opposite the entrance to the Oberoi Mena House. It's usually open daily from 8.30 am to 5 pm. There are other small offices at the Manial Palace and Ramses train station.

The tourist police are on the 1st floor in the alley just to the left of the main tourist office on Sharia Adly.

Money

For general details about banks, foreign exchange bureaus, and transferring funds see the Money section in the Facts for the Visitor chapter. Information on banking hours is given in the Business Hours section in the same chapter, but it's worth knowing that the Banque Masr branches at the Nile Hilton and Shepheard's hotels are open 24 hours a day. Otherwise you could try the city's foreign exchange bureaus, which tend to close at 8 pm.

ATMs For general details about the cards Cairo's ATMs accept see the Money section in the Facts for the Visitor chapter. In central Cairo, Banque Masr ATMs are located at bank branches on Talaat Harb (on the 1st floor of the concrete tower block just south of Midan Talaat Harb); on Qasr al-Ainy (200m south of Midan Tahrir); and on Mohammed Farid (just south of the junc-

tion with Qasr el-Nil). Egyptian British Bank ATMs are located in the foyers of the Cairo Marriott (in Zamalek), Nile Hilton and Semiramis InterContinental hotels; at the main entrance to the Al-Bustan shopping centre on Sharia al-Bustan, Downtown; at the British Council in Agouza; and at the EBB on Abu al-Feda in Zamalek.

American Express American Express (Amex) offices are open from 8.30 am to 5 pm daily (closed Friday). Addresses in Cairo include:

Downtown
(☎ 574 7991, fax 578 4003) 15 Qasr el-Nil
(☎ 578 5001/2) Nile Hilton
Giza
(☎ 570 3411) Nile Tower, 21-23 Sharia al-Giza
Heliopolis
(☎ 290 9158) 72 Omar ibn al-Khattab

Amex also operates a handy 24 hour helpline (☎ 569 3299)

Thomas Cook Thomas Cook offices are open daily from 8 am to 5 pm. Addresses in Cairo include:

Downtown
(☎ 574 3955, fax 576 2750) 17 Mahmoud Bassiouni
Heliopolis
(☎ 414 0625) 7 Sharia Baghdad
Mohandiseen
(☎ 346 7187) 9/10 Sharia 26th of July

Post

Cairo's GPO, on Midan Ataba, is open from 7 am to 7 pm Saturday to Thursday, and from 7 am to noon on Friday and public holidays. The poste restante is down the side street to the right of the main entrance, through the last door (opposite the EMS fast mail office). It's open from 8 am to 6 pm, except Friday and holidays when it's open from 10 am to noon. Mail is held for three weeks.

To send a package abroad you must go to the Post Traffic Centre at Midan Ramses. It is open daily from 8.30 am to 3 pm (except

Friday). Set aside 30 minutes for this process and bring your passport. You'll need to go to the first big room to the left on the 2nd floor. At the counter get form No 13 (E£5), have the parcel weighed and pay for it. Probably customs will have a look at it (for details on these formalities see under Packages in the Post & Communications section in the Facts for the Visitor chapter). After it has been inspected, someone will wrap it for you (E£1.50 per metre of paper used plus E£1.60 for sealing).

Fast mail can be sent through the EMS main office (☎ 393 9796) also down the side street beside the GPO. It's open daily (except Friday) from 8 am to 7 pm.

In addition to EMS, Cairo also has a full complement of international courier services on offer:

DHL
    (☎ 393 8988) 34 Abdel Khalek Sarwat, Downtown
    (☎ 355 7118) 20 Gamal ad-Din Abu al-Mahasin, Garden City
    (☎ 246 0324) 35 Ismail Ramzy, Heliopolis
Federal Express
    (☎ 354 0520) 1079 Corniche el-Nil, Garden City
    (☎ 331 3500) 24 Sharia Syria, Mohandiseen
    (☎ 246 4197) 67 Sharia Hegaz, Heliopolis
TNT Skypak
    (☎ 348 8204) 33 Sharia Doqqi, Doqqi

Telephone

There are several telephone offices (telephone centrales) around Cairo, and most have a few card phones. In central Cairo there are offices on the north side of Midan Tahrir, near the tourist information office in Sharia Adly, and on Sharia Mohammed Mahmoud in Bab al-Luq. In Zamalek there's an office on Sharia 26th of July, near the 15th of May Bridge. These main telephone offices are open 24 hours while branch offices, such as the one just off Sharia Ramses, are open from 8 am to 10 pm. There are also other branch offices in Doqqi and Giza.

For information on rates, making collect calls and telephone services in general, see the Post & Communications section in the Facts for the Visitor chapter.

Fax & Telex

Faxes can be sent to/from the telephone offices on Sharia Adly (fax 393 3909), on Midan Tahrir (fax 578 0979) and also on Sharia Alfy (fax 589 7662). You can also send and receive them from EMS (fax 393 4807) near the GPO. Alternatively, you can receive faxes at Amex (fax 574 7997) at the Qasr el-Nil office.

Telex machines are available at the telephone offices on sharias Adly and Alfy.

Email & Internet Access

Three out of the four central Cairo Internet cafes are operated by InternetEgypt and it's worth checking their Web site (www.internetegypt.com) for the latest information. Addresses of Internet cafes in Cairo include:

InternetEgypt
    (☎ 356 2882) 2 Midan Simon Bolivar, 6th floor, Garden City. Open from 9 am to 10 pm Saturday to Thursday, 3 to 10 pm Friday; one hour for E£12, minimum charge E£3.
Mohandiseen Cybercafe
    (☎ 305 0493) On a side street off Sharia Gamiat ad-Dowal al-Arabiyya, between McDonald's and Arby's. Open daily from 10 am to midnight; one hour for E£12, minimum charge E£3.
Nile Hilton Cybercafe
    (☎ 578 0444 ext 758) In the basement of the Nile Hilton Shopping Mall. Open daily from 10 am to midnight (closed Friday from noon to 2 pm); one hour for E£12, minimum charge E£3.
St@rnet Cyber Café
    (no telephone) In the basement of the Al-Bustan Centre, Sharia al-Bustan, Downtown. Open daily from 10.30 am to 10.30 pm; one hour for E£9.90, minimum charge E£5.50.

Berlin and New Palace hotels both have on-line terminals which guests can use.

Travel Agencies

The area around Midan Tahrir is teeming with travel agencies but don't expect any amazing deals. In fact there are a lot of dodgy operators here; in particular, avoid Metro Travel and Wonder Travel.

For tours of Cairo and surrounds and for trips down to Luxor or Aswan, try Hamis Travel (☎ 574 9275, fax 574 9276, email

...amis@ritsec2.com.eg), with offices on the 1st floor in the annexe just south of the main booking hall at Ramses train station. The company is managed by Anny, a friendly Dutch lady who speaks excellent English. It's open daily from 9 am to 9 pm.

DeCastro Tours (☎ 574 3144, fax 574 3382, email hesham1@brainy1.ie-eg.com) at 12 Talaat Harb is fairly reliable at booking flights. It's always been able to offer some of the best deals in town and can usually secure student discounts. DeCastro can also book hotels throughout Egypt and help with travel arrangements.

One of the best and most reputable agencies in town, though it's way down in Ma'adi, is Egypt Panorama Tours (☎ 350 5880, fax 351 1199, email ept@intouch.com, 4 Road 79) just outside the Al-Ma'adi metro station. They're good on cheap airfares and tours within Egypt and around the Mediterranean region. If you don't want to make the trip down to Ma'adi, Panorama takes bookings over the phone (the staff speak excellent English) and will courier the tickets to you.

The official Egyptian government travel agency, Masr Travel (☎ 393 0168, fax 392 4440), is at 7 Talaat Harb, Downtown.

Bookshops

Cairo has a reasonably good selection of bookshops, particularly if you are searching for Egypt-oriented titles. The best of the lot is the American University in Cairo (AUC) bookshop (enter the campus by the Mohammed Mahmoud gate, and it's in the building to the right). Being an academic outlet, it has stacks of material on the politics, sociology and history of Cairo, Egypt and the Middle East but it also has plenty of guidebooks and some fiction. It's open from 9 am to 4 pm Sunday to Thursday and from 10 am to 3 pm on Saturday. There is also a much smaller branch at the AUC Hostel at 16 Sharia Mohammed ibn Thakeb in Zamalek.

Other bookshops with very good selections of books about Cairo and Egypt are Lehnert & Landrock at 44 Sharia Sherif and Livres d'France at 36 Qasr el-Nil. The for-

mer has plenty of books in German and the latter has shelves of French titles. Lehnert & Landrock is also one of the better places for maps and it has a large collection of old postcards and prints. It's open from 9.30 am to 2 pm and 4 to 7.30 pm, (closed on Saturday afternoon and Sunday). Livres d'France is open from 10 am to 7 pm (closed on Saturday afternoon and Sunday).

L'Orientaliste at 15 Qasr el-Nil, Downtown, opposite Groppi's cafe, is an antiquarian bookshop specialising in Egypt; it also sells 19th century prints. It's open 10 am to 7.30 pm from Monday to Saturday.

Second-Hand Books There's a fairly large second-hand book market on the east side of the Ezbekiyya Gardens, reached from Midan Ataba in central Cairo. Many of its 40 or 50 stalls (cabins, actually) carry English-language books and magazines but half the stock is piled knee-high on the floor, and much of the rest sits on shelves with their spines to the wall.

Newsstands Cairo's three best newsstands are next to each other in Zamalek, at the junction of 26th of July and Hassan Sabry. You can get just about anything from these guys, provided there are no bare breasts or buttocks involved. Downtown, the places with the best selections include a stand on Midan Talaat Harb out front of Groppi's cafe; the newsstand on Mohammed Mahmoud, opposite the entrance to the AUC; and the place on Midan Tahrir, next to TWA and opposite the Nile Hilton. Of the hotel bookshops, those at the Cairo Marriott and Semiramis InterContinental hotels are the best for periodicals and papers.

Libraries

For English readers the best libraries are at the British Council and American Cultural Center (see the Cultural Centres section following). Otherwise, the best public library is the new and very grand Greater Cairo Library (☎ 341 2280) housed in a villa at 15 Mohammed Mazhar, Zamalek. It's stocked with a fantastic collection of art, science and other reference books, mainly in English, and it also has newspapers and magazines for browsing. It's open daily (except Monday) from 9 am to 7 pm (10 am to 8 pm between June and August).

Cultural Centres

Bring your passport as many cultural centres require some ID before they'll allow you to enter.

France
(☎ 355 3725) 1 Madrassat al-Huquq al-Fransiyya, Mounira; open from 9 am to 9 pm Sunday to Thursday
(☎ 414 4824) 27 Sharia Sabry Abu Alam, Midan Ismailia, Heliopolis
Both centres regularly put on films, lectures and exhibitions, have their libraries open to the public and screen French-language news from the satellite TV station TV-5. The institute at Mounira also runs French and Arabic language courses.

Germany
(☎ 575 9877) Goethe Institute, 5 Sharia al-Bustan, Downtown
Presents seminars and lectures in German on Egyptology and other topics. There are also performances by visiting music groups, special art exhibitions and film screenings. The library has more than 15,000 (mainly German) titles. Open from 1 to 7 pm Monday to Thursday and from 8 am to noon on Friday.

Italy
(☎ 340 8791) Italian Cultural Centre, 3 Sheikh Marsafy, Zamalek
The centre puts on films, organises lectures, hosts art exhibitions and has a library.

Netherlands
(☎ 340 0076) Netherlands Cultural Institute, 1 Mahmoud Azmy, Zamalek
Hosts art exhibitions and is well known in the Cairo expatriate community for its weekly lectures – delivered on a wide variety of topics and usually in English.

UK
(☎ 345 3281) British Council, 192 Sharia el-Nil, Agouza
The council's library carries most of the major UK daily and weekly newspapers and has more than 55,000 books and 90 periodical titles. It's open Monday to Thursday from 9 am to 8 pm, (closed 2 pm to 3 pm) and Friday and Saturday from 9 am to 3 pm. Library membership costs E£25, or nonmembers can browse for 20 minutes only (never enforced) free of charge.

USA
(☎ 357 3133) American Studies Library, 5 Latin America, Garden City
Part of the embassy complex, this cultural centre has a library with more than 200 periodical titles and 10,000 books. The reading rooms are open from 10 am to 7 pm on Monday and Wednesday, and from 10 am to 4 pm the rest of the week (closed Saturday).

Film & Photography

There are plenty of labs in central Cairo. One Downtown place we recommend for both quality and price is the Photo Centre (☎ 392 0031) on the 1st floor at 3 Sharia Mahrany, a backstreet off Sherifeen, which itself is a side street off Qasr el-Nil. Also Downtown, there's a Kodak shop on Sharia Adly between Sharia Sherif and Mohammed Farid. In Zamalek there's a Kodak shop on 26th of July and an Agfa outlet at 22 Hassan Sabry. All of these places sell all kinds of film and offer all the services you would expect of a western photo shop.

If you need quick, professional slide processing, the place to go is Antar Photostore (☎ 354 0786) at 180 Sharia Tahrir, just east of Midan Falaki, Bab al-Luq.

There are numerous places to have passport photos done. The cheapest option is to ask one of the photographers in front of the Mogamma. They will use an antique box camera to copy your passport photo or any other photo and make four copies (black-and-white only and often a bit out of focus) for E£4. For colour shots done quickly, your cheapest bet is the instant photo booth (E£6 for four photos) near the ticket windows in Sadat metro station under Midan Tahrir.

Medical Services

Hospitals Many of Cairo's hospitals suffer from antiquated equipment and a cavalier attitude to hygiene but there are several exceptions. They are:

Anglo-American Hospital
(☎ 340 6162/3/4/5) on Sharia Hadayek al-Zuhreyya, to the west of the Cairo Tower, Gezira
As-Salam International Hospital
(☎ 302 9091/2/3) on Corniche el-Nil, Ma'adi
(☎ 363 8050) 3 Sharia Syria, Mohandiseen

Cairo Medical Centre
(☎ 258 1003) Midan Roxy, Heliopolis
Masr International Hospital
(☎ 335 3345) 12 Sharia al-Saraya, near Midan Fini, Doqqi

Pharmacies There is no shortage of pharmacies in Cairo and almost anything can be obtained without a prescription. Pharmacies that operate 24 hours include Isaaf (☎ 574 3369) on the corner of sharias Ramses and 26th of July, Downtown; Al-Ezaby (☎ 414 8167) at 1 Sharia Ahmed Tayseer, Heliopolis; and the Zamalek Pharmacy (☎ 341 6424) at 3 Shagaret ad-Durr, Zamalek.

In the city centre, the Anglo-Eastern Pharmacy on the corner of sharias Abdel Khalek Sarwat and Sherif is open from 10 am to 3 pm and 6.30 to 10 pm (closed Friday).

Health conscious folk might like to check out the Sekem Health Store (☎ 342 4979) at 6 Ahmed Sabry in Zamalek. It stocks organic fruit and vegetables, additive-free jams, honey, herbs and pulses, as well as a range of herbal and homoeopathic teas. It's open daily from 8 am to 9 pm.

CENTRAL CAIRO

Many travellers begin their Egyptian experience in the vicinity of Midan Tahrir and Sharia Talaat Harb. It's the bustling, noisy centre of Cairo where you'll find an amazing variety of shops as well as most of the budget hotels and eating places, banks, travel agencies and cinemas.

Midan Tahrir & Around

Midan Tahrir (Liberation Square) is the fulcrum of modern Cairo. All the city's main roads converge here, resulting in a round-the-clock jam of traffic and pedestrians. But the square is one of the few spaces that isn't tightly hemmed in by buildings or choked by flyovers, making it an excellent spot to stand back, have look around and orient yourself.

One of the best buildings to use as a location aid is the **Nile Hilton**, the distinctive blue and white slab which stands between Midan Tahrir and the Nile. When it was built in 1959 it was the first modern hotel in Cairo, replacing a former British Army barracks. Immediately to the north of the Nile Hilton is the dusky pink neo-Classical bulk of the **Egyptian Museum** (see the special section later in this chapter), while south is the drab **Arab League Building**, occasional gathering place of the leaders of the Arab world.

Continuing around Midan Tahrir anticlockwise, the big white building is Cairo's monstrous, Kafkaesque monument to bureaucracy, the **Mogamma**, home to 18,000 semi-somnolent civil servants – this is where you come for visa extensions. If the Mogamma is a symbol of Egypt's recent socialist-inspired past, then the next building around, across four-lane Qasr al-Ainy, is the beacon for the private initiative-led future.

The **American University in Cairo** (AUC) is the university of choice for the sons and daughters of Cairo's moneyed classes. The campus has an attractive courtyard and a good bookshop. Entrance (ID required) is via the gate on Mohammed Mahmoud, opposite the enterprisingly sited McDonald's.

About 50m north of the AUC is the **Ali Baba Cafeteria** which, until the 1994 knife attack that almost killed him, was a regular morning stop for Nobel Prize-winning author **Naguib Mahfouz** (see under Literature in the Arts section in the Facts about Egypt chapter). It serves chilled Stella beer and the tables beside the window on the upper floor are a good place to watch the goings-on outside.

Buildings around Midan Tahrir then break for Sharia Tahrir, which leads 250m east to a busy square with a bus station in the middle – Midan Falaki.

Bab al-Luq Midan Falaki is at the heart of an area known as Bab al-Luq. It's worth a wander down here to visit the **Souq Mansour**, a covered market of vegetable, meat and fish stalls, and a big favourite with the city's cats. The streets either side of the souq are filled with cheap eating joints, while on the north side of the square is **Cafeteria Horreyya**, a high-ceilinged coffeehouse that is

CENTRAL CAIRO

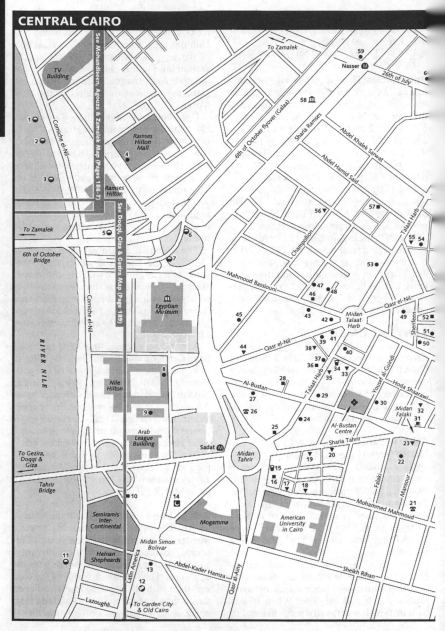

TV Building

Ramses Hilton Mall

Ramses Hilton

See Mohandiseen, Agouza & Zamalek Map (Pages 186-7)

See Doqqi, Giza & Gezira Map (Page 189)

To Zamalek

To Zamalek

6th of October flyover (Galaa)

Nasser Ⓜ

59

26th of July

58 🏛

Sharia Ramses

Abdel Khalek Sarwat

Abdel Hamid Said

Comiche el-Nil

6th of October Bridge

Comiche el-Nil

R I V E R   N I L E

To Zamalek

To Gezira, Doqqi & Giza

Tahrir Bridge

Latin America

1 ◐
2 ◐
3 ◐
4
5 ◐
6
7
8
9
10
11 ◐
12
13
14

Egyptian Museum

Nile Hilton

Arab League Building

Sadat Ⓜ

Midan Tahrir

Mogamma

Semiramis Inter-Continental

Helnan Shepheards

Midan Simon Bolivar

Abdel-Kader Hamza

Qasr al-Ainy

Lazoughli

To Garden City & Old Cairo

Mahmoud Bassiouni

L Champollion

56 ▼

57 ■

55 ▼
54

53 ●

47 ●
46 ■
48

45 ●

43 ●
42 ●

Midan Talaat Harb

49 ●

52 ■
51 ●
50 ●

Sheriffein

Qasr el-Nil

44 ▼

Qasr el-Nil

41 ●
39 ▼
38 ▼
40 ●
37 ▼
36 ▼
34 ▼
33
35 ▼

Talaat Harb

Yousef al-Guindi

Hoda Shaarawi

30 ●

Midan Falaki

32 ▼
31

28 ■

27 ●
☎ 26
29 ●

24 ●

25 ■

Al-Bustan

Al-Bustan Centre

Sharia Tahrir

23 ▼

22 ●

19 ▼
20

15 ▼
16 ■
17 ▼
18 ▼

American University in Cairo

Falaki

Mansour

21 ●

Mohammed Mahmoud

Sheikh Rihan

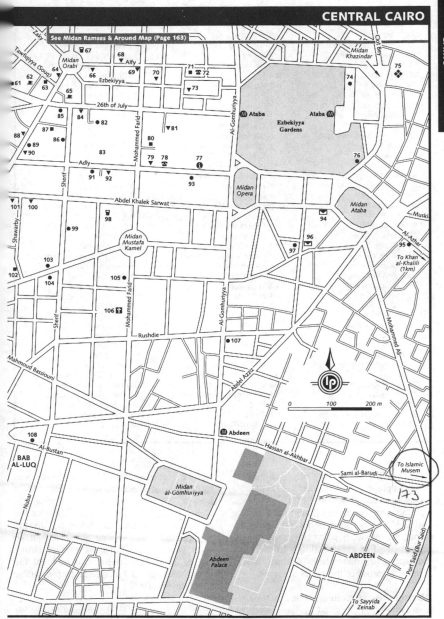

CENTRAL CAIRO

See Midan Ramses & Around Map (Page 163)

CAIRO

CENTRAL CAIRO

PLACES TO STAY
10 Garden City House Hotel
16 Ismailia House Hotel
25 Sun Hotel
28 Magic Hotel
36 Lotus Hotel
46 Dahab Hotel
52 Cosmopolitan Hotel
57 Odeon Palace Hotel
61 Carlton Hotel
63 Sultan Hotel; Safary Hotel;
   Hotel Venice
71 Windsor Hotel
80 Pension Roma
87 Hotel Minerva
102 Berlin Hotel

PLACES TO EAT
17 KFC; Pizza Hut
18 McDonald's
19 Fatatri at-Tahrir
20 At-Tahrir Kushari
23 Lux Kushari
32 Le Bistro
33 Felfela Restaurant
35 Felfela Takeaway
38 Estoril
44 Arabesque
55 El-Abd Bakery
56 Abu Tarek Kushari
64 Casablanca
66 Alfy Bey Restaurant
68 Akher Sa'a
69 International Public Meal
   Kushari
70 Peking Restaurant
73 Ali Hassan al-Hatie
79 La Chesa
81 Ali Hassan al-Hatie
84 Lux Kushari

85 El-Abd Bakery
88 McDonald's
90 Excelsior
92 Restaurant Gad
100 KFC
101 At-Tahrir Kushari

OTHER
1 Maspero River Bus Terminal
2 Qanater Ferries
   (Government)
3 Qanater Ferries (Private)
4 Ramses Hilton Cinema
5 Pyramids Services
6 Local Buses & Minibuses
7 Airport Bus
8 EgyptAir
9 Nile Hilton Mall (Nile Hilton
   Cybercafe)
11 Felucca Mooring Point
12 US Embassy
13 InternetEgypt
14 Omar Makram Mosque
15 Ali Baba Cafeteria
21 Telephone Centrale
22 Souq Mansour
24 Masr Travel
26 Telephone Centrale
27 Goethe Institute
29 EgyptAir
30 Cairo-Berlin Gallery
31 Horreyya Coffeehouse
34 Stella Bar
37 DeCastro Tours
39 American Express
40 Cafe Riche
41 L'Orientaliste Antiquarian
   Books
42 Groppi's
43 Thomas Cook

45 Mashrabia Gallery
47 Townhouse Gallery
48 Atelier du Caire
49 Western Union Money
   Transfer
50 Espace Karim-Francis Gallery
51 Photo Centre
53 Cinema Radio
54 French Cultural Centre
58 Entomological Museum
59 Isaaf Pharmacy
60 Cinema Rialto
62 Ash-Shams Coffeehouse
65 Al-Andalus Coffeehouse
67 Port Tawfiq Bar
72 Telephone Centrale
74 Book Market
75 Sednaoui Department Store
76 Puppet Theatre
77 Tourist Information Office
78 Telephone Centrale
82 Palmyra Nightclub
83 Shar Hashamaim Synagogue
86 Lehnert & Landrock
   Bookshop
89 Cinema Metro
91 Kodak
93 EgyptAir
94 GPO
95 Meat Market
96 Poste Restante
97 EMS Office
98 Cap d'Or
99 Simonds Cafe
103 Livres d'France Bookshop
104 Italian Insurance Building
105 Osiris Auction House
106 St Joseph's Church
107 Egypt Free Shop
108 Antar Photostore

---

one of the few venues for Cairo's enthusiastic chess players. It is also unique (for a coffeehouse anyway) because it serves alcohol.

Continuing east from Midan Falaki, brings you to **Midan al-Gomhuriyya** (Square of the Republic), an empty plaza skirted by speeding traffic. The great building to the east, dominating the square, is the Abdeen Palace, former residence of the rulers of Egypt.

Abdeen Palace Commissioned by the khedive Ismail and designed by the French architect, Rosseau, the Abdeen Palace was started in 1863 and completed 500 rooms later in 1874. It served as the occasional residence of royalty until the abolition of the monarchy in 1952, when Abdeen became the presidential palace. The presidents have since moved out (Mubarak prefers Uruba Palace up in Heliopolis) and parts of the palace are due to be opened to the public some time in 1999.

continued on page 161

EGYPTIAN MUSEUM

More than 100,000 relics and antiquities from almost every period of ancient Egyptian history are housed in the Egyptian Museum (known simply as *Al-Mathaf*, 'the museum'). To put that in perspective, if you spent only one minute at each exhibit it would take more than nine months to see everything.

This collection was first gathered under one roof in Bulaq in 1858 by Auguste Mariette, a French archaeologist who had excavated in Upper Egypt. It was moved to its present purpose-built neoclassical home in 1902. Since then the number of exhibits has completely outgrown the available space and the place is virtually bursting at the seams. A persistent urban legend in Cairo has it that the building's basement is piled so high with uncatalogued artefacts that archaeologists will have to excavate its contents when the long-promised new museum is eventually built.

Box: Detail of a chair found in Tutankhamun's tomb (photo by Chris Mellor).

Right: The Egyptian Museum

ADAM McCROW

Beyond arranging the exhibits chronologically from the Old Kingdom to the Roman Empire, little has been done to present them in any sort of context or to highlight pieces of particular significance or beauty. In fact, since the museum's foundation a century ago, the displays have never been reorganised, despite the ever-increasing number of artefacts. Labelling is poor or nonexistent, while the manner of display – mostly old wood and glass cases with no direct lighting – is hardly the last word in modern museum techniques. But this is slowly starting to change. Two new galleries opened in 1998 equipped with fibre-optic lighting and – taa daa! – labels. Also, new security and lighting systems have been installed following a sensational attempted robbery in 1996, when the authorities belatedly realised that the outmoded security system (basically barred windows and a dog making the rounds after closing) was insufficient protection for the museum's priceless contents. Still, the museum's eccentricity is part of its charm and accidentally stumbling across treasures in its sometimes musty rooms is half the fun.

With so much to see, trying to get around everything in one go is liable to induce chronic pharaonic phatigue. The best strategy is to spread the exploration over at least two visits, maybe tackling one floor at a time.

Admission to the museum is E£20 (E£10 for students). Access to the Royal Mummy Room costs an additional E£40 (E£20 for students); tickets for this can be bought at the 1st floor entrance to the room. The

EGYPTIAN MUSEUM

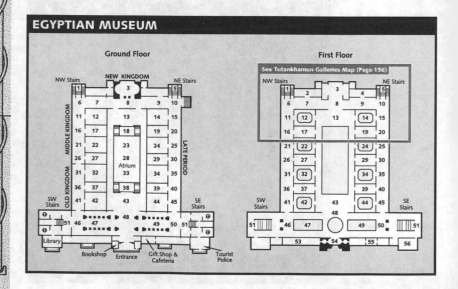

museum (☎ 575 4319) is open daily from 9 am to 4.45 pm, but closes on Friday between noon and 2 pm (11.30 am and 1.30 pm in winter). If you're visiting on Friday morning, note that you can't get back in with the same ticket in the afternoon. The Royal Mummy Room and Room 53 both close at 4.15 pm. Permission to use cameras (without flash) costs E£10; otherwise cameras must be left at the entrance. Use of a video camera costs E£100. There are official guides who will take you around for about E£40 per hour.

Books

It's beyond the scope of this book to provide a comprehensive guide to the museum, but if you do want more help to negotiate this overwhelming storehouse of ancient history there are several specialist publications. There are a couple of official guides produced by the museum but these are very dry and not particularly illuminating. A better bet is *Egyptian Museum Cairo* by Dr Edouard Lambelet (published in English, French and German). It has fairly extensive and generously illustrated descriptions of the main objects of interest, identified by room and catalogue numbers. It sells for around E£60. Less comprehensive but more digestible, *Cairo: The Egyptian Museum & Pharaonic Sites* by Mohammed Saleh (the museum's current director) is a recent publication which focuses on 50 of the most noteworthy exhibits. It makes a good, cheap (E£25) beginner's guide.

An excellent and attractive mummy book is *Royal Mummies in the Egyptian Museum* (E£35) by Salima Ikram and Aidan Dodson. Well illustrated and very readable, this is worth picking up for its explanation of the mummification process, as well as the descriptions of the bandaged, desiccated royals themselves.

All these titles can be bought at the museum bookshop.

Highlights of the Egyptian Museum

For those people who do not have nine months to examine everything in the museum, the following is our list of the top 10 must-see exhibits (also highlighted in the following 'Museum Tour' section).

1 Tutankhamun Galleries
2 Royal Mummy Room
3 Akhenaten Room
4 Graeco-Roman Mummies
5 Royal Tombs of Tanis
6 Old Kingdom Rooms
7 Pharaonic Technology
8 Yuya & Thuyu Rooms
9 Ancient Egyptian Jewellery Room
10 Animal Mummies

Museum Tour: Ground Floor

The ground floor is laid out roughly chronologically in a clockwise fashion starting at the entrance hall. Following are a few of the things to look out for.

ROOM 43 – Early Dynastic Period

The near-life-size limestone statue of a seated pharaoh is of Zoser (Djoser), the Third dynasty pharoah whose architect Imhotep designed the first pyramid, the Step Pyramid of Saqqara. The statue was discovered in 1924 in the north-east corner of the pyramid (a replica now sits in its place, see page 230) and is the oldest statue of its kind in the museum.

ROOMS 47, 46 & 51 – Masterpieces of the Old Kingdom

Look for the three matching black schist triads which depict the pharoah Menkaura (Mycerinus), builder of the smallest of the three Great Pyramids, flanked either side by a female figure. The figure to the pharoah's right is the goddess Hathor, while each of the figures on his left represents a district of Upper Egypt, the name of which is given by the symbol above Hathor's head. Four of these triads were discovered at the pharoah's valley temple, just east of his pyramid at Giza.

ROOMS 42, 37 & 32 – Old Kingdom Rooms

In the centre of Room 42 is what some consider to be the museum's masterpiece: a smooth, black, dioritic, larger than life-size statue of Chephren (Khafre), builder of the second pyramid at Giza. He sits on a lion throne with the wings of the falcon god Horus wrapped around his head in a protective gesture. From the number of statueless bases discovered, archaeologists believe that this is just one of 24 such pieces that originally lined the hall of the pharoah's valley temple on the Giza plateau.

Slightly to the left in front of Chephren is the wooden statue of Ka-Aper. Carved out of a single piece of sycamore (except for the arms) he's amazingly lifelike, especially the eyes which, set in copper lids, have whites of opaque quartz and corneas of rock crystal which have been drilled and filled with black paste to form the pupils. When they dug up this statue at Saqqara, local workmen named him Sheikh al-Balad (headman), because they thought he resembled their own village chief.

Room 32 is dominated by the beautiful double statue of the royal couple, Rahotep and Nofret. Almost life-sized with well-preserved painted surfaces, the limestone sculptures' simple lines make them seem almost contemporary, despite being around for a staggering 4000 years.

Another highlight in here is the slightly bizarre tableau of the chief dwarf Seneb and his family. Seneb is sitting cross-legged in an effort to disguise his short legs and his children have been strategically placed where an ordinary man's legs would be. His (nondwarf) wife has her arms protectively around his shoulders in an immediately recognisable expression of affection. The happy couple and their two kids have been used in recent Egyptian family planning campaigns.

Also in here are the panels known as the Meidum Geese. These are part of a frieze that originates from a mud-brick mastaba at Meidum, near the oasis of Al-Fayoum (to this day, the lakes there are still host to a great variety of bird life). Though painted around 2600 BC, the pigments remain vivid and the degree of realism (while still retaining a distinct pharaonic style) is astonishing – ornithologists have had no trouble identifying the bird types.

ROOM 26 – Mentuhotep II
The seated statue on your right after leaving Room 32, with the black skin and red crown of Lower Egypt, is Mentuhotep II, second ruler of the Middle Kingdom period and the pharaoh who united the north and south. This statue was discovered by Howard Carter under the forecourt of Deir al-Bahri in Thebes in 1910 when the ground gave way under his horse.

ROOMS 21 & 16 – Sphinxes
These grey-granite sphinxes are very different to the great enigmatic Sphinx at Giza – in fact, they look more like the Lion Man from the Wizard of Oz, with a fleshy human face surrounded by a great shaggy mane and big ears. They were sculpted for the pharaoh Amenemhat III during the 12th dynasty and adorned the Delta city of Tanis, which is where they were discovered in 1863.

ROOM 12 – Hathor Shrine
The centrepiece of this room is a remarkably well-preserved sandstone chapel with a vaulted roof painted with reliefs. It was discovered in the temple of Tuthmosis III at Deir al-Bahri in Thebes, complete with the life-size representation of the goddess Hathor in cow form.

Deir al-Bahri is also known as the Temple of Hatshepsut and there's a life-size pink-granite statue of the queen to the left of the chapel. She's represented wearing a pharoah's headdress and a false beard but the face has definite feminine characteristics.

ROOM 3 – Akhenaten Room
This room is devoted to Akhenaten, the 'heretic king' who set up ancient Egypt's first and last monotheistic faith, A quick glance around the room is enough to see that artistic styles changed almost as drastically as the state religion during Akhenaten's 15 year tenure (which ended with the accession of Tutankhamun). Take a look at the four great statues of the pharoah and compare their strangely bulbous bellies, hips and thighs and their elongated heads and thick, Mick Jagger-like lips with the sleek, hard-edged sculpture that you've just seen from the Middle Kingdom. Also worth a look, for their

Left: This broken sandstone bust of Akhenaten (Amenophis IV) was found in Karnak at the temple of Aten. Akhenaten's abandonment of the traditional gods and priesthood in favour of the worship of Aten, god of the sun disk, was not looked on favourably by the priests at Thebes and Karnak. After his death they regained their religious control and did their best to obliterate all record of Akhenaten and his religion.

unusual informality, are the stelae of the king and queen playing with their children, showing an informality and relaxed nature never before seen in royal pharaonic art.

Most striking of all is the unfinished head of Nefertiti, wife of Akhenaten. Worked in light brown quartzite, it's an incredibly delicate and sensitive portrait and shows the queen to be an extremely beautiful woman.

ROOM 10 – Intef
One of the museum's newest exhibits is a piece that was previously displayed in three separate parts until somebody realised they were all bits of the same statue and it was stuck back together again. The reassembled sandstone figure represents Intef, who was head of the army in the 11th dynasty. Displaying a welcome new trend where this museum is concerned, the statue is well labelled.

ROOM 34 – Graeco-Roman Room
The lack of any kind of labelling is acutely felt in this room, which is full of fascinating pieces for which there's no explanation or context provided. But what is evident in many of the exhibits is the assimilation by Egypt's new Greek, then Roman overlords of the indigenous pharaonic style. This is most obvious in the stelae on the back wall, and on the large sandstone panel on the right-hand wall which is inscribed in three languages: in hieroglyphics (the Egyptian literary language),

Demotic (the Egyptian popular language) and at the bottom, in Greek (the official language of the country's then rulers). This trilingually inscribed stone is similar in nature to the more famous Rosetta stone (see the boxed text 'The Rosetta Stone' on page 416), now housed in the British Museum, but of which there's a cast replica back near the museum entrance in Room 48.

ROOMS 50 & 51 – Alexander the Great

On the official museum plan this area is labelled 'Alexander the Great' but currently there's nothing here that relates directly to the Macedonian conqueror. What there is though, is an extremely beautiful small marble statuette of the Greek goddess Aphrodite, who the Egyptians identified with Isis. Carved in the 3rd or 2nd century BC it was found in Alexandria. On the other side of the room is an amazing sarcophagus covered in hieroglyphics made of inlaid coloured glass. The wooden case is also delicately inlaid with semiprecious stones.

Museum Tour: First Floor

The exhibits up here are grouped thematically and can be viewed in any order, but assuming that you've come up the south-east stairs (through Room 51), we'll go anti-clockwise, entering the Tutankhamun Galleries at Room 45. This way, you'll experience the pieces in roughly the same order that they were laid out in the tomb.

TUTANKHAMUN GALLERIES

Without doubt, the exhibit that outshines everything else in the museum is the treasure of the young and comparatively insignificant New Kingdom pharaoh Tutankhamun.

The tomb and treasures of this pharaoh, who ruled for only nine years during the 14th century BC, were discovered in 1922 by English archaeologist Howard Carter. Its well-hidden location in the Valley of the Kings, below the much grander but ransacked tomb of Ramses VI, had prevented tomb robbers and archaeologists from finding it earlier. (For the more complete story see page 292 to 294) The incredible contents displayed here of this rather modest tomb can only make you wonder about the fabulous wealth looted from the tombs of pharaohs far greater than Tutankhamun.

About 1700 items are spread throughout a series of rooms – although, note that most of the 'rooms' are in fact sections of the museum's north and east-wing corridors and room numbers are not displayed, which sometimes makes it hard to find what you're looking for.

ROOM 45 Flanking the doorway as you enter are two life-size statues of the pharaoh found in the antechamber of the tomb. They served as sentries to the burial chamber (a large black-and-white photo on the wall shows the statues *in situ*). Made of wood, they are coated in bitumen – the black skin, identified with Osiris, symbolises rebirth. Also in this room is a wooden statue of the jackal-headed Anubis, protector of the dead, which would also have served as a guardian of the tomb.

ROOM 40 This room has a beautifully painted chest depicting the young pharaoh charging into battle in a chariot, his foes in disorganised chaos before him. As the pharaoh died while still in his teens, it's unlikely he ever led his armies to war, but he may well have gone hunting with his attendants as shown on the chest lid. When this chest was discovered it contained some of the necklaces and belts now displayed in Room 3.

ROOMS 35 & 30 The highlight here is the pharaoh's throne. Covered with sheet gold and inlaid with glass and semiprecious stones, the wooden throne is supported by spindly lions. The colourful tableau on the back of the chair depicts Tutankhamun's queen placing her hand on his shoulder under the rays of the sun (Aten), the worship of which was a hangover from his predecessor, Akhenaten. Their robes are modelled in beaten silver and their hair is glass paste.

The many golden statues found in the tomb were all there to help the pharoah on his journey in the afterlife. They include a series of 28 gilded wooden deities, meant to protect the pharaoh, and 413 *shabti* (only a selection of these symbolic servants are here), who would perform on behalf of the pharoah any labours required of him in the nether world.

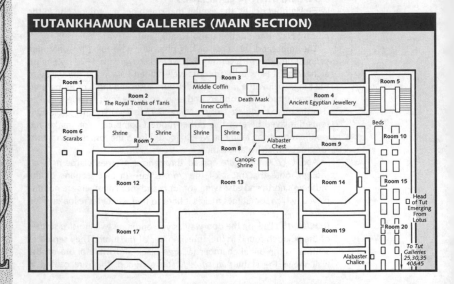

TUTANKHAMUN GALLERIES (MAIN SECTION)

ROOM 25 The gold-plated wooden shrine exhibited here, was found empty, its statues having been stolen in ancient times. But it's of great interest for the royal domestic scenes beaten into the gold leaf, all of which are in an unconventional, realistic style evolved from Ahkenaten's court at Amarna.

ROOM 20 This room contains exquisite alabaster jars, caskets and boxes, including (just south of the door to Room 19) a chalice in which a small light has been inserted to demonstrate the delicacy of its translucent artwork.

ROOM 15 Intricate rigged model ships, to be used by the pharaoh on his voyage through the afterlife, are displayed here. Also, almost unnoticeable against the back wall is a small, beautifully rendered plaster head of the boy-king emerging from a lotus flower.

ROOMS 10 & 9 The northern end of this gallery is filled with the pharoah's three elaborate funerary couches, one supported by two cows, one by two hippos and the third by two lionesses. These couches were for the pharoah to travel on during his journey through the afterlife.

The alabaster chest contains four Canopic jars, the stoppers of which are in the form of Tutankhamun's head. Inside these jars were placed the four miniature gold coffins exhibited in Room 3 which, in turn, contained the pharoah's internal organs. The whole chest and its gory contents was then placed inside the golden Canopic shrine with the four gilded goddesses: Isis, Neith, Nephthys and Selket, all portrayed with similarly protective outstretched arms. If you look closely, you'll see that the alabaster chest is protected by the same four figures at its corners.

Right: An elaborate pectoral made of gold, silver, semi-precious stones and glass was found in the linen wrappings on Tutankhamun's mummy.

ROOMS 8 & 7 These galleries just barely accommodate the four huge gilded wooden shrines that fitted one inside the other like a set of Russian dolls, encasing at their centre the sarcophagi of the boy-king.

ROOM 3 This is the room that everybody wants to see. At peak times you'll have to queue and once inside it feels like you've entered the crush of the Khan al-Khalili bazaar. The central exhibit is the astonishing death mask of Tutankhamun. Made of solid gold and weighing 11kg, the mask was found covering the head of the mummy, where it lay inside a series of three sarcophagi. The mask is an idealised portrait of the young pharoah; the eyes are fashioned from obsidian and quartz, while the outlines of the eyes and the eyebrows are delineated with lapis lazuli.

No less wondrous are the two golden sarcophagi. These are the inner two sarcophagi – the outermost coffin, along with the mummified remains of Tutankhamun, remains in place in his tomb in the Valley of the Kings. The smallest coffin is, like the mask, cast in solid gold and inlaid in the same fashion. It weighs 110kg. The slightly larger coffin is made of gilded wood.

ROOM 4 – Ancient Egyptian Jewellery

The second of the new galleries, this room has finds from all over the place including Saqqara and Giza. The jewellery includes belts, inlaid bead work, necklaces, semiprecious stones and bracelets. Most beautiful of all is a diadem of Set Hathor Iunet, a golden headband with a rearing cobra inset with semiprecious stones. As well as the pharaonic cache there are finds from the Graeco-Roman period from the Western Oases and Red Sea areas including bracelets, another diadem and agate bowls.

ROOM 2 – Royal Tombs of Tanis

One of two new galleries opened in 1998, this room contains a glittering collection of gold and silver encrusted amulets, gold funerary masks, daggers, bracelets, collars, gold sandals and finger and toe coverings from five intact New Kingdom tombs found at the Delta site of Tanis (see page 245). There's also an anthropoid coffin of Psusennes I, unique in being fashioned from solid silver, featuring the head of a falcon.

ROOM 14 – Graeco-Roman Mummies

This room contains a small sample (over 1000 have been discovered) of the stunning portraits found on Graeco-Roman period mummies. These images, whose large watchful eyes seem to follow you around the room, were painted onto wooden panels that were then placed over the mummy's embalmed face – some were even painted directly onto the shrouds themselves. As few other painted portraits from the Graeco-Roman era have survived, this collection is unique both for the number of its paintings and the high quality of its images.

Although the cases are barely lit and are piled with dust, the beautiful and hauntingly realistic faces that stare out from behind the glass bring the personalities of their long-dead owners to life in a way that the stylised elegance of most ancient Egyptian art somehow can't. Take a look at the mummy in front of you as you enter the room; the portrait is of a woman with large brown eyes and it's so life-like you'd recognise her immediately if you saw her on the street. Also, you should peer through the gloom in the case to the right of the entrance and take a look at the portrait of the little girl still affixed to her tiny mummified remains.

Most of these portraits were discovered in the Al-Fayoum Oasis, just south-west of Cairo, but a substantial portion have come from the Nile Valley at sites such as Saqqara and Thebes. (See the boxed text 'Portraits of the Past' on page 237.)

ROOM 34 – Pharaonic Technology

For gadget buffs, this room contains a great number of everyday objects that helped support ancient Egypt's great leap out of prehistory. Everything from combs and mirrors to fishing tackle, ploughs, hoes (that look exactly like the ones still used by Egypt's *fellaheen* today), serious-looking blades and razors can be found here. Hunting paraphernalia includes pharaonic boomerangs that were apparently used for killing birds. (Tutankhamun is depicted using one in the reliefs on the gold shrine in Room 25.)

ROOMS 32 & 27 – Middle Kingdom Models

The lifelike models contained in these rooms were mostly found in the tomb of Meket-Re, a Middle Kingdom notable in Thebes, and together they constitute a fascinating portrait of daily life almost 4000 years ago. The models include fishing boats (complete with fish in the nets), a slaughterhouse, a carpentry workshop, a loom and a model of Meket-Re's house (with figs on the trees and painted columns). Most spectacular is the 1.5m-wide scene of Meket-Re sitting with four scribes and various other hangers-on counting cattle. Plaster model slaves hold the animals by miniature ropes as they pass by the shaded dais on which the boss sits.

ROOM 37 – Model Armies

Discovered in the tomb of a provincial governor and dating from the time of the 11th dynasty (c. 2000 BC), these are two sets of 40 wooden warriors marching in phalanxes. The darker soldiers are Nubians from the south of the kingdom, the lighter-skinned soldiers are Egyptians.

ROOM 43 – Yuya & Thuyu Rooms

Before Tutankhamun, the discovery of the tomb of Yuya and Thuyu (the parents of Queen Tyi) was the most important find in Egyptian archaeology. The tomb was discovered virtually intact in the Valley of the Kings in 1905 and contained a vast number of treasures including five ornate sarcophagi and the remarkably well-preserved mummies of the two royals (which can be seen in the museum's Mummy Room). Among the many other items on display here are such essentials for the hereafter as beds, sandals and a chariot.

ROOMS 53 & 54 – Animal Mummies

Before the rise of pharaonic dynasties in Egypt, animal cults proliferated and the results can be seen in the battered and dust-covered little mummified cats, dogs, birds, rams and jackals in Room 53. More of these bizarre little trussed-up packages can be seen just outside in Room 54, where the better preserved remains of a mummified falcon, a fish, a cat, an ibis, a monkey and a tiny crocodile are on show.

Left: Throughout Egypt falcons were worshipped as representations of Ra (and sometimes Horus), and were used in temple rites and rituals. When they died they were mummified and buried in small clay coffins.

ROOM 56 – Royal Mummy Room

In 1981, the room housing the royal mummies (27 in total) was closed to the public as President Sadat thought it disrespectful to the dead (he had just berated the Iranians for displaying the charred bodies of eight Americans killed during the hostage crisis). But since 1995, after being hidden behind closed doors for 15 years, a selection of Egypt's ancient rulers have been back on public display. The Royal Mummy Room houses the bodies of 11 of Egypt's most illustrious kings and queens from the 18th to 21st dynasties, who ruled Egypt between 1552 and 1069 BC. They include Ramses II, his father Seti I, Tuthmosis II and Queen Meret Amun (wife of Amenhotep I). They lie in individual glass showcases (kept at a constant temperature of 22°C) in a sombre, dimly lit environment reminiscent of a tomb. Talking above a hushed whisper is not permitted (although irreverent tour groups often need to be reminded of this); for this reason, tour guides are not allowed in, making it one of the most peaceful havens in the museum.

It has been announced that the remaining 16 mummies are also to go on display before the year 2000.

For more information there's a booklet on sale at the ticket counter for E£3 or see the book *Royal Mummies in the Egyptian Museum* mentioned in the introduction to this section.

Note, taking young children into the Mummy Room could give them nightmares for months to come.

CHRIS MELLOR

Top: Probably the most familiar visage in ancient Egyptian iconography, Ramses II was responsible for building, among other things, the great temple of Abu Simbel, the Ramesseum and large parts of Luxor Temple – the original location of this larger than life, pink-granite statue of the pharaoh.

Bottom: Carved from wood, this is a burial boat that would have been placed in the tomb of the pharaoh to transport him to the Netherworld. More models like this can be found in rooms 27 and 32 on the 1st floor of the museum.

CHRIS MELLOR

Top: The golden funerary mask of Tutankhamun – arguably the single most stunning artefact held by any museum in the world.

Bottom: A detail from the back of the boy-king's golden throne, depicting Tutankhamun and his wife and composed of gold, other precious metals, semiprecious stones and decorative inlays.

continued from page 148

Downtown

Downtown is the commercial heart of Cairo: it's streets are packed with glitzy shops and above them are a beehive of countless thousands of small, dusty businesses. Talaat Harb and Qasr el-Nil are the two main streets and they intersect at **Midan Talaat Harb**, marked by a tarboosh-wearing statue of Mr Harb, founder of the National Bank. On the midan is **Groppi's**, once the most celebrated patisserie and tearoom this side of the Mediterranean. During the 1920s attendance at Groppi's society functions and nonstop concert dances was *de rigeur* for Cairo's smart set. The only glitter left today is in the beautiful mosaics around the doorway.

Just to the south of the midan, on Sharia Talaat Harb, the **Cafe Riche** used to be a hang-out for Egyptian writers and intellectuals. It's been closed since the late 1980s but is rumoured to be reopening soon.

North of the midan, Qasr el-Nil is devoted to shops selling a drag queen's delight of footwear, but the street is redeemed by some particularly fine architecture, notably the **Italian Insurance building** on the corner with Sharia Sherif and the **Cosmopolitan Hotel**, hidden away just a block to the south of Qasr el-Nil. Talaat Harb has the **Cinema Metro** building, a great 1930s movie palace which when it opened (with *Gone With The Wind*) also had a Ford showroom and a diner. That diner is now the Excelsior restaurant; the food isn't great these days but they serve cold Stella and the view from the large windows is more entertaining than whatever piece of Hollywood junk is being screened next door.

One block east of the Excelsior along Sharia Adly, the building that looks like it strayed from an Indiana Jones movie-set, is the **Shar Hashamaim Synagogue**, the most visible testament to Cairo's once thriving Jewish community. The synagogue can be visited on Saturday, the Jewish holy day of *shabbat*, when it's opened on the off chance there'll be somebody coming by to pray.

A block north of Adly is Sharia 26th of July, named for the date of abdication of Egypt's last king, Farouk. The street's major attraction as far as Cairenes are concerned is **El-Abd Bakery** (corner of Sherif) which is packed-out morning to midnight with folk jostling for cakes, sweets and the best pastries in town (there's a second branch on Talaat Harb). Smoke-filled **Sharia Ezbekiyya**, one block north, is *the* street for kebabs. Newly pedestrianised **Sharia Alfy** is Downtown's nightlife centre with several seedy bars, a couple of belly-dancing joints (see the Entertainment section following) and a good 24 hour eating place in the Akher Sa'a (see under Budget Dining in the Places to Eat section later in this chapter). The nearby **Tawfiqiyya souq** is a late night fruit and vegetable market with several cheap eating places and a couple of good coffeehouses in the surrounding alleyways (see Ahwas in the Entertainment section).

Heading east along 26th of July leads to **Midan Opera**, named for an opera house that burnt down in 1971 and now more notable for a great multi-storey car park. Beyond the car park is Midan Ataba.

Midan Ataba Midan Ataba is the chaotic transition zone where the 'modern European' Cairo runs up against the old medieval Cairo of Saladin, the Mamluks and Ottomans. It's one big bazaar, with all its corners filled with traders and hawkers. In the south-west, behind a clutter of cards and stationary stalls, is the domed **general post office**, with an attractive courtyard interior. A **Postal Museum** on the 1st floor contains a vast collection of commemorative stamps and displays on the history of Egypt's postal service. It's open daily from 9 am to 1 pm (except Friday), admission is 10pt. Heading east along 26th of July leads to **Midan Opera**.

To the east of the midan, behind the ornate building with the green painted shutters, is the **meat market**, fascinating but also not for the squeamish, while just to the north, stalls of cheap clothing mark the beginning of **Sharia Muski**, the long market street that leads into Khan al-Khalili. It's no more than 1km from here to the heart of the bazaar but the way is so crowded it always takes at least 30 minutes of trading elbows to make your way through.

Another good walk from Ataba is to head north to Midan Khazindar, where you should take a look in **Sednaoui**, one of Cairo's famed department stores of earlier this century. Now state-owned and full of tat, the three-storey glass atrium interior nevertheless remains glorious. Running north from Khazindar, arcing its way over 1.5km up to Midan Ramses, is **Sharia Clot Bey** (also known as Sharia Khulud) named after a French physician, Antoine Clot who introduced western ideas about public health into Mohammed Ali's Egypt. Ironically, in WWI this street had become the diseased heart of Cairo's red-light district: the 'Birka', an area of brothels, peepshows and pornographic cabarets. These days it's a shabby but charming street with stone arcades over the pavements sheltering dozens of sepia-toned coffeehouses and eating places.

Midan Ramses & Around The northern gateway into central Cairo, Midan Ramses is a byword for bedlam. The city's main north-south access collides with flyovers and numerous arterial roads to swamp the square with an unchoreographed slew of minibuses, buses, taxis and cars. Commuters swarm from the main train station to add to the melee.

In the middle of it all stands a pharaonic era **statue of Ramses II** discovered near Giza and erected here in 1955. The constant vibrations of the traffic and choking exhaust emissions can't be doing him any good; the statue was scheduled to be removed to a healthier climate in 1997 but he was still there at the time of research.

Ramses station (Mahattat Ramses) is an attractive marriage of Islamic style and industrial-age engineering. At its eastern end it houses the **Egyptian National Railways Museum**, which has a beautiful collection of old locomotives, including one built in 1862 for Princess Eugenie on the occasion of the opening of the Suez Canal. The museum (☎ 763 793) is open daily from 8.30 am to 1 pm (except Monday). Admission is E£1.50 (E£3 on Friday and holidays).

On the south side of the midan is Cairo's pre-eminent orientation aid, the **Al-Fath Mosque**. Completed in the early 1990s the mosque's minaret is visible from just about anywhere in central and Islamic Cairo.

Garden City & Manial

Garden City was developed in the early 1900s along the lines of an English garden suburb. Its curving tree-lined streets were intended to create an air of tranquillity, while the proximity of the **UK embassy** no doubt provided a reassuring veneer of security. The embassy, which anchors the northwestern corner of Garden City, originally had grounds which stretched down to the Nile but the bottom portion of the lawns was lopped off in the 1950s when Nasser had the Corniche ploughed through.

Many of the elegant villas that once characterised the area have fallen prey to quick-buck developers, and 1990s traffic has invaded the narrow avenues. However, enough grand architecture and palm, rubber and mango trees survive to make a walk through the streets still worthwhile.

The Palace Museum Manial is the name for the northern end of Rhoda, the southern of Cairo's two inhabited Nile islands. Separated by just a narrow channel of water from the southern end of Garden City, it's largely a middle-class residential district but it's also home to one of Cairo's least visited and most eccentric tourist sites, the Manial Palace Museum.

The palace was built in the early part of the 20th century as a residence for Prince Mohammed Ali Tawfiq, the uncle of Egypt's last regent, King Farouk. Apparently the prince couldn't decide which architectural style he preferred, so he went for the lot: Ottoman, Moorish, Persian and European rococo are all represented.

Today the palace houses an assortment of collections in five main buildings including Farouk's huge horde of stuffed hunting trophies – not a sight for animal lovers. The

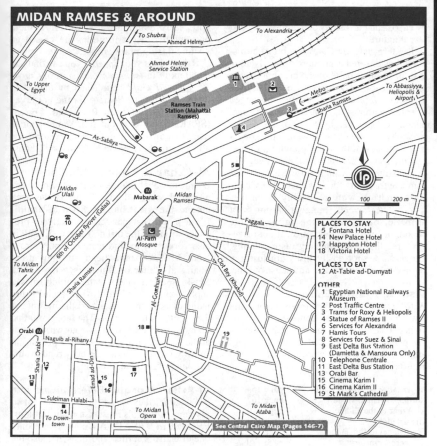

MIDAN RAMSES & AROUND

To Shubra
Ahmed Helmy

To Alexandria

To Upper
Egypt

Ahmed Helmy
Service Station

Metro

To Abbassiyya,
Heliopolis &
Airport

Ramses Train
Station (Mahattat
Ramses)

Sharia Ramses

As-Sabliya

Midan
Ulali

Mubarak

Midan
Ramses

Faggala

To Midan
Tahrir

Al-Fath
Mosque

Sharia Ramses

Al-Gomhuryya

Clot Bey (Khalid)

0   100   200 m

Orabi

Naguib al-Rihany

Sharia Orabi

Emad ad-Din

Suleiman Halabi

To Down-
town

To Midan
Opera

To Midan
Ataba

PLACES TO STAY
5 Fontana Hotel
14 New Palace Hotel
17 Happyton Hotel
18 Victoria Hotel

PLACES TO EAT
12 At-Tabie ad-Dumyati

OTHER
1 Egyptian National Railways
   Museum
2 Post Traffic Centre
3 Trams for Roxy & Heliopolis
4 Statue of Ramses II
6 Services for Alexandria
7 Hamis Tours
8 Services for Suez & Sinai
9 East Delta Bus Station
   (Damietta & Mansoura Only)
10 Telephone Centrale
11 East Delta Bus Station
13 Orabi Bar
15 Cinema Karim I
16 Cinema Karim II
19 St Mark's Cathedral

See Central Cairo Map (Pages 146-7)

largest building contains the prince's collection of manuscripts, clothing, silver objects, furniture, writing implements and other items dating from medieval times to the 19th century. A self-appointed guide likes to show you around this part of the museum, object by object – if you don't want his services let him know.

The palace is open daily from 9 am to 4 pm, admission is E£5 (E£2.50 for students). Photography permits are E£10, video permits are E£150.

The easiest way to get here from Midan Tahrir is to head down Corniche el-Nil and cross the third bridge that you come to; it's a very pleasant 20 minute walk. Alternatively, a taxi from Tahrir (ask for 'Al-Manial') should cost no more than E£2.

ISLAMIC CAIRO

Islamic Cairo is almost another city altogether. Like Alice passing through her looking glass, as the visitor heads east from Midan Ataba all the familiar trappings of the modern world drop away, to be replaced by chaos and curiosities of a completely different nature.

The term Islamic Cairo is a bit of a misnomer, as the area is no more or less Islamic than most other parts of the city but maybe the profusion of minarets on the skyline gives the impression of piety. Unchanged over the centuries to an astonishing degree, Islamic Cairo's neighbourhoods are full of twisting alleyways so narrow that the houses seem to touch at the top. Splendid mosques and crushes of medieval facades hedge in rutted streets on which little Suzuki vans compete for right of way with donkeys, carts and merchants with impossibly laden barrows. The sweet, pungent aromas of turmeric, basil and cumin mix with the odours of livestock and petrol. It's a maze-like area that is completely disorientating, the casual visitor easily loses not just any sense of direction but also any sense of time.

Visiting Islamic Cairo

With more than 800 listed monuments and few signposts or other concessions to the visitor, Islamic Cairo can be a fairly daunting place. We've divided it into six segments, each one of which makes for a half-day's outing:

Al-Azhar & Khan al-Khalili	page 164
North of Khan al-Khalili	page 167
Al-Azhar to the Citadel	page 170
The Citadel	page 174
The Citadel to Ibn Tulun	page 177
Northern Cemetery	page 179

Appropriate dress is necessary for visiting this part of Cairo – legs and shoulders should be decently covered, otherwise custodians may baulk at allowing you inside mosques. Shoes have to be taken off before entering prayer halls so it might be wise to come in footwear that can be easily slipped off and on, but is also robust enough for rutted and rubble-strewn alleyways. Carry lots of small change. You'll need it for tipping guardians and caretakers.

Also note that any given opening times should be interpreted as a rough guide only;

caretakers are usually around from 9 am until early evening but they follow their own whims. Most mosques are closed to visitors during prayer times.

If this whets your appetite you can find out much more in *Islamic Monuments in Cairo: A Practical Guide* published by the AUC Press (E£40). The Society for the Preservation of the Architectural Resources of Egypt (SPARE) also puts out four semi-pictorial maps that are excellent tools for exploration; all are available from most Cairo bookshops.

Al-Azhar & Khan al-Khalili

By far the best place to start becoming acquainted with Islamic Cairo is the area around the great bazaar, Khan al-Khalili. It's a place that panders perfectly to preconceptions of the orient. Khan al-Khalili is also very easy to find from central Cairo – from Midan Ataba head straight along Sharia al-Azhar or Muski (see the Sharia Muski section later). Alternatively, it's a short taxi ride; ask for 'Al-Hussein' – the name of both the midan and the mosque at the mouth of the bazaar. The fare should be no more than E£3 from Downtown. Get out at the Al-Azhar mosque where a pedestrian subway burrows under the busy road to surface just off Midan Hussein.

Al-Azhar Mosque Before diving into the bazaar, it is worth taking time out to visit one of Cairo's most historic institutions. Founded in 970 AD, Al-Azhar is not only one of Cairo's earliest mosques, it's also the world's oldest surviving university. At one time it was the pre-eminent centre of learning, drawing scholars from Europe as well as all over the Arab world. It continues to play a dominant role in Egyptian theological life to this day, with the Sheikh of al-Azhar being the country's ultimate religious authority. However, students are no longer taught in the mosque's courtyard, they attend one of nine campuses around the country.

Architecturally the mosque is a mixture of styles, the result of frequent enlargements over its 1000 year history. The central courtyard is the earliest part, while from

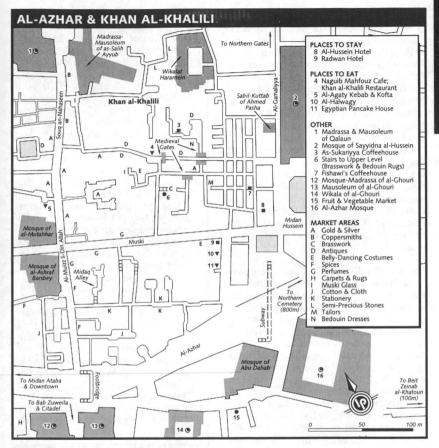

AL-AZHAR & KHAN AL-KHALILI

To Northern Gates

Madrassa-Mausoleum of as-Salih Ayyub

Wikalat Haramein

Khan al-Khalili

Souq an-Nahaseen

Sabil-Kuttab of Ahmed Pasha

Al-Gamaliyya

Medieval Gates

Mosque of al-Mutahhar

Mosque of al-Ashraf Barsbey

Al-Muizz li-Din Allah

Midaq Alley

Muski

Midan Hussein

Footbridge

Subway

To Northern Cemetery (800m)

Al-Azhar

Mosque of Abu Dahab

To Midan Ataba & Downtown

To Bab Zuweila & Citadel

To Beit Zeinab al-Khatoun (100m)

0   50   100 m

PLACES TO STAY
8 Al-Hussein Hotel
9 Radwan Hotel

PLACES TO EAT
4 Naguib Mahfouz Cafe;
   Khan al-Khalili Restaurant
5 Al-Agaty Kebab & Kofta
10 Al-Halwagy
11 Egyptian Pancake House

OTHER
1 Madrassa & Mausoleum
   of Qalaun
2 Mosque of Sayyidna al-Hussein
3 As-Sukariyya Coffeehouse
6 Stairs to Upper Level
   (Brasswork & Bedouin Rugs)
7 Fishawi's Coffeehouse
12 Mosque-Madrassa of al-Ghouri
13 Mausoleum of al-Ghouri
14 Wikala of al-Ghouri
15 Fruit & Vegetable Market
16 Al-Azhar Mosque

MARKET AREAS
A Gold & Silver
B Coppersmiths
C Brasswork
D Antiques
E Belly-Dancing Costumes
F Spices
G Perfumes
H Carpets & Rugs
I Muski Glass
J Cotton & Cloth
K Stationery
L Semi-Precious Stones
M Tailors
N Bedouin Dresses

south to north, the three minarets date from the 14th, 15th and 16th centuries. The tomb chamber, through a doorway on the left just inside the entrance, has a beautiful *mihrab* (niche indicating the direction of Mecca) and should not be missed. The mosque is open daily, admission is E£12.

Leaving the mosque and turning left and then left again brings you into an alley squeezed between the southern wall of Al-Azhar and a row of tiny shops housed in the vaults of a 15th century merchants' build-ing. At the top of this road (see the Al-Azhar to the Citadel map) is **Beit Zeinab al-Kha-toun** (House of Zeinab Khatoun), a restored Ottoman-era house that now serves as a cul-tural centre and sometime gallery. Across a small garden is **Beit al-Harrawi**, another fine piece of 18th century vernacular architecture but too sparse inside to really warrant the E£10 (E£5 for students) admission.

Midan Hussein This was one of the main squares of medieval Cairo, stretching between the two highly venerated mosques of Al-Azhar to the south and Sayyidna al-Hussein to the north. It's still an important space today, particularly at feast times, on Ramadan evenings, and during the *moulids* (religious festivals) of Al-Hussein and An-Nabi Mohammed (see the boxed text 'The Moulid' on page 99). At these times the midan is filled with vast crowds, bright lights and loud music, and the partying goes on until early morning.

On the northern side, the **Mosque of Sayyidna al-Hussein** is one of the most sacred Islamic sites in Egypt (see the boxed text 'Shi'ia Head, Sunni Body' on this page) and, as such, non-Muslims are not allowed inside. The building itself dates only from about 1870 (it replaces an earlier 12th century mosque) and is not of great interest to travellers.

Khan al-Khalili Jaundiced travellers have been known to glibly dismiss Khan al-Khalili as a tourist trap, and it's true that the tour bus-pleasing, travellers cheque-pulling element is well and truly present. But generations of Cairenes have lived their lives in these narrow, canvas covered alleys, plying their trades since the founding of the Khan in the 14th century – the buying and selling did not begin with the arrival of the first tour group.

Today the Khan is an immense conglomeration of markets and shops (many of which are closed on Sunday), where it's possible to find everything from blankets and soap powder to books of magic spells and precious stones – as well, of course, as plenty of stuffed camels and alabaster pyramids. The clumsy 'Hey mister, look for free' touts aside, the merchants of Khan al-Khalili are some of the greatest salespeople and smooth talkers you will ever meet. Almost anything can be bought in the Khan, and if one merchant doesn't have what you're looking for, then he'll find somebody who does. For more details about the unwritten rules and regulations of bargaining see the boxed text 'The Art of Bargaining' on page 112.

Shi'ia Head, Sunni Body

The Mosque of Sayyidna al-Hussein reputedly contains one of the most holy relics of Islam: the head of Al-Hussein, grandson of the Prophet. It was brought here in a green silk bag in 1153 (almost 500 years after his death) out of reach of the Crusaders who were busy desecrating Islamic sites in Palestine. The head is not on view but is buried several metres beneath a shrine.

Al-Hussein was killed by the Umayyad clan who had assumed control of the caliphate after the Prophet Mohammed had died without naming a successor. Ali, the husband of Mohammed's daughter Fatima, put himself forward as the natural successor, claiming the right by marriage. Passed over, he took up arms against the Umayyads, but was assassinated. His son Al-Hussein then led a revolt but was killed at the battle of Kerbala.

The schism is perpetuated in Islam today. The followers of Al-Hussein and Ali became the Shi'ia, who refuse to acknowledge as caliph anyone but descendants of Mohammed. Those who believe that the true line of succession went via the Umayyads are known as Sunnis; they constitute 90% of all Muslims including the Egyptians.

Despite being a Shi'ite martyr, Al-Hussein was a blood relative of the Prophet and as such is regarded as a popular saint in Egypt.

There are few specific things to see in the Khan but a stop off at **Fishawi's Coffeehouse** is a must. Hung with huge ornately framed mirrors and packed day and night, it's been open 24 hours a day for the last 200 years. Entertainment comes in the form of roaming salesmen, women and children who hawk wallets, cigarette lighters in the form of pistols, canes with carved tops, sheesha-style cigarette holders, and packet after packet after packet of Kleenex tissues.

It's easily found: it fills a narrow alleyway with rickety tables and chairs just one block in, off Midan Hussein.

Sharia Muski Sharia Muski is a congested market street that runs parallel to Sharia al-Azhar from Midan Hussein, all the way west to Midan Ataba on the edge of Downtown. It is less overtly 'oriental' than Khan al-Khalili but all the more vivid and boisterous for it. The goods on sale range from plastic furniture and party toys to items like wedding dresses and great mounds of bucket-sized bras at its western end.

North of Khan al-Khalili

From Midan Hussein take the road that leads up along the western side of the Al-Hussein Mosque. Stick to it as it dog-legs left and enters the district known as **Gamaliyya**. This is where Egypt's Nobel-prize winning author Naguib Mahfouz grew up (see the boxed text 'Mahfouz's Cairo' on page 168) Sharia al-Gamaliyya, the main street you are following, was the second most important of medieval Cairo's thoroughfares. Today, it has the appearance of a back alley, rutted and unsealed, barely squeezing between the buildings. These buildings include some fine clusters of Mamluk-era mosques and madrassas, though many of them are partly obscured by forests of crude wooden scaffolding, there to shore up damage inflicted by the 1992 earthquake. Tragically, one of the district's most impressive monuments, the Musafirkhanah Palace, survived the earthquake only to be burnt to the ground in 1998.

At the end of Sharia al-Gamaliyya on the left, just before the street exits through the great city gate, is a former merchants' inn, **Wikala of Qaitbey** (1481), which served as Liam Neeson's storage depot in the film *Ruby Cairo* (see the boxed text 'Egypt at the Cinema' on page 81).

The Northern Walls & Gates The square-towered Bab an-Nasr (Gate of Victory) and the rounded Bab al-Futuh (Gate of Conquests) were built in 1087 as the two

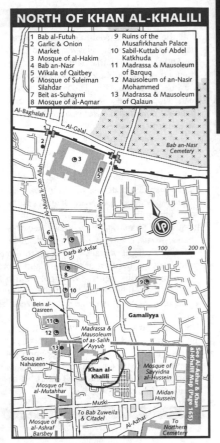

NORTH OF KHAN AL-KHALILI

1 Bab al-Futuh	9 Ruins of the
2 Garlic & Onion	Musafirkhanah Palace
Market	10 Sabil-Kuttab of Abdel
3 Mosque of al-Hakim	Katkhuda
4 Bab an-Nasr	11 Madrassa & Mausoleum
5 Wikala of Qaitbey	of Barquq
6 Mosque of Suleiman	12 Mausoleum of an-Nasir
Silahdar	Mohammed
7 Beit as-Suhaymi	13 Madrassa & Mausoleum
8 Mosque of al-Aqmar	of Qalaun

main northern entrances to the new walled Fatimid city of Al-Qahira. Walk along the outside and you'll see what a hugely imposing bit of military architecture the whole thing is. You can walk along the top of the walls and explore inside the gates via the roof of the Mosque of al-Hakim. Admission to the gates is E£6. You may be asked for E£12: E£6 for the Hakim mosque, E£6 for the gates, but as the mosque can be seen quite well from the walls just say 'Al-Abwab bas' and pay E£6 only.

Mahfouz's Cairo

Until the age of 12, Mahfouz's family occupied a house in a short alleyway called Qasr ash-Shuq, just off Sharia Gamaliyya, and he attended an elementary school behind the Mosque of al-Hussein. Those first dozen years supplied the images and impressions that have coloured the Nobel laureate's writing ever since.

One of his earliest books, not yet translated into English, was called *Khan al-Khalili*, followed a few years later by *Midaq Alley* which focuses on the lives of the people who inhabit a small cul-de-sac within the bazaar. Midaq Alley (Zuqaq al-Midaq) really exists and a film of the same name was shot there. It's just off Sharia al-Muizz li-Din (see the Khan al-Khalili & Al-Azhar map), a little alley with a short flight of stairs leading up to three stubby dead ends. The street sign is kept in a coffeehouse at the foot of the steps and is produced on payment of baksheesh.

Similarly all the events in Mahfouz's *Cairo Trilogy* are rooted in geographical fact and the three separate titles of the trilogy are the names of streets in the area: *Palace Walk* is *Bein al-Qasreen*; *Sugar Street* is near Bab Zuweila; and *Palace of Desire* is Qasr ash-Shuq, the street in which Mahfouz was born.

But while the names may stay the same, in some ways Mahfouz's stories have dated. The mix of upper, middle and working classes that he describes cohabiting in these neighbourhoods is a thing of the past. History and place have lost out to lousy plumbing and lack of amenities. All who could afford it have moved out, including Mahfouz – while Gamaliyya might hold the Nobel laureate's heart his body prefers the comforts of the modern Nileside suburb of Agouza.

Once on the roof, bear left to Bab al-Futuh. Look for the carving above one of the doorways which reads 'Tour Lascalle', evidence that some of Napoleon's troops of occupation were once garrisoned here (Bab an-Nasr bears the graffiti name 'Tour Milhaud'). Continue beyond the tower to the westernmost bastion where you'll find a descending staircase. On the wall as you go down are carved bullocks and pharaonic figures, while at the bottom of the stairs, underneath a window, is a partially eroded hippo – all pointing to the fact that the stone for these fortifications was filched from the ruins of ancient Memphis.

Back up on the ramparts, to the north you are looking out across the former Bab an-Nasr cemetery, nowadays almost completely built over with houses. Somewhere in there, now lost, is the final resting place of Johann Ludwig Burckhardt, the 19th century explorer who rediscovered Petra and the temple of Ramses II at Abu Simbel.

Mosque of al-Hakim Al-Hakim bi-Amr Allah, 'He who rules by God's Command', was only 11 years old when his father died and he became the third Fatimid ruler of Egypt. His tutor nicknamed him 'Little

Lizard' because of his frightening looks and behaviour. Hakim later got his revenge by having the tutor murdered. During his 24 year reign those nearest to him were in constant fear of their lives. A general, forgetting himself in the rush of a victorious encounter, entered the royal apartments unannounced to find a bloodied Hakim standing over a disembowelled page boy. The general was beheaded.

Hakim did, however, take a great interest in the affairs of his people and would on occasion patrol the city's streets on his donkey called Moon. He received petitions and complaints from the city folk and punished dishonest merchants by having them sodomised by a large black servant who accompanied him for this purpose. Hakim also disliked dogs – he had them all slaughtered – and women, whom he forbade to venture out of doors. This latter decree he reinforced by banning the manufacture of women's shoes.

His death was as bizarre as his life. On one of his solitary nocturnal jaunts on Moon up onto the Muqattam Hills, Hakim disappeared and his body was never found. To one of his followers, a man called Al-Darizy, this was proof of Hakim's divine nature. After Hakim's death Al-Darizy travelled widely preaching and founded the sect of the Druze which continues to this day.

Completed in 1010, Hakim's mosque has rarely been used as a place of worship, instead it was used as a prison to hold Crusaders, a stable for Salah ad-Din, Napoleon used it as a warehouse, and Nasser made it into a boys' school. Most fittingly of all, it also served for a time as a madhouse.

Sharia al-Muizz li-Din Allah Al-Muizz li-Din (as it's often shortened to), which takes its name from the Fatimid caliph who conquered Cairo in 969 AD, is the former grand thoroughfare of medieval Cairo. It was the city's main shopping street and a 15th century description tells us that storytellers and entertainers, as well as stalls serving cooked food were to be found along its length. The garlic and onion market beside Al-Hakim's mosque was a slave market until the middle of the 19th century.

Heading south, the produce gives way to a variety of small places selling metal-worked accoutrements for coffeehouses and fuul vendors: sheeshas, braziers and big, pear-shaped cooking pots. On the right, after about 200m, is the **Mosque of Suleiman Silahdar**, built comparatively late in 1839 during the reign of Mohammed Ali and distinguished by its drainpipe-thin minaret. Reflecting the pasha's wider aims of grafting European ideas onto those of traditional Egypt, the mosque mixes a Mamluk-style facade with rococo and baroque forms.

Over the street from the mosque is a side street, Darb al-Asfar, and at No 19 is **Beit as-Suhaymi**, Cairo's finest Ottoman house. With few exceptions, restoration has left many of the city's historic houses feeling completely soulless and looking like reproductions rather than the real thing. By contrast, Beit as-Suhaymi has always had something of a 'Marie Celeste' quality to it, as if its former owner might turn up at any moment. Unfortunately, at the time of research the restorers were in residence and the house was closed to the public; fingers crossed that it comes out unscathed.

Back on Al-Muizz li-Din, just 50m south of the junction with Darb al-Asfar, is the petite **Mosque of al-Aqmar** (the Moonlit). Built in 1125 by one of the last Fatimid caliphs, it's important in terms of Cairo's architectural development because it's the oldest stone-facaded mosque in Egypt. Here, for the first time, appear several features that were to become part of the mosque builders' essential vocabulary: the stalactite carving, for example, and the ribbing in the hooded arch.

Sabil-Kuttab of Abdel Katkhuda A *sabil* is a fountain or tap from which passers-by can take a drink, a *kuttab* is a Quranic school. So, a *sabil-kuttab* provides the two things commended by the Prophet: water for the thirsty and spiritual enlightenment for the ignorant. The building of a sabil-kuttab was a popular way for wealthy people to atone for their sins. This particular example was built in 1744 by a wealthy lord well known for his debauched behaviour. It has some nice ceramic work inside which can't be seen from the street but if you linger the *bawwab* (doorman) may come along with the door key.

Bein al-Qasreen The part of Al-Muizz li-Din immediately south of the sabil-kuttab is known as Bein al-Qasreen, which translates to 'Between the Palaces', a reference to two great royal complexes that flanked the street here during the Fatimid era. The palaces fell into ruin following the fall of the Fatimids but Bein al-Qasreen remained a great public space, off which ran dozens of alleys full of hawkers and traders. The area remained a favourite building place for subsequent rulers whose monuments rose out of the rubble of the former palaces. Today, three great abutting Mamluk complexes line the west of the street, providing one of Cairo's most impressive assemblies of minarets, domes and towering facades. Entrance to each of these complexes is E£6 (E£3 for students).

Northernmost of the three is the **Madrassa & Mausoleum of Barquq**. Barquq seized power in 1382 as Egypt was reeling from plague and famine; his madrassa was completed four years later. It is entered through the bold black-and-white marble portal which leads into a vaulted passageway. To the right, the inner court has a colourful ceiling supported by four pharaonic columns made of porphyry. Although this is called the Mausoleum of Barquq, it's actually his daughter who is buried in the splendid domed tomb chamber here; the sultan himself rests in the Northern Cemetery (see the Khanqah-Mausoleum of ibn Barquq in the Northern Cemetery section later in this chapter).

South of the Barquq complex is the **Mausoleum of an-Nasir Mohammed** (1304). The Gothic doorway was taken from a church in Acre (now Akko, Israel) when An-Nasir and his Mamluk army ended Crusader domination there in 1290. More foreign influence is discernible in the fine

stucco on the minaret which is North African in style. Buried in the mausoleum (on the right as you enter but usually kept locked) is An-Nasir's favourite son; the sultan himself is buried next door in the mausoleum of *his* father, Qalaun.

If you are only going to visit one of the three complexes, make it the **Madrassa & Mausoleum of Qalaun**. The earliest of the trio, the Qalaun complex was completed in just 13 months in 1279. The mausoleum, on the right, is a particularly beautiful assemblage of *mashrabiyya*, inlaid stone and stucco patterned with stars and floral motifs, all lit by stained glass windows. As well as the mausoleum and madrassa, it also includes a *maristan* (hospital). The Arab traveller and historian Ibn Battuta who visited Cairo in 1325 recorded that Qalaun's hospital contained 'an innumerable quantity of appliances and medicaments'. Incredibly, a clinic still occupies a part of the original building, maintaining a tradition of more than 700 years of medical care.

Back to the City Centre Want to buy a minaret top? South of Bein al-Qasreen, the monuments give way to a ramshackle string of shops filled with pots and pans and crescent-shaped finials, which is why this area is popularly known as Sharia an-Nahasseen or the Coppersmiths' Street. After a short stretch, copper gives way to gold signifying that you have re-entered the precincts of Khan al-Khalili. At the junction with Muski, beside the two mosques, a turn left leads to Midan Hussein, while heading off to the right will eventually take you to Midan Ataba (20 to 30 minutes walk); straight ahead is Sharia al-Azhar, the best place to find a taxi.

Al-Azhar to the Citadel

South of Sharia al-Azhar, Al-Muizz li-Din Allah continues as a busy market street running down to the twin-minareted gate of Bab Zuweila; it's a leisurely 10 minute walk. From the gate there are then two possible routes to the Citadel: east along Darb al-Ahmar, or south through Sharia al-Khaya-

AL-AZHAR TO THE CITADEL

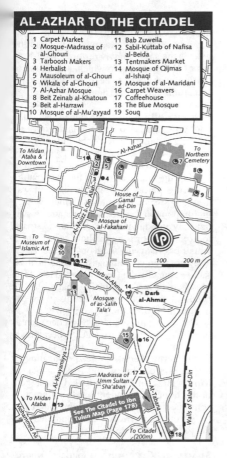

1 Carpet Market
2 Mosque-Madrassa of al-Ghouri
3 Tarboosh Makers
4 Herbalist
5 Mausoleum of al-Ghouri
6 Wikala of al-Ghouri
7 Al-Azhar Mosque
8 Beit Zeinab al-Khatoun
9 Beit al-Harrawi
10 Mosque of al-Mu'ayyad
11 Bab Zuweila
12 Sabil-Kuttab of Nafisa al-Beida
13 Tentmakers Market
14 Mosque of Qijmas al-Ishaqi
15 Mosque of al-Maridani
16 Carpet Weavers
17 Coffeehouse
18 The Blue Mosque
19 Souq

miyya (Street of the Tentmakers). Either way it takes about another 20 minutes to reach the Citadel, where you can then take refreshments, enjoy the view, and exert yourself with a little more sightseeing before picking up a taxi back to town. Alternatively, turning right outside Bab Zuweila will take you the short distance to the Museum of Islamic Art (see that section later).

Al-Ghouri Complex (Al-Ghouriyya)

The grand pair of black and white buildings (dating from 1505) facing each other across the souq on the south side of Sharia al-Azhar are the mosque-madrassa (the one with the red-chequered chimneypot minaret) and mausoleum of Al-Ghouri. Together they form an exquisite monument to the end of the Mamluk era. Qansuh al-Ghouri, the penultimate Mamluk sultan, ruled for 16 years, before, at the age of 78, riding out at the head of his army to do battle with the Ottoman Turks in Syria. The Mamluks were trounced, and soon after the Ottomans began their 281 year rule of Egypt. The head of the defeated Al-Ghouri was sent to Constantinople; his body was never recovered and his Cairo mausoleum instead contains the body of Tumanbey, his short-lived successor, who was captured by the Turks and hanged at Bab Zuweila.

Part of the mausoleum now serves as a theatre where performances of Sufi dancing are held twice-weekly (see the Entertainment section later in this chapter).

Wikala of al-Ghouri About 300m east of the Al-Ghouri complex is another of the doomed sultan's legacies, a *wikala*, built in 1505. Also called a *caravanserai*, this is a medieval merchants' hostel. The traders slept in the upper rooms while their animals were stabled below. The ground floor also had storage areas and business was carried out in the courtyard around the fountain. The gates of the wikala were locked at night to protect the merchandise. In Ottoman times Cairo had more than 360 wikalas but now less than 20 remain, of which this is in by far the best condition.

The courtyard now serves as a theatre and concert hall, while the former stables are artists' ateliers; one houses a small permanent exhibition of peasant and Bedouin crafts. The wikala (☎ 511 0472) is open daily from 8 am to midnight, the entrance fee is E£6.

Souq The area around the Al-Ghouri complex used to be known as Cairo's 'Silk Market', a place where carpets were sold. The passageways behind the mosque-madrassa (slip down the side or enter from Sharia al-Azhar) are still filled with carpet sellers, though their wares are now made of wool or synthetics. South of the Ghouriyya, Al-Muizz li-Din Allah becomes a busy souq given over to household goods, cloth and cheap clothing, particularly gaudy *galabiyyas* (the full-length robe worn by men). On the right, less than 50m south of the Ghouriyya are two of Cairo's last *tarboosh* (fez) makers. You can watch them shaping the hats on their heavy brass presses. Once worn by every respectable *effendi* (gentleman) the tarbooshes are mainly bought now by hotels and theatre troupes. They sell for E£5 to E£30. Further along, on the opposite side of the street, is a herbalist whose shop front is hung with bunches of dried hedgehogs and lizards. All this stuff is used in the preparation of healing compounds, but quite how, we've no idea.

Mosque of al-Mu'ayyad The lord Al-Mu'ayyad was a great intriguer, for which he was arrested and thrown into a lice-infested prison. While incarcerated he vowed that should he survive to see freedom he would one day replace the prison with a 'saintly place'. Not only did he survive, he rose to become sultan. His mosque, completed in 1422 and supposedly built on the site of his former prison, is a typically monumental Mamluk work. The entrance leads into the mausoleum where Al-Mu'ayyad and his son lie in two cenotaphs; beyond that is the mosque itself, an extremely tranquil place with the prayer hall opening on to a large tree-filled garden courtyard. In the far corner of the prayer hall is a small door leading to the mosque's two minarets atop Bab Zuweila. These were added 330 years after the gate was built, it is a mystery how the master masons knew that the gate could take the extra weight. The view from the top of the minarets is about the best in Cairo, offering a panorama of rooftops used as chicken runs, goat pens, pigeon lofts, rubbish dumps and even workshops.

The entrance fee to the mosque is E£12 (E£6 for students) but the caretaker will probably insist on baksheesh to open the door up to the minarets.

Across from the mosque, just before the gate, is the small, newly restored **Sabil-Kuttab of Nafisa al-Beida** which, at the time of writing, was slated to become a visitors' information centre for Islamic Cairo.

Bab Zuweila Built at the same time as the northern gates, Bab Zuweila is the only remaining southern gate of the old medieval city of Al-Qahira. Until the late 19th century it was still closed each evening. The area in front of the gate was one of the main public gathering places in Mamluk times. It was also the site of executions, which were a highly popular form of street theatre. A particularly vicious bunch, the Mamluks used to execute victims by publicly sawing them in half or crucifying them on the great gates. They got their comeuppance – after the massacre at the Citadel (see the boxed text 'The Massacre of the Mamluks' on page 176) the heads of the 500 slain Mamluks were exhibited in front of the gate on spikes.

The gate gained a slightly better reputation in the 19th century when it became associated with Metwalli, a local saint who lived nearby. People in need of healing or divine intercession would leave a lock of hair or piece of clothing nailed to the gate in the hope of his attention. It's a practice continued to this day and if you look carefully you'll see fresh nails hammered into the great wooden doors.

Sharia al-Khayamiyya Sharia al-Khayamiyya (Street of the Tentmakers) takes its name from the artisans who traditionally worked here producing the brightly printed fabrics formerly used to adorn caravans. Nowadays these fabrics are used for the ceremonial tents that are set up for funerals, wakes, weddings and feasts. There's also a lot of appliqué work stitched and sold here. For more information see the Shopping section in the Facts for the Visitor chapter.

Continuing south beyond the covered market, Sharia al-Khayamiyya runs for about 500m before intersecting with Sharia

Mohammed Ali; a left turn here will take you to the great mosque of Sultan Hassan and to the Citadel. However, rather than follow this route, we suggest that you backtrack to Bab Zuweila and head east along Darb al-Ahmar.

Darb al-Ahmar This district, which takes its name from its main street, Darb al-Ahmar (Red Road), was the heart of 14th and 15th century Cairo. During these centuries Cairo had a population of about 250,000, most of whom lived outside the city walls in tightly packed residential districts like this where more than half the narrow, twisting streets ended in cul-de-sacs. As the walled inner city of Al-Qahira was completely built-up, patrons of new mosques, grand palaces and religious institutions were forced to build outside the city gates; most of the structures around here date from the late Mamluk era. The **Mosque of Qijmas al-Ishaqi** (1481) is one of the best examples of architecture from this period. Its plain exterior is quite deceptive, as inside there are beautiful stained glass windows, inlaid marble floors and stucco walls. There's no admission fee here but you'll be expected to offer a few pounds in baksheesh.

About 150m further on the right, the **Mosque of al-Maridani** (1339) is notable for incorporating architectural elements from several different periods: eight granite columns were taken from a pharaonic monument; the arches were made from Roman, Christian and Islamic designs; and the Ottomans added a fountain and wooden housing. The lack of visitors, the trees in the courtyard and the attractive mashrabiyya screening make it a peaceful place to stop at. There is no admission fee here but, as at the Qijmas al-Ishaqi mosque, someone will probably expect baksheesh.

Back on Darb al-Ahmar, known as Sharia at-Tabana at this point, across from the mosque is a small **carpet-weaving workshop**. It's open to the street and you can see the great wooden loom inside, on which they weave rag-rugs from colourful off-cuts.

They weave to specifica[...] colour and name the size[...] something 1m by 1.5m. [...] where the road splits, is[...] open-air coffeehouse, a g[...] break with an iced *limoon*.

Blue Mosque More correctly known as the Mosque of Aqsunqur, this building gets its more popular name from the combination of blue-grey marble on the exterior and the flowery tiling on the interior. The tiles, imported from Syria, were added in 1652 by a Turkish governor but the original and much plainer structure dates from 1347. The minaret affords an excellent view of the Citadel, while over to the east, just behind the mosque, you can see the remains of Salah ad-Din's city walls, now largely covered with rubbish and the detritus of collapsed buildings. Admission to the mosque costs E£12 (E£6 for students).

From here it's about another 400m up to the Citadel. Midan Bab al Khalq Sharia Bur Said

Museum of Islamic Art behind Abdin Pal Overshadowed by the pharaonic crowd-pulling power of the Egyptian Museum, this place, which has one of the world's finest collections of Islamic applied art, receives undeservedly few visitors.

It has to be said though, the museum doesn't do itself any favours. As in the Egyptian Museum the labelling leaves a lot to be desired – 'Statue in the shape of a lion painted blue' reads the printed card beside a statue of a lion painted blue. We recommend that you spend some time walking around Islamic Cairo and visit one or two mosques before coming here to help supply the missing context.

Entrance is through the garden door off Sharia Port Said. This brings you into the central hall containing some of the most beautiful exhibits; so we suggest you immediately turn right, saving the best for later. Rooms 8 and 9 contain woodwork, including some nice coffered ceilings. Room 11 contains metal work and room 12 contains Mamluk weaponry. Room 13 is for

MUSEUM OF ISLAMIC ART

Map labels:
Archaeological Garden
Ticket Office
Entrance
8 7 6
9 10 5
11 4B
12 2 4
13 1 3
14 15 23
Area closed to public
16 22
17 21
18 20
19
To Midan Ataba (800m)
Sharia Mohammed Ali
Sharia Sami al-Barudi
Midan Bab al-Khalq
Sharia Port Said (Bur Said)
To Bab Zuweila (500m)
Sharia Ahmed Mahir

'masterpieces' which include a great door that originally belonged to the Sayyida Zeinab mosque. Beyond are rooms 14 to 16 which are given over to ceramics. There is no tradition of glazed tile making in Egypt so most of what's on display here comes from Persia (modern-day Iran). The cone-topped fireplace in room 16, however, is from Anatolia (now central Turkey).

Walk through rooms 21 (glass) and 20 (Ottoman era) to room 19 which contains a small collection of illuminated manuscripts and ornate Qurans formerly owned by King Farouk. Now make your way back to rooms 4 and 4B which are divided by a row of carved Mamluk columns. The museum's centrepiece is in 4B: an Ottoman fountain combined with beautiful mashrabiyya and a carved wooden ceiling. There's another, more elaborate sunken fountain in room 5 dating from the time of the Mamluks.

The museum (☎ 390 9930) is open daily from 9 am to 4 pm (closed from 11.30 am to 1.30 pm on Friday). Admission is E£16, (E£8 for students).

Getting There & Away The museum is about a 10 minute walk from Midan Ataba, straight down Sharia Mohammed Ali (also called Sharia al-Qala'a). Midan Tahrir is 1.5km west along Sharia Sami al-Barudi and its continuations. Alternatively, a taxi to/from Downtown should cost no more than E£3.

The Citadel

Sprawling over a limestone spur on the eastern edge of the city, the Citadel (Al-Qala'a) was home to Egypt's rulers for some 700 years. Their legacy is a collection of three very different mosques, several palaces housing some fairly indifferent museums, and a couple of terraces with views over the city. Good as these views are, we are inclined to suggest you give the Citadel a miss in protest at the short-sighted greed of the people in charge. The E£20 admission fee is already too high, but on top of that, one part of the Citadel requires you to fork out another (completely unwarranted) E£20, while one of the mosques charges a further E£6 admission. Also, the authorities have recently closed the Citadel's former main entrance (citing security as the reason), forcing would-be visitors to use a rear entrance accessible only by taxi.

Salah ad-Din began building the Citadel in 1176 to fortify the city against the threat of the Crusaders, who were rampaging through Palestine. Following their overthrow of Salah ad-Din's Ayyubid dynasty, the Mamluks occupied the Citadel, extending its area and adding sumptuous palaces and harems. Under the Ottomans (1517-1798) the fortress was further enlarged westwards and a new main gate, the Bab al-Azab, was added, while the Mamluk palaces were allowed to deteriorate. Even so, when Napoleon's French expedition took control of the Citadel in 1798, the emperor's savants regarded these buildings as

THE CITADEL

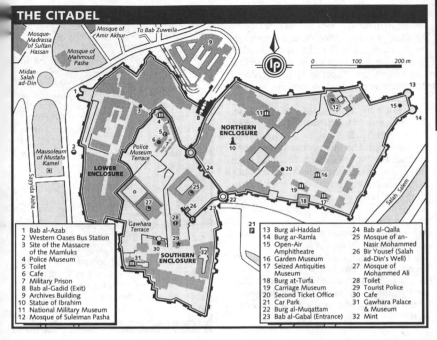

To Bab Zuweila

Mosque-Madrassa of Sultan Hassan

Mosque of Amir Akhur

Mosque of Mahmoud Pasha

Midan Salah ad-Din

Mausoleum of Mustafa Kamel

Sayyida Aisha

Police Museum Terrace

LOWER ENCLOSURE

NORTHERN ENCLOSURE

Gawhara Terrace

SOUTHERN ENCLOSURE

Salah Salem

0   100   200 m

1 Bab al-Azab
2 Western Oases Bus Station
3 Site of the Massacre of the Mamluks
4 Police Museum
5 Toilet
6 Cafe
7 Military Prison
8 Bab al-Gadid (Exit)
9 Archives Building
10 Statue of Ibrahim
11 National Military Museum
12 Mosque of Suleiman Pasha

13 Burg al-Haddad
14 Burg ar-Ramla
15 Open-Air Amphitheatre
16 Garden Museum
17 Seized Antiquities Museum
18 Burg at-Turfa
19 Carriage Museum
20 Second Ticket Office
21 Car Park
22 Burg al-Muqattam
23 Bab al-Gabal (Entrance)

24 Bab al-Qalla
25 Mosque of an-Nasir Mohammed
26 Bir Yousef (Salah ad-Din's Well)
27 Mosque of Mohammed Ali
28 Toilet
29 Tourist Police
30 Cafe
31 Gawhara Palace & Museum
32 Mint

some of the finest Islamic monuments in Cairo. Which didn't stop Mohammed Ali – who rose to power when the French left – from demolishing them. The only Mamluk structure left standing was a single mosque, which was used as a stable. Mohammed Ali completely remodelled the rest of the Citadel and crowned it with the Turkish-style mosque that currently dominates Cairo's eastern skyline.

After Mohammed Ali's grandson and heir Ismail moved the royal presence out of the Citadel (to Abdeen), it was used as a military garrison. The British Army was barracked here in WWII to be replaced by Egyptian soldiers after 1952. The soldiers still have a small foothold but the Citadel has now almost entirely been given over to the tourists.

Anyone interested in knowing more should pick up William Lyster's *The Citadel: A Guide* or a map called *The Citadel*

to Ibn Tulun published by SPARE. Both are widely available in Cairo's bookshops.

The Citadel is divided into the Lower, Southern and Northern enclosures. Entrance is via the Southern Enclosure.

The Citadel is open daily from 8 am to 5 pm in winter (6 pm in summer) but the museums close at 4.30 pm. Admission is E£20. Plus E£20. Plus E£6.

Southern Enclosure This is the main tourist area, presided over by the **Mosque of Mohammed Ali**. Modelled along classic Turkish lines, this mosque took 18 years to build (1830-48) and then the domes had to be demolished and rebuilt later. It's a building that has never found much favour with those who have written about Cairo and has been variously described as being unimaginative, lacking in grace and resembling a great toad. Oblivious to the criticism, the mosque's patron Mohammed Ali lies in the marble tomb on the right as you enter. Note the chintzy clock in the central courtyard, this was a gift from King Louis-Philippe of France in thanks for the pharaonic obelisk that adorns the Place de la Concorde in Paris. It was damaged on delivery and has yet to be repaired.

Dwarfed by Mohammed Ali's mosque, the **Mosque of an-Nasir Mohammed** (1318) is the Citadel's sole surviving Mamluk structure. The interior is a little sparse because the Ottoman sultan Selim I had it stripped of its marble, but the twisted finials of the minarets are interesting for their covering of glazed tiles, something rarely seen in Egypt. The mosque has a separate admission fee of E£6.

Facing the entrance of the An-Nasir Mohammed mosque is a mock Gothic gateway leading out onto a terrace that has superb **views** across Islamic Cairo to the tower blocks of Downtown and, on a clear day, the Pyramids at Giza. The **Police Museum**, at the northern end of the terrace, has an intriguing Assassination Room, with text and photos relating, among other things, to the various attempts on President Nasser's life. Curiously, the somewhat more successful assassination of Sadat fails to get a mention. Immediately below the Police Museum, in the Citadel's Lower Enclosure (closed to the public), is where the infamous massacre of the Mamluks took place (see the boxed text 'Massacre of the Mamluks' on this page).

South of Mohammed Ali's mosque is another terrace with good views, while off the terrace is the very dull **Gawhara Palace & Museum**, a lacklustre attempt to evoke 19th century court life.

Northern Enclosure Entrance to the Northern Enclosure is through the 16th century Bab al-Qalla, which faces the side of the An-Nasir Mohammed mosque. This brings you into a large area of lawn which, at its centre, contains a replica of the equine statue of Ibrahim that stands in Midan Opera. Beyond the statue and the motley as-

Massacre of the Mamluks

In addition to effacing almost all of the Mamluk structures from the Citadel, Mohammed Ali also had a damn good try at eliminating the Mamluks themselves.

On 1 March 1811 he had 500 Mamluk leaders attend a grand day of feasting and revelry at the Citadel in honour of his son's imminent departure for Mecca. When the feasting was over the Mamluks mounted up on their lavishly decorated horses and were led in procession down the narrow high-sided defile below (now the Police Museum towards the Bab al-Azab). But as they approached, the great gates were swung closed before them. Gunfire rained down from above. After the scything fusillades, Mohammed Ali's soldiers waded in with swords and axes to finish the job. Not one Mamluk escaped alive.

There is a popular legend that tells of how one Mamluk survived by jumping his horse over the Citadel walls but in fact the character in question kept his life because he didn't turn up for the feast that bloody day.

sortment of tanks and planes from the Arab-Israeli wars is Mohammed Ali's one-time Harem Palace, now the **National Military Museum**. It's largely devoted to displays of ceremonial garb, but on the top floor is an excellent scale model of the Citadel.

East of the lawns a narrow road leads to a further part of the enclosure for which there's a separate E£20 admission charge. There's little here to justify the extra money. The **Carriage Museum** contains a small collection of 19th century horse-drawn carriages which might occupy 10 minutes of your time; one building east is the pointless **Seized Antiquities Museum** (signposted in Arabic only) which houses a random and unconnected assortment of sarcophagi, jewellery, icons, and other antiquities confiscated from would-be smugglers.

For devotees of Islamic architecture, it may be worth paying the extra charge to

Mosque of Mohammed Ali, Cairo

ADAM McCROW

Entrance to Cairo's modern Opera House.

THOMAS HARTWELL

Greek Orthodox Church of St George, Cairo

EDDIE GERALD

Baron's Palace, Heliopolis, Cairo

EDDIE GERALD

One of the highlights of a trip to Egypt is sailing on a felucca along the Nile River.

The Cairo Tower offers an impressive view of the 'Mother of the World'.

Cairo University, in the heart of Giza on the west bank of the Nile, is the city's largest university.

visit the **Mosque of Suleiman Pasha** (1528), a beautiful little Ottoman-era structure topped by a cluster of domes. The painted woodwork inside has been lovingly restored over the past few years by a local art student. From a point just behind the mosque it may still be possible to get up onto the wall ramparts and walk east towards the **Burg al-Haddad** (Blacksmith's Tower). If the way is now blocked, walk across the new, hideous concrete 'amphitheatre' towards the tower and its companion, the **Burg ar-Ramla** (Sand Tower). These are two of Salah ad-Din's towers and they can be entered at ground level. Although not officially permitted, it is still physically possible to walk either through the walls or along the ramparts around to the **Burg at-Turfa** (Masterpiece Tower).

Getting To/From the Citadel It's a good 3km walk from Downtown to the Citadel. From Midan Ataba go straight down Sharia Mohammed Ali, while from Midan Tahrir the best route is via Midan Falaki to Midan Bab al-Khalq and then down Mohammed Ali. A taxi will cost E£4. By public transport, bus No 174 from Midan Ramses passes by the Citadel as does bus No 173 which starts and terminates at Midan Falaki. Bus No 905 operates between the Citadel and the Pyramids. Bus Nos 57 and 951 go to Midan Ataba and the No 54 minibus travels to Midan Tahrir. Note that all these services stop at Midan Salah ad-Din in front of the Citadel from where it's now necessary to pick up a taxi to take you around to the entrance at the back. Pay no more than E£1.

The Citadel to Ibn Tulun

Anyone visiting the Citadel should also make time for the Mosque-Madrassa of Sultan Hassan, one of Cairo's most awesome pieces of monumental medieval Islamic architecture. The backstreets around this area are also filled with many smaller monuments which, while not justifying a trip on their own, make worthwhile detours if you are in the area. For instance, anyone walking along Sharia Mohammed Ali is strongly advised to swing by the **Madrassa of Sunqur Sa'adi**, knock on the door and ask to see the Mevlevi Theatre, a beautifully restored Dervish whirling space; it's also worth halting at the **Sabil-Kuttab of Qaitbey** to take a look at the intricate marble inlay.

Mosque-Madrassa of Sultan Hassan
Regarded as the finest piece of early Mamluk architecture in Cairo, this great structure (built 1356-63) was designed to fulfil the role of mosque and *madrassa* (theological school), with four iwans off a central court each devoted to one of the main schools of Sunni Islam. At the rear of the eastern iwan is an especially beautiful *mihrab* (niche indicating the direction of Mecca) which is flanked by stolen Crusader columns. To the right is the bronze door which leads through to the sultan's mausoleum.

Note that the minarets are of unequal height. The southernmost of the two is the second highest in Cairo (68m) after that of the new Al-Fath mosque on Midan Ramses; it was originally matched by a twin which collapsed in 1659 and was replaced by the one you see today.

Try to visit this place in the morning when the sun lights up the mausoleum portion of the mosque – the effect is quite eerie. The mosque is open from 8 am to 5 pm (6 pm in summer) daily. Entrance is E£12 (E£6 for students) and the ticket office is at the rear of the mosque.

Mosque of ar-Rifai Built in imitation Mamluk-style, this mosque actually dates from as recently as 1912 (construction began in 1867). Members of modern Egypt's royal family, including Ismail and King Farouk, are buried here as is the last Shah of Iran. Opening hours and ticket prices are the same as for the Mosque-Madrassa of Sultan Hassan. Baksheesh is required to view the tombs of the royals, which lie off to the left of the entrance.

Mosque of ibn Tulun Ibn Tulun was sent to rule Cairo in the 9th century by the

THE CITADEL TO IBN TULUN

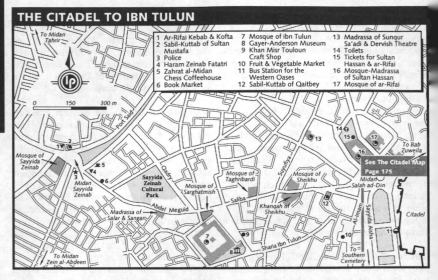

1	Ar-Rifai Kebab & Kofta	7	Mosque of ibn Tulun	13	Madrassa of Sunqur
2	Sabil-Kuttab of Sultan	8	Gayer-Anderson Museum		Sa'adi & Dervish Theatre
	Mustafa	9	Khan Misr Touloun	14	Toilets
3	Police		Craft Shop	15	Tickets for Sultan
4	Haram Zeinab Fatatri	10	Fruit & Vegetable Market		Hassan & ar-Rifai
5	Zahrat al-Midan	11	Bus Station for the	16	Mosque-Madrassa
	Chess Coffeehouse		Western Oases		of Sultan Hassan
6	Book Market	12	Sabil-Kuttab of Qaitbey	17	Mosque of ar-Rifai

Abbasid caliph of Baghdad. He had the mosque built between 876 and 879 AD, making it the city's oldest intact functioning Islamic monument. It's quite unlike any other mosque in Cairo mainly because the inspiration is almost entirely Iraqi – the closest thing to it are the ancient mosques of Samarra.

To the original Iraqi model, Ibn Tulun added some innovations of his own. According to architectural historians this is the first structure to use the pointed arch – a good 200 years before Christianity adopted it for the European Gothic arch. Constructed entirely of mud-brick and timber, the mosque covers 6½ acres in area, large enough for the whole community to assemble for Friday prayers. Although the mosque is still in use, these days the congregation is much more modest and is usually accommodated in just the south-eastern arcaded sanctuary.

After wandering around the massive courtyard, you should climb the spiral minaret reached from the outer, moat-like courtyard which, although originally created to keep the secular city at a distance,

was at one time filled with shops and stalls. The top of the minaret is the best place to appreciate the grandeur and geometric simplicity of the mosque, and the views of the Citadel to the east and Cairo in general are magnificent.

Opening hours for the mosque and minaret are from 8 am to 6 pm; admission is E£6, plus baksheesh for slippers to put over your shoes in the mosque (unless you just want to take your shoes off).

Gayer-Anderson Museum This museum is almost an annexe of the Ibn Tulun mosque, and can be reached from the outer court through a gateway to the south of the main entrance.

Sometimes called Beit al-Kretliya (House of the Cretan Woman), the museum is actually two 16th century houses joined together. It gets its current name from a British major, John Gayer-Anderson, who restored and furnished the houses between 1935 and 1942. The attraction of the museum is not the exhibits themselves but the houses, their puzzle of rooms and the decor. There's a

Persian room with exquisite tiling and a Damascus room with its walls and ceiling patterned with lacquer and gold. There's also an enchanting mashrabiyya gallery that looks down upon a magnificent *qa'a* (reception room) with a central marble fountain, decorated ceiling beams and carpet covered alcoves. The house was used as a location in both *The Spy Who Loved Me* and *Ruby Cairo* (see the boxed text 'Egypt at the Cinema' on page 81).

The museum is open from 8 am to 4 pm daily (closed from noon to 1 pm on Friday). Admission is E£16 (E£8 for students). Those who want to use a camera or video must pay another E£10/25.

Across the street is the Khan Misr Touloun, a good handicrafts emporium, for more information see the Shopping section later in this chapter.

Northern Cemetery

The Northern Cemetery is one half of a vast necropolis known popularly as the City of the Dead. The lurid, arcade-game name refers to the fact that the cemeteries are not only resting places for Cairo's dead and buried but for the living too.

The Northern Cemetery began as an area of desert outside the city walls which offered the Mamluk sultans and emirs the unlimited building space denied them in the already densely packed city. The vast mausoleum complexes they built were more than just tombs, they were also meant as places for entertaining. This is part of an Egyptian tradition which has its roots in pharaonic times when people would picnic among the graves. Even the humblest of family tombs were designed to include a room where visitors could stay overnight. Naturally, the city's homeless took to squatting in the tombs. This was happening as far back as the 14th century, leading to the situation today where the living and dead coexist comfortably side by side. In some tomb-houses cenotaphs serve as tables and washing is strung between headstones. The municipality has running water, gas and electricity, and there's a local police station

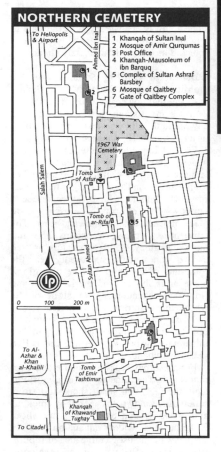

NORTHERN CEMETERY

To Heliopolis & Airport

1 Khanqah of Sultan Inal
2 Mosque of Amir Qurqumas
3 Post Office
4 Khanqah-Mausoleum of ibn Barquq
5 Complex of Sultan Ashraf Barsbey
6 Mosque of Qaitbey
7 Gate of Qaitbey Complex

1967 War Cemetery

Salah Salem

Tomb of Asfur

Tomb of ar-Rifai

Sultan Ahmed

0   100   200 m

To Al-Azhar & Khan al-Khalili

Tomb of Emir Tashtimur

Khanqah of Khawand Tughay

To Citadel

and even a post office. On Fridays and holidays visitors flock here to picnic and pay their respects to the dead.

The easiest way to get to the Northern Cemetery is to walk east along Sharia al-Azhar from Al-Hussein. As you breast the top of the hill, bear right, under the flyover and straight on along the dusty road between the tombs. Follow this road to the left then right. You'll pass by the large crumbling domed Tomb of Emir Tashtimur on your left, about 100m further on a narrow lane goes off to the left passing under a stone archway. This archway is the gate to the former compound of Qaitbey whose splendid mosque is immediately ahead.

Mosque of Qaitbey Sultan Qaitbey, a prolific builder, was the last Mamluk leader with any real power in Egypt. He ruled for 28 years and, though he was as ruthless as any Mamluk sultan, he was also something of an aesthete. His mosque (completed in 1474 and depicted on the E£1 note) is widely agreed to mark the pinnacle of Islamic building in Cairo. The interior has four iwans around a central court that is suffused with light from large, lattice-screened windows. It's one of the most pleasant places in Cairo to sit a while and relax. The adjacent tomb chamber contains the cenotaphs of Qaitbey and his two sisters, as well as two stones which supposedly bear the footprints of the Prophet. The true glory, however, is above in the interlaced star and floral carving adorning the stone dome, which in its intricacy and delicacy was never surpassed here in Cairo or anywhere else in the Islamic world – climb the minaret for the best view. Admission is E£6 (E£3 for students).

From Qaitbey cross the square and continue north. The cemetery has an almost village-like feel with small shops and street sellers, and sandy paths pecked by chickens and nosed around by goats. After about 250m the street widens out and on the right a stone wall encloses a large area of rubble-strewn ground that was formerly the complex of Sultan Ashraf Barsbey.

Complex of Sultan Ashraf Barsbey
Though not as sophisticated as the one topping Qaitbey, the dome here is carved with a beautiful star pattern. Inside, there is some fine marble flooring and a beautiful *minbar* (pulpit) inlaid with ivory. Look for the guard or have one of the children in the area find him, he'll let you in for baksheesh.

Khanqah-Mausoleum of ibn Barquq
Ibn means 'son of', and this is the mau-

soleum of Farag, son of Barquq, whose great madrassa and mausoleum stands on Bein al-Qasreen (see under North of Khan al-Khalili earlier this chapter). Completed in 1411, the khanqah is an imposing fortress-like building with high, sheer facades, and twin minarets and domes. If you go through into the interior courtyard you can see the small monastic cells off the arcades. There's a tomb chamber under each dome, one for women, one for men. Both ceilings have been repainted in recent years and look great. It's also possible to get up onto the roof and climb the minarets. It's open from 8 am to 5 pm, admission is E£6.

Back to Al-Hussein North of Ibn Barquq are two large adjacent complexes, the **Mosque of Amir Qurqumas** (1507) and the **Khanqah of Sultan Inal** (1456), both of which have been the subject of extensive restoration work by a Polish team. Neither are accessible to the public just yet.

Rather than just retracing your steps, from Ibn Barquq, walk straight ahead from the entrance, passing the post office on your left, until you come to a small, elongated mausoleum; turn left immediately after this and a straight walk of 1km down Sharia Sultan Ahmed will bring you back to the road leading to the underpass.

OLD CAIRO

Broadly speaking, Old Cairo (known in Egyptian as 'Masr al-Qadima', with a glottal stop 'Q') incorporates the entire area south of Garden City down to the quarter known to foreigners as Coptic Cairo. Most people visiting this area head straight to the latter, from where it is possible to explore sights further to the north-east, such as the Mosque of Amr ibn al-As and the archaeological site of ancient Fustat. The Early Islamic-era Nilometer on the island of Rhoda is also best visited from Coptic Cairo.

This is a very traditional part of Cairo and appropriate dress is essential. Visitors of either sex wearing shorts or with bare shoulders will not be allowed into churches or mosques.

OLD CAIRO

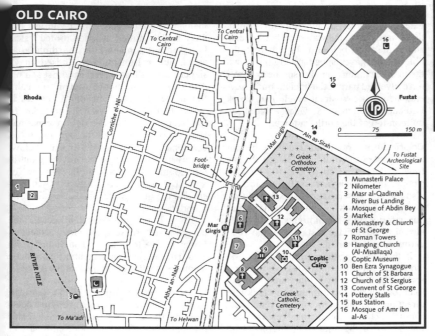

1 Munasterli Palace
2 Nilometer
3 Masr al-Qadimah
    River Bus Landing
4 Mosque of Abdin Bey
5 Market
6 Monastery & Church
    of St George
7 Roman Towers
8 Hanging Church
    (Al-Muallaqa)
9 Coptic Museum
10 Ben Ezra Synagogue
11 Church of St Barbara
12 Church of St Sergius
13 Convent of St George
14 Pottery Stalls
15 Bus Station
16 Mosque of Amr ibn
    al-As

Coptic Cairo

Coptic Cairo is the heartland of Egypt's Christian community, as well as being the oldest part of modern-day Cairo. Seemingly oblivious to the growth and chaos which it has spawned, the tightly walled enclave remains a haven of tranquillity and peace.

Archaeologists claim that there was a small Nile-side settlement on this site as far back as the 6th century BC on which the Romans later established a fortress, called Babylon-in-Egypt, early in the 2nd century AD. The name Babylon is most likely a Roman corruption of 'Per-hapi-en-on' or 'Estate of the Nile God at On', a pharaonic name for what was the former port for On (ancient Heliopolis).

Predating the arrival of Islam in Egypt, Babylon has always been a stronghold of Christianity (see the History section in the Facts about Egypt chapter). At one time there were more than 20 churches clustered within less than one square kilometre, although the number is down to only five today. They are linked by narrow cobbled alleyways running between high stone walls, and the feel of the place is quite similar to parts of the Old City of Jerusalem. In fact, after the Jews were exiled from their holy city in 70 AD, some found refuge in Egypt and the country's oldest existing synagogue is here in Coptic Cairo.

There are two entrances to the Coptic Cairo compound: a sunken staircase beside the footbridge over the metro gives access to most churches and the synagogue, while the main entrance is for visiting the Coptic Museum and Church of the Virgin. Eventually, when restoration work is finished, the two parts of the compound will be reconnected.

Roman Towers The main entrance to the compound is between the remains of the two round towers of Babylon's western gate. Built in 98 AD by Emperor Trajan, these were part of the waterside battlements and at the time, before it shifted west, the Nile would have lapped up right against them. Excavations on the southern tower have revealed part of the ancient quay, several metres below street level. The Greek Orthodox Church of St George has been built on top of the northern tower.

Coptic Museum Founded in 1908 the museum houses Coptic art from Graeco-Roman times to the Islamic era (300 to 1000 AD) in a collection drawing not just from Cairo but also from the desert monasteries and Nubia. It's split into two wings, the old and the new but unfortunately the old wing is currently closed while damage sustained in the 1992 earthquake is repaired.

In the new wing the exhibits (stonework, woodwork, manuscripts, glass and ceramics) are housed on two floors and arranged in chronological order in an anti-clockwise direction. Explanations are in French and English. The rooms themselves are very much part of the attraction, adorned with elaborately painted ceilings, fountains and mashrabiyya screens.

The museum is open daily from 9 am to 5 pm. Admission is E£16 (E£8 for students); photography permits are E£10, video permits are E£100.

There's a pleasant but expensive cafe in the southern part of the garden where there is also a gate leading through to the Hanging Church. If this gate is locked, go back out onto the main street running parallel to the metro and there's another entrance south of the Roman tower.

Hanging Church Dedicated to the Virgin Mary, this church is more popularly called the Hanging Church ('Al-Muallaqa', The Suspended) because it is built on top of the Water Gate of Roman Babylon. It's the most famous, the most beautiful and possibly even the oldest Christian place of worship in Cairo, dating back in all likelihood to the 4th century.

The interior of the church, renovated many times throughout the centuries, has three barrel-vaulted, wooden-roofed aisles. Ivory inlaid screens hide the three altar areas, but in front of them, raised on 13 slender pillars that represent Christ and his disciples, is a fine pulpit, used only on Palm Sunday each year. One of the pillars is darker than the rest, symbolising Judas. In the baptistery off to the right a panel has been cut out of the floor through which you can look down on the Water Gate below; however, it's hard to make anything out in the gloom so also look out the window for a good view of one of the gate's twin towers and the green water stagnating about its foundations.

There is no admission fee because the church is still in use. Coptic mass is held on Friday from 8 to 11 am and on Sunday from 7 to 10 am. The ancient liturgical Coptic language is still used in most of the services.

Monastery & Church of St George Back on Sharia Mar Girgis, the first doorway north of the main entrance leads through to the Greek Orthodox Monastery and Church of St George (in Arabic he's called Mar Girgis), named after one of the most popular Christian saints in the Middle East. He was a conscript in the Roman army who was executed in 303 AD for tearing up a copy of the Emperor Diocletian's decree that forbade the practice of Christianity. There has been a church dedicated to him in Coptic Cairo since the 10th century but this particular one dates from 1909. The interior is a bit gutted from past fires, but the stained glass windows are bright and colourful. The monastery next door is closed to the public.

Convent of St George If you descend the sunken staircase by the footbridge, then the first doorway on your left along the alleyway leads into the courtyard of the Convent of St George. The convent is closed to visitors but you can step down into the main hall and the chapel. Inside the latter is a beautiful, wooden door, almost 8m high, behind which is a small room still used for the chain-wrapping ritual which symbolises the persecution of St George during the Roman occupation. Visitors wishing to be blessed are welcome to be wrapped by the patient nuns who will then intone the requisite prayers.

Churches of St Sergius & St Barbara

To get to St Sergius, also called Abu Serga, leave the Convent of St George by the same door you entered, turn left and walk down the lane, following it around to the right and then take a left for the church entrance. This church is supposedly built over one of the spots where the Holy Family rested after fleeing from King Herod; the crypt in question is reached by descending some steps to the right of the altar but it's been flooded for some time now. Every year, on 1 June, a special mass is held here to commemorate the event. The church is open from 8 am to 4 pm daily.

Continuing on along the alley brings you to Ben Ezra on the right and to the Church of St Barbara on the left. St Barbara's is dedicated to the saint who was beaten to death by her father for trying to convert him to Christianity. Her relics supposedly rest in a small chapel to the left of the nave.

If you walk on past the church, an iron gate on the left leads through to a large **Greek Orthodox cemetery** the peace of which is usually shattered by the shouts and cheers from a neighbouring football pitch and sports field.

Ben Ezra Synagogue Ben Ezra, Egypt's oldest synagogue, dates from the 9th century, though it occupies the shell of a 4th century Christian church. In the 12th century the synagogue was restored by Abraham Ben Ezra, Rabbi of Jerusalem, from whom it takes its name. Several legends are connected with the synagogue. It is said that the temple of the prophet Jeremiah once stood on the same spot and that this is where he gathered the Jews after they fled from Nebuchadnezzar, destroyer of their Jerusalem temple. There is also a spring which is supposed to mark the place where the pharaoh's daughter found

Moses in the reeds, and where Mary drew water to wash Jesus.

Fustat

Fustat was founded in 642 AD as a garrison for the conquering armies of Amr ibn al-As. It gradually took on a more permanent aspect and became a thriving commercial city and the first Islamic capital of Egypt. Fustat was razed during the reign of the Fatimids and under the Mamluks it became a rubbish dump. It has remained an uninhabited wasteland ever since.

The fact that Fustat has lain dormant and largely uninhabited for the 600 years since its destruction makes it one of the most important Islamic archaeological sites in the world. It was first excavated early this century and most of the finds (predominantly pottery) are on display in the Museum of Islamic Art. Although it takes enormous leaps of the imagination to make anything of the sun-baked earthen mounds and trenches, it's possible to identify traces of alleyways, houses, wells and water-pipe systems surrounded by a low wall. It costs E£6 to visit the site.

To get there from Coptic Cairo's main entrance, head north along Sharia Mar Girgis, and take the first road to the right (Sharia Ain as-Sirah), follow it for about 500m until you see a large unmarked gate on your left that opens onto a short path leading to the ruins.

Potters Fustat has always been home to potters. The smoke you see rising across the moonscape is from kilns. Nestled beneath the smouldering mounds are hundreds of workshops turning out pots, urns, dishes and pipes for sewers and drainage. The pottery factories line the entire length of Sharia Ain as-Sirah and though they look unwelcoming the inhabitants don't mind visitors wandering around and observing. If you are looking to buy, then Sharia Mar Girgis in the area around the Mosque of Amr is lined with pottery stalls.

Mosque of Amr ibn al-As

Although hardly any of the original structure remains, this mosque can claim direct descent from the first mosque ever built in Egypt. It was constructed in 642 AD by the victorious invader Amr (the general who conquered Egypt for Islam) and was founded on the site where he'd first pitched his tent. The original structure is said to have been made of palm trunks thatched with leaves but it was rebuilt and expanded until it reached its current size in 827 AD. The reconstruction didn't end there and the mosque has continued to be amended and reworked until as recently as 1983. There's little of interest to see inside, although of the 200 or so columns supporting the ceiling no two are said to be the same. Admission is E£6.

Beside the mosque is a bus station from which several buses run up to Midan Tahrir including Nos 134, 135, 412, 444 and 814; the fare is 25pt.

Rhoda

Rhoda has a history that dates back to pharaonic times when it was part of the territory of ancient Heliopolis. During the Roman era it was the site of a fortress, twin to that at Babylon, while in the 13th century, the island contained palaces, mosques, more than 50 towers and extensive gardens (the name Rhoda means 'garden' in Arabic). As a result of power shifts, Rhoda was abandoned and later quarried for stone. Until the middle of this century the island remained undeveloped and largely agricultural but during the post-Revolution period it experienced a building boom. Today it's an extremely drab and shabby residential district notable only for the Manial Palace Museum at the northern end and the Nilometer in the south. The distance between the two is quite substantial and Manial is best visited from Garden City (see the Garden City & Manial section earlier in this chapter) while the Nilometer is best reached from Old Cairo.

Nilometer Built in the 9th century to measure the rise and fall of the Nile, the Nilometer helped predict the state of the annual harvest. If the Nile rose to 16 cubits (a cubit is about the length of a forearm) this held great promise for the crops, and people would celebrate. The conical dome was added when the Nilometer was restored in the 19th century. The measuring device, a graduated column, is well below the level of the Nile in a paved area at the bottom of a flight of steps. The admission fee is E£6.

Umm Kolthum Museum Occupying a riverside site next to the Nilometer, the Munasterli Palace (built 1851) has served in recent years as a lacklustre arts centre but at present it's undergoing a major refitting for its new role as a museum dedicated to the life of legendary songstress Umm Kolthum (see under Music in the Arts section in the Facts about Egypt chapter). The museum will contain photographs and personal effects as well as an audio library of every performance and interview the great diva ever gave. The museum is due to open in December 1999.

Getting There & Away

By far the easiest way of getting down to Old Cairo is on the Metro: Mar Girgis station is right outside the Coptic compound. The ride costs 30pt from Midan Tahrir and trains run every few minutes. There are buses running between Tahrir and Old Cairo but they are incredibly crowded. However, the bus trip back to Tahrir isn't as bad because you can get on at the terminal, beside the Amr ibn al-As mosque, before the bus fills up.

The slow way, but the most pleasant way if you have the time, is to get a river bus from the Maspero terminal near the Radio & Television building, just north of the Ramses Hilton in central Cairo. Check it's going to Masr al-Qadima as not all do (see under River Bus in the Getting Around section later in this chapter for route details). The ride takes about 50 minutes and costs 25pt. The last boat back to Maspero leaves at 4.15 pm. From the landing at Old Cairo cross the Corniche and head down the street with the Marlboro-emblazoned shop on the corner; at the end of the street turn left and walk straight along Sharia Athar an-Nabi for about 250m until you come to the footbridge over the metro line.

GEZIRA & ZAMALEK

Uninhabited until the mid-19th century, Gezira (which means 'island') was a 3.5km by 1km strip of alluvial land rising up out of the Nile opposite Bulaq. Following the creation of a new city (modern-day Downtown) on the flood plain of the river's west bank, the khedive Ismail built a great palace on the island and had much of it landscaped as a vast royal garden. In the early years of this century, as Cairo was experiencing a land development boom, the palace grounds were partitioned, sold off and built upon.

The island today divides almost equally into two: the southern part is largely green and leafy and retains the name Gezira, while the north is an upmarket residential district known as Zamalek.

Gezira

Gezira is best approached across the Tahrir Bridge from Midan Tahrir, which brings you to the small Midan Saad Zaghloul presided over by a statue of a stout man in a tarboosh, representing Saad Zaghloul the nationalist leader of the 1930s. To the right of the bridge is the beginning of a new Nileside **pedestrian Corniche** which will soon allow you to walk north up the shore of the island into Zamalek. Between the promenade and the main road is a narrow strip of greenery known as the **Andalusian Garden**, a small park complete with pharaonic obelisk that costs 50pt to enter.

Opera House & Museum of Modern Art

Immediately west of Midan Saad Zaghloul are the immaculately groomed grounds of the Opera House, a US$30 million complex that includes the Museum of Modern Art, the Hanagar Art Gallery, a music library, a planetarium (closed at the time of research) and various performance spaces. Opened only in 1988, the Opera House itself is a modern take on traditional Islamic design, and was a gift from the Japanese. You can only enter the Opera House itself during performances but the grounds are pleasant to walk around. They contain the Museum of Modern Art (☎ 342 0592), home to a fairly limited collection of 20th century Egyptian painting, some of which is certainly worth seeing (see Art in the Facts about Egypt chapter). There are also temporary exhibitions. The museum is open daily (except Monday) from 10 am to 1 pm and from 5 to 9.30 pm. Admission is E£10 (E£5 for students).

Mahmoud Mokhtar Museum At the time of writing, this museum had failed in its search for a new home and, consequently, was closed. Mokhtar (1891-1934) was the sculptor laureate of Egypt; he was responsible for Saad Zaghloul on the nearby midan and for the Mother of Egypt statue outside the entrance to the zoo. The museum's collection contains some of his lesser works. Check with the tourist office for its new location.

Cairo Tower The story has it that the tower, completed in 1961 and looking like a 185m-high wickerwork tube, was built as a thumb to the nose at the Americans who had given Nasser the money used for its construction to buy US arms. After the Pyramids it's now the city's most famous landmark. The view from the top is excellent – clearest in the early morning or late afternoon. There's an expensive revolving restaurant on top as well as a cheaper cafeteria. The entrance fee for the tower, if you're going to the top, is E£10 (plus E£10 for a video permit). It's open daily, hours for the viewing area are 9 am to midnight. You might be greeted with quite a long queue at dusk.

Zamalek

Occupying the northern part of the island of Gezira, Zamalek is an attractive residential district with a continental European tinge. It has few tourist sites but it's a pleasant place to wander and an even better place to eat

CAIRO

MOHANDISEEN, AGOUZA & ZAMALEK

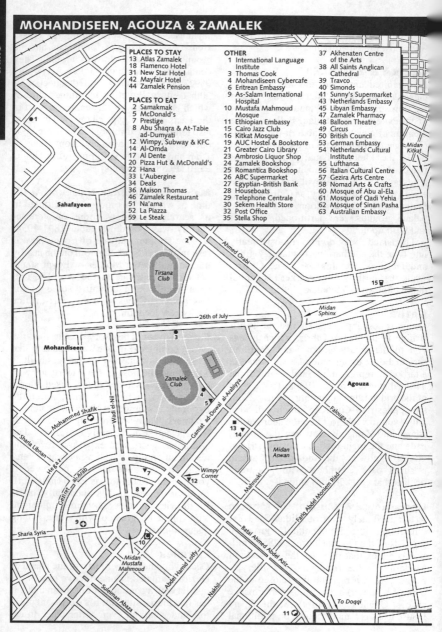

PLACES TO STAY
13 Atlas Zamalek
18 Flamenco Hotel
31 New Star Hotel
42 Mayfair Hotel
44 Zamalek Pension

PLACES TO EAT
2 Samakmak
5 McDonald's
7 Prestige
8 Abu Shagra & At-Tabie
   ad-Dumyati
12 Wimpy, Subway & KFC
14 Al-Omda
17 Al Dente
20 Pizza Hut & McDonald's
22 Hana
33 L'Aubergine
34 Deals
36 Maison Thomas
46 Zamalek Restaurant
51 Na'ama
52 La Piazza
59 Le Steak

OTHER
1 International Language
   Institute
3 Thomas Cook
4 Mohandiseen Cybercafe
6 Eritrean Embassy
9 As-Salam International
   Hospital
10 Mustafa Mahmoud
   Mosque
11 Ethiopian Embassy
15 Cairo Jazz Club
16 Kitkat Mosque
19 AUC Hostel & Bookstore
21 Greater Cairo Library
23 Ambrosio Liquor Shop
24 Zamalek Bookshop
25 Romantica Bookshop
26 ABC Supermarket
27 Egyptian-British Bank
28 Houseboats
29 Telephone Centrale
30 Sekem Health Store
32 Post Office
35 Stella Shop

37 Akhenaten Centre
   of the Arts
38 All Saints Anglican
   Cathedral
39 Travco
40 Simonds
41 Sunny's Supermarket
43 Netherlands Embassy
45 Libyan Embassy
47 Zamalek Pharmacy
48 Balloon Theatre
49 Circus
50 British Council
53 German Embassy
54 Netherlands Cultural
   Institute
55 Lufthansa
56 Italian Cultural Centre
57 Gezira Arts Centre
58 Nomad Arts & Crafts
60 Mosque of Abu al-Ela
61 Mosque of Qadi Yehia
62 Mosque of Sinan Pasha
63 Australian Embassy

MOHANDISEEN, AGOUZA & ZAMALEK

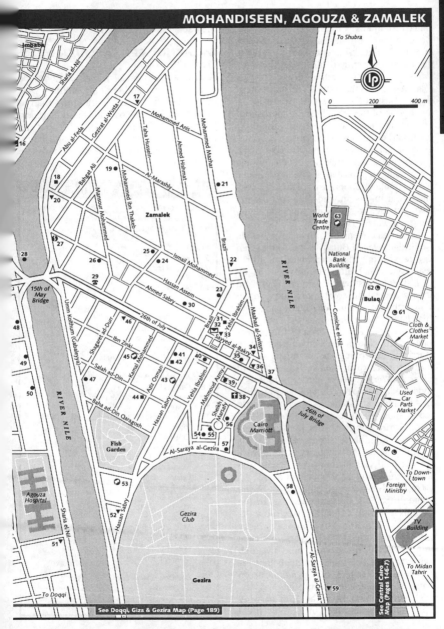

To Shubra

0   200   400 m

Imbaba

Sharia el-Nil

16

Abu al-Feda

Gezirat al-Wusta

Bangat Ali

Mansour Mohammed

17

Mohammed Anis

Mohammed Mazhar

Taha Hussein

Ahmed Hishmat

Al-Marashly

19

Mohammed Ibn Thaleb

Zamalek

21

18

20

27

28

25

26

24

Ismail Mohammed

Brazil

22

29

Hassan Assem

23

Ahmed Sabry

30

World Trade Centre

63

National Bank Building

62

61

RIVER NILE

Coniche el-Nil

Bulaq

Cloth & Clothes Market

15th of May Bridge

48

49

50

Umm Kolthum (Gabalayya)

26th of July

Shagaret ad-Durr

Ibn Zinki

Kamal Mohammed

Salah ad-Din

Aziz Osman

46

45

47

44

43

41

42

40

Brazil

Yehia Ibrahim

31

32

33

Sayyed al-Bakry

34

35

36

37

Maahad al-Swissy

Mahmoud Azmy

39

38

Baha ad-Din Qaragosh

Hassan Sabry

Yehia Ibrahim

Sheikh Marsafy

Used Car Parts Market

26th of July Bridge

RIVER NILE

Fish Garden

54 55

56

57

Cairo Marriott

60

To Down-town

Foreign Ministry

Agouza Hospital

53

52

Hassan Sabry

Al-Saraya al-Gezira

58

TV Building

51

Gezira Club

Al-Saraya al-Gezira

To Midan Tahrir

To Doqqi

Gezira

59

See Doqqi, Giza & Gezira Map (Page 189)

See Central Cairo Map (Pages 146-7)

(Le Steak, L'Aubergine, Maison Thomas or Hana restaurants) or drink (L'Aubergine, Deals or the Cairo Marriott), see the Places to Eat and Entertainment sections later in this chapter for more details.

The main street is 26th of July which cuts east-west across the island. The junction of sharias Hassan Sabry and Al-Brazil is the focal point of the area. There's good shopping around here, particularly at Sunny's (a supermarket on Aziz Osman that is something of an institution among Cairo's expat community), and three of the city's best newsstands are located at the crossroads. Just a couple of doors east of Hassan Sabry on 26th of July is Simonds, the best cafe in town at which to read your papers – if you can get a seat.

At the eastern end of 26th of July, beside the bridge over to Bulaq, is the **Akhenaten Centre of Arts** housed in a luxurious European-style villa built earlier this century by an Egyptian aristocratic family. There are always several different exhibitions on, so it's worth dropping in; see Activities later in this chapter for opening hours.

Immediately south of 26th of July, overlooking the Nile is the salmon-pink **Cairo Marriott**, occupying the premises of Ismail's former royal palace. It has a good bakery and an attractive garden, which is a good place for a beer. Behind the Marriott, on Al-Saraya al-Gezira, is a beautiful little neo-Islamic villa that opened in spring 1999 as the **Gezira Centre of Arts**, housing a permanent exhibition of Islamic ceramics plus several galleries for temporary exhibitions – see Art Galleries in the Activities section later in this chapter for opening hours.

On the Nile-side road on the west of the island is the **Fish Garden**, once part of the grounds of Ismail's Gezira Palace (now the Marriott). It's a small area of grassy hillocks and tree-shaded lovers' benches with an aquarium grotto where the fish swim (or float belly up) in tunnels that resemble bomb shelters. It's open daily from 9 am to 3.30 pm, entry costs 50pt.

The **view** north from the 15th of May Bridge contains a sweep of the Nile lined with houseboats and the Kitkat mosque in the background is beautiful.

MOHANDISEEN, AGOUZA & DOQQI

A map of Cairo in Baedecker's 1929 guide to Egypt shows nothing on the Nile's west bank other than a hospital and the road to the Pyramids. The hospital is still there, set back off the Corniche in Agouza, but it's now hemmed in on all sides by an unsightly rash of mid-rise housing blocks that shot up

DOQQI, GIZA & GEZIRA

PLACES TO STAY
11 Pyramisa Hotel
24 HI Manial Youth Hostel

PLACES TO EAT
20 KFC
22 TGI Friday's
26 KFC
29 Abu Shaqra

OTHER
1   Agricultural Museum
2   Syrian Embassy
3   Masr International Hospital
4   Kenyan Embassy
5   Anglo-American Hospital
6   Casanova's Disco
7   Museum of Modern Art
8   Opera House
9   Mahmoud Mokhtar Museum
10 Police
12 Mahmoud Khalil Museum
13 Jordanian Embassy
14 Cinema Tahrir
15 TNT Skypack
16 University River Bus Stop
17 Saudia Arabian Embassy
18 Lebanese Embassy
19 Israeli Embassy
21 French Embassy
23 Manial River Bus Stop
25 Mosque
27 MSC (Student Cards)
28 Manial Palace Museum
30 Western Union/Federal Express
31 Canadian Embassy
32 DHL
33 Dok Dok Felucca Point
34 UK Embassy
35 Feluccas

DOQQI, GIZA & GEZIRA

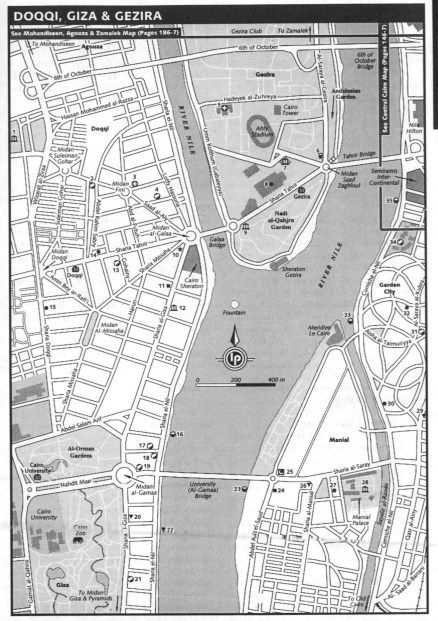

See Mohandiseen, Agouza & Zamalek Map (Pages 186-7)

See Central Cairo Map (Pages 146-7)

Gezira Club   To Zamalek

To Mohandiseen   Agouza

6th of October

6th of October

Gezira

6th of October Bridge

Hassan Mohammed al-Razza

Doqqi

Midan Suleiman Gohar

Hadeyek al-Zuhreya

Cairo Tower

Andalusian Garden

Nile Hilton

Ahly Stadium

RIVER NILE

Umm Kolthum (Gabalayya)

Tahrir Bridge

Midan Saad Zaghloul

Semiramis Inter-Continental

Midan Fini

Midan al-Galaa

Sharia Tahrir

Gezira

Nadi al-Qahira Garden

Galaa Bridge

Midan Doqqi

Cairo Sheraton

Sheraton Gezira

RIVER NILE

Garden City

Midan Al-Missaha

Fountain

Meridien Le Caire

Al-Orman Gardens

Cairo University

Nahdit Masr

0   200   400 m

Manial

Cairo University

Midan al-Gamaa

University (Al-Gamaa) Bridge

Sharia al-Saray

Manial Palace

Cairo Zoo

Giza

To Midan Giza & Pyramids

To Old Cairo

during the 1960s and 70s when Mohandis-een, Agouza and Doqqi were created as new suburbs for Egypt's emerging professional classes. The three districts remain bastions of the middle classes, home largely to those families who made good during the years of Sadat's open-door policy. Unless you happen to find concrete and traffic stimulating, the sole attraction of these areas is that they contain many of the city's better eating places (see the Places to Eat section later).

What little history there is here is on the river in the form of the **houseboats** moored off Sharia el-Nil just north of 15th of May Bridge. Known as *dahabiyyas*, these floating two storey wooden structures used to line the banks of the Nile all the way up from Giza to Imbaba forming an extensive waterborne neighbourhood. During the 1930s they were something of a tourist attraction, especially when some of the boats were converted into casinos, music halls and bordellos. Many of the houseboats continue to be rented out and they're popular with teachers at the British Council, which is just a few hundred metres south down the street.

Nile-side attractions these days are a little more sedate: there's just the **Balloon Theatre**, a venue for farcical Egyptian plays, and the big top of the **Cairo Circus**. These are both in summer only (June to August), check with the tourist office or *Egypt Today* for more details.

Agricultural Museum

It sounds dull but this one is actually quite fascinating, verging on the bizarre. Apart from stuff on life in Egyptian villages, it has giant plastic fruits, glass cases packed full of stuffed birds, and a pharaonic-era mummified bull from Memphis. The gardens are also quite relaxing. The museum is off Sharia Wizarat al-Ziraa in Doqqi, to the west of 6th of October Bridge. It's open daily (except Monday) from 9 am to 2 pm, admission is a mere 25pt.

Mahmoud Khalil Museum

This museum (☎ 336 2379) houses one of the Middle East's finest collections of 19th

century European art, including numerous sculptures by Rodin and a rich selection of French works by the likes of Delacroix, Gauguin, Lautrec, Monet and Pissaro. There are also some Reubens, Sisleys and a Picasso. The paintings are housed in a recently renovated villa that used to be the home of Mohammed Mahmoud Khalil, a noted politician during the 1940s, and was later taken over by Sadat as the official residence of the President of Egypt. It's on Sharia al-Giza on the border of Doqqi and Giza. The museum is open daily (except Monday) from 9.30 am to 6 pm, admission is an unrealistic E£25 (E£5 for students).

GIZA

A former village on the west bank of the Nile, Giza is now a vast governorate in its own right. It stretches from the Nile 18km westwards to the Pyramids, adjoining Doqqi to the north and petering out into fields then desert to the south. To Cairenes it's best known as the home of their largest university, **Cairo University**. The plaza in front of the domed main building is a favoured gathering point for demonstrations, directed more often than not against Israel which has an embassy about 500m north-east of here.

Cairo Zoo

Though bedraggled and short on funds, Cairo's zoo has managed to struggle through more than 100 years of existence – it celebrated its centennial in 1994. It remains a popular excursion for local families and couples, especially on Friday and Saturday. It's not, however, a good place for anybody who cares about animals.

The zoo is near Cairo University, between Sharia Gamiat al-Qahira (Cairo University St) and Sharia al-Giza. It's open from 9.30 am to 6 pm, admission costs E£1.

Across the road from the zoo are the small but well kept Al-Orman Gardens.

Sharia al-Haram

Sharia al-Haram, or Pyramids Rd, starts just south of Midan Giza and runs 10km south-west to the site of the great monuments. The road was laid down in the 1860s for the benefit of the Empress Eugenie, who was visiting Egypt for the inauguration of the Suez Canal. Wayside houses and places of refreshment sprang up along the route to cater to the carriage loads of tourists that followed. These were soon joined by the nightclubs and casinos for which Pyramids Rd has long been notorious. The most famous were burnt down in the 1972 riots but they were replaced, and in the 70s the strip boomed, providing girlie entertainment for the oil-rich Arabs from the Gulf who began to flock over every summer. The Gulfies still come and Pyramids Rd is still full of dodgy nightclubs, but the shows these days are not so much risqué as rip-off.

Kerdassa

Many of the scarves, galabeyyas, rugs and weavings sold in the bazaars and shops of Cairo are made in this touristy village near Giza. There is one main market street along which you'll find all of the above as well as a hideous collection of stuffed animals such as gazelles, jackals and rabbits. In fact, Kerdassa is almost as well known for its illegal trade in Egyptian wildlife as it is for crafts. The Egyptian Environmental Affairs Agency periodically raids the bazaar to try and halt this.

To get to Kerdassa, head down Al-Haram towards the Pyramids, turn right at the Maryutia Canal, and follow the road for about 5km to the village. The minibus from Midan Tahrir to the Pyramids begins and ends its trips at the junction of the canal and Al-Haram, and a local microbus does the stretch along the canal for 25pt. You can also get bus No 116 from Midan Giza all the way to Kerdassa, the trip takes 20 minutes and costs 25pt.

Wissa Wassef Art Centre

This tranquil art centre is next to the Motel Salma in Harraniyya, on the Saqqara Rd, about 4km south of Al-Haram. It specialises in woollen and cotton tapestries, as well as batiks and ceramics, and features a museum, workshops and sales gallery.

The centre is open da... pm in summer and from... winter; admission is fr... want to see tapestrie... come on Friday when th... closed. To get there, take a microbus for... Sir down the Saqqara Rd from Al-Haram. It's the same stop as for the Motel Salma.

THE PYRAMIDS

The sole survivors from the ancient Greek-listed Seven Wonders of the World, the Pyramids are the planet's oldest tourist attraction. They were already more than 2000 years old when Herodotus the Greek historian visited them, and more than 2500 years old at the time of the birth of Jesus Christ.

In the days of Herodotus (5th century BC) the Pyramids were covered with a polished white limestone casing and they must have gleamed. Unfortunately, right up until the 19th century successive builders in Egypt stripped away these outer blocks to build their palaces and mosques, exposing the softer inner core stones to the elements. Had it not been for this, the Pyramids might still stand today exactly as they were built, defying time to shift them.

But, even more than their age, the wonder of the Pyramids lies in their twin mysteries: What were they built for? And how were they built? The traditionally accepted notion that they are tombs built on the order of the pharaohs by vast teams of workers tens of thousands strong is constantly being challenged, and new theories ranging from the highly unlikely through to the wild and wacky are constantly being propounded.

Pyramidologists – for the study of the vast structures has become a science in its own right – point to the millimetre-precise carving, placement of the stones and the cosmological significance of the structures' dimensions as evidence that the Pyramids were variously constructed by angels, the devil or visitors from another planet. It's easy to laugh at such seemingly out-there ideas but visit the Giza Plateau and gaze on the Pyramids and you'll immediately see why so many people believe that such

1 Post Office
2 Oberoi Mena House
3 Tourist Office
  & Tourist Police
4 Ticket Office
5 Horse Stables
6 Tourist Police
7 Rest House
8 Solar Boat Pits
9 Eastern Cemetery
10 Queens' Pyramids
11 Solar Barque Museum
12 Western Cemetery
13 Chephren's Mortuary
   Temple
14 Sphinx Temple
15 Chephren's Valley
   Temple
16 Ticket Office
17 Cheops' Pavilion
18 Mycerinus' Valley
   Temple
19 Tomb of Khenthawes
20 Mycerinus' Mortuary
   Temple
21 Queens' Pyramids

awesome structures could only have come from unearthly origins.

The Pyramid Builders

It was neither an obsession with death, nor a fear of it, that led the ancient Egyptians to build such incredible mausoleums as the Pyramids: it was their belief in eternal life and their desire to be one with the cosmos. A pharaoh was the son of a god, and the sole receiver of the *ka* (life force), that emanated from the god. The pharaoh, in turn, conducted this vital force to his people, so in life and death he was worshipped as a god.

A pyramid was a sanctum for the preservation of the ka, and the apex of a much larger funerary complex that provided a place of worship for his loyal subjects. It also provided a visible reminder of the absolute and eternal power of the gods and their universe.

The mortuary complexes of Cheops (Khufu), Chephren (Khafre) and Mycerinus (Menkaure), who were father, son and grandson, included: a pyramid, which was the pharaoh's tomb as well as a repository for all his household goods, clothes and treasure; a funerary temple on the east side of the pyramid; pits for the storage of the pharaoh's solar boats (known as barques), which were his means of transport in the afterlife; a valley temple on the banks of the Nile; and a causeway from the river to the pyramid.

In the case of the Pyramid of Cheops, the biggest of the trio, it supposedly took 10 years to build the causeway and the massive earth ramps used as a form of scaffolding, and 20 years to raise the pyramid itself. The stone was quarried locally and from the Muqqatam Hills. Napoleon calculated that the 2½ million blocks of stone used in Cheops' Pyramid alone were enough to

What They Said About the Pyramids

We will also mention the Pyramids ... that idle and foolish exhibition of royal wealth. For the cause by most assigned for their construction is an intention on the part of those kings to exhaust their treasures, rather than leave them to successors or plotting rivals, or to keep the people from idleness.

Pliny the Elder, circa 50 AD

Soldiers, 40 centuries of history look down upon you from these Pyramids.
Napoleon, readying his forces for battle at Giza, 1798

Back to the tent, skirting the base of the Pyramid of Khephren, which seems to me inordinately huge and completely sheer; it's like a cliff, like a thing of nature, a mountain – as though it had been created just as it is, and with something terrible about it as if it were going to crush you.

Gustave Flaubert, 1849

The Pyramids looked as if they would wear out the air, boring holes in it all day long.
Florence Nightingale, 1840s

The Pyramids were a quarter of a mile away, impressive by sheer bulk and reputation; it felt odd to be living at such close quarters with anything quite so famous – it was like having the Prince of Wales at the next table in a restaurant; one kept pretending not to notice, while all the time glancing furtively to see if they were still there.

Evelyn Waugh at the Mena House Hotel, 1929

I discovered that the marvels of the Pyramids at Gizeh and the sphinx had been degraded into commodities for an enormous tourist trade.

Cecil Beaton, 1942

Very big. *Very* old.

camel owner, 1999

build a 3m-high wall around all of France. The job was done by a highly skilled corps of masons, mathematicians, surveyors and stonecutters as well as about 100,000 slaves who carried out the back-breaking task of moving and laying the stones.

Giza Plateau Basics

There are two entrances to the Plateau: the main entrance is via a continuation of Pyramids Rd which runs up past the Oberoi Mena House to the foot of the Pyramid of Cheops; the second is through the village of Nazlet as-Samaan which pushes right up to the foot of the Sphinx.

If you come by bus or taxi you're most likely to be dropped off at the end of Pyramids Rd by the Mena House Oberoi hotel. As you follow the road up to the Giza Plateau on which the Pyramids are sited, you'll pass the tourist office (open daily from around 9 am to 5 pm) off to the left, where you can check on the official rates for horse and camel rides. If anyone around here starts steering you towards the unmistakable stench of a stable, backtrack fast and ignore all the jabbering about them being able to get you onto the Plateau area without a ticket.

There's an admission fee of E£20 for the Plateau and then the same again to enter each of the Pyramids, plus another E£20 for the Solar Barque Museum (plus E£10/100 for cameras/video permits). The Pyramid chambers are open from 8.30 am to 4 pm, but the site itself is open from about 7 am to 7.30 pm. The Solar Barque Museum is open from 9 am to 4 pm (5 pm in summer).

Note that the Pyramids are closed on a rotating basis, and only two are open for the public to clamber inside at any one time. This is to allow for necessary periodic restoration work.

The Hassle

Since the time of Mark Twain, who visited in 1866 – and even before – tourists at the Pyramids have 'suffered torture that no pen can describe from the hungry appeals for baksheesh that gleamed from Arab eyes'. Every visitor to the Giza Plateau has to run the gauntlet of camel and horse hustlers, souvenir and soft drink hawkers, would-be guides, agonisingly persistent shop owners and sundry beggars. As writer Tony Horwitz comments in *Baghdad Without a Map*, it's difficult to gaze in awe at these ancient wonders with modern Egypt tugging so persistently at your sleeve.

The good news is that on our last visit most of the touts were actually being kept away from the tourists by armies of flustered young policemen. It was actually possible to walk around the Pyramids with next to no hassle. Whether the policing is a permanent measure or not though, one can only hope.

In the case that the scourge has resumed at the time of your visit, all we can say is be firm in your refusals and don't be drawn – 'No' is enough, so don't feel that you have to justify yourself.

Camels & Horses

One strategy to avoid the hassle is to hire a horse or camel and gallop, glide, or jolt through the desert around the Pyramids. At present the beasts can't be avoided as the area in front of the Pyramids resembles a chaotic, sandy paddock but there are plans for that to change and all animals to be shifted away from the immediate vicinity of the monu-

ments. This may well have happened by the time you read this. Wherever they are, beware of the camel owners, who are a pretty unscrupulous lot. Bargain fiercely and be sure of what you have agreed on. A camel should not cost more than E£15 to E£20 an hour but more than a few people have found themselves paying ridiculous amounts of money at the end of the ride to be let *off* their mounts. Women should be particularly careful – *do not* allow the camel or horse owner to climb on the animal behind you.

Hiring a horse is a better option as once you're mounted you are away and off on your own. There are stables near the tourist office on Pyramids Rd but the animals here are often not in very good condition. If you head south of the entrance by the Sphinx, you'll come across several stables. MG (☎ 358 3832) and AA are the two stables we would recommend, both are places that look after their horses well. Tell them if you are an experienced rider and you'll get a better steed. Again, the hire of a horse should cost no more than E£20 per hour. The best time to go for a ride is at sunset, ending at the Cheops Pavilion just as the sound and light show illuminates the Pyramids and the Sphinx. Alternatively, some of the stables are open through the night and it's exhilarating to ride out at dawn and watch the sun rise over the desert.

Great Pyramid of Cheops (Khufu)

The oldest at Giza and the largest in Egypt, the Great Pyramid of Cheops stood 146.5m high when it was completed around 2600 BC. After 46 centuries its height has been reduced by only 9m. About 2½ million limestone blocks, weighing around six million tonnes, were used in the construction.

Although there is not much to see inside the pyramid, the experience of climbing through such an ancient structure is unforgettable though completely impossible if you suffer from even the tiniest degree of claustrophobia. The entrance, on the north face, leads to a descending passage which ends in an unfinished tomb (usually closed) about 100m along and 30m below the pyramid. About 20m from the entrance, however, there is an ascending passage, 1.3m high and 1m wide, which continues for about 40m before opening into the Great Gallery, which is 47m long and 8.5m high. There is also a smaller horizontal passage leading into the so-called Queen's Chamber.

As you ascend the Great Gallery to the King's Chamber notice how precisely the blocks were fitted together at the top. Unlike the rest of the pyramid, the main tomb chamber, which is just over 5m wide and 10m long, was built of red granite blocks. The roof, which weighs more than 400 tonnes, consists of nine huge slabs of granite, above which are another four slabs separated by gaps designed to distribute the enormous weight away from the chamber. There is plenty of air in this room, as it was built so that fresh air flowed in from two shafts on the north and south walls. Entry costs E£20.

Climbing the outside of the Great Pyramid was, for centuries, a popular adventure despite the fact that every year a few people fell to their death. Scaling the pyramid is now forbidden.

On the eastern side of the pyramid are the Queens' Pyramids, three small structures about 20m high, which resemble little more than pyramid-shaped piles of rubble. They were the tombs of Cheops' wives and sisters.

Solar Barque Museum Along the eastern and southern sides of the Pyramid of Cheops are five long pits which once contained the pharaoh's boats. These solar barques may have been used to bring the mummy of the dead Pharaoh across the Nile to the valley temple, from where it was brought up the causeway and placed in the tomb chamber. The boats were then buried around the pyramid to provide transport for the king in the next world.

One of these ancient wooden vessels, possibly the oldest boat in existence, was unearthed in 1954. It was restored and a glass museum was built over it to protect it from damage from the elements. For the same rea-

son, visitors to the museum must don protective footwear in order to keep sand out.

The barque is 43m long and 8m high and sits in a 5m-deep pit. Entry costs E£20 (plus E£10/100 for camera/video permits).

Pyramid of Chephren (Khafre)

South-west of the Great Pyramid, and with almost the same dimensions, is the Pyramid of Chephren. At first it seems larger than his father's because it stands on higher ground and its peak still has part of the original limestone casing which once covered the entire structure. It is 136.5m high (originally 143.5m).

The chambers and passageways of this pyramid are less elaborate than those in the Great Pyramid, but are almost as claustrophobic. The entrance leads down into a passage and then across to the burial chamber, which still contains the large granite sarcophagus of Chephren. Entry costs E£20.

Among the most interesting features of this pyramid are the substantial remains of Chephren's mortuary temple outside to the east. Several rooms can be visited and the causeway, which originally provided access from the Nile to the tomb, still leads from the main temple to the valley temple.

Pyramid of Mycerinus (Menkaure)

At a height of 62m (originally 66.5m), this is the smallest of the three pyramids. Extensive damage was done to the exterior by a 16th century caliph who wanted to demolish all the pyramids.

Inside, a hall descends from the entrance into a passageway, which in turn leads into a small chamber and a group of rooms. There is nothing particularly noteworthy about the interior, but at the very least you can have the thrill of exploring a seldom-visited site; it's another E£20 to enter. Outside are the excavated remains of Mycerinus' mortuary temple and, further east, the ruins of his valley temple, still lying beneath the sand.

The Sphinx

Legends and superstitions abound about the Sphinx and the mystery surrounding its long-forgotten purpose is almost as intriguing as its appearance. English playwright Alan Bennett, however, was disappointed, noting in his diary, 'The Sphinx, like a personality seen on TV and then met in the flesh, is smaller than one had imagined'.

Known in Arabic as Abu al-Hol (Father of Terror), the feline man was called the Sphinx by the ancient Greeks because it resembled the mythical winged monster with a woman's head and lion's body who proposed a riddle to the Thebans and killed all unable to answer correctly.

Carved almost entirely from one huge piece of limestone left over from the carving of the stones for Cheops' Pyramid, the Sphinx is about 50m long and 22m high. It is not known when it was carved but one theory is that it was Chephren who thought of shaping the rock into a lion's body with a god's face, wearing the royal headdress of Egypt. Another theory is that it is the likeness of Chephren himself that has been staring out over the desert sands for so many centuries.

One legend about the Sphinx is associated with the fact that it was engulfed and hidden by sand for several hundred years. The sun-god Ra appeared to the man who was to become Tuthmosis IV and promised him the crown of Egypt if he would free his image, the Sphinx, from the sand. A stele found between the paws of the Sphinx recorded this first known restoration.

During the period of the Ottoman Empire the Turks used the Sphinx for target practice (though other sources have it that it was Napoleon), and its nose and beard were blasted off. Part of the fallen beard was carted off by 19th century adventurers and is now in the British Museum in London.

These days the Sphinx has potentially greater problems from its ordinance-inflicted injuries of the past. It's suffering the stone equivalent of cancer and is being eaten away from the inside. By what, the experts don't quite know – pollution and rising ground water are the two likeliest diagnoses. A succession of restoration attempts have been made throughout the 20th century, several of which disastrously speeded up the decay

rather than halting it. The Sphinx's shiny white paws are the result of the latest effort.

Other Sites

Tomb of Khenthawes This rarely visited but imposing structure, opposite the Great Pyramid and north of Mycerinus' causeway, is the tomb of the daughter of Pharaoh Mycerinus. The tomb is a rectangular building cut into a small hill. You can go down a corridor at the back of the chapel room to the burial chambers, but the descent is a bit hazardous.

Cemeteries Private cemeteries with several rows of tombs are organised around the Pyramids in a grid pattern. Most of the tombs are closed to the public, but those of Qar, Idu and Queen Mersyankh III, in the eastern cemetery, are accessible, although it's sometimes difficult to find the guard who has the keys.

The Tomb of Iasen, in the western cemetery, contains interesting inscriptions and wall paintings which present a glimpse of daily life during the Old Kingdom.

Sound & Light Show

The Sphinx takes the role of the narrator in this show, which is designed with the tourist in mind but is definitely worth seeing. The booming narrative that accompanies the colourful illumination of the Pyramids and the Sphinx is an entertaining way to learn a little of Egypt's ancient history.

There are two or three shows each evening, each in a different language, but one is always in English. Show times are 6.30, 7.30 and 8.30 pm in winter and one hour later in summer. At the time of writing, the schedule was as follows:

day	show 1	show 2	show 3
Mon	English	French	
Tues	English	Italian	French
Wed	English	French	
Thurs	Japanese	English	Arabic
Fri	English	French	
Sat	English	Spanish	
Sun	Russian	French	German

There is open-air seating on the terrace of the Cheops' Pavilion, near the Sphinx and facing Chephren's valley temple. Admission costs E£33 (E£17.50 for students). During Ramadan performance times can be different. If you are unsure call ☎ 385 2880/7320, or ask at the tourist office.

Getting There & Away

The most comfortable way of getting to the Pyramids is to make use of the new No 355 service, a big air-con bus that runs from Heliopolis via Roxy, Abbassiyya and Midan Tahrir, where it picks up from a stand beside the Egyptian Museum (see the Central Cairo map). It runs every 20 minutes and costs E£2. Alternatively, you can take a microbus from Midan Abdel Moniem Riad station. These go near the Ramses Hilton hotel – there are no signs, just ask for 'Haram' and somebody will point you to the right line of vehicles. The fare is 25pt and you'll be dropped off about 500m short of the Oberoi Mena House, which is straight ahead. Or you can take a left to follow the 'Pizza Hut 600m' sign which will take you through the village of Nazlet as-Samaan to reach the Giza Plateau via the Sphinx entrance.

Coming back the No 355 bus and microbuses pick up from the junction of the Desert Highway and Pyramids Rd (see the Giza Plateau map), or from the junction of Saqqara and Pyramids Rds.

Taking a taxi from Downtown costs E£15 one way.

Ride to Saqqara If you're after adventure you could rent a camel or horse for the ride across the desert to Saqqara. This trip is not really for inexperienced riders. By the end of the day you will have spent about six to seven hours atop a horse or camel and a few more hours roaming around the sites at Saqqara.

The trip takes about three hours each way, and costs anything from E£30 to E£50 for a horse and E£30 to E£70 for a camel, depending on how desperate the owners are and how well you can bargain. Don't forget that a camel can carry two people.

HELIOPOLIS

It's only a suburb of Cairo, but were it to stand alone as a town in its own right, Heliopolis would be considered one of the gems of North Africa.

It was conceived as an exclusive 'garden city' in the desert, miles to the north-east of the squalor of Cairo, which would house the European officials who ruled Egypt; construction began in 1906. The architectural style was an odd European-Moorish mix – a European fantasy of the Orient set in stone. In addition to Europeans, the new suburb, known in Egyptian as Masr al-Gedida or 'New Cairo', attracted the Egyptian upper classes and spawned large Coptic, Jewish and Islamic communities. In the 1950s, however, overcrowding in Cairo caught up with this not-so-distant neighbour and the former desert suburb was breached by a creeping tide of middle-income highrises. Ranks of apartment buildings festooned with satellite TV dishes now greatly outnumber the graceful, old villas, but Heliopolis remains a fairly upmarket address; the president resides here as do most of his ministers and the odd deposed head of an African state.

A Walk Around Heliopolis

If you are heading to Heliopolis by tram the place to jump off is Roxy. The way you'll know it's Roxy is that the tram stops twice here, after halting for a minute it moves forward 100m then stops again. This is where you jump off. Ask if you aren't sure: 'Fi Roxy?' Follow the tram tracks (do not branch off left) until the major traffic junction at which point you want to swing left along the wide avenue which leads up to **Midan Roxy**, which takes its name from the cinema on its east side. Following the road as it curves round to the right brings you on to **Sharia Ibrahim Laqqany** with its fantastic colonnaded facades book-ended by teardrop turrets.

After 300m Ibrahim Laqqany intersects with Sharia al-Ahram, the one-time main street of Heliopolis with a tram line running up the centre. (This is where you get off if

CAIRO

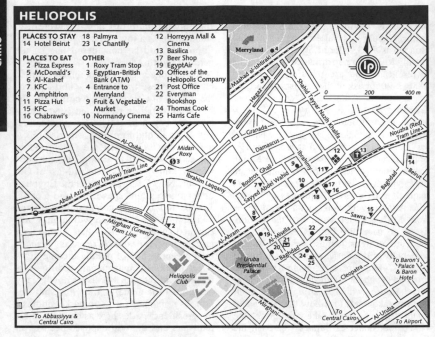

HELIOPOLIS

PLACES TO STAY	18 Palmyra	12 Horreyya Mall &
14 Hotel Beirut	23 Le Chantilly	Cinema
		13 Basilica
PLACES TO EAT	OTHER	17 Beer Shop
2 Pizza Express	1 Roxy Tram Stop	19 EgyptAir
5 McDonald's	3 Egyptian-British	20 Offices of the
6 Al-Kashef	Bank (ATM)	Heliopolis Company
7 KFC	4 Entrance to	21 Post Office
8 Amphitrion	Merryland	22 Everyman
11 Pizza Hut	9 Fruit & Vegetable	Bookshop
15 KFC	Market	24 Thomas Cook
16 Chabrawi's	10 Normandy Cinema	25 Harris Cafe

you're coming up to Heliopolis by bus.) At this point, on your left is the **Amphitrion cafeteria** while over Sharia Al-Ahram to the right is the former Heliopolis Grand Hotel now the **Uruba Palace**, the official residence of Egypt's president.

Sharia al-Ahram has suffered particularly badly from rapacious developers but further east up the street around the junction with Ibrahimy a cluster of grand old buildings remain including that housing the **Palmyra cafeteria**. Both the Palmyra and the Amphitrion cafeteria, back down the street, are as old as Heliopolis itself and were popular watering holes for the allied soldiers back during WWI and WWII. Today they're two of the very few places in Cairo where it's possible to drink a beer without having to skulk in some dingy room away from public eyes. Both terraces serve food and are great places to relax and street watch on a balmy evening.

Two blocks further east on Al-Ahram is the **Basilica** designed as a miniature version of Istanbul's famous Aya Sofia. Its distinctive shape has caused it to be known as the 'jellymould' by local expats. Baron Empain, the Belgian industrialist who founded Heliopolis, is buried in the crypt. Unfortunately the place is usually kept locked. From the Basilica head south (right) down Al-Shahid Tayyar Nazih Khalifa; a six minute walk brings you to Sharia al-Uruba, the airport road, facing the Baron's Palace.

The Baron's Palace Just off the modern-day airport road, the Baron's Palace (Qasr al-Baron) makes for a bizarre and incongruous sight: a Hindu-style temple looming up among the faceless apartment blocks. This was the personal residence of Baron Empain, modelled – for no known reason – on the temples of Angkor Wat in Cambodia.

Three generations of the Empain family inhabited the palace until it was sequestered by the state in the 1950s and allowed to fall into ruin. While a rich collection of sandstone Buddhas, geishas, elephants and serpents still adorns the exterior, the interior has been gutted and is now home to large colonies of bats. Entry is not permitted but if you tip the bawwab (who lives in a shack in the grounds) a couple of pounds, he'll let you walk around the outside.

After the Baron's Palace retrace your steps until the point at which the road forks and bear left along Sharia Sawra until Baghdad; 200m west is **Le Chantilly**, about the best place up here to eat or just to take a beer in the garden out back. Continue on down Baghdad turning right at the bottom, two or three doors along on your right are the former **Offices of the Heliopolis Company** with a beautifully restored main chamber – the attendants are usually happy for visitors to poke their heads in.

You can catch a tram or bus back Downtown on Sharia al-Ahram.

October War Panorama
Built with help from North Korean artists, this memorial to the 1973 'victory' over the Israeli occupation of Sinai is quite an extraordinary propaganda effort.

Inside at the centre of the cylindrical building, you climb two flights of stairs to a revolving dais which carries the audience around a 3D mural depicting the breaching of the Bar Lev Line on the Suez Canal by Egyptian forces and the initial retreats by the Israelis. A stirring commentary recounts the heroic victories but is short on detail on the successful Israeli counterattacks that pushed the Egyptians back before both sides accepted a UN-brokered cease-fire. Sinai was eventually liberated by negotiation six years later.

The Panorama (see the Greater Cairo map) is open daily (except Tuesday). Admission is E£8 and performances, usually with an Arabic commentary, begin at 9.30 and 11 am and 6 pm. Groups can request a performance with an English commentary.

It's located about 2km south-west of the Baron's Palace, further in towards the city, in the suburb of Medinet Nasr (Victory City). Coming in from the airport, it's off to the left on Sharia al-Uruba.

Getting There & Away
The best way to get to Heliopolis is to take the airport bus (No 356) from Midan Abdel Moniem Riad, behind the Egyptian Museum. It goes along Mirghani, then left at the presidential palace and up Sharia al-Ahram. The fare is E£2 and it runs every 20 minutes. Alternatively, there's the tram which goes from just north of Midan Ramses (see Getting Around later this chapter). The journey up to Roxy takes about 30 minutes and costs 25pt.

ACTIVITIES
For more details of activities in Cairo check the 'What's On' section of the monthly *Egypt Today* magazine.

Art Galleries
In addition to the Museum of Modern Art (see the Gezira section earlier this chapter) there are numerous small galleries around town where contemporary local and foreign artists and sculptors exhibit. *Al-Ahram Weekly*, as well as *Egypt Today*, has fairly comprehensive listings of what's hanging, or check some of the places below, which tend to show the most interesting stuff:

Akhenaten Centre of Arts
   (☎ 340 8211) 1 Maahad al-Swissry, Zamalek. Open 10 am to 1 pm and 5 to 7 pm daily (closed Friday). These are the official Ministry of Culture exhibition halls (four of them) housed in a grand villa on the banks of the Nile.
Atelier du Caire
   (☎ 574 6730) 2 Karim ad-Dawla, off Mahmoud Bassiouni, one block west of Midan Talaat Harb. Open 10 am to 1 pm and 5 to 11 pm daily (closed Friday). Official artists' union exhibition halls.
British Council
   (☎ 354 3281) 192 Sharia el-Nil, Agouza Small gallery that often hosts visiting exhibitions from abroad.

Cairo-Berlin
(☎ 393 1764) 17 Yousef al-Guindi, Downtown. Open 11 am to 9 pm daily (closed Saturday). Along with the Mashrabia, this place consistently hosts the most exciting works in town.

Espace Karim-Francis
(☎ 393 1699) 1 Sherifeen, off Qasr el-Nil, Downtown. Open 10 am to 2 pm and 5 to 8 pm (closed Friday). Up on the 3rd floor of an apartment block.

Gezira Centre of Arts
(☎ 341 8672) Al-Saraya al-Gezira, Zamalek. Open from 10 am to 1.30 pm and 5.30 to 9 pm daily (5.50 to 8 pm on Friday) except Monday. Museum of Islamic ceramics plus several galleries with temporary exhibitions of anything from ceramics to pottery to painting.

Hanager Arts Centre
(☎ 340 6861) Opera House grounds, Gezira. Open 10 am to 10 pm daily. Spacious venue for big-name shows.

Mashrabia
(☎ 578 4494) 8 Champollion, off Midan Tahrir. Open 11 am to 9 pm daily (closed Saturday). Cairo's most attractive gallery and one of the two best in terms of its stable of artists.

Townhouse Gallery
(☎ 575 5901) Hussein Pasha, off Mahmoud Bassiouni. Open 10 am to 2 pm and 6 to 9 pm daily (closed Thursday and Friday morning). New privately owned gallery.

Billiards & Bowls

Billiards (pool), snooker and 10-pin bowling have really taken off in Cairo in a big way in the last couple of years. Most of the venues are in the more wealthy suburbs like Ma'adi and Medinat Nasr, away from the city centre. But right in the middle of Downtown in the Al-Bustan Centre, there's bowling (E£12, 10 lanes) and pool (E£20 per hour) on the 9th floor and more pool tables on the 2nd floor. Also, on the top floor of the Ramses Hilton Mall there's a snooker hall (E£25 per hour) and a pool hall (E£20 per hour), both of which serve beer. They're open from 11 to 3 am.

Felucca Rides

Feluccas are the ancient broad-sail boats that are seen everywhere up and down the Nile. They can be hired out by the hour from several places along the Corniche. One of the most pleasant things to do in Cairo is to go out on a felucca with a supply of beer and a small picnic just as sunset approaches. The best spot for hiring is the Dok Dok landing stage on the Corniche at Garden City just north of the Meridien Le Caire. A boat and captain should cost about E£15 per hour irrespective of the number of people on board. This rate is, of course, subject to haggling. Other felucca mooring points are the southeast end of Gezira just north of the Tahrir Bridge; opposite the Helnan Shepheard's hotel (captains here tend to be more voracious in their demands for money); and in Ma'adi just north of the Felfela.

Horse Riding

A horse ride out by the Pyramids, especially in the evening, can be a great way to escape the clamour of Cairo and vent some pent-up aggro. For details, see the Pyramids section earlier in this chapter.

Swimming

Finding a place to cool off is not easy in Cairo. Sporting clubs, the places that most Cairenes who can afford to go to swim, restrict access to members only for insurance reasons. The only option is to make for a hotel. At the cheaper end of the scale the Atlas Zamalek has a high-rise postage stamp-sized plunge pool which costs E£28.50 per day (of which E£25 is a minimum charge against refreshments). Cheapest of all is the pool on the roof of the Fontana Hotel on Midan Ramses which is just E£10 for a day's use, trouble is it's not big enough to actually swim in.

Most of the five-star hotels allow nonguests to use their pools. The best value is the pool at the Meridien Le Caire which has a fantastic Nile-side location and costs E£39 per person per day. The Cairo Marriott has a nice pool out in the garden and charges E£63 per day, but the one at the Mena House Oberoi is unbeatable, surrounded by palm trees and with views of the Pyramids; it costs E£175 for two people.

ORGANISED TOURS

Some of the budget hotels in central Cairo arrange tours to various places around the city such as the Pyramids, Saqqara and Memphis. The price is usually about E£20 and includes transport only – there's no guide and admission is extra. The stories about these trips have often been negative, so forewarned is forearmed.

If you do want a guide then perhaps the best option is to call Salah Mohammed Abdel Hafez (☎ 298 0650, mobile 012-313 8446, email samo@intouch.com). This genial chap runs a full day excursion to the already mentioned places, as well as to the Wissa Wassef Art Centre at Harraniyya, for E£18 per person (once again, lunch and admission prices are extra). If you're staying at one of the city centre hotels, he'll pick you up at around 9 am. You'll need to arrange the tour at least one day in advance – leave a message on the answering machine if he's not there.

A third option is to go through a travel agency like Masr Travel or American Express. They both do half-day sightseeing tours to the Pyramids and Sphinx, Memphis and Saqqara, Old Cairo, and the Egyptian Museum for US$26 to US$30. See under Travel Agencies in the Information section earlier in this chapter for contact details.

PLACES TO STAY

For general information about accommodation in Cairo see the Accommodation section in the Facts for the Visitor chapter.

PLACES TO STAY – BUDGET

There's a plethora of inexpensive hotels and pensions, concentrated mainly in the busy city centre area. Prices for these places can be deceiving, because they aren't always accurate indicators of the hotel's quality and because prices can also often be negotiated. So consider the listed room rates as estimates – we got these rates from the hotels themselves but at the same time we met other travellers who had paid less for the same accommodation and some who'd paid more.

Camping

The only camping in all of Cairo is at *Motel Salma* (☎ 384 9152, fax 385 1010), next to

the Wissa Wassef Art Centre at Harraniyya, south of Giza. Although inconvenient in that it's miles and miles from anywhere, it does have views of the Pyramids from the back of the site. Overland tour companies occasionally stop here. Be prepared for a mosquito attack at sunset. Camping costs E£7 per person with your own tent or camper van. You can also get a stuffy two/four person cabin for E£30/40, or E£50 with your own shower.

To get to the Salma, take a microbus for Abu Sir from Sharia al-Haram (Pyramids Rd). It's about a 4km trip; ask the driver about the best place to alight.

Hostels

Again, there's only one place that actually calls itself a hostel. *HI Manial Youth Hostel* (☎ 364 0729, fax 398 4107, 135 Abdel Aziz el-Saud, Manial) is in reasonable nick with clean toilets, although the beds are nothing great. Each dorm room sleeps either three or six people. There are no rooms for couples or families. Mosquitoes and cats are plentiful enough to ensure constant companionship of a sort. For HI members it costs E£12 in three-bed dorms or E£8 in six-bed dorms; nonmembers pay E£4 more. Breakfast is included and there's an 11 pm curfew. From Midan Abdel Moniem Riad, take minibus No 82 to the Al-Gamaa Bridge and then head down the riverside street.

Hotels & Pensions

The inexpensive hotels and pensions are concentrated Downtown, mainly on and around Sharia Talaat Harb (see the Central Cairo map). This is the most convenient place to be for getting around, eating and entertainment. Most of the hotels are on the upper floors of old, and often fairly decrepit, apartment blocks. Rooms tend to be large, but are also musty and sparsely furnished. In this price range there is no air-con (except where noted), but sometimes there may be a ceiling fan. Shared bathrooms are the norm, usually with pharaonic-era plumbing that delivers a highly erratic water supply.

The following list, while far from exhaustive, covers what we consider to be the

The Great Hotel Scam

The most perpetrated scam of all in Cairo is the one in which a local convinces the newly arrived traveller that the hotel they are heading for is closed/horrible/very expensive and leads them off to another 'better' place, for which they earn a commission.

The main culprits are the taxi drivers at Cairo airport. They have fixed commission rates with many of the Downtown hostels and will always take you to whichever is offering the best rate at that time. (Any hostel that refuses to pay the taxi drivers' commission can find itself blackballed and suffer a decline in trade as a consequence.) And it's not just the taxi drivers. On arrival at the airport, if you're not with a group, you may be approached by a man or woman with an official-looking badge that says 'Egyptian Chamber of Tourism' or something similar. These people are not government tourism officials, they are hotel touts. There are also a couple of touts that ride the buses from the airport. As a final hurdle, there are also touts who attempt to latch onto new arrivals on the street – they'll offer to lead you to your hotel where they can 'check everything is OK' and, of course, unbeknown to you, claim credit and cash for bringing you in.

The problem with all of this is that, in the worst case scenario, you could be waylaid into checking into some very dodgy fleapit which may be way out of the centre. Secondly, whatever commission was paid out will ultimately find its way onto your bill. Worse still, often your 'local friend' will also negotiate a higher than normal price for the room, thus increasing their cut.

The simple rule is do not be swayed by anyone who tries to dissuade you from going to the hotel of your choice. Hotels do not open and close with any great frequency in Cairo and if it's listed in this book then it is very unlikely to have gone out of business in the meantime. Some taxi drivers will stall by telling you that they don't know where your hotel is – in that case tell them to let you out at Midan Tahrir (or the Nile Hilton) and it's a short walk to almost all the budget hotels from there. And if you find yourself with a new 'friend' walking you to your hotel, stop them at the door – if they begin to protest, then bear in mind that no decent, ordinary Egyptian would ever dream of accompanying a foreigner into their hotel.

better options. The cheapest beds are provided first.

Sultan Hotel (☎ 577 2258, 4 Souq at-Tawfiqiyya) off the top end of Talaat Harb, Downtown. At last visit, there were a total of three Sultan hotels, plus **Safary Hotel** (☎ 575 0752) and **Hotel Venice**, all occupying one building, forming a small backpackers' ghetto on a colourful market street. Give or take a pound, there's little between them. They offer grubby cramped dorms (from E£5 to E£9 for a bed), one or two of the places have doubles (E£16 to E£20), and in all cases over-burdened, unsanitary bathroom facilities are shared. Recommended only for those on the tightest of budgets.

Dahab Hotel (☎ 579 4400, 26 Mahmoud Bassiouni, Downtown) is supposed to recreate the feel of a Sinai beach camp. This place (opened in 1998) is a collection of whitewashed huts on a Downtown rooftop, with cushioned communal spaces open to the sky, bamboo screens and Bob Marley on the cassette deck. Totally laid-back, but the downside is the number of street hustlers the management allows to hang around – female travellers have complained about not being able to escape the unappreciated attention of local males. Beds in dorms are E£12 (shared showers), while a sparse double with private shower is E£35.

Hotel Minerva (☎ 392 0600/1/2, 39 Talaat Harb, Downtown) has a ground floor reception hidden down the alley opposite the Al'Américaine cafe, while the hotel itself occupies the 6th and 7th floors. The not-so-obvious location means this old place is often overlooked, but the rooms are kept clean, as are the communal showers and toilets, and it's good value with singles/doubles at E£16/28, or doubles with shower at E£32.

New Palace Hotel (☎ 575 1283, email *mony@starnet.com.eg, 17 Suleiman Halabi, 6th floor)* in central Cairo, opened in 1998. This is a vast place located a few minutes walk north of Downtown (see the Midan Ramses & Around map). Rooms are variable in size and quality, but all are clean. There's an excellent, partly open-air, rooftop communal area complete with pigeon roosts and cafeteria serving cheap meals. The hotel also has an online terminal for guests' use. Dorm beds cost E£12 while doubles range from E£30 for a basic room to E£50 to E£60 for one with air-con and shower. Prices seemed negotiable. Note that while we have received many positive comments about this place, we have also received more than one complaint from single female travellers.

Ismailia House Hotel (☎ 356 3122, 1 *Midan Tahrir, 8th floor, Downtown)* gets by on its great location (west facing rooms have fantastic views over the midan) but the rooms and bathrooms are very grubby and the management is obnoxious. Singles, some of which are really dingy, cost E£25. Doubles without/with private bathroom are E£40/50. A bed in a share room (a double room with two extra rickety beds crammed in) costs from E£12 to E£15.

Sun Hotel (☎ 578 1786, 2 Talaat Harb, *9th floor, Downtown)* is in a good location just off Midan Tahrir but has no views. It has decent-sized but still dingy singles/doubles for E£25/40, or you can pay E£15 per person in a four-bed room. The clean, communal bathrooms have hot water and there's a lounge room with satellite TV and an OK kitchen. A major drawback is that the elevator only works from 3 pm to 8 am.

Magic Hotel (☎ 579 5918, 10 Sharia al-Bustan, 3rd floor, Downtown)* is slightly better run than its two sister establishments, the Sun and Ismailia House – bedrooms and bathrooms are that little bit cleaner and the place has a cosier, less traveller-worn feel. Singles/doubles with fans cost E£25/40.

Pension Roma (☎ 391 1088, fax 579 6243, 169 Mohammed Farid, 6th floor, *Downtown)* is down a side alley next to the Gattegno department store. This hotel is the city's most charming budget option, long popular for its old world elegance including shiny hardwood floors, antique furniture, a splendid breakfast room and proprietress Madam Cressaty herself. It has recently been repainted and spruced up. Reservations are necessary. Single/double/triple rooms without bath are E£25/45/60, or E£5 more with private shower.

Berlin Hotel (☎/fax 395 7502, email *berlinhotelcairo@hotmail.com, 2 Shawarby, 4th floor, off Qasr el-Nil, Downtown)* is a bit more pricey than most other budget options but in our opinion well worth it for clean, air-con rooms all with their own shower. Rare among Cairo's budget hotels, the English-speaking owner/manager Hisham Yousef actually seems to care about offering good service. An online computer is also available for guests' use. Singles/doubles/triples are E£60/80/90.

Mayfair Hotel (☎ 340 7315, 9 Aziz *Osman)* is in Zamalek which is a more relaxing and greener place than central Cairo with lots of good eating and drinking places and it's still only a five minute taxi ride from Downtown. The Mayfair is quiet and tranquil with a great shady terrace, but with a good supermarket next door and a busy shopping street nearby. Singles/doubles without bath are E£25/30, or air-con doubles with bath are E£50 to E£60.

Zamalek Pension (☎ 340 9318, 6 Salah *ad-Din)* in Zamalek is great for quiet and privacy. There are only about five rooms and you feel like a house guest rather than a hotel resident. Plus it's located on a leafy street in an attractive neighbourhood. Price wise it's really heading into the mid-range, with singles/doubles costing from E£50/70. You will pay more if you want air-con.

PLACES TO STAY – MID-RANGE

The hotels in this section are organised by area then listed alphabetically.

Central Cairo

Carlton Hotel (☎ 575 5022, fax 575 5323, 21 Sharia 26th of July) in Downtown (entered via the side street that runs down by the Rivoli cinema) is a nice old place, though now showing its age around the edges (ask for one of the newly renovated rooms). There's a pleasant rooftop dining terrace but no beer is served. Singles/doubles cost E£65/85.

Cosmopolitan Hotel (☎ 392 3663, fax 393 3531, Sharia ibn Taalab) off Qasr el-Nil, Downtown is a gorgeous, old Art Deco building with dark lacquered antique furniture and tiled bathrooms with tubs, supplemented by some mod-cons such as central air-con. Singles/doubles cost E£135/175.

Garden City House Hotel (☎ 354 4969, 23 Kamal ad-Din Salah, Garden City) opposite the back of the Semiramis InterContinental (look for the small sign at 3rd floor level) is a longtime favourite among Egyptologists and Middle Eastern scholars, but now more popular with young students from the nearby American University in Cairo. It's noisy, a bit dusty and definitely overpriced, but a lot of people love it and keep coming back. Singles/doubles range from E£51/94 (without bath) to E£64/102 (with bath), breakfast and supper included.

Lotus Hotel (☎ 575 0966, fax 575 4720, 12 Talaat Harb, 7th floor, Downtown) is reached via an elevator at the end of an arcade almost opposite the Felfela Takeaway. Rooms are clean and comfortable and they all have air-con and large balconies. Singles without/with bath are E£47/67 and doubles are E£67/87.

Odeon Palace Hotel (☎/fax 577 6637, 6 Abdel Hamid Said) off Talaat Harb, Downtown is a very comfortable, upper mid-range hotel where all rooms have a mini-fridge, TV, telephone and air-con. The rooftop 24 hour bar is popular with night owls. Singles/doubles cost E£115/146, breakfast is E£10 extra.

Windsor Hotel (☎ 591 5277, fax 592 1621, 19 Sharia Alfy, Downtown) was the British Officers' Club before 1952. It retains a colonial air, particularly in the reception area with its beautifully ornate lift, and in the lounge bar, which is one of the best spots in town for a beer. In 1991, former Monty Python member, Michael Palin, stayed here while filming the BBC series *Around the World in 80 Days*; he described the place as possessing an 'almost unreal individuality'. There's a wide variety of rooms with all combinations of bathroom types, cramped or the size of a tennis court, with or without shower/toilet/tub, newly tiled or well-worn antique, hot water or no water. Singles range from E£75 to E£102, doubles from E£102 to E£140.

Around Midan Ramses

Midan Ramses is a little north of the city centre – about 10 minutes walk or two stops on the metro.

Fontana Hotel (☎ 592 2321, fax 592 2145, Midan Ramses) on the north-west corner of the midan, high above the traffic and fumes, has clean rooms, a pleasant roof-top cafe/bar with a small pool for cooling off and a disco on the floor below. The views are great but the location is not really convenient for anywhere except the train station. Singles/doubles cost E£57/84.

Happyton Hotel (☎/fax 592 8671/00, 10 Ali al-Kassar) is halfway between Midan Ramses and Downtown, tucked away down a quiet backstreet off Emad ad-Din (behind the Karim Cinema). It's a relaxed, good value-for-money option with its own restaurant and a small, open-air rooftop bar. Rooms with air-con cost E£40/52.

Victoria Hotel (☎ 589 2290, fax 591 3008, 66 Al-Gomhuriyya) in central Cairo, dates back to the 1930s and still retains plenty of period charm, particularly in the foyer area. There's also a nice garden cafe with a fountain. Rooms cost E£120/170.

Islamic Cairo

Islamic Cairo (see the Al-Azhar & Khan Al-Khalili map) is the liveliest and most fascinating part of the city, but noise levels are high and once you have managed to get off to sleep you're almost sure to be woken soon after by the early morning calls to prayer.

Al-Hussein Hotel (☎ 591 8089, Midan Hussein) is right in the thick of things in the Khan al-Khalili bazaar. The rooms are clean and the restaurant on the roof has a fantastic view of medieval Cairo (pity that the food is so lousy). Air-con singles/doubles with bath and views over the midan cost E£60/70; smaller rooms without bath or views cost E£35/45.

Radwan Hotel (☎ 590 1311, Midan Hussein) is a passable second choice if Al-Hussein is full. It has OK rooms for E£45/70 with breakfast and bath.

Zamalek

Only a five minute taxi ride from Downtown, Zamalek is more relaxing and greener than Central Cairo.

Flamenco Hotel (☎ 340 0815, fax 340 9312, 2 Geziret al-Wusta, Zamalek) is highly recommended for anyone who does not mind being a little out of the centre. It overlooks the branch of the Nile between Zamalek and Mohandiseen and the views from the balconies are excellent. The service is good and there are two OK bars and a good restaurant. Singles/doubles cost E£220/292.

New Star Hotel (☎ 340 0928, fax 341 1321, 34 Yehia Ibrahim, Zamalek) is tucked away on a backstreet near the junction of 26th of July and Hassan Sabry. It has fully carpeted air-con doubles with modern bathrooms and large balconies with Nile views for E£170.

Heliopolis

About 40 minutes north of the city centre by taxi, bus or tram, staying in Heliopolis is not a viable option for a casual visitor to Cairo, but if you have business up here or want to be close to the airport and don't wish to spend top dollars, there are a couple of reasonable three-star options.

Baron Hotel (☎ 291 5757, fax 290 7077, 8 Mahaad al-Sahari) off Al-Uruba, over-

looks the incredible Hindu-styled Baron's Palace and has a decent bar and restaurant. Rooms cost E£135/170.

Hotel Beirut (☎ 291 6048, 43 Sharia Baghdad) is a fairly sombre place, but it's very convenient for exploring central Heliopolis and the bar is popular with local expats. Singles/doubles cost E£204/272.

PLACES TO STAY – TOP END

All Cairo's five-star hotels come with the complete complement of amenities such as restaurants, bars, executive suites, business centres, shops and banks, plus a few Egyptian touches like belly-dancing nightclubs and weekly wedding receptions in the foyer. The following prices generally don't include breakfast and taxes (typically 19% plus a further 5% service tax).

Cairo Marriott (☎ 340 8888, fax 340 8240, Al-Saraya al-Gezira, Zamalek) is the best of the city's top-end hotels. The Marriott is a former royal palace which has been tastefully extended and added to. It boasts a classy reception, exquisite dining areas and a serene garden with bar, cafe, pool and tennis courts. Single/double rooms are all US$180.

Cairo Sheraton (☎ 348 8600, fax 336 4601, Midan al-Galaa, Doqqi) is on the wrong side of the Nile, which means it's a good 15 minute walk to the city centre. The interior of the hotel is very 70s and unattractive to boot. Rooms start from US$152/176.

Sheraton Gezira (☎ 341 1333, fax 340 5056, Sharia al-Orman, Gezira) is on the very southern tip of the island of Gezira where views are superb both from the rooms and from the numerous riverside restaurants and bars. Standard rooms cost US$185/210.

Helnan Shepheard's (☎ 355 3800, fax 355 7284) on Corniche el-Nil in central Cairo is a gloomy, badly-aged place with little to recommend it apart from the good location just south of the Midan Tahrir. Rooms fronting the Nile cost US$134/160, while those at the back cost US$90/105, including tax included.

Oberoi Mena House (☎ 383 3444, fax 383 7777) on Pyramids Rd in Giza is rated

CAIRO

by many as Cairo's best hotel. However it's 10km out of the city centre, but staying next to the Pyramids might prove more than ample compensation for some. The interior is like an opulent oriental fantasy, and there are beautiful gardens with a large, deep pool from which the Pyramids can be seen while floating on your back. Rooms start at US$130/160.

Meridien Le Caire (☎ 362 1717, fax 368 1555) on Corniche el-Nil in Manial is at the northern tip of the island of Rhoda. The views from the rooms are fantastic. Its restaurant, the *Champollion*, is reckoned to be one of the three best in town, while the poolside terrace is a great place for a sunset cocktail. However, the hotel is showing its age and it's a 1.5km walk up to Midan Tahrir and central Cairo. Spacious single/double rooms with all facilities cost US$180.

Nile Hilton (☎ 578 0444, fax 578 0475, email nhilton@brainy1.ie-eg.com) Midan Tahrir, Downtown, remains one of the best places to stay (despite its age) for those with the money. It has the best location in the city, on Midan Tahrir next to the Egyptian Museum, and it has terrific river views from the Nile-facing rooms. *Ibis Cafe* on its terrace is popular with city residents and its secluded pool is one of the best in town. Rooms are large and clean, although the plumbing can be unreliable. The better singles/doubles cost about US$180/210.

Pyramisa (☎ 336 7000, fax 360 5347, 60 Sharia al-Giza, Doqqi), despite a poor location in the shadow of the towering Cairo Sheraton, is a small, intimate place with very reasonable rates for a five star hotel at US$100/120.

Ramses Hilton (☎ 574 4400, fax 575 7152, 115 Corniche el-Nil) in central Cairo is modern but bland and characterless. Worse still, it's surrounded by flyovers and is adjacent to a city bus station – unless you take a taxi from the door every time, walking anywhere involves negotiating at least half a dozen of Cairo's most lethal roads. Rooms range from US$155/187 for a standard single/double to US$2030 for a three bed suite.

Semiramis InterContinental (☎ 355 7171, fax 356 3020, email cairo@inter conti.com) on Corniche el-Nil in central Cairo is in a good location just south of Midan Tahrir, and there is only one road to be crossed to get to the Egyptian Museum or Downtown. The foyer area is the most attractive of all the newer hotels and the places to eat are very pleasant with lots of glass, greenery and Nile views. Rooms with Nile views cost US$190/220, rooms overlooking the city are US$20 cheaper.

PLACES TO EAT

For general descriptions of food types plus hints on ordering and prices, see the Food section in the Facts for the Visitor chapter.

Fuul & Ta'amiyya

There are fuul and ta'amiyya places on nearly every street in Cairo but, of course, some are better than others. Three stand out as perennial favourites with Cairenes.

At-Tabie ad-Dumyati at 31 Orabi, north of Midan Orabi (see the Midan Ramses & Around map), is a personal favourite. It does fuul with tomatoes and onions, egg and pasturma, or clarified butter. You can takeaway or there's a restaurant section (see Budget Dining following). There's also a branch in Mohandiseen on Midan Mustafa Mahmoud.

Felfela Takeaway on Talaat Harb beats all other competition Downtown. Place your order, pay at the tills, then present your ticket at the busy counter, way at the back, to get your food.

Na'ama on the Corniche in Agouza, just north of the 6th of October Bridge, is the other really good one. It's a bit out of the way, but then most of its trade seems to come from taxi drivers. It's open 24 hours.

Kushari

Cairo's best kushari joints are all Downtown and include: *At-Tahrir* at 19 Abdel Khalek Sarwat, east off Talaat Harb, with another shop on Sharia Tahrir, in Bab al-Luq; *Abu Tarek* at 40 Champollion is reckoned to be *the* best; the *Lux* on Sharia 26th of July and also on the south side of Midan

Falaki; and the *International Public Meal Kushari*, distinguishable by its red-painted window frames on the corner of Emad ad-Din and Alfy.

Kofta & Kebab

While kofta and kebab dominate many Cairo menus, there are several places which sell nothing else. Each evening, Sharia Ezbekiyya, just north of 26th of July, Downtown, is choked with smoke from the charcoal braziers of half a dozen meat merchants. None, however, are particularly good. Serious carnivores should head for the Zein al-Abdeen district which was, until recently, the site of the city's slaughterhouses.

Ouf, on Midan Zein al-Abdeen (see the Greater Cairo map), is a fairly straightforward kebab house distinguished by fine meat and excellent offal, particularly the *kellawi* (kidneys). You can dine upstairs or out on the pavement in the evening. It's open until 2 am or later.

Abu Ramy's is a meat-eating experience not to be missed. It's an open-air restaurant on waste ground beside the old slaughterhouses. The abattoirs are no longer in use so you no longer get to see your meal tethered nearby but the meat is still the freshest and best in Cairo. As well as kofta and kebab, they serve *kebda* (liver), kidneys, sausage and strongly flavoured, succulent *rayesh* (lamb chops). This place only opens after evening prayers (about 8 pm) and serves food until dawn. A 250g portion of meat plus complimentary salads will come to about E£10. To get there, take a taxi to Ouf on Midan Zein al-Abdeen; at the bottom of the street, past the stalls selling butchers' knives, bear left and Abu Ramy's is 50m on the right.

Al-Agaty is by far the best of Khan al-Khalili's kofta and kebab joints, most of which are centred on Midan Hussein and are to be avoided as they're too used to overcharging unwitting tourists for poor quality food. Instead, Al-Agaty is a modest little place tucked away down a side street, Sharia Makassisse, just off Sharia al-Muizz li-Din Allah, close to the junction with Muski. There's no outdoor seating unfortu-

nately, but the food is good and reasonably priced. It's open from noon to midnight.

Ar-Rifai (see The Citadel to Ibn Tuluu map), just off Midan Sayyida Zeinab, is another good late night place, very popular with Cairo's small but growing band of clubbers who taxi down here in the early hours of the morning for post-rave meat fests. It's up the alleyway to the left of the garish sabil-kuttab of Sultan Mustafa, opposite the Sayyida Zeinab mosque.

Fast Food

Fast-food chains are mushrooming in Cairo quicker than you can say 'Big Mac and fries'. There are now more than 30 international franchises in town. The term fast food is something of a misnomer though, as young Egyptians spend hours at a time hogging the tables in these joints, which are considered some of the trendiest places in town to hang out. Mohandiseen's Gamiat ad-Dowal al-Arabiyya has become the street to cruise down – Cairo's smog-choked, six lane, concrete Sunset Boulevard – largely because of its heavy concentration of fast-food outlets.

The following list of fast-food outlets covers only the central Cairo branches.

KFC
Mohammed Mahmoud, just off Midan Tahrir opposite the AUC
21 Abdel Khalek Sarwat, just off Talaat Harb
McDonald's
42 Talaat Harb
Mohammed Mahmoud, just off Midan Tahrir opposite the AUC
Ramses Hilton mall, 6th floor
Pizza Hut
16 Midan Tahrir, across from the AUC
Texas Fried Chicken
31 Sharia 26th of July, west of Talaat Harb
Wimpy
Sharia Hoda Shaarawi, near Midan Falaki
Talaat Harb, just south of Midan Talaat Harb
Sharia Sherif, north of the junction with Qasr el-Nil

Vegetarian

Although there are few vegetarian restaurants (just two in fact), nonmeat-eaters shouldn't have too much trouble. The menus at places like *At-Tabie ad-Dumyati* or *Felfela Restaurant* in central Cairo, *Maroosh* in Mohandiseen, or *Chabrawi's* in Heliopolis feature lots of nonmeat dishes (see elsewhere in this Places to Eat section for more information on all these places).

L'Aubergine (☎ 340 6550, 5 Sayyed al-Bakry, Zamalek) is Cairo's sole veggie restaurant and luckily it's a good one. The menu is constantly changing but last time we visited it included things like blue cheese and leek lasagne (E£17), aubergine moussaka (E£16) and vegetables in coconut, ginger and green coriander sauce (E£17). There are also salads and soups, and beer is served. It's open from noon to 1 am.

Al-Omda, which is along the side street beside the Atlas Zamalek in Mohandiseen, is a popular kushari and shwarma place that has an upstairs salad-only restaurant. We heard about this only after our last visit so we haven't been there but reviews in the local press were favourable.

Budget Dining

North of Midan Talaat Harb There are a few kushari joints around here (mentioned earlier in this section), as well as the best-avoided kebab shops along Sharia Ezbekiyya. There are also a few places like the *Casablanca* just off Midan Orabi which are fine if you stick to the rotisserie-grilled chicken (a half with bread and tahina goes for E£10). For something better, head for one of the following.

Akher Sa'a at 8 Sharia Alfy (the sign is in Arabic only but look for the Christian bookshop next door) is a hugely popular fuul and ta'amiyya takeaway joint with a no-frills restaurant next door. The menu is limited but you can get things like omelettes (with pasturma is good) and tahina and bread. The bill is never more than E£3 to E£4. It's open 24 hours.

At-Tabie ad-Dumyati (☎ 575 4211, 31 Sharia Orabi) 200m north of Midan Orabi (see the Midan Ramses & Around map) is absolutely one of the best places for a good cheap meal in Cairo. Like Akher Sa'a, it's

basic (it resembles a canteen), but it's clean, the portions are large, the service is fast and friendly and the food is excellent. It's predominantly vegetarian and has a wonderful salad bar where you can choose four from about 30 different prepared salads and mezze for just E£3. Other specialities include fuul (numerous different types), ta'amiyya and a very tasty lentil soup. A filling meal for two here can come to as little as E£10.

Excelsior on the corner of Talaat Harb and Adly, serves terrible, overpriced food, but the macaroni and cannelloni (both around the E£5 mark) are digestible. Most people just order a beer and grab a seat at the window to watch the goings-on outside.

Restaurant Gad on Sharia Adly, opposite the synagogue, is popular at lunch time with Downtown office workers. Though gloomy and grim inside it has an extensive menu of Egyptian dishes and you can eat for less than E£10 if you forgo the meat. The 'special Gad rice' (E£11) which is done with nuts, sultanas, vegetables and chicken is good, if a bit oily.

South of Midan Talaat Harb The area around Midan Falaki and the Souq Mansour is dotted with plenty of juice stands, bakeries, fuul and ta'amiyya, fiteer and kushari places (the best of which are mentioned earlier this section), while Mansour Mohammed, which runs down the side of the AUC, is lined with fast food joints.

Fatatri at-Tahrir at 166 Sharia Tahrir, close to Midan Tahrir, is a 24 hour sit-down restaurant which specialises in *fiteer* (the Egyptian pancake/pizza); sweet or savoury, it's E£6 for small fiteer, E£8 for medium and E£10 for large.

Felfela Restaurant (☎ 392 2751, 15 Sharia Hoda Shaarawi) is perpetually packed with tourists, coach parties and locals, but it does deserve its popularity. The quirky decor (tree-trunk tables, stuffed animals, aquariums and lanterns) creates a fun dining environment and, depending on your choices, the all-Egyptian food is excellent and moderately priced. Give the meat

EDDIE GERALD

For the lounge room wall perhaps? Portraits of famous faces for sale in Downtown Cairo.

EDDIE GERALD

Billboards for Egyptian films make a bold backdrop for this busy Cairo thoroughfare.

The Pyramids of Mycerinus, Chephren and Cheops, with the smaller Queen's Pyramids in front.

The Sphinx's origins are unknown, but it remains one of the most recognisable monuments of Egypt.

dishes a miss, as they are all overpriced and done better elsewhere. Instead order a selection of fuul, ta'amiyya, salads and other side dishes like tahina and baba ghanoug. A bill for two can come in at less than E£20. You can also get beer here.

Islamic Cairo This is not a good part of town in which to be looking for a feed. Although there are plenty of places around Midan Hussein, they're mostly rip-off joints. *Al-Agaty* is about the only decent cheap restaurant in this area (see Kofta & Kebabs earlier). Otherwise, the options are to splash out at the *Naguib Mahfouz Cafe*, described later in this section, or snack on fiteer or fuul and ta'amiyya.

Egyptian Pancake House just off Midan Hussein is quite good value with a medium fiteer, (choose from cheese, egg, tomato, olives and ground meat, or raisins, coconut and icing sugar) for E£8. One fiteer is usually enough for a complete meal.

Al-Halwagy (☎ 591 7055) just along from the Pancake House, is a good ta'amiyya, fuul and salad place (E£10 for a meal for two) which has been around for nearly a century. You can eat at pavement tables or secrete yourself upstairs where one of the tables has a veiled view over the bazaar below. It's open 24 hours.

Naguib Mahfouz Cafe (☎ 590 3788) is actually the foyer of the Khan al-Khalili Restaurant in Islamic Cairo (see later in this section). The surroundings are extremely pleasant and almost justify the grossly inflated prices of the tea, coffee, shwarma and sandwiches on the menu.

Zamalek Cheap dining is not one of Zamalek's fortes but there are a few possibilities.

Al Dente (☎ 340 9117, 26 Bahgat Aly) is a tiny Italian place frequented by students from the nearby AUC hostel. It's pasta only – choose the type and the sauce. Portions are generous and cost between E£6 and E£10.

Maison Thomas (☎ 340 7057, 157 26th of July) is Cairo's only continental-style deli. It does by far the best pizza in Cairo,

with prices ranging from E£15 to E£20 for a 'regular', which is easily enough for two. It also has excellent though pricey sandwiches and salads. Eat in or take out, it's open 24 hours.

Zamalek Restaurant near the junction of 26th of July and Shagaret ad-Durr is a cheap little kebab house that does kofta and kebab or half a spit-roasted chicken, with bread or rice for less than E£10.

Heliopolis Traditional Egyptian fare such as kebab, kofta, shwarma and spit-roasted chicken is served at *Amphitrion* and *Palmyra*, the two terrace cafeterias on Sharia al-Ahram; and at *Al-Kashef*, at the bottom of Sharia Damascus, near the intersection with Ibrahim Laqqany.

Chabrawi's is a fuul and ta'amiyya place with a 1st floor dining room. It also has an extensive salad bar and serves some more unusual dishes like egg-fried cauliflower and *agah*, which is a cross between a puffed-up omelette and a giant ta'amiyya. Other than pasturma the place is completely vegetarian. It's extremely clean, cheap and highly recommended.

Harris Cafe at 6 Sharia Baghdad is a very pleasant Continental-style cafe, with outdoor seating, that in addition to cappuccinos, hot chocolate and the like, also does decent turkey, roast chicken, smoked salmon and club sandwiches. It's open until 12.30 am.

Restaurants

Downtown There are few really good restaurants in central Cairo, those mentioned here are the best of a fairly uninspiring bunch.

Alfy Bey Restaurant (☎ 577 4999) on Sharia Alfy has been in business since 1938 and following a recent refurbishment it's looking in good shape. The food, while basic, is very good and represents excellent value with most mains in the E£8 to E£12 range. Choose from dishes like lamb chops, kebab, grilled chicken or stuffed pigeon; but there's no beer. It's open from 11 to 1 am.

Ali Hassan al-Hatie (☎ 591 6055, 391 8829) has two branches, the one just south of the Windsor Hotel has a gem of a dining hall that almost feels like the interior of a mosque, with chandeliers suspended from a 5m-high ceiling and a menu which is an absolute delight (drilled shops?), but the food is appalling. Instead, head for the branch tucked away down an alley off Sharia 26th of July – the interior is utilitarian but the traditional Egyptian food is good and filling. Try the *moza*, roast lamb on rice (E£15).

Arabesque (☎ *574 7898, 6 Qasr el-Nil*), between Midan Talaat Harb and Midan Tahrir, scores highly for its decor and surroundings – you enter through a small art gallery into a cosy dining area divided by mashrabiyya screens and columns with a small gurgling fountain as a centrepiece. Unfortunately the dishes – a mix of traditional Egyptian fare, seafood and steaks – are very hit and miss and it's wise to steer clear of anything ambitious. Main meals range from E£25 to E£30.

Da Mario at the Nile Hilton is one of the better value hotel restaurants. It serves a variety of very well presented pastas in gigantic portions for E£18 to E£25. The courtyard garden setting is also pleasant and wine and beer are available. It's open noon to 2 am.

Estoril (☎ *574 3102*) at 12 Talaat Harb (down the alley next to the Amex office) is an old-style eatery with traditional Egyptian grills and salads plus Lebanese mezze. Quality is very variable but if you stick with a selection of starters accompanied by beer then you'll come away happy.

Le Bistro at 8 Hoda Shaarawi, 200m on beyond the Felfela, has cooking that is sufficiently Gaelic to ensure that the place is heavily patronised by Cairo's French-speaking community. The menu features some good salads (all less than E£10) and plenty of beef and chicken-in-sauce dishes for around the E£20 mark. It's open daily from 11 am to 11 pm, busy at lunch but like a morgue in the evenings.

Peking Restaurant (☎ *591 2381, 14 Sharia Ezbekiyya*) just north of 26th of July is a very passable Cantonese restaurant. Don't be put off by the shabby exterior, in-

side the place is smart, if a little dark. The food is reasonably authentic and if you've been in Egypt for any length of time it is refreshingly non-Egyptian. Expect to spend between E£20 to E£30 per person, without drinks.

Islamic Cairo Almost the only good restaurants in Islamic Cairo are the kofta and kebab places described earlier in this section.

Khan al-Khalili Restaurant (☎ *590 3788, 5 Sikket al-Badestan*) in the heart of the bazaar is run by the Oberoi hotel people so, while it's certainly classy, the 'Disney-fied Orientalism' of resident musicians and chintzy decor can come across as a bit phoney. The menu is limited and the food, though good, is overpriced. It's open from 11 am to midnight.

Zamalek One of Cairo's best restaurants is *L'Aubergine*, described in the earlier Vegetarian section, which also has a nonveggie element upstairs called *Cafe Kurnovsky*. Again the menu is ever changing but the food is invariably good with prices similar to those downstairs.

Deals (☎ *341 0502, 2 Maahad al-Swissry*) is a busy little bar that moonlights as a restaurant. The food ranges from burgers and chilli con carne to calamari and large salads. Check the blackboard for daily specials. As bar food goes, it's very good and not expensive, but if you're planning to eat make sure you get there before 8 pm to stand a chance of finding some table space.

Hana (☎ *341 3197*) on Sharia Brazil, about 400m north of 26th of July, is an unpretentious, smoky, little Korean restaurant that serves up fairly authentic South-East Asian food (the menu includes some Japanese and Chinese dishes). *Kimchi* (fermented pickles) comes complimentary, as does fruit at the end of the meal. Dishes are substantial and cost around E£20, rice is another E£3. Beer is available. It's open from 11 am to 11 pm.

La Piazza at 4 Hassan Sabry is part of a complex of restaurants under the collective title Four Corners. It has a light and airy dining room with plenty of greenery, and some of the items on the menu are quite good (though not the pastas). The onion soup is excellent as is the liver pâté mousse, and the salads are usually a good bet.

Le Steak is part of a clutch of restaurants on board the Le Pacha, a boat moored off the Corniche in Zamalek. It's one of the most exclusive establishments in town, notable for the excellent service as much as for the food. Besides steaks, the menu is a mix of Continental European with Middle Eastern favourites. It's pricey but not ridiculously so – you'll be looking at E£40 for two courses.

Mohandiseen & Doqqi Though bland and flavourless in appearance, Cairo's grey concrete suburbs contain some of the city's better restaurants and if you have the cash it's worth taxiing out here to eat.

Abu Shaqra (☎ 344 2299, 17 Gamiat ad-Dowal al-Arabiyya) is renowned for its (pricey) kebabs but it also has a variety of other dishes, such as pigeon stuffed with rice and served with chips, and *fatta moza tagen* (lamb on a bed of baked rice with pieces of bread in a vinegary sauce), both of which cost less than E£12. It's open from 9 am to 2 am. There's also a branch near Garden City at 69 Qasr el-Nil.

Tabasco (☎ 336 5583, 8 Midan Amman) in Doqqi (see the Greater Cairo map) is run by the same people as Zamalek's L'Aubergine and is every bit as popular, especially with the city's smart young set. Again, the menu changes regularly, but ranges over a wider culinary field stretching beyond the Mediterranean to include, on occasion, dishes from Mexico and Eastern Europe. Prices are more expensive here (in the E£25 to E£40 range), and you usually need to make reservations. It's open from noon to 2 am.

Maroosh (☎ 345 0972, 64 Midan Libnan) (see the Greater Cairo map), has excellent mezze which can be enjoyed while lounging in rattan chairs on a street-side terrace. Skip the main meat dishes (which shouldn't be too difficult in the case of the 'lamb scrotum sandwich') and fill with bread and dips which cost from E£5 each. For those who don't know th tabouleh from their fatoush, everything i well described in English on the menu. It's open from 8 am to 2 am.

Prestige (☎ 347 0383, 43 Sharia Geziret al-Arab) is two restaurants in one – a cheerful, cheap pizzeria (prices in the E£12 to E£20 range) and a more expensive Italianish place specialising in steaks and fresh fish (E£30 to E£40) with pavement seating under large sun umbrellas. Beer is served here, but only inside. Prestige is open from noon to 2 am.

Samakmak (☎ 347 8232, 92 Ahmed Orabi) in Sahafayeen is a branch of the well-respected Alexandrian fish restaurant (see under Places to Eat in the Alexandria section in the Alexandria & the Mediterranean Coast chapter for more details). It has an odd setting, on a paved terrace between two apartment blocks off a busy road, but the fish and seafood are excellent. You can expect to pay about E£40 for a two course meal.

Tia Maria (☎ 335 3273, 32 Sharia Jeddah) (see the Greater Cairo map) has an incredibly chintzy interior, all frilly, pink curtains and whatnot, but the Italian food is superb. We can thoroughly recommend the spaghetti carbonara (E£12), the seafood pasta (E£18), served in an enormous clam shell and the crespelle Argentine (crepes with ice cream smothered in caramel sauce). It's open from noon to 1 am.

Giza & Pyramids Rd There are very few places to eat in Giza itself. Pyramids Rd is lined with fast food joints; at the Pyramid end there are several options but most of these are overpriced and not particularly good.

TGI Friday's (☎ 570 9690) exists in Cairo on a boat moored at 26 Sharia el-Nil, between the University and Giza bridges. It's a shamelessly manufactured American feel-good franchise and the Egyptians love it. The menu offers a broad range of American cuisine and it's possible to eat for less

resist dessert. Reser-
...ded at the weekend
...st and loudest.

...ed open-air chicken
...th of Pyramids Rd.
...arge garden, which
...could be quite pleasant if it weren't for the
constant attention of clouds of mosquitoes
– last time we were there, one of our party
who had come in sandals had to spend the
evening with her feet in her handbag. There
is no menu: it's spit-roasted chicken only
(sometimes quail too) with a selection of
very good mezze as starters. The cost is
about E£20 per person. If you're taking a
taxi here from central Cairo, you can expect
it to cost about E£15 or about E£2 from the
Mena House area.

Heliopolis *Le Chantilly* at 11 Sharia
Baghdad is about the best up here. The food
is fine, if unexciting, but the surroundings
are very pleasant if you can find seating in
the garden at the back. Entrees are in the
E£25 to E£35 range, although there are a
few cheaper options, and beer is served.

Pizza Express (☎ 450 5871) on Mirghani, in front of the Heliopolis Club, is a
franchise of the UK chain. It's several cuts
above the likes of Pizza Hut, boasting a
cool, classy interior and very good food –
salads are crisp with good dressings and the
pizzas (17 varieties) are made in view of the
diners. Prices range from E£8.50 to E£17.

Self-Catering
Cairo's few western-style supermarkets are
all located out of the city centre. Probably
the most convenient is *Sunny's Supermarket* at 11 Aziz Osman in Zamalek. This
place is something of an institution among
expats and has a community notice board
displaying flats for rent, positions vacant,
missing pets and the like. Also in Zamalek
is the new *ABC Supermarket* on Mansour
Mohammed, but despite being a lot bigger
than Sunny's it doesn't offer any more in
terms of variety.

For fresh fruit and vegetables try the
Tawfiqiyya souq off the top end of Talaat

Harb, Downtown or *Souq Mansour*, off
Midan Falaki and close to Midan Tahrir. Of
the two, the Tawfiqiyya souq has a larger
range of produce and it's open until late at
night. It's also home to several bakeries and
numerous *ba'als*, the all-purpose grocers at
which you can stock up on things like
bread, cheese and yoghurt.

For bread, there are bakeries all over
town, especially around the markets, but if
you want something resembling the bread
you buy at home try the bakeries at the Nile
Hilton and Cairo Marriott hotels. For pastries and sweets the very best are found at
El-Abd which has two branches Downtown, one at 35 Talaat Harb and one on the
corner of 26th of July and Sharia Sherif.
Both are open until midnight.

ENTERTAINMENT
Western-style discos, cinemas showing
English-language films and nightclubs with
floor shows abound in Cairo. With bucks to
burn you can head to the casinos at many of
the five-star hotels or, if you've already
blown the budget, there are thousands of
ahwas (coffeehouses) where you can while
away the hours over a game of backgammon and a glass of *shai* (tea).

Ahwas
Other than in the newer suburbs like Mohandiseen, Doqqi and Agouza, almost
every street in Cairo has at least one ahwa.
One of the oldest, and certainly the most famous, is *Fishawi's*, a few steps off Midan
Hussein in Khan al-Khalili. Despite frequently being swamped by foreign tourists
and equally wide-eyed Egyptians from out-
of-town, Fishawi's manages to shrug it all
off (no waiters in fancy headgear or
Fishawi keyrings for sale) and play the role
of a regular ahwa, serving up tea, coffee
and sheesha to all comers. The place is
open 24 hours and the best time to visit is
late at night.

More colourful than Fishawi's in terms
of decor, if not atmosphere, is *Ash-Shams*,
tucked in a courtyard alleyway between the
26th of July and the Tawfiqiyya souq in

Downtown with walls adorned with gilt stucco and kitschy faux-classical paintings. However because of its popularity with travellers from the neighbouring hotels waiters have a bad tendency to overcharge and the sheesha here is terrible. Much better is the nearby *Al-Andalus*, tucked away behind the Grand Hotel on the corner of Talaat Harb and 26th of July. This place is kept spotlessly clean, prices are displayed (and we've never been cheated by staff here) and, most unusually, upstairs is a 'family room' where women can go to smoke sheesha away from masculine eyes.

Although *domina* (dominoes), *towla* (backgammon) and occasionally cards are the standard games played at ahwas, there are a couple of places popular with the chess crowd, notably the *Horreyya* on Midan Falaki in Bab al-Luq and *Zahrat al-Midan* (see The Citadel to Ibn Tulun map) on Midan Sayyida Zeinab at the junction with Sharia Abdel Meguid.

Bars

Local Bars There are several local bars on and around Sharia Alfy in Downtown but they're fairly unwelcoming. Exceptions are *Cafeteria Port Tawfiq* on Midan Orabi and *Cafeteria Orabi* (see Midan Ramses & Around map) just 150m north on the left-hand side of Sharia Orabi. *Cap d'Or* on Abdel Khalek Sarwat is a little more salubrious and is possibly the best of central Cairo's local bars. The staff and regulars here are quite used to seeing foreigners. The same applies to the cramped *Stella Bar* on the corner of Hoda Shaarawi and Talaat Harb. None of these places are suitable for women on their own and the toilets are pretty foul in all of them (at the Stella you can at least nip a few doors down to use the ones at the Felfela Restaurant).

Although primarily a coffeehouse, *Cafeteria Horreyya Coffeehouse* on Midan Falaki also serves Stella (the cheapest in town at E£5.25), while on nearby Midan Tahrir *Ali Baba Cafeteria* is a great place to sink a cold one (E£6.25), especially if you can get the upstairs table by the window.

Western-Style Bars Like any other busy city, bars and hang-outs open and close and go in and out of favour. At the time of writing the most popular place to go is upstairs at *L'Aubergine* at 5 Sayyed al-Bakry in Zamalek. The crowd is largely thirtysomething, expat residents, and the atmosphere is cool jazz and candlelight. A beer costs E£9.50. It gets busy from 11 pm onwards and closes about 2 am. Just up the street, *Deals* is a small cellar bar which gets too packed for comfort late in the evening and at weekends but is pleasant enough at quieter times.

Tabasco at 8 Midan Amman and *El Gato Negro* at 32 Sharia Jeddah, both in Doqqi (see the Greater Cairo map), pull in a young, trendy and mainly Egyptian crowd. The music is usually good and the decor is smart and hip. The drawback is that both places have hefty minimum charges. A good night out at either of these places is going to set you back at least E£40 or E£50.

All the larger hotels have bars, almost all of which are bland and very pricey. Bucking the trend and, in fact, one of the most relaxing places to drink in Cairo, is the creaky *Lounge Bar* at the Windsor Hotel (see the Central Cairo map). Seating is on sofas or remodelled padded barrels and the decor is post-colonial. A lot of locals use the place, particularly those in the theatre and cinema business and solo women travellers should feel quite comfortable here. It's open until 1 am and beer is E£6.50.

The rooftop bar at *Odeon Palace Hotel* on Abdel Hamid Said (off Talaat Harb) draws a local crowd similar to that at the Windsor, though its main appeal is that it's open 24 hours. The minimum charge is E£10 and a beer is just more than half that. There is also a rooftop terrace bar at *Fontana Hotel*, which has a fantastic view of the chaos down below on Midan Ramses.

Live Music Cairo's live music scene is next to nonexistent. It's largely limited to crooners doing covers in restaurants. For instance, every night at *TGI Friday's* (see under Giza & Pyramids Rd in the Places to

Eat section) at 10 pm there's a live music spot; it's pretty unexciting stuff. The one blip of activity is at *Cairo Jazz Club (☎ 345 9939, 197 26th of July, Agouza)*. There's live jazz or blues here every night and the club is just as suitably smoky and seedy as a jazz club should be. Unfortunately there's a minimum charge of E£30.

Liquor Stores Takeaway alcohol supplies can be bought from the liquor stores irregularly dotted around the city. There are several at the top end of Talaat Harb including *Nicolakis*, next to the Casablanca restaurant. In Zamalek there's a dedicated Stella shop a few doors along on 26th of July near the Marriott, or *Ambrosio* on Sharia Brazil. Foreign beers are not available except at duty-free stores (see the Customs section in the Facts for the Visitor chapter).

Casinos

Nearly all Cairo's five-star hotels have casinos, open to non-Egyptians only (take your passport). All games are conducted in US dollars or other major foreign currencies, with a minimum stake of US$1. Smart casual attire is required. These casinos are not to be confused with local *casinos*, the name given for certain restaurants popular with families on a day out.

Cinemas

For general information on cinema-going in Egypt see under The Cultural Scene in the Entertainment section in the Facts for the Visitor chapter. For details of what's showing check the *Egyptian Gazette*, *Middle East Times* or *Al-Ahram Weekly* newspapers. The following of Cairo's cinemas regularly screen English-language films:

Cairo Sheraton
(☎ 360 6081) Sharia al-Giza, Doqqi
The closest Cairo has to an arthouse cinema, in that it tends to forgo blockbusters for Merchant Ivory films and the like.
Horreyya I & II
(☎ 452 9980) 6th floor Horreyya Mall, Sharia al-Ahram, Heliopolis.
Cairo's best cinema in terms of sound and

comfort though closed at the time of writing due to fire.
Karim I & II
(☎ 591 6095) Emad ad-Din, central Cairo
This old cinema has been recently refurbished. The programming and cheap tickets make it popular with young Egyptian males – it's not a place for women to go unaccompanied.
Metro
(☎ 393 7566) Talaat Harb, Downtown
Once Cairo's finest, now one of its scruffiest.
Normandy
(☎ 258 0254) 32 Sharia al-Ahram, Heliopolis
One of Cairo's older cinemas, with open-air screenings in summer.
Radio
(☎ 575 6562) 24 Talaat Harb, Downtown
See comments on Karim I & II.
Ramses Hilton I & II
(☎ 574 7436) 7th floor, Ramses Hilton Mall
Two relatively new screens, well maintained, although II is a bit small.
Rennaisance
(☎ 578 4915) World Trade Centre annexe, Corniche el-Nil, Bulaq
Cairo's newest and swishest cinema.
Tahrir
(☎ 335 4726) 122 Sharia Tahrir, Doqqi
Good comfortable cinema where single females shouldn't receive any hassle.

Discos & Nightclubs

Opened in 1998, *Crazy House Disco (☎ 366 1082)* is part of a huge new entertainment complex called Cairo Land, bizarrely located on the edge of the city's ancient Southern Cemetery. The club (Cairo's only purpose-built dance venue) is huge with three dance floors. Admission is E£50 on Thursdays, E£25 every other night, including two free beers. It opens about midnight and goes through to 6 am. It's at 1 Salah Salem and to get there you'll have to take a taxi (about E£5 from central Cairo).

The other 'in' place at the time of writing is Thursday night at *El Gato Negro (☎ 361 6888)* at 32 Sharia Jeddah in Doqqi. The place is loud and the dance floor crushed, despite some lousy music. There's a E£20 admission charge which gets you one free beer. At about 2 am a courtesy mini bus shuttles all comers over to the Crazy House Disco.

Much more interesting and much more fun is *Africana* on Pyramids Rd, where sounds south of the Sahara make up the play list. A place for Cairo's huge communities of African students and refugees to let off steam, it's hot and sweaty with frequent brawls and 'high velocity chair shows' – but that's all part of the charm. It's open Thursday to Saturday from around midnight. Admission is E£25 which gets you one beer. The club is not easy to find: it's on the right as you head towards the Pyramids, beyond the Haram Theatre and then one block past KFC.

Belly-Dancing The best dancers perform at Cairo's five-star hotels. Dina, reckoned to be the best, and the legendary Fifi Abdou perform at the *Meridien Le Caire* (Dina on Wednesday and Saturday; Fifi on Thursday and Friday). The shows begin at midnight and cost E£175, including a buffet but not drinks. Another big name, Lucy, dances at the *Semiramis* on Tuesday and Saturday. The show is from 11pm to 4 am and costs E£190, not including drinks. She's also at the *Parisienne* club on Pyramids Rd on Thursday nights.

At the other end of the scale, it is possible to watch belly-dancing for just a few pounds. There are several places Downtown plus plenty more along Pyramids Rd (generally expensive rip-off joints) that cater mainly to local Egyptians rather than the oil-rich Gulf Arabs who make up the five star audiences. It has to be said that these places are fairly seedy and most of the dancers have the appearance and grace of amateur wrestlers, but it can be fun especially when the inebriated patrons join in as they invariably do. The *Palmyra*, just off 26th of July, is a cavernous place with the full Arab music contingent, belly-dancers (from about 1 to 4 am) and occasionally other acts like acrobats. There is an entry charge of E£3 and a Stella costs E£12. Alternatively, there's also the *New Arizona* and the *Shererazad Nightclub*, both on Sharia Alfy (the latter is above the Alfy Bey Restaurant), but neither of these is as entertaining as the Palmyra.

Music, Theatre & Dance

Cairo Opera House (☎ 342 0598) on Gezira is the city's premier performing arts venue.

Well-known international troupes sometimes perform here (the Bolshoi Ballet visits almost annually) and at other times the recitals by local companies, such as the Cairo Opera Ballet Company and the Cairo Orchestra, are worth catching. In addition to a main hall and small hall, the Opera House also has an open-air theatre and summer amphitheatre. Check *Egypt Today* and *Al-Ahram Weekly* for what's on, or pass by and pick up a program. Jacket and tie are required by males for main hall performances, but less well-dressed travellers have been known to borrow them from staff.

There are often music recitals and plays of varying quality at the Ewart Hall and Wallace Theatre, both part of the American University in Cairo (AUC) campus. In Islamic Cairo theatre performances and music evenings are held at the House of Zeinab Khatoun and the Al-Ghouri complex, especially during Ramadan. It's worth attending something at each of these places at least once, if only for the setting. Also worth checking, especially if you have kids, is the *Cairo Puppet Theatre* in the Ezbekiyya Gardens, just north of Ataba. Performances are usually held late in the morning from Sunday to Thursday between October and May. Again, check the two publications mentioned earlier for notices of events.

Sufi Dancing

On Wednesday and Saturday nights from 9 pm (9.30 pm in winter) the Al-Tannoura Egyptian Heritage Dance Troupe gives a 1½ hour display of Sufi dancing in the Mausoleum of al-Ghouri in Islamic Cairo. The troupe has toured overseas, and their colourful performances are extremely popular. Admission is free and it's advisable to come early, especially in winter, as the small auditorium can get quite crowded.

SHOPPING

The Shopping section in the Facts for the Visitor chapter gives some idea of what to look out for in Egypt. And if it's available anywhere in Egypt it will be found in Cairo.

For regular, run-of-the-mill tourist souvenirs the sprawling Khan al-Khalili bazaar is definitely the place to head for (see that section earlier this chapter).

For more general shopping, including clothes, try the Ramses Hilton Mall which has seven floors of all kinds of stores, or the World Trade Centre, which houses a lot of Benetton-type outlets as well as a few more one-off shops.

For something more unusual, as a gift or memento, definitely take a look in Khan Misr Touloun (☎ 365 2227) which is opposite the entrance to the Ibn Tulun mosque in Islamic Cairo (see The Citadel to Ibn Tulun map). Run by a French lady and her Egyptian husband, it's a beautiful shop that carries handicrafts from the villages and oases of Egypt including wooden chests, bowls and plates, marionettes, blown glass, clay figurines, scarves and woven clothing. It's open from 10 am to 5 pm Monday to Friday.

Marketing Link (☎ 341 5123) is a fairtrade shop with merchandise produced in income-generating projects throughout Egypt. Items on sale include Bedouin rugs from Sinai and the northern Western Desert embroidery from Sinai, handmade paper from Muqattam, Bedouin beadwork and Upper Egyptian shawls. The prices are competitive and often better than you can get in the souq, plus there is quality control to ensure that you're getting good stuff. It's at 27 Yehia Ibrahim, apartment 8, Zamalek.

Nagada (☎/fax 594 3249) has beautiful handwoven textiles from the town of the same name (about 28km north of Luxor), as well as handmade pottery from Al-Fayoum and clothes, lamps and jewellery. It's at 8 Sharia Dar al-Shefa, 3rd floor, Garden City. To get here head south along the Corniche and take the left immediately opposite the turn-off on the right for Le Meridien hotel; follow the street that veers to the right, then take the first right and it's the second or third building along.

Also worth a look is Nomad (☎ 341 1917) at 14 Al-Saraya al-Gezira, up on the 1st floor of an apartment building down the street from the Cairo Marriott. This is a small, well-hidden gem of a place that specialises in jewellery and traditional Bedouin craft and costumes. It's open from 10 am to 3 pm Monday to Saturday.

GETTING THERE & AWAY
See the Getting Around chapter for information on the best modes of transport between Cairo and the rest of the country.

Air
EgyptAir has a number of offices around town including their main sales office on Sharia Adly (☎ 392 7649), another office on the corner of Talaat Harb and Sharia al-Bustan (☎ 393 2836), one in the garden courtyard of the Nile Hilton (☎ 576 5200), and one at 22 Ibrahim Laqqany up in Heliopolis (☎ 291 5461). All are open from 8 am to 8 pm. For general EgyptAir information call ☎ 245 0270.

For international air fare details see the Getting There & Away chapter, for domestic flights, see the Getting Around chapter.

You can call Cairo airport for flight information (☎ 291 4255). The addresses of some of the airlines represented in Cairo include:

Air France
    (☎ 275 8899) 2 Midan Talaat Harb
Air Malta
    (☎ 575 6022) 2 Talaat Harb
Air Sinai
    (☎ 577 2949) Nile Hilton
Alitalia
    (☎ 578 5823) Nile Hilton
Austrian Airlines
    (☎ 392 1522) 22 Qasr el-Nil
British Airways
    (☎ 578 0743) 1 Sharia al-Bustan, Midan Tahrir
EgyptAir
    See above
Emirates
    (☎ 340 1142) Cairo Marriott, Zamalek
Ethiopian Airlines
    (☎ 574 0603) Nile Hilton
Gulf Air
    (☎ 574 3336) 21 Mahmoud Bassiouni
Japan Airlines (JAL)
    (☎ 574 7233) Nile Hilton
Kenya Airways
    (☎ 579 8529) Nile Hilton
    (May soon move in to share offices with KLM)
KLM (Royal Dutch Airlines)
    (☎ 574 7004) 11 Qasr el-Nil

Lufthansa
(☎ 342 0471) 6 Al-Sheikh al-Marsafi, Zamalek
Middle East Airlines
(☎ 574 3422) 12 Qasr el-Nil
Olympic Airways
(☎ 393 1459) 23 Qasr el-Nil
Royal Jordanian Airlines
(☎ 575 0614) 6 Qasr el-Nil
Scandinavian Airlines (SAS)
(☎ 575 3627) 2 Champollion, Midan Tahrir
Singapore Airlines
(☎ 578 0321) Nile Hilton
Sudan Airways
(☎ 578 7145) 1 Sharia al-Bustan, Midan Tahrir
Swissair
(☎ 392 1522) 22 Qasr el-Nil
Syrian Air
(☎ 392 8284) 35 Talaat Harb
Turkish Airlines
(☎ 578 4634) 3 Midan Mustafa Kamel
TWA
(☎ 574 9904) 1 Qasr el-Nil, Midan Tahrir

Bus

Bus Stations The city is in the process of being reordered and part of that process is the relocation of its bus stations. In an attempt to keep the big buses out of the Downtown area, a big new bus station is under construction in the Bulaq district, just north of the centre. Called the Turgoman garage, it's located on Sharia al-Gisr, 1km north-west of the intersection of sharias Galaa and 26th of July (see the Greater Cairo map). It's an awkward location in that it's too far to walk to from central Cairo and the only way to get there is by taxi (E£2 from Downtown). At the time of writing the station has no facilities and is nothing more than a series of prefab ticket huts on a vast, partly asphalted wasteland. From here buses go to Alexandria, Marsa Matruh, Hurghada, Safaga, Al-Quseir, Marsa Alam, Sharm el-Sheikh, Dahab, Nuweiba, Luxor and Aswan, as well as Amman, Benghazi, Riyadh and Tripoli.

There are further bus stations at Midan Ulali, just south of Midan Ramses (see the Midan Ramses & Around map), from where buses depart for the Delta and the Suez towns and at Ahmed Helmy bus station, immediately north of the train station,

which has local services to Middle Egypt towns like Beni Suef, Minya and Asyut.

Sinai buses mostly go from the Sinai terminal in Abbassiyya (see the Greater Cairo map). This is some distance north of the city centre and to get here you need to take bus Nos 983 or 948 or minibus No 32 from the station at Midan Abdel Moniem Riad. Alternatively, a taxi to/from Downtown should cost E£6. Sinai buses also usually stop at the Al-Mazar garage in Heliopolis.

Alexandria & the Mediterranean Coast Superjet's mega-comfy buses will whisk you from Turgoman garage to Alexandria's Sidi Gaber bus station in about 2½ hours. There are departures every 30 minutes, starting at 5 am and finishing at 9 or 10 pm; the fare is E£20.

The West Delta Bus Co also has services to Alexandria from Turgoman garage with departures every 30 minutes from about 5.30 am onwards. Fares cost from E£16 to E£20, depending on the type of bus. Buses depart for Marsa Matruh (E£25 to E£35, five hours), at 7.15, 7.45 and 8.30 am and 4.30 pm.

The Nile Delta, Suez Canal & Red Sea Coast The East Delta Bus Co's white and yellow-green striped buses leave from two depots on Midan Ulali. Buses depart from the parking lot opposite the telephone centrale every 30 minutes to Mansura (E£6 to E£7, 2½ hours) and hourly to Damietta (E£9 to E£10.50, 3½ hours). From around the corner there are hourly buses to Port Said (E£13 to E£15, three hours), buses every 30 minutes to Ismailia (E£6, 2½ hours) and services every 15 minutes to Suez (E£6, 1½ to two hours).

To get to Tanta (E£6) and other smaller Delta destinations, you can take a Middle Delta Bus Co bus from the Turgoman garage. They depart hourly between 7 am and 9 pm.

Hurghada and other Red Sea buses also all go from Turgoman garage. Superjet has three daily Hurghada services (E£45 to E£47, six hours) departing at 8.30 am, and 2.30 and 10.30 pm. Upper Egypt Travel has at least nine, the first departing at 9 am, the latest at 11.30 pm. The 10 am, noon, 8.30 and 9.40 am services all continue to Safaga (E£50). There's one daily bus to Al-Quseir (E£55) at 10 pm (stopping at Safaga) and one to Marsa Alam (E£65) at 6.30 pm.

Upper Egypt Upper Egypt Travel has luxury buses from Turgoman garage to Luxor (E£50, 10 to 11 hours) departing daily at 8.30 pm and to Aswan (E£55, 12 hours) at 5.15 pm. The same company's ordinary buses (cheap no-frills green buses) leave from the Ahmed Helmy bus station behind Ramses train station and go to destinations such as Beni Suef (E£4.50), Al-Minya (E£8 to E£11, four hours), Asyut (E£10 to E£15, six to seven hours), Luxor and Aswan. Buses to destinations such as Minya and Asyut run every 30 to 60 minutes from about 6 am to 6 pm.

Sinai Nearly all East Delta Bus Co buses to the Sinai leave from the Sinai terminal (☎ 482 4753) in Abbassiyya. These buses are considerably more expensive than those in the rest of the country. They run to Sharm el-Sheikh (E£35 to E£65, seven hours) 10 times per day between 7 am and midnight. The 8 pm bus is the cheapest (E£35); services between 8.30 am and 5pm cost more (E£50); and the final three buses between 11.30 pm and midnight are the most expensive (E£65). The 8.30 am and 2 and 5 pm and midnight buses go on to Dahab (E£55, but E£70 on the midnight bus, nine hours). There are two buses daily to Nuweiba (nine hours) at 8 am (E£50) and 11 pm (E£55), both of which carry on to Taba (E£50/70, 10 hours). The early morning bus goes via St Katherine's Monastery and there's an additional St Katherine's service (E£35, 7½ hours) at 11.30 am.

East Delta Bus Co buses to Al-Arish and Rafah leave from Midan Ulali but also pick up passengers at the Sinai terminal. There are buses to Al-Arish (five hours) at 8 and 8.30 am (E£35) and at 12.30 and 4.30 pm (E£25). The 8.30 am and 4.30 pm buses go on to Rafah (E£35, six hours).

Superjet also has a nightly service to Sharm el-Sheikh (E£55, seven hours) which leaves at 11 pm from the Turgoman garage.

Western Oases All Western Oases buses go from a small station tucked tight against the western wall of the Citadel, just south of Midan Salah ad-Din. The buses also stop near Midan Giza at the 6th of October City minibus stop where the flyover forks and Pyramids Rd begins to pick up additional passengers, however if you want to be sure of a place it's best to reserve tickets 24 hours in advance and catch the bus from the main terminal.

Note, there are no direct buses from here to Siwa – to get there take a bus to Alexandria or Marsa Matruh, and then another onwards.

To Bahariyya (Bawiti) (six hours) there are buses at 7 and 8 am (E£12.25) and 3 and 6.30 pm (E£18.25), on Friday there's one service only at 9 am. Take some food and water as sometimes the oases buses don't stop anywhere useful for breaks.

For Farafra (10 to 11 hours) take the 7 am (E£25.50) or 6.30 pm (E£30.50) Bahariyya bus. The road linking Farafra and Bahariyya is still partly unpaved which makes this leg of the journey long and dusty.

To Dakhla (Mut) there are three daily buses via Asyut and Al-Kharga. All of these buses have air-con (if it works), the priceyer ones also have video. They leave at 7 and 8 am and 6.30 and 8 pm (E£42.50, 12 to 14 hours). The evening services are supposedly direct and do not stop in Asyut itself.

To Al-Kharga (E£37.50, nine hours) there are two buses a day (via Asyut) at 9 am and 9 pm (E£32 with air-con and video). The three daily buses to Dakhla also go via Al-Kharga but, according to the Upper Egypt Bus Co, these are direct buses for Dakhla and do not pick up or set down passengers in Al-Kharga.

Al-Fayoum Buses for Al-Fayoum leave from the Ahmed Helmy bus station and a separate station in the vicinity of Midan Giza. For the latter, take a Pyramids minibus from Midan Abdel Moniem Riad and get off just after Midan Giza, immediately after passing under a railway bridge, then walk north along the canal, the bus station is 500m ahead. Buses go every 15 minutes and the fare is E£3.50 on the newer air-con buses or E£2.50 on the old nonair-con heaps.

Israel & the Palestinian Territories For details on buses to Tel Aviv and Jerusalem, see the Getting There & Away chapter.

Jordan Superjet has a daily 7 am Amman service departing from the Turgoman garage. The fare, including the ferry, is US$66. The East Delta Bus Co also has a daily Amman service, this one departing at 8 am from Abbassiyya's Sinai terminal; the fare is E£63 plus US$32 (or roughly US$50 in total).

Libya Superjet has a daily 7 am Libya service departing from the Turgoman garage. The fare to Benghazi is E£100, while to Tripoli it's E£205. The East Delta Bus Co runs a bus to Tripoli (E£180) at 10 am every Monday and Thursday.

Train

Ramses station (Mahattat Ramses), on Midan Ramses, is Cairo's main train station and it's 100% pure confusion. If you need help there is a tourist office with tourist police just inside the main entrance on the left, open daily from 8 am to 8 pm. In a secondary entrance to the right is a small post office and next to it is the left-luggage area (marked 'cloak room'), which is open 24 hours and charges E£1 per piece.

For general details about the types of trains and tickets that are available, including student discounts, see the Train section in the Getting Around chapter. For travel information call ☎ 147 or ☎ 575 3555.

Luxor & Aswan If you can afford it, the wagons-lit sleeper is the way to travel (see the Getting Around chapter for a description of this service). It departs Cairo at 7.45 pm each evening, arriving in Luxor at 5.10 the next morning (the perfect hour to head off sightseeing) and Aswan at 9.30 am. An evening

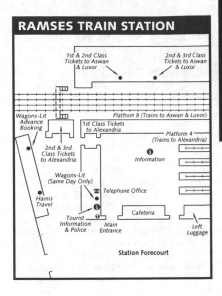

meal and early breakfast are included in the fare of E£314.50 one way or E£579 return. The same fare applies to both Luxor and Aswan; if you want to go to both places you have to use the Luxor-Aswan leg within 72 hours. There is no student discount.

The wagons-lit booking office (☎ 574 9474, fax 574 9074) is in a building just south of the main station building, across the car park – follow the blue on yellow signs which read 'Res. Office'. Unfortunately, they don't take credit cards or travellers cheques – it's cash only. The office is open from 9 am to 3 pm (Friday until 2 pm). After 3 pm you can use the wagons-lit office in the main hall of the station, although this office is really for same-day travel only. In the high season (from about October to April) it is best to book two or three days in advance. If you want to book your tickets in advance of your arrival in Egypt you could try using Hamis Travel (see Travel Agencies earlier this chapter).

Tickets for this train can also be booked at the wagons-lit office at Shepheard's Hotel in central Cairo.

Other Trains Aside from the wagons-lit train, there are only two other services that foreigners are currently allowed to travel on down to Upper Egypt; these are the No 980, departing Cairo daily at 7.30 am, and the No 996, leaving at 10 pm. First/2nd class fares on the night train are E£51/31 to Luxor, while to Aswan it's E£63/37. Fares on the morning train are E£3 cheaper. Students pay two-thirds the full fare. The journey time is about 10 hours to Luxor and a further five on to Aswan.

Tickets can be bought from the ticket office beside platform 11, that is, on the other side of the tracks from the main hall (see the Ramses Station map). The trains themselves, at the time of writing, go from platform eight.

You must buy your tickets at least a couple of days in advance.

Alexandria & Northern Destinations

The best trains running between Cairo and Alexandria are the Turbini (also known as the Spanish trains). They make only one stop, at Sidi Gaber station in Alexandria, and they take 2½ hours. Second class in this train is about as good as 1st class in most others. You can't mistake the train, it looks a little like the high-speed European TGVs. They depart Cairo at 9 am and 3 and 6 pm and tickets for 1st/2nd class air-con cost E£22/17.

The next best trains are the Faransawi, the 'French-line' services, which take at least 2¾ hours and cost E£20/12 in 1st/2nd class. They stop at Benha, Tanta (E£9/6) and Damanhur on the way and leave at 6, 8.30 and 11 am, noon (this train stops in Tanta only) and 2.10, 4, 5, 8 (does not stop in Tanta) and 9.30 pm.

All other Alexandria services take hours and hours making innumerable stops.

For 1st class tickets head for the windows directly in front of you in the main entrance, past the tourist office and the telephones. For 2nd class ordinary tickets, bear left at the telephones, down the steps and into the small hall just to the right.

Suez Canal & Eastern Destinations

Four trains make the trip from Cairo to Port Said (four hours), stopping en route at

---

Ticket Scams

Some readers have reported being told they cannot buy tickets all the way to Aswan, but that they must pay for as far as, say, Edfu, and worry about the rest later. They then found themselves paying rather a lot for another ticket on the train to complete the journey. Don't fall for this – insist on a ticket all the way through. Conversely, we've had a letter from another reader who wanted to buy a ticket to Luxor but was told all they had left were tickets for Aswan – which is just absolute nonsense. If you have any problems, go and see the tourist office in the main hall.

There have also been problems caused by touts buying up large blocks of tickets and holding them to resell at a premium. Hence, when you go along to the station there are no seats left. In this case, staff at some of the Downtown hostels can get the tickets for you for about E£10 more than the official price.

Zagazig, Ismailia and Qantara. They leave at 6.20 and 11.30 am and 2.30 and 6.30 pm. There are six other trains for Ismailia (three hours). Those making the fewest stops leave at 5.35 and 8.45 am. There is no 1st class service; the 2nd class air-con fare to Port Said is E£14 and to Ismailia it will set you back E£8.

Service Taxi

Most service taxis depart from lots around Ramses station and Midan Ulali. Just north of Ulali, to the right of the Shubra road, is the area for Delta and Suez services. From here they depart for Mansura, Qantara, Damietta, Suez and Ismailia (E£5), Port Said (E£8), Al-Arish (E£12, five hours) and Rafah (E£15, six hours). Fares are determined by the distance, so keep an eye out for what others pay to get the set price.

Service taxis for Alexandria leave from in front of Ramses station, at the time of research the set fare was E£10.

Taxis for destinations in and around Al-Fayoum (E£4) leave from the Al-Fayoum bus stop near Midan Giza (see under Al-Fayoum in the Bus section earlier this chapter).

GETTING AROUND

Overcrowded buses and minibuses are the most common form of transport for the majority of Cairenes, but for anyone who prefers breathing while travelling, taxis are the only option. By western standards they are very cheap and there's never one far away. The only time when taxis aren't the best bet is when you are travelling a fair distance, say north to Heliopolis or south down to Ma'adi, in which case they become a little expensive. In such cases, the alternatives are the bus to Heliopolis or the metro to Ma'adi.

It's also wise to avoid taking taxis between about 2.30 and 4 pm (that's always supposing that you can find one free at this time of day) as this is when everyone slinks off home for the day and the roads are even more congested than usual.

To/From the Airport

Bus Don't believe anyone who tells you that there is no bus to the city centre – there are two, plus a minibus.

The best is the new No 356 airport service. These are big white, modern, air-con buses that run from Midan Abdel Moniem Riad behind the Egyptian Museum in central Cairo up via Abbassiyya and Heliopolis to Terminal II, where they stop for just a few minutes, then go on to Terminal I. The buses run at 20 minute intervals from 5.45 am to 11 pm and the fare is E£2, plus E£1 per large luggage item. To find the buses at either terminal, head out into the car park and you'll spot the stand, if not a waiting bus.

In addition to the No 356, there's local bus No 400 (25pt) and minibus No 27 (50pt), which both follow the same route as the No 356 airport service.

Taxi Cairo's is not the easiest of airports to get away from. Although there are bus services they are far from obvious and you may well just decide to grab a taxi. If you do,

then the going rate to central Cairo is around E£25 to E£30. Heading up to the airport from the centre there are more taxis around so you can afford to bargain harder – you shouldn't pay more than E£20 to E£25. Avoid the large 'official' airport taxis as they have a fixed rate of E£46. It's generally better to get out of the arrivals hall and away from all the touts before starting to bargain with anyone. Walking away often tends to bring the price down. Triple check the agreed fare, as there is an irritating tendency for drivers to nod at what you say and hit you with an out-of-the-world fare later on.

In the traffic-free early hours of the morning (when so many flights seem to arrive) the journey to central Cairo takes 20 minutes but at other, busier times of the day it can take well over an hour.

Bus & Minibus

See the Getting Around chapter for general information on Egypt's city buses.

Cairo's main local bus and minibus stations are at Midan Abdel Moniem Riad, behind the Egyptian Museum. From here, services leave for just about everywhere in the city.

Microbus

Increasingly, Cairenes are using private microbuses (as opposed to the public minibuses) to get around. Destinations are not marked in any language, so they are hard to use unless you are familiar with their routes. What you do is position yourself beside the road that leads where you want to go and when a microbus passes, yell out your destination – if it's going where you want to go and there are seats free it'll stop.

Metro

The Metro system is startlingly efficient, and the stations are cleaner than any other public places in Cairo. It's also extremely inexpensive and, outside rush hours, not too crowded. At the time of writing there were two lines in operation with a third under construction and a fourth on the planning board. The main line, with 32 stations,

CAIRO

THE CAIRO METRO

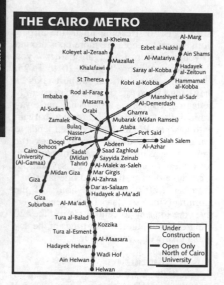

Shubra al-Kheima
Al-Marg
Koleyet al-Zeraah
Ezbet al-Nakhl
Ain Shams
Mazallat
Al-Matariya
Khalafawi
Saray al-Kobba
Hadayek al-Zeitoun
St Theresa
Kobri al-Kobba
Hammamat al-Kobba
Rod al-Farag
Imbaba
Masarra
Manshiyet al-Sadr
Al-Sudan
Orabi
Al-Demerdash
Zamalek
Ghamra
Bulaq
Mubarak (Midan Ramses)
Nasser-Gezira
Ataba
Doqqi
Port Said
Behoos
Abdeen
Salah Salem
Cairo University (Al-Gamaa)
Sadat (Midan Tahrir)
Saad Zaghloul
Al-Azhar
Sayyida Zeinab
Midan Giza
Al-Malek as-Saleh
Giza
Mar Girgis
Al-Zahraa
Giza Suburban
Al-Ma'adi
Dar as-Salaam
Hadayek al-Ma'adi
Tura al-Balad
Sakanat al-Ma'adi
Kozzika
Tura al-Esment
Al-Maasara
Hadayek Helwan
Wadi Hof
Ain Helwan
Helwan

Under Construction
Open Only North of Cairo University

stretches for 43km from the southern suburb of Helwan up to Al-Marg, near Heliopolis. You are most likely to use the Metro if you're going down to Old Cairo (served by a station called Mar Girgis). The second line connects the working class district of Shubra with Cairo University (convenient for the zoo), stopping off at the Opera House complex enroute. This line will eventually be extended south through Midan Giza to Giza train station. A new line, travelling underneath the Nile, links Cairo University to Tahrir Square 5km away in the centre of the city.

Metro stations are easily identified by signs with a big red 'M' in a blue star.

It costs 30pt to ride up to nine stops; 50pt for up to 16 stops; 70pt for up to 22 stops; E£1 for up to 28 stops; and E£1.20 to ride the length of the line. The service starts at about 5 am and closes around 11.30 pm.

Men should note that the first carriage is reserved for women only. Women who want to ride in this carriage should make sure they're standing at the right place on the platform (near where the front part of

the train will stop) as the trains don't hang around in the station for long.

Tram

Most of Cairo's trams (known to Cairenes, confusingly, as 'metros') have been phased out. The remaining line a visitor to the city might use is that which connects central Cairo to Heliopolis. This runs from just north of Midan Ramses up to Midan Roxy on the southern edge of Heliopolis, at which point the line divides into three: Nouzha, Mirghani and Abdel Aziz Fahmy. For further details see the Heliopolis section earlier in this chapter.

Car

Driving in Cairo is not for the faint-hearted. It's like the chariot race in Ben Hur only with Fiats. The roads are always crowded – the city's rush hour begins at about 8 am each morning and doesn't slack off until about midnight. Lane markings are ignored as Cairo drivers treat other vehicles like obstacles on a slalom, and a favourite manoeuvre is to suddenly sweep across multiple lanes of traffic to make a turn on the opposite side of the carriageway. Brakes are scorned in favour of the horn. Traffic lights are discretionary unless enforced by a policeman, who is equally likely to wave you through on a red light and halt you on green. Driving at night is particularly hazardous as headlights are reserved exclusively for flashing oncoming vehicles.

It is a wonder that the roads aren't strewn with shattered glass and crumpled bits of car bodywork. But in fact there are very few accidents. Cairo drivers have their own road rules, they look out for each other and they are extremely tolerant of the type of driving that anywhere else would spark an epidemic of road-rage. Things only tend to go awry when an inexperienced driver is thrown into the mix – something anyone considering driving here should bear in mind.

For more information see the Road Rules section in the Getting Around chapter.

Rental If you are crazy enough to want to battle the traffic in Cairo, there are a number of car rental agencies in the city, including the big three: Avis, Hertz and Budget.

You need to be over the age of 25 and have an international driving permit. However, the rental agencies don't care whether you have a permit or not and will rent you the car regardless but you can cop a heavy fine if you're caught driving without one.

As an indication of prices, for a small car like a Suzuki Swift you'll be looking at about US$40 per day, plus up to US$0.20 for each extra kilometre. A Toyota Corolla is about US$56 to US$60 per day, plus around US$0.25 per kilometre. Remember that a 10% to 17% tax will be added to your bill. It's usually possible to pay with travellers cheques or by credit card.

Avis
  (☎ 354 7400, fax 356 2464) 16 Mamal as-Sukkar, Garden City
  (☎ 576 6432) Nile Hilton
  (☎ 291 4288) Cairo international airport, ask for Avis
  (☎ 291 0223) Heliopolis Sheraton
  (☎ 290 5055) Meridien Heliopolis
Budget Rent-a-Car
  (☎ 340 0070, fax 341 3790) 5 Makrizy, Zamalek (head office)
  (☎ 340 6667) Cairo Marriott
  (☎ 265 2395) Cairo international airport
Europcar
  (☎ 347 4712/3, fax 303 6123) 27 Sharia Libnan, Mohandiseen
  (☎ 291 4288) Cairo international airport, ask for Europcar
Hertz
  (☎ 303 4241, fax 347 4172) 195 Sharia 26th of July, Mohandiseen
  (☎ 574 4400) Ramses Hilton
  (☎ 354 3239, fax 356 3020) Semiramis Inter-Continental
  (☎ 291 4288) Cairo international airport, ask for Hertz
J Car
  (☎ 335 0521, fax 360 3255) 33 Sharia Missaha, Doqqi
  (☎ 291 4288) Cairo international airport, ask for J Car
Thrifty
  (☎/fax 266 3313) 1 Al-Entesar, Heliopolis
  (☎ 265 2620) Cairo international airport

Taxi

If it's too far to walk, then the easiest way of getting around in Cairo is to flag down a taxi. They're cheap enough to make the hassle of the buses redundant. Use the following as a rough guide to what you should be paying for taxi rides around Cairo:

Downtown to the Airport	E£25
Downtown to Heliopolis	E£10
Downtown to Khan al-Khalili	E£3
Downtown to Zamalek	E£3
Midan Tahrir to the Citadel	E£4
Midan Tahrir to Midan Ramses	E£2
Midan Tahrir to the Pyramids	E£15

Note, these fares are generous and are more than a local would pay. For comprehensive information on taxi etiquette see the Getting Around chapter.

Hantour

These horse-drawn carriages and their insistent drivers hang around on the Corniche near the Helnan Shepheard's hotel and on Gezira near the Cairo Tower. They aren't a feasible means of getting around the city and are there for pleasure rides only.

River Bus

The river bus terminal is at Maspero, on the Corniche in front of the big round TV building. From here, boats depart every 15 minutes or so between 6.30 am and 3.45 pm for University, a landing over on the Giza side of the river just north of the University Bridge. Every second boat continues south on to Manial, Rhoda, Giza and Masr al-Qadima (Old Cairo). The last stop is convenient for Coptic Cairo. The complete trip takes 50 minutes and the fare is 50pt.

Immediately south of the river bus terminal at Maspero is the departure point for boats to Qanater (see the Nile Delta section in the Around Cairo chapter).

Around Cairo

Most of the destinations described in this chapter can be visited on day trips from Cairo, except for Al-Fayoum, where, if you don't have your own transport, you'll have to reckon on staying the night.

MEMPHIS

Memphis, once the glorious Old Kingdom capital of Egypt, has almost completely vanished. It is believed that the city was founded around 3100 BC, probably by King Menes, when Upper and Lower Egypt were first united. It had many splendid palaces and gardens, and was one of the most renowned and populous cities of the ancient world. Even as late as the 5th century BC, long after Thebes had taken over as capital of Egypt, Memphis was described by the Greek historian Herodotus as a 'prosperous city and cosmopolitan centre'. Its enduring importance, even then, was reflected in the size of its cemetery on the west bank of the Nile, an area replete with royal pyramids, private tombs and sacred animal necropolises. This city of the dead, centred at Saqqara, covers 30km along the edge of the desert, from Dahshur in the south to Giza in the north.

Centuries of annual floods have inundated the city with Nile mud, while other ancient buildings and monuments have long since been ploughed over so that today there are few signs of the grandeur of Memphis – in fact, it's extremely difficult to imagine that a city once stood where there is now only a small museum and some statues in a garden.

The partly open-air museum contains a colossal limestone statue of Ramses II, similar to the one that stands at the centre of Midan Ramses in Cairo. This one, however, is lying down and is a lot more neglected and damaged. In the garden there is an eight tonne alabaster sphinx, more statues of Ramses II, the sarcophagus of Amenhotep and the alabaster beds on which the sacred Apis bulls were mummified before being placed in the

HIGHLIGHTS

- **Saqqara** This is where you get to feel like Indiana Jones and explore half-buried ruins in the peaceful solitude of the desert.

- **Dahshur** Older but smaller cousins of the Pyramids of Giza, these are worth visiting for their stark, isolated location and because you'll be one of the very few who ever makes it out here.

- **Birqash Camel Market** Pretty it isn't but a visit to Birqash makes for a wild contrast with Cairo city life.

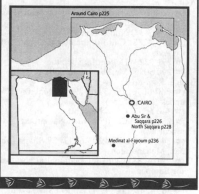

Around Cairo p225

CAIRO

Abu Sir &
Saqqara p226
North Saqqara p228

Medinat al-Fayoum p236

Serapeum at Saqqara. Admission is E£14/7 for adults/students, plus E£5/25 for a camera/video. It's open from 8 am to 5 pm. There is an extraordinarily overpriced cafeteria across the road.

Maybe the simplest way to visit Memphis is to take a guided tour from Cairo. This solves the transport issue (getting to Memphis is a pain in the neck) and you have expert help in trying to recreate in your mind's eye, from what is a very disappointing site, what was once one of the world's greatest cities. Memphis can very easily be tied in with a trip to Saqqara – see

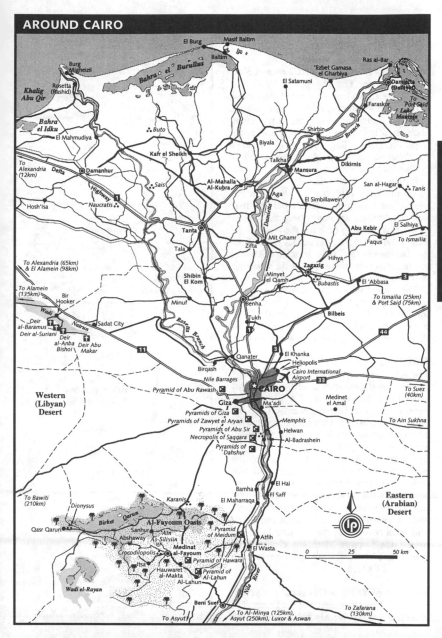

AROUND CAIRO

El Burg · Masif Baltim
Baltim
'Ezbet Gamasa
el Gharbiya
Ras al-Bar
Burg
Migheizil
El Satamuni
Damietta
(Dumyat)
Rosetta
(Rashid)
Khalig
Abu Qir
Bahra el Burullus
Faraskor
To
Port Said
Lake
Manzala
Bahra
el Idku
Shirbin
El Mahmudiya
·.· Buto
Biyala
Branch
To
Alexandria
(12km)
Delta
Damanhur
Kafr el Sheikh
Talkha
Mansura
Dikirnis
Highway 1
Sais
Al-Mahalla
Al-Kubra
Aga
San al-Hagar
·· Tanis
Hosh'Isa
Naucratis ·.·
El Simbillawein
Abu Kebir
El Salhiya
Tanta
Mit Ghamr
Faqus
To Ismailia
To Alexandria (65km)
& El Alamein (98km)
Tala
Zifta
Hihya
Zagazig
To Alamein
(135km)
Shibin
El Kom
Minyet
el Qamh
Bubastis
El 'Abbasa
Bir
Hooker
Wadi
Natrun
Minuf
Benha
Bilbeis
To Ismailia (25km)
& Port Said (75km)
Deir
al-Baramus
Deir al-Suriani
Sadat City
Tukh
1
44
Deir
al-Anba
Bishoi
Deir Abu
Makar
Rosetta Branch
11
Qanater
3
El Khanka
Heliopolis
To Suez
(40km)
Western
(Libyan)
Desert
Birqash
Nile Barrages
Cairo International
Airport
33
Pyramid of Abu Rawash
CAIRO
To Ain Sukhna
Giza
Ma'adi
Medinet
el Amal
Pyramids of Giza
Pyramids of Zawyet el Aryan
Memphis
Pyramids of Abu Sir
Helwan
Necropolis of Saqqara
Al-Badrashein
Pyramid of
Dahshur
Eastern
(Arabian)
Desert
Bamha
El Hai
To Bawiti
(210km)
Dionysus
Karanis
El Maharraqa
El Saff
Qasr Qarun
Birket
Qarun
Al-Fayoum Oasis
Sanhur
Ain
Pyramid
of Meidum
Atfih
Abshaway
As-Siliyiin
Medinat
al-Fayoum
El Wasta
0   25   50 km
Crocodilopolis
Isa
Hauwaret
al-Makta
Pyramid of Hawara
Pyramid of
Al-Lahun
Wadi el-Rayan
Al-Lahun
Beni Suef
To Al-Minya (125km),
Asyut (250km), Luxor & Aswan
To Zafarana
(130km)
To Asyut

the Organised Tours section of the Cairo chapter for details of local tour operators.

Getting There & Away

Memphis is 24km south of Cairo and 3km from Saqqara. The cheapest way to get there from Cairo is to take a 3rd class train from Ramses station to Al-Manashi, and get off at Al-Badrashein village; the trip takes about two hours (to go 24km!) and costs 35pt. From the village, you can then walk for about half an hour, catch a Saqqara microbus for 25pt, or take a taxi.

Rather than catch the slow train, you could just as easily go via Helwan on the metro, get a microbus (don't believe it if you're told there are none) from the station to the boat landing (ask for the *markib lil-Badrashein*), take a boat across the Nile to Al-Badrashein, and then another microbus to Memphis from there. This way, however, will still take you a good 1½ hours.

The easiest way is to gather six or seven people and hire a service taxi for about E£80 for the trip. For more details on this, and transport to and from this area in general, see the Saqqara Getting There & Away section.

ABU SIR

The four pyramids of Abu Sir, at the edge of the desert and surrounded by a sea of sand dunes, formed part of a 5th dynasty necropolis, a northern extension of the Saqqara necropolis. Originally there were 14 pyramids at Abu Sir; those that remain are badly damaged. The exception is the Pyramid of Sahure, which opened to the public for the first time in mid-1996. For years the pyramid was difficult to find and seldom visited by tourists but at the beginning of 1999 the site was officially 'opened' and the enormous asphalt road leading to it will soon be used by the big tour buses on their Giza-Saqqara-Memphis circuit. The site is open between 8 am and 5 pm and admission is E£10/5.

Pyramid of Sahure This is the most complete and the northernmost of the group. The entrance corridor is only half a metre high

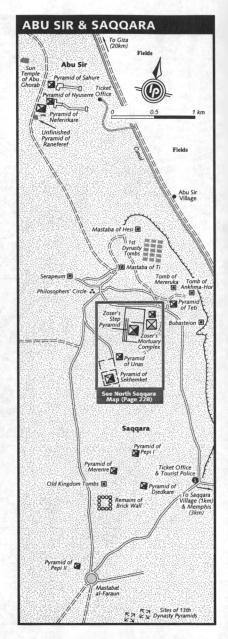

ABU SIR & SAQQARA

and slopes down to a small room, from where you go through a 75m corridor before crawling the last two metres on your stomach through pharaonic dust and spider webs to get into the burial chamber. The remains of Sahure's mortuary temple stand nearby. The limestone walls of the temple originally contained some 10,000 sq metres of reliefs, but when it was excavated only 150m were left. The fragments depict a military campaign against the Libyans and boats arriving from Syria and departing for Punt.

From this pyramid, on a clear day, you can see as many as 10 other pyramids stretching out before you to the horizon.

Pyramid of Nyuserre This is the most dilapidated of the three complete pyramids at Abu Sir. Nyuserre took over his father Neferirkare's causeway, which you can still see linking up with what's left of Nyuserre's mortuary temple (built on top of his father's valley temple foundations) to the south-east.

Pyramid of Neferirkare Neferirkare's tomb is one of the best in the area and stands 45m high. It now resembles Zoser's Step Pyramid but, like the Giza pyramids, originally had an outer casing of stone. It was near here that the so-called Abu Sir papyri – describing schedules of ceremonies and festivals, listing temple furnishings and equipment, recording financial transactions and temple inspections – were found in the 19th century. An invaluable source of information to Egyptologists, most are now housed in the British Museum.

Pyramid of Raneferef On a diagonal just west of Neferirkare's pyramid are the remains of the unfinished pyramid of Raneferef. Czech archaeologists working here recently found papyrus fragments, similar to the Abu Sir papyri, in the mud-brick mortuary temple.

Other Monuments North of the temple there are some interesting monuments, including several *mastabas* (the flat tomb superstructures common at the time). If

you're travelling to Abu Sir by camel, horse or donkey across the desert from Giza, then stop off at the 5th dynasty Sun Temple of Abu Ghorab. Built by King Nyuserre in honour of the sun-god Ra, it is one of only two Old Kingdom sun temples discovered by Egyptologists. The huge altar is made from five big blocks of alabaster and once served as the base of a large solar obelisk. Very few travellers ever make it this far off the beaten track.

SAQQARA

When Memphis was the capital of Egypt, Saqqara was its necropolis. Deceased pharaohs, family members and sacred animals were ceremoniously transported from Memphis to be permanently enshrined in one of the myriad temples, pyramids and tombs at Saqqara.

In the 3000 years between the foundation of Memphis and the end of Greek rule under the Ptolemies, the necropolis grew until it covered a 7km-stretch of the Western Desert. In terms of the value of what has been and has yet to be uncovered, there are few archaeological sites in the world that compare with Saqqara; yet, apart from the Step Pyramid, the necropolis was virtually ignored by archaeologists until the mid-19th century, when Auguste Mariette found the Serapeum. Even the massive mortuary complex surrounding Zoser's Step Pyramid wasn't discovered and reclaimed from the sand until 1924, and it is still being restored.

A worthwhile visit to Saqqara will take more than one day. Because of its size it seems that other visitors are few and far between, apart from the organised tour groups that are rushed through in the mornings. You'll find here, in the middle of the desert, a peaceful quality rarely found at other ancient sites in Egypt.

Orientation & Information

The main places of interest are in North Saqqara, the area around Zoser's Step Pyramid. Most travellers start their visit here and then, if they are up to it, continue by taxi, donkey or camel north to Abu Sir

NORTH SAQQARA

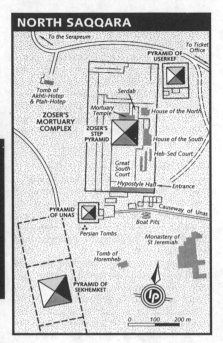

lected only at the entrance to Zoser's Step Pyramid. Before setting off, check at the ticket office which monuments are open.

Zoser's Step Pyramid

Constructed by Imhotep, the pharaoh's chief architect, in 27 BC, the Step Pyramid of King Zoser was the largest stone structure ever built. It is still the most noticeable feature of Saqqara. Imhotep's brilliant use of stone, and his daring break with the tradition of building royal tombs as underground rooms with the occasional mud-brick mastaba, was the inspiration for Egypt's future architectural achievements.

The pyramid began as a simple mastaba, but Imhotep added to it five times. With each level of stone he gained confidence in his use of the new medium and mastered the techniques required to move, place and secure the huge blocks. This first pyramid rose to over 62m, in six steps, before it was sheathed in fine limestone.

The Step Pyramid dominates Zoser's mortuary complex, which is 544m long and 277m wide and was once surrounded by a magnificent bastioned and panelled limestone wall. Part of the enclosure wall survives, to a height of over 4.5m, and a section near the south-eastern corner has been restored using stones found in the desert, to its original 10m elevation. In the enclosure wall, the many false doors which were carved and painted to resemble real wood, hinges and sockets allowed the pharaoh's *ka*, or attendant spirit, to come and go at will.

For the living, there is only one entrance, on the south-eastern corner, via a vestibule and along a colonnaded corridor into the broad hypostyle hall. The 40 pillars in the corridor are the original 'bundle columns', ribbed to resemble a bundle of palm or papyrus stems. The walls have been restored, but the protective ceiling is modern concrete. The roof of the hypostyle hall is supported by four impressive bundle columns and there's a large, false, half-open ka door. Here you will be accosted by a bevy of 'guides' eager to show you around.

and/or down to South Saqqara. It's imperative to have some form of transport to get around as the tombs and sites are spread over a vast distance and walking is not feasible. Make sure you bring some water as it gets very hot. The site's rest house was recently pulled down because it was leaking water into the surrounding monuments and although another one is planned at a new location, at the time of writing construction had not yet begun and there was nowhere selling drinks.

Most of the pyramids and tombs at Saqqara can be 'officially' visited between 8 am and 5 pm. The guards start locking the monument doors at about 4.30 pm, although some have been known to lock up even earlier – with tourists inside – in order to extract some baksheesh. The admission fee for all North Saqqara sights is E£20/10. There is a E£5 fee for using a camera, col-

Saqqara Itinerary

With its vast size and huge collection of monuments and tombs there is too much at Saqqara to be seen in one visit. The following is a sample itinerary including the most important monuments:

- Enter through the hypostyle hall and gaze on the Step Pyramid of Zoser, the world's oldest pyramid.
- Wander around Zoser's Funerary Complex, through the huge South Court, into the houses of the North & South and in front of the eerie serdab, where you can stare into the stone eyes of Zoser. Continue around through the ruins of the mortuary temple and around the back of the Step Pyramid.
- Walk south along hill above the western edge of the funerary complex and down the Causeway of Unas, where you can visit some of the beautiful tombs dotted on either side or peer into the huge boat pits.
- Head over to the Pyramid of Teti – the place to see the famous Pyramid Texts.
- Descend into the Serapeum. Peer through the gloom and into the gigantic sarcophagi of the 25 huge Apis bulls that were entombed in this bizarre place.
- Walk over to the tombs of Akhi-Hotep & Ptah-Hotep to see some beautiful reliefs showing this 5th dynasty father and son building boats, hunting wild animals and having manicures.
- If you've still got the energy, enter the Mastaba of Ti and see how royal hairdressers lived 5000 years ago through the fascinating tomb reliefs of daily life in the Old Kingdom.

The hall leads into the Great South Court, a huge open area flanking the south side of the pyramid, with a rebuilt section of wall featuring a frieze of cobras. The cobra, or uraeus, was a symbol of Egyptian royalty, a fire-spitting agent of destruction and protector of the king. A rearing cobra, its hood inflated, always formed part of a pharaoh's headdress.

Near the frieze is a shaft that plunges 28m to the floor of Zoser's Southern Tomb, which is similar in decoration to the main tomb beneath the Step Pyramid. Originally, it probably stored the Canopic jars containing the pharaoh's preserved internal organs.

In the centre of the Great South Court are two stone altars representing the thrones of Upper and Lower Egypt. During the 30th year of a pharaoh's reign it was traditional for him to renew his rule by re-enacting his coronation. In a ritual called the Heb-Sed Race, he would sit first on one throne and then on the other to symbolise the unification of Egypt. He would also, during the five day jubilee, present all the provincial priests with gifts, obliging them to recognise his supremacy over their local gods. The jubilee would actually have been held in Memphis, while these altars in the Great South Court perpetuated in stone the cosmic regeneration of the pharaoh's power and ka.

On the eastern side of the pyramid are two 'houses' representing the shrines of Upper and Lower Egypt which symbolise the unity of the country. The House of the South, which is faced with proto-Doric columns, features the oldest known examples of tourist graffiti. The vandalism of visiting 12th century BC Theban scribes, who scrawled their admiration for Zoser on the wall in a cursive style of hieroglyphs, is now protected under a piece of transparent plastic just inside the entrance. The House of the North is similar to its southern counterpart, except that sculpted papyrus flowers grace the capitals of its columns. To the north of the pyramid is the Pyramid of Userkef, now little more than a mound of rubble.

The *serdab*, a stone structure right in front of the pyramid, contains a slightly tilted wooden box with two holes drilled into its north face. Look through these and you'll have the eerie experience of coming face to face with Zoser himself. Inside is a life-size, lifelike painted statue of the long-dead king, gazing stonily out towards the stars. Although it's only a copy (the original is in the Egyptian Museum), it's still quite haunting. Serdabs were designed so that the pharaoh's ka could communicate with the outside world. The original entrance to the Step Pyramid is directly behind the serdab, but is closed to the public.

Pyramid & Causeway of Unas

What appears to be a big mound of rubble to the south-west of Zoser's tomb is actually the Pyramid of Unas, the last pharaoh of the 5th dynasty. Built only 350 years after the inspired creation of the Step Pyramid, and after the perfection of the Great Pyramids of Giza, this unassuming pile of loose blocks and dirt marked the beginning of a trend in design. Until Unas' time (24 BC), pyramid interiors had been unadorned – so while the outside of his tomb looks more like Zoser's than Cheops', the inside is of immense historical importance.

In 1881, Thomas Cook & Sons sponsored the excavation of the tomb by Gaston Maspero, who found the walls covered in hieroglyphs. Carved into the huge slabs of white alabaster, these so-called Pyramid Texts are the earliest known examples of decorative writing in a pharaonic tomb chamber. The texts record the rituals, prayers and hymns that accompanied the pharaoh's burial to enable the release of his ka, and list the articles, like food and clothing, necessary for his existence in the afterlife.

Unfortunately, the deterioration of the reliefs inside led the Supreme Council for Antiquities to close the pyramid permanently in 1998.

Part of the 1km causeway, which ran from the east side of the Pyramid of Unas, has been restored. On either side of it more than 200 mastabas have been excavated and there are several well-preserved tombs, some of which can normally be visited. The beautiful tomb of the 5th dynasty princess Idut, who was probably a daughter of Unas,

is next to the southern wall of Zoser's complex. On the walls of its 10 chambers are colourful scenes of oxen, gazelle, ibex, hippopotamus and other animals. The Mastaba of Queen Nebet and the Mastaba of Mehu are also beautifully decorated, and the Tomb of Nebkau-Her, which may be closed, is worth visiting if you can gain access.

Egyptologists debate whether the huge, sculpted boat pits, made of stone and located south of the causeway, actually held the royal barges which took the pharaoh on his journey to the afterlife, or whether they merely represented these solar boats. Nothing was found when the 40m-long crescent-shaped trenches were excavated.

Persian Tombs

The tombs of three Persian noblemen, just south of the Pyramid of Unas, are some of the deepest subterranean burial chambers in Egypt. The entrance is covered by a small, inconspicuous wooden hut, to which a guard in the area has the key. If you don't have your own torch he will lead you to the 25m down the winding staircase to the vaulted tombs of Psamtik, Zenhebu and Pelese. According to the ancient wall drawings, which are colourful and fantastic, Zenhebu was a famous Persian admiral and Psamtik was chief physician to the pharaoh's court. The tombs were sunk so deep to prevent grave robbers from stealing the contents. It didn't work: it was thieves who cut the spiral entrance passage.

Monastery of St Jeremiah

The half-buried remains of this 5th century AD monastery are up the hill from the Causeway of Unas and south-east of the boat pits. There's not much left of the structure because it was ransacked by invading Arabs in 950 AD, and more recently Egyptian antiquities officials took all the wall paintings and carvings to the Coptic Museum in Cairo.

Pyramid of Sekhemket

The unfinished Pyramid of Sekhemket is a short distance to the west of the ruined monastery. It was abandoned before completion, for unknown reasons, when it was only 3m high. There's an unused alabaster sarcophagus in one of the underground passageways, but no one is permitted to enter this pile of rubble because of the danger of a cave-in.

Tomb of Akhti-Hotep & Ptah-Hotep

Akhti-Hotep and Ptah-Hotep, father and son officials during the reign of Djedkare (a 5th dynasty pharaoh), designed their own tomb complex consisting of two burial chambers, a chapel and a hall of pillars. The Hotep duo were judges, overseers of the priests of the pyramids, and chiefs of the granary and treasury. The reliefs in their chambers are some of the best at Saqqara and depict everyday life during the 5th dynasty. You'll see: Akhti-Hotep in the marshes building boats, fighting enemies and crossing rivers; a splendid scene of wild animals with Ptah-Hotep and other hunters in hot pursuit; people playing games, collecting food and eating; and Ptah-Hotep having a manicure while being entertained by musicians. The dual tomb is south of the main road.

Philosophers' Circle

On the way to the Serapeum several statues of Greek philosophers and poets are arranged in a circle, set up during the Ptolemaic period, beneath a protective roof. From left to right, the statues are: Plato (standing), Heraclitus (seated), Thales (standing), Protagoras (seated), Homer (seated), Hesiod (seated), Demetrius of Phalerum (standing against a bust of Serapis) and Pindar.

Serapeum

The sacred Apis bulls were by far the most important of the cult animals entombed at Saqqara. The Apis, it was believed, was an incarnation of Ptah, the god of Memphis, and was the calf of a cow struck by lightning from heaven. Once divinely impregnated, the cow would never again give birth and her calf was kept in the Temple of Ptah and worshipped as a god. The Apis was always portrayed as black, with a distinctive white diamond on its forehead, a sun disc between its horns, the image of an eagle on its back and a scarab on its tongue. When it died, the bull was mummified, then carried on an alabaster bed to the subterranean galleries of the Serapeum at Saqqara, and placed in a huge sarcophagus.

The Apis catacombs date from 13 BC when Ramses II began construction of the first gallery, which reached a length of 68m. The catacombs were subsequently added to and remained in use until around 30 BC. Twenty-five Apis were embalmed here in monolithic granite coffins weighing up to 70 tonnes each; only one mummified bull, now in the Cairo Agricultural Museum, was found when the Serapeum was excavated.

Until 1851 the existence of the sacred Apis tombs was known only from classical references. Having found a half-buried sphinx at Saqqara, and following the description given by the Greek historian Strabo in 24 BC, the French archaeologist Auguste Mariette uncovered the avenue of sphinxes leading to the Serapeum. His great discovery sparked the extensive and continuing excavation of Saqqara. In 1856 Mariette wrote that he'd been so profoundly astonished on first gaining access to the Apis vaults, five years before, that the feeling was still fresh in his mind. Only one chamber, walled up during the reign of Ramses II, had escaped the notice of tomb robbers. Finding it intact, Mariette wrote:

The finger marks of the Egyptian who had inserted the last stone in the wall built to conceal the doorway were still recognisable on the lime. There were also the marks of naked feet imprinted on the sand which lay in one corner of the tomb chamber. Everything was in its original condition in this tomb where the embalmed remains of the bull had lain undisturbed for 37 centuries.

The Serapeum is just off the main road, west of the Philosophers' Circle. It's very likely you'll experience the same feeling as Mariette: this place is definitely weird and gets stranger still as you wander along galleries lit only by tiny lanterns casting a murky light over the vaults and the enormous, macabre black sarcophagi they contain. The largest sarcophagus, at the end of the main gallery, was carved from a single piece of black granite and is covered in hieroglyphs.

At the time of writing the Serapeum was closed for renovation and was due to open in early 2000.

Mastaba of Ti

This tomb, or mastaba, is one of the main sources of knowledge about life in Egypt towards the end of the Old Kingdom. Ti, an important court official who served under three pharaohs, collected titles like his kings collected slaves. He was Lord of Secrets, Superintendent of Works, Overseer of the Pyramids of Abu Sir, Counsellor to the Pharaoh and even Royal Hairdresser. He married a woman of royal blood and the inscriptions on the walls of his tomb reveal that his children were rated as royalty. One of the best reliefs depicts Ti standing regally on a boat sailing through papyrus marshes, while others show men and women at various jobs like ploughing, shipbuilding, reaping grain and feeding cranes.

The tomb, discovered by Mariette in 1865, is a few hundred metres to the northeast of the Philosophers' Circle.

Pyramid of Teti

The avenue of sphinxes excavated by Mariette in the 1850s has again been engulfed by desert sands, but it once extended as far east as the Pyramid of Teti. Teti was the first king of the 6th dynasty and his pyramid was built in step form and then filled and encased in limestone. Unfortunately, the pyramid was robbed both for its treasure and its stone and little remains but a mound. However, the burial chamber is still intact and Teti's basalt sarcophagus is inside. Now that the Pyramid of Unas is closed this is where you can see the famous pyramid texts. To get to this somewhat weathered tomb you must follow the road from the Serapeum, heading a little to the north once you've passed the Step Pyramid.

Tombs of Mereruka & Ankhma-Hor

Nearby Teti's pyramid is the Tomb of Mereruka, which has 31 rooms, many with magnificent wall inscriptions. Egyptologists have learned a great deal about the wildlife of ancient Egypt from these drawings. As you enter the tomb, notice on one of the walls the large-mouthed, sharptusked hippopotamuses.

The Tomb of Ankhma-Hor, a little further east, contains some very interesting scenes depicting 6th dynasty surgical operations, including toe surgery and a circumcision.

Mastabat al-Faraun

The oldest structure in the South Saqqara area is the unusual mortuary complex of the 4th dynasty king Shepseskaf, believed to be a son of Mycerinus. Shepseskaf's tomb is neither a mastaba nor a pyramid. The Mastabat al-Faraun, or 'pharaoh's bench', is an enormous stone structure resembling a sarcophagus topped with a rounded lid. The complex once covered 700 sq metres and the interior consists of long passageways and a burial chamber. It is possible to enter the tomb if you can find a guard.

A little north-west of the Mastabat al-Faraun is the **Pyramid of Pepi II**, a 6th dynasty pharaoh who allegedly ruled for 94 years. Pepi II's tomb contains some fine hieroglyphs. The ruins of his mortuary temple, which was once connected to the pyramid by a causeway, can also be explored.

Organised Tours

For details on organised tours to this area see the Organised Tours section in the Cairo chapter.

Getting There & Away

Saqqara is about 25km south of Cairo and about 3km north-west of Memphis. Although it is possible to get within 1.5km of the Saqqara ticket office using public transport, this is a very time consuming business and, once there, you'll be stuck for getting around unless you try to hitch a ride up onto the plateau and then haggle for a camel or donkey. The site is best covered in a taxi, combined with a visit to Memphis and Dahshur. You'll have to arrange this option in Cairo as there are no taxis hanging around the site.

If you're coming from Cairo or Giza and are determined to do it on your own you have several options.

Bus One of the cheapest ways of getting to Saqqara without going via Memphis is to take a bus or minibus (25 to 50pt) to the Pyramids Rd (see the Giza section in the Cairo chapter) and get off at the Saqqara Rd stop. From there you can get a microbus to the turn-off to the Saqqara site (don't ask for Saqqara village as you'll end up in the wrong place), from where you'll probably have to walk the last 1.5km to the ticket office. Once at the ticket office, you'll have to try and hitch.

Train Refer to the Memphis Getting There & Away section for details on the train. The train from Cairo to the village of Al-Badrashein also goes to Dahshur; a taxi from either to North Saqqara should cost about E£5. You can arrange a microbus from Memphis, to the turn-off to the Saqqara site on the Giza-Memphis road, from where it's about a 1.5km walk to the Saqqara ticket office. There is usually a bit of traffic along the Giza-Memphis road.

From Al-Badrashein, by the way, there are (sometimes) direct microbuses to Giza.

Taxi This is one of the best ways to get to and around the Saqqara site. A taxi from central Cairo will cost about E£15 an hour shared among a maximum of seven people. However, make sure you know what you want to see and stipulate how long you want to be out – it's not unknown for taxi drivers to simply skip the main sights (like the Step Pyramid!) and dump unsuspecting visitors at a few of the lesser monuments before whisking you back to Cairo. Also, if you're going to be out for the day, don't let the taxi driver decide where you're going to have lunch or you may well end up paying through the nose to cover his commission.

Camel The most adventurous (although physically strenuous) option is to hire a camel, donkey or horse and cross the desert from the Great Pyramids of Giza to Saqqara. This takes about six to seven hours for a round trip so make sure you're prepared for it. Many of the better stables will allow you to go one way, but you'll have to pay for the animals' return journey (usually the equivalent of a one hour fee).

Unless you're accustomed, that amount of time spent in a saddle will make sitting down rather difficult for a few days to follow. Also keep in mind that you won't have much time left to explore Saqqara unless you start off very early and make it a long day.

Animals can be hired from the stables south of the Sphinx – see the Pyramids section in the Cairo chapter.

Getting Around
It is not feasible to explore Saqqara on foot and, as there are no taxis near the ticket office, your only option for getting around, if you do arrive independently, is to attempt to hitch or to hire (from near the Serapeum) a camel, horse or donkey; a trip around North Saqqara should cost, after bargaining, E£8 – but don't be surprised if it's more as the handlers are well aware that you're in need of the extra legs so your bargaining power is diminished.

The only taxis you'll find around here are those coming from Cairo and they're usually already full.

DAHSHUR
Situated some 20km south of Saqqara in a quiet patch of desert, Dahshur is an impressive 3.5km-long field of 4th and 12th dynasty pyramids. The site was an off-limits military zone until mid-1996, and the camel drivers, guides and other touts who infest Giza and Saqqara have yet to find enough of a market here, so you can enjoy the monuments in peace.

There were originally 11 pyramids at Dahshur, although only four remain intact. Of the two remaining Middle Kingdom pyramids, only the oddly shaped Black

Pyramid of Amenemhet III is worth a look. The tower-like structure appears to have completely collapsed due to the pilfering of its limestone outer-casing in medieval times but in fact, the mud-brick remains contain a maze of corridors and rooms designed to deceive tomb robbers. And while thieves did manage to penetrate its burial chambers, they left behind a number of precious funerary artefacts that were discovered in 1993.

However, the site is most famous for the fascinating Bent and Red pyramids, both of which were built by Sneferu, the father of Cheops and founder of the 4th dynasty. Why Sneferu had two pyramids, and possibly a third at Meidum, remains a mystery. As Sneferu's body has not been found in any of his tombs, nobody even knows which, if any, was his final resting place.

Dahshur is open from 8 am to 5 pm. Admission costs E£10/5.

Red Pyramid

The world's oldest true pyramid, the Red Pyramid – so called because of red graffiti that was scribbled on its outer casing in ancient times – is only 10m smaller than the great pyramid at Giza. Perhaps Cheops wanted to make sure that he outdid his father. It is the only pyramid at Dahshur that is open to the public and the entrance is up 125 stone steps, some 28m off the ground. A 65m-long passage takes you down to three chambers, the first two with stunning 15m-high corbelled ceilings. The third is up some steps and is not as well preserved.

Bent Pyramid

With its distinctive rhomboidal form, the Bent Pyramid has been puzzling Egyptologists since the 19th century. For some reason, almost half way up its 101m height, the angle of its slope changes from 54.31° to 43.21°. The popular theory for this is that halfway through its building Sneferu's architect realised the structure would have collapsed if it continued at the same angle. Others say the incline was changed to speed up construction when the pharaoh died suddenly. Whatever the reason, it and the Pyramid of Meidum,

also built (or at least completed) by Sneferu, demonstrate the design transition from step pyramid to true pyramid.

Rare among the pyramids around Cairo in that it still has its outer casing intact, the Bent Pyramid is also unique for its two entrances (on the north and west walls). Inside there are reportedly cedar beams that are thought to have come from Lebanon, but until the Supreme Council for Antiquities finishes restoration work, it remains off-limits to visitors.

There is a small subsidiary pyramid to the south of the Bent Pyramid and the remains of a small mortuary temple against its east side. About halfway toward the cultivation to the east you can also see the ruins of Sneferu's valley temple, which yielded some interesting reliefs. About 1.5km to the south-east, at the edge of the cultivation is Dahshur Lake, the last remaining pyramid harbour lake and a nesting ground for birds. If you walk there over the desert, prepare to be surrounded by village children clamouring for baksheesh.

Getting There & Away

See the Saqqara Getting There & Away section for details. You can get a microbus to Dahshur on the road from Saqqara or from the Giza-Memphis road.

AL-FAYOUM OASIS

About 100km south-west of Cairo is Al-Fayoum, Egypt's largest oasis. The region of Al-Fayoum is about 70km wide and 60km long, including the lake known as Birket Qarun. Home to more than two million people, it is an intricately irrigated and extremely fertile basin watered by the Nile via hundreds of capillary canals.

The region was once filled by Birket Qarun and during the reign of the 12th dynasty pharaoh Amenemhet III a series of canals were built linking the lake to the Nile. Amenemhet also drained marshes in an early effort at land reclamation. Later the Nile was diverted to the agricultural land and the lake, which lies 45m below sea level, suffers from increasing salinity; only a few varieties of fish remain and the water level is slowly decreasing.

The oasis was a favourite vacation spot for pharaohs of the 13th dynasty, and many fine palaces were built in the area. The Greeks later called the area Crocodilopolis, because they believed the crocodiles in Birket Qarun were sacred. A temple was built in honour of Sobek, the crocodile-headed god, and during Ptolemaic and Roman times pilgrims came from all over the ancient world to feed the sacred beasts.

Al-Fayoum has been called the garden of Egypt: lush fields of vegetables and sugar cane, and groves of citrus fruits, nuts and olives produce abundant harvests; the lake, canals and vegetation support an amazing variety of bird life (some of which is unfortunately hunted by groups of tourists); and life in the mud-brick villages throughout the oasis appears to have changed very little over the centuries.

Getting There & Away

Bus Buses to Cairo (E£4; three hours) leave every half hour between 7 am and 7 pm from the station under Kubri al-Misalla. They take you to the Ahmed Helmy station behind Ramses train station in Cairo, stopping en route at Giza. From a separate station in an area called Hawatim to the south-west of the town, buses leave regularly for Beni Suef (E£1; one hour), plus there are buses at 7.30 am and 2.30 pm for Minya (E£4.25).

There are two separate bus/service taxi stations for Abshaway and Ain as-Siliyiin/Lake Qarun. Both are on the west side of town.

Train For the 3rd class train buff, there are four daily departures to Cairo (E£1.60), leaving at 7.30 and 11.30 am, and 3.15 and 7.30 pm. Progress is so slow as to be barely perceptible – the journey takes more than four hours.

Service Taxi Service taxis leave from the bus stations. To Cairo, they cost E£4 from Giza or E£5 from Midan Ramses. You can get to Beni Suef for E£1.50.

Getting Around

For details of how to get to the various sights around the oasis, see the respective entries over the next few pages. Note that departures of these buses are pretty unreliable. Green-and-white minibuses cover all areas of Medinat al-Fayoum, between the western and eastern bus stations and the centre of town (wust al-balad) for 25pt.

Medinat al-Fayoum

All the tradition and fertility of Al-Fayoum Oasis surrounds the rather grimy Medinat al-Fayoum, or 'town of the Fayoum', which sadly is a microcosm of everything that is bad about Cairo: horn-happy drivers, choking fumes and dust, crowded streets and a population of more than 400,000.

The canal acts as the city's main artery; most of the commercial activities take place around it and the further you wander away from the canal, the quieter things become. The bus and taxi stations, unfortunately, are all a bit of a hike from the centre.

There is a tourist office (☎ 342 313), open from 8 am to 2 pm daily except Friday, at the rear of the governorate building. There's also a tourist information booth (☎ 342 586), open from 8 am to 5 pm daily, by the water wheels in the centre of town.

Close by one another, across the canal from the tourist information booth, are the Banque Masr, the Banque du Caire and, on the same side of Amenemhet as the tourist office, the Bank of Alexandria. All keep the usual hours. You can change money at these places but they won't give cash advances on credit cards. A 24 hour telephone centrale is also located by the canal, and there's a post office on Sharia an-Nasr, open from 8 am to 2 pm, closed Friday.

As far as things to see goes, there's the **Obelisk of Senusert** which you'll pass coming in from Cairo at the centre of a roundabout to the north-east of town. Although it looks lost amongst the cars and buses, it's supposedly the only obelisk in Egypt with a rounded top, and also features a cleft in which a golden statue of Ra was placed, reflecting the sun's rays in the four directions

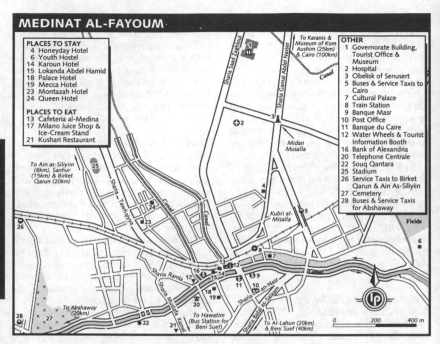

MEDINAT AL-FAYOUM

PLACES TO STAY
4   Honeyday Hotel
6   Youth Hostel
14 Karoun Hotel
15 Lokanda Abdel Hamid
18 Palace Hotel
19 Mecca Hotel
23 Montazah Hotel
24 Queen Hotel

PLACES TO EAT
13 Cafeteria al-Medina
17 Milano Juice Shop &
    Ice-Cream Stand
21 Kushari Restaurant

OTHER
1   Governorate Building,
    Tourist Office &
    Museum
2   Hospital
3   Obelisk of Senusert
5   Buses & Service Taxis to
    Cairo
7   Cultural Palace
8   Train Station
9   Banque Masr
10 Post Office
11 Banque du Caire
12 Water Wheels & Tourist
    Information Booth
16 Bank of Alexandria
20 Telephone Centrale
22 Souq Qantara
25 Stadium
26 Service Taxis to Birket
    Qarun & Ain As-Siliyiin
27 Cemetery
28 Buses & Service Taxis
    for Abshaway

To Karanis &
Museum of Kom
Aushim (25km)
& Cairo (100km)

Midan
Musalla

To Ain as-Siliyiin
(8km), Sanhur
(15km) & Birket
Qarun (20km)

Kubri al-
Misalla

Fields

To Abshaway
(20km)

To Hawatim
(Bus Station for
Beni Suef)

To Al-Lahun (20km)
& Beni Suef (40km)

0   200   400 m

---

of the wind. In the governorate building is a small **museum** with a variety of interesting displays on the history and fauna of the oasis, and on its future as a tourist destination. Opposite the tourist office are four functioning models of the **water wheels** still in use around Al-Fayoum (in total, there are about 200 dotted around the oasis).

Places to Stay Better to spend as little time here as possible and head straight out to the oasis.

Hostels *Youth Hostel* (☎ 343 682) just more than 1km east of the centre of town, costs E£3 for members and E£5 for non-members for a bed in a room of six. The building looks like it has been bombed-out.

Hotels The cheapest (and smelliest) accommodation in town is the horrible *Karoun*

Hotel, opposite the Cafeteria al-Medina. It has doubles for E£3 and is to be avoided.

Trying hard to meet the same grimy standards is *Lokanda Abdel Hamid* (just 'Hotel' in English), around the corner facing the canal. Doubles cost E£5, triples E£9. They have hot water.

The quiet *Montazah Hotel* (☎ 348 662), about 500m north-west of the centre, one block in from Sharia Tawfiqiyya, has fairly good singles/doubles without bath, fan and breakfast for E£20/25, and doubles with bath for E£35.

A block north, also off Sharia Tawfiqiyya, is *Queen Hotel* (☎ 346 819, fax 346 233) with older rooms for E£85/120, and new rooms for E£120/150. All rooms have air-con, telephone, TV and fridge. Breakfast is included.

Back on the canal is *Palace Hotel* (☎ 351 222) which is keeping its standards up by providing soap and towels. It has good, clean singles/doubles (including breakfast) without bath for E£20/35, or with bath for E£30/45. For E£15 more you can have air-con. The staff here are friendly, but check the rooms first as some are better than others. The management also runs the more basic *Mecca Hotel* (☎ *351 223*) just behind. Rooms here without bath are E£10/18. Meals are not available.

Honeyday Hotel (☎ *341 205, fax 340 105*) at the bottom of Sharia Gamal Abdel Nasser, has a bar, coffeehouse and restaurant and offers good rooms for E£55/75, including breakfast.

Places to Eat There's not much to choose from in Medinat al-Fayoum. Aside from the standard *fuul*, *ta'amiyya* and *kushari stands* (there's a good one on Sharia Mustafa Kamel, not far in from Sharia al-Horreyya), there's *Cafeteria al-Medina*, built around the water wheels, which serves kebabs and a few other meat and chicken dishes. It charges a pricey E£25 for a generous but unoriginal meal and it also has beer. *Milano* juice shop serves good juices, and the neighbouring ice-cream stand doesn't do a bad job either. There is also a restaurant at *Queen Hotel*, where you can get the ubiquitous escalope panée as well as kofta and chicken, for around E£15.

Karanis

At the edge of the oasis depression, 25km north of Medinat al-Fayoum on the road to Cairo, is the ruin of the 3rd century city of Karanis, where Ptolemy II's mercenaries lived. You can still see the remains of their bathhouse among the ruins.

There are two Graeco-Roman temples in the southern part of the town. The larger one, built around the end of the 1st century BC, was dedicated to two local crocodile gods, Pnepheros and Petesouchos, and has inscriptions dating from the reigns of the Roman emperors Nero, Claudius and Vespasiun. Some of the painted portraits found here are now in the Egyptian Museum in Cairo. Entry to the site is E£16 (E£8 for students).

The nearby Museum of Kom Aushim has good displays of Old and Middle Kingdom objects including sacred wooden boats, Canopic jars, and wooden and ceramic statuettes entombed to serve the deceased in the afterlife. Items from the Graeco-Roman period, and later history, are exhibited on the 1st floor. The museum is open daily from 8 am to 4 pm; entry is E£6/3.

Places to Stay – Camping You can pitch a tent in the grounds of the Museum of Kom Aushim for E£4.

Portraits of the Past

Al-Fayoum may not be famous for much these days, but it was here that the world's first known portraits were found. These extraordinarily lifelike pictures, known as the Fayoum Portraits, were painted on wooden panels and put over the face of mummies, or painted directly onto the linen shroud covering the corpse, in a fusion of ancient Egyptian and Graeco-Roman funerary practices.

Dating back to between the 1st and 3rd centuries BC, the portraits are the only surviving examples of a Graeco-Roman method of painting using wax or tempura and are remarkable for the superb skill of the anonymous artists who painted them. The beautifully rendered and eerily modern-looking faces bridge the centuries and look like they were painted yesterday. The haunting images are made all the more poignant by their youth (some are only babies) – a reflection of the high mortality rates at the time. They are thought to be descendents of soldiers who accompanied Alexander the Great and settled in Egypt, marrying Egyptians, and mixing Egyptian religious beliefs with their own.

More than 1000 of these pictures have been found in Egypt, and a large number of them came from the cemetery at Hawara. They are now in museums around the world.

It used to be possible to camp at the lake but the tourist police are reluctant to give permits since the massacre in Luxor. Ask at the tourist office to see if this has changed.

Getting There & Away There's a bus (50pt) to Karanis at 7 am and 2.30 pm, or simply take one of the Cairo-bound buses.

Pyramid of Hawara & Labyrinth

About 12km south-east of Medinat al-Fayoum, off the road to Beni Suef, is the dilapidated 58m mud-brick Pyramid of Hawara, also known as the Pyramid of Amenemhet III (12th dynasty). Amenemhet's once-vast mortuary complex is now nothing but rubble, and even its temple, which had quite a reputation in ancient times, has suffered at the hands of stone robbers. Herodotus said the temple (300m by 250m) was a 3000 room labyrinth that surpassed even the pyramids; while Strabo claimed it had as many rooms as there were provinces, so that all the pharaoh's subjects could be represented by their local officials in the offering of sacrifices. In 24 BC, Strabo wrote:

There are long and numerous covered ways, with winding passages communicating with each other, so that no stranger could find his way in or out of them without a guide. The roofs of these dwellings consist of a single stone each, and the covered ways are roofed in the same manner with single slabs of stone of extraordinary size, without the intermixture of timber or any other material.

The area was also used as a cemetery by the Greeks and Romans; it was here that they adopted the Egyptian practice of mummification, and also where many of the famous Fayoum Portraits were found (see the boxed text 'Portraits of the Past' on page 237 for more information on these fascinating paintings). All that remains now are pieces of mummy cloth and human bones sticking through the mounds of rubble. There's also a crocodile cemetery north-east of the pyramid. At the time of writing, it was not possible to go into the pyramid as rising ground-water had blocked the entrance. The site is open from 7 am to 5 pm; entry is E£16/8.

Getting There & Away The buses between Beni Suef and Medinat al-Fayoum pass through Hawarat al-Makta, from where it's a short walk to the pyramid. Just ask the driver to let you off.

Pyramid of Al-Lahun

About 10km south-east of Hawara, on the Nile side of the narrow fertile passage through the desert connecting Al-Fayoum to the Nile, are the ruins of a small mud-brick pyramid. Once cased in limestone, it was built by Senusert II in the Middle Kingdom period, around 1885 BC. The pyramid was stripped of all its treasures by ancient tomb robbers but modern excavators found the one thing they missed: an amazing solid gold cobra.

The Uraeus of Sesostris II, 12th dynasty, was found at the Pyramid of Al-Lahun. Its head is made of lapis lazuli, and its body contains lapis lazuli, feldspar and carnelian. The uraeus would once have been attached to a ceremonial headdress.

The Pyramid of Al-Lahun is definitely off the beaten track. Although there's not much of it left, you can climb to the top for a great view of the surrounding area. The people in the neighbouring village will probably be so surprised to see you that they'll invite you to tour their fields and houses. The hitch is the entry price – E£16/8.

Getting There & Away You can hitch from Beni Suef or Medinat al-Fayoum, or take the local bus between the two cities, to the village of Al-Lahun from where it's a 2km walk to the pyramid.

Ain as-Siliyiin

The spring waters and gardens of Ain as-Siliyiin, about 8km north-west of Medinat al-Fayoum, merit an excursion if only to see their location amidst a lovely lush valley. The spring water itself is sweet to taste and is said to help in the prevention of arteriosclerosis because of the traces of titanium found in it. One of the springs recently dried up, supposedly due to the earthquake of 1992. There are a few cafes, restaurants and little stores where you can buy water, biscuits and the like. Farmers from the adjacent gardens sell their seasonal produce along the walkway. It costs 25pt to get in.

Places to Stay *Hotel-Chalet Ain as-Siliyiin* (☎ 522 113) is pleasantly located amidst the greenery near the springs. Its simple rooms are quite big and boast a terrace, of sorts. They cost E£38 to E£50 with air-con, not including breakfast.

Getting There & Away From Medinat al-Fayoum, get a Sanhur service taxi or a bus (50pt; hourly) from the station in the west of the town and tell the driver where you want to get off.

Birket Qarun

This is another pleasant enough spot where there is really nothing to do, except sit at one of the lakeside cafes or hire a boat for about E£5 an hour.

You can use the beach for 50pt on Fridays and public holidays.

Places to Stay Arriving at the lake, the place you'll pass first is the four star *Auberge du Lac* (☎ 700 002, fax 700 730). World leaders met at the original hotel on this site after WWI to decide on the borders of the Middle East. It later served as King Farouk's private hunting lodge. These days it is often taken over by hunting groups targeting ducks and geese, or by Cairenes looking for some fresh air. Singles/doubles are a pricey US$70/105, including breakfast.

Another 500m further west is the three star *Panorama Shakshouk Hotel* (☎ 701 746, fax 701 757) where rooms are available for E£180/280 on an obligatory half-board basis. There's a swimming pool built out over the lake.

A third, cheaper option is *Oasis Motel* (☎ 701 565) but it was closed for renovation at the time of our last visit.

Places to Eat At the lake many restaurants are only open during high season and most are attached to big hotels. The *Auberge* is a favourite weekend lunching place for daytrippers from Cairo and serves Fayoum's famed duck, but like all big hotels, is not cheap (you're looking at around E£40 to E£50 for a full meal).

Getting There & Away To get here, take a Sanhur to Shakshouk pick-up (E£1). When you see the lake and Auberge du Lac, you've arrived; get off wherever you choose. It's easy enough to get another pick-up going either way along the south bank road.

Qasr Qarun

The ruins of the ancient town of Dionysus, once the starting point for caravans to the oasis of Bahariyya in the Western Desert, are just near the village of Qasr Qarun at the western end of Birket Qarun.

The Ptolemaic temple, erected in 4 BC to Sobek, the god of Al-Fayoum, is just off to the left of the road shortly before the village. It was partly restored in 1956. You can ask to go down to the underground chambers and climb up to the top for a view of the desert, the sparse remains of Ptolemaic and Roman settlements and the oasis. To the west of the temple is the ruined fortress that gives the area its name and used to guard the caravans as they arrived at the town. Inside are the remains of a Christian basilica with a few stone capitals. Entry is E£16/8.

Getting There & Away Getting out here is a bit of an ordeal, considering the relatively small distances involved. From Medinat al-Fayoum, take a service taxi or pick-up to the town of Abshaway (55pt; one hour) and change there for Qasr Qarun (E£1.20; one hour). There are also some pick-ups plying the road along the south side of the lake to Qasr Qarun, but they are few and far between.

Wadi Rayan

In the 1960s, the Egyptian authorities followed in the footsteps of their ancestors and carried out extensive irrigation works, creating a series of lakes in a depression called Wadi Rayan, south-east of Lake Qarun. Filled with excess water from the oasis, it was designed to be the first step in an ambitious land-reclamation project. Stocked with fish, it is also a major nesting ground for birds. There are waterfalls linking the lakes and they have become a weekend picnic spot for Cairenes. If you avoid Fridays and national holidays, Wadi Rayan is a peaceful spot to spend an afternoon birdwatching or picnicing in the desert.

Getting There & Away There is no public transportation to Wadi Rayan so you'll have to either hire a taxi or use your own vehicle. To get there follow the road to the end of Lake Qarun and take the wide asphalt road to the left just after you see the mud-brick domes of the village of Tunis (rural retreat for Cairo's artists and westernised intelligentsia) on a ridge to your left. An asphalt road leads right to the lake. There is an entrance fee of E£5 per person and E£5 per vehicle.

PYRAMID OF MEIDUM

About 32km north-east of Medinat al-Fayoum and 45km north of Beni Suef, beyond the vegetation belt, is the ruin of the first true pyramid attempted by the ancient Egyptians. The Pyramid of Meidum is impressive, although it looks more like a stone tower than a pyramid, rising abruptly as it does from a large hill of rubble. This is one case, however, where the apparent state of disrepair was not caused by time or centuries of stone robbers, but rather the result of one instantaneous accident. The pyramid began as an eight-stepped structure; the steps were then filled in and the outer casing was added, forming the first true pyramid shell. However, there were serious design flaws and sometime after completion (possibly as late as the time of the Ptolemaic rulers in the last centuries BC) the pyramid's own weight caused the sides to collapse, leaving just the core that still stands today.

The pyramid, started by King Huni, was completed by his son Sneferu, the founder of the 4th dynasty. Sneferu's architects obviously learnt from the mistakes that eventually led to the disaster of Meidum, as he also built the more successful Bent and Red pyramids at Dahshur, and his son Cheops built one of the Great Pyramids at Giza.

Entrance to the site is E£16/8. Ask the guard at the nearby house to unlock the entrance of the pyramid for you. You can follow the steps 75m down to the empty underground burial chamber.

Getting There & Away

It's actually much easier to get to the pyramid from Beni Suef, about 45km to the south, than from Medinat al-Fayoum. Get a pick-up (75pt; 45 minutes) from Beni Suef to Al-Wasta, and then another to Meidum village (35pt), from where you'll have to walk a couple of kilometres, unless you can get a ride.

Alternatively, you could get one of the service taxis or buses running between Beni Suef and Cairo and ask to get off at the Meidum turn-off, from where you still have

An open-air potter's workshop at El-Nazla in Al-Fayoum, Egypt's largest oasis.

MARK ECCLESTON

This massive limestone statue of Ramses II lies neglected and damaged at a Memphis museum.

GREG ELMS

Beautifully preserved, the Temple of Hathor at Dendara is a sight to behold with its massive stone roof, dark chambers, underground passages and towering columns inscribed with hieroglyphs.

about 6km to go. The reverse of this is probably the easiest way to get back to Beni Suef (or to Cairo for that matter) – just flag down a service taxi, but be prepared to wait.

BIRQASH CAMEL MARKET

Egypt's largest Souq al-Gamaal (camel market) is held at Birqash, about 35km north-west of Cairo. Up until 1995, this famous market was located among run-down tenements and overcrowded streets in Imbaba, one of Cairo's western suburbs. But a burgeoning population has made land, even on the city's periphery, a valuable commodity – too precious for camels – and so one of Cairo's age-old institutions was relocated to the edge of the Western Desert, an area deemed more suitable for camel trading.

The market is an easy half-day trip from Cairo but, like all of Egypt's animal markets, it's not for animal lovers or the faint-hearted. Hundreds of camels are sold here every day, most having been brought up the 40 Days Road from western Sudan to just north of Abu Simbel by camel herders (for more information, see the boxed text 'Taking Camels to Market' on page 325). From here, most are sold to traders at the market in Daraw, from where they're hobbled and crammed into trucks for the 24 hour journey to Birqash. By the time they arrive, many are emaciated while others are fit only for the knackery. Traders stand no nonsense and camels that get out of line are beaten relentlessly. The sound of bawling beasts is sickening.

In addition to those from Sudan, there are camels from various parts of Egypt (including Sinai, the west and the south) and sometimes as far away as Somalia. They are traded for other livestock such as goats, sheep and horses, or sold for farm work and for slaughter. If you're interested in buying a camel, smaller ones cost about E£1500 while the bigger beasts fetch E£3000. The market is most lively on Friday and Monday mornings, from about 7 to 9 am. As the day wears on, the bargaining activity subsides and by early afternoon it becomes quite subdued.

For a long time a question mark has hung over whether or not there is an official entrance fee for tourists, but the practice has established itself and you are issued with a ticket saying, in Arabic, 'Government souq'. Admission is E£3, plus E£2 for a camera and E£15 for a video.

Getting There & Away

There are several options for getting to and from Birqash. If you are driving, take Pyramids Road and turn right onto the Mansuriyya Canal road for 25km. Turn left at a sign for Nimos nursery and when the road forks after 2km, bear left. After about a kilometre you'll find the market.

Using public transport, the cheapest way involves getting yourself to the site of the old camel market at Imbaba, from where microbuses filled with *galabiyya*-clad (robe) traders and potential buyers shuttle back and forth to Birqash. To get to the old camel market take bus No 99 from Midan Abdel Moniem Riad, or minibus No 72 from Midan Ramses to Midan Libnan (in Mohandiseen) and then catch a microbus from there. Or, easier still, take a taxi from central Cairo all the way to the old site – ask for Imbaba airport *(matar Imbaba)* as it's the closest landmark. Expect to pay about E£3 to E£5. Microbuses to Birqash (E£1) leave from a cafe (look for the sign 'Modern Cairo House') opposite the old souq site (which has become, for the time being, a garbage dump-cum-playground).

From Imbaba, the road winds through fields dotted with date palms, dusty villages and orange orchards before climbing the desert escarpment to the market. In all, it's a 45 minute taste of rural Egypt. Microbuses from Birqash back to Imbaba leave when full so, depending on the time of the day, you may have to wait an hour or so.

Alternatively, on Friday only, the Sun Hotel (see Places to Stay in the Cairo chapter) organises a minibus tour to the souq, leaving from the hotel at 7 am and returning at about noon. The charge is E£20 per person (minimum five people); you must book a day or two in advance.

The final option is to hire a taxi to take you all the way there and back. Depending on your bargaining skills, you'll be looking at around E£70; make sure to negotiate waiting time.

WADI NATRUN

About 100km north-west of Cairo, Wadi Natrun is a partly cultivated valley now strongly connected to the Coptic church. In ancient times the valley was important to the Egyptians as it was a source of natron, used in the mummification process. The natron comes from large deposits of sodium carbonate left when the valley's salt lakes dried up every summer – those deposits are now used on a larger scale by the chemical industry.

A visit to the monasteries of Wadi Natrun should explain the endurance of the ancient Coptic Christian sect. It is the desert, in a sense, that has been the protector of the faith, for it was there that thousands of Christians retreated to escape Roman persecution in the 4th century AD. They lived in caves, or built monasteries, and developed the monastic tradition that was later adopted by European Christians.

The focal point of the monasteries was the church, around which were built a well, storerooms, a dining hall, kitchen, bakery and the monks' cells. These originally isolated, unprotected communities were fortified after destructive raids in 817 AD by Arabs who were on their way to conquer North Africa. Of the 60 monasteries that were scattered over the valley, only four remain. But the religious life they all protected is thriving. The Coptic pope is still chosen from among the Wadi Natrun monks, and monasticism is experiencing a revival, with younger Copts again donning robes and embroidered hoods to live within these ancient walls in the desert.

Apart from the solitude and serenity of the monasteries, they are also worth visiting for the Coptic art they contain, particularly the Deir as-Suriani monastery.

As a general rule, you can visit all of the monasteries with the exception of Deir Abu Makar (Makarios). If you wish to stay overnight, you need written permission from the monasteries' Cairo residences for permission: Deir Anba Bishoi (☎ 591 4448); Deir as-Suriani (☎ 592 9658); Deir al-Baramus (☎ 592 2775); Deir Abu Makar (☎ 577 0614). Women are generally not allowed to stay overnight.

Deir Anba Bishoi

St Bishoi founded two monasteries in Wadi Natrun: this one (which bears his name) and the nearby Deir as-Suriani. Deir Anba Bishoi – a great place to watch a desert sunset – contains the saint's body, which is said to be perfectly preserved under a red cloth, and the remains of Paul of Tamweh, who made quite a name for himself by committing suicide seven times. The monks there claim that it is not uncommon for St Bishoi to perform miracles for true believers.

Deir as-Suriani

Deir as-Suriani, or the 'monastery of the Syrians', is named after a group of wandering Syrian monks who bought the monastery, with the help of one of their wealthy countrymen, from the Copts in the 8th century – although it's been occupied solely by Coptic monks since the 16th century. It's worth visiting for its superb art. A series of remarkable wall paintings has recently been discovered under the plaster in the monastery's Church of the Virgin. Some of the paintings can be viewed through small 'windows' cut in the plaster covering them.

Deir as-Suriani is about 500m north-west of Deir Anba Bishoi.

Deir Abu Makar (Makarios)

This monastery is nearly 20km south-east of Deir Anba Bishoi and was founded around the cell where St Makarios spent his last 20 or so years. Although structurally it has suffered worst at the hands of raiding Bedouins, it is perhaps the most renowned of the four monasteries, as over the centuries most of the Coptic popes have been selected from among its monks. It is the last resting place of many of those popes and also contains the remains of the '49 Martyrs', a group of monks killed by Bedouins in 444 AD. It is also the most secluded of the monasteries, and permission even to visit must be organised in advance.

Deir al-Baramus

Deir al-Baramus was the most isolated of the Wadi Natrun monasteries until recently, when a good road was built between it and Deir Anba Bishoi to the south-east. Despite this, it still has an isolated feel, and is probably the best monastery to stay at, as it's a little less austere than the others. The special feature of St John's church is a superb iconostasis of inlaid ivory.

Getting There & Away

You can get a West Delta Bus Co bus to the village of Wadi Natrun for E£3 from Cairo's Turgoman garage. Departures are every hour from 6.30 am. From the village you have to negotiate for a taxi. If you go on a Friday or Sunday, when the monasteries are crowded with pious Copts, you shouldn't have any trouble picking up a lift.

If you have your own vehicle and you're coming from Cairo, take Pyramids Rd and turn onto the Desert Highway just before the Mena House. At about 95km from Cairo (just after the rest house) turn left into the wadi, go through the village of Bir Hooker and continue on, following the signs indicating the monasteries. The first one is Deir Anba Bishoi. Deir as-Suriani is about half a kilometre to the north-west, Deir Abu Makar is 20km further via a sealed road to the south-east, and Deir al-Baramus is off to the north-west.

THE NILE DELTA

If you have the time, it's well worth the effort to explore the lush, fan-shaped Delta of Egypt between Cairo and Alexandria. This is where the Nile divides in half to flow north into the sea at the Mediterranean ports of Damietta and Rosetta. The Delta is also laced with several smaller tributaries and is reputedly one of the most fertile and, not surprisingly, most cultivated regions in the world.

The Delta region played ju a part in the early history of did Upper Egypt, although fe ical remains record this. While the desert and dryness of the south helped preserve its pharaonic sites, the amazing fertility of the Delta region had the opposite effect. Over the centuries, when the ancient cities, temples and palaces of the Delta were left to ruin, they were literally ploughed into oblivion by the *fellaheen* (peasant farmers). The attraction of this area, then, is the chance of coming across communities rarely visited by foreigners, where you can gain a little insight into the Egyptian peasant farmer's way of life. If you do intend spending any time in this region then we strongly recommend that you read Amitav Ghosh's excellent *In An Antique Land* – see Books in the Facts for the Visitor section.

Service taxis and buses crisscross the region from town to town, but if you want to explore this incredibly green countryside you'll have to hire a car. Theoretically, you're not supposed to leave the main roads, but in the unlikely event of being hassled by the police you can always say you're lost.

Nile Barrages (Qanater)

The Nile Barrages and the city of Qanater (which simply means barrages) lie 16km north of Cairo where the Nile splits into the eastern Damietta branch and the western Rosetta branch. The barrages, begun in the early 19th century, were successfully completed several decades later. The series of basins and locks, on both main branches of the Nile and two side canals, ensured the vital large scale regulation of the Nile into the Delta region, and led to a great increase in cotton production.

The Damietta Barrage consists of 71 sluices stretching 521m across the river; the Rosetta Barrage is 438m long with 61 sluices. Between the two is a 1km-wide area filled with beautiful gardens and cafes. It's a superb place to rent a bicycle or a felucca and take a relaxing tour.

The town of Qanater, at the fork of the river, is officially the start of the Delta region.

If you want to meet the locals, take a boat up to the Nile Barrages and make three dozen friends on the way.

Getting There & Away To get to the barrages from Cairo you can take a river bus for 50pt from the water-taxi station in front of the Radio & Television building (Maspero station), just north of the Ramses Hilton. The trip takes about two hours. A faster but less relaxing way to get there is by taking bus No 930 from Midan Ataba bus station or No 950 from Ahmed Helmy bus station behind Ramses train station.

Zagazig

Just outside this town, founded in the 19th century, are the ruins of Bubastis, one of the most ancient cities in Egypt. There's not much to see in Zagazig itself, but as it's only 80km north-east of Cairo it's an easy day trip to the ruins (though there's also a hotel or two in town should you want to stay overnight). The train heading for Port Said from Cairo takes about 1½ hours to Zagazig and a service taxi (E£4) from Midan Ahmed Helmy in Cairo takes about one hour.

Bubastis

The great deity of the ancient city of Bubastis was the elegant cat-goddess Bastet. Festivals held in her honour are said to have attracted more than 700,000 revellers, who would sing, dance, feast, consume great quantities of wine and offer sacrifices to the goddess. The architectural gem of Bubastis was the Temple of Bastet, sited between two canals, surrounded by trees and encircled by the city, which was built at a higher level to look down on it. The temple was begun by Cheops and Chephren during the 4th dynasty, and pharaohs of subsequent dynasties made their additions over about 17 centuries. The temple is now just a pile of rubble, and the most interesting site at Bubastis is the cat cemetery 200m down the road. The series of underground galleries, where many bronze statues of cats were found, is great to explore.

Tanis

Just outside the village of San al-Hagar, 70km north-east of Zagazig, are the ruins of ancient Tanis, which many believe to be the Biblical city where the Hebrews were persecuted by the Egyptians before fleeing through the Red Sea in search of the Promised Land. (It's also where Indiana Jones discovered the 'Lost Ark'.) It was certainly of great importance to a succession of powerful pharaohs, all of whom left their mark through the extraordinary buildings or statues they commissioned. For several centuries Tanis was one of the largest cities in the Delta.

The site covers about 4 sq km, only part of which has been excavated. The monuments uncovered date from as early as the 6th dynasty reign of Pepi I, around 2330 BC, through to the time of the Ptolemies in the 1st century BC. The excavation of the city so far has revealed sacred lakes, the foundations of many temples, a royal necropolis and a multitude of statues and carvings. There are a few royal tombs that can be visited (there's an admission fee), though they're not particularly impressive and all the finds from them are now on display in Cairo's Egyptian Museum.

Although it's less impressive than other archaeological sites in the country, the Egyptian government has been promoting Tanis as a tourist destination for the past few years.

Tanta

The largest city in the Delta, Tanta is 90km from Cairo and 110km from Alexandria. There's nothing much of interest here, although it is a centre for Sufism. There's a mosque here dedicated to Sayyed Ahmed al-Badawi, a Moroccan Sufi who fought the Crusaders in the 13th century, and the *moulid* (religious festival) held in his honour following the October cotton harvest is one of the biggest in Egypt, drawing crowds of one to two million.

While there are no actual structural remains in this area of the western Delta, there are the sites of three ancient cities. North-west of Tanta, on the east bank of the Nile, is **Sais**, Egypt's 26th dynasty capital. Sacred to Neith, the goddess of war and hunting and protector of embalmed bodies, Sais dates back to the start of Egyptian history and once had palaces, temples and royal tombs.

West of Tanta, more then half way along the road to Damanhur, is the site of **Naucratis**, an ancient city where the Greeks were allowed to settle and trade during the 7th century BC. The city of **Buto**, north-east of Damanhur and north-west of Tanta, was the cult centre of Edjo, the cobra-goddess of Lower Egypt, always represented on a pharaoh's crown as a uraeus.

Tanta is easily reached from Cairo, either by service taxi from Midan Ahmed Helmy, by Middle Delta Bus Co buses from Turgoman garage, or on nearly all Cairo-Alexandria trains (except the Turbos and one or two others).

Mansura

Mansura is known as the 'city of victory' for the part it played in Egypt's early Islamic history. In 1249 the Egyptians retreated from the coast and set up camp at Mansura after the Crusader forces, under Louis IX of France, had captured the port of Damietta. When the Crusaders decided to make their push inland, they charged straight through the Muslim camp, only to be cut down on the other side of Mansura by 10,000 Mamluk warriors. Louis himself was captured and ransomed for the return of Damietta.

In more recent times, Mansura has played an important role at the centre of Egypt's cotton industry. However, for the casual visitor there's absolutely nothing to see or do here.

There are regular train connections with Cairo, and a service taxi from Midan Ahmed Helmy costs E£8. The East Delta Co bus from Midan Ulali costs about E£7 and takes 2½ hours.

Damietta (Dumyat)

Once a prosperous Arab trading port, Damietta's fortunes suffered greatly with the construction of the Suez Canal and the subsequent development of Port Said. During the Middle Ages, its strategic position on the north coast of Egypt, at the mouth of the Nile, meant it was regularly being threatened by foreign armies. When it wasn't being attacked by marauding Crusaders, Damietta (Dumyat to the locals) did a roaring trade in coffee, linen, oil and dates, and was a port of call for ships from all over the known world.

Besides a few old Delta-style mansions, there's not much to see here. Should you want to stay, try *Al-Manshi Hotel* (☎ 323 308, 5 Sharia Nokrashi*) which has singles/doubles from E£20/27.

East Delta Co buses leave from Midan Ulali in Cairo (E£10) every hour from 6 am to 6.30 pm.

Nile Valley – Beni Suef to Qus

He who rides the sea of the Nile must have sails woven of patience.

Egyptian Proverb

The ancient Greek traveller and writer Herodotus described Egypt as 'the gift of the Nile'; the ancient Egyptians likened their land to a lotus – the Delta being the flower, the oasis of Al-Fayoum the bud and the river and its valley the stem. Whichever way you look at it, Egypt is the Nile. The river is the lifeblood of the country and the fertile Nile Valley is its main artery.

As the world's longest river, the Nile cuts through an incredible 6680km of Africa as it winds its way north towards the Mediterranean. It begins its journey from two separate sources, 1500km apart: Lake Victoria in Uganda, from which the White Nile journeys almost 3000km, and Lake Tana in the Ethiopian Highlands. The two rivers converge at Khartoum in Sudan and the Nile then flows north without a single tributary contributing to the waters.

But Egypt is the main beneficiary of this mighty river. Rain seldom falls in the Nile Valley but prior to this century the river would break its banks each summer and flood the surrounding land, covering it with a rich layer of silt. As the waters subsided farmers would simply plant seeds on their newly fertilised land and wait for the crops to grow. As Herodotus (who had a sound-bite for every occasion) put it, the Egyptians 'gather in the fruits of the earth with less labour than any other people'.

But while it may have been a relatively easy life for farmers, the Nile was not always reliable. Some years the river would not rise high enough to flood all the land, causing famine. At other times the flood would be too high, washing away villages and precious topsoil. So from the earliest times the Egyptians recognised that controlling the river's flow was the key to prosperity. To this end they developed a highly

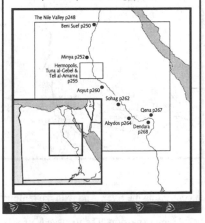

The Nile Valley p248
Beni Suef p250
Minya p252
Hermopolis,
Tuna al-Gebel &
Tell al-Amarna
p255
Asyut p260
Sohag p262
Qena p267
Abydos p264
Dendara
p268

sophisticated irrigation system with a complex system of canals and reservoirs to try and conserve water and squeeze more than one crop out of the silt each year.

It was not until the completion of the High Dam at Aswan in 1971 (see the High Dam section in the Nile Valley – Esna to Abu Simbel chapter) that Egypt finally succeeded

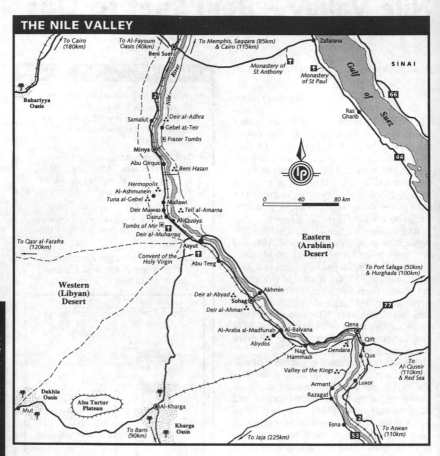

THE NILE VALLEY

in controlling the river. And with the taming of the Nile, the countryside has seen a huge population explosion. The thousands of villages that dot the edges of the old flood plain are now the size of small towns in Europe. The provincial capitals, like Minya, Asyut and Qena, are in many ways just large extensions of these villages.

Still, as you head south from Cairo, you are struck by the lush green fields contrasting with the desert beyond. Farmers still practice flood irrigation and occasionally

you can catch a glimpse of a *sakia*, or waterwheel, being turned by a blindfolded donkey, or a *shadouf*, the age-old implement for lifting water. You also see peasants working the land by hand, often using tools modelled on designs thousands of years old.

All this makes the countryside extremely picturesque. But, as with so much in Egypt, there is another side to this rural idyll. Labour-intensive as it may be, agricultural work cannot employ all of the area's burgeoning population and the lack of any real

Troubles in the Nile Valley

In 1992, the current round of Islamist-instigated violence broke out in Cairo and Upper Egypt. Although massive police action crushed the movement's radical wings in Cairo, it has proved far more difficult to do the same in the Nile Valley area between Minya and Qena. Easy escape routes to the desert and the hiding places afforded by crops such as sugar cane make it difficult for the police to fully control the area. Also, while the majority of the population has never supported the violence, mass arrests and police brutality have fuelled resentment against the government and the conflict has taken on some aspects of a traditional feud, with police and militants as the opposing 'families'.

These days, few foreigners travel this stretch of Upper Egypt and partly as a result of this the assaults on tourists that took place in the early 1990s have all but stopped. Ironically, it was in the supposedly safe area of Luxor that militants were able to pull off their most brutal attack on tourists yet, when they massacred 58 foreigners at the Temple of Hatshepsut in November 1997. Since then, the police have visibly tightened up their protection on tourists throughout the country. However, the area between Minya and Qena remains by far the most tense and violence continues, even if tourists are not always the victims. The high profile of the police, the constant checkpoints along the highway up and down the Nile, and the anxious assertions by officials and others that there are no problems and that tourists are well liked combine to give a slight feel for the kind of troubles most visitors, thankfully, never have any direct experience.

At this point in time independent travel is definitely *not* recommended anywhere between Minya and Qena, and it is quite likely that anyone who attempts to visit ancient sites such as Tuna al-Gebel, Tell al-Amarna, the monasteries near Sohag, or Abydos will be escorted out of the area by the local police, whether they like it or not. Make sure that you check the safety of the area with your embassy before attempting to travel here.

industrial base south of Cairo has caused severe economic hardship. Worst hit of all are young people, who suffer extremely high rates of unemployment and have little hope of finding long-term work. Add to this a historic distrust of the distant authorities in Cairo and a tradition of violent vendettas, and it is understandable how resentment against the state's perceived neglect of the area was exploited by Islamist leaders in the late 1980s and early 1990s, resulting in the violence that continues in parts of Middle and Upper Egypt today (see the boxed text 'Troubles in the Nile Valley' on this page).

BENI SUEF

Beni Suef is a provincial capital 120km south of Cairo. There's little to keep a traveller here these days; it is close to the Pyramid of Mei-

dum and the oasis area of Al-Fayoum but both of these places can be just as easily visited from Cairo (see the Around Cairo chapter). There's also a small, newly inaugurated museum next to the governorate building with artefacts found in the area.

Should you find yourself here, there is a 24 hour telephone centrale in the train station building, a post office just past it, and yet another telephone office after that. The Bank of Alexandria has a branch just off the central Midan al-Gomhuriyya.

Places to Stay & Eat

Near the train station is *Semiramis Hotel* (☎ 322 092, fax 326 017), the two star premier establishment in town. It has good singles/doubles with en suite bath, TV and breakfast for E£39/57.

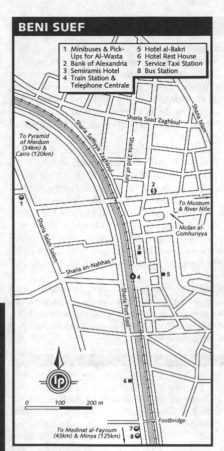

BENI SUEF

1 Minibuses & Pick-Ups for Al-Wasta	5 Hotel al-Bakri
2 Bank of Alexandria	6 Hotel Rest House
3 Semiramis Hotel	7 Service Taxi Station
4 Train Station & Telephone Centrale	8 Bus Station

BENI SUEF TO QUS

A block back from the square is *Hotel al-Bakri*. Its singles/doubles with bath cost E£16/20 or E£13/16 without. Breakfast is included.

Close to the bus and service taxi stations is *Hotel Rest House* (☎ 322 116). It's a bit musty, but has reasonable rooms with bath for E£14/16.50.

There's not an awful lot to choose from food-wise. A filling kebab meal will cost you about E£15 at *Semiramis Hotel*, or below *Hotel al-Bakri* there's a cheap kushari place. Otherwise, there are a few fuul and ta'amiyya stands about.

Getting There & Away

The bus station is along the main road, south of town. Buses run from about 6 am to 6 pm to Ahmed Helmy bus station behind Ramses station in Cairo. There are also frequent buses to Minya and Al-Fayoum. Beni Suef is also a departure point for the trek across the desert to the Monastery of St Anthony, which is about 150km east, near the Gulf of Suez (see the Monastery of St Anthony in the Red Sea Coast chapter for details). There is a bus to Zafarana, the closest Red Sea town to the monastery, once a day.

There are frequent train connections north to Cairo and Giza, and south to Minya. There are also (slow) trains to Al-Fayoum. Prices are posted in Arabic.

GEBEL AT-TEIR & FRAZER TOMBS

The main feature of the small Christian hamlet of Gebel at-Teir, 93km south of Beni Suef, is **Deir al-Adhra** (the Monastery of the Virgin). Established as a church/monastery in the 4th century AD by the Byzantine empress Helena, it was built on one of the sites where the Holy Family supposedly rested while fleeing Palestine. Gebel at-Teir and its church are perched on a hill 130m above the east bank of the Nile.

It is much more quickly reached from Minya, about 20km to the south, than from Beni Suef. Get a service taxi or microbus from Minya to Samalut and from there take a pick-up to the Nile boat landing (25pt), where you can take the car ferry for E£1 or the felucca for the same. On the other side is a pick-up going to Deir al-Adhra, but you may find yourself paying about E£1 to get it moving, as there are not always a lot of passengers going that way. When you arrive, ask for the *kineesa*, or church, and someone will appear with the keys and give you a short tour. There are some interesting 400-year-old icons inside.

About 5km south of Gebel at-Teir are the Frazer Tombs, which date back to the 5th and 6th dynasties. These Old Kingdom tombs are hewn into the desert cliff on the east bank of the Nile and overlook the plain and fields. The four tombs are very simple, containing eroded statues and carved hieroglyphs but no colourful scenes. If you're attracted to places where other tourists rarely go, these are for you.

To get there from Minya, take a pick-up (25pt) from the bridge 500m south-east of town. It will head north along the east bank road until a turn-off at two white pillars. From the turn-off, you must walk to the cliffs (a short cut through the fields – along the path starting at the pump house – will halve the distance).

MINYA

They call it the 'Bride of Upper Egypt' (Arous as-Sa'id), as Minya more or less marks the divide between Upper and Lower Egypt. A semi-industrial provincial capital 245km south of Cairo, it is a centre for sugar processing and the manufacture of soap and perfume. It has also acquired the unfortunate reputation of being a centre for Islamist opposition to the government. Because so many of the 'troubles' have been based in the countryside around here, Minya has become something of an armed fortress, with nervous policemen patrolling in tanks and personnel carriers. Even with this, it remains a pleasant town with a long Corniche along the Nile and some great, if shabby, early-20th century buildings testifying to its former prosperity as a centre of the cotton industry. Keep in mind that while you can usually (but not always) wander around the town relatively freely, the police will want to accompany you to monuments in the countryside.

Information

Should you need to extend your visa, the passport office is on the 2nd floor of the post office. There's a tourist office (☎ 320 150) in the governorate building and another in the train station (☎ 342 044) – the latter is open until 8 pm.

The Banque Masr branch on Midan as-Sa'a does Visa card cash advances – it takes some

time, though. There are a couple of other banks for cash and travellers cheque transactions, including the National Bank on the corner of Al-Gomhuriyya and the Corniche.

The post office is open from 8 am to 2 pm daily except Friday. The telephone office is in the train station and sells phone cards.

Things to See

Although Minya is a pleasant place the town itself doesn't have that much to see. Other than the interesting architecture in the town centre, there's the tree-lined Corniche along the Nile, which is a relaxing place for a picnic or a ride in a *hantour* (horse-drawn carriage). There is also a lively souq at the southern end of the town centre.

About 7km south-east of the town, near the ferry landing on the east bank, is a large Muslim and Christian cemetery called **Zawiyyet al-Mayyiteen** (Place of the Dead). The cemetery consists of several hundred mud-brick mausolea stretching for 4km from the road to the hills and is said to be one of the largest cemeteries in the world.

Places to Stay

Hotels *Majestic Hotel* (☎ 364 212) on Al-Gomhuriyya is the cheapest place in town (and maybe the dustiest too) – a three-bed room costs E£13.50.

Palace Hotel (☎ 324 071) on Midan Tahrir is worth a look-in for the decor even if you don't intend staying – a huge painted Nefertiti greets you at the bottom of the stairs, while the rooms have very high-ceilings and the central lobby is big and airy, if a little shabby. Singles/doubles are E£12/16 without bath or E£21/28 with.

Hotel Seety (☎ 363 930, 71 Saad Zaghloul) is half a block south of the train station and despite its run-down appearance, has clean and comfortable rooms that are quite cheap at E£8/10 without bath or E£10/14 with.

Savoy Hotel (☎ 363 270) directly opposite the train station on Midan al-Mahatta exudes decrepit grandeur with a big hall and high, painted ceilings. The rooms are large but rather run down and singles/doubles/triples

BENI SUEF TO QUS

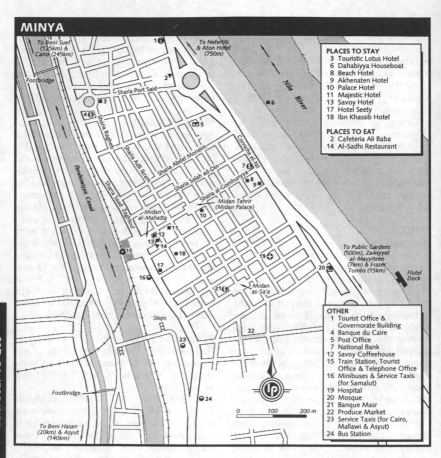

MINYA

PLACES TO STAY
3 Touristic Lotus Hotel
6 Dahabiyya Houseboat
8 Beach Hotel
9 Akhenaten Hotel
10 Palace Hotel
11 Majestic Hotel
13 Savoy Hotel
17 Hotel Seety
18 Ibn Khassib Hotel

PLACES TO EAT
2 Cafeteria Ali Baba
14 Al-Sadhi Restaurant

OTHER
1 Tourist Office &
   Governorate Building
4 Banque du Caire
5 Post Office
7 National Bank
12 Savoy Coffeehouse
15 Train Station, Tourist
   Office & Telephone Office
16 Minibuses & Service Taxis
   (for Samalut)
19 Hospital
20 Mosque
21 Banque Masr
22 Produce Market
23 Service Taxis (for Cairo,
   Mallawi & Asyut)
24 Bus Station

cost E£20/30/36 with bathroom, or E£15/25/30 without.

Ibn Khassib Hotel (☎ 364 535) at 5 Sharia Ragheb, a side street near the train station, is another aged building. It has 12 doubles and six singles, all with high ceilings and Victorian-style furniture, but check the rooms first, some have tiny bathrooms/showers. Singles/doubles with breakfast, air-con and bath go for E£34/44; without bath or air-con, they come down to E£30/38. There's a restaurant and bar with beer and a new billiard area.

On Al-Gomhuriyya *Beach Hotel* (☎ 322 307) is a clean, pleasant place down near the river. Singles/doubles without bath go for E£21/28 or E£28/35 with.

Akhenaten Hotel (☎ 365 917/8) on the Corniche has 42 clean, carpeted rooms with air-con, some of which have great views of the Nile. Get one of these rooms and in terms of value for money, this is the best place to stay. Singles/doubles are E£33.10/42.50 without breakfast, or a few pounds extra with air-con.

Dahabiyya (☎ *325 596*) is an old house-boat owned by the Coptic Evangelical Organisation with four small rooms and reportedly dodgy shared bathrooms for E£25/50, including breakfast.

Touristic Lotus Hotel (☎ *364 541, fax 364 576, 1 Sharia Port Said*) is about a 10 minute walk north of the train station. It used to be popular with German groups and has singles/doubles, all with air-con and TV, for E£43.90/63.20, including breakfast.

Nefertiti & Aton (☎ *331 515, fax 326 467*) is on the Corniche about 1km north of the town centre. It's a four star hotel that has rooms facing the Nile for US$51/61, not including taxes. It also has three restaurants and two bars.

Places to Eat

There are a lot of the usual cheap fuul and ta'amiyya stands scattered around Midan al-Mahatta, Midan Tahrir and along the market street stretching south off the latter. Otherwise, *Cafeteria Ali Baba*, on the Corniche just north of Sharia Port Said, serves a satisfying meal of the usual favourites – kebabs or another meat dish, salad, tahina and a soft drink for about E£10. This is also a good place for a morning cup of coffee and a pastry.

Al-Sadhi, to the right of Savoy Hotel, has good meals for around E£12. Other than that, most of the restaurants are at the hotels. The restaurants on top of *Touristic Lotus Hotel* and *Akhenaten Hotel* both serve simple filling meals for about E£15 to E£20. They also have good views. The restaurant at *Ibn Khassib Hotel* serves a large chicken followed by an orange for about E£12. They have Stella beer for E£6.

Savoy Coffeehouse is good for a cup of tea and a game of backgammon.

Getting There & Away

Bus The police usually insist that foreigners travel only by train but there is a bus station 500m south of the train station from where there's a service every hour to Cairo (E£12; four hours) from 5 am to 4 pm. You can book ahead or try your luck on the day. Buses also depart for Beni Suef (E£7) every

20 to 40 minutes, and for Asyut (E£5.50; two to three hours) every 30 minutes, and there's a daily bus to Hurghada (E£30). In summer there is a morning bus right through to Alexandria (E£35).

Train The trip from Cairo (four hours) costs E£23 in 1st class or E£14/6.50 in 2nd class with/without air-con. Trains heading south depart fairly frequently, with the fastest trains leaving Minya between about 11 pm and 1 am. Five go all the way to Aswan and six to Luxor. Although foreigners are only supposed to take the two 'special' trains that come from Cairo, in practice no one stops you from taking the one you want. Fares from Minya are (1st class/2nd class with air-con/2nd class without): Asyut E£13/8/3.40; Sohag E£21/13/5.80; Qena E£31/19/9; Luxor E£31/24/10; and Aswan E£49/30/13.20.

Service Taxi From Cairo, service taxis take three to four hours to Minya and cost E£10. From Minya, they still have departures as late as 8 pm. There are also service taxis to Asyut and Mallawi, but you're unlikely to be allowed to take them. The depot is about a five minute walk south from the train station (just past the bridge).

BENI HASAN

Beni Hasan is a necropolis on the east bank of the Nile about 20km south of Minya. More than 30 distinctive Middle Kingdom tombs of varying sizes are carved into a limestone cliff. Only a few of them are accessible. The site is open from 7 am to 5 pm but you should get there by 3 pm at the latest. It's a good idea to start earlier because it can get quite hot here towards the end of the day. Admission is E£12 (half for students). You are expected to give the guard a bit of baksheesh for unlocking the tombs.

There are various tombs at Beni Hasan, the best of which (and the only ones open to the public) are the following:

Tomb of Kheti (No 17) Kheti was a governor of the *nome* (district) of Oryx during

In Middle Egypt you'll find the fastest way to get around is by the shared, long-distance taxis known as 'ser-vees'.

the time of Egypt's 11th dynasty (about 2000 BC). Wall scenes in his tomb show daily life in the Middle Kingdom.

Tomb of Baqet (No 15) Baqet was the father of Kheti. His tomb has some interesting wall paintings: wrestlers doing more than just wrestling with each other, gazelles doing the same, and a hunt for unicorns and winged monsters.

Tomb of Khnumhotep (No 3) This is a beautiful tomb. Khnumhotep served as a governor under Amenemhet III (about 1820 BC). The walls show colourful scenes of Khnumhotep's family life, and above the door are some interesting scenes of acrobats.

Tomb of Amenemhet (No 2) This has the unusual addition of a false door facing west. The dead are supposed to enter the underworld only from the west. Amenemhet was a nomarch, or governor, and commander in chief of the Oryx nome.

Getting There & Away
From Minya, take the Mallawi service taxi or microbus, which costs E£1, and get the driver to let you off at Abu Qirqus. Alternatively, walk past the bus station and over-

pass, cross the railway tracks and veer left until you find another microbus station from where you can take an Abu Qirqus microbus (50pt). The journey takes about 30 minutes. Once there, walk across the Ibrahimiyya Canal and railway tracks and on for about 200m. There you take a pick-up (25pt) to the river. At the river you'll find an office, where round trip boat tickets cost E£6 if there's less than eight people, E£8 if you're by yourself. The price drops to E£2 per person if there are eight or more.

MALLAWI
Mallawi is 48km south of Minya. There is not much in town, except for a small museum that houses a collection of artefacts from Tuna al-Gebel and Hermopolis. It's open daily except Wednesday from 9 am to 4 pm (Friday until noon) and entry is E£6. However, as the focus of many of the worst battles between the police and Islamist militants in recent years you're unlikely to be allowed to stop here at all.

Getting There & Away
All buses to or from Minya and Asyut stop here. A service taxi from Minya costs E£1; from Asyut it's about E£2 for the one hour trip.

HERMOPOLIS

Little remains of this ancient city, 8km north of Mallawi, that was once the centre for the cult of Thoth, the ibis-headed god of wisdom, healing and writing.

The Greeks associated Thoth with their own Hermes – hence the city's Hellenic name – but in ancient times the city was known as Khmunu. Khmun was one of the eight all-powerful deities of the primordial chaos that preceded creation, and this city was believed to be sited where the sun first rose over the earth. The Arabic name for the present-day village, and the area surrounding the ruined city of Hermopolis, is Al-Ashmunein, a derivation of Khmun.

Apart from a few Middle and New Kingdom remains, the only real monument at Hermopolis is a ruined Roman agora and its early Christian basilica – the largest of its type still standing in Egypt. There is a small museum near two large sandstone statues of Thoth unearthed in the area.

At the time of writing, Hermopolis was closed – the tourist office in either Asyut or Minya should know if it has reopened.

Getting There & Away

To get to Hermopolis from Mallawi, take a local microbus or service taxi to the village of Al-Ashmunein; the turn-off to the site is 1km from the main road. From the junction you can either walk the short distance to Hermopolis or coax your driver to go a bit further.

TUNA AL-GEBEL

Apart from bordering on Akhetaten, the pharaoh Akhenaten's short-lived capital, Tuna al-Gebel was also the necropolis of Hermopolis. The area's oldest monument is one of the six stelae that marked the

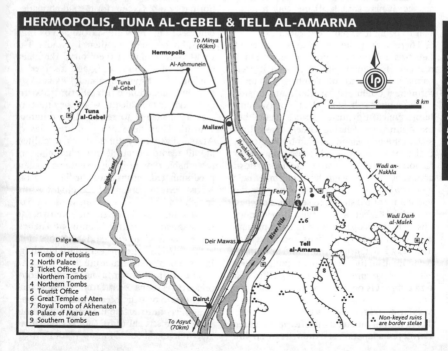

HERMOPOLIS, TUNA AL-GEBEL & TELL AL-AMARNA

1 Tomb of Petosiris
2 North Palace
3 Ticket Office for Northern Tombs
4 Northern Tombs
5 Tourist Office
6 Great Temple of Aten
7 Royal Tomb of Akhenaten
8 Palace of Maru Aten
9 Southern Tombs

Non-keyed ruins are border stelae

BENI SUEF TO QUS

boundary of Akhetaten – in this case the western perimeter of the city's farmlands and associated villages. The stele, a rockhewn shrine and some statues, show Akhenaten and Nefertiti in various poses.

To the south of the stele, which is about 5km past the village of Tuna al-Gebel, are the catacombs and tombs of the residents and sacred animals of Hermopolis. A German team has been working at Tuna al-Gebel since 1979.

The most interesting things to see there are the dark catacomb galleries once filled with thousands of mummified baboons, ibises and ibis eggs – baboons and ibises were sacred to Thoth. Most of the animals have been destroyed by robbers, and in fact only one of the baboons was found fully intact by archaeologists. Most of the mummification was done in the Ptolemaic and Roman periods. The subterranean cemetery extends for at least 3km, but Egyptologists suspect it may stretch all the way to Hermopolis. You definitely need a torch if you're going to explore the galleries.

There's also the interesting **Tomb of Petosiris**, a Ptolemaic tomb designed in the manner of a temple and dedicated to Petosiris, a high priest of Thoth. It's entered through a columned vestibule and inside tomb paintings show a mixture of two cultures: typical Egyptian farming scenes but the figures are wearing Greek dress. In a small building behind the Tomb of Petosiris is the extremely well-preserved **mummy of Isadora**, a woman who drowned in the Nile in about 150 AD. Her teeth, hair and fingernails are clearly visible. You'll need to give the guard a bit of baksheesh to see her though.

Tuna al-Gebel is 7km west of Hermopolis. The site is open from 7 am to 5 pm and admission costs E£12 (half for students). The very few tourists who come here these days are usually escorted by police from Minya. Make sure you check with the tourist office that it is open before you set out.

Getting There & Away

There's a fair amount of traffic between the Hermopolis junction and the village, so you could flag down a pick-up truck but as you'll probably be there with the police, they will take you there and back.

TELL AL-AMARNA

The scant remains of this once-glorious city, 12km south-west of Mallawi, are a little disappointing when compared to its fascinating, albeit brief, history.

In the 14th century BC, the rebellious pharaoh Akhenaten and his queen Nefertiti abandoned the gods, temples and priests of Karnak at Thebes to establish a new city and a new religion. There they and their followers, through their worship of Aten, god of the sun disc, developed what many scholars believe was the first known form of monotheism.

The city, in the area now known as Tell al-Amarna, was built on the east bank of the Nile on a beautiful, yet solitary, crescent-shaped plain, extending about 12km from north to south. Except for the side bounded by the river, the palaces, temples and residences of the city were surrounded by high cliffs, broken here and there by wadis. The royal couple named their city Akhetaten (Horizon of the Sun Disc), and it served as the capital of Egypt for about 14 years.

It was abandoned for all time shortly after Akhenaten's death, when the priests of Karnak managed to regain their religious control. They desecrated the temples of Aten and generally did their best to obliterate all record of the heretic pharaoh's objectionable new religion. Polytheism again predominated throughout the land as the Karnak priests persuaded Akhenaten's son-in-law and successor Tutankaten, or Tutankhamun as he became known, to re-establish the cult of Amun at Thebes. Akhetaten fell into ruin, and the stones of its palaces and temples were used for buildings in Hermopolis and other cities.

The Tell al-Amarna necropolis comprises two groups of cliff tombs, one at each end of the city, which feature colourful wall paintings of life during the Aten revolution. Akhenaten's royal tomb (admission E£16) is in a ravine about 13km up Wadi Darb al-

Malek, the valley that divides the north and south sections of the cliffs. He was not buried there, however, and no other tomb bearing his name has ever been found.

Due to the city's sudden demise, many of the tombs were never finished and very few were actually used.

Orientation & Information

The site is open from 7 am to 4 pm in winter; 5 pm in summer.

The admission pricing system here is extremely confusing. To start with, you have three options to cross the Nile – the local passenger launch (50pt), the car ferry (50pt) or the blue tourist boat (E£4 return for one or two people; E£1 each for three or more). Tickets for the latter are bought from the tourist office on the east bank – you cross the river before paying for your ticket.

Once you've crossed the river, you pay the E£12 fee to enter the site at the tourist office. What you pay from here on depends on how many of you there are, which sites you wish to visit, and what mode of transport you used to cross the river. All payments are made to the staff at the tourist office except the admission fee to the north tombs which must be paid near the site.

For less than eight people, you'll be looking at E£8 for a two hour bus tour around the northern tombs and the palace; for three or more people you each pay E£3.75. On arrival at the northern tombs, everyone must pay a E£12 (E£6 for students) entry fee.

Those wishing to take a bus tour to the southern tombs and the Great Temple of Aten must pay E£23 (shared among one to eight people) or E£3.75 each for groups of more than eight. It takes about 30 minutes to drive to the south tombs and you can supposedly stay as long as you want. To the Royal Tomb of Akhenaten it costs E£35 for the bus (one to eight people) or E£5 each when there are more than eight people.

The northern tombs are about 3km from the ferry crossing at At-Till, the southern ones about 8km away. Other remains of temples and private or administrative buildings are scattered about a wide area.

Tombs

In all, there are 25 tombs cut into the base of the cliffs, numbered from one to six in the north, and seven to 25 in the south. Those worth visiting are described here.

Tomb of Huya (No 1) Huya was the superintendent of Akhenaten's royal harem. The pharaoh and his family are depicted just inside the entrance on the right.

Tomb of Mery-Re II (No 2) Together with tomb No 1, this is the most distant of the northern tombs and guides are often keen to skip them unless you really insist on visiting. The tomb has just been restored.

Tomb of Ahmose (No 3) Ahmose was one of the king's versatile fan-bearers; his statue is at the back of the tomb.

Tomb of Merirye (No 4) Merirye was the high priest of Aten. The tomb paintings show the pharaoh riding around town in his chariot and visiting the Temple of Aten.

Tomb of Panehse (No 6) Panehse was vizier of Lower Egypt and a servant of Aten. Most of the scenes in this tomb show Akhenaten and his family attending ceremonies at the Sun Temple.

Tomb of Mahu (No 9) This southern tomb is one of the best preserved, and the wall paintings provide interesting details of Mahu's duties as Akhenaten's chief of police.

Tomb of Ay (No 25) This is the finest tomb at Tell al-Amarna. The wall paintings show street and palace scenes, and one depicts Akhenaten and Nefertiti presenting Ay and his wife with golden collars.

Getting There & Away

If you've somehow evaded the police, you can get to Tell al-Amarna from Mallawi, by taking a service taxi or a covered pick-up from the south depot to the ferry crossing at At-Till. From Asyut, it's easiest to take a service taxi to Mallawi (about E£2.50) and then backtrack using one of the pick-ups previously mentioned.

When leaving, you may find you have to pay more for a pick-up from the west bank ferry landing back to either Mallawi or Deir Mawas as not many vehicles head in those directions after about 3 pm.

DAIRUT

Dairut is about 10km south of Deir Mawas, but there is not a lot of interest to most travellers here. It has a large Christian population and over the years has been the scene of numerous bloody clashes. In the past several travellers were attacked here and the police are unlikely to let you stay.

AL-QUSIYA

About 8km south-west of the small rural town of Al-Qusiya, 35km south of Mallawi, is the Coptic complex of Deir al-Muharraq. About 7km further west, on an escarpment at the edge of the desert, lie the Tombs of Mir. There are no hotels in Al-Qusiya, but there's a large guesthouse just outside the pseudo-medieval crenellated walls of Deir al-Muharraq and the monks sometimes allow groups of travellers to stay there (but not usually individuals). In any event, both sites can be visited in an easy day trip from Minya or Asyut providing you have your own wheels.

Deir al-Muharraq

The 100 or so monks who reside in Deir al-Muharraq (the Burnt Monastery) claim that Mary and Jesus inhabited a cave on this site for six months and 10 days after fleeing from Herod into Egypt – their longest stay at any of the numerous places they are said to have rested during that flight. For 10 days every year (usually 18 to 28 June), thousands of pilgrims attend feasts to celebrate the consecration of the Church of al-Adhra (Church of the Virgin) which was built over the cave. Coptic Christians believe Al-Adhra to be one of the first churches in the world.

The religious significance of this place, they say, is given in the Old Testament; remember to remove your shoes before entering.

In that day there will be an altar to the Lord in the midst of the land of Egypt, and a pillar to the Lord at its border. It will be a sign and a witness to the Lord of Host in the land of Egypt; when they cry to the Lord because of oppressors he will send them a saviour, and will defend and deliver them. And the Lord will make himself known to the Egyptians; and the Egyptians will know the Lord in that day and worship with sacrifice and burnt offering, and they will make vows to the Lord and perform them. (Isaiah 19:19)

Next to Al-Adhra is a square tower, a 5th century structure built for the monks to use as added protection in case of attack. It has four floors, an old sundial on an outer wall, and a church inside.

The Church of St George (or Mari Girgis), built in 1880, is behind Al-Adhra and is decorated with paintings of the 12 apostles and other religious scenes. Again, be sure to take off your shoes.

Guided tours usually finish with a brief visit to the new church built in 1940 and the nearby gift shop, and sometimes with a cool drink in the monastery's reception room. Donations are appreciated.

Tombs of Mir

The necropolis of the governors of Cusae, or the Tombs of Mir as they're also known, were dug into the barren escarpment during the Old and Middle Kingdoms. Nine of the tombs here are decorated and open to the public; six others were never finished and remain unexcavated.

Tomb No 1 and the adjoining tomb No 2 are inscribed with 720 pharaonic deities but, during early Christian times, the Copts used the tombs as cells and many faces and names of the gods were destroyed. In tomb No 4 you can still see the original grid drawn on the wall to assist the artist in designing the layout of the tomb art. Tomb No 3 features a cow giving birth.

Admission to the tombs is E£16 (E£8 for students) and there's a E£10 camera fee per tomb, or E£150 for video.

Getting There & Away

The Asyut to Minya bus will drop you at Al-Qusiya (E£1.25; about 50 minutes from

Asyut), otherwise, you could take a service taxi. From there, you may be able to get a local microbus to the monastery, or the police, worried about your welfare, may take you there themselves.

Few vehicles from Al-Qusiya go out to the Tombs of Mir, so you'll have to hire a taxi to take you there. Ideally, you could combine this with a visit to the monastery.

ASYUT

Asyut, 375km south of Cairo, was settled during pharaonic times on a broad fertile plain bordering the west bank of the Nile. It's the largest town in Upper Egypt and the region's chief agricultural centre, dealing in cotton and grain. There is also a small carpet-making industry. It was also once the end of the line for great caravan routes – for several centuries, the camel caravans that travelled up the 40 Day Road from Darfur province in Sudan ended their trip in Asyut, and as recently as 150 years ago the town boasted the largest slave market in Egypt.

Asyut has a high number of Copts and it was one of the earliest centres of Islamist foment. It was here that sectarian violence first began in the early 1990s. Although the town has been quiet for several years, the countryside around it still has incidents from time to time, although – as in other troublespots in Upper Egypt – attacks are usually directed towards the police rather than Christians. As a result you will almost certainly have the police on your back when you arrive.

Although Asyut is still a transit point for people coming from the oases, few people stay here longer than a few hours.

Information

There is a tourist office (☎ 310 010) on Sharia ath-Thawra on the 1st floor of the governorate building. The staff is very friendly and willing to help. The office is open daily except Friday from 8.30 am to 2 pm.

You can change money at the cluster of banks on Midan Talaat Harb. Banque Masr, which does Visa and MasterCard cash advances, has two branches and the Bank of Alexandria, good for changing Eurocheques, has one. Just up the road is the Banque du Caire.

The GPO is opposite the Badr Hotel behind the train station. The telephone centrale is to the right of the entrance of the train station.

Things to See

At the end of Sharia Salah Salem is 'Banana Island' *(Gezirat al-Moz)* which is a pleasant place to picnic. You'll have to bargain with a felucca captain for the ride across.

At the northern edge of town is the 19th century Asyut barrage, which was built across the Nile, under British supervision, to regulate the flow of water into the Ibrahimiyya Canal and assist in the irrigation of the valley as far north as Beni Suef. It's an impressive structure but you're not allowed to walk on or around it. Taking photographs anywhere around here would be unwise.

On the east bank of the Nile, about 200m to the right after you've crossed the barrage, is the Lillian Trasher Orphanage. Born in Jacksonville, Florida, in the USA, Lillian Trasher came to Egypt in 1910 at the age of 23 and the following year she founded an orphanage in Asyut. It has since grown to be the biggest and most well known of its type in Egypt. Trasher never left, but died in her adopted country in 1961. The orphanage is something of a symbol of Christian charity in a city with a heavy concentration of Copts and welcomes interested visitors. Donations are appreciated. Microbuses will take you close to it from the centre of town for 25pt; a taxi will cost E£1. Ask for 'Malga Trasher'.

Places to Stay & Eat

Because of security concerns we did not visit Asyut while researching the latest edition of this book, and the information here dates from earlier visits. But prices have been updated by telephone.

Youth Hostel (☎ 324 846, Lux Houses, 503 Sharia al-Walidiyya) charges E£5.10 for a bed in a crowded dorm of eight. The entrance to this place is off a side street.

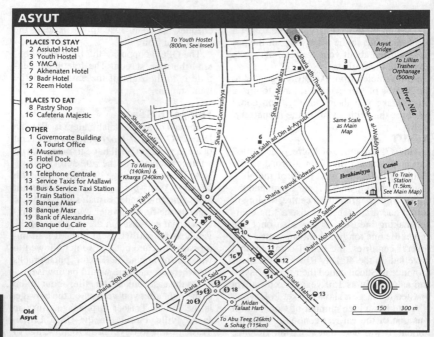

ASYUT

PLACES TO STAY
2 Assiutel Hotel
3 Youth Hostel
6 YMCA
7 Akhenaten Hotel
9 Badr Hotel
12 Reem Hotel

PLACES TO EAT
8 Pastry Shop
16 Cafeteria Majestic

OTHER
1 Governorate Building
    & Tourist Office
4 Museum
5 Flotel Dock
10 GPO
11 Telephone Centrale
13 Service Taxis for Mallawi
14 Bus & Service Taxi Station
15 Train Station
17 Banque Masr
18 Banque Masr
19 Bank of Alexandria
20 Banque du Caire

To Youth Hostel
(800m, See Inset)

Asyut Bridge

To Lillian Trasher Orphanage (500m)

River Nile

Same Scale as Main Map

Sharia al-Walidiyya

Canal

Ibrahimiyya

To Train Station (1.5km, See Main Map)

Sharia ath-Thawra

Sharia al-Mohafaza

Sharia al-Gomhuriyya

Sharia al-Galaa

Sharia al-Gomhuriyya

Sharia Salah ad-Din al-Ayyubi

Sharia Farouk Kidwani

To Minya (140km) &
Kharga (240km)

Sharia Tahrir

Sharia Talaat Harb

Sharia Salah Salem

Sharia Mohammed Farid

Sharia 26th of July

Sharia Port Said

Sharia Nahda

Old Asyut

Midan Talaat Harb

To Abu Teeg (26km) & Sohag (115km)

0   150   300 m

YMCA (☎ 323 218), about 500m down Salah ad-Din al-Ayyubi, used to get rave reviews in the days that travellers stayed in Asyut. It has singles/doubles with air-con, TV, mini-fridge and private bath for E£25/35 a single/double.

Akhenaten Hotel (☎ 337 723, fax 331 600) has pretty reasonable singles/doubles with bathroom for E£31/37. Some rooms are tiny so ask to see one first. Breakfast is available.

Reem Hotel (☎ 311 421, fax 311 424) on Sharia Nahda next to the railway tracks has singles for E£38.50 and doubles for E£58.50, including taxes, TV and breakfast. The rooms overlooking the railway are very noisy.

Assiutel Hotel (☎ 312 121, fax 312 122) on Sharia ath-Thawra, overlooking the Nile, is a good mid-range option with comfortable rooms for E£130/160, including breakfast.

Badr Hotel (☎ 329 811, fax 322 820) on Sharia Nahda, near the train station, is a centrally located western-style hotel with singles/doubles for E£82/90. Breakfast is extra (E£9.50) and there's a restaurant and bar.

All the bigger hotels have their own restaurants. At the cheaper end of the scale, the air-con restaurant at **Akhenaten Hotel** does an escalope as well as good pizza and soup. Beer is also served. **Cafeteria Majestic** opposite the train station has some decent food and there are a few of the usual fuul and ta'amiyya stands scattered around.

Getting There & Away
Asyut is a major hub for all forms of transport but the police will encourage you to take the train.

Bus From Asyut buses depart for Cairo (E£16.25 to E£20.25; six to seven hours) almost every other hour between 7 am and midnight. There are buses to Alexandria (E£28; 10 hours) regularly departing between 7 am and 7 pm and buses for Minya (E£3, two to three hours) every two hours from 6 am to 5 pm. At 8 am there's a bus for Esna and Luxor (E£10.50) and there are also five buses a day to Qena and frequent departures to Sohag. If you are heading out to the oases, there are eight daily buses to Kharga (E£6 to E£8), four of which go on to Dakhla (E£14 to E£17).

Train Trains arrive and depart for destinations north and south of Asyut frequently. There are about 20 trains throughout the day to Cairo and Minya, and about half that number to Luxor. The 1st and 2nd class fares to Cairo are E£31 and E£19 (E£21/14 for students).

The same fares to Minya (two to three hours) are E£13/8 (E£9/6 for students). To Luxor (four to six hours) it costs E£29/19 (E£20/14). There are very slow regular trains to the next main centre down the line, Sohag, but the police are unlikely to let you get on.

Service Taxi Service taxis gather around the bus station. There are services to Cairo (E£15), Minya (E£4.50, two hours) and to Kharga (E£8). Microbuses and service taxis to Mallawi (E£2) leave from the big lot near the mosque.

AROUND ASYUT
Convent of the Holy Virgin
About 10km south-west of Asyut in an area known as Dirunka, is this convent, built near a cave which Coptic Christians believe the Holy Family sought refuge in during their flight into Egypt. Some 50 or so nuns and monks live at the convent, which is built into a cliff about 120m above the valley. One of the monks will happily show you around. During the Moulid of the Virgin (7 to 22 August), tens of thousands of pilgrims descend on the place and there are daily parades with portraits of Mary and Jesus carried around.

Groups and individuals are welcome to stay in the *rest house* just outside the main gate, but food is not available. A dorm bed costs E£3 or E£5 per bed in one of the smaller rooms. The convent is open from 6 am to 6 pm.

SOHAG
The city of Sohag, 115km south of Asyut, is the administrative centre for the governorate of the same name and one of the major Coptic Christian areas of Upper Egypt. The main reason to visit is to see the White and Red monasteries just outside Sohag, and the town of Akhmin across the river. However, as in Minya and Asyut, there is a strong police presence on the streets here. They take their job of protecting the few tourists who do pass through very seriously. If they know you're in town they will insist on escorting you everywhere and you'll probably be banned from leaving your hotel after dark. It's probably better to visit as a day-trip from Luxor.

There's no tourist office but you can change cash or travellers cheques at the Bank of Alexandria or the Banque du Caire, both on Al-Gomhuriyya. The post office is a little way down the road from the Banque du Caire along the Nile.

White & Red Monasteries
Deir al-Abyad, the White Monastery, was built in 400 AD by the Coptic saint Shenouda, with chunks of white limestone from a pharaonic temple. It once supported a community of 2000 monks; today there are just four. Its fortress walls still stand, but most of the interior is in ruins, though you can see the several types of arches used in its construction. The monastery is 12km north-west of Sohag and is open from 8 am to 8 pm.

Deir al-Ahmar, the Red Monastery, is 4km from Deir al-Abyad and is hidden at the rear of a village so you'll need to ask directions. It was founded by Bishoi, a thief who converted to Christianity. He built this and two monasteries in Wadi Natrun and eventually became a Coptic saint. There are two chapels on the grounds, Santa Maria

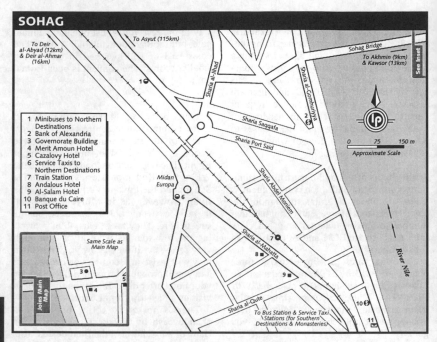

SOHAG

To Deir
al-Abyad (12km)
& Deir al-Ahmar
(16km)

To Asyut (115km)

Sohag Bridge
To Akhmin (9km)
& Kawsor (13km)

See Inset

Sharia al-Jihad

Sharia al-Gomhuryya

Sharia Saqqafa

Sharia Port Said

Sharia Abdel Moniem

0   75   150 m
Approximate Scale

1 Minibuses to Northern
   Destinations
2 Bank of Alexandria
3 Governorate Building
4 Merit Amoun Hotel
5 Cazalovy Hotel
6 Service Taxis to
   Northern Destinations
7 Train Station
8 Andalous Hotel
9 Al-Salam Hotel
10 Banque du Caire
11 Post Office

Midan
Europa

Sharia al-Mahatta

Sharia al-Qute

River Nile

Same Scale as
Main Map

Joins Main Map

To Bus Station & Service Taxi
Stations (for Southern
Destinations & Monasteries)

Chapel and the St Bishoi Chapel. Be sure to see the remains of a 10th century fresco in a frame on a side altar – it contains a 1000 year old icon. There are interesting though fading frescoes on the walls, unusual pillars and old wooden peg locks on the doors.

To get to the monasteries you'll have to take a taxi (about E£10 there and back) unless you're visiting sometime during the first two weeks of July, when you can catch a bus for about E£1 with the thousands of other pilgrims.

Akhmin

The town of Akhmin, on the east bank of the Nile, is well known for its unique woven carpets and wall hangings and, more recently, the discovery of the **statue of Meret Amun**. This is the tallest statue of an ancient queen to have been discovered in Egypt. Meret Amun (Beloved of the God Amun)

was one of the daughters of Ramses II and wife of Amenhotep. She was also a priestess of the Temple of Min, which was dedicated to a local deity and god of fertility. Little is left of the temple itself, and the statue of Meret Amun now stands in a huge excavation pit among the houses in the middle of town. Accidentally unearthed in 1982 during excavations to build a new school, it was not until recently that the statue was raised and the site was opened to the public. Admission costs E£10 (half for students) and the site is open daily from 9 am to 5 pm. As the statue is so tall, you can get a good view of it without even entering the site.

Opposite the statue of Meret Amun is a tiny post office and, across the road from this, a small **weaving factory**. It's the house with the green door – just knock to be led through to the showroom where you can buy silk and cotton handwoven textiles straight from the bolt or packets of ready-made tablecloths and serviettes. Ask to see the men and boys who make the products at work – you'll hear the 25 looms clattering away before you even climb the stairs.

A microbus from Sohag to Akhmin takes 15 minutes and costs 20pt.

Places to Stay & Eat

Travellers are discouraged from staying in Sohag. Some hotels will quote outrageous amounts in an effort to dissuade you from staying, others will simply refuse to take you. Wherever you do stay, you will probably be forbidden from going out after dark.

Andalous Hotel (☎ 324 328) is on Sharia al-Mahatta, directly across from the train station. Basic singles/doubles with shared bathrooms are E£7/10 or E£9/14 with private facilities but they aren't keen to have foreigners stay and some travellers have reported being charged as much as E£50 for a room.

Al-Salam Hotel (☎ 333 317) is on the same street as the Andalous and it has basic singles/doubles without bath for E£15/25 or E£18/45 with bath.

Merit Amoun Hotel (☎ 601 985, fax 603 222) over on the east bank of the river is a big place with a fanciful three star rating. Singles/doubles are E£70/88 including taxes.

Cazalovy Hotel (☎ 601 185) also on the east bank, about 100m beyond the Merit Amoun, offers the best value in town, with air-con rooms for E£38.80/55. Soap and towels are provided and breakfast is included.

There's not much choice in the way of food in Sohag. As well as the usual fruit and vegetable stands, there are a few fuul and ta'amiyya places near the train station. If you follow Sharia al-Mahatta south of the train station (left as you walk out the entrance) to a big square, and cross this, there is an OK kebab restaurant. There are also restaurants in the *Cazalovy* and *Merit Amoun* hotels; the former is probably the better of the two.

Getting There & Away

Bus The main bus station is around the corner from the big square south of the train station. There are seven buses a day for Cairo (E£17). The first leaves at 5 am and the last at 10 pm. There is a bus to Aswan (E£13) via Luxor (E£6.50) at 6 am. If you miss this one, get a bus or service taxi to Qena where there are many services each day. Buses to Asyut (E£2.75; 1½ to two hours) depart every 30 to 40 minutes.

Train Trains north and south stop fairly frequently at Sohag. The 1st/2nd class fare to Asyut is E£10/6. The train to Al-Balyana generally makes a lot of stops (E£1.50 in 3rd class).

Service Taxi There are several service taxi stations in Sohag but the police are unlikely to let you take one. Should they lighten up, cars to Asyut and other northern destinations, including Cairo, can be found north of the train station on Midan Europa. Service taxis for Qena and Nag Hammadi leave from the southern depot, which is on the main road south, just after a canal. There are also stations for local taxis to the monasteries and to Akhmin – on some of these local routes wonderful vintage cars are used as service taxis.

AL-BALYANA

The only reason to go to this town is to visit the village of Al-Araba al-Madfunah, 10km away. There you'll find the necropolis of Abydos and the magnificent Temple of Seti, one of the most beautiful monuments in Egypt. The police here tend to be somewhat heavy-handed in their efforts to protect you and if you haven't been escorted thus far, you'll certainly pick up some policemen here.

Should you need to change money, there's a tiny Banque Masr kiosk at the entrance to Abydos but don't rely on it being open.

Abydos

The temples at Abydos served several dynasties of Egyptians and its huge necropolis was, for a long time, *the* place to be buried. Excavations indicate that it was a burial place as far back as the last predynastic

BENI SUEF TO QUS

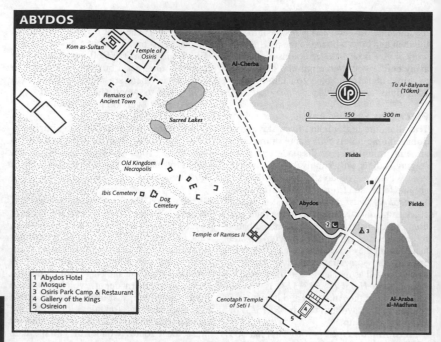

ABYDOS

Kom as-Sultan
Temple of Osiris
Al-Cherba
To Al-Balyana (10km)
Remains of Ancient Town
0   150   300 m
Sacred Lakes
Fields
Old Kingdom Necropolis
Fields
1
Ibis Cemetery
Dog Cemetery
Abydos
2
3
Temple of Ramses II
1 Abydos Hotel
2 Mosque
3 Osiris Park Camp & Restaurant
4 Gallery of the Kings
5 Osireion
Cenotaph Temple of Seti I
Al-Araba al-Madfuna
4
5

kings, before 3100 BC, while Seti I and Ramses II, two of the last pharaohs, built the most important temples of the complex in the 13th century BC. And Abydos was still important during Roman times.

Abydos maintained its importance for so many centuries because of the cult of Osiris, god of the dead. The area was a natural shrine for the worship of this ruler of the netherworld because, according to mythology, it was here that the head of Osiris was buried after his brother Seth had murdered him – see the boxed text 'The Cult of Osiris' on page 265. The temple at Abydos was the most important of the shrines to Osiris and became a place of pilgrimage. Most Egyptians would have made the journey there at least once in their lifetime.

Abydos is open from 7 am to 5 pm daily. The admission fee for both temples is E£12, or E£6 for students. Bring a torch (flashlight).

Should you want more information, there's a booklet on sale at the Osiris Park Camp shop for E£10. There's also *Abydos – The Holy City in Ancient Egypt* written by a fascinating woman by the name of Dorothy Eady, but better to known to many as Umm Seti. She was an English woman who believed she was a temple priestess and lover of Seti I and for 35 years, until her death in 1981, she lived at Abydos. *The Search of Umm Seti* by Jonathan Cott is a biography of her life there.

Cenotaph Temple of Seti I The first structure you'll see at Abydos is one of Egypt's most complete – and beautiful – temples. A cenotaph temple was a secondary mortuary temple dedicated to one or more gods and honouring the deified, deceased pharaoh who built it. Pharaoh Seti's splendid temple honours seven gods: Osiris,

The Cult of Osiris

Of all ancient Egypt's myths, the one we are most familiar with today is that of Osiris. This is because it was recorded for posterity by the Greek writer Plutarch in about 1 AD.

According to Plutarch, Osiris brought Egyptians out of a state of barbarity. He taught them how to grow crops and ensured that the laws were obeyed. Together Osiris and his consort/sister Isis ruled the country, and all seemed well. However, Seth, Osiris' brother, began to plot against them. Seth's plan was to have a chest made to Osiris' measurements and then hold a banquet where the person who could fit into the chest could claim it as a prize. At the banquet, Osiris climbed into the chest and, as he did so, Seth's collaborators slammed it shut, sealed it and flung it into the Nile. The chest washed up on the shores of Lebanon (Byblos) where it was eventually found by Isis and returned to Egypt. Seth, however, intercepted the chest, hacked Osiris' body into 14 parts and scattered them throughout the Nile Valley. Isis sought out each part and, when she discovered one, held a burial ceremony at that place. This is why, according to Plutarch, so many temples in the Nile Valley lay claim to Osiris' tomb.

From earliest times Osiris was regarded as god or king of the dead (although in the New Kingdom he is referred to as lord of the living). The incumbent pharaoh was regarded as the living Horus (Osiris' son, and credited with avenging his father's death). When the pharaoh died, his name was prefaced with 'Osiris', the implication being that he would take his place on Osiris' throne from where he could give orders to the living.

Osiris is typically depicted holding the crook and flail which represent kingship.

Isis, Horus, Amun, Ra-Harakhty, Ptah and Seti I himself. Unusually, each one has its own chapel. The temple is also unique in that it is L-shaped instead of rectangular. The Osiris Sanctuary was especially important; it opens into an area extending the width of the temple, with two halls and two sets of three chapels dedicated to Osiris, Isis and Horus.

As you roam through Seti's dark halls and sanctuaries a definite air of mystery, an almost tangible impression of ancient pomp and circumstance, surrounds you. The colourful hieroglyphs on the walls, describing the rituals that were carried out there, make it easy to imagine the ceremonies honouring the death and rebirth of Osiris and the great processions of cult worshippers that passed in and out of the temple.

In a corridor known as the Gallery of the Kings to the left of the sanctuaries, a list of Egypt's pharaohs up to Seti I was found. Though not complete, the 76 cartouches greatly assisted archaeologists in unravelling Egypt's long history from Menes onwards.

It's possible to enter the Osireion, directly behind the main temple, but only if you wade through ankle-deep water. It is sited lower than the main temple and, since the rise of the water table, it has been permanently under water. Here you'll find excerpts from the *Book of the Dead* and the *Book of Gates*, and images of Horus holding a scale in front of Osiris.

Temple of Ramses II North-west of Seti's temple his son Ramses II built another temple dedicated to Osiris – and himself. The roof of the Temple of Ramses II has collapsed, and only 25% of the huge statues and pillars remain, but the hieroglyphs on the walls are interesting. You have to get the guard to unlock the gate.

Places to Stay & Eat
You are unlikely to be allowed to stay in Al-Balyana, given the police's nervousness. Should the situation change, there's *Wadi Melouk Hotel*, which has very basic doubles for E£5. There are some cafes and food stands around the town.

Osiris Park Restaurant & Camp (☎ 812 200), right in front of the temple was open for food at the time of writing, but almost nobody was allowed to stay overnight. It's managed by Horus, a protege of Umm Seti. The only other option is *Abydos Hotel (☎ 812 102)* 200m before Osiris Park.

Getting There & Away
Al-Balyana is serviced by buses, trains and service taxis, and their respective stations are conveniently close to each other. However, you're unlikely to be given much choice in your mode of transport. If you haven't come in convoy, the police will usually take you to the train station. Occasionally they will stick you on the bus of a tour group coming from Luxor with an armed police escort. Arriving at Al-Balyana train station, you will be met by police who will put you in a local taxi and then escort you there and back. This costs about E£5.

QENA
Qena, a provincial capital 91km east of Al-Balyana and 62km north of Luxor, is at the intersection of the main Nile road and the

road across the desert to the Red Sea towns of Port Safaga and Hurghada.

Unless you're on your way to or from the Red Sea and don't have a through connection, the only reason to stop in Qena is to visit the spectacular temple complex at Dendara, just outside the town. There are two service taxi stations quite a long way apart from one another, one for northern destinations and places across the Nile, the other for southern destinations. If you need money, there is a Bank of Alexandria and a Banque du Caire in town. Again, you are likely to be met by policemen here and could well be escorted to the temple and then put on the first train to Luxor.

Dendara
Although it indicates the decline of a purely Egyptian style of art, the wonderfully preserved complex at Dendara is a sight to behold. The almost intact main Temple of Hathor is complete with a massive stone roof, dark chambers, underground passages and towering columns inscribed with hieroglyphs.

While the Dendara necropolis includes early dynastic tombs and evidence that Cheops and later pharaohs built there, the temple complex, as it stands today, was built by the Ptolemies and the Romans. Its very design, however, suggests that it was built on the site of an older temple and, as was the custom of the day, reproduces the character and mythology of the original. So, despite the apparent shortcomings in the quality of its design and decoration, and the fact that it was raised during foreign occupation, it is an impressive, beautiful monument to an ancient goddess of great renown.

Hathor was the goddess of pleasure and love; she was usually represented as a cow, or a woman with a cow's head, or a woman whose headdress was a sun disc fixed between the horns of a cow. She was the beneficent deity of maternal and family love, of beauty and light; the Greeks associated her with Aphrodite. She was also the wet nurse of Horus, before becoming his mate and bearing Ihy, the youthful aspect of the creator-gods.

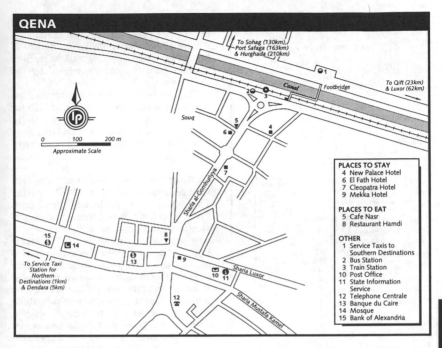

QENA

To Sohag (130km),
Port Safaga (163km)
& Hurghada (210km)

Canal Footbridge

To Qift (23km)
& Luxor (62km)

Souq

0   100   200 m

Approximate Scale

Sharia al-Gomhuriyya

Sharia Luxor

Sharia Mustafa Kamel

To Service Taxi
Station for
Northern
Destinations (1km)
& Dendara (5km)

PLACES TO STAY
4   New Palace Hotel
6   El Fath Hotel
7   Cleopatra Hotel
9   Mekka Hotel

PLACES TO EAT
5   Cafe Nasr
8   Restaurant Hamdi

OTHER
1   Service Taxis to
    Southern Destinations
2   Bus Station
3   Train Station
10 Post Office
11 State Information
    Service
12 Telephone Centrale
13 Banque du Caire
14 Mosque
15 Bank of Alexandria

BENI SUEF TO QUS

Dendara was the ritual location where Hathor gave birth to Horus' child, and her temple stands on the edge of the desert as if awaiting her return.

Hathor's head forms the capital of all 24 columns in the temple's **Outer Hypostyle Hall**. On the walls, there are strange scenes showing the Roman emperors Augustus, Tiberius, Caligula, Claudius and Nero as pharaohs, making offerings to Hathor. The ceiling portrays vultures flying among the sun, moon and stars of the Egyptian zodiac, with the sky-goddess Nut among other deities sailing their solar boats across the heavens.

The hieroglyphs in the **Inner Hypostyle Hall** deal with the temple's foundation. Beyond is the Hall of Offerings and sanctuary of the temple proper, surrounded by a gallery of **chapels** and the east and west staircases to the roof.

The **Hall of Offerings**, where the daily rituals of the cult were carried out, shows the pharaoh and others making offerings to Hathor. During the New Year Festival, images of the goddess were carried from here to the roof to be looked on by Ra, the sun-god. Views of the surrounding countryside from the roof are magnificent. The graffiti on the edge of the temple was left by Napoleon's commander Desaix, and other French soldiers, in 1799.

The **sanctuary** was usually kept bolted and only the pharaoh, or priests acting on his behalf, could enter. Reliefs on the walls depict the special rituals of the pharaoh entering the sanctuary to show his adoration for the goddess.

From the chapel behind the sanctuary Hathor would embark each New Year on her annual journey to Edfu, where she would lie in blissful union with Horus.

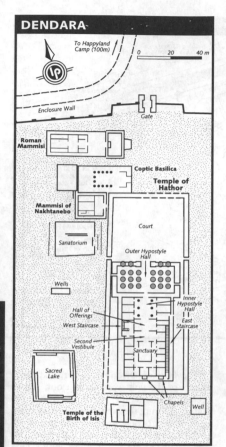

DENDARA

To Happyland Camp (100m)

0   20   40 m

Enclosure Wall

Gate

Roman Mammisi

Coptic Basilica

Temple of Hathor

Mammisi of Nakhtanebo

Court

Sanatorium

Outer Hypostyle Hall

Wells

Inner Hypostyle Hall

Hall of Offerings

West Staircase

East Staircase

Second Vestibule

Sanctuary

Sacred Lake

Chapels

Well

Temple of the Birth of Isis

The reliefs on the exterior of the temple's south wall show various Roman emperors such as Nero and Caesarian – son of Julius and Cleopatra – and the great Egyptian queen herself making offerings to the head of Hathor.

Behind the main temple is the smaller **Temple of the Birth of Isis** built by Emperor Augustus. North of the main temple, the second structure on your left is a **Roman mammisi**, or birth house, which is dedicated to Hathor and her son Ihy.

A 5th century **Coptic basilica** is squeezed between the mammisi, the court of Hathor's temple and another birth house. The birth house was begun by Nakhtanebo, a 30th dynasty pharaoh, and completed by the Ptolemies.

The Dendara complex is open from 7 am to 6 pm and admission is E£12, or E£6 for students. There are several souvenir stalls, public toilets, a phone, an ambulance base and a cafe where you can get an expensive soft drink.

Getting There & Away Dendara is 4km west of Qena on the other side of the Nile. These days most people arrive here from Luxor in convoy. If you want to hire a service taxi from Luxor to do this trip, it will cost you about E£100 to E£120 return. From Qena you can take a local microbus to the northern service taxi station, and from there another microbus along the main road. It drops you at the turn-off just after a new railway bridge, from where you have about a 20 minute walk to the temple. If you haven't already met up with the police, you will at the temple and they are likely to escort you back to town after your visit.

Places to Stay & Eat

If you must stay in Qena, there's **Happyland Camp** 100m from the temple, basically a hotel with overpriced beds. There's a possibility of camping in its messy garden. Other not great choices in town include **New Palace Hotel** (☎ 322 509), just behind the Mobil petrol station, plus a few other cheap dives along Sharia al-Gomhuriyya.

Cafe Nasr has good cheap food such as spinach, tahina, salad and tea for E£2.50, while **Restaurant Hamdi** serves full meals of chicken and vegetables for around E£7. There are several kushari, kofta and ta'amiyya places along the main street.

Getting There & Away

Bus The bus station is in front of the train station. However, buses not originating or terminating here pass along the main road and drop (and might pick up) passengers at the bridge over the canal. There are two Superjet buses to Cairo (E£25) at 7 am and 8 pm. Eleven buses go to Aswan (E£7) from 6.30 am to 7.45 pm, and most stop in Luxor (E£2). A few other buses only go as far as Edfu or Luxor. There are nine buses to Hurghada and six of them go on to Suez (E£22 to E£38; nine to 10 hours). Superjet also has services to Hurghada (E£15) and Suez (E£40). There are also buses for coastal destinations such as Al-Quseir (E£7) and Port Safaga (E£7 to E£10).

Other buses serve Nile destinations such as Sohag, Asyut and Minya. Often, you can transfer from the Cairo buses for these. These buses all pass through Al-Balyana, where you can change for Abydos.

Train This is not a very practical way to get to and from Qena, as generally only the slower trains stop here. There are 1st and 2nd class air-con trains to Luxor and 2nd and 3rd class trains to Al-Balyana, if you want to visit Abydos.

Service Taxi Service taxis to destinations north of Qena leave from a T-junction 1km outside town. For destinations to the south of Qena, such as Luxor, service taxis leave from a taxi station that is on the other side of the canal from the train station.

Getting Around
There is a local microbus that shuttles from town to the northern service-taxi station. You can pick it up near the train station or, if you're coming up from the south, at the canal bridge near the southern service taxi station. It costs 25pt.

QIFT
In Graeco-Roman times Qift was a major trading town on the Arabia-India trade route and an important starting point for expeditions to the Red Sea and Sinai. The town lost its importance as a trading centre from the 10th century onwards.

At the time of writing the police were not letting foreigners visit Qift.

QUS
During medieval times this was the most important Islamic city in Egypt, after Cairo. Founded in 1083, it served as a port and transit point for goods coming and going between the Nile and Al-Quseir on the Red Sea. Today, the town is the site of a US$246 million Egyptian-German paper mill project that converts bagasse – the waste product of sugar cane refining – into paper products.

At the time of writing the police were not letting foreigners visit Qus.

BENI SUEF TO QUS

Nile Valley – Luxor

The sheer grandeur of Luxor's monumental architecture, and its excellent state of preservation, have made this village-city one of Egypt's greatest tourist attractions. Built on and around the 4000 year old site of ancient Thebes, Luxor is one of the world's greatest open-air museums, a time capsule of a glorious long-gone era.

Its attraction for tourists is by no means a recent phenomenon: travellers have been visiting Thebes for centuries, marvelling at the splendid temples of Luxor, Karnak, Ramses II and Hatshepsut. As far back as Graeco-Roman times visitors would wait to hear the mysterious voice of Memnon emanating from the colossal statues of Amenhotep III, while in the past hundred years or so, since archaeology became a respectable science, curious travellers have been following the footsteps of the excavators into the famous tombs of the Valley of the Kings.

With such a huge proportion of the town's economy derived from tourists, Luxor has been heavily hit by Egypt's severe downturn in tourism in recent years. The massacre at Hatshepsut's temple in 1997 was a disaster for the local economy and it has yet to recover.

Nevertheless, travellers in Luxor still complain of the almost incessant hassle from vendors, street hawkers and felucca middlemen. In the steamy summer months, when business is slack, it can be enough to tip a temper already frazzled by the heat. In winter, it's easier to bear in mind that they are just trying to make a living. And also keep in mind that behind the sometimes sleazy tourist facade, the town and its environs are filled with ordinary, friendly people.

HISTORY

Following the collapse of centralised power at the end of the Old Kingdom period, the small village of Thebes, under the 11th and

HIGHLIGHTS

- **The Hypostyle Hall, Karnak** Lose yourself in a stone papyrus forest.

- **Valley of the Kings** See how Egypt's ancient rulers tried to confound both thieves and mortality with spectacular tombs dug deep into the desert mountains.

- **Temple of Hatshepsut** Walk through this temple that was carved out of the Theban hills in honour of one of the few women to rule ancient Egypt.

- **Tomb of Nefertari** Get some idea of how Theban tombs looked before they were dulled by time and the breath of thousands of tourists.

- **Felucca Ride** Glide along the Nile as you watch the sun set behind the mountains of Thebes.

- **Gurna** Wander between colourful mud-brick houses of this mountainside village and see how modern Thebans coexist with the remains of their ancestors.

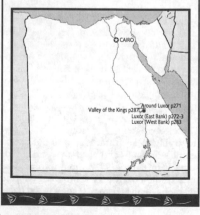

CAIRO

Valley of the Kings p287
Around Luxor p271
Luxor (East Bank) p272-3
Luxor (West Bank) p283

AROUND LUXOR

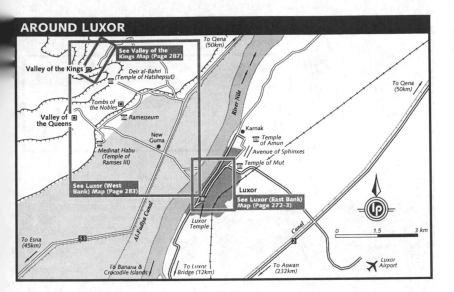

To Qena (50km)

See Valley of the Kings Map (Page 287)

Valley of the Kings

Deir al-Bahri (Temple of Hatshepsut)

To Qena (50km)

River Nile

Tombs of the Nobles

Valley of the Queens

Ramesseum

Karnak

Temple of Amun

New Gurna

Avenue of Sphinxes

Temple of Mut

Medinat Habu (Temple of Ramses III)

See Luxor (West Bank) Map (Page 283)

Luxor

See Luxor (East Bank) Map (Page 272-3)

Al-Fadiya Canal

Luxor Temple

Canal

0   1.5   3 km

To Esna (45km)

To Banana & Crocodile Islands

To Luxor Bridge (12km)

To Aswan (232km)

Luxor Airport

12th dynasty pharaohs, emerged as the main power in Upper Egypt. Rising against the northern capital of Heracleopolis, Thebes reunited the country under its political, religious and administrative control and ushered in the Middle Kingdom period. The strength of its government also enabled it to re-establish control after a second period of decline; liberate the country from foreign rule; and bring in the New Kingdom dynasties.

At the height of its glory and opulence, from 1570 to 1090 BC, all the New Kingdom pharaohs (with the exception of Akhenaten who moved to Tell al-Amarna) made Thebes their permanent residence; the city had a population of nearly one million and the architectural activity was astounding.

Because so many kings left their mark at Thebes it can quickly become very confusing trying to keep track of who built what temples or tombs and when they did so; for some help putting everything into context refer to the boxed text 'Chronology of the Pharaohs' in the History section in the Facts for the Visitor chapter.

ORIENTATION

What most visitors today know as Luxor is actually three separate areas: the city of Luxor itself, the village of Karnak a couple of kilometres to the north-east, and the monuments and necropolis of ancient Thebes on the west bank of the Nile.

In the town there are only three main thoroughfares: Sharia al-Mahatta, Sharia al-Karnak and the Corniche. Another road you may want to know if you're looking for cheap accommodation is Sharia Television, around which are clustered many, although by no means all, of the cheap hotels.

Sharia al-Mahatta – the street directly in front of the train station – runs perpendicular to the Nile all the way to the gardens of Luxor Temple. Sharia al-Karnak (or Sharia Maabad al-Karnak, 'Karnak Temple Street') runs one block in from, and parallel to, the river, from Luxor Temple to Karnak Temple. To confuse matters Sharia al-Karnak, where it meets Sharia al-Mahatta, is also known as Sharia al-Markaz; to the south, around the temple to the river, it's known as Sharia al-Lokanda.

LUXOR

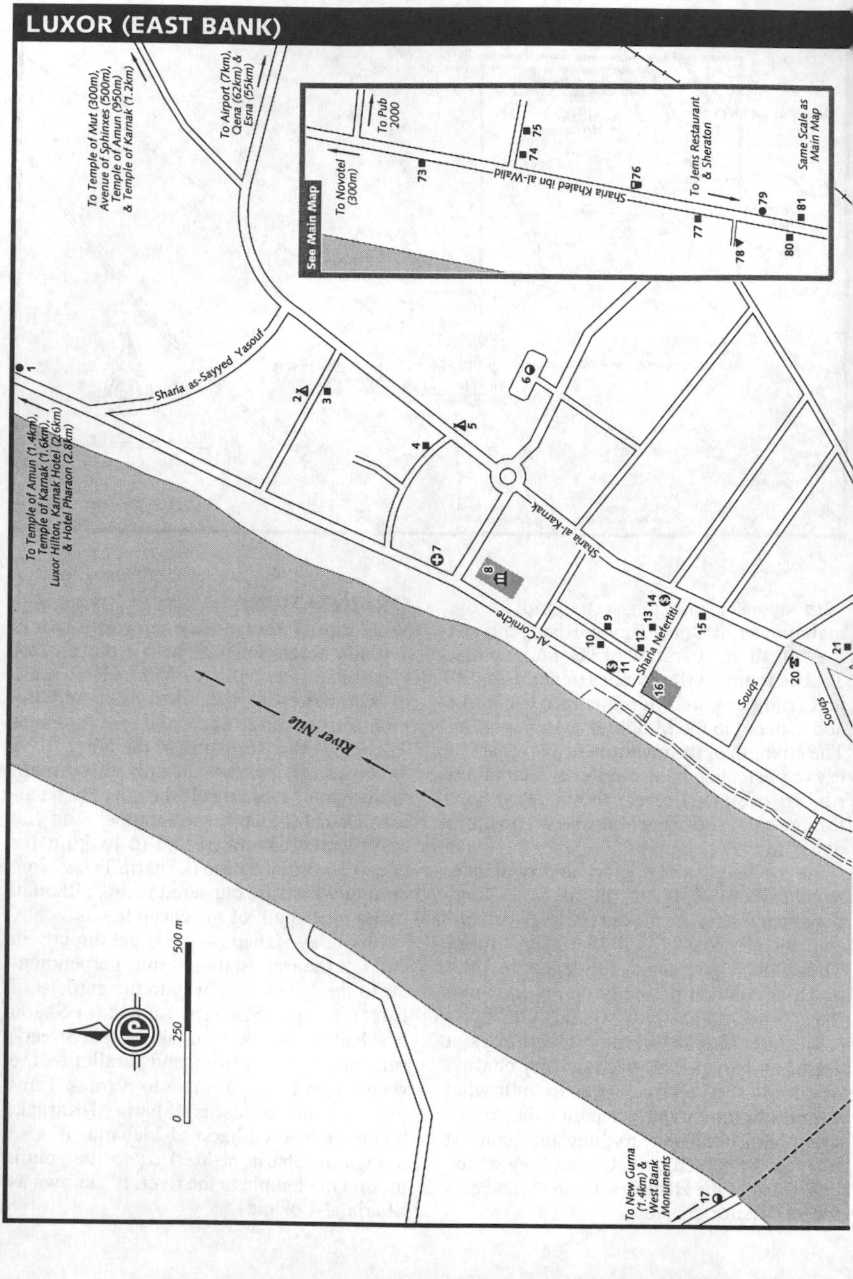

LUXOR (EAST BANK)

See Main Map

To Airport (7km), Qena (62km) & Esna (55km)

To Novotel (300m)

To Pub 2000

Sharia Khaled ibn al-Walid

73

74 75

76

77

78

79

80 81

To Jems Restaurant & Sheraton

Same Scale as Main Map

To Temple of Mut (300m), Avenue of Sphinxes (500m), Temple of Amun (950m) & Temple of Karnak (1.2km)

To Temple of Amun (1.4km), Temple of Karnak (1.5km), Luxor Hilton, Karnak Hotel (2.64km) & Hotel Pharaon (2.88km)

Sharia as-Sayyed Yasouf

1

2

3

4

5

6

7

8

9

10

11

12

13 14

15

16

17

20

21

Sharia al-Karnak

Sharia Nefertiti

Souqs

Souqs

Al-Corniche

River Nile

To New Gurna (1.46m) & West Bank Monuments

0   250   500 m

LUXOR

LUXOR (EAST BANK)

PLACES TO STAY

2 Rezeiky Camp
3 Pola Hotel
4 Youth Hostel
5 YMCA Camping Ground
9 Windsor Hotel
10 Merryland Hotel
12 Nile Hotel
13 Philippe Hotel
15 St Mark Hotel
16 Hotel Mercure
19 Mina Palace Hotel
21 Emilio Hotel
22 Pyramids Hotel
23 Nobles Hotel
24 St Catherine Hotel
25 Sphinx Hotel
26 Venus Hotel
33 Horus Hotel
39 Saint Mina Hotel
44 Anglo Hotel
45 New Radwan Hotel
46 New Everest Hotel
47 Akhenaten Hotel
48 Arabesque Hotel
50 Luxor Wena Hotel
52 Mercure Inn & Dawar
   al-Umda Restaurant
56 Old Winter Palace
58 Sherif Hotel
59 Shady Hotel
60 Santa Maria Hotel
61 Everest Hotel
63 Oasis Hotel
64 Grand Hotel
65 Atlas Hotel
66 Fontana Hotel
69 Moon Valley Hotel
70 Happy Land Hotel
71 Tutotel
72 Novotel
73 Club Med Belladona
   Resort
74 St Joseph Hotel
75 Flobater Hotel
77 Sonesta St George Hotel
80 Isis Hotel
81 Gaddis Hotel

PLACES TO EAT

30 Amoun & Al-Hussein
   Restaurants
38 Mensa Restaurant
43 Salt & Bread Cafeteria
49 Ali Baba Cafe
62 Sayyida Zeinab Kushari
   Restaurant
67 Mish Mish Restaurant
78 Ritz Restaurant

OTHER

1 Rainbow Internet Cafe
6 Service Taxi Station
7 Hospital
8 Luxor Museum
11 Bank of Alexandria
14 Banque Masr
17 Taxis & Donkeys to
   West Bank Monuments
18 Mummification Museum
20 Telephone Centrale
27 Student Card Office
28 Police
29 Brooke Hospital for Animals
31 Entrance to
   Luxor Temple
32 Luxor Temple
34 Bus Station
35 Mosque
36 GPO
37 Cassette Shop
40 Stella Outlet
41 Fuel Station
42 Train Station
51 Tourist Bazaar (Tourist
   Office, Tourist Police
   & Aboudi Bookshop)
53 Bakery
54 New Winter Palace
55 Thomas Cook, EgyptAir,
   American Express,
   Masr Travel & AA
   Gaddis Bookshop
57 Barghouti
68 National Bank of Egypt
76 King's Head Pub
79 Passport Office

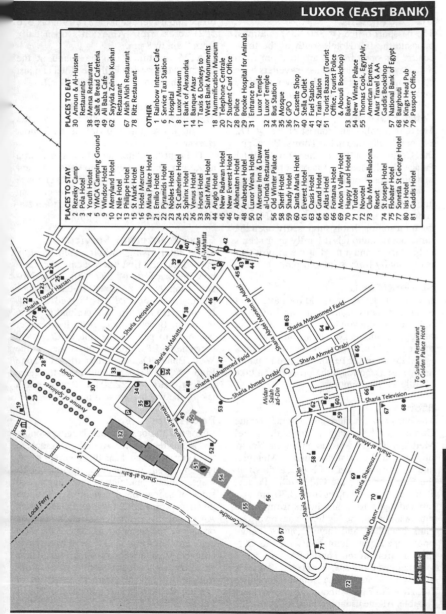

LUXOR

INFORMATION
Visa Extensions
The passport office (☎ 380 885) is almost opposite the Isis Hotel, south of the town centre. It's open from 8 am to 2 pm from Saturday to Thursday. Some travellers have commented that it's much easier to get a visa extension here than in Cairo.

Tourist Offices
The tourist police and tourist office (☎ 372 215 or 373 294) are in the Tourist Bazaar on the Corniche, next to the New Winter Palace Hotel. The office is open from 8 am to 8 pm, except on Friday when it closes at 1 pm. Travellers can leave messages on a notice board next to the main information counter. There is another tourist office at the train station that is supposedly open the same hours, although it hardly ever seems to be staffed, and a third at the airport that is open daily from 8 am to 8 pm.

Student Cards
If you're under 30 years old (or have proof of student status) you can get an ISIC card in Luxor, giving you half-price access to all of Egypt's sites and discounts on travel. An office (☎ 372 625) next to the Venus Hotel issues the cards for E£40. You need a photo and your passport and the process can take as little as five minutes.

Money
The Bank of Alexandria has a branch on the Corniche, a little way up from the Hotel Mercure. Banque Masr is on Sharia Nefertiti, around the corner from the Mercure, and the National Bank of Egypt is down on the Corniche near the Old Winter Palace. Banks are usually open from 8.30 am to 2 pm and again for a few hours from 5 or 6 pm. In addition, the big hotels have various bank branches, and there is an exchange booth open quite long hours on the Corniche in front of the Tourist Bazaar.

American Express (Amex) (☎ 372 862) is at the Old Winter Palace Hotel and operates from 8 am to 7 pm, although the hours seem flexible. All the usual services are available.

There's also a Thomas Cook exchange office and travel agent (☎ 372 196, fax 376 502) across from Amex; it's open daily from 8 am to 8 pm.

ATM machines can be found at the Banque Masr beside Philippe Hotel and just outside the doorway of Gaddis Hotel.

Post & Communications
The GPO is situated on Sharia al-Mahatta and there's a branch office in the Tourist Bazaar.

The central telephone office is on Sharia al-Karnak and is open 24 hours; there's another branch below the resplendent entrance of the old Winter Palace Hotel (open from 8 am to 10 pm) and a third at the train station (open from 8 am to 8 pm).

Email & Internet Services
Some enterprising military men recently opened Luxor's first Internet cafe, the Rainbow Internet Cafe (☎ 377 800) at the Officers' Club (Nadi az-Zubaat) on the Corniche slightly north of Sharia as-Sayyed Yasouf. It's open from 9 am to 2 pm and 6 pm to midnight. Because there is no local server you have to pay for the line to Cairo and they charge E£45 for an hour's use. On the West Bank, Osman International Phone Line (☎ 310 110), just up from the ferry landing, charges E£22.50 for 30 minutes and is open between 7 pm and midnight.

Bookshops
Luxor has the best English language bookshops outside of Cairo. Aboudi Bookshop, in the Tourist Bazaar near the Tourist Office, has an excellent selection of guidebooks, maps, postcards and fiction, including a good stock of second-hand novels. A few doors down towards the Old Winter Palace Hotel, AA Gaddis has a smaller selection of books on Egypt. The larger hotels, such as the Mercure and the Sheraton also have bookshops, although their prices are often high. There are also newsstands that stock reasonably up-to-date foreign newspapers in front of Aboudi Bookshop and outside the Winter Palace.

LUXOR MUSEUM

This great little museum on the Corniche, about halfway between the Luxor and Karnak temples, has a small but well-chosen collection of relics from the Theban temples and necropolis. The displays, which include pottery, jewellery, furniture, statues and stelae, were arranged by the Brooklyn Museum of New York.

To the right just after you enter is a well-preserved cow-goddess head from Tutankhamun's tomb. The showpiece of the 1st floor is exhibit No 61, a finely carved statuette of Tuthmosis III that dates from at least 1436 BC.

The most interesting exhibit is the Wall of Akhenaten on the 2nd floor, which is actually a set of 283 sandstone blocks found within the ninth pylon of the Karnak Temple. The reliefs show the rebel pharaoh and his queen, Nefertiti, making offerings to Aten.

Also on the 2nd floor, check out Tutankhamun's well-preserved funerary boats and the box of animal-headed Canopic jars that once contained the internal organs of the priest of the god Montu.

On the left, just before the exit, is the entrance to a relatively new hall, which contains 16 of the 24 statues that were uncovered in Luxor Temple in 1989. Some of them, such as that of Amenhotep III, are exquisite pieces of art.

The museum is open daily from 9 am to 1 pm and 4 to 9 pm (winter) or 5 to 10 pm (summer). Entry costs E£30 (E£15 for students); the last tickets are sold 30 minutes before closing time. Photography permits cost E£10 (no flash or tripod allowed), while video costs E£100.

MUMMIFICATION MUSEUM

Down the steps just opposite the Mina Palace Hotel on the Corniche is the recently opened Mummification Museum. Although small, its well presented displays tell you everything you ever wanted to know about mummies and mummification (although the explanations of the process itself could be a little more detailed). The well-preserved mummy of a 21st dynasty official, Maser-harti, as well as a host of mummified animals (including a ram, crocodile, cat and baboon) are all on display. More interesting to those who are tired of desiccated bodies are the exhibits showing the tools and materials used in the mummification process – check out the small but particularly gruesome spoon and metal spatula that were used for scraping the brain out of the skull. A number of artefacts that were crucial to the mummy's journey to the afterlife have also been included, as well as some picturesque painted coffins. Presiding over the entrance/exit is a beautiful little statue of the jackal-god, Anubis, who was considered to be the inventor of the mummification process.

The museum is open from 9 am to 1 pm and 4 to 9 pm in winter, 5 to 10 pm in summer. Admission will set you back E£20 (E£10 for students).

LUXOR TEMPLE

Built by the New Kingdom pharaoh Amenophis III, the Luxor Temple is a strikingly graceful piece of architecture on the banks of the Nile. Originally joined to Karnak by an avenue of sphinxes, the temple sits on the site of an older sanctuary dedicated to the Theban triad of Amun, Mut and Khons.

Amun, one of the gods of creation, was the most important god of Thebes. As Amun-Ra, the fusion of Amun and the sun-god Ra, he was also a state deity worshipped in many parts of the country. Once a year from his Great Temple at Karnak the images of Amun and the other two gods in the local triad – Amun's wife, the war-goddess Mut, and their son, the moon-god Khons – would journey down the Nile to Luxor Temple for the Opet Festival, a celebration held during the flood season.

Amenophis rededicated the massive temple as Amun's sacred 'harem of the south', and retained what was left of the original sanctuary built by Tuthmosis III and Hatshepsut 100 years earlier. The temple was added to over the centuries by Tutankhamun, Ramses II, Alexander the Great and various Romans. At one point the Arabs

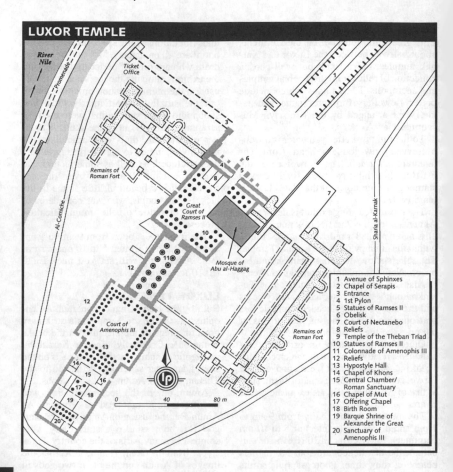

LUXOR TEMPLE

1 Avenue of Sphinxes
2 Chapel of Serapis
3 Entrance
4 1st Pylon
5 Statues of Ramses II
6 Obelisk
7 Court of Nectanebo
8 Reliefs
9 Temple of the Theban Triad
10 Statues of Ramses II
11 Colonnade of Amenophis III
12 Reliefs
13 Hypostyle Hall
14 Chapel of Khons
15 Central Chamber/
   Roman Sanctuary
16 Chapel of Mut
17 Offering Chapel
18 Birth Room
19 Barque Shrine of
   Alexander the Great
20 Sanctuary of
   Amenophis III

built a mosque in one of the interior courts, and there was also once a village within the temple walls. Excavation work has been going on since 1885, and has included removing the village and clearing the forecourt and 1st pylon of debris, and exposing part of the avenue of sphinxes leading to Karnak.

Tour The temple is entered from the Corniche. From here you proceed along a path that was once part of the avenue of sphinxes until you find yourself standing before the enormous **1st pylon**. In front of this 24m-high wall are some colossal **statues of Ramses II** and a pink granite **obelisk**. There were originally six statues, four seated and two standing, but only two of the seated figures and the westernmost standing one remain. The obelisk, too, was one of a pair; its towering counterpart now stands in the Place de la Concorde in Paris.

Behind the pylon, which is decorated with Ramses' victorious exploits in battle, is another of his additions to the main complex: the **Great Court of Ramses II**. This is surrounded by a double row of columns with lotus-bud capitals, more reliefs of his deeds of derring-do and several huge statues. In the western corner of the court is the original Middle Kingdom **Temple of the Theban Triad** and south of that is the 13th century **Mosque of Abu al-Haggag**, dedicated to a local sheikh and holy man.

Beyond the court, 14 papyrus columns form the **Colonnade of Amenophis III**. The walls behind the splendid columns were decorated during the reign of the young pharaoh Tutankhamun and celebrate the return to Theban orthodoxy following the wayward reign of the previous pharaoh, Akhenaten. The Opet Festival is depicted in great detail, with the king, the nobility and the common people joining the triumphal procession of Amun, Mut and Khons from Karnak.

The colonnade takes you into the **Court of Amenophis III**. This was once enclosed on three sides by double rows of towering columns, of which the best preserved, with their architraves extant, are those on the east and west sides.

The **Hypostyle Hall**, on the south side of the court, is the first inner room of the temple proper and features four rows of eight columns each.

Beyond are the main rooms of the **Temple of Amun**, the central chamber of which was once stuccoed over by the Romans and used as a cult sanctuary. Through this chamber, on either side of which are chapels dedicated to Mut and Khons, is an **Offering Chapel** with four columns.

The interesting inscriptions in the birth room, to the eastern side of the chapel, show scenes of how mortal Amenophis claimed divine status by coming up with the notion that Amun had visited his mother Mutemuia in the 'guise' of his father Tuthmosis IV, with the result that he, Amenophis III, was actually the god's son.

Alexander the Great rebuilt the **Barque Shrine**, beyond the Offering Chapel, adding to it reliefs of himself being presented to Amun. The **Sanctuary of Amenophis III** is the last chamber on the central axis of the temple.

Luxor Temple is open daily from 6 am to 9 pm in winter and 10 pm in summer. Summer hours begin on 1 May. Entry costs E£20 (E£10 for students) at all times of the day. Taking photographs is free. The best time to visit is in the evening, when the temperature is lower and the temple is lit up, creating an eerie spectacle as shadow and light play off the reliefs and many structures.

TEMPLES OF KARNAK

Karnak is more than a temple; it is a spectacular complex of sanctuaries, kiosks, pylons and obelisks, all dedicated to the Theban gods – and to the greater glory of Egypt's Middle and New Kingdom rulers. Everything here is on a gigantic scale: the site measures about 1.5km by 800m, large enough to contain about 10 cathedrals, while the 1st pylon is twice the size of the one at Luxor Temple. Built, added to, dismantled, restored, enlarged and decorated over a period of nearly 1500 years, Karnak was the most important place of worship in all Egypt during the height of Theban power and was called 'The Most Perfect of Places' (Ipet-Isut).

Trying to describe this immense monument has vexed travellers for centuries. As Amelia Edwards, the 19th century writer and artist who journeyed up the Nile, succinctly put it:

It is a place that has been much written about and often painted; but of which no writing and no art can convey more than a dwarfed and pallid impression ... The scale is too vast; the effect too tremendous; the sense of one's own dumbness, and littleness, and incapacity, too complete and crushing.

At the centre of this remarkable place is the enormous Amun Temple Enclosure (sometimes referred to as the Precinct of Amun), dominated by the Great Temple of Amun and containing a large Sacred Lake. This was the main place of worship of the Theban triad (Amun-Re, Mut and Khonsu), and contains

LUXOR

KARNAK: AMUN TEMPLE ENCLOSURE

1	Avenue of Ram-Headed Sphinxes
2	1st Pylon
3	Chapel of Mut
4	Chapel of Amun
5	Chapel of Khons
6	Temple of Seti II
7	Kiosk of Taharqa
8	Colonnade
9	Statues of Ramses II
10	Colonnade
11	Pylon
12	Court
13	Vestibule
14	Hypostyle Hall
15	Barque Chapels
16	2nd Pylon
17	3rd Pylon
18	4th Pylon
19	Hypostyle Hall
20	Obelisks of Hatshepsut
21	5th Pylon
22	6th Pylon
23	Sacred Barque Sanctuary
24	Wall of Records
25	Great Festival Temple of Tuthmosis III
26	Botanic Garden
27	Nilometer
28	Refreshment Stand
29	Fallen Obelisk of Hatshepsut
30	Giant Scarab
31	7th Pylon
32	8th Pylon

the famous hypostyle hall, a spectacular forest of giant papyrus-shaped columns.

Flanking the Amun Temple Enclosure on the south side is the Mut Temple Enclosure, which was once linked to the main temple by an avenue of ram-headed sphinxes. To the north is the Montu Temple Enclosure, which honoured the original local god of Thebes. A canal once connected the Amun and Montu enclosures with the Nile, providing access for the sacred boats in the journey to the Luxor Temple during the Opet Festival. A paved avenue of human-headed sphinxes also once linked Karnak, from Euergetes' Gate on the south side of the Mut Temple Enclosure, with Luxor Temple. Only a small section of this sacred way, where it leaves the Great Temple of Amun and enters the forecourt of his Southern Harem, has been excavated. The rest of the 3km avenue lies beneath the city and paved roads of modern Luxor.

Although the original sanctuary of the Great Temple of Amun was built during the Middle Kingdom period, when the Theban pharaohs first came to prominence, the rest of the temples, pylons, courts, columns and reliefs were the work of New Kingdom rulers. The further into the complex you venture the further back in time you go.

The oldest parts of the complex are the White Pavilion of Sesostris I and the 12th dynasty foundations of what became the most sacred part of the Great Temple of Amun, the Sacred Barque Sanctuary and Central Court of Amun (behind the 6th pylon). The limestone fragments of the demolished pavilion, or chapel, were recovered from the foundations of the 3rd pylon, built five centuries after Sesostris' reign, and expertly reconstructed in the open-air museum to the north of the Great Court.

The major additions to the complex were constructed by pharaohs of the 18th to 20th dynasties, between 1570 and 1090 BC. The pharaohs of the later dynasties extended and rebuilt the complex, and the Ptolemies and early Christians also left their mark on it.

Wandering through this gigantic complex is one of the highlights of any visit to

Egypt and it demands more than one visit if you want to make sense of the sometimes overwhelming jumble of ancient remains. Apart from its sheer size, the fact that almost every pharaoh left his (or her) mark here means that if you take the time you get a crash-course in the evolution of ancient Egyptian artistic and architectural styles.

General admission to the temples of Karnak is between 6 am and 5.30 pm in winter and 6 pm in summer, and tickets cost E£20, or E£10 for students. Photography is free.

Amun Temple Enclosure – Main Axis

From the entrance you pass down the processional avenue of ram-headed sphinxes, which once led to the Nile, to the massive **1st pylon**. You used to be able to climb the stairs on your left to the top of the pylon's north tower, from where there is an amazing view of Karnak and the surrounding country but the stairs were closed off when a tourist fell to the ground and died.

You emerge from the 1st pylon into the **Great Court**, the largest area of the Karnak complex. To the left is the **Temple of Seti II**, dedicated to the Theban triad. The three small chapels held the sacred barques of Amun, Mut and Khons during the lead-up to the Opet Festival.

The north and south walls of the court are lined with columns with papyrus-bud capitals. The south wall is intersected by the **Temple of Ramses III**, which was built before the court. Obligatory scenes of the pharaoh as glorious conqueror adorn the pylon of this 60m-long temple which also features an open court, a vestibule with four columns, a hypostyle hall of eight columns and three barque chapels.

In the centre of the Great Court is the one remaining column of the **Kiosk of Taharqa**. A 25th dynasty Ethiopian pharaoh, Taharqa built his open-sided pavilion of 10 columns, each rising 21m and topped with papyrus-form capitals.

The **2nd pylon** was originally built by Horemheb, an 18th dynasty general who headed a military dictatorship and became the last pharaoh of his dynasty. Ramses I and II added their names and deeds to the pylon above that of Horemheb. Ramses II also raised two colossal pink granite statues of himself on either side of the entrance.

Beyond the 2nd pylon is the awesome **Great Hypostyle Hall**. It was built by Seti I and finished by Ramses II. Covering an area of 6000 square metres (which is large enough to contain both St Peter's in Rome and London's St Paul's), the hall is an unforgettable forest of 134 towering stone papyrus-shaped pillars. It is impossible to get an overall idea of this court; there is nothing to do but stand and stare up at the dizzying spectacle.

Between the **3rd pylon**, built by Amenophis III, and the **4th pylon**, raised by Tuthmosis I, is a narrow court. Tuthmosis I and III raised two pairs of obelisks in front of the 4th pylon, which was, during their reign, the entrance to the temple proper. Only one of the four is still standing, but parts of the others lie in the court.

Beyond the 4th pylon is the oldest preserved part of the complex, its 14 columns suggesting that it was originally a small hypostyle hall. It was constructed by Tuthmosis III in his attempt to eradicate or hide all signs of the reign of his stepmother, Queen Hatshepsut (see the section on Deir al-Bahri later in this chapter). In this hall, around the two magnificent **Obelisks of Hatshepsut**, the vengeful king built a 25m-high sandstone structure. The upper shaft of one of the obelisks, which Hatshepsut raised to the glory of her 'father' Amun, lies on the ground by the Sacred Lake; the other obelisk still stands, reclaimed from the sandstone, in front of the 5th pylon. It is the tallest obelisk in Egypt, standing 29.2m high, and was originally covered in electrum (a commonly used alloy of gold and silver) from its pyramidal peak to halfway down the shaft.

The **5th pylon** was constructed by Tuthmosis I, with little space between it and the now ruined 6th pylon (built at a later date). The latter, the smallest pylon at Karnak, was raised by his son Tuthmosis II (Hat-

shepsut's husband and half-brother). In the small vestibule beyond the 6th pylon are two pink granite columns on which the emblems of Egypt are carved in high relief: the lily of Upper Egypt on the north pillar and the papyrus flower of Lower Egypt on the south pillar. Nearby are two huge statues of Amun and his female counterpart Amunet, which date from the reign of Tutankhamun.

Also among the ruins of this area around the temple's original Central Court are a **Sacred Barque Sanctuary** and at least two well-preserved walls.

Hatshepsut's wall and its colourful reliefs survived the years well because once again Tuthmosis III chose to cover her structure with one of his own rather than destroy it once and for all.

Although the king was no match for his powerful though peace-loving stepmother, he made up for Hatshepsut's domination during his teenage years by setting out, almost immediately after her death, to conquer the known world. His reputation as a great hero and empire builder was justly deserved, as portrayed in the relief work on what is known as the **Wall of Records**. Though unrelenting in his bid for power, he had a penchant for being fairly just in his treatment of the people he conquered. This wall was a running tally of the organised tribute he exacted in honour of Amun from his subjugated lands.

East of the foundations of the original Temple of Amun stands the **Great Festival Temple of Tuthmosis III**. It contains several fine reliefs of plants and animals in the so-called Botanic Garden. Of the temple's many columns, 20 are unique in Egypt in that they are larger at their peak than their base.

Between the Great Festival Temple and the eastern gate of the enclosure are the ruins of two other structures – a portico built by Taharqa and a smaller temple that was built by Tuthmosis III. The world's largest obelisk once stood on the base in front of this temple. The so-called Lateran Obelisk, which was 32.2m high, was removed from Karnak in 357 AD on the orders of the Roman emperor Constantine. Although it was bound for Constantinople, it ended up in the Circus Maximus in Rome and finally, in the 1580s, was re-erected in the Piazza San Giovanni in Laterano, Rome.

Against the northern enclosure wall of the precinct of Amun is the cult **Temple of Ptah**, started by Tuthmosis III and finished by the Ptolemies. Access to the inner chambers is through a series of five doorways, which lead you to two of the temple's original statues. The headless figure of Ptah, the creator-god of Memphis, is in the middle chapel behind a locked door – the custodian will unlock it for the usual remittance. To his left is the eerily beautiful, bare-breasted and lioness-headed, black granite statue of his goddess-wife Sekhmet (the Spreader of Terror).

Amun Temple Enclosure – Southern Axis

The secondary axis of the Amun Temple Enclosure runs south from the 3rd and 4th pylons. It is basically a processional way, bounded on the east and west sides by walls, and sectioned off by a number of pylons that create a series of courts. Just before you get to the **7th pylon**, built by Tuthmosis III, is the **Cachette Court**, so named because of the thousands of stone and bronze statues discovered there during excavation work in 1903. Seven of the statues, of Middle Kingdom pharaohs, stand in front of the pylon. Nearby are the remains of two colossal statues of Tuthmosis III.

The well-preserved **8th pylon**, built by Queen Hatshepsut, is the oldest part of the north-south axis of the temple. Four of the original six colossi are still standing, the most complete being the one of Amenophis I.

The **9th** and **10th pylons** were built by Horemheb, who used some of the stones of a demolished temple that had been built to the east by Akhenaten (before he decamped to Tell al-Amarna).

To the east of the 7th and 8th pylons is the **Sacred Lake**, where the priests of Amun purified themselves before performing ceremonies in the temple. On the north-west side of the lake is the top half of Hatshepsut's fallen obelisk, and a huge stone statue of a scarab beetle dedicated by Amenophis III to Aten, the disc of the rising sun. Tour guides tell visitors to walk around the scarab – once for good luck, three times for marriage and seven times for a first child.

There are the ruins of about 20 other chapels within the main enclosure. In a fairly good state of repair in the south-west corner is the **Temple of Khonsu**, god of the moon and time, and son of Amun and Mut. The pylon faces Euergetes' Gate and the avenue of sphinxes leading to Luxor Temple, and provides access to a small hypostyle hall and ruined sanctuary. The temple was started by Ramses III, and added to by other Ramessids, Ptolemies and also Herihor. Herihor, like Horemheb, had pushed his way up through the ranks of the army to claim power, declaring himself not only pharaoh but high priest of Amun as well.

Nearby is the small, finely decorated **Temple of Opet**, dedicated to the hippopotamus-goddess Opet, mother of Osiris.

Mut Temple Enclosure

From the 10th pylon an avenue of sphinxes leads to the partly excavated southern enclosure – the precinct of Mut. The badly ruined Temple of Mut was built by Amenophis III and consists of a sanctuary, a hypostyle hall and two courts. The Temple of Ramses III stands south-west of the lake, which partly surrounds the main temple. Throughout the area are granite statues of Sekhmet, with her leonine head crowned by a solar disc. At one time, more than 500 of these statues stood here.

Montu Temple Enclosure

A usually locked gate on the wall near the Temple of Ptah (Amun Temple Enclosure) leads to the Montu Temple Enclosure. Montu, the falcon-headed warrior-god, was the original deity of Thebes. The main temple was built by Amenophis III and modified by others. The complex is very dilapidated.

Open-Air Museum

Just before the 2nd pylon, off to the left, is an open-air museum that contains a collection of statuary found throughout the temple complex. A separate ticket is required for the museum, which closes at 5.30 pm. Entry is E£10 (half for students).

Sound & Light Show

Karnak Temple's sound and light show is a 1½ hour Hollywood-style extravaganza that recounts the history of Thebes and the lives of the many pharaohs who built sanctuaries, courts, statues or obelisks in honour of Amun. The show starts at the avenue of ram-headed sphinxes, passes through the 1st pylon to the Great Court and on through the Great Hypostyle Hall to the grandstand at the Sacred Lake for the show's finale. The overly dramatic text and booming music veer into kitsch for much of the show but it is almost worth the E£33 (no discount) just for a specially lit night-time walk through the temple.

There are three performances per night with sessions starting at 6.30, 7.45 and 9 pm; or about one hour later in summer. The following language schedule was correct at the time of writing but check at the tourist office:

day	show 1	show 2	show 3
Monday	English	French	Spanish
Tuesday	Japanese	English	Italian
Wednesday	German	English	French
Thursday	English	French	Arabic
Friday	French	English	Spanish
Saturday	French	English	Italian
Sunday	German	English	French

Getting There & Away

To get to Karnak you can take a microbus from Luxor station or from behind Luxor Temple for 25pt or hire a *hantour* (horse-drawn carriage) for around E£5. Give the driver baksheesh if you want him to wait. It's a quick bicycle ride to the temple or you can easily walk.

BROOKE HOSPITAL FOR ANIMALS

Although not really a tourist sight, the hospital, part of a worldwide UK network of clinics aiming to provide at least minimum care for animals, especially those put to work, is interesting. It's up the road from the Mina Palace Hotel, and has been operating in Luxor for more than three decades (although the original hospital was on a different site). You might like to visit and see what they do for the horses which used to pull the hantours through the streets of Luxor – they have a notice board of dos and don'ts on treatment of horses, including not tipping drivers for pushing the animals into going too fast. It's open daily from 8 am to 1.30 pm and 4 to 6 pm (winter) or 6 to 8 pm (summer).

If you are particularly interested in its work, it also has clinics in Cairo, Alexandria, Edfu and Aswan.

WEST BANK

Arriving on the West Bank of Luxor you meet with one of the most striking vistas in Egypt. As you pass through the lush green fields, desert mountains dotted with brightly coloured houses loom ahead. When you get closer you begin to make out gaping black holes among the houses and giant sandstone forms on the edge of the cultivation below. These are the tombs and temples of the necropolis of ancient Thebes, where magnificent temples were raised to honour the cults of pharaohs entombed in the nearby cliffs, and where queens, royal children, nobles, priests, artisans and even workers built tombs which ranged, in the quality of their design and decor, from the spectacular to the ordinary.

During the New Kingdom, the necropolis also supported a large living population. In an attempt to protect the valuable tombs from robbers, the artisans, labourers, temple priests and guards devoted their lives to the construction and maintenance of this city of the dead. They perfected the techniques of tomb building, decoration and concealment, and passed the secrets down through their own families.

The desire for secrecy greatly affected tomb design. Instead of a single mortuary monument like a pyramid, which was both a venue to worship the immortal pharaoh and

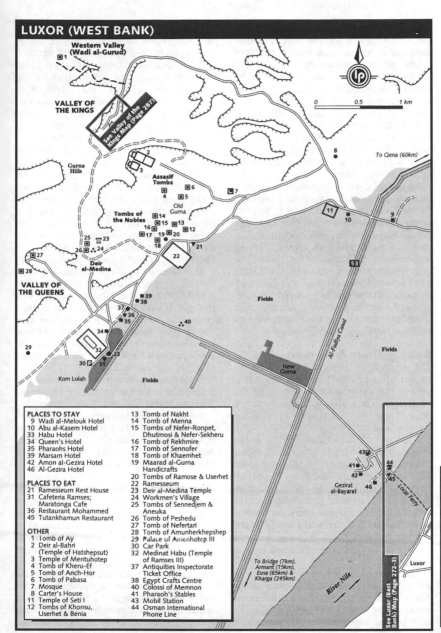

LUXOR (WEST BANK)

Western Valley
(Wadi al-Gurud)

VALLEY OF
THE KINGS

See Valley of the
Kings Map (Page 287)

Gurna
Hills

Assasif
Tombs

Old
Guma

Tombs of
the Nobles

Deir
al-Medina

VALLEY OF
THE QUEENS

Kom Lolah

Fields

Fields

Fields

New
Guma

Al-Fadiya Canal

To Qena (60km)

0   0.5   1 km

53

To Bridge (7km),
Armant (15km),
Esna (65km) &
Kharga (245km)

Gezirat
al-Bayarat

River Nile

Local Ferry

Luxor

See Luxor (East
Bank) Map (Page 272-3)

PLACES TO STAY
9 Wadi al-Melouk Hotel
10 Abu al-Kasem Hotel
33 Habu Hotel
34 Queen's Hotel
35 Pharaohs Hotel
39 Marsam Hotel
42 Amon al-Gezira Hotel
46 Al-Gezira Hotel

PLACES TO EAT
21 Ramesseum Rest House
31 Cafeteria Ramses;
   Maratonga Cafe
36 Restaurant Mohammed
45 Tutankhamun Restaurant

OTHER
1 Tomb of Ay
2 Deir al-Bahri
   (Temple of Hatshepsut)
3 Temple of Mentuhotep
4 Tomb of Kheru-Ef
5 Tomb of Anch-Hor
6 Tomb of Pabasa
7 Mosque
8 Carter's House
11 Temple of Seti I
12 Tombs of Khonsu,
   Userhet & Benia

13 Tomb of Nakht
14 Tomb of Menna
15 Tombs of Nefer-Ronpet,
   Dhutmosi & Nefer-Sekheru
16 Tomb of Rekhmire
17 Tomb of Sennofer
18 Tomb of Khaemhet
19 Maarad al-Gurna
   Handicrafts
20 Tombs of Ramose & Userhet
22 Ramesseum
23 Deir al-Medina Temple
24 Workmen's Village
25 Tombs of Sennedjem &
   Aneuka
26 Tomb of Peshedu
27 Tomb of Nefertari
28 Tomb of Amunherkhepshep
29 Palace of Amenhotep III
30 Car Park
32 Medinat Habu (Temple
   of Ramses III)
37 Antiquities Inspectorate
   Ticket Office
38 Egypt Crafts Centre
40 Colossi of Memnon
41 Pharaoh's Stables
43 Mobil Station
44 Osman International
   Phone Line

LUXOR

the resting place of his mummified remains, the New Kingdom Theban rulers commissioned their funerary monuments in pairs.

Magnificent mortuary temples were built on the plains, where the illusion of the pharaoh's immortality could be perpetuated by the devotions of his priests and subjects, while the king's body and worldly wealth were laid in splendidly decorated secret tombs excavated in the hills. The prime location for the latter was an isolated canyon to the north-west, surrounded on three sides by high rugged cliffs.

However, even though there was only one way into the Valley of the Kings and the tombs were well hidden, very few escaped the vandalism of the grave robbers.

Nowadays, ancient and modern coexist on the West Bank, with several thriving communities built among the ruins. The most famous of these is the village of Gurna (see the boxed text 'Guardians or Thieves?' on page 297) which has existed for hundreds of years and whose residents, some claim, continued the practice of grave robbing until well into the 20th century.

Getting There & Around

The recent completion of Luxor's controversial bridge across the Nile has transformed the experience of getting to the West Bank. The tourist and car ferries have been dropped, so if you want to cross the river by boat (still the quickest way to go), you have the choice of either the *baladi* or popular ferry, or one of the small motor launches (called *lunches* locally) that moor all along the banks of the Nile. The baladi ferry costs E£1 for foreigners (10pt for locals) and leaves from a dock in front of Luxor Temple. Launches leave from wherever they can find customers and will take you across for E£5, or will charge you E£1 per person if there are more than five in your group.

The advantage of the latter is that you can go immediately, rather than wait for an indeterminate period of time; on the other hand, sitting among the villagers on the ferry is a far more interesting experience.

Once you arrive on the West Bank, you will be greeted by a cacophony of voices calling out the destinations of pick-up truck taxis. If you listen for Gurna you'll be on the right road to the ticket office (25pt). There are lots of service taxis running back and forth between the villages, so you can always flag one down and find your way to one of the sites, although you might have to walk from the main road to the entrance.

Alternatively, if you haven't already been nabbed by the brother, cousin or friend of a taxi driver on the boat, you can also find a Peugeot taxi at the ferry landing, but be prepared to bargain hard. If you want to rent one for the day, you'll be looking at anywhere between E£40 and E£70, depending on the season, the state of tourism and your bargaining skills. Still, it'll be cheaper than bringing one from the town.

If you walk up the hill from the ferry landing, you will find bicycles for rent for between E£6 and E£10, but keep in mind that you'll usually get a better deal, and a better bike, in town. Almost all of the sites on the West Bank can be seen by bicycle but it can get very hot during the day so don't push yourself. You will need plenty of water and a good hat.

Donkeys and camels with guides can be rented here – for more information, see the Donkey, Horse & Camel Rides section.

As an idea of distances, from the local ferry landing it is 3km straight ahead to the ticket office, past the Colossi of Memnon, 4km to the Valley of the Queens and 8km to the Valley of the Kings.

Information

What to Bring Bring a torch (flashlight) and, more importantly, your own water because although drinks are available at some sites, they can be relatively expensive. At the noisy rest house just outside the Valley of the Kings, for instance, meals and drinks (including bottled water) are vastly overpriced.

Also, bring plenty of small change for baksheesh. Although it can be annoying when the tomb and temple guards tag along and give you explanations in broken English, remember that their salaries are pathetic and they are expected to augment them through tips. About 25pt or 50pt will be enough to either get rid of them, or to open a door or shine a light on a particularly beautiful painting. Your other option is to destroy the ambience of the place completely by tagging along with a group in each tomb or temple.

Tickets If you wanted to see everything on offer in Thebes, you would end up spending more than US$65 on tickets (without a student card). Add to that the cost of the various sites on the East Bank and to the north and south of Luxor, and sightseeing can become prohibitively expensive for the traveller on a tight budget.

Tickets are bought at the Antiquities Inspectorate ticket office, which is about 3km inland from the local ferry landing. It is open daily from 6 am to 4 pm (5 pm in summer). The various sites are officially open from 7 am to 5 pm in winter (though you can often get in from 6 am) and 6 am to 7 pm in summer. The exception to this is the Tomb of Nefertari, which has its own opening hours (see the Valley of the Queens section for details).

Permits for taking photographs cost E£10 (E£5 for students) for *each* tomb, although many travellers have reported getting around this with a little baksheesh. Using a flash destroys the already deteriorating colours in the tombs and is not permitted; resist the temptation to use one.

With the exception of Tutankhamun's tomb, you cannot pay for admission at the sites, and individual tickets are required for each tomb, temple or group of sites, so you need to know exactly what you want to see before you set off. Tickets are valid only for the day of purchase and no refunds are given. They are numbered and priced (half for students) as follows:

1	Valley of the Kings (three tombs only)	E£20
2	Tomb of Tutankhamun	E£40
3	Deir al-Bahri (Temple of Hatshepsut)	E£12
4	Medinat Habu (Temple of Ramses III)	E£12
5	Ramesseum	E£12
6	Assasif Tombs (Kheru-Ef & Anch-Hor)	E£12
7	Tombs of the Nobles (Menna & Nakht)	E£12
8	Tombs of the Nobles (Sennofer & Rekhmire)	E£12
9	Tombs of the Nobles (Ramose, Userhet & Khaemhet)	E£12
10	Deir al-Medina Temple & Tombs	E£12
11	Valley of the Queens (excluding Tomb of Nefertari)	E£12
12	Tomb of Nefertari	E£100
13	Temple of Seti I	E£12
14	Assasif Tombs (Tomb of Babasa)	E£12
15	Tomb of Peshedu (Deir al-Medina)	E£10
16	Tomb of Ay (Western Valley)	E£10
17	Tombs of the Nobles (Khokha, Nefer-Renpet, Dhutmosi & Nefer-Sekheru)	E£12
18	Tombs of the Nobles (Khonsu, Userhet & Benia)	E£12

Colossi of Memnon

The massive pair of statues known as the Colossi of Memnon are the first monuments that most tourists see when they arrive on the West Bank. They are all that remain of the temple of the hedonistic Amenophis III. Rising about 18m from the plain, the enthroned, faceless statues of Amenophis have kept a lonely vigil on the changing landscape around them, surviving the annual flooding of the Nile which gradually destroyed the temple buildings behind them.

Over the centuries, the crumbling rubble of what was believed to have been one of the most splendid of the Theban temples was ploughed into the fertile soil. A stele, now in the Egyptian Museum, describes the temple as being built from 'white sandstone, with gold throughout, a floor covered with silver, and doors covered with electrum'.

The colossi were among the great tourist attractions of Egypt during Graeco-Roman times because the Greeks believed they were actually statues of the legendary

Where First?

Because of the incredible heat and desolate mountain landscape around most of the archeological remains, a series of early morning visits – ideally between sunrise and 1pm – is the best way to see the West Bank's many sites. Unfortunately, this is when everybody else goes and you can find yourself in a hot stuffy tomb with a busload of tourists. Still, you'll have your afternoons free to loll beside a pool or have a siesta and can visit Luxor and Karnak temples, or one of the museums, in the evening.

If you don't have the luxury of several days in Luxor, choosing what to miss can be difficult. If you only have one day (and a lot of energy), the best plan is to head over to the West Bank as early as possible. It is feasible to spend a couple of hours at the Valley of the Kings, have a quick visit to Deir al-Bahri and then head over to Medinat Habu. You can have a drink in one of the cafeterias before heading over to the Valley of the Queens and, if you can get a ticket, visiting Nefertari's colourful tomb. Then you can head back to the east bank for a quick look around Luxor Temple before heading to Karnak Temple; try to arrive by 4.30 pm and spend a couple of hours there before rounding off the day with the sound and light show.

If you've got more time, the above should be done over two or three days. You could add a hike over the mountain between the Valley of the Kings and Deir al-Bahri.

See the highlights at the beginning of this chapter for further suggestions of other things that should be done in Luxor, time permitting.

Memnon, a king of Ethiopia and son of the dawn-goddess Eos, who was slain by Achilles during the Trojan War.

It was the northern statue that attracted most of the attention because at sunrise it would emit a haunting, musical sound that the Greeks believed was the voice of Memnon greeting his mother each day. Eos in turn would weep tears of dew for the untimely death of her beautiful son.

Actually, the phenomenon of the famous vocal statue was probably produced by the combined effect of a simple change in temperature and the fact that the upper part of the colossus was severely damaged by an earthquake in about 30 BC. As the heat of the morning sun baked the dew-soaked stone, sand particles would break off and resonate inside the cracks in the structure. Certainly, after a well-meaning Roman governor repaired the statue some time in the 2nd century AD, Memnon's plaintive greeting to his mother was heard no more.

The colossi are just off the road, west of New Gurna and are usually being photographed by an army of tourists – you won't miss them.

Temple of Seti I

Seti I, the father of Ramses II, expanded the Egyptian empire to include Cyprus and parts of Mesopotamia. His imposing mortuary temple, dedicated to Amun, was an inspiring place of worship for his own cult and also served as a treasure house for some of the spoils of his military ventures.

Although the first two pylons and courts are in ruins, the temple itself is in reasonable repair and the surviving reliefs, in the hypostyle hall, chapels and sanctuary, are superbly executed and some of the finest examples of New Kingdom art. This temple, just off Sharia Wadi al-Melouk (the road to the Valley of the Kings) is seldom visited by tourists, so is well worth the effort.

Carter's House

On a barren hill, where the road from Deir al-Bahri to the Valley of the Kings meets the road from Seti's temple, there is a domed house where Howard Carter lived during his search for the tomb of Tutankhamun. There is talk of turning this into a museum describing the process of finding the famous tomb but as yet nothing has come of it.

Valley of the Kings

Once called the 'Gates of the Kings' or the 'Place of Truth', the canyon now known as the Valley of the Kings is at once a place of death – for nothing grows on its steep, scorching cliffs – and a majestic domain befitting the mighty kings who once lay there in great stone sarcophagi, awaiting immortality.

The isolated valley, behind Deir al-Bahri, is dominated by the natural pyramid-shaped mountain peak of Al-Qurn (the Horn). It consists of two branches, the east and west valleys, with the former containing most of the royal burial sites.

All the tombs (except the newly discovered Tomb of the Sons of Ramses II) followed a similar design, deviating only because of structural difficulties or the length of time spent on their construction. The longer the reign of the pharaoh, the larger and more magnificent his tomb. Two groups of workers and artisans would live, in alternating shifts, in the valley itself for the duration of the work, which usually took many years.

The tombs were designed to resemble the underworld, with a long, inclined rock-hewn corridor descending into either an antechamber or a series of sometimes pillared halls, and ending in the burial chamber. Once the tomb was cut its decoration was started; this dealt almost exclusively with the afterlife and the pharaoh's existence in it.

The colourful paintings and reliefs are extracts from ancient theological compositions, or 'books', and were incorporated in the tomb to assist the pharaoh into the next life. Texts were taken from the *Book of Amduat* – 'the book of him who is in the netherworld'; the *Book of Gates*, which charted the king's course through the underworld; and the *Book of the Litany of Ra*, believed to be the words spoken by Ra, the sun-god, on his own journey through the caverns of death.

The worshippers of Amun or Amun-Ra (the fusion of the two deities and king of the gods) believed that the Valley of the Kings was traversed each night by Ra, and it was

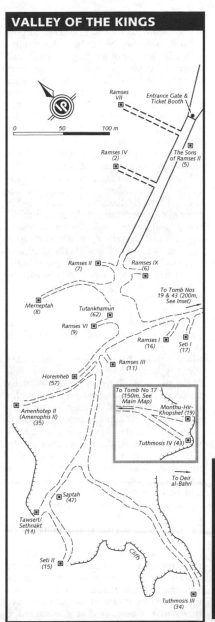

VALLEY OF THE KINGS

LUXOR

the aim of those who had been buried that day to secure passage on his sacred barque.

To do this, they had to be well equipped with a knowledge of the magic texts (hence the tomb decorations) before they could enter the boat of the god. Once aboard, they were brought to the kingdom of Osiris, god of the dead, where they were judged. Those kings who passed the ordeal would then board a second sacred barque for the journey to the east, where, having overcome the powers of darkness and death, they would live again, immortal in the company of Amun-Ra.

In all, more than 60 tombs have been excavated in the valley, although not all belong to pharaohs. Each tomb is numbered in order of discovery but not all are open to the public and there are often some tombs closed for renovation work. It's worth having your own torch (flashlight) to illuminate badly lit areas. Sometimes the guards have the endearing habit of switching off the lights if you won't give them baksheesh – and they wait until you're halfway in to leave you in the dark.

The road into the Valley of the Kings is a gradual, dry, hot climb, so be prepared if you are riding a bicycle. There is a rest house before the entrance to the valley where you can buy mineral water, soft drinks and meals. It's expensive and usually crowded. There is a *tuf-tuf* – a noisy tractor dressed up to look like a train – which ferries visitors between the entrance and the tombs (it can be hot during summer). You're charged an absurd E£1 for the ride.

If you want to avoid the inevitable crowds that tour buses bring to the tombs, head for the tombs outside the immediate area of the entrance. There are many to choose from, but among the better ones are the tombs of Ramses VI (No 9), Queen Tawsert/Sethnakt (No 14), Tuthmosis III (No 34) and Saptah (No 47).

You cannot buy tickets for the tombs at the entrance to the valley itself (see the Tickets section, earlier in this chapter). Note that any one ticket is for three tombs only. If you want to visit more, you'll have to buy more tickets (and if you wanted to

visit, say, four tombs, you'd still have to buy two tickets). The Tomb of Tutankhamun has been deemed worth a ticket on its own (E£40) and this can be bought at the entrance to the site.

Tomb of Ramses IV (No 2) This is the second tomb on the right as you enter the Valley of the Kings. Its whereabouts was known even by the Ptolemies, as is evident from the graffiti dating back to 278 BC which can be seen on the walls. Only recently opened to the public, it's not one of the finest tombs – many of the paintings in the burial chamber have deteriorated, although the painting of the goddess Nut, stretched across the blue ceiling, is still in good condition.

Tomb of Ramses IX (No 6) This tomb consists of a long, sloping corridor, a large antechamber decorated with animals, serpents and demons, then a pillared hall and short hallway before the burial chamber. The goddess Nut is the feature of the ceiling painting; she is surrounded by sacred barques full of stars. Just before the staircase down to the burial chamber are the cartouche symbols of Ramses IX.

Tomb of Ramses II (No 7) This tomb, the burial place of Egypt's longest reigning pharaoh, is being excavated by French archaeologists. It's expected to be opened to the public in about the year 2000.

Tomb of Merneptah (No 8) Reliefs of Isis, the wife of Osiris and divine mourner of the dead, and Nepthys, the sister of Isis and guardian of coffins, adorn the entrance to this tomb. Merneptah was the son of Ramses II and the pharaoh mentioned in the biblical book *Exodus*. The walls of the steep corridor, which descends 80m to his burial chamber, are decorated with texts from the *Book of Gates*.

Tomb of Ramses VI (No 9) The early excavation of this tomb forestalled the discovery of Tutankhamun's tomb below it.

Gurna's colourful old mud-brick houses may soon be demolished as part of a new planning scheme.

With a million new mouths to feed each year, crops like this near Luxor are an important resource.

Osiride pillars at the Ramasseum in Luxor.

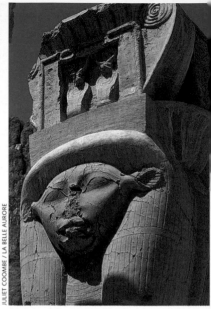

Temple of Queen Hatshepsut, Luxor.

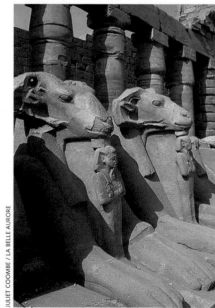

Ram-headed sphinxes at the Amun Temple.

Statues honouring Amun at the Amun Temple.

Usually the first monument tourists see on Luxor's West Bank is the imposing 18m-high Colossi of Memnon. Sadly, they're all that remains of the temple of the hedonistic Amenophis III.

GREG ELMS

GREG ELMS

TM FLOWER

TM FLOWER

Decorative elements of tombs in the Valley of the Kings.

GREG ELMS

The Luxor Temple casts an eerie spectacle at night when shadow and light contrast and highlight the many reliefs and statues.

Originally built for Ramses V but usurped by his successor, who saved time and money by appropriating the site, this tomb extends 83m into the mountain. The passageway is decorated with scenes from the *Book of the Dead* and the *Book of the Caverns* and the complete text of the *Book of Gates*.

Ramses VI's smashed sarcophagus lies in the pillared burial chamber at the end of the corridor. The burial chamber has a beautiful and unusual ceiling that details the *Book of Day & Night* and features the goddess Nut twice, stretched across the morning and evening sky.

Tomb of Ramses III (No 11) The burial chamber of this tomb, which is one of the largest in the valley, remains unexcavated and is closed to the public.

There is, however, plenty to see in the three passageways and 10 side chambers in the first part of the tomb. Also known as the Tomb of the Harpers, because of the painting of two musicians playing to the gods in a room off the second passage, it is interesting because the colouring of its sunken reliefs is still quite vivid. The side chambers are decorated with pictures of their former contents, while other walls depict daily happenings in Egyptian life.

Tomb of Queen Tawsert/Sethnakt (No 14) Queen Tawsert was the wife of Seti II. Her tomb was later taken over by Sethnakt after he had trouble building his own tomb. The tomb is decorated with well-preserved paintings showing scenes from the *Book of the Dead*, the *Book of the Gates* and the ceremony of the Opening of the Mouth. Sethnakt's granite sarcophagus is in the tomb. At the time of writing the tomb was closed for restoration.

Tomb of Seti II (No 15) Adjacent to Queen Tawsert's tomb is that of her husband, Seti II. The tomb entrance starts with some fine reliefs but it was abruptly abandoned before completion. During the excavation of Tutankhamun's tomb it was used by Howard Carter for preliminary storage and restoration work on the finds. Today the mummy of an unknown person can be seen in the tomb, although at the time of writing it was temporarily closed.

Tomb of Ramses I (No 16) Although the tomb next to Seti's belongs to the founder of the 19th dynasty, it is a very simple affair because Ramses I only ruled for a couple of years.

The tomb, which has the shortest entrance corridor of all the royal resting places in the valley, has a single, almost square, burial chamber, containing the king's open pink-granite sarcophagus. The chamber is the only part of the tomb that is decorated; it features the pharaoh in the presence of deities such as Osiris, Ptah, Anubis and Maat set on a blue-purple background.

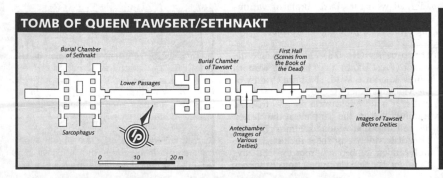

TOMB OF QUEEN TAWSERT/SETHNAKT

Burial Chamber of Sethnakt

Lower Passages

Sarcophagus

Burial Chamber of Tawsert

First Hall (Scenes from the Book of the Dead)

Antechamber (Images of Various Deities)

Images of Tawsert Before Deities

0   10   20 m

LUXOR

Tomb of Seti I (No 17) The longest, deepest and most splendid tomb in the Valley of the Kings is the burial site of Seti I, which plunges more than 100m down into the hillside. The detail of the enchanting, finely executed reliefs rivals even the renowned decorations in his Cenotaph Temple at Abydos.

Three long passages, intersected by decorated chambers, culminate in the large, two-part burial chamber. Colourful scenes include Seti appearing before Ra-Harakhty (god of the morning sun) beneath a ceiling of flying vultures and texts from the *Litany of Ra*.

In the first chamber Seti is shown in the presence of deities and in another passage the walls feature the Opening of the Mouth ritual which ensured that the mummy's organs were functioning.

The first section of the burial chamber is a pillared hall decorated with texts from the *Book of Gates*, while the second part, which contained Seti's magnificent alabaster sarcophagus, features texts from the *Amduat* and an astronomical ceiling.

At the time of writing, this tomb was closed for restoration but it is due to open again in March 2000.

Tomb of Monthu-Hir-Khopshef (No 19) The Tomb of Ramses IX's son, whose name translates as 'the Arm of Montu is Strong', is one of several newly opened tombs in the valley. Located high up in the valley's eastern wall, its entrance corridor is adorned with life-sized reliefs of various gods, including Anubis and Horus, receiving offerings from the young prince.

Tomb of Ay (No 23) This tomb (see the Luxor (West Bank) map) is in the western valley, known as Wadi al-Gurud (Valley of the Monkeys) after the baboons on the tomb walls. It is accessed by a rough dirt road leading off from the car park at the Valley of the Kings that winds for almost 2km up a desolate valley past sheer rock cliffs. The well-hidden tomb dates from the 18th dynasty and is noted for its paintings of scenes depicting daily life in ancient Egypt – hunting, gathering reeds and so on – and the wall featuring 12 baboons.

Before making your way up to this tomb, ask at the ticket office to ensure that it's open. Those on bikes should note that it is not feasible to cycle up here unless you happen to have a good mountain bike.

Tomb of Tuthmosis III (No 34) Hidden in the hills between high limestone cliffs and reached only via a steep staircase that crosses an even steeper ravine, this tomb demonstrates the lengths to which the ancient pharaohs went to thwart the cunning of the ancient thieves.

Tuthmosis III was one of the first to build his tomb in the Valley of the Kings. As secrecy was his utmost concern, he chose the most inaccessible spot and designed his burial place with a series of passages at haphazard angles and a deep shaft to mislead or catch potential robbers – all to no avail, of course.

The shaft, now traversed by a narrow gangway, leads to an antechamber supported by two pillars, the walls of which are adorned with a list of more than 700 gods and demigods.

The burial chamber, which is oval-shaped like a cartouche, is decorated in a fairly restrained manner. The roof is supported by two pillars, next to which is the king's empty, red sandstone sarcophagus; his mummy was found at Deir al-Bahri.

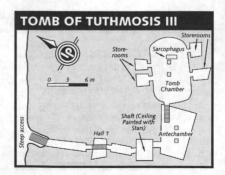

TOMB OF TUTHMOSIS III

Tomb of Amenhotep II (Amenophis II) (No 35) One of the deepest structures in the valley, this tomb has more than 90 steps that take you down to a modern gangway built over a deep pit designed to protect the inner, lower chambers from thieves.

Stars cover the entire ceiling in the huge burial chamber and the walls feature, as if on a giant painted scroll, the entire text of the *Book of Amduat*. This was indeed the final resting place of Amenophis II, for although thieves did manage to make off with everything of value, they did no damage to the interior and left the king himself undisturbed.

When the huge tomb was excavated, by the French in 1898, a total of 13 mummies were found, including that of Amenhotep lying *in situ* in his sarcophagus, a garland of flowers still around his neck. Nine of the other mummies, hidden there by priests, were also of royal blood, including those of Tuthmosis IV, Seti II, Amenohotep III and his wife Queen Tiy.

A word of warning: this tomb can sometimes be exceedingly hot and humid; drink lots of water.

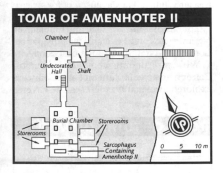

Tomb of Tuthmosis IV (No 43) This is one of the largest and deepest tombs constructed during the 18th dynasty. It's above the Tomb of Monthu-Hir-Khopshef and accessed by a separate path (though the guardians will probably show you a short cut up the hill). Two long flights of steps lead down and around to the burial chamber where there's an enormous sarcophagus covered in hieroglyphs. Most of the walls in this tomb were never finished. However there are two, well-preserved painted sections where various gods, such as Osiris and Hathor, are shown presenting the pharaoh with the key of life.

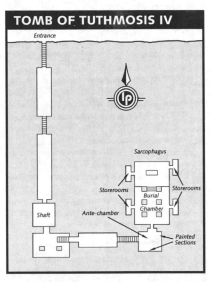

Tomb of Saptah (No 47) The entry corridor is lined with hieroglyphs while the azure ceiling is decorated with vultures. Notice the sun disc above your head as you enter. Pieces of the funerary furniture found in this tomb now grace the Metropolitan Museum of Art in New York. Saptah's mummy was one of those found in the Tomb of Amenophis II.

Tomb of Horemheb (No 57) Horemheb, a general of the Egyptian army in about 1320 BC, became a military dictator and eventually the last pharaoh of the 18th dynasty.

From the entrance a steep flight of steps and an equally steep passage leads to a

TOMB OF HOREMHEB

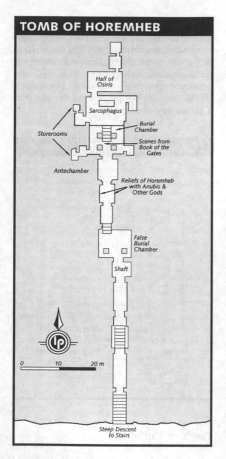

Hall of Osiris

Sarcophagus

Burial Chamber

Storerooms

Scenes from Book of the Gates

Antechamber

Reliefs of Horemheb with Anubis & Other Gods

False Burial Chamber

Shaft

0   10   20 m

Steep Descent to Stairs

Tomb of Tutankhamun (No 62) The story behind the celebrated discovery of this, the most famous tomb in the Valley of the Kings, and the fabulous treasures it contained, far outshines its actual appearance, making it dubious whether or not it warrants the E£40 charged for entry (half for students).

Tutankhamun's tomb is neither large nor impressive and bears all the signs of a rather hasty completion and inglorious burial. The extraordinary contents of this rather modest tomb built for a fairly insignificant boy-king can only make you guess at the immense wealth that must have been laid to rest with the likes of the powerful Seti I or Ramses II.

For years archaeologists believed that if, in fact, Tutankhamun was buried in the valley, his tomb would contain little of interest. The nephew of Akhenaten, he was merely a puppet pharaoh of the priests of Amun, supporting their counter-revolution against the parvenus of the late rebel king's desertion from Thebes. He died, young, with no great battles or buildings to his credit.

The English Egyptologist Howard Carter, however, believed he would find the young pharaoh buried among his ancestors with his treasures intact. He slaved away for six seasons in the valley, excavating thousands and thousands of tonnes of sand and rubble from possible sites, until even his wealthy patron, Lord Carnarvon, tired of the obsession.

With his funding about to be cut off Carter made one last attempt at the only unexplored area that was left – a site covered

chamber with fine festive reliefs and then a false burial chamber supported by two pillars. This attempt to fool any potential grave robbers didn't work, as ancient thieves managed to find and uncover the stairway which leads steeply down to the real tomb; they left nothing but Horemheb's red granite sarcophagus.

The wall paintings of the burial chamber were never finished, indicating an untimely death, but are interesting because they reveal the different stages of decoration.

TOMB OF TUTANKHAMUN

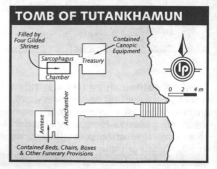

Filled by Four Gilded Shrines

Contained Canopic Equipment

Sarcophagus

Treasury

Chamber

Annexe

Antechamber

0   2   4 m

Contained Beds, Chairs, Boxes & Other Funerary Provisions

by workers' huts just under the already excavated Tomb of Ramses VI.

On 4 November 1922 he uncovered steps and then a door, its seals untouched, and wired Lord Carnarvon to join him in Egypt immediately for the opening of what he believed was the completely intact Tomb of Tutankhamun.

The discovery proved sceptics wrong, and the tomb's priceless cache of pharaonic treasures, which had remained undisturbed by robbers, vindicated Carter's dream beyond even his wildest imaginings.

Sadly, in perhaps the last great irony in the history of tomb robbing in the Valley of the Kings, evidence came to light some years later that clouded the discovery of the tomb. This suggested that prior to the tomb being officially opened in the presence of experts from the Metropolitan Museum of Art, Carter and Carnarvon themselves broke in, stole several articles and resealed the door.

The tomb is small and for the most part undecorated. Three small chambers were crammed with furniture, statues, chariots, musical instruments, weapons, boxes, jars

The Greatest Find Since Tutankhamun

In May 1995, American archaeologist Kent Weeks announced to the world his discovery of the largest tomb ever to be unearthed in Egypt. Believed to be the burial place of more than 50 sons of Ramses II – one of Egypt's most prolific pharaohs (in terms of producing both offspring and monuments) – it was immediately hailed as the greatest find since that of Tutankhamun. Or, as one London newspaper succinctly put it: 'The Mummy of all Tombs'.

The story of the tomb's discovery dates back to 1987 when the Egyptian Antiquities Organisation announced plans to level a hillside at the entrance to the Valley of the Kings in order to expand the paved car park. Weeks was familiar with the area and knew that there was a tomb entrance hidden somewhere in the hill. Indeed, Howard Carter had uncovered it earlier this century and, believing it to be insignificant, used it as a dump while clearing the debris out of Tutankhamun's tomb.

A year later, after moving mountains of rubble, Weeks finally located the entrance to the tomb, known only as KV5 (Kings Valley No 5). Together with his wife and a small team of workers, he then set about clearing the entrance chambers. Remnants of pottery, fragments of sarcophagi and, more importantly, wall decorations led Weeks to believe it was the tomb of the sons of Ramses II.

However, it wasn't until 1995 that Weeks unearthed a doorway leading to a long corridor flanked by dozens of rooms and heading in the direction of Ramses II's tomb. In the three years since then Weeks and his team have discovered an incredible 110 chambers and corridors, making the tomb many times larger and more complex than any other ever found in Egypt. The symmetrical nature of many of the corridors leads Weeks to suspect that there are many more rooms still buried in debris. Just as significant are the mummified remains of four adult males that have also been found. DNA tests will be carried out to determine if they are related – if so, it will go a long way towards confirming Weeks' theory that these are the sons of Ramses II. If not, the mystery surrounding this astounding find will continue.

Weeks estimates it will take at least 10 years to study the tomb, although this is likely to increase along with the tomb's size. Apart from the time needed for excavation, the tomb's structure is weak, so extensive engineering work will have to be carried out, too. As for visitors, for the next few years they'll just have to be content with reading about KV5 in Weeks' new book *The Lost Tomb* or following progress on the Web site (www.kv5.com).

and food, all of which are now in the Egyptian Museum in Cairo. Only the outermost coffin of gilded wood containing the decaying, mummified body of Tutankhamun, still lies within the carved granite sarcophagus in the burial chamber of his tomb, the walls of which are decorated with texts from the *Book of the Dead*.

Walk to Deir al-Bahri

From the tombs of Seti I and Ramses I you can continue south-east and hike over the hills to Deir al-Bahri (or vice versa, of course). The walk takes about 45 minutes through an amazing lunar-type landscape.

From the top, there are various views of the Temple of Hatshepsut in the amphitheatre setting of Deir al-Bahri below and excellent views across the plain towards the Nile.

In summer you should start this hike as early as possible, partly to catch the changing colours of the barren hills as the sun rises, but also because it gets mighty hot there later in the day. If you tire on the ascent there are donkeys available to carry you to the top. You're also likely to run into one of the many policemen who man the tents erected on strategic points of the mountain in the aftermath of the 1997 massacre at Deir al-Bahri. Sometimes they insist on following you, other times they'll leave you alone.

If you plan to visit the sites, however, you will need tickets, which can only be obtained when the ticket offices open. There's also a much longer trail from the Valley of the Kings to the Valley of the Queens via Deir al-Medina.

Alternatively, if you're just hankering for a view, you can scramble up the hill from the Valley of the Kings to the viewpoint overlooking Deir al-Bahri then return to the valley.

Deir al-Bahri (Temple of Hatshepsut)

Rising out of the desert plain, in a series of terraces, the Mortuary Temple of Queen Hatshepsut merges with the sheer limestone cliffs of the eastern face of the Theban

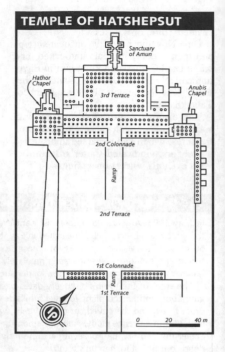

Mountain as if nature herself had built this extraordinary monument.

The partly rock-cut, partly freestanding structure is one of the finest monuments of ancient Egypt, although its original appearance, surrounded by myrrh trees, garden beds and approached by a grand sphinx-lined causeway, must have been even more spectacular.

Discovered in the mid-19th century by Auguste Mariette, it wasn't completely excavated until 1896 and it's still in the process of being restored.

Unfortunately, over the centuries the temple has been vandalised. Akhenaten removed all references to Amun, before taking his court off to Tell al-Amarna; and the early Christians who took it over as a monastery (hence the name Deir al-Bahri, or Monastery of the North), also defaced the pagan reliefs. The worst damage, however, was done out of pure spite by Hatshepsut's successor, Tuthmosis III.

Following the death of Tuthmosis I in 1495 BC, a great controversy arose, between the late pharaoh's daughter Hatshepsut and his grandson Tuthmosis III, over the rights of succession. The struggle for ultimate control was eventually won by the formidable Hatshepsut. As well as being only the third queen ever to rule ancient Egypt, Hatshepsut declared herself pharaoh – which made her the first woman ever to reign as king. She won over the priesthood by claiming divine birth (as most pharaohs did) and by assuming the dress and manner of a man – she's depicted wearing the traditional Pharaonic beard in reliefs.

Hatshepsut ruled for 20 years, and for Egypt it was a time of peace and internal growth. It is not known how she died, whether it was of natural causes or something more sinister, but when Tuthmosis III finally took his place on the throne he obliterated or covered her name or image wherever he found it. Even in her own mortuary temple, where he and Hatshepsut were always represented together, as co-rulers, he hacked out her likeness.

The temple's 37m-wide causeway leads on to the three huge terraced courts, each approached by ramps and separated by colonnades. The renowned delicate relief work of the lower terrace features scenes of birds being caught in nets, and the transport from the Aswan quarries to Thebes of a pair of obelisks commissioned by Hatshepsut.

The central court contains the best preserved reliefs. There Queen Hatshepsut recorded her divine birth and told the story of an expedition to the Land of Punt to collect myrrh trees needed for the precious myrrh incense used in temple ceremonies. There are also two chapels at either end of the colonnade. At the northern end the colourful reliefs in the Chapel of Anubis show the co-rulers, Hatshepsut and Tuthmosis III (with the queen's image again disfigured by her nephew), in the presence of Anubis, the god of embalming, Ra-Harakhty, the falcon-headed sun-god, and

Mummy Find

In 1876 the greatest mummy find in history was made just north of the Temple of Hatshepsut in tomb No 320. After many antiquities began showing up in the marketplace the authorities realised someone had found, and was plundering, an unknown tomb (see the boxed text 'Guardians or Thieves?' on page 297). After investigations they discovered a massive shaft at the foot of the cliffs containing the mummies of 40 pharaohs, queens and nobles.

It seems that the New Kingdom priests realised that the bodies of their kings would never be safe from violation in their own tombs, no matter what precautions were taken against grave robbers, so they moved them to this communal grave. The mummies included those of Amenophis I, Tuthmosis II and III, Seti I and Ramses I and III, most of which are now on display at the Egyptian Museum in Cairo.

Their removal from the tomb and procession down to the banks of the Nile, from where they were taken by barge to Cairo, is said to have been watched by local villagers, with the black-clad women ululating to give a royal send-off to the illustrious remains. The episode has made for one of the most stunning scenes in Shadi Abdel Salam's 1975 epic *The Mummy (Al-Mumia)* – incidentally, one of the best films ever to come out of Egypt.

his wife Hathor. In the Hathor Chapel you can see (if you have a torch) an untouched figure of Hatshepsut worshipping the cow-headed goddess.

Although the 3rd terrace is out of bounds while a Polish-Egyptian team works on its restoration, you can see the pink granite doorway leading into the Sanctuary of Amun, which is hewn out of the cliff.

You can hike over the mountain to the Valley of the Kings from here (see the previous Walk to Deir al-Bahri section).

LUXOR

A situlae of Pediamum-neb-nesut-tawy, a high priest and official of the 30th dynasty. It is one of a pair bought by Belzoni who, by befriending the tomb robbers at the time, managed to aquire a wide range of artefacts for the British Museum.

Assasif Tombs

This group of tombs, situated between Deir al-Bahri and the Tombs of the Nobles, dates back to the 18th dynasty and is under excavation by archaeologists. Of the many tombs here, several may be open to the public including Kheru-Ef, Anch-Hor and Pabasa. Like the Tombs of the Nobles further south, the artwork here concentrates on everyday life, with scenes depicting such things as fishing and hunting, viticulture and bee keeping, rather than more noble themes.

Tombs of the Nobles

The tombs in this area are some of the best, though least visited, attractions on the West Bank. Nestled in the foothills and among the houses of the old village of Gurna (Sheikh Abd al-Gurna) are at least 400 tombs that date from the 6th dynasty to the Graeco-Roman period. The tomb chapels in the area date from the 18th to the 20th dynasties.

Of the hundred or so tombs that have something of interest, 13 are highly recommended. They have been numbered and divided into five groups, each requiring a separate ticket (for details see the earlier Tickets section). It's possible some of the tombs may be closed; the ticket office people will know.

There are no signs indicating the tombs, so you'll need to ask the locals or look out for the modern stone walls built around the entrances to some of the tombs. If you're on your own, most of the guardians here will give you a guided tour whether you want it or not.

Tombs of Khonsu, Userhet & Benia (Nos 31, 51 & 343)

Khonsu was an adviser to Tuthmosis III. Scenes inside his colourful tomb include a boat carrying the dead to Abydos and, before the final shrine, Khonsu offering incense to Osiris and Anubis. The ceiling is adorned with birds and eggs.

The Tomb of Benia, just behind that of Khonsu, is more colourful than its neighbour. Benia was a child of the royal nursery during the 18th dynasty. At the end of the tomb, there's a *ka* statue (substitute body) of Benia flanked by his parents. Statues such as these are typical of tombs in this area, but the faces of this trio have been destroyed.

The Tomb of Userhet (not to be confused with Userhet No 56) was closed at the time of writing.

Tombs of Menna & Nakht (Nos 52 & 69)

Situated close to Khonsu, Userhet and Benia, the wall paintings in the tombs of Menna and Nakht (which may be closed to the public) emphasise rural life in the 18th dynasty. Menna was an estate inspector and Nakht was an astronomer of Amun. Their finely detailed tombs show scenes of farm-

Guardians or Thieves?

Surrounding and, in some cases, covering the hundreds of tombs lining the West Bank's barren mountainsides are the colourful houses that make up the village of Gurna. These bright mud-brick dwellings have been here for generations but if the authorities have their way they will soon be knocked down and their inhabitants moved to modern apartment blocks north of the road to the Valley of the Kings. Officialdom claims that the villagers steal antiquities and destroy the tombs, an accusation that goes back to the 19th century, when a then notorious tomb-robbing family, the Abdel Rassouls, discovered the cache of royal mummies near Hatshepsut's temple (see the boxed text 'Mummy Find' on page 295). Stunning amulets and cartouches found their way on to the black market but the suspicious antiquities officials could not discover the source until a disagreement caused a disgruntled family member to lead them to the stash.

Nowadays, however, the Gurnawis insist that whatever tomb-robbing did exist is finished. They maintain that their presence protects the remaining monuments from unwanted intruders and believe that the government wants them out because it does not want tourists to see the poverty in which they live.

Attempts to relocate the village are not new. In the 1940s the government sponsored the then up-and-coming architect Hassan Fathy to create a new village for the Gurnawis. Using traditional materials and building techniques, Fathy built New Gurna, just off the main road to the east of the Colossi of Memnon. It still exists but you have to search through a forest of concrete in order to see the remaining domes and beautifully proportioned public buildings that he designed. Fathy himself acknowledged that New Gurna was a failure soon after it was built, although he blamed the authorities' disdain for the Gurnawis rather than any flaw in his rather naive attempts at social engineering.

Now it seems that history is repeating itself as officials try to force the villagers into tiny public-housing units, disregarding the size of their extended families and their need for livestock pens to supplement meagre incomes. The villagers are digging in and refusing to leave, knowing that the government will not risk using force and alienating the population in an area so important to tourism. Who will win this battle of wills remains to be seen.

ing, hunting, fishing and feasting. The Tomb of Nakht has a small museum area in its first chamber. Although this tomb is so small that only a handful of visitors can squeeze in at a time, the walls have some of the best known examples of Egyptian tomb paintings, including familiar scenes like the three musicians that show up on a million T-shirts, posters, postcards and papyrus paintings.

Tombs of Ramose, Userhet & Khaemhet (Nos 55, 56 & 57)

The Tomb Chapel of Ramose, who was a governor of Thebes during the reigns of Amenophis III and Akhenaten, is fascinating. It's one of the few monuments dating from that time, when the cult power of the priests of Karnak was usurped by the new monotheistic worship of Aten. Exquisite paintings and low reliefs grace the walls, showing scenes from the reigns of both kings and the transition between the two forms of religious worship. The reliefs of Ramose, his wife and other relatives are extraordinarily lifelike and clearly show their affectionate relationships. The tomb was never actually finished because Ramose deserted Thebes to follow the rebel pharaoh Akhenaten to his new city at Tell al-Amarna.

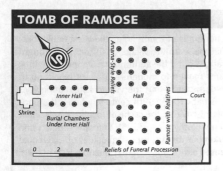

TOMB OF RAMOSE

Amarna-Style Reliefs

Inner Hall

Shrine

Burial Chambers
Under Inner Hall

Hall

Court

Ramose with Relatives

Reliefs of Funeral Procession

0   2   4 m

The Tomb of Userhet, who was one of Amenophis II's royal scribes, is next to Ramose's. Its distinctive features are the wall paintings depicting daily life in ancient Egypt. Userhet is shown presenting gifts to Amenophis II; there's a barber cutting hair on another wall; and there are men making wine, and hunting gazelles from a chariot.

The third tomb belongs to Khaemhet, who was Amenophis III's royal inspector of the granaries and court scribe. Scenes on the walls show Khaemhet offering sacrifices; the pharaoh depicted as a sphinx; the funeral ritual of Osiris; and images of daily country life and official business.

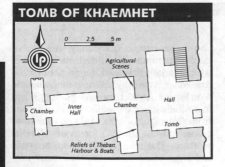

TOMB OF KHAEMHET

0   2.5   5 m

Agricultural Scenes

Chamber

Inner Hall

Chamber

Hall

Tomb

Reliefs of Theban
Harbour & Boats

Tombs of Sennofer & Rekhmire (Nos 96 & 100)
Prince Sennofer of Thebes worked for Amenophis II as a supervisor of the gardens of the Temple of Amun. The most interesting parts of his tomb are deep underground in the main chamber. The ceiling there is covered with clear paintings of grapes and vines, while most of the scenes on the surrounding walls and columns depict Sennofer with his sister. The guard usually has a kerosene lamp, but bring a torch just in case.

The Tomb of Rekhmire, a governor during the reigns of Tuthmosis III and Amenophis II, is one of the best preserved in the area. In the first chamber, to the extreme left, are scenes of Rekhmire receiving gifts from foreign lands. The panther and giraffe are gifts from Nubia; the elephant, horses and chariot come from Syria; and the expensive vases come from Crete and the Aegean Islands.

Tombs of Nefer-Ronpet, Dhutmosi & Nefer-Sekheru (Nos 178, 295 & 296)
This trio of tombs is not far from Khonsu, Userhet and Benia, and is surrounded by a new stone wall, so it's not too difficult to recognise. Nefer-Ronpet, commonly known as Kenro, was an official scribe of the treasury. Discovered in 1915, the highlight of this brightly painted tomb is a scene showing Kenro overseeing the weighing of gold at the treasury. Next door, the Tomb of Nefer-Sekheru is equally rich in yellow hues and, like Kenro's tomb, features a ceiling painted with a riot of geometric designs. From this long tomb, a small passage leads into the Tomb of Dhutmosi, which is in poor condition.

The Ramesseum
The Ramesseum is yet another monument raised by Ramses II to the ultimate glory of himself. The massive temple was built to impress his priests, his subjects, his successors and of course the gods, so that he, the great warrior king, could live forever. Many of his other works were rather crudely constructed but in this, his mortuary temple, he demanded perfection in the workmanship so that it would stand as an eternal testimony to his greatness.

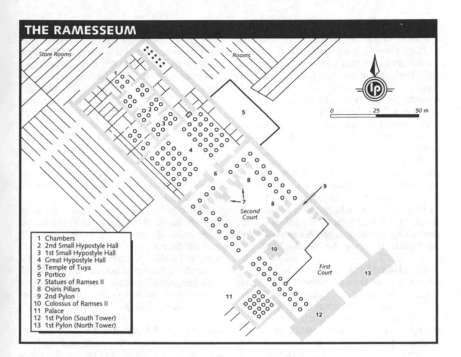

THE RAMESSEUM

Store Rooms

Rooms

0   25   50 m

1 Chambers
2 2nd Small Hypostyle Hall
3 1st Small Hypostyle Hall
4 Great Hypostyle Hall
5 Temple of Tuya
6 Portico
7 Statues of Ramses II
8 Osiris Pillars
9 2nd Pylon
10 Colossus of Ramses II
11 Palace
12 1st Pylon (South Tower)
13 1st Pylon (North Tower)

Second Court

First Court

Of course, it has done no such thing. It's mostly in ruins. This fact no doubt disappoints Ramses II more than it does modern-day visitors to the site. He dared all those who questioned his greatness in future centuries to gaze on the magnificence of his monuments in order to understand his power over life and death. The scattered remains of the colossal statue of the king and the ruins of his temple prompted the English poet Shelley to cut this presumptuous pharaoh down to size by using the undeniable fact of Ramses' mortality to ridicule his aspirations to immortality.

I met a traveller from an antique land
Who said: Two vast and trunkless legs of stone
Stand in the desert ... Near them, on the sand,
Half sunk, a shattered visage lies, whose frown,
And wrinkled lip, and sneer of cold command,
Tell that its sculptor well those passions read
Which yet survive, stamped on these lifeless things,

The hand that mocked them, and the heart that fed:
And on the pedestal these words appear:
'My name is Ozymandias, king of kings:
Look on my works, ye Mighty, and despair!'
Nothing beside remains. Round the decay
Of that colossal wreck, boundless and bare
The lone and level sands stretch far away.

Although a little more elaborate than other temples, the fairly orthodox layout of the Ramesseum, with its two courts, hypostyle hall, sanctuary, accompanying chambers and storerooms, is uncommon in that the usual rectangular floor plan was altered to incorporate an older, smaller temple – that of Ramses' mother, Tuya, which is off to one side.

The **1st and 2nd pylons** measure more than 60m across and feature reliefs of Ramses' military exploits. Through them are the ruins of the huge **First Court**, including the double colonnade that fronted the royal palace.

Near the western stairs is part of the **Colossus of Ramses II**, the Ozymandias of Shelley's poem, lying somewhat forlornly on the ground. When it stood, it was 17.5m tall. The head of another granite statue of Ramses, one of a pair, lies in the **Second Court**. Twenty-nine of the original 48 columns of the **Great Hypostyle Hall** are still standing. In the smaller hall behind it, the roof, which features astronomical hieroglyphs, is still in place.

There is a rest house/restaurant next to the temple which is called, not surprisingly, *Ramesseum Rest House*. It is owned by Sayyed Hussein, whose father was a friend of Howard Carter. The rest house is a great place to relax and have a cool drink or something to eat. You can leave your bike here while exploring the surroundings.

Deir al-Medina

About 1km off the road to the Valley of the Queens and up a short, steep paved road is Deir al-Medina (Monastery of the Town). It is named after a temple here that was occupied by early Christian monks. Near the temple is a ruined settlement known as the Workmen's Village, for it was here that many of the workers and artists who created the royal tombs lived and were buried. Although less frequently visited than many of the other tombs on the West Bank, some of the small tombs here have exquisite reliefs, making it well worth a visit.

Temple The small Ptolemaic temple of Deir al-Medina is just north of the Workmen's Village, along a rocky track. The temple was built between 221 and 116 BC by Philopator, Philometor and Euergetes II. It was dedicated to Hathor, the goddess of pleasure and love, and to Maat, the goddess of truth and the personification of cosmic order.

Workmen's Village Archaeologists have been excavating this settlement for most of this century and at least 70 houses have been uncovered. Three tombs in the village's terraced necropolis are now open to the public.

The beautifully adorned **Tomb of Aneuka (No 359)** belonged to a 19th dynasty servant who worked in the so-called Place of Truth – the Valley of the Kings. The tomb has only one chamber, but the wall paintings are magnificent. One of the most famous scenes shows a cat killing a snake; it's on the left of burial chamber. Right next to it is the **Tomb of Sennedjem (No 1)**, a 20th dynasty tomb that contains two small chambers and some equally exquisite paintings. Due to the popularity and small size of both these tombs, only 10 people at a time are allowed inside; it's likely you'll find yourself in a sizeable queue.

While you wait, take a look at the 19th dynasty **Tomb of Peshedu (No 3)** just up the slope from the other two tombs. Peshedu was another servant in the Place of Truth and can be seen in the burial chamber praying under a palm tree beside a lake. Most of the other tombs in the area also belonged to the servants, overseers and labourers who worked in the valley.

Valley of the Queens

There are at least 75 tombs in Biban al-Harim, the Valley of the Queens. They belonged to queens of the 19th and 20th dynasties and other members of the royal families, including princesses and the Ramessid princes. Only tomb Nos 43, 44, 52, 55 and 66 are open.

Tomb of Nefertari (No 66) Hailed as the finest tomb in the Theban necropolis – and in all of Egypt for that matter – the Tomb of Nefertari was first opened to the public in November 1995 and has been solidly booked ever since. Entry costs E£100, or E£50 for students, making it by far the most expensive monument in Egypt.

Nefertari was one of the five wives of Ramses II, the New Kingdom pharaoh known for his colossal monuments of self-celebration. However, the tomb he created for his favourite queen is a shrine to her beauty and, without doubt, an exquisite labour of love. Every inch of the walls in the tomb's three chambers and connecting

Preserving Egypt's Finest Tomb

Since the Tomb of Nefertari was discovered in 1904 by Italian archaeologist, Ernesto Schiaparelli, Egyptian and foreign archaeologists have pondered the best way to restore and keep it preserved. It wasn't until 1986 that the Egyptian Antiquities Organisation, together with the Getty Conservation Institute in the USA, embarked on a program to safeguard this magnificent tomb.

During the years since its discovery, the tomb paintings had suffered due to dehydration of the plaster and a build-up of salt crystals under the paintings, causing the images to flake off the limestone walls. Using minimal intervention and ensuring the reversibility of materials used, the paintings were cleaned and adhesion between the plaster and rock reinforced. No colours were added to the paintings. The restoration work, estimated to cost about US$6 million, lasted for five years, after which the tomb was prepared for visitors. Devices to monitor the temperature, humidity and salt levels were installed and wooden floors to keep dust at bay were laid. As breathing can raise humidity levels which in turn can activate salt crystallisation, a limit of 150 visitors per day was set. However, even this figure has been subject to controversy, with some archaeologists believing only two people per day should be allowed to view Egypt's finest tomb.

TOMB OF NEFERTARI

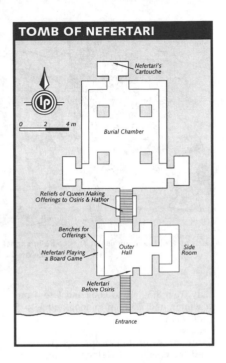

corridors is adorned with colourful scenes of Nefertari in the company of the gods and with associated text from the *Book of the Dead* nearby. Invariably 'the most beautiful of them', as Nefertari was known, is depicted wearing a divinely transparent white gown and a golden headdress featuring two long feathers extending from the back of a vulture. The ceiling of the tomb is festooned with golden stars.

Some of the best scenes in the tomb are in the side room off to your right at the bottom of the first set of stairs. In one panel here, the queen is shown with her arms outstretched next to the mummiform body of Osiris. At the top of the second staircase, which leads to the burial chamber, is another of the tomb's highlights – Nefertari offering two bowls of milk to Hathor, the goddess of pleasure and love.

Like most of the tombs in the Valley of the Kings, this one had been plundered by the time it was discovered by archaeologists. Only a few fragments of the queen's pink granite sarcophagus remained.

In order to preserve the tomb's exquisite artwork, ticket sales are limited to 150 per day, so get to the ticket office early if you want to go. A maximum of 10 people are allowed in at any one time for a maximum of 15 minutes, and photography is strictly prohibited. You may be required to wear shoe covers and nose masks. The tomb is open

LUXOR

Just as well the mummies of Thebes lie in silence in Cairo's Egyptian Museum because there's no peace on the West Bank.

daily from 8.30 am to noon and 1 to 4 pm in winter, and 7.30 am to noon and 1 to 5 pm in summer.

Tomb of Amunherkhepshep (No 55)

Until the opening of Nefertari's tomb, the Tomb of Amunherkhepshep was the valley's showpiece. Now thoroughly overshadowed, it is still a worthwhile option for those who can't afford, or who miss out on, tickets to Nefertari.

Amun was the son of Ramses III and was nine years old when he died. The scenes on

the tomb walls show his father grooming him to be pharaoh by introducing him to various gods. Amun's mother was pregnant at the time of his death and in her grief she aborted the child and entombed it with Amun. A five-month-old mummified foetus was discovered there. Wall paintings also show Ramses leading his son to Anubis, the jackal-headed god of the dead, who then takes the young Prince Amun down to the entrance of the Passage of the Dead.

Medinat Habu

Second in size only to the Great Temple at Karnak, the magnificent temple complex of Medinat Habu is one of the most underrated sites on the West Bank, and is usually bypassed by tourists in favour of the more famous Ramesseum. With the Theban mountains as a backdrop and the sleepy village of Kom Lolah in front, it is a wonderful place to spend a few hours.

The site was one of the first places in Thebes to be closely associated with the local god Amun. Although most famous for the large mortuary temple built by Ramses III, Hatshepsut and Tuthmosis III also constructed buildings in the complex. They were

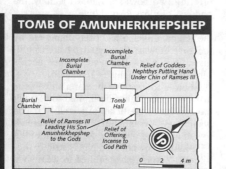

TOMB OF AMUNHERKHEPSHEP

Incomplete Burial Chamber

Incomplete Burial Chamber

Relief of Goddess Nephthys Putting Hand Under Chin of Ramses III

Burial Chamber

Tomb Hall

Relief of Ramses III Leading His Son Amunherkhepshep to the Gods

Relief of Offering Incense to God Path

0   2   4 m

LUXOR

later added to and altered by a succession of rulers right through to the Ptolemies. At Medinat Habu's height there were temples, storage rooms, workshops, administrative buildings and accommodation for the priests and officials. It was the centre of the economic life of Thebes for several centuries and was still inhabited as late as the 9th century AD, when a plague was thought to have decimated the town. You can still see the mud-brick remains of the medieval town which gave the site its name (*medina* means town or city) on top of the site's enclosure walls.

The original **Temple of Amun**, built by Hatshepsut and Tuthmosis III, was later completely overshadowed by the enormous **Mortuary Temple of Ramses III**, which is the dominant feature of Medinat Habu.

Ramses III was inspired in the construction of his shrine by the Ramesseum of his illustrious forebear, Ramses III. His own temple and the smaller one dedicated to Amun are both enclosed within the massive outer walls of the complex.

Also just inside, to the left of the gate, are the **Tomb Chapels of the Divine Adorers**, which were built for the principal priestesses of Amun. Outside the eastern gate, one of only two entrances, was a landing quay for a canal which once connected Medinat Habu with the Nile.

You enter the site through the unique **Syrian Gate**, a large two storey building modelled after an Asiatic fortress. If you follow the wall to the left you will find a staircase leading to the upper floors. There's not much to see in the rooms but you get some great views over the village in front of the temple and across the fields to the south.

The well-preserved **1st pylon** marks the front of the temple proper. Ramses III is portrayed in its reliefs as the victor in several wars. Most famous are the fine reliefs of his victory over the Libyans (who you can recognise by their long robes, sidelocks and beards). There is also a gruesome scene of scribes tallying the number of prisoners taken by counting severed hands and genitals.

To the left of the **First Court** are the remains of the **Pharaoh's Palace**; the three

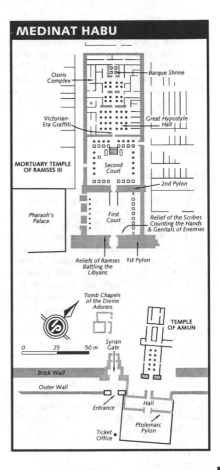

MEDINAT HABU

Osiris Complex

Barque Shrine

Victorian-Era Graffiti

Great Hypostyle Hall

MORTUARY TEMPLE OF RAMSES III

Second Court

2nd Pylon

Pharaoh's Palace

First Court

Relief of the Scribes Counting the Hands & Genitals of Enemies

Reliefs of Ramses Battling the Libyans

1st Pylon

Tomb Chapels of the Divine Adorers

TEMPLE OF AMUN

0   25   50 m

Syrian Gate

Brick Wall

Outer Wall

Entrance

Hall

Ticket Office

Ptolemaic Pylon

rooms at the rear were for the royal harem. There is a window between the First Court and the Pharaoh's Palace known as the **Window of Appearances**, which allowed the king to show himself to his subjects.

The reliefs of the **2nd pylon** feature Ramses III presenting prisoners of war to Amun and his vulture-goddess wife, Mut. Colonnades and reliefs surround the **Second Court**, depicting various religious ceremonies.

If you have time to wander about the extensive ruins around the mortuary temple

LUXOR

you will see the remains of an early Christian basilica as well as a small sacred lake.

Medinat Habu is off the road on your right as you return from the Valley of the Queens or can be reached by an asphalt road that turns off just east of the ticket office. After you have finished wandering around the you come out in the small village of Kom Lolah, where Richard Critchfield's book *Shahhat: An Egyptian* takes place.

New Gurna

For architecture buffs, Hassan Fathy's mudbrick architectural masterpiece, New Gurna, lies just past the railway track on the main road from the ferry to the ticket office. It was built to rehouse the inhabitants of Old Gurna (see the boxed text 'Guardians or Thieves?' on page 297) but most of them stayed where they were. The new, purpose-built village gradually filled up with the overflow from the surrounding area. Sadly, many of the domed mud-brick houses have been replaced with concrete buildings – Fathy did not plan his buildings to allow for extensions to accommodate growing extended families, sowing the seeds of the project's failure. However, the beautiful mud-brick mosque and theatre still survive, and you can still see the venerable architect's own house. Just ask for someone from the Abu al-Haggag family and they will show you around.

ACTIVITIES
Felucca Rides

One of the best things to do in Luxor in the late afternoon or early evening is to relax aboard a felucca. Local feluccas cruise the river throughout the day and cost around E£3 per person per hour or E£10 per boat per hour. In the low season, you may be able to do even better. Feluccas can be caught on either side of the Nile (below the Corniche, on the water or around the ferry landing).

An enjoyable outing is the trip upriver to Banana Island. The tiny isle, dotted with palms, is about 5km from Luxor and the trip takes two to three hours. Plan it in such a way that you're on your way back in time to watch a brilliant Nile sunset from the boat.

Ballooning

Two companies – Hod Hod Suleiman (☎ 370 116) and Balloons Over Egypt (☎ 376 515) – offer early-morning balloon flights over Luxor's West Bank. It costs about US$200 for the flight plus a champagne breakfast and some folkloric dancing. Trips are usually arranged through hotels or travel agencies.

Donkey, Horse & Camel Rides

Almost all the smaller hotels organise donkey treks around the West Bank. These trips, which start at about 7 am (sometimes 5 am) and finish about lunch time, cost a minimum of about E£20 per person, and may be more expensive. The hotels push these trips pretty hard, and although a lot of travellers have reported being pleased with them, you can probably organise it more cheaply yourself with some hard bargaining when you cross the river.

If you just want to loll about on the back of a camel and take in the sights of the Nile, the boys at the local ferry dock on the West Bank ask for E£25 for an hour. Some of the bigger hotels offer camel trips, which include visits to nearby villages for a cup of tea.

Pharaoh's Stables (☎ 310 015), which is reached by turning left just before the Mobil Station, about 500m along the road leading to the Colossi of Memnon, has horses as well as camels and donkeys. A sunset ride in the desert is an unforgettable experience and owners Bakri and Nasser rent out their horses for between E£15 and E£20 per hour (less if you're in a group) and a guide will take you through the fields, alongside Habu Temple and out towards the mountains.

Swimming

Many of the bigger hotels and even some at the budget hotels have swimming pools. The Karnak, Windsor, Emilio and Arabesque hotels and the Rezeiky Camp all charge E£7. The St Joseph and Flobater hotels, next to each other on the way out to the Sheraton, ask E£10 per person, as do the Shady and Wena Luxor hotels. The Novotel and Club Med Belladona Resort charge E£15. The Sheraton, Isis and Mercure hotels all charge E£20.

ORGANISED TOURS

Masr Travel (☎ 380 951), Thomas Cook and other travel agencies around the Old Winter Palace will organise half and full-day tours to the West Bank in air-con buses. In summer this might be worth considering, as there are hefty reductions. Otherwise, it's generally an expensive option at around US$40 for a half/full-day trip. Almost all of the small hotels aggressively promote their own tours. Some of these are better than others and there have been complaints by a number of travellers that they ended up seeing little more than papyrus shops and alabaster factories from a sweaty nonair-con car. If you do decide to take one of these tours, you're looking at about E£45 to E£65 per person.

The Novotel organises full-day cruises on its Lotus Boat to Dendara or Esna for E£150 per person, including lunch, guide and admission.

SPECIAL EVENTS

Luxor's premier tourist event is the Opet Festival, a modern-day recreation of the ancient festival in which images of the local deities – Amun, Mut and Khon – were paraded from Karnak Temple by boat upriver to Luxor Temple. Traditionally held during the inundation season, it's now usually celebrated on 4 November, although in 1998 it was cancelled due to a lack of tourists. Check with the tourist office to see if it's still on.

The town's biggest traditional festival is the Moulid of Abu al-Haggag. One of Egypt's largest moulids, it is held in honour of Luxor's patron sheikh, Yousef Abu al-Haggag, a 12th century Iraqi who settled in Luxor. The moulid takes place around the Mosque of Abu al-Haggag, the town's oldest mosque, which is actually on top of the

Moulids Around Luxor

Moulids (see the boxed text 'The Moulid' on page 99) are the place to hear real Saidi music, see traditional Saidi stick dancing (tahtib), or watch mirmah, where riders on Arabian horses gallop to and fro in what looks like a type of jousting.

There are a number of moulids in the Luxor area, most of them smaller and more manageable than the moulid of Abu al-Haggag (see Special Events), which draws hundreds of thousands of visitors. Most take place in the month of Sha'aban, the month immediately before Ramadan. Although many take place outside the cordon sanitaire around Luxor and are therefore all but impossible to visit these days, a few remain accessible.

Abu al-Gumsan, named after a religious man who died in 1984, is a small moulid that takes place on the 27th of Shaaban near the West Bank village of Taref, just south of the road to the Valley of the Kings. **Sheikh Musa** and **Abu al-Jud** both take place in the sprawling village of Karnak, the latter on 30th of Ashura. Other local moulids include **Sheikh Hamid** on the 1st of Sha'aban and **Sheikh Hussein** a couple of days later.

One of the only accessible Christian moulids is **Mar Girgis** (St George), which takes place at the monastery of the same name and has its climax on 11 November, although the celebrations go on for most of the week before. The monastery is at the village of Razagat, just south of Armant at the turn-off for the road to Kharga oasis. Although this area is officially forbidden to foreigners, service taxis ferrying the hundreds of people attending the moulid will often avoid the checkpoint on the main road and go via a desert track.

Bakri, at the Pharaoh's Stable, is often performing with his horses at moulids and he is more than willing to give you more information.

north-east corner of Luxor Temple. It's a raucous five day event that takes place in the third week before Ramadan. For more information see the boxed text 'Moulids Around Luxor' on page 305.

On 23 February each year a marathon is held on the West Bank. It begins at Deir al-Bahri and loops around the main antiquities sites before ending back where it began. You can ask at the tourist office for information.

PLACES TO STAY
Perhaps more than at any tourist destination in Egypt, the cost of accommodation in Luxor fluctuates seasonally. There is no hard-and-fast rule on how much rates might increase in winter, or drop in summer. Some hotels drop their charges by 50% in the low season, others barely alter them. Where only one rate is given, it's the low-season rate.

Due to the slump in tourism, many places have not raised their prices much in recent years, although this could change.

PLACES TO STAY – BUDGET
Luxor is full of budget places to stay, though a few of them have had a tough time staying afloat during the last couple of years. Many hotels boast both roof gardens and washing machines – although 'roof garden' can mean anything from an attractive rooftop restaurant to a concrete platform with chunks of cement and swirls of twisted iron all over the place. Most hotels offer breakfast, which almost universally means bread, butter, jam, cheese and maybe an egg, and a cup of tea or coffee. Unless stated otherwise, the prices below include breakfast.

Another common feature is the notice board. The quality of these varies considerably – some have a lot of useful information, others are more of a token effort.

Avoid the hotel touts who pounce on travellers as they get off the train/bus – they get a 25% to 40% commission for bringing you in which is added on your bill.

Warning
Female travellers should use extreme caution when looking for accommodation in Luxor. Several have reported being sexually assaulted after being given spiked drinks by hotel staff.

Camping
YMCA (☎ 372 425) camping ground on Sharia al-Karnak costs E£4 per night, including the use of its 20 showers. This place was once popular with overland travel groups, but it has lost business to the more expensive Rezeiky Camp, further up the road towards the temple.

Rezeiky Camp (☎ 381 334, fax 381 400) charges E£10 per person to pitch a tent and E£10 for a vehicle, for which you get access to the swimming pool and showers. The camp is in the midst of transforming itself into a hotel by the addition of air-con motel-style rooms for E£30/50 a single/double, but you're paying for the privilege of having the pool on your doorstep. The owners are currently adding 15 more rooms in a poorly designed concrete addition. There's a large garden with a restaurant and bar (E£6 for a beer), as well as a washing machine for which you pay E£10 for a 4kg load – all in all, not a great deal given the variety on offer in town.

Hostels
Youth Hostel (☎ 372 139), in a street just off Sharia al-Karnak has slightly dingy rooms have at least three beds and the showers tend to get swampy. With a membership card the cost is E£8.10, or E£10.10 without. Breakfast is E£2.50 extra. It is beside a school, which means lots of early morning noise.

Hotels – South of Sharia al-Mahatta
Anglo Hotel (☎ 381 679) is the closest place to the train station. It costs E£10/20 for a single/double room with breakfast and shared bathroom. At the time of writing, 10 new rooms with private baths, telephones, TVs and air-con were being added and doubles were supposed to be going for about E£30. It's fairly clean and the management is friendly, but the proximity of the train station means it can be noisy.

Sharia Abdel Moneim al-Adasi leads away from the train station to Sharia Mohammed Farid and then on to Sharia Television. Around these two streets teems a growing family of little budget pensions and hotels. You'll see the signs to some as you reach Sharia Mohammed Farid, which is about three minutes walk from the station.

Oasis Hotel (☎ *381 699*) on Sharia Mohammed Farid has spacious double rooms and more poky singles. Quite a few travellers stay here, and their reports have invariably been good (though the breakfast is skimpy). Some rooms have their own bath but all rooms have fans and comfortable beds. The bathrooms are clean, and there's plenty of hot water. Singles/doubles with air-con cost E£6/13.

Two streets past the Oasis then down a dead-end alley off to the right is *Grand Hotel* (☎ *382 905*) – it's signposted. Clean and welcoming, it has a small rooftop terrace with great views, and decent shared bathrooms with hot water. Singles/doubles with fan go for E£6/10, but make sure you check the prices on arrival; some travellers have reported being charged more than they thought. The owner, a local schoolteacher named Nobi, is very friendly and keeps a room off the lobby where people can leave their belongings after checking out if they have a long wait for their train or bus. Bikes are for hire at E£6 per day.

Heading towards the Nile on Sharia Mohammed Farid is *Akhenaten Hotel* (☎ *373 979*), which looks fancier on the outside than most other hotels and pensions around here, but has quite modest, cramped rooms. Singles without/with bath cost E£8/10; doubles are E£13/15.

Back on Sharia Abdel Moneim, if you head down another block you'll arrive at the intersection with Sharia Ahmed Orabi. The next main street running more or less parallel to it is Sharia Television. Between and around these two streets hotels abound, most of them budget places.

If you turn left into Sharia Ahmed Orabi and then right into the second dusty laneway, you'll find *Atlas Hotel* (☎ *373 514*). At E£8 per person (plus E£2 for breakfast) for a room with bath, some also with air-con, this is not a bad place and with 40 rooms it's rarely full.

Continue down this lane, turn left and take the next two lefts, and you'll find one of the better deals in Luxor. The 25 room *Fontana Hotel* (☎ *380 663*) is popular with backpackers. The owner asks for E£6 per person for a room with a fan and E£8/15 for singles/doubles with air-con and private bathroom. However he has been known to come down to E£5 for rooms with shared baths, as well as to raise his prices for the unwary – so sharpen your haggling skills. None of the bathrooms (all of which have full bathtubs as well as showers) are shared by more than three rooms and toilet paper and towels are provided. The rooms are spotlessly clean and there's a kitchen (of sorts), rooftop terrace and washing machine for guests to use. The main complaint from travellers is that the owner can be a little too aggressive in promoting his tours.

On Sharia Nozha, a dead-end lane running off Sharia Television, is *Everest Hotel* (☎ *373 260*). The renovated rooms are OK and come with air-con or fan and attached bathrooms (with toilet paper), and are a reasonable deal at E£10/20. Like many other small hotels, the management is anxious to get you on one of its tours of the West Bank.

If none of these appeal and you find your way out of the rabbit warren, there are more on the west side of Sharia Television. The closest is the homey *Sherif Hotel* (☎ *370 757*) on a small street off the very beginning of Sharia Television. Run by a pleasant English teacher named Amr, it has 15 rooms, six with their own bathroom and four with air-con. Singles/doubles with shared bathrooms and fans go for E£7/14; and E£12/19 with air-con. It's a good deal and very conveniently located.

On Sharia Shamouz, a few blocks south of the Sherif is *Moon Valley Hotel* (☎ *375 710*) on your right. With photos of the owner in the lobby and a common living room with a VCR and videos available, it is homey, although some of the rooms are better than others. Rooms that come with air-con or fan plus private shower and toilet cost E£10 per person.

On Sharia Qamr is *Happy Land Hotel* (☎ 371 828) run by Mr Ibrahim. Here is where you see the fierce competition among budget hotels in Luxor at work. The rooms are spotless and toilet paper, soap and mosquito coils are provided, as well as free laundry. Mr Ibrahim also claims that his is the only budget hotel in town that offers cornflakes and real fruit with his breakfast. The cheapest rooms are E£6 per person in a dormitory with fan, including breakfast, while a good single with private bath costs E£10. It's about a 10 minute walk from the train station. Alternatively, take a minibus from the station to one stop south of the Novotel on the Corniche. The hotel is signposted.

A good option just south of Sharia Al-Mahatta is the new *New Everest Hotel* (☎ 370 017), on a small side street on the other side of Sharia al-Mahatta from the El-Salam. It has 12 clean rooms, four of which have air-con. Singles/doubles with shared facilities cost E£5/10 without breakfast; air-con doubles with bath are E£20, including breakfast.

Hotels – North of Sharia al-Mahatta

The friendly *Saint Mina Hotel* (☎ 375 409) is an excellent deal if you've got a little extra money. The hotel's 20 rooms, half of which have private bathrooms, are very clean with air-con or fans, although some travellers have complained about noisy plumbing. Singles/doubles with bath are E£30/50, and without bath are E£25/45. These prices drop considerably in summer. It's as good a place as some of the mid-range places with double or more room rates.

Sphinx Hotel (☎ 372 830) has singles/doubles for E£12/16 which may or may not include breakfast depending on how well you can haggle. The rooms are musty and run-down although the staff is friendly.

With its less-than-friendly staff, *Nobles Hotel* (☎ 372 823) is not quite as good, but is not a terrible deal either, at E£15/25 with a fan. If you want air-con, a double costs E£30.

Across the road, *Venus Hotel* (☎ 382 625) has 30 reasonable rooms with bath. Popular with backpackers, singles/doubles with their own bathrooms cost E£15/20 and the hotel has a restaurant with blaring satellite TV and bar. There's also a 6th floor terrace where you can down a cold Stella for E£6. They can also arrange donkey trips to the West Bank and have bicycles that they rent for E£3 per day.

Almost opposite the Venus is *Pyramids Hotel* (☎ 373 243). A bed here costs E£15/20 with bath, including breakfast and taxes. The location is good, there's hot water and most of the rooms have air-con.

Hotels – West Bank

Although the West Bank is a more pleasant place to be than the town, there is only a limited selection of budget accommodation.

Opposite the Medinat Habu temple complex is *Habu Hotel* (☎ 372 477). With its small, vaulted rooms and stunning views over the entrance to the temple, this could be a gem of a hotel if the management bothered to take care of it. The three upstairs rooms with a terrace overlooking the temple gate almost make it worthwhile to stay here, despite the filthy bathrooms and reports of thriving insect life. But it's probably better to pay E£6 for a beer up here rather than shell out the E£25/40 they're asking for the single/double rooms.

Maratonga Restaurant just across the road also has a couple of rooms that it sometimes rents out to people for E£20 per person – a bit much for the clean but basic facilities on offer.

The nearby *Queen's Hotel* (☎ 384 835) has slightly better rooms than those at the Habu but the view is not the best. However, the roof restaurant has a very good panorama.

The best place to stay on the West Bank in this price range is *Marsam Hotel* (☎ 382 403) also known as Ali Abd al-Rasul Hotel or Sheikh Ali Hotel. A local institution, the hotel was originally built for American archeologists in the 1920s. In the 1960s it became a retreat for Egyptian artists (*Marsam* means 'a place for drawing' in

Arabic) – you can still see the odd sculpture in the shady courtyard/garden. It belonged to Sheikh Ali Abdul Rasul, a cantankerous old guy with a bone-cracking handshake and an aggressive sense of hospitality that kept you riveted to your seat, whether you liked it or not. Sheikh Ali was a member of the clan that helped discover the Tomb of Seti I. Following his death, his son took over the hotel and it is currently under the management of an Austrian/Czech woman and has improved vastly in the past couple of years. There are 23 rooms altogether, 10 in the main concrete building and the remainder in two mud-brick buildings. Six are currently closed for renovation. Very simple but clean singles/doubles with shared bathrooms cost E£25/35, including breakfast.

Abu al-Kasem Hotel (☎ 310 319) is near the Temple of Seti I on Sharia Wadi al-Melouk. It has 20 dusty singles/doubles with fans and bathrooms for E£35/50. Although it's basically clean, it's looking a bit scruffy these days. The best rooms overlook the mountains and there's a great view from the roof. The owners, the Abu al-Kasem family, also have an alabaster factory attached to the hotel and rent bicycles for E£5 a day, or donkeys for E£10.

Wadi al-Melouk Hotel (☎ 310 175), on the east side of Al-Fadlya canal, is run-down and overpriced. Rooms have balconies but no fans, and cost E£15 per person. There is a wonderful roof terrace but it doesn't offset the state of the bathrooms. Bargaining with the old man who runs it might be possible.

PLACES TO STAY – MID-RANGE

Many mid-range places have dropped their prices substantially in the last few years following the decline in tourism; in some cases this hasn't helped them attract the few visitors that come here and they have become musty and run-down. If visitors start returning, prices will no doubt increase again.

East Bank

About 3km north of the town centre, opposite the Hilton, is *Karnak Hotel* (☎ 374 155). If you want to be out of the bustle of Luxor, but stay on the East Bank, this is a great place to be. It has a garden plus a clean pool and has received rave reviews from some travellers. Prices in winter are US$40/50, including breakfast, but they go down by 20% in the summer.

About 200m north, down on the banks of the Nile, is *Hotel Pharaon* (☎ 381 177, fax 376 477), which has pretty good air-con rooms with TVs and telephones for US$15/28 in the winter, half this in the summer. There is a large pool and great Nile views.

Heading back into town, the high-rise *Pola Hotel* (☎ 380 551, fax 380 552), just off Sharia al-Karnak opposite the Rezeiky Camp, has wonderful views from the roof, plus a pool, bar and restaurant. The shoddily-built rooms go for US$28/35, but the management is desperate to fill the hotel and at the time of writing was offering discounts of up to 50%.

Windsor Hotel (☎ 375 547, fax 373 447) is in a small alley just off Sharia Nefertiti. It's a reasonable 120 room hotel, although some of the rooms are a little shabby and others are decidedly gloomy and dark. It's popular with European tour groups and singles/doubles cost E£60/70. This place's particular boast, aside from its pool, is that it is the biggest three star establishment in Luxor.

Just across the way is *Merryland Hotel* (☎ 381 746). Its 32 rooms are in better shape than the Windsor, and with singles/doubles with TV, phone, air-con, bath and balcony, for E£40/60 it is very reasonable. Its rooftop bar has spectacular Nile views.

Philippe Hotel (☎ 373 604, fax 380 050) on Sharia Nefertiti, between the Corniche and Sharia al-Karnak, is an upper mid-range hotel with clean, carpeted rooms, although those in its new wing are far superior to the old. All the rooms have powerful air-con, TV, mini-fridge and bathrooms with bathtubs. There's a pleasant roof garden with a small bar and pool. Including breakfast a single/double costs

US$30/36. As this was one of the few hotels to be full during the recent tourist slump, reservations are recommended.

Next door to the Philippe is the run-down *Nile Hotel* (☎/fax 372 859), which has 50 double rooms that look as though they've been vacant for a long time. Singles/doubles cost E£60/70 in winter – 20% less in the summer – but there are much better deals in town.

Emilio Hotel (☎ 373 570, fax 370 000) at the northern end of Sharia Yousef Hassan is a very good upper mid-range hotel. It has 48 rooms, all with bathrooms, air-con, TV, mini-fridge and a hotel video channel. The astroturf roof terrace has plenty of shade, reclining chairs and a popular pool. Singles/ doubles cost US$50/55, including taxes and breakfast. Reservations are needed here in winter, because it is often taken over by travel groups.

Around the corner on Sharia al-Karnak is the new *St Mark Hotel* (☎/fax 383 403) which is a good deal at E£35/60 for air-con single/double rooms with bath, TV and fridge. The rooms are small but clean and the staff is friendly. There's also a small roof bar where beer is served.

Mina Palace Hotel (☎ 372 074) is on the Corniche just opposite the entrance to the Mummification Museum. Although it is getting slightly run-down, the Nile views are great. It has singles/doubles with air-con and private bathrooms for E£76/86, although at the time of writing the management was willing to drop the price to almost half this. Make sure you ask for a corner room with two balconies – one looking towards Luxor Temple and the other over the Nile.

The two star *St Catherine Hotel* (☎/fax 372 684, 2 Sharia Yousef Hassan) is sometimes spelled 'Catreen' or 'Cathrine'. It has little to recommend it except the price. It has halved its prices in recent years to E£27/36 a single/double but you can probably bargain this down.

On Sharia al-Karnak, about a block north of Sharia al-Mahatta, you'll see *Horus Hotel* (☎ 372 165, fax 373 447). Rooms seem rea

sonably comfortable, but some travellers have complained that the plumbing leaves a lot to be desired and the place needs a facelift. The asking price is E£30/40. The front rooms are definitely better than the others but they face a mosque which could mean waking up with the early morning call to prayer.

Up beside the train station at the beginning of Sharia Abdel Moneim al-Adasi is the newly opened *New Radwan Hotel* (☎ 385 502, fax 385 501). With full bathrooms and air-con it is an excellent deal at E£50/60 for singles/doubles. There is a roof terrace and a bar.

Arabesque Hotel (☎ 371 299, fax 372 193) on Sharia Mohammed Farid, not far from the GPO, has slashed the prices of its air-con rooms with very small beds to E£50/60. The roof garden has good views over Luxor Temple and the Nile, and there's a pool, but the rooms suffer a little from street noise.

Down on Sharia Television, there are several mid-range places offering comfortable rooms with all the necessary mod cons. *Shady Hotel* (☎/fax 374 859) charges E£50/70 for clean rooms on the street side, E£10 extra for the supposedly quieter pool side, although as the pool is surrounded by buildings it is probably just as noisy. Taxes are extra. Across the street, the more rundown *Santa Maria Hotel* (☎/fax 380 430) offers singles/doubles for E£49/66.

Further down Sharia Television is the blue and yellow *Golden Palace Hotel* (☎ 382 972, fax 382 974). At only E£40/70 for clean, air-con singles/doubles with TV, fridge and telephone, it is an excellent deal. There is also a reasonable sized pool and plans for a roof garden.

A couple of three-star hotels are situated past the Club Med on Sharia Khaled ibn al-Walid. *St Joseph Hotel* (☎ 381 707, fax 381 727) costs about US$25/35 for a single/double with TV, air-con, phone and bath. Breakfast is E£10 extra. There is also a pool and basement bar. Next door, the rather oddly named *Flobater Hotel* (☎ 374 223, fax 370 618) is similarly priced, at US$28/35 for sin gles/doubles. It has a token pool and a pleasant roof garden.

West Bank

Pharaohs Hotel (☎/fax 310 702) is the oldest mid-range place to stay on the West Bank. It has 14 old rooms (which are currently being used by police officers billeted in the area) and 15 new ones, all with aircon and bathrooms. Although it's not beautiful, the location can't be beat. Singles/doubles in the new building cost E£55/110. There is also a garden restaurant that serves Stella for E£6 and has kebab meals starting at E£10.

Far better, but further from the monuments, are two new hotels that have recently opened in the area known as the Gezira, just up from the ferry landing. *Amon al-Gezira Hotel (☎ 310 912)* is a small, spotlessly clean family-run hotel presided over by Ahmed Mahmoud Suleiman. Five of the nine rooms here have their own bathrooms and there is a terrace on each floor as well as a great roof terrace and a garden. Doubles go for E£60 to E£70 with air-con. To get there follow the signs to the Pharaoh's Stables.

The other new addition on the West Bank is *Al-Gezira Hotel (☎/fax 310 034)*. The hotel has 11 rooms, some with great Nile views, and all with their own bathrooms and either air-con or ceiling fans. Singles/doubles cost E£40/60. There is also a very pleasant roof restaurant overlooking the Nile where you can eat a filling Egyptian meal for E£20. Stella is available for E£7. To get to the hotel take the small track that goes beside the bicycle hire and video rental shop just up from the local ferry landing. The hotel is about 50m away on the left.

PLACES TO STAY – TOP END

The dramatic slump in tourism that followed the massacre at the temple of Hatshepsut in 1997 has put a brake on the frenzy of five star hotel building that had begun in Luxor in the early 1990s. There are currently several hotel projects on hold but there's still enough choice to suit most tastes.

The hotels in this price range start at about US$50 for a single and generally have all the usual attributes of the big international hotels. Unless specified, the rates do not include breakfast or taxes of up to 26%. Some of the top end options include (listed alphabetically):

Club Med Belladona Resort (☎ 380 850, fax 380 879) is a four star resort charging E£180/234 for singles/doubles including taxes and breakfast. Half and full board are available.

Gaddis Hotel (☎ 382 838, fax 382 837) is almost opposite the Isis Hotel on Sharia Khaled ibn al-Walid. Rooms at this recently built hotel start at US$60/79. It has three restaurants, a bar and pool.

Hilton Hotel (☎ 374 933, fax 376 571) is 1km north of Karnak Temple and has singles/doubles from US$55/70 including breakfast. Buses are on hand to shuttle guests into the centre of town.

Hotel Mercure (☎ 580 944, fax 384 912) is a four star place on the Corniche with two categories of rooms. Those overlooking the Nile cost US$99/120 in winter (including breakfast and taxes) while rooms facing the garden are US$81/103. In summer prices are reduced by 10% to 15%.

Isis Hotel (☎ 372 750, fax 372 923) is an eyesore of a building set in a lush garden setting with manicured hedges and two pools. Singles/doubles at this five star hotel start at US$70/85 for rooms overlooking the street, or US$80/100 for a Nile view.

Luxor Wena Hotel (☎ 380 018, fax 379 849) on Sharia al-Karnak near Luxor Temple, is at the centre of a long-running court battle and as a result is looking a bit dilapidated. Rooms go for US$100/120, including breakfast and taxes. There's a swimming pool and a variety of restaurants.

Mercure Inn (☎ 373 321) is another four star hotel belonging to the French chain. Singles/doubles cost US$55/70, including breakfast and taxes.

Mövenpick Jolie Ville (☎ 374 855, fax 374 936) is on Crocodile Island, 4km south of town. It's a five star Swiss-managed place with swimming pool, tennis courts and sailboats. There is also a mini zoo and a playground, making it popular for families with young children. There are 320 modern, well-appointed rooms set out in bungalow style amidst tropical gardens. Singles/doubles range from US$110/150 to US$140/190. The hotel motorboat shuttles guests to and from the centre of town.

Novotel Luxor (☎ 380 925) is a squat high-rise at the southern tip of the Corniche with great Nile views and a floating swimming pool. Singles/doubles are US$95/121, including breakfast.

Sheraton Luxor Resort (☎ 374 544) is a secluded three storey low-rise at the southern end of Khaled ibn al-Walid St, the Sheraton sits on the edge of the Nile and has some great views. It also has one of the best pools in town. Singles/doubles start at US$55/80 for a garden view and US$75/100 for a Nile view. Prices include breakfast and taxes.

Sonesta St George Hotel (☎ 382 575, fax 382 571) had the distinction of opening its doors only days before the 1997 massacre decimated tourism in Luxor. Rooms in this marble-filled 224 room building go for US$123/150, including breakfast and taxes.

Tutotel (☎ 377 990, fax 372 671) is a new four star hotel, with singles/doubles for US$60/80 including breakfast and taxes. There is a rooftop pool and all the usual facilities.

Winter Palace & New Winter Palace (☎ 380 422, fax 374 087) stand side by side on the Corniche, but the new section is not nearly as interesting and romantic as the old, which was built to attract the aristocracy of Europe and is one of Egypt's famous historic hotels. Standard rooms in the old section cost US$158/175 with a Nile/garden view, while deluxe rooms start at US$272/289. In the new wing, prices start at US$149/160. There's a large garden, a swimming pool, table-tennis and a tennis court.

PLACES TO EAT
Budget Dining
Sharia al-Mahatta has a number of good sandwich stands and other cheap eats possibilities, as well as a few juice stands at its Luxor Temple end. The other cheap eats area is Sharia Television, which is where you'll find **Sayyida Zeinab**, one of Luxor's best kushari joints. A large plate of kushari goes for E£2.50, a small one for E£1.50.

Salt & Bread Cafeteria on Midan al-Mahatta across from the train station serves cheap meals for about E£5. It offers many entrees, including kebab, pigeon and chicken. The menu also includes six kinds of omelette – one wonders how different they can be.

Mensa Restaurant on Sharia al-Mahatta has basic food that's slightly overpriced. Dishes include sandwiches, chicken and pigeon stuffed with rice. You can have almost a full meal for about E£8.50.

Al-Hussein on Sharia al-Karnak does a good fish in a tomato and basil sauce and the pizzas are acceptable, if smallish, for E£7. The soups are sometimes good, sometimes watery. Most main dishes cost E£7 to E£10 before service is added on.

Amoun Restaurant also on Sharia Karnak serves oriental kebab, chicken, fish and various rice and vegetable dishes for similar prices to those at the neighbouring Al-Hussein. These are two of the town's most popular eating houses for tourists.

Ali Baba Cafe on the corner of sharias Mohammed Farid and al-Karnak is popular with locals and tourists alike. Although part of the Luxor Wena hotel, it has its own street entrance and has reasonably priced mezze and meals such as shish kebab and shish tawouk. You can also get sheeshas for about E£3.

Mish Mish on Sharia Television serves good basic meals for less than E£10. Try the Mish Mish salad, a mixed platter with homous and cold meats, enough to constitute a light meal, for E£6.

Sultana Restaurant, which is also on Sharia Television, is a tiny place, popular with travellers, where a reasonable vegetable stew or *bram*, served steaming in a clay pot, costs only E£7.50 and pizzas go for between E£9 and E£11.

Restaurants
East Bank Unfortunately there are no really fine restaurants in Luxor – the food at the Winter Palace does not live up to expectations and if you want a culinary treat you'd be better off at one of the other five-star hotels. **Mövenpick Jolie Ville** is famous for its breakfast buffets but its other meals are also highly recommended. For something totally different, the new **Sonesta St George** has a Japanese restaurant that has received excellent reviews from the local residents.

Peace Abouzeid Restaurant (☎ 372 419) on the Corniche by Karnak Temple is one of Luxor's few Nileside restaurants that isn't part of a hotel. Although the lunch time buffet tends to be mobbed by dazed tourists on day bus trips from Hurghada, at night its tables are frequented by Egyptians and foreigners who want dinner and a sheesha by the Nile. A grilled pigeon meal costs about E£30 and there is a wide selection of seafood and Egyptian specialties.

Kings Head Pub (☎ 371 249) on Sharia Khaled ibn al-Walid, near the passport office, continues to be one of Luxor's most popular bar/eateries. This place is England through and through – except that it's open 24 hours and the king in question is Akhenaten wearing a Tudor hat. It's a laid-back place to spend an afternoon catching up on foreign newspapers or tucking into toasted sandwiches and chips. They even have a E£20 roast beef and Yorkshire pudding lunch time special on Sundays. Beer is reasonably priced and there's a huge array of cocktails (E£12 each) and spirits.

Ritz Restaurant (no phone) in a small alleyway off Sharia Khaled ibn al-Walid between the Sonesta St George and Isis hotels, is a new place that offers a variety of mains starting from E£15 and has soups starting at E£3.50.

Jem's (☎ 383 604), also on Khaled ibn al-Walid (which has become Luxor's restaurant strip), does very good Egyptian or European meals, including a vegetarian set menu for E£30. Filling appetisers and salads are cheaper at about E£8.

Tudor Rose (no phone), which is underneath Jem's, is presumably hoping to cash in on the success of the King's Head – it also offers English food like roast beef and Yorkshire pud. Prices are similar to those at the King's Head but it lacks the ambience.

La Mama (☎ 374 544) Italian restaurant on the terrace at the entrance to the Sheraton is a good bet if you've got kids in tow. Apart from a good range of the usual Italian specialties like pizza and pasta for about E£20, there's a pelican that wanders around and chases you if you get too close.

West Bank Some of the best, or at least most atmospheric, meals in Luxor can be found on the West Bank rather than across the river in town.

Tutankhamun Restaurant (☎ 310 118) down by the local ferry dock is run by Aam Mahmoud, a former cook at one of the French archaeological missions in Luxor. He serves up excellent stews and other dishes. A meal usually costs about E£10 to E£15.

Al-Gezira Hotel also serves Egyptian specialties like the infamous *molokhiyya* (see Food in the Facts for the Visitor chapter) and stuffed cabbage leaves. The surroundings are pleasant and its roof restaurant looks out over the Nile and the bright lights of Luxor beyond. Meals here cost E£20 and beer is available for E£7.

Marsam Hotel (☎ 382 403) serves surprisingly good, fresh food on its tree-filled terrace and dishes range from Egyptian specialties such as stuffed pigeon and lentil soup to stir-fried vegetables. It's a set menu and it is a good idea to order ahead. There is no beer available.

Restaurant Mohammed (☎ 311 014) is basically a large room in owner Mohammed Abdel Lahi's mud-brick house, which is just along from the Pharaohs Hotel. It is very popular with French archaeologists and other foreign residents in the area. You can get good, basic Egyptian food, as well as standard chicken and french-fry platters. A full kofta meal costs E£8 and duck goes for E£15. Portions are generous and Stella is available for E£7. It opens around noon and closes when the last patrons leave, which is usually about 10 pm.

Self-Catering

If you want to buy your own food for meals or snacks, you will find a wide range on sale in Luxor. The best place for fruit and vegetables is the *souq*, although the good stuff sells out early in the morning. On either side of the main street are little shops selling fruit and veg throughout the day.

On these streets you'll also find small *grocery shops*, or *ba'als*, that stock canned goods, some western-style cereals, imported cheese such as Edam (called *felamenk*) as well as local white cheese and *gibna rumi*. If you're over by Sharia Television, look for the grocery store named **Barghouti** on the west side of the street, just south of Mish Mish restaurant. It has a good selection of yoghurts, cheeses kept in clean, functioning fridges, as well as an excellent selection of dry foods.

Luxor has a number of **bakeries** but one of the best is a no-name bakery at the beginning of Sharia Ahmed Orabi that makes delicious cookies and breads, and has prices in English.

Those in search of a few takeaway beers can go to the **Stella outlet** just north of the train station. Look for the yellow sign with the blue star. It's open from 8.30 am to 2 pm and 5 to 11 pm. It's not open on Sunday.

ENTERTAINMENT

The downturn in tourism has dampened nocturnal activities in Luxor but you still have a few options.

Bars

If you want a drink, there are several bars in Luxor. Apart from **Kings Head Pub** (see the previous Places to Eat section for details), **Pub 2000** (☎ *370 076*) on a side street parallel to Sharia Khaled ibn al-Walid, about 200m south of the Novotel, has a popular happy hour between 7.30 and 8.30 pm where Stellas go for E£4.50. It also has a good selection of meals, including reasonably priced daily specials. **St Joseph Bar** bar at the St Joseph Hotel has its own happy hour between 10 and 11 pm. Beer is reduced by 30% and spirits by 50%. In addition, most of the mid-range hotels have roof bars, many overlooking the Nile.

Over on the West Bank beer is available at **Habu Hotel**, in the garden of **Pharaohs Hotel** and at **Restaurant Mohammed**.

Nightclubs, Discos & Shows

Dawar al-Umda restaurant, in the garden of the Mercure Inn, has a folkloric show that includes a belly-dancer, *rababa* music, and occasionally a snakecharmer. With its rea-

sonably priced Egyptian food, it is very popular. The show starts between 8 and 9 pm every Thursday.

The other big hotels all offer some kind of evening entertainment. **Mövenpick Jolie Ville** presents a quite extravagant floor show. You are dressed in a galabiyya, taken for a felucca ride at sunset, introduced to 'peasants', and then fed and entertained in a tent by the Nile.

Isis and **Winter Palace** hotels have folkloric and belly-dance performances as well as discos. With the current drop in tourism, belly-dancing is not held as often as it was in the past, so check with the hotels beforehand. **Tutotel** hotel's disco is one of the more popular options, while at **Hotel Mercure**, nonguests must pay a minimum charge of E£20 to get into the Sabil disco. This covers you for the belly-dancer at 11.30 pm too.

Away from the tourist establishments is **Mandaria**, a nightclub/restaurant frequented by local businessmen and the few Arab tourists that venture to Luxor. Regular patrons buy an entire bottle of Johnny Walker which sits in the centre of the table and goes down as the evening progresses. The show starts sometime around midnight and continues into the pre-dawn hours. It's down an alleyway almost opposite Isis Hotel.

If you want to avoid the bright lights of the town, the West Bank is the place to be, although the jumpy police have put a damper on some of the more interesting night-time experiences to be enjoyed here. Pharaoh's Stables used to arrange evening desert barbecues for groups of 10 or more and sometimes would put on a horse-dancing show. Bakri or Nasser will be able to tell you if this is possible again (for telephone number see details in the Donkey, Horse & Camel Rides section earlier in this chapter).

On Thursday nights, especially in the summer, you can often hear the music from a local wedding or a Sufi *zikr* wafting across the fields – if you follow your ears you will usually be welcomed.

Saidi Music

Upper Egyptians (or 'Saidis') may be ridiculed as country bumpkins by the relatively sophisticated Cairenes, but their sometimes stubborn adherence to tradition has preserved some of Egypt's most distinctive regional culture. This is especially true when it comes to music, and with its strong rhythms and simple instruments Saidi music is a welcome change from the tinny Cairo pop that you hear throughout the country.

People in Luxor will tell you of four different types of Saidi music, although categories blur. First is the very popular *medah*, which comes from traditional Sufi zikr and often involves repetitive chanting. Second is *kaff al-Saidi*, which is usually one or two singers accompanied by handclapping *(kaff* means palm) instead of instruments. Third is *muzmar*, named after a reed instrument and often used to accompany horse-dancing or belly-dancing. Finally, there's *rababa*, named after an instrument which looks and sounds a bit like a homemade, single-string violin.

Many of the musicians come from the small towns around Luxor and get their start at village weddings or Sufi zikrs and sometimes you can hear their music on weekend nights on the West Bank.

A few of the most famous and, to western ears, most accessible Saidi musicians include Sheikh Ahmed Birrin, a blind sheikh hailing from Esna with an addictive, reedy voice; Rayyis Nessim, a student of Birrin; Yousef Bakash, a famous rababa musician who's been 'discovered' and is now famous in France (and is one of the few Saidi musicians available on CD); Gamal al-Esnawi, one of the younger generation of medah singers; and Sayyed ad-Dawy, who sings the famous epic, the *Sira al-Hilalawi*.

Their cassettes (which cost about E£7) can be bought in Luxor at the Hani w'Hanafon tape shop opposite the post office on Sharia al-Mahatta. The owners are happy to let you listen before you buy.

SHOPPING

Pretty much the whole range of standard Egyptian souvenirs can be bought in Luxor, although the variety is not nearly as great as in Cairo. One exception is alabaster. You will notice a plethora of alabaster shops on the West Bank. The alabaster is mined about 80km north-west of the Valley of the Kings, and some of the handmade cups, vases and other articles make sturdy and original souvenirs.

A more unusual buy are the clay pots *(tawagen,* singular *tagen)* that are used in local cooking. Extremely practical, they can be used to cook on top of the stove or in the oven and they look good on the table too. Before they are used they must be 'cured' using a mixture of molasses and oil in a very low oven for about 30 minutes. They aren't exactly light, but come in various sizes and go from E£5 and more. They are on sale just beside the police station in Luxor.

A very welcome addition to the West Bank's oversupply of tourist bazaars are two new handicraft shops. One, Bedouin Market (☎ 311 152) is just beside Marsam Hotel and is open between 9 am and 5 pm. It stocks well-made products from all over Egypt and is associated with the Marketing Link centre in Cairo (see the Shopping section in the chapter). The second shop, Maarad al-Gurna is almost directly in front of the tomb of Ramose in the Tombs of the Nobles. Run by Golo, the artist responsible for a number of the illustrations in this book, and Edith Pointeau, it stocks specially designed, locally produced items, most with an interesting twist.

LUXOR

GETTING THERE & AWAY
Air

The EgyptAir (☎ 380 580) office is on the Corniche, next to Amex. EgyptAir flies daily between Cairo, Luxor and Aswan. A one-way ticket to Luxor from Cairo costs E£419 and there are frequent daily departures. There are also daily flights from Luxor to Aswan (E£190 one way) and three flights per week to Sharm el-Sheikh (E£415 one way). In the high season, there are several flights a day to Abu Simbel (E£832 return) via Aswan and one flight a week to Hurghada (E£190 one way).

Bus

The bus station is behind Luxor Temple on Sharia al-Karnak (the garage on Sharia Television is not an official pick-up point).

From Luxor, there is only one daily departure to Cairo and it leaves at 7 pm (E£50.25; 10 to 11 hours). Seven buses leave for Aswan (E£6.50 to E£8; four to five hours) between 6.30 am to 2.30 pm but only the last one has air-con. Some of these are through-services from Qena and Hurghada, so there may not always be seats. The same buses go to Esna (E£2.50) and Edfu (E£4).

To Hurghada, the first bus is at about 6.30 am and costs E£12.25 (five hours). There is another at 10.30 am (E£14.25), a third at 2.30 pm (E£17.25), which may be full as it comes up from Aswan, and at 7 pm there's a deluxe service, costing E£20.25. All of the buses to Hurghada go on to Suez (E£30.25 to E£40.25).

There are 10 buses to Qena from 6 am to 7 pm that cost from E£3 to E£5, but you may not be allowed to take them because of the jittery police.

Three buses go to Kharga each week: Saturday, Monday and Wednesday at 8.30 am. Tickets cost E£22, but the buses do not use the new Armant-Kharga road and instead go via Asyut.

From time to time there is a 'direct' bus to Dahab on offer for E£80. However, some travellers have reported that 'direct' means going via Cairo on a nightmarish 24 odyssey. When tourism is up, some tourist companies offer direct air-con coaches that are more expensive but far more reliable. The tourist office will know if either has started again.

Train

The train station at Luxor has a post office (which has express mail service, card phones, left-luggage, telex and telegraph facilities) and an often-closed tourist information office.

If you want a sleeper to Cairo, the only option is the wagons-lit train (see the Getting Around chapter for details). Berths have to be booked two or three days in advance. The ticket window (☎ 372 015) for these is open only between 9 am and 2 pm and 5 and 8 pm and the fare is E£314.35 one way. The train leaves Luxor at about 8.30 pm and reaches Cairo at 6.30 am. There is no student discount.

Otherwise there are only two other Cairo trains that foreigners are allowed to take. One departs at 8.15 am with 1st and 2nd class fares of E£51/28, while the other departs at 11.30 pm and its fares are E£51/31. The 8.15 am train stops at Balyana if you want to go Abydos. Student discounts are available on both these services.

First and 2nd class tickets to Aswan (four hours) cost E£20/12 on the 6 am train and E£22/14 on the 5.15 pm service. Heading in the other direction, fares to Minya are E£34/21 on the 8.15 am train and E£37/27 more for the 11.30 pm train.

There is a train to Kharga every Thursday at 7 am, 3rd class only, and it has no air-con and is supposed to take seven hours but reportedly can take up to 10. Tickets cost E£9.80 (E£4.90 for students).

For tickets, the 3rd class window is on your left when facing the tracks; other tickets are sold at the windows on the right.

Service Taxi

The service taxi station is on a street off Sharia al-Karnak, a couple of blocks inland from the Luxor Museum. Regular destinations include Aswan (E£8; 3½ hours), Esna (E£2; 45 minutes), Edfu (E£4; two hours),

Kom Ombo (E£8; 2½ hours) and Qena (E£2).

The drivers are always ready to bargain for special trips down the Nile to Aswan, stopping at the sights on the way – reckon on about E£100 for the car. Keep in mind that you may have to travel in a convoy. The times are listed below and you should arrive at the service taxi station about 30 minutes beforehand.

Those planning a trip from Luxor to the New Valley oasis of Kharga via the new direct road will have to go via Asyut until the police deem the road secure. Taxis are reluctant to undertake the trip and their current asking price is E£700 for the car (maximum seven people). You're better off suffering the long bus or train ride.

Convoys
No matter where you want to go these days, getting out of Luxor by road usually involves going in police convoy. Current convoy times are listed below but you should check with the tourist office before travelling:

To Hurghada 6 am   8 am 2 pm   5.30 pm
To Aswan   7 am   11 am 3 pm

Hurghada-bound vehicles congregate at the road behind the Pola Hotel about 30 minutes before the convoy time. Those heading south meet at the checkpoint just before the bridge.

Cruise Ship
For information on the 250 cruise boats that ply the Nile between Luxor and Aswan see the Getting Around chapter.

Felucca
You can no longer take a felucca from Luxor to Aswan. For more information see the boxed text 'Felucca Trips' on page 341.

GETTING AROUND
To/From the Airport
Luxor airport is 7km east of town and the official price for a taxi is E£10, although they'll usually ask for more. There are no buses to and from the airport into town.

Motorcycle
A few hotels have started renting out motorcycles for about E£40 to E£60 per day. If you are interested, hunt around a bit and check the condition of the bikes carefully.

Bicycle
Luxor is bursting with bicycle rental shops and almost all hotels have bikes too. Depending on the quality of the bike, how good business is and the determination of your bargaining, they can cost from E£4 to E£10 per day. You are often asked to leave your passport or student identification card.

Bicycles can also be rented on the West Bank, near the local ferry landing, but the choice of bicycle is better in the town itself and the prices on the West Bank are sometimes inflated.

It's sometimes possible to rent children's bicycles.

Hantour
For about E£6 per hour you can get around town by horse and carriage. Rates are, of course, subject to haggling, squabbling and, occasionally, screaming.

Felucca
There are, of course, a multitude of feluccas to take you on short trips around Luxor. They leave from various points all along the river. How much you pay depends on your bargaining skills, but you're looking at about E£15 to E£20 for a couple of hours sailing.

LUXOR

Nile Valley – Esna to Abu Simbel

Following the death of Alexander the Great, his huge empire was divided between his Macedonian generals. For 300 years the Greek-speaking Ptolemies ruled Egypt in the guise of pharaohs, respecting the traditions and religion of the Egyptians and setting an example to the Romans who succeeded them.

Their centre of power tied them to Alexandria and the coast but they also pushed their way south, extending Graeco-Roman power into Nubia (the land that straddles what is now the Egypt-Sudan border) through their politically sensible policy of assimilation rather than subjugation.

In Upper Egypt they raised temples honouring the local gods, building them in grand pharaonic style to appease the priesthood and earn the trust of the people. Somehow, though, these archaic imitations lost something in the translation; in many ways they were stilted, unimaginative edifices lacking the artistic brilliance that marked the truly Egyptian constructions they copied.

In southern Upper Egypt, south of Luxor, the major Graeco-Roman works were a series of riverside temples at Esna, Edfu, Kom Ombo and Philae, admirable as much for their location as their actual artistic or architectural merit.

Beyond Edfu the ribbon of cultivation on the east bank gives way to the Eastern Desert. At Silsila, 145km south of Luxor, the Nile passes through a gorge, once thought to mark a cataract. Beyond here there are early dynastic and New Kingdom ruins, including Elephantine and Abu Simbel; there's also the city of Aswan, the great High Dam and Lake Nasser, which mark the end of Egypt proper.

ESNA

The Graeco-Roman Temple of Khnum is the main attraction of Esna, a busy little farming town on the west bank of the Nile,

HIGHLIGHTS

- **Abu Simbel** Stand in awe of ancient and modern engineering in front of the Great Temple of Ramses II, arguably Egypt's single most stunning monument.

- **Nubian Museum** Get a small idea of what was lost when the High Dam was built.

- **Take a felucca trip** Spend a day or two seeing one of the world's greatest rivers up close as you drift through Upper Egypt.

- **Cruise Lake Nasser** A trip on the MS *Eugénie* doesn't come cheap but it's worth it.

- **The Temple of Horus at Edfu** Wander through one of the last great monuments to be built in pharaonic Egypt.

- **Daraw camel market** Watch as 2000 camels are bought and sold at the end of one of the world's historic camel caravans.

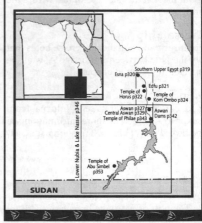

SOUTHERN UPPER EGYPT

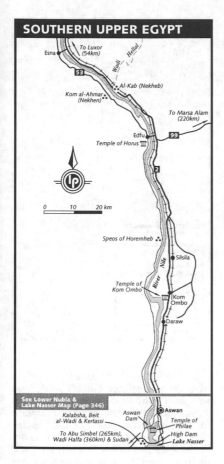

To Luxor (54km)
Esna
53
Al-Kab (Nekheb)
Kom al-Ahmar (Nekhen)
To Marsa Alam (220km)
Edfu
Temple of Horus
99
2
0   10   20 km
Speos of Horemheb
Silsila
Temple of Kom Ombo
Kom Ombo
Daraw
See Lower Nubia & Lake Nasser Map (Page 346)
Kalabsha, Beit al-Wadi & Kertassi
Aswan Dam
Aswan
Temple of Philae
To Abu Simbel (265km), Wadi Halfa (360km) & Sudan
High Dam
Lake Nasser
River Nile

54km south of Luxor. Wandering around the town's dusty streets it's hard to believe that only 100 years ago, Esna was the den of iniquity where Flaubert encountered the famous erotic dancer Kuchuk Hanem and forced her to dance The Bee – a striptease where the dancer removes her clothes to release a fictitious trapped bee. Nowadays there's not much happening apart from the usual relentless hassle of the bazaar touts.

The post office and a branch of the Bank of Alexandria are on the street that leads to the Nile from the canal. On Saturday, there's an animal market here too. The tourist police are in the bazaar near the temple.

Temple of Khnum

All that actually remains of the temple is the well-preserved Great Hypostyle Hall built during the reign of the Roman emperor Claudius. This sits rather incongruously in its huge excavation pit among the houses and narrow alleyways in the middle of town.

Dedicated to Khnum, the ram-headed creator-god who fashioned humankind on his potter's wheel using Nile clay, the temple was begun by Ptolemy VI and built over the ruins of earlier temples. The hall, as it stands today, was built later; it was excavated from the silt that had accumulated through centuries of annual Nile floods and is about 9m below the modern street level.

The intact roof of the hall is supported by 24 columns decorated with a series of texts recording hymns to Khnum and relating the annual sacred festivals of Esna. The texts also refer to other temples in the area and one from the same era has been excavated at Kom Mer, 12km south of Esna. The west wall of the Roman-built hall is also the only remaining part of the original Ptolemaic temple and features reliefs of Ptolemy VI, Philometor and Euergetes II.

The ticket booth is on the river itself, about 1km upriver from the main bridge across the Nile. You buy your ticket and follow the tourist bazaar through to the temple. It's open from 6 am to 5.30 pm (an hour longer in summer), and admission costs E£8, or E£4 for students.

Places to Stay & Eat

About 800m south of the temple and then 100m inland, via another covered bazaar, is Esna's only accommodation option, the basic *Hotel Haramein*. But as Esna is an easy day's trip from Luxor, there is no need to stay here.

There are a few of the usual food stands around for a cheap snack, although you should watch out for the odd rip-off in the small tourist bazaar. Basic food and drinks are available at the service taxi station, and there's a *coffeehouse* that's good for some small talk with the locals along the canal.

Getting There & Away

Trains are a pain, because the station is on the east bank of the Nile. However, there are frequent buses and service taxis from Luxor. The bus stops a lot on the way making a service taxi (sometimes in the form of a microbus) the best option. These take 45 minutes from Luxor and cost E£2. In Esna, the service taxi station is next to the canal, however, arrivals are generally dropped on the main thoroughfare into town along which *hantour* (horse and carriage) drivers congregate in the hope of picking up a fare. They ask E£2 each way for the five to 10 minute ride to the temple.

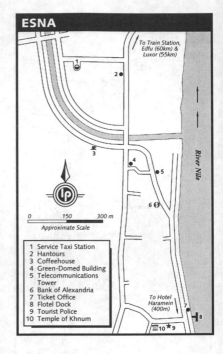

ESNA

To Train Station, Edfu (60km) & Luxor (55km)

River Nile

0   150   300 m
Approximate Scale

To Hotel Haramein (400km)

1 Service Taxi Station
2 Hantours
3 Coffeehouse
4 Green-Domed Building
5 Telecommunications Tower
6 Bank of Alexandria
7 Ticket Office
8 Flotel Dock
9 Tourist Police
10 Temple of Khnum

Should you prefer to walk to the temple from the service taxi drop-off point, head straight (south) down the main road, cross a small bridge over the canal and continue for 50m until you come to a small green-domed building on your left. Turn left after the building and follow this lane for 100m until you get to a telecommunications tower. Turn right and continue along this road (which eventually meets up with the Nile) for about 800m. You'll see the ticket office next to the mooring for the Nile cruisers. The temple is 50m inland, up through the tourist bazaar.

AL-KAB & KOM AL-AHMAR

Between Esna and Edfu are the scattered ruins of two settlements dating from predynastic to late dynastic times. The earliest remains in the area, now known as Al-Kab, on the east bank of the Nile, are about 6000

Built in the 3rd century AD, the Temple of Philae near Aswan is a majestic sight.

Up to 2000 camels are sold in the Bedouin camel market at Daraw on a busy Sunday.

Coffee anyone? A friendly stallholder in Edfu satisfies that craving for caffeine.

CHRIS MELLOR

Four statues of Ramses II stand like sentinels at the huge Abu Simbel temple.

TM FLOWER

A seated statue of Ramses II (2nd from right) with three gods in the Abu Simbel complex.

A 21m-high tribute to the great king himself, Ramses II, at Abu Simbel.

Ptolemies and Romans contributed to the spectacular relief carvings at the Temple of Kom Ombo.

Statues at Wadi as-Subua, near Lake Nasser.

Horus statue at the Temple of Horus in Edfu.

years old. Much of what is visible, however, dates from later than that, when the ancient settlement of Nekheb was capital of the *nome*. The town of Nekheb was enclosed by massive mud-brick walls and still contains the remains of a Roman temple, a sacred lake and cemeteries, and the ruins of the main Temple of Nekhbet with its several pylons, hypostyle hall and *mammisi* (birth house). The temple was probably begun before 2700 BC but was enlarged considerably by numerous pharaohs of the 18th to 30th dynasties including Tuthmosis III, Amenophis II and the Ramessids.

A few kilometres east of the town enclosure are three desert temples. At the entrance to Wadi Hellal is the rock-hewn Ptolemaic Sanctuary of Sheshmetet. To the south-east of that is a chapel built during the reign of Ramses II, restored under the Ptolemies and dedicated to a number of deities. About 3.5km from Nekheb is the Temple of Hathor and Nekhbet, built by Tuthmosis IV and Amenophis III. North of Nekheb are a number of rock-cut tombs with fine reliefs.

On the opposite side of the river, the remains of the ancient town of Nekhen, which predated Nekheb as capital of the nome, stretch for about 3km along the edge of the desert. Now known as Kom al-Ahmar (the Red Mound), the area features the ruins of Predynastic settlements and cemeteries and in the nearby wadis there are several Middle and New Kingdom tombs. The local god was Nekheny, a falcon with two long plumes on his head, who was later associated with Horus.

Al-Kab and Kom al-Ahmar are 26km south of Esna, and north of Edfu.

EDFU

The largest and most completely preserved pharaonic, albeit Greek-built, temple in Egypt is the extraordinary Temple of Horus at Edfu. One of the last great Egyptian attempts at monument building on a grand scale, the structure dominates this west bank riverside town, 53km south of Esna. The town and temple were established on a

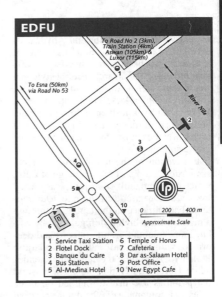

EDFU

To Road No 2 (3km),
Train Station (4km),
Aswan (105km) &
Luxor (115km)

To Esna (50km)
via Road No 53

River Nile

0   200   400 m
Approximate Scale

1	Service Taxi Station	6	Temple of Horus
2	Flotel Dock	7	Cafeteria
3	Banque du Caire	8	Dar as-Salaam Hotel
4	Bus Station	9	Post Office
5	Al-Medina Hotel	10	New Egypt Cafe

rise above the broad river valley around them, and so escaped the annual Nile inundation that contributed to the ruin of so many other buildings of antiquity.

Edfu, a sugar and pottery centre, is also a very friendly place.

Just before you get to the temple you cross a square that appears to be the nerve centre of town. Approaching the square, the post office is along the first street off to the left. The bus station is about 100m along the street to the right. The service taxi station is at the entrance to town, next to the bridge over the Nile.

Temple of Horus

Construction of this huge complex began under Ptolemy III Euergetes I in 237 BC and was completed nearly 200 years later during the reign of Ptolemy XIII (the father of Cleopatra) in the 1st century BC. In conception and design it follows the traditions of authentic pharaonic architecture, with the same general plan, scale and ornamentation, right down to the Egyptian attire worn by the Greek kings depicted in the temple's reliefs. Though it is much newer than the temples of Karnak, Luxor and Abydos, its excellent state of preservation fills in a lot of historical gaps because it is, in effect, a 2000 year old replica of an architectural style that was already archaic during Ptolemaic times.

Being a copy it lacks artistic spontaneity. Where the Greek influence does penetrate, however, it produces a strangely graceful effect, which is most obvious in the fine line of the columns.

Excavation of the temple from beneath sand, rubble and part of the village of Edfu, which had been built on its roof, was started by Auguste Mariette in the mid-19th century. The entrance to the temple is through a massive 36m-high pylon guarded by two huge and splendid granite falcons and decorated with colossal reliefs of pharaoh Ptolemy XIII pulling the hair of his enemies while Horus and Hathor look on. Beyond the pylon is a court surrounded on three sides by a colonnade of 32 columns covered in reliefs.

Before you enter the temple proper, through the 12 enormous columns of the first of two hypostyle halls, check out the areas on either side. On your left is the **Hall of Consecrations** where, according to the wall inscriptions, Horus poured sacred water on the king; on your right is the so-called **library**, which features a list of books and a relief of Seshat, the goddess of writing. On either side of the second hall are doorways leading into the narrow **Passage of Victory**, which runs between the temple and its massive protective enclosure walls.

Once through the magnificent **Great Hypostyle Hall** there are two **antechambers**, the first of which has a staircase of 242 steps leading up to the rooftop and a fantastic view of the Nile and surrounding fields. You may have to pay the guard a bit of baksheesh if you want to go up because the stairs are usually closed.

The second chamber, which is beautifully decorated with a variety of scenes, leads to the **Sanctuary of Horus**, where the live falcon, the god and his wife reigned and received offerings. Around the sanctuary,

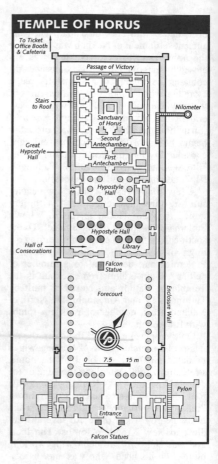

TEMPLE OF HORUS

To Ticket Office Booth & Cafeteria

Passage of Victory

Stairs to Roof

Nilometer

Sanctuary of Horus

Second Antechamber

Great Hypostyle Hall

First Antechamber

Hypostyle Hall

Hypostyle Hall

Hall of Consecrations

Library

Falcon Statue

Forecourt

Enclosure Wall

0   7.5   15 m

Pylon

Entrance

Falcon Statues

there are a number of smaller chambers with fine reliefs and, off the Passage of Victory, a staircase leads down and passes under the outer wall of the temple to a Nilometer.

The Temple of Horus is open from 7 am to 4 pm in winter and 6 am to 6 pm in summer. Admission is E£20, or E£10 for students.

Places to Stay & Eat

Al-Medina Hotel (☎ 701 326) in the centre of town costs E£10/15 a night for simple rooms without/with bathroom. Though a very basic hotel, several travellers have sung its praises. Another option is *Dar as-Salaam Hotel*, further down the road towards the temple. It has similar rooms, but charges E£15 for single occupancy. The hot water is unreliable, but the rooms have fans and are OK. The other hotels dotted around town aren't recommended.

Apart from the expensive cafeteria in the temple grounds, there are a few kebab places on the square, as well as *New Egypt* cafe opposite the post office which serves watery soup, tasty beans and spinach and roast chicken. At all these eateries you should ask how much dishes are first.

Getting There & Away

Trains, buses and service taxis stop frequently in Edfu. However, the train station is on the east bank of the Nile, about 4km from town. Buses travelling between Luxor and Aswan sometimes only stop on this side too, which can be a real pain. Leaving is not so bad, as you can at least take a bus from the station in town. The fare is E£4 to Luxor or E£2.50 to Aswan.

Service taxis are again the best option. From Esna, the trip takes about an hour and costs E£2, direct taxis from Luxor (E£5) take about two hours, and from Aswan (E£3.50) they take 1½ hours. They will drop you at the station just over the bridge on the west bank; from here you can get a covered pick-up to the temple.

If you've had enough of the Nile, tombs and temples, you can exit east and head straight for Marsa Alam on the Red Sea. The daily bus servicing this route originates in Aswan and passes Edfu at about 8 to 8.30 am. However, it does not usually stop at the bus station in town. Instead, it pulls up for 30 minutes at a cafe on the east bank of the river at the start of the desert road. It takes three hours to Marsa Alam and costs E£7.

Most feluccas end their journey at Edfu on their way north from Aswan. Very patient travellers who prefer to travel against the current can get a felucca heading south.

SILSILA

At Silsila, about 42km south of Edfu, the Nile narrows considerably to pass between steep sandstone cliffs which are cluttered with ancient rock stelae and graffiti. Known in pharaonic times as Khenu (Place of Rowing), the gorge also marks the change from limestone to sandstone in the bedrock of Egypt. The local Silsila quarries were worked by thousands of men throughout the New Kingdom and Graeco-Roman periods to provide the sandstone used in temple building.

On the west bank of the river is the Speos of Horemheb, a rock-hewn chapel dedicated to pharaoh Horemheb and seven deities, including the local god Sobek.

KOM OMBO

The fertile, irrigated sugar cane and corn fields around Kom Ombo, 65km south of Edfu, support not only the original community of fellaheen but also a large population of Nubians displaced from their own lands by the creation of Lake Nasser. It's a pleasant little place easily accessible en route between Aswan and Luxor. If you're not stopping here on a felucca trip it's possibly best visited on a day trip from Aswan, which is 40km to the south.

In ancient times Kom Ombo was strategic as a trading town on the great caravan route from Nubia, and was the meeting place of the routes from the gold mines of the Eastern Desert and the Red Sea. During the Ptolemaic period it served as the capital of the Ombite *nome*, and elephants were brought up from Africa to Kom Ombo to train with the armies to defend the region. The main attraction these days, however, is the unique riverside Temple of Kom Ombo, about 4km from the centre of town.

Temple of Kom Ombo

The Temple of Kom Ombo or, more precisely, the dual Temple of Sobek and Haroeris, stands on a promontory at a bend in the Nile, where in ancient times sacred crocodiles basked in the sun on the riverbank. Although substantially ruined by the changing tides of the river and later by

TEMPLE OF KOM OMBO

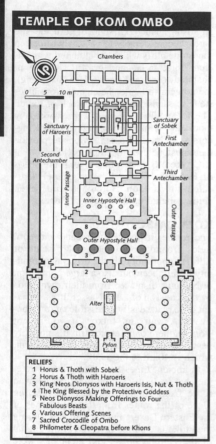

Chambers

0   5   10 m

Sanctuary of Haroeris

Sanctuary of Sobek

First Antechamber

Second Antechamber

Third Antechamber

Inner Passage

Inner Hypostyle Hall

7

8   6

Outer Hypostyle Hall

3   4   5

2   1

Court

Alter

Outer Passage

Pylon

RELIEFS
1 Horus & Thoth with Sobek
2 Horus & Thoth with Haroeris
3 King Neos Dionysos with Haroeris Isis, Nut & Thoth
4 The King Blessed by the Protective Goddess
5 Neos Dionysos Making Offerings to Four Fabulous Beasts
6 Various Offering Scenes
7 Sacred Crocodile of Ombo
8 Philometer & Cleopatra before Khons

headed sky-god; the right half was dedicated to Sobek, the local crocodile-headed god, who was also worshipped in Al-Fayoum.

The Graeco-Roman structure faces the Nile. The entrance pylon, the outer enclosure wall and part of the court, all built by Augustus after 30 BC, have been either mostly destroyed by pilfering stonemasons or eroded by the river. The temple proper was actually begun by Ptolemy VI Philometor in the early 2nd century BC; Ptolemy XIII (also known as Neos Dionysos) built the outer and inner hypostyle halls; and subsequent Ptolemies and Romans contributed to the relief decoration.

South of the main temple is the **Roman Chapel of Hathor**, dedicated to the wife of Horus, which is used to store a collection of mummified crocodiles dug up from a nearby sacred animal cemetery. Four of the collection are on display.

The temple is open from 8 am to 4 pm; admission costs E£10 (E£5 for students).

Places to Stay & Eat

Cleopatra Hotel (☎ 500 325) next to the local pick-up station is the best option in town. It's basic but quite adequate with singles/doubles at E£12.50/24 and triples/quads at E£27/32. The rooms have fans and the shared facilities are spotless. There's hot water, and towels are provided; breakfast is not.

The only alternative is the rather grimy *Radwan Hotel* (☎ 501 827) just south of the service taxi station on the main road. A bed costs E£4, but you can smell the bathrooms from outside the front door.

Al-Noba Restaurant on the main road a little way north of the service taxi station is the only sit-down eatery in this part of town. It's cheap and relatively clean, and serves chicken, rice and vegetables. Otherwise, there are the usual ta'amiyya and kebab stands.

Snacks can be had at one of the cafeterias situated on the bank of the Nile between the temple and the boat landing. Of the two, *Cafeteria Venus* has the best atmosphere, serving burgers, kofta and beer in a pleasant garden setting.

builders who used many of its stones for new buildings, Kom Ombo is, nevertheless, a stunning sight.

It is also unusual in that, architecturally, everything is doubled and perfectly symmetrical along the main axis of the temple. There are twin entrances, twin courts, twin colonnades, twin hypostyle halls, twin sanctuaries and, in keeping with the dual nature of the temple, there was probably a twin priesthood.

The left side of the temple was dedicated to Haroeris, or Horus the Elder, the falcon-

Getting There & Away

A service taxi or minibus from Aswan to the town of Kom Ombo takes between 45 minutes and one hour, and costs E£1.50. Trains and buses also frequently stop in the town; trains are slower, and both trains and buses are much less frequent than service taxis.

As you approach Kom Ombo from Aswan, you can ask the driver to drop you off at the road leading to the temple – look for the sign. From here it's about a 2km walk or hitch. If you are heading back to Aswan, it shouldn't be hard to get a lift or flag down a passing service taxi or microbus once on the highway.

Otherwise, to get to the temple from Kom Ombo, take a covered pick-up (25pt) to the boat landing on the Nile about 800m north of the temple, then walk the remainder of the way. Pick-ups to the boat landing leave from opposite Cleopatra Hotel.

A private taxi between the town and temple should cost about E£7 return. Feluccas travelling between Aswan and Luxor often stop at the temple itself.

Should you want to head to the Red Sea from here, the daily bus from Aswan to Marsa Alam calls in at about 7 am. Tickets are E£12.

DARAW

The main reason to stop in this otherwise unremarkable village 8km south of Kom Ombo is to see its famous camel market (Souq al-Gamaal). Most of the camels are brought up in caravans from Sudan along the 40 Days Road to just north of Abu Simbel, from where they're trucked to Daraw. Others walk to the market in smaller groups, entering Egypt at Wadi al-Alagi and making their way through the Eastern Desert.

Although camels are sold here each day of the week, Sunday is the day when the main group of camels (sometimes as many as 2000) that have come up from Abu Simbel are put on the market.

Wandering around among the hobbled camels and giving some order to the chaos of men yelling as they go about the buying and selling of the animals is the 'sheikh' of the

Taking Camels to Market

For hundreds of years camels from Sudan have been brought to Egypt in large caravans along the Darb al-Arba'een (the 40 Days Road), the treacherous desert route thought to have been named for the number of days it took for the journey from Sudan's Darfur province to southern Egypt.

In the centuries following their introduction into the region – thought to have been by the Persians in the 6th century BC – the camels brought slaves, ostrich feathers, precious stones, animal skins and other goods to Egypt, where they were used by the country's pharaonic overlords or, in later times, distributed to the great empires in Greece, Persia, Rome and Europe. But by the 18th and 19th centuries the gradual introduction of steamers and trains in Egypt and Sudan meant that camels were no longer the most efficient way to get goods from south to north. The establishment of airlinks between the two countries this century seemed to seal the fate of the caravans as relics of a bygone age.

But the camels have continued to come. Now, however, they themselves are the cargo. Some are used for agricultural work, others are exported to other Middle Eastern countries, but many – if not most – are destined for the dinner tables of poor Egyptians (yes, that cheap kebab does taste a bit strange ...).

Once they get to Daraw they spend two days in quarantine, where they are inoculated against a number of diseases. After they have been sold, most go on to the camel market in Birqash, about 35km north-west of Cairo, from where they are either shipped on to other countries in the region or are sent to the slaughter house.

market, Badawi, a character born in 1925. He speaks English, Greek and a smattering of other languages and loves to relate stories about how he worked for (and sometimes against) the British during their occupation of

Egypt earlier this century. He walks around the market with a long stick covered in what looks suspiciously like donkey fur and will give you a self-addressed envelope to send back the photos he insists you take of him.

Getting There & Away

The service taxis and minibuses running between Aswan and Kom Ombo stop in Daraw (if passengers indicate they want to get off). The fare is E£1.50 – the same as for the entire stretch. The market is 2km off the east side of the main road.

Aswan

Over the centuries Aswan, Egypt's southernmost city, has been a garrison town and frontier city, the gateway to Africa and the now inundated land of Nubia, a prosperous marketplace at the crossroads of the ancient caravan routes and, more recently, a popular winter resort.

In ancient times the area was known as Sunt; the Ptolemaic town of Syene stood to the south-west of the present city; and the Copts called the place Souan, which means 'trade', from which the Arabic 'Aswan' is derived.

The main town and temple area of Sunt was actually on the southern end of the island called Yebu (meaning both 'elephant' and 'ivory'), which the Greeks later renamed Elephantine Island. A natural fortress protected by the turbulent river, Aswan was then capital of the first Upper Egyptian nome and a base for military expeditions into Nubia, Sudan and Ethiopia. From those foreign parts, right up into Islamic times, the city was visited by the great caravans of camels and elephants laden with slaves, gold, ivory, spices, cloth and other exotic wares.

Pharaonic and Ptolemaic leaders took their turn through history to guard the southern reaches of Egypt from the customary routes of invasion; their fleets patrolled the river as far as the Second Nile Cataract at Wadi Halfa and their troops penetrated several hundred kilometres into Sudan. Aswan

was also, to a certain extent, the Siberia of the Roman Empire, one of those far-flung garrisons where troublesome generals were sent to protect the interests of the emperor while staying out of the Forum.

The modern town of Aswan, which is the perfect place for a break from the rigours of travelling in Egypt, lies on the east bank of the Nile opposite Elephantine Island. The town is at the northern end of the First Nile Cataract, one of six rocky outcrops (the remaining five are all in Sudan) situated between Aswan and Khartoum.

Although its ancient temples and ruins are not as outstanding as others in the country, Aswan does have a few things to offer the traveller, one of which is the town's superb location on the river. The Nile is magically beautiful here as it flows down from the dams and around the giant granite boulders and palm-studded islands that protrude from the cascading rapids of the First Nile Cataract. The Corniche is one of the most attractive of the country's Nileside boulevards.

So, while you can visit pharaonic, Graeco-Roman, Coptic, Islamic and modern monuments, a good museum, superb botanical gardens, the massive High Dam, Lake Nasser and one of the most fascinating souqs outside Cairo, by far the best thing to do in Aswan is sit by the Nile and watch the feluccas gliding by at sunset.

The best time to visit Aswan is in winter, when the days are warm and dry, with an average temperature of about 26°C. In summer, the temperatures are around 38°C to 45°C and it's too hot to do anything other than sit by a fan and swat flies or flop into a swimming pool.

ORIENTATION

It's quite easy to find your way around Aswan because there are only three main avenues and most of the city is along the Nile or parallel to it. The train station is at the northern end of town, only three blocks east of the river and its boulevard, the Corniche el-Nil.

The street running from north to south in front of the train station is Sharia as-Souq

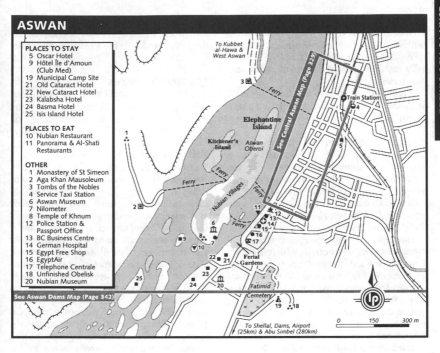

ASWAN

PLACES TO STAY
5 Oscar Hotel
9 Hôtel Île d'Amoun
   (Club Med)
19 Municipal Camp Site
21 Old Cataract Hotel
22 New Cataract Hotel
23 Kalabsha Hotel
24 Basma Hotel
25 Isis Island Hotel

PLACES TO EAT
10 Nubian Restaurant
11 Panorama & Al-Shati
   Restaurants

OTHER
1 Monastery of St Simeon
2 Aga Khan Mausoleum
3 Tombs of the Nobles
4 Service Taxi Station
6 Aswan Museum
7 Nilometer
8 Temple of Khnum
12 Police Station &
   Passport Office
13 BC Business Centre
14 German Hospital
15 Egypt Free Shop
16 EgyptAir
17 Telephone Centrale
18 Unfinished Obelisk
20 Nubian Museum

See Aswan Dams Map (Page 342)

To Kubbet
al-Hawa &
West Aswan

Elephantine
Island

Kitchener's
Island   Aswan
            Oberoi

Train Station

See Central Aswan Map (Page 325)

Nubian Villages

Ferial
Gardens

Fatimid
Cemetery

To Shellal, Dams, Airport
(25km) & Abu Simbel (280km)

0   150   300 m

(also occasionally signposted as Sharia Saad Zaghloul), Aswan's splendid market street, where the souqs overflow with colourful, tempting and aromatic wares. Running parallel to it is Sharia Abtal at-Tahrir where you'll find the Youth Hostel and a few hotels. Most of Aswan's government buildings, banks, travel agencies, restaurants and top-end hotels are on the Corniche, and from there you can see the rock tombs on the west bank, as well as Elephantine Island.

INFORMATION
Visa Extensions
The passport office is on the Corniche and is open Saturday to Thursday from 8.30 am to 1 pm and 6 to 8 pm.

Tourist Offices
There are two tourist offices; one (☎ 312 811) is next to the train station and the other

(☎ 323 297) is on a side street, one block in from the Corniche. Shukri Saad, who can usually be found at the office next to the station, is one of the most helpful tourist officials in Egypt. He and his staff will assist in booking accommodation and can give you official prices for taxis and felucca trips – although lower prices are usually obtainable with some haggling.

Both offices are open Saturday to Thursday from 8.30 am to 2 pm and again from 6 to 8 pm; Friday opening hours are from 10 am to 2 pm and 6 to 8 pm.

Money
The main banks have their branches on the Corniche. Banque Masr and the Banque du Caire will issue cash advances on Visa and MasterCard. There is also an ATM beside the Banque du Caire (although it doesn't always work). The Bank of Alexandria accepts

Eurocheques. Banque Masr also has a foreign-exchange booth (open daily from 8 am to 3 pm and 5 to 8 pm) next to its main building.

An American Express office (☎ 322 909) is in the Old Cataract Hotel but it only offers travel services.

Thomas Cook (☎ 304 011, fax 306 209) is on the Corniche and is open daily from 9 am to 5 pm.

Post & Communications

The GPO is also on the Corniche, next to the municipal swimming pool. However, poste restante must be collected from the smaller post office on the corner of sharias Abtal at-Tahrir and Salah ad-Din (go around the back, opposite the Victoria Hotel). Both are open daily, except Friday, from 8 am to 2 pm.

International telephone calls can be made from the telephone centrale, which is on the Corniche towards the southern end of town, just past the EgyptAir office. There are card phones here (and usually stocks of cards). The office is open daily from 8 am to 10 pm. In the same office is a post office stamp counter that is occasionally open, and telexes and faxes can also be sent from here.

Back up the road, next to Photo Sabri, is the BC Business Centre, from where you can also send faxes. There are also a couple of the orange card phones at the train station.

Email & Internet Access

There are two places where you can send and receive email in Aswan. The governorate has five computers that it currently lets you use for free between 9 am and 1.30 pm. The computers can be found at the governorate's Information & Decision Support Center – it's hard to miss, just look for the big sign saying 'Internet' beside the cinema. Also, the Rosewan Hotel has recently started its own cybercafe. As in Luxor, the connection is through Cairo so you're paying for a long-distance call. There is a flat rate of E£1.50 per minute.

Bookshops

Only the top-end hotels such as the New Cataract have bookshops selling foreign-language material. If you're just after international newspapers and magazines, try the newsstand near the Philae Hotel on the Corniche.

Medical Services

The German Hospital (☎ 317 176) has staff who speak foreign languages and is the place to go if you get ill in Aswan. It's on the Corniche next to the Egypt Free shop.

THE TOWN & EAST BANK

The exotic atmosphere of Aswan's back-street souqs is definitely one of the highlights of the city. Although the fabulous caravans no longer pass this way, the colour and activity of these markets and stalls recall those romantic times. Just wander through the small, narrow alleyways and you'll see, hear, smell and, if you want, taste life as it has been for many centuries in these parts. (There are too many of these small passageways to show on our map.)

Unfortunately, Sharia as-Souq itself is very much a tourist market nowadays. Nubian baskets, T-shirts, perfume, spices, beaded *galabiyyas* and grotesquely stuffed crocodiles and desert creatures are all for sale. Although the traders here are not as persistent as those in Luxor they can still be irritating.

Fresh and live produce, such as fruit and vegetables and chickens or pigeons, are traded in the street running between the Aswan Palace and Happi hotels.

Walking along the Corniche and watching the sun set over the desert across on the far side of the Nile is another favourite pass-time in Aswan. If you want to sit down to watch the sun work its magic, the Ferial Gardens at the southern end of the Corniche are a peaceful place and best of all entrance is free.

Nubian Museum

The long awaited Nubian Museum finally opened its doors in November 1997. Showcasing the history, art and culture of Nubia from prehistoric times down to the present, it is a very small and belated thanks to the

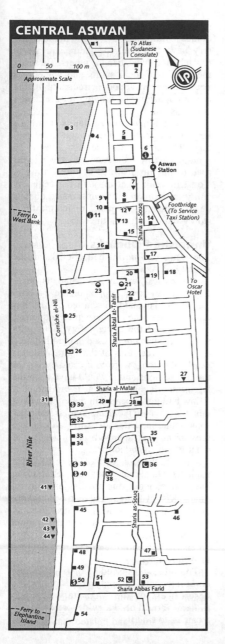

CENTRAL ASWAN

PLACES TO STAY
1 New Abu Simbel Hotel
2 Mena Hotel
5 Rosewan & As-Saffa Hotels
8 Marwa Hotel
10 Youth Hostel
14 Noorhan Hotel
15 Al-Amin Hotel
16 Ramses Hotel
18 Bob Marley Hotel
19 New Brethren Hotel
20 Cleopatra Hotel
22 Nubian Oasis Hotel
24 Abu Simbel Hotel
28 Aswan Palace Hotel
29 Happi Hotel
31 Isis Hotel
33 Al-Salam Hotel
34 Hathor Hotel
37 Victoria Hotel
45 Horus Hotel
46 Keylany Hotel
47 Hotel Orabi
48 Memnon Hotel
49 Philae Hotel
51 Al-Amir Hotel
53 Abu Shelib Hotel

PLACES TO EAT
7 Restaurant Derwash
9 Al-Dar Restaurant
12 An-Nasr
13 Esraa (Kofta Place)
17 Medina Restaurant
27 Al-Masry Restaurant
35 Al-Sayyida Nefissa Restaurant
41 Saladin Restaurant
42 Aswan Moon Restaurant
43 Emy Restaurant
44 Monalisa Restaurant

OTHER
3 Governorate Building
4 Governorate Internet Centre
6 Tourist Office
11 Tourist Office & Nile Valley Navigation Office
21 Bus Station
23 Share Taxi Stand
25 Cultural Centre
26 GPO
30 Banque Masr
32 Card Phones
36 Mosque
38 Post Office (Poste Restante)
39 Banque du Caire
40 Bank of Alexandria
50 Banque du Caire
52 Mosque
54 Thomas Cook

sacrifice made by the Nubian people for the Aswan Dam. The exhibits are beautifully displayed and clearly written explanations take you from 4500 BC through to the present day.

Among the highlights are the 6000 year old painted pottery bowls, a stunning quartzite statue of a 25th dynasty Kushite priest of Amun, and a fascinating display tracing the development of irrigation along the Nile, from the earliest attempts to control the flow of the river, right up to the building of the Aswan Dam.

All this is housed in a well-designed modern building, loosely based on traditional Nubian architecture. In the museum garden there is a reconstructed Nubian house (which you can't enter, unfortunately) and a small newly-built 'cave' where fragments of prehistoric rock paintings have been placed. The site also incorporates an 11th century Fatimid tomb.

The museum entrance is opposite the Basma Hotel, about a 10 minute walk from the EgyptAir office. It is open from 9 am to 1 pm and then from 5 pm to 9 pm. Entrance costs E£20, E£10 for students.

Fatimid Cemetery

Behind the Nubian Museum, to the left of the road to the airport, is a vast cemetery with a collection of low mud-brick buildings with domed roofs. Many of the graves here are modern but some of the mausoleums clustered towards the back of the cemetery date from the 9th century. Although in very bad shape, they show the progression of tomb architecture from simple open enclosures to complex domes built on cubes. In a feature unique to southern Egypt, some of the domes are built on a drum with corners sticking out like horns. Many of the tombs had marble inscriptions attached to them until the late 19th century, when a freak rainstorm made them fall away. In a sloppy attempt to preserve them they were collected and taken to Cairo without any record of which tomb they were originally attached to, thus losing forever the actual dates of their construction and the

names of their inhabitants. A few of the domes towards the outer edges of the cemetery have flags outside them, and are in much better shape than the others. These are the graves of local saints and sometimes you can see local people circumambulating the sarcophagus and praying for the saint's intercession.

The municipality of Aswan is building a large green metal fence around the cemetery. The main entrance is a five to 10 minute walk from the roundabout where the road to the airport forks off the Corniche. You can walk right through the cemetery and join the road to the unfinished obelisk on the other side – just aim for the three storey building facing the back.

Unfinished Obelisks

There are two unfinished obelisks in the vicinity of Aswan.

The closest, and most visited, is about 1.5km from town, opposite the Fatimid Cemetery. This huge discarded obelisk lies on the edge of the northern granite quarries that supplied the ancient Egyptians with most of the hard stone used in pyramids and temples. Three sides of the shaft, which is nearly 42m long, were completed except for the inscriptions and it would have been the largest single piece of stone ever handled if a flaw had not appeared in the granite. So it lies there, where the disappointed stonemasons abandoned it, still partly attached to the parent rock and with no indication of what it was intended for.

Entry to the site costs E£20, or E£10 for students. No service taxis run past the site, but you can get one to the junction on Sharia Kisr al-Haggar and then walk (about 10 minutes). Private taxis will charge about E£2. You can also walk through the Fatimid Cemetery. Most people simply visit the obelisk at the end of an organised day trip to Abu Simbel.

The other unfinished obelisk – this time complete with hieroglyphics – is in the desert west of the Monastery of Saint Simeon. You'll need a guide, preferably on a camel, to find it.

THE RIVER
Feluccas & Ferries

As you will quickly discover if you spend any time near the Nile, feluccas are the traditional canvas-sailed boats of the Nile. The river is at its most picturesque in Aswan and no visit would be complete without at least an hour spent sailing around the islands in one of these graceful little boats. One of the most scenic sections of the river is around the southern end of Elephantine Island. Here you'll probably encounter a troop of young boys furiously hand-paddling their minuscule self-made boats in pursuit of larger vessels in order to score some baksheesh from passers-by. One enterprising 10 year old sings in whichever language the tourists in the nearest boat speak, belting out everything from Italian arias to *Three Blind Mice*.

In case you've miraculously avoided them, felucca touts hang out on the Corniche. The prices for boats are negotiable and vary widely according to the effectiveness of your bargaining and the time of year – if they're having a bad season, they may be willing to take people out for less than they would normally find acceptable. The best strategy is to first show that you are interested and then begin to walk away. The official government price for hiring a felucca capable of seating one to eight people is E£15 per hour, but with a bit of bargaining you should be able to hire a boat for five or six hours for a reasonable price. A shorter three or four hour tour costs about E£35 to E£45. A three hour trip down to Sehel Island is about E£35.

If you simply want to get from A to B, the best deal in town is the public ferry. For only 25pt, you can get to Elephantine Island, either the landing opposite the telephone centrale or the one across from Thomas Cook. There is another ferry that leaves from a landing in front of the governorate building and takes you over to the Tombs of the Nobles on the west bank for 50pt. When the river is low it leaves from in front of the Abu Simbel Hotel. Note that women sit up front, men towards the back.

To get to Kitchener's Island you can either incorporate it into a felucca tour or you can take the northernmost ferry to Elephantine and walk through the edge of the village to the other side of the island. You'll find a couple of little feluccas at the edge of the lush palm gardens overlooking the entrance to Kitchener's Island. From here you can also go to the landing for St Simeon monastery on the west bank. You'll have to bargain hard, though; you're a captive audience and will be unlikely to get the captain down to less than E£4 or E£5 for a one way trip.

For details on taking a three day sail down the Nile to Edfu see the boxed text 'Felucca Trips' on page 340.

Elephantine Island

Perhaps elephants once roamed the banks of the Nile here. They certainly passed through in the great caravans or with various armies. But it is more likely that Aswan's longest inhabited area was named Yebu after the numerous giant grey granite boulders, in the river around the island, which resemble a herd of elephants bathing.

As well as being Egypt's frontier town, where the island officials were known as 'Keepers of the Gate of the South', Elephantine produced most of the pharaohs of the 5th dynasty. It was also the centre of the cult of the ram-headed Khnum, creator of humankind and god of the cataracts who controlled the Nile's water level, and his companion goddesses Satis (his wife) and Anukis (his daughter).

Excavation of the island's ancient town, which began at the start of this century, is still being carried out by a German team, although most of the area is open to visitors and numbered plaques help you around the extensive ruins. These include a small 3rd dynasty step pyramid, a tiny chapel reconstructed from the Temple of Kalabsha, which is just south of the High Dam, and a temple devoted to Khnum. It's a great place to wander about in the late afternoon.

The inhabitants of the three colourful Nubian villages on the east side of Elephantine are friendly and the alleyways are worth exploring. You can also wander through the beautiful palm gardens that separate the two southern villages.

Taking up much of the northern end of the island, the deluxe and famously ugly Aswan Oberoi Hotel has its own private ferry and a 3m fence around it to keep the tourists in, and away from the local Nubians. Construction on an extension to the hotel on the island's northern tip has been stopped by a lawsuit, but the concrete shell looks set to remain for several years while the matter is fought out in the courts.

Aswan Museum At the south-eastern end of the island, overlooking the ruins of the original town and situated next to an attractive flower and spice garden, this modest, dusty little museum houses a collection of antiquities discovered in Aswan and Nubia. Most of the Nubian artifacts were found and rescued before the construction of the old Aswan Dam. The weapons, pottery, utensils, statues, encased mummies and sarcophagi date from predynastic to late Roman times and everything is labelled in Arabic and English. The sarcophagus and mummy of a sacred ram, the animal associated with Khnum, are in a room by themselves to the right of the main entrance, while four mummies can be seen in the left of the museum.

The building itself dates back to 1898 and was a rest house for Sir William Willcocks, the architect of the Aswan Dam. It has been a museum since 1912. The museum is open Sunday to Thursday from 8 am to 5 pm, 6 pm in summer. Admission is E£10 (E£5 for students). You'll probably be shepherded around the well-tended gardens, for some baksheesh of course.

Nilometer Heavenly portents and priestly prophecies aside, the only sure indication in ancient times of the likelihood of a bountiful harvest was that given by the Nilometer. Descending to the water's edge from beneath a sycamore tree near the museum, the shaft of the ancient Nilometer measured the height of the Nile. Although it dates from

pharaonic times, and bears inscriptions and cartouches from the reigns of Amenophis III and Psammetichus II, it was rebuilt by the Romans, and restored last century.

When the Nilometer recorded that the level of the river was high it would mean that the approaching annual flood would be heavy and therefore sufficient for the irrigation vital to a good harvest. It also affected the taxation system, for the higher the river, the better the crop season and the more prosperous the fellaheen and merchants – and therefore the higher the taxes.

You can enter the Nilometer from the river or down steps from near the Aswan Museum or just view it from a felucca on the water.

Kitchener's Island

One of the most delightful places in Aswan, this island to the west of Elephantine was given to Lord Horatio Kitchener in the 1890s when he was consul-general of Egypt and commander of the Egyptian army. Indulging his passion for beautiful flowers, Kitchener turned the entire island into a botanic garden, importing plants from the Far East, India and parts of Africa. The only ugly part of the island is the area with caged animals, including monkeys. The gardens are perfect for a peaceful stroll except on Friday when the island is invaded by picnic crowds with ghetto blasters. Entry is E£5 and there is no student reduction. See Feluccas & Ferries earlier for information on how to get to the island.

THE WEST BANK
Mausoleum of the Aga Khan

Aswan was the favourite wintering place of Mohammed Shah Aga Khan, the 48th imam, or leader, of the Ismaili sect of Islam. When he died in 1957 his wife, the Begum, oversaw the construction of his domed granite and sandstone mausoleum, which is partway up the hill on the west bank opposite Elephantine Island.

Modelled on the Fatimid tombs of Cairo, the interior, which incorporates a small mosque, is more impressive than the exterior. The sarcophagus, of Carrara marble, is inscribed with texts from the Quran and stands in a vaulted chamber in the interior courtyard. Part of the sarcophagus has been reserved for the Begum.

Now in her 90s, the Begum still lives for some of the year in the white villa (below the mausoleum) which used to be their winter retreat. Every day she places a red rose on his sarcophagus; a ritual that is carried on in summer by her gardener.

At the time of writing the tomb was closed to visitors. Nobody knows whether it will open again but its old hours were 8 am to 4 pm Tuesday to Sunday and admission was free. Should you be able to visit, dress modestly and remove your shoes.

Monastery of St Simeon

Deir Amba Samaan is a 7th century monastery which, although unused for over 800 years, is one of the best preserved of the original Christian strongholds in Egypt. Confusingly, the original monastery foundations were dedicated to a local saint named Hadra but the monastery survived under the name of St Simeon until Salah al-Din destroyed it in 1173.

Surrounded by desert sands, except for a glimpse of the fertile belt around Aswan in the distance, the monastery has stunning views and bears more resemblance to a fortress than a religious sanctuary. It once provided accommodation for about 300 resident monks plus a further 100 or so pilgrims. Built on two levels, the lower of stone and the upper of mud-brick, it was surrounded by 10m-high walls and contained a church, stores, bakeries, offices, a kitchen, dormitories, stables and workshops. Mud-brick architecture buffs will love the long vault in the upper enclosure. Off this are the monks' cells with their *mastaba* beds. The last room on the right still has graffiti from the Muslim pilgrims who were put up here en route to Mecca.

The monastery is open from 7 am to 4 pm; admission is E£12 (half for students).

Getting There & Away For information on boats to the Mausoleum and St Simeon,

see Feluccas & Ferries earlier. If you're heading up to the monastery you can either negotiate with the camel drivers at the boat landing (expect to pay about E£25 for an hour) or scramble up the desert track (about 25 minutes).

Alternatively, you can take the ferry to the Tombs of the Nobles and ride a camel or donkey from there.

Tombs of the Nobles

The high cliffs opposite Aswan, just north of Kitchener's Island, are honeycombed with the tombs of the princes, governors, 'Keepers of the Gate of the South' and other dignitaries of ancient Yebu. They date from the Old and Middle kingdoms and although most of them are in a sorry state of repair, there are a few worth visiting.

Admission to the tombs is E£12, or E£6 for students. Hours are from 8 am to 4 pm (winter) and 5 pm (summer).

For details on how to get to the tombs see Feluccas & Ferries earlier.

Tombs of Mekhu & Sabni (Nos 25 & 26) These tombs are of roughly around 6th dynasty construction. The reliefs in No 26 record a tale of tragedy and triumph. Mekhu, one of the 'Keepers of the Gate', was murdered on an expedition into Africa, so his son Sabni led the army into Nubia to punish the tribe responsible. Sabni recovered his father's body and sent a messenger to the pharaoh in Memphis to inform him that the enemy had been taught a lesson. On his return to Aswan he was met by priests, professional mourners and some of the royal embalmers, all sent by the pharaoh himself to show the importance that went with the keepers of the kingdom's southern frontier.

Tomb of Prince Sarenput II (No 31)
Dating from the 12th dynasty, this is one of the best preserved tombs. There are statues of the prince and wall paintings depicting Sarenput and his son hunting and fishing.

Tomb of Prince Sarenput I (No 36)
This tomb also dates from the 12th dynasty

but it's older than No 31. On the rear wall of a columned court, to the left of the door, the prince is shown being followed by his dogs and sandal-bearer, and there are other scenes of his three sons and of women bearing flowers.

Tomb of Heqaib (No 35) The Tomb of Heqaib, the deified official whose temple stood on Elephantine, has a columned facade and some fine reliefs showing fighting bulls and hunting scenes.

Kubbet al-Hawa
Also on the west bank is Kubbet al-Hawa, a small tomb constructed for a local sheikh at the top of the hill. If you climb up to it, you'll be rewarded with fantastic views of the Nile and the surrounding area.

ACTIVITIES
Swimming
Aswan is a hot place, and sometimes a swim seems just the way to escape the worst of it. Short of joining the local kids and jumping into the Nile to cool off (which you should definitely not do – see boxed text 'Bilharzia' on page 88) there are a few hotels with swimming pools open to the public, generally from 9 am to sunset. The cheapest by far is the small pool at the Cleopatra Hotel, which costs E£10. The Basma Hotel has a pool which nonguests can use for E£25, while the Aswan Oberoi and Isis Island charge E£30. The municipal pool next to the GPO does not admit tourists.

ORGANISED TOURS
For details on tours to Abu Simbel, see Getting There & Away under Abu Simbel at the end of this chapter. Small hotels and travel agencies also arrange day tours of the area's major sights, usually incorporating Philae Temple, the unfinished obelisk and the Nubian Museum.

PLACES TO STAY
As in Luxor, prices for accommodation vary greatly with the season. The high season officially extends from October to April, however, its zenith is December and January when many Egyptians come here in groups. In the low season, and even until early November, you'll have no trouble finding a room, and haggling is part of the game. All the prices below are low-season rates, so expect prices to be higher if you're here in winter.

Arriving by train, you'll invariably be met by hotel touts each postulating the best deal in town and often claiming to be the owner of a particular place. Unless you want to be hassled by them for the rest of your stay in Aswan, it's best to give these guys a wide berth and find your own place to stay.

PLACES TO STAY – BUDGET
The hotel rates given in this section include breakfast, unless otherwise specified.

Camping
There's an official *camping ground* next to the unfinished obelisk, which is a 20 to 25 minute walk from the area around EgyptAir. Facilities are basic (filthy toilets and cold showers only) but there are grassy spaces for setting up tents and a few trees to provide shade. Bright lamps and guards keep the place secure, but the lights can make it difficult to sleep. It costs E£3 per person plus E£5/2 for a car/motorcycle.

Hostels
Youth Hostel (☎ 322 235) is on Sharia Abtal at-Tahrir, not far from the train station at the side entrance of the governorate-run hostel which, just to confuse you, also calls itself a youth hostel. The 'real' youth hostel charges members E£7.60 for a bed in a dorm, while nonmembers pay E£8.60. Breakfast is not available. The rooms have fans, the showers and toilets are clean and, if you avoid Egyptian university breaks, the place is generally empty. They make a point of keeping foreigners separate from locals.

Hotels – North of Aswan Station
Rosewan Hotel (☎ 304 497) has been popular with budget travellers for quite a few years

but the rooms are now a bit overpriced. It has fairly clean, simple, rather small singles/doubles/triples with shower/toilet combinations for E£12/22/33. All rooms have fans and tiled floors. The staff are very friendly and the owner, Farouk Nasser, is a self-taught artist, poet and all-round character.

Hotel As-Saffa (☎ 302 172), next door to the Rosewan, has deteriorated and seems to be a favorite with local construction workers. Prices start at E£7/10 for singles/doubles without baths but it's not recommended.

Mena Hotel (☎ 304 388) has carpeted rooms with air-con, TV, phone, shower, toilet and small balcony for E£25/35. (There are also a few cheaper rooms with poor air-con or just fans.) There's a colourful roof garden with cushioned chairs which is ideal for an evening beer (E£5). To get to the Mena, follow the street that runs parallel to the railway line for about four minutes.

Hotels – South of Aswan Station

Marwa Hotel is entered from an alley off Sharia Abtal at-Tahrir, directly across the street from the Youth Hostel. The rooms are simple and a little cramped, but at E£5 a person in a share room of three or four beds, it is fairly popular. Each room has a fan and there's hot water in the communal showers. A few rooms have air-con, for which you pay E£2 more. Breakfast is E£1 extra.

Al-Amin Hotel (☎ 302 298) is an inexpensive hotel (not to be confused with the dark, uninviting Al-Eman Hotel two blocks south) that lists itself as being on Sharia Abtal at-Tahrir, but is actually on a side street just across from the Ramses Hotel. The rooms are somewhat dusty and the toilet/shower combinations are rather small. They charge E£11/22 for singles/doubles with bath, not including breakfast.

Abu Simbel Hotel (☎ 302 888), not far from the tourist office on the Corniche, used to be a mid-range place but went downhill in the late 1980s. Some much-needed renovations have been carried out improving things slightly. Singles/doubles with showers cost E£29.50/38.50. The view of the Nile from the tiny balcony of each room is fantastic,

and for some people makes up for the tiny bathrooms and shabby state.

Nubian Oasis Hotel (☎ 312 126) just off Sharia as-Souq remains one of Aswan's most popular travellers' haunts, although from complaints we've received about rude and aggressive staff and theft, it seems this popularity is being abused. Some staff also use hard-sell tactics to attempt to sell tours and felucca trips. Otherwise, it has reasonable, clean singles/doubles at E£10/15 without baths, or doubles with baths and air-con for E£20. There's a large lounge area and a roof garden where Stellas cost E£6.

Noorhan Hotel (☎ 316 069) on the eastern side of Sharia as-Souq has had mixed reviews from travellers. Their touts can be aggressive and will try to sell you their organised trips, but OK rooms with fans cost E£6 per person or E£7.50 with private bath. There are also some rooms with air-con that go for E£10 per person. Stellas are available for E£5.50.

Bob Marley Hotel, one block east of the Medina restaurant, is a longstanding cheapie that has had bad press from travellers. For E£6 per person you get a scruffy double room with fan and balcony; E£1.50 more gets a private bathroom. Make sure you ask for a room with a lock that's working.

New Brethren Hotel (☎ 310 466) on Sharia as-Souq may have an off-putting Islamic name but it's not too bad at E£10/20 for singles/doubles with shared bath.

Aswan Palace Hotel (☎ 313 664) in the midst of the souq is certainly no palace and at E£10/12 for noisy singles/doubles, it's no great deal either.

Victoria Hotel (☎ 303 870) boasts rickety wooden balconies, high ceilings, iron bed frames and a wonderful sweeping staircase. Unfortunately the shared facilities are full of a less welcome kind of character. Large rooms cost E£7/12.

Abu Shelib Hotel (☎ 303 051) at the southern end of Sharia as-Souq is next to a mosque. Rooms are clean and simple, with fans and/or air-con, and toilet/shower combinations (big bathrooms in some). Singles/doubles are E£20/30, but you may be able to negotiate, depending on the size of the rooms and whether or not they have showers. It's popular with overland travel groups.

Hotel Orabi (☎/fax 317 578) on a quiet side street just off the souq is relatively new and its central location is an advantage for exploring the souq and the Corniche. The staff are friendly, the rooms are modern and comfortable, and the communal bathrooms are clean (though prone to flooding). Some rooms have big balconies. The cost is E£10/15 for singles/doubles with air-con but shared bathroom. A bed in a triple with a fan is E£6 per person.

Keylany Hotel (☎ 317 332) has recently been expanded and the 21 brand new rooms have ceiling fans and pine furniture and their own spotless bathrooms. Singles go for E£7 and doubles cost E£14. This is definitely one of the better options in this range.

PLACES TO STAY – MID-RANGE

Ramses Hotel (☎ 324 000, fax 315 701) on Sharia Abtal at-Tahrir is a good deal and, according to some, the best value hotel in Aswan. Singles/doubles with showers, toilets, air-con, colour TV, mini-fridge and Nile views cost about E£35/55. This hotel is popular with tour groups from Europe.

Happi Hotel (☎ 314 115), also on Sharia Abtal at-Tahrir, a few blocks down from the Ramses, has 64 clean rooms with spotless bathrooms for E£35/50. The rooms have air-con and some also have balconies, TV and double beds. Ask for one with a Nile view. The owner also runs the Cleopatra Hotel, so guests can use the Cleopatra's pool for a discount.

Oscar Hotel (☎/fax 306 066) has become a travellers' favourite. Rooms cost E£40/70, but can be bargained down. Some have balconies and bedside reading lights. There's also a rooftop terrace where beers (E£6) are available.

New Abu Simbel Hotel (☎ 306 096) is several blocks north of the train station and though it's out of the centre, the management is friendly, towels and toilet paper are provided and there's a pleasant garden where you can cool off with a beer. At E£25/35, the screened rooms with private bathroom and air-con, are good value.

Al-Salaam Hotel (☎ 302 651, 303 649) on the Corniche can be considered a fair deal for the price. Singles/doubles cost E£25/40 with fans, E£35/50 with air-con. Most of the freshly-painted rooms have private bathrooms and some have great views of the Nile.

Hathor Hotel (☎ 314 580, fax 303 462), on the Corniche, has 36 singles/doubles, most with air-con, for E£20/40, but some of the rooms are tiny. The roof terrace has spectacular views over the Nile and a small swimming pool.

Horus Hotel (☎/fax 313 313), also on the Corniche, has large and comfortable singles/doubles with air-con and bath for E£40/50. Some rooms have great Nile views. Ask for a room that has been renovated. There is a rooftop bar and restaurant.

Philae Hotel (☎ 312 090) has just been renovated and has raised its prices accordingly. Three-quarters of the rooms overlook the Nile and you pay extra for the view. Singles with/without a Nile view are E£55/70; doubles are E£70/90. Taxes are extra.

Memnon Hotel (☎ 300 483) is above the National Bank of Egypt on the Corniche but can only be entered through the back alley. The reception is on the 2nd floor. All the rooms are clean, have air-con and comfortable beds and the management is installing a pool on the roof. The staff can be a bit pushy when it comes to trying to sell felucca trips. Singles/doubles with private bath cost E£35/40.

Al-Amir Hotel (☎ 314 735) is a three star hotel a street back from the Corniche on Sharia Abbas Farid. It's popular with Egyptians and offers 28 rooms with all the essentials such as thick mattresses, bathroom slippers, TV, air-con and phones. It's next to a mosque, and somewhat overpriced considering that it's not on the Nile – singles/doubles cost E£85/115.

Cleopatra Hotel (☎ 314 003, fax 314 002) on Sharia as-Souq not far from the train station is well situated for exploring the old market area. All 109 rooms are clean and comfortable with air-con, private bathroom and telephone, although they don't quite live up to the promise of the newly renovated lobby. There's also a rooftop pool. Singles/doubles go for E£94.50/126.

PLACES TO STAY – TOP END

Old Cataract Hotel (☎ *316 000, fax 316 011*) is one of Egypt's most famous and historic hotels. An impressive Moorish-style building it is surrounded by gardens on a rise above the river, with splendid views of the Nile and across the southern tip of Elephantine Island to the Mausoleum of the Aga Khan. Doubles here cost US$110/150 for a standard room with a garden/Nile view, or US$240 for a deluxe room with terrace, plus 23% in taxes and service charges. Suites range from US$350 to US$900. There is no discount for single occupancy. The hotel is worth visiting just to partake of a cool Stella or a cocktail on the verandah, however, a minimum charge of E£25 is imposed and if the hotel is full the management closes the terrace to nonresidents. The hotel's exterior was used in the movie of Agatha Christie's *Death on the Nile*, in part because Christie once did some writing here.

New Cataract Hotel (☎ *316 000, fax 316 011*) is a high-rise lump next door to the old hotel. Singles/doubles with a garden view are US$65/80; with a Nile view US$75/90. This hotel has none of the style of the Old Cataract though its setting is also sublime and it has a big pool.

The four star *Kalabsha Hotel* (☎ *322 666, fax 325 974*) is another modernist affair, with an excellent view of the First Nile Cataract. Singles/doubles are US$27/33 at the back and US$39/50 at the front, plus the usual taxes. Guests can use the swimming pool at the New Cataract Hotel for free.

Another four star, *Basma Hotel* (☎ *310 901, fax 310 907*) is at the top of the hill just past the Kalabsha Hotel. Its garden terrace has great views over the southern end of Elephantine Island and the Aga Khan's mausoleum. Less offensive aesthetically than the Kalabsha and New Cataract, it has

the usual four star amenities. Single/double rooms go for US$65/85, not including breakfast or taxes.

Aswan Oberoi (☎ *314 667, fax 313 538*) is the disfiguring blot that rises from Elephantine Island. It has two hotel launches that ferry guests and visitors from the east bank. The views from the tower are, of course, magnificent and the gardens are pleasant to hang around and watch the feluccas, or to have a dip in the pool. Rooms, however, start at US$75/106 (without breakfast or taxes) up to about US$300.

The four star *Isis Hotel* (☎ *315 100/200/ 300*) has singles/doubles for US$80/106, including taxes. Although its shoddily built rooms are hardly beautiful, it has a prime location on the river in the centre of town.

The same people have recently opened a 400 room monstrosity, *Isis Island Hotel* (☎ *317 400, fax 317 405*), on one of the islands south of Elephantine. Controversy surrounded the construction of this place as it was built within a few metres of a group of islands which are home to the only original Nile vegetation remaining in Egypt and which have been designated a protected area. An ostentatious launch ferries guests (and outsiders wanting to use the pool) from in front of the EgyptAir office.

The salmon-toned *Hôtel Île d'Amoun* (☎ *313 800, fax 317 193*) is on a neighbouring islet. It's operated by Club Med, which took over the original building years ago and transformed it into an idyllic garden paradise. Rooms (including taxes but not breakfast) cost US$33/46. The hotel's modest motor boats leave from in front of EgyptAir.

PLACES TO EAT
Budget Dining
Along Sharia as-Souq is a smorgasbord of small restaurants and cafes in the midst of the lively atmosphere of the souqs. There are also plenty of cafes by the train station. *Restaurant Derwash* on the south side of the midan in front of the station has been recommended by some travellers. A block from the station is *Samah*, a little ta'amiyya

stall. Down a side street, a bit further, is *An-Nasr* which has pizza, as well as fried fish and chicken.

Next to the Youth Hostel is an OK place called *Al-Dar*, which does full meals for E£6. Alternatively you could try *Esraa*, a tiny kofta place just down the road.

Medina Restaurant on Sharia as-Souq, across from the Cleopatra Hotel, is recommended for its kofta and kebab deals, and is often patronised by travellers. They also do a vegetarian meal for E£4.50.

Al-Sayyida Nefissa tucked away in a side alley in the heart of the souq is a good-value place serving kofta for E£6, soup for E£1, and a meal of rice, salad, vegetables and bread for E£2.50.

Restaurants

Al-Masry Restaurant (☎ 302 576) on Sharia al-Matar is one Aswan's better-known restaurants. It serves kebabs and kofta only, but it's clean with attractive Arabesque tiled walls, and the meat is excellent and comes with bread, salad and tahina. It's a popular place with local families. Expect to pay around E£16.

There are three places on the Corniche where you can sit out on a barge in the river and get decent food and beers.

Aswan Moon Restaurant (☎ 316 108) is the best of the trio and a popular hang-out for both foreigners and Egyptians. After a few days in Aswan you're likely to recognise the regulars. Main courses go for about E£15 and a beer is E£7. It serves generous soups and pizzas (E£10), but the salads tend to be small. The atmosphere is particularly laid-back and the service is excellent.

Emy Restaurant, next door to the Aswan Moon, prepares especially nice fruit cocktail drinks, as well as serving the usual selection of meals. The view from the top deck at sunset is bliss, and there is a discount available for those with student cards.

The third barge is owned by *Saladin Restaurant* and while it's pleasant enough for a drink, the food is nothing to rave about. It's less popular than the other two and rarely full.

The tiny *Restaurant el-Nil* is on the Corniche a few doors along from Thomas Cook. A full meal with fish (carp from Lake Nasser), chicken or meat with rice, vegetables, salad, tahina and bread should cost about E£9.

On the Nile side of the Corniche there are several other restaurants floating on pontoons on the river, all offering a similar range of dishes at virtually the same prices. They include *Monalisa Restaurant*, *Panorama* and *Al-Shati*. Panorama has some greenery and is particularly nice for a riverside lunch. They cook most of their meals in the huge, local clay pots and have a wide selection of herbal teas on offer.

With its huge dome, orientalist motifs and muted lighting, the Old Cataract Hotel's *1902 restaurant* has the most dramatic decor in Aswan, but is closed to outsiders if the hotel is full. The four-course set menu is a pricey E£102, not including service and taxes. Still, with restrained oriental music and a French chef doing the cooking, it is worth it for a special occasion.

Alternatively, you can partake in a buffet dinner at either *Kalabsha Hotel* (E£40) or *Hôtel Île d'Amoun* (E£56).

Nubian Restaurant on Essa Island serves meals for about E£35; it seems to mainly cater to groups.

Self-Catering

The souq is the best place to head if you want to buy your own food. On the main street as well as some of the small alleyways there are a number of small grocery shops that stock canned goods, cheese and UHT milk. As you can see after a quick stroll through the market, fruit and vegetables are abundant, if seasonal. They are best bought in the morning, when they are fresh.

ENTERTAINMENT

Aswan's world-famous folkloric dance troupe is supposed to perform from 9.30 to 11.30 pm nightly (except Friday) at the cultural centre (☎ 313 390) on the Corniche between October and February. However, with the lack of tourists following the Luxor massacre, the performances have been suspended. Check with the centre or the tourist office to see if they've resumed. (When they're running, admission is E£10.) The centre also sometimes presents other traditional Upper Egyptian and Nubian music performances.

Otherwise, strolling along the Corniche, watching the moon rise from a rooftop terrace, and having a beer at one of the floating restaurants is about all that most travellers get up to in Aswan at night. The top-end hotels all have discos and nightclubs, but they're fairly empty.

SHOPPING

Aswan's famous souq may be more touristic than it used to be but it's still a good place to pick up souvenirs and crafts. Colourful Nubian skullcaps are popular and go for about E£5 each. More bulky are the baskets and trays that you can see around town. Prices of these vary with their size and age; expect to pay about E£40 for an old, medium-sized tray. Small round disks go for around E£10. The spices and indigo powder prominently displayed are also good buys and most of the spice shops sell the hibiscus flowers used to make karkadey (see Entertainment in the Facts for the Visitor chapter). Aswan is also famous for the quality of its henna powder and its delicious roasted peanuts. The higher grade of the latter go for E£6 a kilogram.

GETTING THERE & AWAY
Air

The EgyptAir office (☎ 315 000) is at the southern end of the Corniche. There are daily flights from Cairo to Aswan (E£576 one way; 1¼ hours nonstop). The one-way hop to Luxor is E£190; to Hurghada via Luxor it's E£374. The return flight from Aswan to Abu Simbel costs E£290 and includes bus transfers between the airport and the temple site. This fare has been reduced because the police have forbidden foreigners to drive to Abu Simbel; should this change the air fare will probably be almost double.

Bus

The bus station is in the middle of town on Sharia Abtal at-Tahrir. In their zeal to 'protect' foreigners, some policemen have been forbidding foreigners even from taking buses out of Aswan. There seem to be no hard and fast rules, although at the time of writing Abu Simbel buses were definitely off-limits. Check with Shukri at the tourist office or ask around before you buy your ticket.

A direct bus for Cairo (12 hours) leaves at 3.30 pm and costs E£55. A second bus leaving three hours later costs E£14 less. They both supposedly have air-con, video and toilet, so the difference is anybody's guess.

Should the security measures relax, there are two daily buses to Abu Simbel (E£20 return). You should book in advance. Take note – neither of these buses has air-con.

There are hourly buses to Kom Ombo (E£1.50/5 without/with air-con; one hour), Edfu (E£3/10; two hours), Esna (E£4.50/15; three hours) and Luxor (E£6.50/15; four to five hours).

There are five buses going right through to Hurghada (seven hours). At 6 and 8 am tickets cost E£25 and the bus continues to Suez (E£37); the 3.30 pm is a Pullman (E£40) which goes on to Cairo but doesn't stop in Suez. The 5 pm (E£35) stops in Suez (E£45) and the 6.30 pm (E£25) goes on to Cairo via Suez (E£40) – a 15 hour haul. A bus for Marsa Alam (E£12; five hours) departs at 6 am.

Train

There are a handful of trains running daily between Cairo and Aswan but only three of them can be used by foreigners. However, if you try climbing aboard another train and buying your ticket on board then usually nobody will stop you. If you want to stop off in Daraw or some of the other smaller towns between Aswan and Luxor this is probably the best way outside of the convoy.

The most expensive is the wagons-lit train (No 85) which costs E£300 one way to Cairo and departs at 3 pm. See Getting There & Away in the Cairo chapter for more details.

Felucca Trips

Watching the dark waters of the Nile slide by from the deck of a felucca is one of the highlights of any trip to Egypt, and Aswan is the best place to arrange overnight trips, largely because you'll be going with the current and won't find yourself marooned if the wind dies. Trips north of Edfu have been forbidden for security reasons. So, unless things change, you are limited to trips to Kom Ombo (two days, one night) or, the most popular option, Edfu (three days, two nights).

A typical itinerary is to set sail in the morning and spend the day heading towards the town of Kom Ombo. Many of the captains are Nubian and will take you for tea in their village along the way. Nights are spent on the boat or camping on an island in the Nile. Night-time entertainment ranges from star-gazing to partying, depending on you and your fellow passengers. Once you arrive you can either return to Aswan or head up to Luxor by service taxi.

Arranging a felucca trip can seem daunting when you face the legions of touts on Aswan's Corniche. The small hotels can be just as aggressive in trying to rope you in. While it is easier to let them do the organising, remember that they get a percentage, which either comes out of the captain's fee or your food allowance. If you want to be sure of what you're getting it's best to do it yourself.

Officially, feluccas can carry a minimum of six passengers and a maximum of eight, for E£25 per person to Kom Ombo, E£45 to Edfu. On top of this add E£5 for police registration, plus there's the cost of food supplies. You can get boats for less than the official price, but take care: if it's much cheaper you'll either have a resentful captain and crew, or you'll be eating little more than bread and fuul for three days.

Finding a good captain is essential, especially if you are a single woman or a group of women. Some women travellers have reported sailing with felucca captains who had groping hands and there have been some rare reports of assault. Many of the better captains can be found having a sheesha in Nileside restaurants like the Aswan Moon. Others, such as the British felucca owner, Jon Cairo, moor further north, in front of the Abu Simbel Hotel. If you want help, Shukri Saad at the tourist office can recommend some reputable people.

Express train Nos 981 and 997 to Cairo leave at 5 am and 8.45 pm. The 1st/2nd class fare is E£63/37; student discounts are available. These trains have air-con and a restaurant. The trip to Cairo is scheduled to take about 15 hours but has been known to take more than 20 hours. Reservations are needed for all these trains. If you don't want to dine on the train, ask for a ticket without meals or they'll automatically issue meal tickets.

Tickets for the train to Luxor (four hours) cost E£22/12 in 1st/2nd class on the afternoon service, and a few pounds more on the morning train. Both trains also stop at Kom Ombo (E£7/4) and Edfu (E£12/6).

Service Taxi

At the time of writing the police in Aswan were forbidding foreigners from taking service taxis, often turning them back at the checkpoint just north of town. As with all such directives, people do get around the rules but in general it's better to take the bus or train, or else get a group of people together and hire a private taxi. If this changes (check with the tourist office), the service taxi station is across the train tracks on the east side of town. Just off Sharia as-Souq, one block south of the train station, is an overpass over the tracks. Climb the overpass and walk to the end of the street on the other

Felucca Trips

When dealing with a felucca captain, there are a few things to look out for:

- Ensure that he has what appears to be a decent, functioning boat, with some blankets and cooking implements, a sunshade and something comfortable to sit on. There should also be a place to lock up valuables. If a different boat is foisted on you at the last minute, be firm in refusing to take it. Likewise with the captain himself – many travellers agree to sail with one man and find themselves with someone else when they get on the boat.
- Establish whether the price includes food and, if so, go with whoever does the shopping to see just what you are getting. Otherwise, set a price without food and get your own.
- Agree on the number of passengers before you go and don't be talked into taking 'a few others on board later downriver', otherwise you'll find yourselves sharing limited supplies of food, water and space.
- Decide on the drop-off point before you sail. Although you may think you're going to Edfu, many felucca captains stop 30km short of the town, in the villages of Hammam, Faris or Ar-Ramady and arrange for 'special' share taxis – which take you straight to a hotel of the captain's choice in Luxor for E£10 per person (instead of the E£5 it usually costs).
- *Don't* hand over your passports. Often captains, or more likely middlemen, like to take them so that they have a couple of passengers in the bag. They then scour around for other people. A photocopy will do for the permit. It's advisable to accompany the captain to the police when organising permission too.
- Take plenty of bottled water for the trip; otherwise the captain will dip into the Nile for cooking and drinking water.
- Bring a sleeping bag – it can get bitterly cold at night, and the supply of blankets on board won't be enough. Insect repellent is a good idea. A hat is essential.
- Take your rubbish with you when you leave if you camp overnight on an island or beach. As one person put it after encountering piles of plastic bottles and beer cans left by previous travellers: 'I'm not old or fussy or picky – I just enjoy sitting on a clean beach, not on a garbage dump'.

side (about 10 minutes). Turn right and walk about 500m to the service taxi station. Alternatively, just follow the tracks south until the tunnel: the service taxi station is on the other side of the railway line.

Car & Motorcycle
All foreigners are forbidden to use the road to Abu Simbel. Driving north means going in a police convoy. These congregate in front of the Officer's Club, just north of the governorate building on the Corniche and leave at 8 am and 1 pm. You should be there about 15 minutes in advance. Check with the tourist office to see if the rules have been relaxed.

Cruise Ship
For details about the five star cruisers, the MS *Eugénie* and *Qasr Ibrim*, which sail between Aswan High Dam and Abu Simbel, see the Lake Nasser section later in this chapter.

Boat to Sudan
See under Sea in the Getting There & Away chapter for details on boat transport to Sudan.

Although the Sudanese consulate in Aswan has been officially closed for many years, a representative from the embassy in Cairo, Mohammed Amin, shuttles back and forth to handle the consular business of the many Sudanese in Aswan. Visas are currently unavailable here, but he is friendly and may be able to advise you about travelling south. He can be found at flat 1, building No 20 (no phone number) in the area of Atlas, just behind New Abu Simbel Hotel. As most of the buildings here look the same, ask for 'qunsuliya sudaniya' and someone will direct you.

GETTING AROUND
To/From the Airport
The airport is 25km south-west of town and the taxi fare is about E£20.

Taxi
A taxi tour including the Philae Temple, High Dam and unfinished obelisk near Fatimid Cemetery costs around E£30 for five to six people. Taxis can also take you on day trips to Daraw and/or Kom Ombo for about E£40.

Bicycle
There are a few places at the train station end of Sharia as-Souq where you can hire bicycles for about E£5 a day – try around the Marwa and Ramses hotels.

Around Aswan

ASWAN DAM
When the British constructed the Aswan Dam above the First Nile Cataract at the turn of the century it was the largest of its kind in the world. The growing population of Egypt had made it imperative to put more land under cultivation and the only way to achieve this was to regulate the flow of the Nile. Measuring 2441m across, the dam was built between 1898 and 1902 almost entirely of local Aswan granite.

Although its height had to be raised twice to meet the demand, it not only greatly increased the area of cultivable land but also provided the country with most of its hydroelectric power. Now completely surpassed both in function and as a tourist attraction by the High Dam 6km upstream, it is still worth a brief visit, as the area around the First Nile Cataract below it is extremely fertile and picturesque.

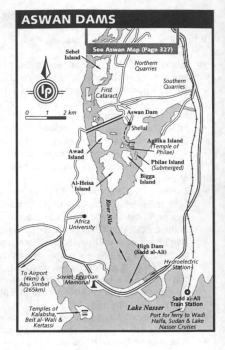

ASWAN DAMS

See Aswan Map (Page 327)

Sehel Island
Northern Quarries
Southern Quarries
First Cataract
0   1   2 km
Aswan Dam
Shellal
Agilika Island (Temple of Philae)
Awad Island
Philae Island (Submerged)
Bigga Island
Al-Heisa Island
River Nile
Africa University
High Dam (Sadd al-Ali)
Hydroelectric Station
To Airport (4km) & Abu Simbel (265km)
Soviet-Egyptian Memorial
Temples of Kalabsha, Beit al-Wali & Kertassi
Lake Nasser
Sadd al-Ali Train Station
Port for Ferry to Wadi Halfa, Sudan & Lake Nasser Cruises

The road to the airport and, when the road is open, all trips to Abu Simbel include a drive across this dam.

SEHEL ISLAND
Sehel, the large island north of the old Aswan Dam, was sacred to the goddess Anukis and her husband Khnum. As a destination for an extended felucca trip on this part of the Nile, Sehel Island is a good choice, although there isn't much to see apart from a friendly Nubian village and a great many rock inscriptions, dating from Middle Kingdom to Graeco-Roman times.

TEMPLE OF PHILAE
The romantic and majestic aura surrounding the temple complex of Isis on the island of Philae (pronounced fee-LI) has been luring pilgrims for thousands of years. During the 19th century the ruins were one of Egypt's

TEMPLE OF PHILAE

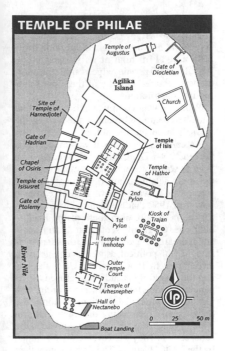

legendary tourist attractions. From the turn of this century, Philae and its temples became swamped for six months of every year by the high waters of the reservoir created by the construction of the old Aswan Dam. It seemed that they were destined to be lost forever and travellers took to rowboats to glide among the partly submerged columns and peer down through the translucent green to the wondrous sanctuaries of the mighty gods below.

In the 1960s, with the approaching completion of the High Dam, a rescue was organised by UNESCO. The massive complex was disassembled and removed stone by stone from Philae between 1972 and 1980. The temples were reconstructed 20m higher on nearby Agilika Island, which was even landscaped to resemble the sacred isle of Isis, in positions corresponding as closely as possible to their original layout.

The oldest part of Philae dates from the 4th century BC but most of the existing structures were built by the Ptolemies and the Romans up to the 3rd century AD. The early Christians also added their bit by transforming the main temple's hypostyle hall into a chapel, building some churches and defacing the pagan reliefs. Their inscriptions were in turn vandalised by the early Muslims.

At first it was the cults of Isis, Osiris and Horus, and the Graeco-Roman temple raised in honour of the goddess, that drew devotees from Egypt and the whole Mediterranean.

The boat to Agilika Island, which is where the temple is located, leaves you at the base of the **Hall of Nectanebo**, the oldest part of the Philae complex. Heading north, you walk down the **Outer Temple Court**, which has colonnades running along both sides, to the entrance of the Temple of Isis marked by the 18m-high towers of the **1st Pylon**.

In the Central Court of the **Temple of Isis** is the mammisi (birth house) dedicated to Horus. Successive pharaohs reinstated their legitimacy as the mortal descendants of Horus by taking part in the mammisi rituals, which celebrated the god's birth.

The **2nd Pylon** provides access to the vestibule and the **Inner Sanctuary of Isis**; a staircase, on the western side, leads up to the **Osiris Chambers**, which are decorated with scenes of mourners; and everywhere there are reliefs of Isis, her husband and son, other deities and, of course, the Ptolemies and Romans who built or contributed to the temple.

On the northern tip of the island are the **Temple of Augustus** and the **Gate of Diocletian**; east of the 2nd Pylon is the delightful **Temple of Hathor** decorated with reliefs of musicians and Bes, the god of singing and pleasure; and south of that, the elegant, unfinished pavilion by the water's edge is the **Kiosk of Trajan**. The completed reliefs on the kiosk feature Emperor Trajan making offerings to Isis, Osiris and Horus.

The temple complex is open from 8 am to 4 pm (winter) and 7 am to 5 pm (summer), and admission is E£20, or E£10 for students. Tickets are purchased from the small office before the boat landing at Shellal.

There is a sound and light show in the evening which costs E£33 (no student discount) for the ticket plus the cost of the boat (see Getting There & Away, later) to Agilika Island. If you're going to see a sound and light show in Egypt, this is one of the least kitschy, and just being on the island at night almost makes it worth the money. Times vary according to the season. In winter (27 September to 24 April) they're at 6, 7.30 and 9 pm; in summer (26 April to 26 September) at 8, 9.30 and 11 pm; and during Ramadan at 8.30, 10 and 11 pm. Double-check the following schedule at the tourist office:

day	show 1	show 2	show 3
Monday	English	Italian	-
Tuesday	French	English	-
Wednesday	English	Spanish	French
Thursday	French	Arabic	-
Friday	English	French	-
Saturday	English	French	-
Sunday	French	German	-

Getting There & Away

The boat landing for the Philae complex is at Shellal, south of the old Aswan Dam. The only easy way to get there is by taxi or organised trip (arranged by most travel agencies and major hotels in town, but possibly for more money than you may pay otherwise). The round-trip taxi fare for a group of six costs about E£30 without bargaining. It is possible, if you can get a ride to the old Aswan Dam, to walk along the water's edge to Shellal. From here, a small motorboat to the island costs E£14 (during the day) or E£16 (in the evening) divided between however many of you there are (maximum eight). If there are more than eight, each person simply pays E£2 for the return trip. These amounts are paid directly to the boatmen.

HIGH DAM

Egypt's contemporary example of building on a monumental scale contains 18 times the amount of material used in the Great Pyramid of Cheops. The controversial Sadd al-Ali, the High Dam, 17km south of Aswan, is 3600m across, 980m wide at its base and 111m high at its highest point. About 35,000 people helped build this enormous structure, and 451 of them died during its construction.

When it was completed the water that collected behind it became Lake Nasser, the world's largest artificial lake.

As early as the 1940s it was evident that the old Aswan Dam, which only regulated the flow of water, was not big enough to counter the unpredictable annual flooding of the great river. But it wasn't until Nasser came to power in 1952 that the plans were drawn up for the new dam, 6km south of the British-built one. Originally scoffed at as an impossible dream, the building of the dam was fraught with political, as well as engineering, difficulties. In 1956, after the USA, the UK and the World Bank suddenly refused the financial backing they had offered for the project, Nasser ordered the nationalisation of the Suez Canal precipitating the Suez Crisis in which France, the UK and Israel invaded the canal region. They were eventually restrained by the United Nations. The Soviet Union then offered the necessary funding and expertise, and work began on the High Dam in 1960. It was completed in 1971.

The benefits of building the dam have been enormous. Egypt's area of cultivable land has increased by 30%; the High Dam's hydroelectric station has doubled the country's power supply and a rise in the Sahara's water table has been recorded as far away as Algeria.

On the other hand, the dam prevents the flow of the silt that was so critical to the Nile Valley's fertility. The effects of this are being felt all over Egypt. Heavy use of artificial fertilisers has led to increasing salinity of the ground water in agricultural areas. At the Nile's mouth in the Mediterranean, shrimp beds and fishing grounds have almost disappeared. The now perennially-full irrigation canals have led to endemic infection of the bilharzia parasite, a huge public-health problem. In turn, the authorities are faced with the problem that silt could eventually fill the lake.

Most people get to the High Dam as part of an organised trip to sites around Aswan. For the privilege of driving part of the way along the dam to a small pavilion with a couple of displays detailing the dimensions and the construction of the dam, you pay E£5. If you come by foot from the train station you'll still have to pay 50pt.

Many visitors are disappointed by the visit, expecting views more spectacular than they actually get, so perhaps you should not hope for too much. Video cameras and zoom lenses cannot be used, though nobody seems to police this.

On the west side of the dam, there is a stone monument honouring Soviet-Egyptian friendship and cooperation.

Getting There & Away

The cheapest way to get to the High Dam, which is 13km south of Aswan, is to take a train (almost every hour from 6 am to 4 pm; E£1) to Sadd al-Ali station, the end of the Cairo-Aswan line. The station is near the docks for the boat to Sudan and from there you can either walk for a long way or try to get a service taxi to the dam.

If you're planning to take a taxi across the top of the dam, then you might also consider continuing on to the Temple of Kalabsha, which is visible from the dam on the west side of Lake Nasser. It's about 3km from the western end of the dam.

Lower Nubia & Lake Nasser

For countless centuries before the Aswan and High dams irrevocably changed the topography of the area, the rocky cataract at Aswan marked the dividing line between Egypt and its southern neighbour, Nubia. As the Nile changed here, so too did the territory along its shores. Whereas the land to the north was under continuous cultivation, to the south it was more rugged, with rocky

desert cliffs and sand forcing its way down to the water's edge and separating the pockets of agricultural land.

HISTORY

The Ancient Egyptians called Nubia *Ta-Seti*, The Land of the Bow, after the weapons for which the Nubians were famous, but the modern name is thought to come from the ancient Egyptian word for gold *(nbw)*, which was extensively mined in the north-eastern part of the country in pharaonic and Graeco-Roman times. It is ironic that our name for this now lost land comes from ancient Egyptian, as much of Nubia's long history was dominated by its more powerful northern neighbour. When Egypt was strong it either annexed or aggressively exploited the natural resources of its weaker neighbour; by contrast, times of turmoil and anarchy in Egypt tended to be periods of indigenous growth and development in Nubia.

There is evidence of settlements in northern Nubia as early as 12,000 BC, and until 3500 BC it seems that Nubia and Southern Egypt developed in roughly similar ways, with the growing domestication of animals, the development of crops and the gradual adoption of permanent settlements. But there were also important differences. Although the two were ethnically linked, the darker-skinned Nubians had more African features than the Egyptians. Their language was Nilo-Saharan, while Ancient Egyptian was Afro-Asiatic.

With its unification in around 3100 BC, Egypt developed rapidly. Throughout the Old Kingdom trading and mining expeditions were sent to extract Nubian mineral wealth, establishing the pattern that was to last nearly 5000 years. When centralised authority collapsed in Egypt during the First Intermediate Period, a new culture began to establish itself in Nubia and relations between the two neighbours appear to have been good. But with the reunification of Egypt at the start of the Middle Kingdom, Lower Nubia (roughly the area between the first and second cataracts) was once again

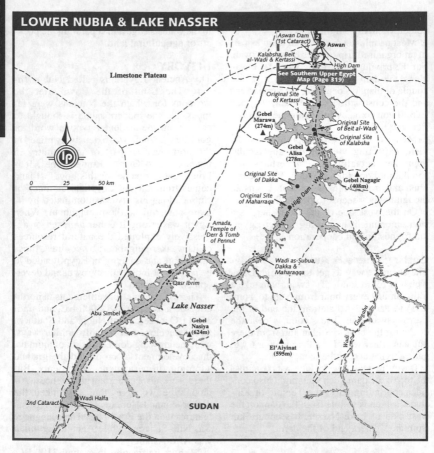

LOWER NUBIA & LAKE NASSER

annexed as a province. A chain of mud-brick fortresses was built on strategic points along the Nile to safeguard trade with the south and establish a buffer between Egypt and the independent Kingdom of Kush, with its capital at Kerma near the 3rd cataract.

When central government in Egypt once again collapsed with the Hyksos invasion during the Second Intermediate period, the Kushites seized the fortresses and other strategic sites and allied themselves with the Hyksos in the Delta. With the establish-

ment of the New Kingdom, the Egyptians invaded Nubia once again and divided it into two provinces, Kush in the south and Wawat in the north.

A couple of hundred years after the collapse of the New Kingdom in 1070 BC, a series of southern power centres emerged in Nubia. The first of these was in Napata in southern Nubia and it was later followed by the Ethiopian kingdom of Meroe, which controlled important trade routes into Africa and held on to the area until about 350 AD.

In the 5th century, after nearly 200 years of instability, Ballana culture had a brief 200 year fluorescence in Lower Nubia. Although its origins were obscure the graves from this period were the richest ever found in Nubia, with jewellery, weapons, furniture and even soldiers, servants and horses found buried with their owners. Some of the treasures found there can now be seen in the Nubian Museum in Aswan.

Christianity gradually spread in Nubia after the 5th century AD and by 652 the newly Islamised authorities in Egypt made a peace treaty with the Christian kingdoms in Nubia. However, attacks on Nubia grew in the 12th and 13th centuries and in 1315 the last Christian king of Nubia was replaced with a Muslim and most of the population converted to Islam. Once again Lower Nubia reverted to a transit point between Egypt to the north and Africa to the south. Finally, with the establishment of the Anglo-Egyptian government in Sudan in 1899 a border between Egypt and Sudan was established 40km north of Wadi Halfa and the land of Nubia was divided for the last time.

MODERN NUBIA

Following the completion of the first Aswan Dam in 1902, and again after its height was raised in 1912 and 1934, the water level of the Nile in Lower Nubia gradually rose from 87m to 121m, partially submerging many of the monuments in the area and, by the 1930s, totally flooding a large number of Nubian villages. With their homes flooded, many Nubians moved north into Egypt where, with government help, they bought land and built villages based on their traditional architecture. Most of the Nubian villages close to Aswan, such as Elephantine, West Aswan, and Sehel, are made up of people who moved at this time.

However, the majority of Nubians, assuming that the Nile's new shoreline would not change again, decided to stay in their homeland and build new houses on higher land. The rising waters imposed huge changes on those who stayed: the date plantations that had been central to their econ-omy were destroyed by the rising waters and would take years to replace, so many Nubian men were forced to search for work in the north, leaving the women behind to run the communities.

Then, less than 30 years later, the building of the High Dam meant that those who had stayed were forced to move again. In the 1960s 50,000 Egyptian Nubians were relocated to government-built villages around Kom Ombo, 50km north of Aswan.

NUBIAN CULTURE

There is no doubt that the Nubians have paid an extremely high price for Egypt's greater good. After first losing their homes, and then their homeland, they are now faced with losing their distinctive identity as new generations grow up as Egyptians.

Perhaps because it is so vulnerable, Nubian culture is also very vibrant. Nubian music is famous the world over for its unique sound. This was popularised in the west by musicians like Hamza ad-Din, whose oud melodies are ethereally beautiful. Apart from the oud, two basic instruments give the music its distinctive rhythm and harmony: the *douff* is a kind of wide but shallow drum or tabla that musicians hold

The traditional and highly distinctive Nubian mud-brick houses are often painted with bold designs.

Nubian Music

It's one of those strange quirks, but it's almost easier to hear and buy Nubian music in the west than it is in Egypt. The city folk of Cairo and Alexandria have an aversion to anything that comes from south of the capital and, with few exceptions, Nubian music is conspicuously absent from national TV and radio. You won't find it in the downtown cassette shops either. Yet while mainstream Egyptian pop icons like Amr Diab dream of reaching an audience beyond the Arab world, Nubian artists sell CDs by the rack load in Europe and play to sell out audiences.

The biggest name is Ali Hassan Kuban, a septuagenarian former tillerman from a small village near Aswan. He grew up playing at weddings and parties and made the leap to a global audience after being invited to perform at a Berlin festival in 1989. Since then, he's toured all over Europe as well as in Japan, Canada and the USA. He has several CDs out on the German Piranha label (www.piranha.de) including *From Nubia to Cairo* and *Walk Like a Nubian*.

What makes Kuban's music appealing to a western audience is that unlike Arabic music with its jarring use of quarter tones, the Nubian sound is extremely accessible. It has a rhythmic quality that's almost African, which mixes with simple melodies and soulful vocals. It's an incredibly warm sound. This can be heard at its best on a series of CDs by a loose grouping of musicians and vocalists recording under the name Salamat. Look out especially for *Mambo al-Soudani* (again on Piranha).

A slightly different facet of Nubian music is represented by Hamza ad-Din, a Nubian composer born in Wadi Halfa in 1929 and widely respected in the west for his semi-classical compositions written for the oud. Inspired by his Sufi beliefs, Ad-Din's work is extremely haunting, especially *Escalay (The Waterwheel)*, which you can find in a recording by the composer himself, or there's an excellent version of it by the Kronos Quartet on their CD *Pieces of Africa*.

Other names to look out for are the now retired Sayyed Gayer, who sings poems and love songs accompanied only by the *douff*, and Ahmed Monieb and Mohammed Hamam.

The one place in Egypt you might be able to pick cassettes by some of these artists is in Aswan; there are several cassette shops in the souq and the sales assistants are happy to pull out their Nubian collections and let you listen.

in their hands, while the *kisir* is a type of stringed instrument. See the boxed text 'Nubian Music'.

Less well-known abroad is Nubia's distinctive architecture. As in Upper Egypt, traditional Nubian houses are made with mud-brick. But here the similarities end. Lower Nubian houses sometimes have domed or vaulted ceilings and houses from further south usually have a flat split-palm roof. They are plastered or whitewashed and covered with pictures and decorations, including ceramic plates. The basic forms can be seen in the Nubian villages around Aswan and in Ballana near Kom Ombo.

Nubians also have their own marriage customs. Traditionally, wedding festivities lasted up to 15 days but nowadays they have devolved to a three-day affair. On the first night, the bride and groom celebrate separately with their respective friends and families. On the second night, the bride takes her party to the groom's home and both groups dance to traditional music until the wee hours. Then the bride returns home and her hands and feet are painted in beautiful designs with henna. The groom will also have his hands and feet covered in henna but without any design. On the third day, the groom and his party walk slowly to the bride's house in a procession, or *zaffa*, singing and dancing the whole way. Traditionally the groom will stay at the bride's house for three days before seeing his family. The couple will then set up home.

Women visitors who want to get a taste of Nubian culture can have their hands 'tatooed' with henna at some of the Nubian villages around Aswan – it looks great and you get to spend time with Nubian women. Try asking around west Aswan, just north of the Tombs of the Nobles. You're looking at anywhere between E£15 and E£30 depending on the size of the design.

LAKE NASSER

Looking out over Lake Nasser's wide expanses of calm green-blue water, it's hard to believe that it is a manmade creation. As the world's largest artificial lake, its statistics are staggering: with an area of 5250 sq km, it stretches 510km in length and between 5km and 35km in width. On average it contains some 135 billion cubic metres of water, of which an estimated six billion is lost each year to evaporation. Its maximum capacity is 157 billion cubic metres of water. This was reached in 1996 after heavy rains in Ethiopia and occasioned the opening of a special spillway at Toshka, about 30km north of Abu Simbel, for the first time since the dam was built. The Egyptian government has since embarked on a controversial project to build a new canal and irrigate thousands of acres in what is now the Nubian Desert between Toshka and the New Valley.

Numbers aside, the contrast between this enormous body of water and the remote desert stretching away on all sides makes Lake Nasser a place of austere beauty. Because the level of the lake fluctuates it has been difficult to build any settlements around its edges. Instead it has become a place for migrating birds to rest on their long journeys north and south. Gazelle, fox and several types of snake (including the deadly horned viper) live on its shores. Many species of fish live in its waters, including the enormous Nile Perch. Crocodiles – some reportedly up

Warning

Lake Nasser is a restricted area and in order to take a safari or sailing trip you need a permit. If you intend to take one of the trips listed here you must contact the companies at least two weeks in advance and supply them with the relevant passport details.

to 5m long – and monitor lizards also live in its shallows. The main human presence here, apart from the few tourists who visit, is limited to the 5000 or so fishermen who spend up to six months at a time in small rowing boats, altogether catching about 50,000 tons of small fish each year.

Apart from the beauty of the lake itself, the main attraction is the temples that were so painstakingly moved in the 1960s. Although all but Qasr Ibrim have roads leading to them, foreigners are currently forbidden to drive to any except Kalabsha, Beit al-Wali and Kertassi. For the moment the rest can only be reached by boat or, in the case of Abu Simbel, plane.

Kalabsha, Beit al-Wali and Kertassi

As a result of the massive UNESCO effort, these three temples were transplanted from a now submerged site about 60km south of Aswan. The new site is on the west bank of Lake Nasser just south of the dam.

The Temple of Kalabsha was erected during the reign of Emperor Augustus, between 30 BC and 14 AD, and was dedicated to the Nubian god Mandulis. Isis and Osiris were also worshipped there and during the Christian era the temple was used as a church.

The then-West German government financed the transfer and reconstruction of the 13,000 blocks of the temple and was presented with the temple's west pylon, which is now in the Berlin Museum. During the rescue operation, evidence was found of even older structures, dating from the times of Amenophis II and Ptolemy IX.

Saving Nubia's Monuments

As plans for building the Aswan Dam were drawn up, attention worldwide focussed on the antiquities that would be lost by the creation of a huge lake behind the dam. A great many valuable and irreplaceable ancient monuments were doomed to be drowned by the waters of Lake Nasser.

Teams from the Egyptian Department of antiquities and archeological missions from many countries descended on Nubia to set in motion the UNESCO-organised projects aimed at rescuing as many of the threatened treasures as possible. Necropolises were excavated, all portable artefacts and relics were removed to museums and, while some temples disappeared beneath the lake, 14 were salvaged and moved to safety.

Ten of them, including the temple complexes of Philae, Kalabsha and Abu Simbel, were dismantled stone by stone and rebuilt, all but Philae in groups of three, on higher ground in Egypt. The other four were donated to the countries which contributed to the rescue effort; they include the splendid Temple of Dendur, which has been reconstructed in a glass building in the Metropolitan Museum of Art in New York.

The preservation of the temples at Abu Simbel, 280km south of Aswan, must rank as the greatest achievement of the UNESCO rescue operation. And, hewn as they were out of solid rock, the modern technology involved in cutting, moving and rebuilding the incredible temples and statues at least paralleled the skill of the ancient artisans who chiselled them out of the cliff face in the first place.

A worldwide appeal for the vital funding and expertise needed to salvage these Abu Simbel monuments was launched in the 1960s. The response was immediately forthcoming and a variety of conservation schemes were put forward. Finally, in 1964 a cofferdam was built to hold back the already encroaching water of the new lake, while Egyptian, Italian, Swedish, German and French archaeological teams began to move the massive structures.

At a cost of about US$40 million the temples were cut up into more than 2000 huge blocks, weighing from 10 to 40 tonnes each, and reconstructed inside a specially built mountain 210m away from the water and 65m higher than the original site. The temples were carefully oriented to face in the correct direction and the landscape of their original environment was recreated on and around the concrete, dome-shaped mountain.

The project took just over four years. The temples of Abu Simbel were officially reopened in 1968, while the sacred site they had occupied for over 3000 years disappeared beneath Lake Nasser. A plaque to the right of the temple entrance eloquently describes this achievement: 'Through this restoration of the past, we have indeed helped to build the future of mankind'.

An impressive stone causeway leads from the lake up to the 1st pylon of the temple, beyond which are the colonnaded court and the hypostyle hall, which has 12 columns. Inscriptions on the walls show various emperors and pharaohs cavorting with the gods and goddesses. Just beyond the hall are three chambers, with stairs leading from one up to the roof. The view of Lake Nasser and the High Dam, across the capitals of the hall and court, is fantastic. An inner passage, between the temple and the encircling wall, leads to a well-preserved Nilometer.

The Temple of Beit al-Wali (House of the Holy Man) was rebuilt with assistance from the US government and placed just north-west of the Temple of Kalabsha. Most of Beit al-Wali, which was carved from the rocks, was built during the reign of

Ramses II. On the walls of the forecourt are several fascinating reliefs, detailing the pharaoh's victory over the Nubians (on the south wall) and his wars against the Libyans and Syrians (the north wall). Ramses is shown pulling the hair of his enemies while women plead for mercy. The most beautiful scenes are those detailing the tribute being paid by the defeated Nubians. Ramses is shown sitting on his throne and receiving, among other things, leopard skins, gold, elephant tusks, feathers, cattle, a monkey and an ostrich.

Just north of the Temple of Kalabsha are the remains of the Temple of Kertassi. Two Hathor (cow-headed) columns, a massive architrave and four columns with intricate capitals are the only pieces which were salvaged from Lake Nasser.

Strewn about the area between these two temples are a jumble of rocks with prehistoric carvings and paintings, some amazingly well-preserved, that were salvaged along with the temples.

Kalabsha is open from 8 am to 4 pm and costs E£12 to enter (E£6 for students). When the water level is high, you'll need a boat to get to the temple; the motorboats can be found near the shipyard on the western side of the dam. It costs about E£25 to hire a boat to take you there and back.

Wadi as-Subua

The temples of Wadi al-Subua, Dakka and Mahararaqa were all moved to this site, about 4km west of the original Wadi al-Subua, by the Egyptian Antiquities Organisation between 1961 and 1965.

Wadi al-Subua means 'valley of lions' in Arabic and refers to the avenue of 10 sphinxes that stood in front of the **Temple of Ramses-Mery-Amun**. Yet another monument dating to the reign of the energetic Ramses II, the rear part of the temple was hewn from rock and the front portion was free-standing. At the entrance to the temple itself are the remains of colossal statues of Ramses, and scenes on the towers portray the pharaoh making offerings to the gods. The rear of the temple was converted to a church, but the original reliefs showing Ramses making yet more offerings to the gods, some with traces of colour, are well preserved. In what was the sanctuary the statues that originally stood in the niche in the west wall were destroyed by the Christians and the reliefs were covered with plaster and then painted with Christian figures. Most of these have now disappeared, showing the Ramesside reliefs underneath, but if you look carefully you'll see a contrast that could only ever exist in Egypt: a finely-etched Ramses who appears to be offering flowers to the haloed, fragmentary upper body of St Peter.

About 1km to the north are the remains of the **Temple of Dakka**, a Ptolemaic structure dating back to the 3rd century BC. Originally situated 40km north of here, it is dedicated to the god of wisdom, Thoth of Pnubs (or 'sycamore-fig tree') and is notable for its 12m-high pylon, which you can climb for great views of the lake and surrounding temples.

The **Temple of Mahararaqa**, the smallest of the three at this site, originally stood 50km north of here near the village of Ofendina. Thought to have been dedicated to Serapis, the Alexandrian god, its decorations were never finished and the walls seem very bare. In the north-east corner of the main hall a spiral staircase leads up to the roof, the only spiral staircase in any ancient Egyptian structure. There is some evidence that the temple was later used as a church, but little of it remains. Entrance to the site is E£12 (E£6 for students).

Amada

Standing 2.6km from its original site, the **Temple of Amada** is the oldest surviving monument on Lake Nasser, dating back to the 18th dynasty. Dedicated, like many temples in Nubia, to the gods Amun-Re and Re-Harakhti, it has some of the finest reliefs in any Nubian monument and contains two important historical inscriptions. The first, on the left of the entrance, tells how a Libyan-backed rebellion in Nubia was quashed by the kings; the second, on the back wall of the temple, describes a campaign by the New Kingdom pharaoh Amenophis II against the Asiatics and details his ruthless murder of prisoners of war. All this was no doubt designed to impress upon the Nubians that political opposition to the powerful Egyptians was useless. Later the temple was converted into a church and a mud-brick dome was built on the roof.

On the very top of the temple facade you can see crudely-carved camels that are thought to have been made either by Bedouin or travellers during the middle ages.

The **Temple of Derr**, was the only pharaonic temple to be situated on the east bank of the Nile and originally stood 11km south-west of its present site. Although the front of the building is damaged, there are some well-preserved reliefs in the pillared hall, portraying Ramses II once again, worshipped as a living god, as at Abu Simbel. In the scenes on either side of the doorway you can see him killing his enemies, followed by his famous pet lion.

Five minutes walk from the Temple of Derr is the small rock-cut **Tomb of Pennut**, which was originally situated at Aniba, 40km south of Amada. Pennut was the chief administrator of Lower Nubia during the reign of Ramses VI. Consisting of a small offering chapel with a niche at the rear, some of the reliefs still have traces of colour and depict events and personalities from Pennut's life, including a scene showing him being presented with a gift by Ramses VI himself. Entrance to the Amada site costs E£12 (E£6 for students).

Qasr Ibrim

The only Nubian monument visible on its original site, Qasr Ibrim sits with water lapping at its edges on what was once the top of a 70m-high cliff about 60km north of Abu Simbel. The unusual name of this fortress is derived from the Meroitic name, *Pedeme*, which became Primis in Greek, Phrim in Coptic and finally Ibrim in Arabic.

Early history of the site is obscure. Situated at a strategic point overlooking the Nile, archeologists have so far found evidence of a fortification here dating back to 1000 BC, but it is possible that there was some sort of garrison at the site as much as 800 years earlier, when the Egyptians built a series of mud-brick fortresses along the Nile to maintain their control over Lower Nubia.

In about 680 BC the 25th dynasty Nubian king of Egypt, Taharka, built a mud-brick temple here and about 700 years later the first fortification wall was built. During Roman times the area seems to have been a bastion of paganism as Christianity spread in Nubia. As many as six temples, including a mud-brick temple to Isis, are thought to have existed on its five-acre site. The area finally converted to Christianity more than 200 years after Egypt and Taharka's temple became a church. By the 13th century, Ibrim had become one of Lower Nubia's principal Christian centres and held out against Islam until the 16th century, when a group of Bosnian mercenaries working for the Ottomans came and occupied the site. They stayed on and married into the local Nubian community, using part of the cathedral as a mosque. Their descendants were driven out by panicked Mamluks fleeing Mohammed Ali's purges in the early 19th century (see the boxed text 'Massacre of the Mamluks' on page 176).

Apart from the structural remains, of which a 7th century sandstone cathedral is the most prominent, many written documents have been found at Qasr Ibrim, but at the time of writing extensive archeological work was being carried out and the site was closed to visitors.

Abu Simbel

While the fate of his colossal statue at the Ramesseum in Luxor no doubt gnaws at the spirit of Ramses II, the mere existence, in the 20th century AD, of his great temple at Abu Simbel must make him shake with laughter and shout 'I told you so'.

Carved out of the mountain on the west bank of the Nile between 1290 and 1224 BC, the temple was dedicated to the gods Ra-Harakhty, Amun and Ptah and, of course, to the deified pharaoh himself. But

The crumbling mud-brick remains of Shali, the 13th century fortress, dominate modern-day Siwa.

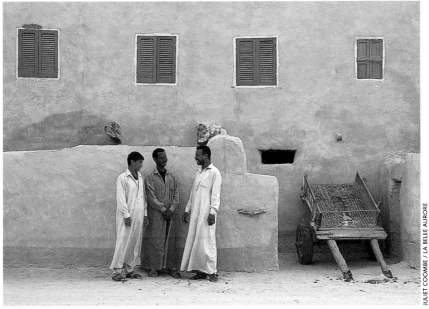

Brightly coloured buildings are a feature of Siwa's unique charm and character.

Several hundred mud-brick tombs are housed in the Necropolis of Al-Bagawat in Kharga Oasis.

Temple remains and entrance to the Roman tomb Qasr El-Labaka near Kharga Oasis.

The White Desert's bizarre, 'otherworldly' rock formations are shaped by constant wind erosion.

TEMPLE OF ABU SIMBEL

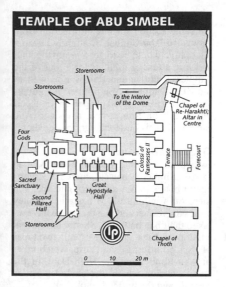

Storerooms

Storerooms

To the Interior
of the Dome

Chapel of
Re-Harakhti;
Altar in
Centre

Four
Gods

Colossi of
Ramesses II

Terrace

Forecourt

Sacred
Sanctuary

Great
Hypostyle
Hall

Second
Pillared
Hall

Storerooms

Chapel of
Thoth

0   10   20 m

Each statue is more than 20m high and is accompanied by smaller, though much larger than life-size, statues of the king's mother Queen Tuya, his wife Nefertari and some of their children.

Above the entrance to the Great Hypostyle Hall, between the central throned colossi, is the figure of the falcon-headed sun-god Ra-Harakhty. Unfortunately, the sun-god has been subjected to the trials of time and now lacks part of a leg and foot.

The roof of the hall is supported by eight columns, each fronted by a 10m-high statue of Ramses; the roof is decorated with vultures representing Osiris; and the reliefs on the walls depict the pharaoh in various battles, trampling over his enemies, victorious as usual. In the next hall, the four columned vestibule, Ramses and Nefertari are shown in front of the gods and the solar barques that carry the dead to the underworld.

The innermost chamber is the Sacred Sanctuary, where the four gods of the Great Temple sit on their thrones carved in the back wall and wait for the dawn. The temple is aligned in such a way that on 22 February and 22 October every year (speculated to be the anniversaries of Ramses' coronation and birth), the first rays of the rising sun reach across the Nile, penetrate the temple, move along the hypostyle hall, through the vestibule and into the sanctuary, where they illuminate the somewhat mutilated figures of Ra-Harakhty, Ramses II and Amun. Ptah, to the left, is never illuminated. (Until the temples were moved, this phenomenon happened one day earlier.)

mostly, with its colossal statues of Ramses II addressing the river, it was designed as a show of strength, an awesome great quarteted sentinel watching over any boats sailing into the pharaoh's lands from the south.

However, over centuries both the Nile and the desert sands imperceptibly shifted until the temple was lost to human memory. It was rediscovered by chance in 1813 by the Swiss explorer John Lewis Burkhardt – only one of the heads was completely showing above the sand, the next head was broken off, and of the remaining two, only the crowns could be seen. There's a superb and often reproduced etching of this scene made by David Roberts, who visited about 25 years after Burkhardt. It wasn't until the British began excavating, around the turn of this century, that the temple's full glory was revealed.

From the great temple's forecourt, a short flight of steps leads up to the terrace in front of the massive rock-cut facade, which is about 30m high and 35m wide. Guarding the entrance, the four famous colossal statues of Ramses II sit majestically, staring out across the desert as if looking through time itself.

Temple of Hathor The other temple at the Abu Simbel complex is the rock-cut Temple of Hathor, which is fronted by six massive standing statues, about 10m high. Four of them represent Ramses, the other two represent his beloved wife Queen Nefertari and they are all flanked by the smaller figures of the Ramessid princes and princesses.

The six pillars of the hypostyle hall are crowned with Hathor capitals and its walls are adorned with scenes depicting: Nefertari before Hathor and Mut; the queen honouring her husband; and Ramses, yet again, being valiant and victorious. In the vestibule and adjoining chambers there are colourful scenes of the goddess and her sacred barque. In the sanctuary there is a weathered statue of a cow, the sacred symbol of Hathor, emerging from the rock.

Admission for both temples is E£36 (E£18 for students) including the mandatory fee for a guide, whether you want one or not.

Places to Stay & Eat

There are two hotels at Abu Simbel. The four star *Nefertari Hotel* (☎ 400 508/9) is about 400m from the temples in a relatively lush setting overlooking Lake Nasser. It has singles/doubles for US$72/90 including breakfast but not taxes. The rather small rooms have lake views, air-con, full carpeting and, in some, a mini-fridge. There's also a swimming pool. The *restaurant* stays open all year, and offers breakfast for E£11 and lunch/dinner for E£31/37. During winter, reservations are recommended. They will also let you camp for about E£20 – you get to use the showers, pool and mosquitoes.

The three star *Nobaleh Ramses Hotel* (☎/fax 400 380) is in the town of Abu Simbel, about 1.5km from the temple site. The 39 singles/doubles cost US$50/82.50 half-board, including tax, although deals are possible. The large rooms are bright and clean, come with en suite bath and toilet and are equipped with TV, air-con and fridge. The buffet breakfast here costs E£10, lunch is E£19 and dinner E£25.

The line-up of cheap cafes in town, such as *Nubian Oasis* and *Wadi el-Nil* offers little incentive to dine there.

Getting There & Away

Although there is a perfectly good road between Aswan and Abu Simbel, at the time of writing the police had deemed it off limits to all foreigners. As a result, EgyptAir halved its fare and most visitors see the temple in the company of a planeload of package tourists. (See the Aswan Getting There & Away section for flight details.)

Should the police change their policy, see the same section for bus information from Aswan to Abu Simbel. A slightly cheaper alternative would be to get a group together and hire a taxi or minibus for a tour of the temples at Philae and Kalabsha as well as the High Dam and Abu Simbel. A minibus should cost about E£30 per person (transport only). But be forewarned, a visit to Abu Simbel alone is quite enough for one day.

Organised Tours

Even though you can't actually take the road to Abu Simbel at present, there's no shortage of hotels in Aswan offering to take you there on a minibus. *Don't* pay any money until you've checked that the police have relaxed their ban on travel. Should the current situation change, there are usually two types of trips on offer: a 'short' trip, which takes in Abu Simbel and the High Dam, or the 'long' version which also includes Philae Temple and the unfinished obelisk.

Generally the trips begin between 4 and 5 am, with minibuses picking up guests from various hotels around town. They aim to get to the temple by about 8.30 am, before it gets too hot, and leave about 10 am. In general, those on the short trip will be back by about 2.30 pm; long haulers will be looking at about 5 pm. Admission fees are not included in the price of the trip. Many minibuses do not have air-con, which can be extremely uncomfortable in summer, especially if the organisers have packed in too many people (which they often try to do). Travellers have also complained that they have very little time in Abu Simbel, making it hardly worth the long drive.

Alternatively, most of the larger travel agents in Aswan are likely to resume sending air-con coaches to Abu Simbel if the road opens. Try Thomas Cook or one of the other reputable agencies in town.

Cruising Lake Nasser There are other ways of seeing Lake Nasser and its monuments. One of the best, and certainly the most luxurious, is a cruise. There are five boats currently sailing on Lake Nasser and the ministry of tourism has promised to limit the number to six, although whether they can resist the temptation to overdevelop this area like they have much of the rest of Egypt remains to be seen. Of the five currently on offer, two stand out far above the rest. The *Eugénie* and *Qasr Ibrim* are both run by the same company, Belle Epoque Travel, and were the brainchild of Mustafa al-Guindi, a Cairene of Nubian origin who is almost singlehandedly responsible for getting Lake Nasser opened to tourists. The boats are stunningly designed: *Eugénie* is modelled on a turn-of-the-century hunting lodge; Qasr Ibrim is all 1930s art deco elegance. Both have pools, jacuzzis and fantastic French cuisine. In addition, passengers are pampered with such treats as evening cocktails and classical music in front of Abu Simbel Temple. Trips on the cruises can be arranged through the company's Cairo office (☎ 518 1857/8, fax 353 6114). A standard room is at least US$90 per person per day on a three or four-day trip, including all meals and temple visits.

Fishing Safaris The size of the fish in Lake Nasser is legendary (the record for a Nile Perch is almost 100kg) and it is beginning to attract the attention of fishing enthusiasts around the world. At the moment there are two companies running fishing trips on the lake. The African Angler is run by a former Kenyan safari guide, Tim Bailey. He has seven fishing boats and two supply boats and runs weekly safaris from September to December and February to June. All of the fish caught by anglers are returned to the lake and he is trying to promote environmental conservation in the area. He can be contacted between safaris at the Basma Hotel in Aswan (☎ 316 052). He also operates through Abercrombie & Kent in Cairo (☎ 394 7735) and through agencies specialising in fishing throughout Europe and Australia. Bohayrat Orascom (☎/fax 314 090) is the other company and they're based in Aswan. They charge about US$90 per person, per day, including all food and equipment. The company also runs 'crocodile safari' day trips out of Aswan for US$35 per person.

Sailing Another new option for seeing Lake Nasser is by sailboat. Cairo-based Hermes Travel (☎ 303 5105, fax 345 4711) has a 15m yacht, the only one currently on the lake, with five double cabins and an auxiliary engine (for those times when the wind does not cooperate). With the boat's shallow draft, it can get to places that the cruise ships cannot reach, and as well as travelling to all the temples on the lake it sails to the Eastern Desert protectorate of Wadi al-Alagi, linking up with 4WDs that can take you across the desert to the usually off-limits Red Sea port of Berenice. Prices are in the range of US$50 per person per day.

Western Oases

'There are deserts and there are deserts,' explorer Ralph Bagnold famously said. But the Western (or Libyan) Desert, a vast expanse that starts at the western banks of the Nile and continues well into Libya, is the desert of deserts. Covering a total of 2.8 million square kilometres and bordered by Libya in the west, Sudan in the south and the Mediterranean in the north, it is a vast world of desolation and beauty – and one of the few places in Egypt where you can go for days at a time without seeing a soul.

Five isolated but thriving oases dot this otherwise uninhabited expanse: Kharga, Dakhla, Farafra, Bahariyya and, to the north-west, Siwa. Herodotus called these small settlements the Islands of the Blest and after a long camel trek through the desert, they must certainly have appeared so for, despite their remoteness, the five have long and surprisingly rich histories. Recent research in the area has unearthed a wealth of prehistoric artefacts, pointing to habitation at the very dawn of human history. In late pharaonic and Roman times the oases were the bustling hubs on trade routes between Africa and the Mediterranean.

In more recent history, since the time of Nasser, the Egyptian authorities have formulated grandiose plans to conquer the desert through land-reclamation and intensive agriculture. The oases were to form a new alternative to the Nile Valley for Egypt's burgeoning population and landless farmers and inner-city families were encouraged to settle there. In the late 1950s the oases of Kharga, Dakhla and Farafra were grouped into the New Valley governorate, and the first new inhabitants arrived on 3 October 1959 – this date is now an annual public holiday throughout the New Valley. But although some of the New Valley projects were successful, many were not and as of 1996, only 143,000 people lived within the governorate boundaries, far short of original plans.

HIGHLIGHTS

- **White Desert** The only desert in the world where the sand looks like snow and surreal white sculptures arise from the sand.

- **Siwa** This palm-filled, tranquil oasis is unique in Egypt thanks to its historic isolation and fiercely independent inhabitants.

- **Al-Qasr** Wander through the labyrinthine streets of Dakhla's ancient mud-brick town, built to keep out sandstorms and invaders.

- **Roman fortresses** The hilltop ruins dotting Kharga Oasis once protected lucrative slave caravans from Africa.

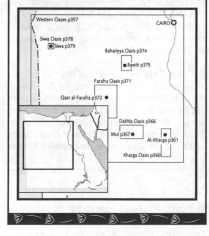

Although the oases are attracting more and more travellers, their increased popularity has not diminished the adventure of exploring this remote region. The towns and villages are dotted with archaeological sites easily accessible to most travellers, while a safari into the open desert beyond is one of the last great trips that can be taken

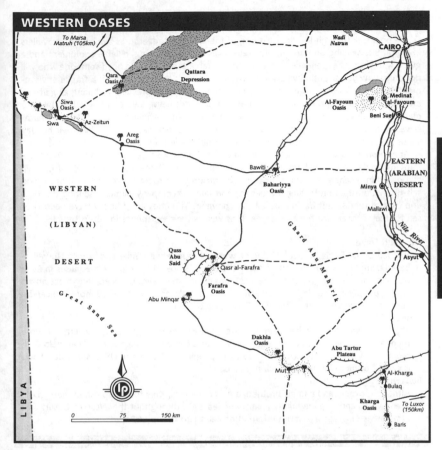

WESTERN OASES

To Marsa
Matruh (105km)

Qattara
Depression

Qara
Oasis

Wadi
Natrun

CAIRO

Al-Fayoum
Oasis

Medinat
al-Fayoum

Siwa
Oasis

Beni Suef

Siwa

Az-Zeitun

Areg
Oasis

WESTERN

Bawiti

Bahariyya
Oasis

EASTERN
(ARABIAN)
DESERT

Minya

(LIBYAN)

Mallawi

DESERT

Nile River

Ghard Abu Muharik

Quss
Abu
Said

Qasr al-Farafra

Asyut

Great Sand Sea

Farafra
Oasis

Abu Minqar

Dakhla
Oasis

Abu Tartur
Plateau

Mut

Al-Kharga

LIBYA

0   75   150 km

Bulaq

Kharga
Oasis

To Luxor
(150km)

Baris

in Egypt. The ideal time to visit is in late autumn or early spring, because summer temperatures can soar as high as 52°C (125°F), though humidity rarely exceeds 9%. Winter is very pleasant with average daytime highs of between 20°C and 25°C between December and February and sometimes March, but it can get very nippy (down to 2°C at times) at night.

Asphalt roads link all the oases. Kharga is also linked by road to Luxor and Asyut. Note, however, that while you can drive from Kharga to Luxor, you cannot do the reverse, due to the nervous Luxor police.

Siwa is usually reached by road from Marsa Matruh on the north coast. Although there is road access from Bahariyya to Siwa, there is as yet no public transport. For more information see Getting There & Away in the Siwa section.

KHARGA OASIS

Kharga, the largest and most developed of the oases, lies in a desert depression about

Desert Safaris

Going on a trek through the desert is one of the last great adventures available to travellers in Egypt. But heading off into remote areas takes serious planning, reliable equipment and a guide with years of experience. For a truly memorable safari you also need someone who will not only show you beautiful vistas, but who understands that the desert is a fragile environment. As well as following such basic environmentally friendly practices as taking all garbage away with you and burning all toilet paper, this includes being aware of the vulnerability of many antiquities sites that dot remote areas in Egypt. Guides who allow tourists to help themselves to flint arrowheads or spray water on prehistoric rock paintings so that their holiday snaps look clearer are destroying a link to mankind's earliest history.

Apart from local guides available from the oases themselves (see the Organised Tours sections in Dahkla, Farafra, Bahariyya and Siwa), a number of other adventure travel outfits have sprung up in recent years. Unfortunately, the majority are more concerned with profit and self-promotion than protecting the desert, and tales of company names inscribed on rocks and piles of rubbish left behind are all too common. The ones listed below have been chosen for their concern for the environment, as well as their experience in desert travel.

Abanoub Travel
   Headed by Dr Rabia, a medical doctor who fell in love with Sinai and whose Nuweiba-based company has been leading tours there ever since. His company specialises in Sinai but also takes small groups to the Eastern and Western Deserts. Jeep tours cost about US$35 per person per day, including food. Camel treks are about US$10 more. He can be contacted in Nuweiba at ☎ 062-520 201, fax 520 206.
Amr Shannon
   Shannon is an artist who has been leading small groups through Egypt's deserts for more than 20 years. He has his own Jeep Cherokee and camping equipment and can help with rental of 4WDs. He'll take groups of up to 12 people at a flat rate of US$300 per day. Food is extra. For more information call ☎ 519 6894.
Badawiyya
   Although owner Saad and his brothers are from Farafra, they have also established an office in Cairo and arrange highly recommended treks throughout the Western Desert and other areas of Egypt. For more information call Cairo ☎ 345 8524.

30km wide and 200km long. The chief town is Al-Kharga, 233km from Asyut. It was originally a way station on the 40 Day Road, the caravan route between Sudan and Egypt. But unlike the other oasis towns, which have retained something of their original character, this place, capital of the New Valley, reflects the dreams of Egyptian planners in the 1960s. Enormous concrete-and-glass modernist structures stand on wide, shadeless boulevards that speak of a brave new world of agri-business and mass population movement rather than desert heat and date plantations.

Even though the town itself is pretty much faceless and uninteresting, there are several things worth seeing.

Orientation

The bus station is in the south-east of the town, near what's left of the old centre, and it's a fair hike to most of the hotels. If you're coming from Dakhla, decide where you want to stay before arriving – you may

Desert Safaris

WESTERN OASES

Lama Expeditions
  Samir Lama is the undisputed king of the Western Desert explorers. Although he now lives in Germany he organises several long-range desert expeditions each year. Lasting from 15 to 21 days the trips head into the far south-west of Egypt and beyond into Sudan. Lama usually takes small groups of six to eight people but will take special groups of up to 12 people. He can be reached in Frankfurt at ☎ 49-69-447 897, fax 499 0767.
Max Adventure Travel
  One of the first companies in Cairo to organise desert trips, Max takes groups out to the Western Desert and South Sinai. Trips to the latter cost US$120 per day per person and include all meals, mineral water. Western Desert trips cost about US$100 per person. For more information, call Supriya Chawla in Cairo ☎ 303 5125, fax 303 6123.

want to be let off at Sharia al-Adel rather than having to trudge all the way back again.

Those arriving from the Nile Valley will be treated to a spectacular panorama as the road descends the escarpment before passing one of Egypt's most notorious prisons at Al-Munira, about 23km north of Al-Kharga. Once in town you'll come to Midan Nasser, marked by a large statue of a woman (representing Egypt) holding her children (the oases).

Information
The tourist office (☎ 921 206, fax 921 205) on Midan Nasser is open daily except Friday from 8.30 am to 3 pm and again for variable periods in the evening. The staff are friendly but they don't always have the most recent information. Another source of local information is the New Valley Tourist Friends Association (☎ 921 451) at Midan Basateen, near the Ministry of Culture. It's open daily from 5 to 10 pm but it is closed on Friday.

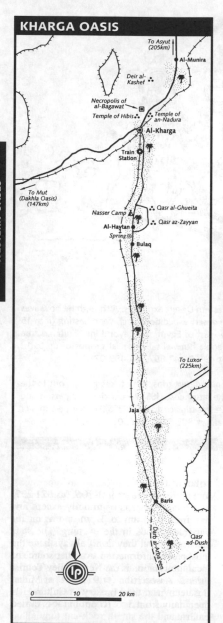

KHARGA OASIS

To Asyut
(205km)

Al-Munira

Deir al-
Kashef

Necropolis of
al-Bagawat

Temple of Hibis

Temple of
an-Nadura

Al-Kharga

Train
Station

To Mut
(Dakhla Oasis)
(147km)

Nasser Camp

Qasr al-Ghueita

Qasr az-Zayyan

Al-Haytan

Spring

Bulaq

To Luxor
(225km)

Jaja

Baris

Qasr
ad-Dush

Darb al-Arba'een

0   10   20 km

The local branches of the Banque du Caire and Banque Masr both change cash and travellers cheques, while the latter also does credit card cash advances – the only place in the oases to do so. The post office is open from 8 am to 2.30 pm; closed Friday. The telephone centrale, on Sharia al-Gomhuriya, is open 24 hours a day.

Duaa's Studio, a little place between the Waha Hotel and the square on Sharia al-Adel, usually has some Kodak and Agfa film.

Museum

Down the road from the tourist office is a museum housing archaeological exhibits from various ancient sites around Kharga and Dakhla oases. Particularly good is the small display in the room to the right of the entrance hall. Sponsored by a Canadian museum, it traces the prehistory of the oases in both English and Arabic and has four vitrines filled with prehistoric artefacts. As well as this there is a wide selection of pharaonic, Ptolemaic and early Christian displays. Museum hours are from 8 am to 4 pm; entry is E£20; E£10 for students.

Temple of Hibis

This 6th century BC structure dedicated to the god Amun was built mostly by the Persian emperor Darius I. Dedicated to the Theban triad Amun, Mut and Khonsu, it was the centre of the town of Hibis, capital of the oasis in ancient times. In the hypostyle hall, graffiti from 19th century European travellers, including the famous Western Desert explorer, Gerhard Rohlfs, can still be seen. The temple is 2km north of town just to the left off the main road. Tickets are E£16/8 for adults/students.

Temple of an-Nadura

This temple, to the north-east of the town, also doubled as a fortress and was built to protect the oasis by the Roman emperor Antonius Pius in 138 AD. You can't miss the ruins, perched on a rise off to the right of the main road, shortly before the turn-off to Hibis Temple. Follow the road to the right for 500m and scramble up the potsherd-strewn hill. Although the temple is ruined it has sweeping views of the desert and oasis, and is a great place to watch the sunset.

Necropolis of al-Bagawat

About 1km on from the Temple of Hibis, this necropolis is probably the most interesting of the three sights clustered just north of the town. Most of the several hundred mud-brick tombs in this Christian cemetery date from the 4th to the 6th centuries AD. They are traditional domed Coptic tombs, some of which have interesting, but rapidly disappearing wall paintings of biblical scenes. Admission is E£20 (E£10 for students). You will be dogged by someone anxious to become your guide; if you want to get inside some of the more colourful tombs, he's your man. Ask to see the Chapel of Peace, which has figures of the apostles on the squinches of the domes, just visible through the Greek graffiti. The Chapel of the Exodus has the best-preserved paintings, with a dome full of Old Testament biblical stories and graffiti dating back to the 9th century. Also worth seeing are tomb No 25 and a small tomb that the site-guard has named the Chapel of the Grapes (Anaeed al-Ainab) after the grapevines that cover the walls. The site is open from 8 am to 5 pm (6 pm in summer).

If you're on foot, just cut across the desert when you see the necropolis to your left. By car, you'll have to drive 1km or so up the road to the entrance.

Deir al-Kashef

Dominating the cliffs to the north of Bagawat is the ruined monastery of Mustafa al-Kashef, or Mustafa the Tax Collector. Strategically placed to overlook what was once one of the most important crossroads of the Western Desert, the point where the Darb al-Ghabari from Dakhla crossed the Darb al-Arba'een, the magnificent remains date back to the early Christian era, although the site was occupied as early as the Middle Kingdom. Once five storeys high, much of it has collapsed but you can just see the tops of the arched corridors that crisscrossed the

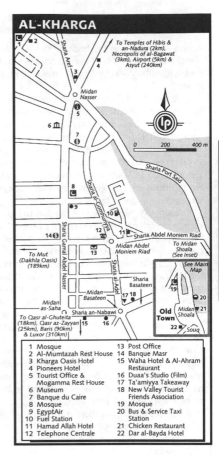

AL-KHARGA

1	Mosque
2	Al-Mumtazah Rest House
3	Kharga Oasis Hotel
4	Pioneers Hotel
5	Tourist Office & Mogamma Rest House
6	Museum
7	Banque du Caire
8	Mosque
9	EgyptAir
10	Fuel Station
11	Hamad Allah Hotel
12	Telephone Centrale
13	Post Office
14	Banque Masr
15	Waha Hotel & Al-Ahram Restaurant
16	Duaa's Studio (Film)
17	Ta'amiyya Takeaway
18	New Valley Tourist Friends Association
19	Mosque
20	Bus & Service Taxi Station
21	Chicken Restaurant
22	Dar al-Bayda Hotel

WESTERN OASES

building. On the plain below are other ruins, including a small church with some barely visible wall paintings on the west wall and the remains of tiny cells where the monks once slept.

To get there, either walk or drive on the left-hand track from the ticket office at the Necropolis of al-Bagawat. It snakes behind the hill on which the cemetery is built, passing below the ugly concrete rest house of the famous oasis archaeologist Ahmed Fakhry and the small, rock-cut tombs that

WESTERN OASES

The Real English Patient (& Other Desert Explorers)

Anyone familiar with the book or film *The English Patient* may be intrigued to know that the character played by Ralph Fiennes – the 'English Patient' of the title – is not a fictional creation; neither was he English, nor was he ever a patient crippled by burns and a broken heart.

Ladislaus 'Laszlo' Almasy was a Hungarian aristocrat who arrived in Cairo during the interwar years. Adventurer, explorer and sometime spy, he worked for the British-run Egyptian Desert Survey Department conducting arial surveys. Flying above the Western Desert in his Gypsy Moth, Laszlo did make the discoveries attributed to him in the book and the film, most notably a way to the top of the Gilf Kebir and the Cave of the Swimmers in Uwaynat. When WWII broke out Almasy enlisted with the pro-German Hungarian air force and found himself attached to Rommel's Afrika Korps teaching desert survival. Famously, in 1942 Almasy led a German spy on a gruelling overland trek across the Western Desert to get him into Egypt undetected by the British.

But although Almasy has received all the attention in recent years, he was only one among many extraordinary modern heroes of the Western Desert. Even as recently as the late 19th century vast swathes of this huge and mysterious territory remained uncharted because the distance between water sources was too great for camels to manage. In 1874 the German geographer Gerhard Rohlfs began to map the area, in the process making an epic and near-fatal journey of 420 miles through the Great Sand Sea without being able to water his camels. In what is now a classic moment in the annals of desert travel he had given himself up for dead when a freak rainstorm saved his party and his camels. He and his companion built a cairn on the top of the nearest dune and named it Regenfeld (Rainfield). In 1876 he published an account of his explorations *Drei Monate in der Libyschen Wust*, still one of the most important works on the Western Desert.

In 1923, the Egyptian explorer Ahmed Hassanein made the first crossing of the Western Desert in modern times, travelling an incredible 3572km from Sallum on the Mediterranean coast to Fasher in the Sudan via the oasis of Kufra (now in Libya). In between his long marches he managed to discover Gebel Uwaynat in the south-west corner of the country, later describing it in his book *Lost Oasis*.

But it was the introduction of the car that allowed desert exploration to really take off. In 1923 another Egyptian, Prince Kamal al-Din, took three custom-made Citroen caterpillars into the Great Sand Sea. Over the next couple of years he mapped the remote south-west corner of the desert.

Like Almasy, British employees of the Desert Survey, such as PA Clayton and GW Murray, did much to chart the desert. During WWII Clayton was joined by other desert enthusiasts who formed the Long Range Desert Group, the gang loosely portrayed in *The English Patient*. The group spent the war years patrolling the Western Desert for the allies, using the expertise they'd gained in years of travel in the area to mount daring raids and help prevent the German and Italian armies from advancing into Egypt. One of its members, Ralph Bagnold, tells how he and his army buddies got started on their desert trips in the classic *Libyan Sands: Travel in a Dead World*. He later went back to England and continued his desert exploration by building a wind-tunnel and studying the effect of wind on sand. The outcome was his book *The Physics of Blown Sand and Desert Dunes*, which was later used by NASA to interpret satellite pictures of Mars.

honeycomb the mountain. After about 1km you will come upon the imposing mud-brick ruins.

Places to Stay

Camping You can camp in the grounds of the Kharga Oasis Hotel for E£7 per person and use the toilet and shower inside.

Hotels The newly built *Dar al-Bayda Hotel* (☎ 921 717) is a much-needed addition to Kharga's small pantheon of hotels. Just to the right off Midan Shoala, where the buses and service taxis are based, it has clean, pleasant rooms, most with fans. A third floor is under construction and there are plans for a bar/restaurant on top. Singles are E£14 and doubles with bath cost E£20. Breakfast is E£4 extra. Rooms on the new floor, scheduled to open in 1999, are supposed to be cheaper.

Waha Hotel (☎ 920 393) is a reasonable cheapie but the singles are cramped and windowless and the shared bathrooms can be filthy. On the plus side, the rooms have fans, the water is hot and the staff are friendly. If you're coming in from Dakhla, the bus can drop you off at the entrance. Singles/doubles without bath cost E£7/14 or E£15/20 with bath.

There are several government rest houses in Al-Kharga. *Mogamma*, behind the tourist office, is the best, comprising four chalets, one of which can sleep 10 people. The rooms cost E£17.30 per person, have fridge, kitchen and TV and are very clean. *Al-Mumtazah* rest house, a huge modernist affair with five large rooms, is another option but it's not nearly as good and is inconveniently located, though it's cheaper at E£9 for a bed. To get rooms at either place you can contact the tourist office.

Hamad Allah Hotel (☎ 920 638, fax 925 017) is popular with overland tour groups. Singles/doubles with bath, fridge, TV and breakfast cost E£31/53 or E£45/75.25 with air-con. The rooms are clean but a bit dark and in need of a coat of paint.

Kharga Oasis Hotel (☎ 921 500) is another modern homage to concrete, but has a nice palm-filled garden and terrace. A favourite stopping-off point for desert adventurers, it's a good place, although it often seems sadly empty. Singles/doubles cost E£55/77 without air-con, or E£61/83 with. Prices include breakfast and taxes.

The first five star hotel in the oases, *Pioneers Hotel* (☎ 927 982, fax 927 983) opened its lacquered doors in November 1998. A salmon pink, 90-room low-rise, it is more appropriate to the mass-tourism of the Nile Valley than the oases, and bills itself as 'a short-cut to modern life'. If you can't live without satellite TV and central air-con, singles/doubles on half-board basis will set you back US$95/124.

Places to Eat

Restaurants are few and far between in Kharga and the best places to eat are the hotels. At *Hamad Allah Hotel* set lunch (E£17) and dinner (E£19) are available and there's a bar. *Kharga Oasis Hotel* restaurant has lunch for E£21 and dinner for E£24. There's an outdoor bar overlooking the tranquil garden. *Pioneers Hotel* has the usual overpriced Egyptian five-star hotel food, as well as a bar and outdoor terrace.

Otherwise, try *Al-Ahram* at the front of the Waha Hotel, which sells chicken, and vegetable dishes, or there's a cheap chicken (only) place a few doors down from the bus station on Midan Shoala. There's also a ta'amiyya takeaway joint on Sharia al-Adel near the roundabout, and a juice stand just opposite.

Getting There & Away

Air EgyptAir flies from Cairo to Al-Kharga and back again on Sunday and Wednesday; the fare is E£450 each way. The EgyptAir office is on Sharia Nasser, just by the big mosque. The airport is 5km north of town.

Bus There are buses leaving Al-Kharga daily heading for Cairo: 6 am (E£23.25), and 9, 10.30 and 11 pm (E£37/32/37 respectively). The 9 and 11 pm buses originate in Dakhla and take the desert road all the way, making the trip from Kharga in seven to eight hours. The other two go into Asyut and take the Nile Valley agricultural road, allowing you to stop in Minya or Beni Suef, but lengthening the trip to Cairo to 11 hours or more.

There are several buses from Al-Kharga to Asyut (E£6 to E£7; three to four hours) leaving at 6, 7, 8.30 and 11 am, noon, 2 and 7 pm and at 1 am. Two other buses pass through Al-Kharga en route from Dakhla to Asyut.

Buses to Dakhla (E£5 to E£7; three hours) leave at 7 am, noon and 2.30 pm.

There is a bus to Luxor each Friday, Sunday and Tuesday at 7.30 am. It originates at Dakhla and you buy your ticket on the bus.

Service Taxi A service taxi is a convenient way to travel to Al-Kharga from Asyut. The trip takes from three to four hours and costs E£8 per person. To Dakhla, the trip takes three hours and costs E£7.

Special Taxi At the time of writing special taxis are about the only vehicles using the new Kharga-Luxor road (via Jaja). You'll be looking at about E£500 for the trip (maximum seven people). There might be the odd truck going this way but hitching isn't recommended.

Train There is a train from Kharga to Luxor every Friday at 7 am. The trip takes about seven hours and tickets (3rd class only) cost E£9.80 (students E£4.90). A branch line has been inaugurated to Baris but there is no scheduled service as yet.

Getting Around

Covered pick-up trucks act as the local transport in Al-Kharga. They run up and down Sharia Gamal Abdel Nasser, and between Midan Shoala and the Midan Nasser, as well as servicing various other routes around town. Expect to pay between 25pt and 50pt, depending on the distance travelled.

SOUTH TO BARIS

Heading south from Al-Kharga is an asphalt road leading to the southernmost town in the oases, Baris. The road passes through a number of newly established villages with

names like Revolution – all part of the numerous projects designed to turn the desert around here green. As you follow the road there are a number of easily accessible sites.

Dominating the hillside on the east side of the Baris road, about 18km south of Al-Kharga, are the remains of **Qasr al-Ghueita**, or Palace of the Beautiful One, a temple from the 25th dynasty dedicated to the Theban triad Amun, Mut and Khonsu. Inside the mud-brick walls there is a well-preserved Ptolemaic temple with reliefs showing scenes of Hapi, god of the Nile. An asphalt road leads the 2km to the temple from the main road. Entry is E£16, or E£8 for students. About 7km further south are the remains of **Qasr az-Zayyan**, another Roman temple built inside a fortress. Close to a modern village it doesn't have the remote feel of most of the other temple-fortresses in the area but is still worth a visit. Entry is E£16 (E£8 for students).

If you don't have a vehicle you can get to the temples by taking a bus heading for Baris or a covered pick-up going to Bulaq. Ask the driver to let you off at the asphalt road leading to the temples. There is also an asphalt road linking the two, but 7km is a long hike if you're on foot. If you are planning to do this, take lots of water.

Baris

Baris, 90km south of Al-Kharga, is the fourth town of the New Valley governorate, but there is little here to remind you that it was once one of the most important trading centres along the Darb al-Arba'een. Other than a few kiosks selling fuul and ta'amiyya there is little of note apart from the uninhabited mud-brick houses of Baris al-Gedida, about 2km north of the original town. Designed in traditional oasis style by Egypt's most famous modern architect, Hassan Fathy, the village was supposed to be a model for other new settlements. However, the 1967 war intervened and the village was never completed.

About 23km to the south-east of Baris is **Qasr ad-Dush**, a temple/fortress built by the Romans. Originally the gateway to Egypt from the south, it was an important stopping point on the Darb al-Arba'een and may also have been used to guard an east-west track to the Esna and Edfu temples in the Nile Valley, known as the Darb al-Dush. The sandstone temple abutting the eastern side of the fortress is dedicated to Osiris and was built by Domitian in the 1st century AD. Few decorations remain but the temple was renowned for once having been partially covered with gold. As in other temples throughout Egypt, the European travellers who visited Dush in the 19th century left their names inscribed for posterity and they can still be seen in the gateway, next to the original inscriptions to Roman emperors.

There is an asphalt road to the temple and to get there from Baris you can either get dropped off by the bus from Al-Kharga, leaving you without a way of getting back to town, or negotiate for a special ride out with a covered pick-up, usually available for about E£20, including waiting time. Admission costs E£16/8.

Places to Stay

Just south of Qasr al-Ghueita, 20km south of Al-Kharga is *Nasser Camp*. Newly acquired by the ever-expanding empire of the Pioneers Hotel, it has overpriced tents and bungalows set in a straggling garden beside a spring. Prices start at E£12 per person in a canvas tent and a ridiculous E£80 per person for a stuffy room in one of their prefab bungalows.

There are *government rest houses* in Baris and Bulaq, but they have just been bought by a private sector company and may be renovated so rooms (currently E£15) may be more. In the very spartan rest house at Baris, a bed costs E£5, but meals are not available. Check with the tourist office in Al-Kharga that they are actually open. One of the employees at the Al-Kharga tourist office, Farhat Shaera, spends Thursday to Saturday in Baris and you can also call him there (☎ 963 054) for more information.

Getting There & Away

There are two buses each day between Al-Kharga and Baris (E£1.75), leaving Al-Kharga at 7 am and 2 pm and Baris at 6 am and 3 pm. At 7 am and 2 pm each day a local bus heads down to Baris, stopping at all the villages on the way, and will take you to Dush and other outlying villages (also for E£1.75). The frequent microbuses and pick-up trucks are a more convenient option between Al-Kharga and Baris and cost about E£3.

DAKHLA OASIS

Dakhla, about 189km west of Kharga, was created from more than 600 natural springs and ponds. Its picturesque mud-brick villages, many built upon much older settlements, sit among impossibly lush fields and orchards. The oasis is home to about 70,000 people and produces rice, wheat, mangoes, oranges, olives and dates as well as apricots, the latter being dried and then sold mainly during Ramadan. As they drive about on donkey carts and work the fields, farmers wear straw hats, giving the place a strange, Latin American air.

Recent research in Dakhla has shown it to be lived in continuously since prehistory. In Neolithic times it was the site of a huge lake and prehistoric rock paintings show that elephants, buffaloes and ostriches wandered along its shores. As the lake dried up, the human population is thought to have migrated eastwards and been among the early settlers in the Nile Valley.

The bus from Asyut and Kharga drops you off at Mut (population 13,000), the largest town in the oasis, from where you can take a service taxi to Al-Qasr, the other town of interest in the area. The bus coming from Farafra can drop you at Al-Qasr or Mut.

Information

Omar Ahmed is one of the most helpful tourist information officers in Egypt. He is a mine of knowledge about the oases and very obliging. There are two tourist offices and Omar flits between them. The new one (☎ 821 686) is in Mut on Sharia as-Sawra al-Khadra and the other (☎ 820 404) is in the same building as the Government Rest House, also in Mut, just by the bus station. Both are open from 8 am to 3 pm.

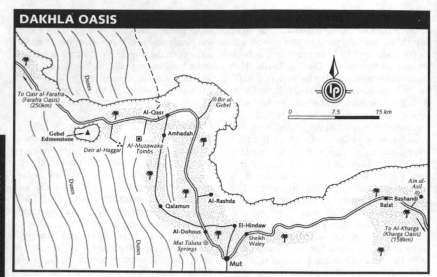

DAKHLA OASIS

WESTERN OASES

The Banque Masr in Mut exchanges cash and travellers cheques. It is open from 8 am to 3 pm and 6 to 9 pm; closed Friday. The post office is behind the mosque at the bus station and is open from 8 am to 2 pm, except Friday. The 24 hour telephone centrale handles international traffic (but there are no card phones).

Ethnographic Museum

This museum is attached to the Dar al-Wafdeen Hotel. If you want to see displays on oasis life, ask at the tourist office to have it opened. Or you can go to the Cultural Palace on Sharia al-Wadi and ask for the museum's manager, Ibrahim Kamel (☎ 821 311). He is usually in his office between 8 am and 2 pm.

Old City of Mut

Often ignored by passing travellers, the labyrinth of mud-brick houses and winding lanes which clings to the slopes of the hill leading to the old citadel is worth exploring. You can climb up to the remains of the **citadel**, which used to be the town proper

(but is now used as a dump and has been taken over by goats), for views of the oasis town against the backdrop of desert cliffs and dunes. On the right of the street leading into the new town centre is a former medieval Islamic **cemetery**.

Hot Springs

There are several hot sulphur pools around the town of Mut, but the easiest to reach is the official touristic one 3km down the road to Al-Qasr from Mut. Called Mut Talata (Mut Three) the spring is the site of a small new hotel (see Places to Stay later in this chapter), so unless you can afford to pay the inflated prices to stay there, you have to dip in the very exposed 1.5m deep pool just outside the hotel's pink walls. The pool's rust-coloured water may not look very inviting (and it can stain clothes) but it is very hot and relaxing.

Sand Dunes & Camel Rides

A few kilometres out past the bus station you can have a roll around in sand dunes said to have been there since Roman times.

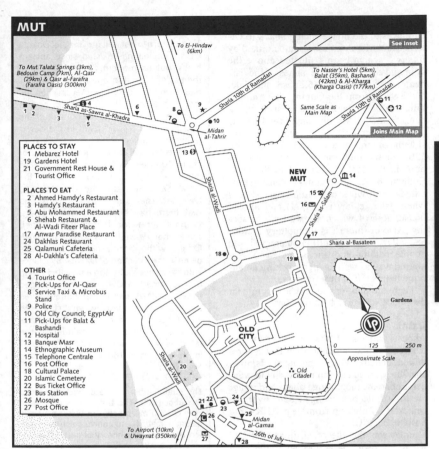

MUT

To El-Hindaw
(6km)

To Mut Talata Springs (3km),
Bedouin Camp (7km), Al-Qasr
(29km) & Qasr al-Farafra
(Farafra Oasis) (300km)

Sharia as-Sawra al-Khadra

To Nasser's Hotel (5km),
Balat (35km), Bashandi
(42km) & Al-Kharga
(Kharga Oasis) (177km)

See Inset

Same Scale as
Main Map

Joins Main Map

Midan
al-Tahrir

NEW
MUT

Sharia as-Salam

Sharia al-Basateen

Sharia al-Wadi

Gardens

**OLD
CITY**

Old
Citadel

0   125   250 m
Approximate Scale

Midan
al-Gamaa

26th of July

To Airport (10km)
& Uwaynat (350km)

PLACES TO STAY
1 Mebarez Hotel
19 Gardens Hotel
21 Government Rest House &
   Tourist Office

PLACES TO EAT
2 Ahmed Hamdy's Restaurant
3 Hamdy's Restaurant
5 Abu Mohammed Restaurant
6 Shehab Restaurant &
   Al-Wadi Fiteer Place
17 Anwar Paradise Restaurant
24 Dakhlas Restaurant
25 Qalamuni Cafeteria
28 Al-Dakhla's Cafeteria

OTHER
4 Tourist Office
7 Pick-Ups for Al-Qasr
8 Service Taxi & Microbus
   Stand
9 Police
10 Old City Council; EgyptAir
11 Pick-Ups for Balat &
   Bashandi
12 Hospital
13 Banque Masr
14 Ethnographic Museum
15 Telephone Centrale
16 Post Office
18 Cultural Palace
20 Islamic Cemetery
22 Bus Ticket Office
23 Bus Station
26 Mosque
27 Post Office

WESTERN OASES

They are not the most spectacular of dunes,
but are easy to reach for people without their
own transport. Sunset camel rides out to the
dunes can also be arranged – ask at the
Bedouin Camp (see Places to Stay), Abu
Mohammed Restaurant or the tourist office.

Al-Qasr

Situated on the edge of lush vegetation at
the foot of high limestone cliffs is the medieval town of Al-Qasr, a charming little
place that reminds you what the other oasis

towns must have been like before New Valley development projects changed the face
of the area. Some 700 people live in the
town though at one time it contained 4500.
It is now forbidden for newcomers to settle
in the old section of Al-Qasr.

The town was built on Roman foundations and its architecture has retained
much of its medieval character. The narrow covered streets retain their cool in the
hot summer months and also serve to protect, to some extent, their inhabitants from

desert sandstorms. You can see quite a few entrances to old houses that go back to Ottoman and Mamluk times, some marked by *lintels* – acacia beams situated above the door and carved with the names of the carpenter, the owner of the house, the date, and a verse from the Quran. There are 54 lintels in the village, the earliest of which dates from 924 AD, but one of the finest is above the tomb of Sheikh Nasr ad-Din inside the old mosque, which is marked by a 12th century mud-brick minaret (it was rebuilt in the 19th century). The Supreme Council for Antiquities has recently renovated the town's old *madrassa* (school where Islamic law is taught) and an old house, both of which are well worth seeing. Also of interest is the pottery factory and a huge old corn mill. You can still see people making mud-bricks in the time-honoured way as well as men working an antique bellows in a tiny foundry.

There are pick-ups to Al-Qasr from near the police station in Mut for 50pt.

Balat

About 35km east of Mut on the road to Al-Kharga is Balat, another town that has retained much of its medieval Islamic character. There is not much to do but wander around the picturesque alleys and imagine how little has changed here over the centuries. A pick-up from near Al-Kharga hospital costs E£1.

Balat was the site of an important Old Kingdom town and if you have your own vehicle you may want to explore a couple of nearby sites which date back to Pharaonic times. The Al-Adaba tombs are about 200m after Balat on the road to Al-Kharga then 1km into the desert. About 2km south of here, still in the desert, is Ain al-Asil. Entry to both sites costs E£20.

Other Sights

From Mut on the road to Al-Qasr and Farafra Oasis, there are several places worth visiting if you are in no hurry, although for some you'll need your own transport or have to bargain with locals.

The Long Dry Walk

The eastern-most village in the Dakhla oasis, Teneida has existed since ancient times, but its modern fame comes from the part it played in one of this century's most incredible desert journeys. When the Italians took over the Kufra oasis, now in Libya, in 1930, some of the nomads of the area preferred to risk death in the desert rather than subjection to foreign rule. With no time for real preparation, a group of about 500 men, women and children set out on a risky 322km journey across the Great Sand Sea and the Gilf Kebir to Uwaynat. They arrived there only to find that there had been no rain for years. Without food for themselves or their camels many gave themselves up for dead. Others, without knowing the area, wandered in the direction of Dakhla. By chance a British patrol found the emaciated group that remained in Uwaynat and managed to save most of them. After 21 days, three of the men who'd left Uwaynat staggered into Teneida and a rescue operation was mounted to find the remainder of the refugees wandering in the desert. According to a report in *The Times* of London in May 1931:

The total number of Arabs reaching Dakhla was about 300. The first arrivals must have covered 420 miles between water over arid desert, a feat of endurance which can have few parallels in the history of desert travel.

On the west side of the Kharga-Dakhla road, about 55km south of Mut you can see **prehistoric rock paintings**. At a bend in the road beyond Teneida you can see strangely shaped rock formations, just next to the last of Dakhla's cultivated land. One of the largest and closest to the road has well-preserved pictures of giraffes, antelope and fish. The place was a major caravan stop and marked an intersection between two major trade routes, the Darb al-Ghabari, which ran between Dakhla and Kharga and another, now lost track that linked the village of Teneida with the Darb al-Arba'een to the south.

About 25km north of Mut there is a turn-off to the right to **Bir al-Gebel** where there is a pleasant spring about 5km off the main road. A sign states that there is a rest house, but it is not operating.

About 4km west of Al-Qasr, you'll find a turn-off to the left (south) to the beautifully coloured **Al-Muzawaka tombs** which date back to pharaonic times. From the road they are 1km into the desert (signposted in Arabic only). The custodian will probably delight in showing you a rough-cut tomb – just to the left of the two main tombs – which contains four adult mummies. Baksheesh is expected, of course.

About 7km west of Al-Qasr, at the checkpoint on the road to Farafra, there's a signposted turn-off to **Deir al-Haggar**. From the turn-off it's another 5km to the sandstone temple which was built during the reign of Nero (45-68 AD) and has recently been restored and opened to the public (for a hefty fee of E£20 or half for students). The temple has been enclosed by a wall to help prevent wind and sand erosion, and at the entrance is a display room outlining its history and the restoration process.

On a secondary road leading back to Mut, you can visit several **tombs** near the ruined village of Amhadah, dating from the 22nd century BC. About 15km further towards Mut is the Mamluk village of **Qalamun** with a cemetery from where there is a good view of the surrounding area.

Organised Tours

Like every other oasis, Dakhla has its share of would-be desert guides. Most of the hotels and restaurants can dig up 4WDs to take you on a trek about the area. As an example, Hamdy at the Ahmed Hamdy restaurant will take you on a day trip around Dakhla which includes Alamun, Al-Gedida, a drive through the dunes, visits to a spring, Al-Qasr and the Muzawaka tombs, among other things, for E£100. He takes up to six

people. An overnight trip around the same area, with Bedouin music, will cost about E£300, including food. The owner of the Bedouin Camp (see Places to Stay), Hag Abdel Hamid, also arranges camel and jeep trips into the desert around Dakhla. You're looking at about E£100 to E£150 per person per day including a guide, all meals and bedding.

Places to Stay

Camping It's possible to camp near the dunes west of Mut or in Al-Qasr, on a desert plateau just north of town, where the night sky is a spectacular field of stars; but you should check with the tourist office first.

Rest Houses There are two rest houses in Mut. *Government Rest House* near the bus station (in the same building as the tourist office) is pretty basic, and the question of running water problematic, but it's cheap at E£4.35 per person. *Dar al-Wafdeen Government Hotel* is reserved for officials only.

Hotels The only option in Al-Qasr is the friendly *Al-Qasr Hotel* (☎ 876 013) on the main road near the entry to the old town. It has four big screened rooms with narrow balconies for E£5 per person; breakfast is E£2 extra. Shared bathrooms are clean and, contrary to the norm, have hot water only. It's run by the amiable Mohammed, who also manages the ground-floor coffeehouse and restaurant. It serves good basic fare such as chicken, rice, fuul and salad.

A reasonable deal in Mut itself is *Gardens Hotel* (☎ 821 577) where singles/doubles without bath or fan cost E£12/16; with bath E£15/20 (triples E£24). Breakfast is extra. The showers sometimes have piping-hot water but the shared bathrooms can be pretty dire. The palm-filled courtyard out the back is a peaceful spot to relax. The hotel rents bikes for E£5.

Another cheap alternative is *Nasser's Hotel*, on the edge of Sheikh Waley, a village about 5km east of Mut on the road to Kharga Oasis (or 20 minutes by bicycle from Mut). It's about 400m off the main road to the left and is signposted. The young and likeable owner, Nasser, built this simple, peasant-style mud-brick house over a period of two years. He has five rooms for E£10 per person, including breakfast. Nasser usually meets the buses from Kharga and Farafra but if you don't find him and are interested in staying there, you can contact him at his brother Ahmed Hamdy's restaurant in Mut (☎ 820 767).

There are two new places between Mut and al-Qasr. *Bedouin Camp* (☎ 830 604/5) (currently signposted as Bedwen Camp) is 7km north of Mut, on a desert hilltop near the small desert village of Al-Dohous. Run by Bedouin who settled in the area a generation ago, the eight reed huts and three mud-brick rooms are simple but very clean and quiet and have great views. The shared bathrooms are also clean but have cold water only. A large sitting area with rugs and cushions on the floor serves as the dining area and is sometimes used for parties where Bedouin music is played. Rooms are E£15 per person, including breakfast.

The other new place is the three star *Mut Talata* (☎ 821 530). Operated by the Pioneers Hotel in Al-Kharga, with what are evidently its signature salmon pink walls, it has six 'chalets', three canvas tents with mattresses and a villa with five rooms and a restaurant. At US$39/58 a single/double for half-board, it's overpriced but it does have a pleasant deep pool fed by the warm water of the nearby spring.

A slightly less expensive option is *Mebarez Hotel* (☎/fax 821 524). It's past Hamdy's Restaurant on the road to Al-Qasr, and is popular with groups. Singles/doubles with bath and air-con cost E£44/58. Without bath, the rooms are E£28/42. There's an international phone line (but there's a 30% mark-up on normal tariffs).

Places to Eat

There aren't too many restaurants or cafes in Mut. *Al-Dakhla's Cafeteria* is on the square where the buses stop and has a few dishes or, better, is *Qalamuni Cafeteria* on the same square which has a wide choice of cheap eats.

Ahmed Hamdy's Restaurant (☎ 820 767) is popular with travellers and serves chicken, kebab, vegetables and a few other small dishes plus excellent, freshly squeezed lime juices and beer. Confusingly, there are two restaurants with almost the same name, a result of a dispute between two brothers. Ahmed Hamdy's is the original – it's the one closest to Mebarez Hotel.

The nearby *Abu Mohammed Restaurant* is the place to go for an E£8 to E£10 meal that will fill you to bursting point. Seemingly unending serves of soups, vegetables, rice, kebab, salads, sweets and nonalcoholic Stella emerge from a pristine kitchen.

Down by Gardens Hotel is *Anwar Paradise Restaurant* which serves up ta'amiyya and fuul, and is quite popular with the locals.

Gardens Hotel Restaurant serves a range of meat dishes, rice, omelettes and salad plus a very tasty mixed vegetable dish baked and served in an earthenware pot. Prices are cheap but it's best to eat here in the evening when the head chef is around.

Mebarez Hotel Restaurant is quite OK, but more expensive. Breakfast is E£5, lunch costs E£14 and dinner is E£16.

Other places worth investigating are *Shehab Restaurant* and *Al-Wadi Fiteer Place* next door where you can get a sweet fiteer.

Getting There & Away

Air EgyptAir flies from Mut to Cairo every Sunday and Wednesday at 8 am. A one-way ticket will cost you E£500. The airport is 10km from Midan al-Gamaa on the road to Uwaynat.

Bus The services to Cairo via Kharga Oasis (E£8) and Asyut (E£15) leave every day at 7 pm and 8 pm. The fare to Cairo (supposedly eight to 10 hours) is E£42. You can also go to Cairo via Farafra and Bahariyya Oasis at 6 am and 6 pm for E£35. Other buses to Asyut (E£15) via At-Kharga (E£8) leave every day at 6 and 8 am and 5 pm. There is also a bus to Luxor via Al-Kharga and Asyut every Friday, Sunday and Tuesday at 5 am.

Service Taxi Service taxis leave from the bus station, and cost E£7 to Al-Kharga and E£15 to either Farafra Oasis or Asyut. There are not a lot of them, so try in the morning. There are also microbuses to Farafra Oasis for E£12 to E£15.

Getting Around
Bus There are buses from Mut to Al-Qasr at 7 and 10.30 am and 1 and 2 pm. There are two buses a day to Balat at 11 am and 2 pm. Services are very unreliable so don't count on them.

Pick-Ups Most of the small towns and villages are linked by pick-up, but working out where they all go can be difficult and they can be ridiculously crowded. To Al-Qasr (50pt) they depart from near the police station. You can take pick-ups to Balat and Bashandi from in front of the hospital for E£1. It may prove easier on occasion to bargain for a 'special' pick-up.

Bicycle Abu Mohammed Restaurant and Gardens Hotel rent out a few clattering bicycles for E£5.

FARAFRA OASIS
The main town of Farafra, the smallest oasis in the Western Desert, is Qasr al-Farafra. It's named after the town's fort of which little remains. As in the other old oasis towns, the villagers would retreat into the fort when they were attacked, and each family was assigned a room where they stored provisions. Although linked by a 300km paved road to Mut (Dakhla) and another 185km stretch to Bahariyya, the 2900 people of this oasis are still quite isolated from most of the world. For better or for worse, that is starting to change as the population increases annually by about 1.8% and new constructions, in the New Valley breeze-block, four storey mould, start to take shape.

Many of the Farafrans are Bedouins and still adhere to some of the age-old traditions of their culture. The small mud-brick houses of the town all have wooden doorways with medieval peg locks, and some of

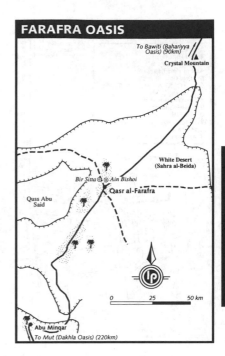

FARAFRA OASIS

the walls are painted with verses of the Quran and murals of ships and planes – references to their haj journeys. The Bedouin women of Farafra produce beautifully embroidered dresses and shirts, although most of the work is for their own personal use and not for sale. Olives and olive oil are a specialty of the region, but the rich oasis also produces dates, figs, apricots, guavas, oranges, apples and sunflower seeds. Wheat and rice are the main crops.

There are more than 100 springs and wells around the oasis, many sunk in the mid 1960s as part of the government's program to attract outsiders to the region. Not all of the springs are open to travellers but there are some that can be visited.

The calm and simplicity of this place will enchant you, especially if you're coming from Cairo or Kharga. There's precious little to do but wander around the town and

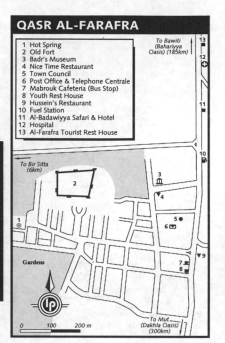

QASR AL-FARAFRA

1 Hot Spring
2 Old Fort
3 Badr's Museum
4 Nice Time Restaurant
5 Town Council
6 Post Office & Telephone Centrale
7 Mabrouk Cafeteria (Bus Stop)
8 Youth Rest House
9 Hussein's Restaurant
10 Fuel Station
11 Al-Badawiyya Safari & Hotel
12 Hospital
13 Al-Farafra Tourist Rest House

To Bawiti
(Bahariyya
Oasis) (185km)

To Bir Sitta
(6km)

Gardens

To Mut
(Dakhla Oasis)
(300km)

0   100   200 m

its beautiful gardens and then head out into the desert.

Information
There is no tourist office as such but Farafra's mayor, Mohammed Rifaat, is an informed chap who can be of great assistance to travellers and often extends an invitation to his chambers at the town council. The nearby post office is open from 8.30 am to 2.30 pm; closed Friday. The telephone centrale next door is open daily from 6 am to noon for national calls only.

There is nowhere to change money here.

Badr's Museum
This is Farafra's only 'sight', and it's worth checking out. The museum is the showpiece of Badr, a very expressive artist who paints and sculpts not-so-subtle works of village people in everyday life. His distinctive style

has won him foreign admirers, and he has had successful exhibitions throughout Europe in the early 1990s and, more recently, in Cairo. His most recent addition to the museum is a desert garden.

Bir Sitta
A popular stop on most itineraries is Bir Sitta or Well Number Six, a sulphurous hot spring just 6km from Qasr Al-Farafra. Hot water gushes from a pipe into a jacuzzi-sized concrete pool and then spills out into a larger tank. A great place for a night-time soak under the stars, you can also camp there, although a cluster of stone, domed rooms looking suspiciously like a hotel are under construction on the nearby hill and may change this.

Ain Bishoi
This roman spring bubbles forth on a hillock to the north-west of the Al-Farafra Tourist Rest House. It has been developed into an irrigated grove of date palms together with citrus, olives, apricots and carob trees, and is a cool haven amidst the arid landscape. Several families tend the crops here; you should seek someone out and ask permission before wandering around.

White Desert
The White Desert, or Sahra al-Beida, is an otherworldly region of blinding-white rock formations shaped by wind erosion. As you approach the white outcroppings they take on surreal forms – you can make out ostriches, camels, hawks and other bizarre shapes. They are best viewed at sunrise or sunset, when the sun turns the white chalk pink and orange, or under a full moon, which gives the landscape an eerie arctic appearance.

About 20km from Qasr al-Farafra on the road to Bahariyya you can see the first formations on the south side of the road. Regular vehicles can drive the first 1km or so off the road but only 4WD vehicles can advance deeper into the area. Some travellers simply get off the bus and take themselves off into the desert – but be sure to have adequate supplies, and remember that traffic either way is not very heavy.

Otherwise various locals organise overnight excursions into the White Desert. Try at Al-Badawiyya Safari & Hotel (see Places to Stay & Eat); the three Bedouin brothers who run this place have years of experience in desert travel and offer trips by camel or 4WD.

Places to Stay & Eat

For now you can camp at Bir Sitta but once the new hotel opens there you many not be allowed. Ask in town before heading out there.

There are only two places to stay in town. The government-run *Al-Farafra Tourist Rest House* is next to the new hospital, about 1km out along the road to Bahariyya. It costs E£10 per person in not-great rooms, each with a fan and three beds. There's cold water only and breakfast is not available.

Far better is the tastefully designed mud-brick *Al-Badawiyya Safari & Hotel (☎ 345 8524 in Cairo)* which is one of the best hotels in the oases. The rooms come in different styles and start with large quads with shared bathrooms for E£10 per person. Double rooms with shared baths are E£15 per person, while you're looking at E£50 to E£70 for large double and triple rooms, with their own bathroom, sitting area and TV. All rooms are spotlessly clean. Breakfast is E£5 to E£8. It's popular with small safari groups as well as individual travellers, so you may need to reserve in advance.

Youth Rest House on the same road is for Egyptians only.

The choice of where to eat is limited in Farafra. *Hussein's* is the larger of the two restaurants in town but even here most of the pots are empty by 7 pm, so come early. Check the prices beforehand – he's been known to charge E£2 for a cup of tea.

Close to Badr's museum is the tiny *Nice Time* restaurant, which is off the main road and has become something of a traveller's hang-out.

Other than that, your best option is *Al-Badawiyya* hotel where the food is more

expensive but fresh and good. A plate of spaghetti (with fresh tomato sauce, not just the usual tomato paste) can be had for E£5. A chicken meal is about E£25. They can also scrounge up a beer, if you like.

Shopping

'Mr Socks' is a local character who knits socks, scarves and other woollies out of camel hair. He and his wares can be found at the Al-Badawiyya hotel, where camel and sheep-hair rugs are also on sale.

Getting There & Away

There is a bus from Farafra to Cairo (E£25; 10 to 11 hours) via Bahariyya (E£10; 2½ hours) every day between 10 and 11 am. Another leaves Farafra at about 11 pm and arrives in Cairo at 6 am. Every Saturday, Monday and Thursday there is a third bus at 9 am. There are two buses a day from Farafra to Dakhla (E£12; four to five hours) – the first leaves between 1 and 2 pm and the other between 1 and 2 am. The bus originates in Cairo so the times are approximate.

You can flag down all buses in front of the Al-Badawiyya hotel or at the Mabrouk Cafeteria, a sheesha and tea joint at the south end of town. Tickets are bought from the conductor. As usual, you should check the latest schedules for all these buses, or you may end up staying longer in one of the oases than you want.

Microbuses to Dakhla leave from in front of the Mabrouk Cafeteria whenever they have a full load and a seat costs about E£15. There's not a lot of traffic between the two oases, however, and you're better off going early in the morning. Sometimes you can hitch a ride from Farafra to Dakhla, but don't count on this.

BAHARIYYA OASIS

Situated in a 2000 sq km depression about 330km south-west of Cairo is the oasis of Bahariyya. A major agricultural centre in ancient times the oasis was famous for its wine as far back as the Middle Kingdom. Most of the ancient monuments around Bahariyya date from later, however, when the

WESTERN OASES

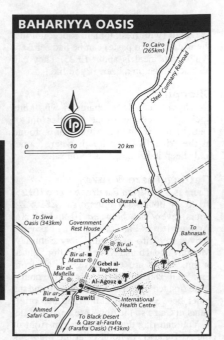

BAHARIYYA OASIS

To Cairo
(265km)

Steel Company Railroad

0   10   20 km

Gebel Ghurabi ▲

To Siwa
Oasis (343km)   Government
Rest House

To
Bahnasah

Bir al-
Ghaba

Bir al- ■
Mattar
Bir al-
Muftella   Gebel al-
Ingleez

Al-Agouz

Bir ar-
Ramla   Bawiti   International
Health Centre

Ahmed
Safari Camp   To Black Desert
& Qasr al-Farafra
(Farafra Oasis) (143km)

oasis sat on the route that kept the 26th dynasty Libyan rulers in touch with their homeland. Although none of the main ancient trade routes passed through the oasis it was prosperous until the 4th century, when attacks from marauding tribes and the decline of Roman rule left much of its once-rich agricultural land to be reclaimed by the surrounding desert.

Nowadays Bahariyya is part of Giza governorate, unlike the oases to the south, and is linked to both Cairo and Qasr al-Farafra by paved roads across the desert. There is also a road to Siwa.

There are several little villages spread throughout the oasis, but the main one, with a population of about 30,000, is Bawiti. The main street of the town has got the same squat modern buildings as the rest of the oases but a walk in almost any direction will lead you to the more traditional mud-

brick houses that many of the inhabitants still live in.

Information

The tourist office is in the town council building opposite the police station and is open, more or less, from 8 am to 2 pm and 5 to 8 pm.

There is a National Bank, open Sunday to Thursday from 8 am to 2 pm, where you can change cash only. The telephone centrale is open from 8 am to midnight. At the time of writing there was no international line.

Oasis Heritage Museum

The Oasis Heritage Museum is a smaller, newer version of the museum in Farafra, and is about 1km from the police station on the road to Cairo. Set up in a small house by a young artist called Mahmoud Eed, it features unbaked clay figurines set in scenes from traditional village life, such as men playing *siga* (a game played in the dirt with clay balls or seeds) and a man crying in agony as his injured leg is treated. There is also a display of old oasis dresses and jewellery.

Hot & Cold Springs

The closest springs to central Bawiti are the so-called Roman springs, known as Al-Bishmu, about a 10 minute walk from the Popular Restaurant. The view over the oasis gardens and the desert beyond is wonderful, but the spring is not suitable for swimming. An equally useless place for swimming is Bir al-Muftella, about 3km from the centre of town. It's an interesting walk out through the town, but don't go for the water alone. Take the Siwa road and keep asking. If you pass a big, white conical structure (a sheikh's tomb) on your right, you'll know you're on the right track.

The hot sulphurous spring of Bir ar-Ramla is OK if you're into scalding (45°C) baths, but you may feel a bit exposed to the donkey traffic to and fro. Women especially should think twice and stay well covered. It's about a 3km walk from the centre of the town.

The best spot is quite possibly Bir al-Ghaba, about 15km north-east of Bawiti.

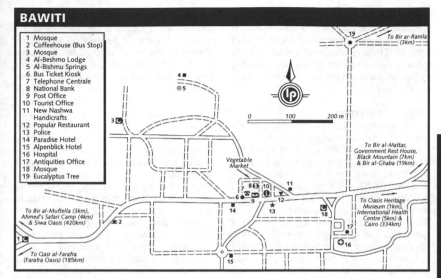

BAWITI

1 Mosque
2 Coffeehouse (Bus Stop)
3 Mosque
4 Al-Beshmo Lodge
5 Al-Bishmu Springs
6 Bus Ticket Kiosk
7 Telephone Centrale
8 National Bank
9 Post Office
10 Tourist Office
11 New Nashwa
    Handicrafts
12 Popular Restaurant
13 Police
14 Paradise Hotel
15 Alpenblick Hotel
16 Hospital
17 Antiquities Office
18 Mosque
19 Eucalyptus Tree

To Bir ar-Ramla (3km)

To Bir al-Mattar, Government Rest House, Black Mountain (7km) & Bir al-Ghaba (19km)

Vegetable Market

To Oasis Heritage Museum (1km), International Health Centre (5km) & Cairo (334km)

To Bir al-Muftella (3km), Ahmed's Safari Camp (4km) & Siwa Oasis (420km)

To Qasr al-Farafra (Farafra Oasis) (185km)

0   100   200 m

There is nothing quite like a moonlit hot bath on the edge of the desert. The Alpenblick Hotel runs a rudimentary camp site there, so you can often arrange with them to get down there for a bath, or you may prefer to just stay in the camp for a couple of days. Be sure to bring supplies with you, though, there's nothing here.

At Bir al-Mattar, 7km north-east of Bawiti, cold springs pour into a viaduct and then down into a concrete pool where you can splash.

Gebel al-Ingleez

The area around Bawiti is not bad territory for walking. You can't miss Gebel al-Ingleez: it's a flat-top hill with the remains of a WWI castle built by Capt. Williams in order to monitor the movements of Libyan Senussi tribesmen. To get there go out along the road to Cairo and turn off onto the track heading to Bir al-Ghaba and the Government Rest House at Bir al-Mattar. Keep the mountain in sight and follow village tracks out to it. The walk takes about an hour.

Black Desert

About 20km south of Bawiti on the way to Farafra you will notice black, volcano-shaped mountains. This is the beginning of the Black Desert, formed over the millennia as wind eroded the mountains and spread a fine black powder over the ground.

White Desert

The first piece of advice is simply not to do the trip to the White Desert from here (as it's so expensive to arrange from Bawiti) but wait until you get to Farafra (see the previous section for details). However, if you feel you have to make an overnight trip to the desert from here, there are plenty of people trying to encourage you, occasionally even travellers themselves hoping to get a free ride for rounding up a few people.

Other Attractions

Bahariyya is not renowned for its ancient sites, although in Bawiti there are the remains of a temple and settlement dating back to the 17th dynasty. There is also a special hill, south-west of the town, known as Qarat al-Firakhi (Ridge of the Chicken Merchant). The hill features several underground galleries containing signs of bird burials. There are several ancient tombs around, too. If you are interested, go to the antiquities office to get permission and help to see them.

Organised Tours
There is fierce competition among the few hotels in town to arrange desert trips but somehow everyone charges more or less the same price – the big distinction is whether or not you stay near the asphalt road. A trek in a 4WD with one night and two days in the White Desert is E£350, with a maximum of four people, if you stay on or near the road. This rises to E£800 or E£900 for three days and two nights off-road, including food, blankets and tents. Most of the operators in town also offer three or four day trips to Siwa for about E£700 for a maximum of four, but this does not necessarily include camping in the desert. Badri at the New Nashwa Handicrafts shop is one of the more reliable guides but whoever you pick, ensure that you see the car before you head out into the sand, and check that you have adequate water in case of a breakdown.

Places to Stay & Eat
Travellers arriving by bus are generally met by a team of hotel touts who, in an unusual attempt not to be pushy, will give you the business cards of each of their establishments and then sit back while you make up your mind.

Government Rest House is 7km out of town near Bir al-Mattar. For E£5 per night (including transport) you can stay here, but it is very basic and in need of renovation. Ask at the tourist office or the Paradise Hotel.

Paradise Hotel (☎ 802 600) in the centre of town has recently been renovated, although it remains basic. There are six rooms with three beds and it costs E£3.50 per person. Breakfast on the small vine-covered terrace is an extra E£1.50.

Ahmed's Safari Camp (☎ 802 090) about 4km west of the centre has become a

bit of a favourite among travellers and trans-Africa groups. It has a range of options (prices are per person): cool, pleasant, domed double rooms with private bathroom for E£12.50 including breakfast; rooms with shared facilities for E£5 per person; basic reed huts at E£3; or a roof where you can sleep under the stars for E£2. Breakfast is not included in the last three options. Two large new rooms with vaults and full bathrooms cost E£25 on a double occupancy basis. Meals of sorts are available, as are beers. If you can't get a lift and want to walk, take the Siwa fork and keep asking your way there. Alternatively you could try to rent a bike from the New Nashwa Handicraft shop in town.

Alpenblick Hotel (☎ 802 184) which is a relatively attractive, but more expensive, two storey place with a variety of clean rooms. Large doubles without/with private bath (and hot water) cost E£35/46 including breakfast. The budget rooms cost E£17 (breakfast is E£5 extra).

The Alpenblick also has 15 huts with mattresses out at Bir al-Ghaba. The enclosure is watched by a warden, who will help out with tea and firewood. It costs E£10 a night and is very peaceful, but you must bring your own food.

The brand new *Al-Beshmo Lodge* (☎/fax 802 177) is situated beside the Al-Beshmo springs and has 20 comfortable singles/doubles for E£35/50 without bath or E£55/80 with. The price includes a buffet breakfast. All rooms have fans and some have air-con. The shared bathrooms are big and spotless and there is also a cafe just outside the hotel entrance.

About 5km outside town on the road to Cairo is *International Health Centre* (☎ 802 322), a three star spa resort with forgettable architecture. It has 27 rooms and eight chalets built around a hot spring. Singles are US$40 or it's US$35 per person for a double on a half-board basis. As well as a deep pool of therapeutic spring water there's a gym, sauna and restaurant.

Unless you make your own meals, your food will be limited to the hotels or the town's one restaurant, *Popular Restaurant* (also known as Bayoumi's), which serves a selection of dishes like chicken, soup, rice and vegetables for around E£12. It's also open for breakfast.

There are several grocery stores where you can pick up supplies for a few nights out in the desert.

Shopping
New Nashwa Handicrafts shop (☎ 802 276) opposite the Popular Restaurant sells white camel-hair blankets for about E£100, as well as camel-hair woollies and rugs. Badri, the owner also rents bicycles for E£10 per day.

Getting There & Away
Bus There are daily buses to Cairo at 7 am and 3 pm and another sometime between midnight and 1 am. Tickets cost E£12 – E£10 is payable at the bus office and the remainder on the bus. Each Saturday, Monday and Thursday at about 11.30 am, you can catch a bus originating in Farafra on its way to Cairo for the same price.

Heading to Farafra (E£18.25) you can pick up one of the buses from Cairo which are supposed to leave Bahariyya at 8 am, noon and 3 and 6.30 pm. Passengers are usually dropped off at the Popular Restaurant before the bus continues down the street to a new coffeehouse where it stops for about 30 minutes.

Note that only some bus tickets can be booked from the Bahariyya ticket office (a kiosk in front of the telephone office). As most of the buses don't originate here, you either have to book in Cairo or take your chances on standing. Ticket office opening hours are erratic – try from 9 am to 1 pm or after the evening prayer until about 11 pm.

Service Taxi Supposedly, there's always a service taxi going to Sayyida Zeinab in Cairo between 3 and 4 pm, but this could be earlier or later and not every day. Ask at Popular Restaurant. A service taxi to Farafra (and they're not very frequent) will also cost E£15. Microbuses to either place cost about the same but are more frequent.

They can be caught opposite the police intelligence office or, again, ask at Popular Restaurant.

If you want to get a taxi to Siwa, expect to pay at least E£550.

SIWA OASIS
The lush and productive Western Desert oasis of Siwa, famous throughout the country for its dates and olives, is 305km southwest of Marsa Matruh and 550km west of Cairo, near the Libyan border. It lies 12m below sea level in a depression (ranging from 9km to 28km in width) which stretches for 80km.

It is undoubtedly one of the most picturesque and idyllic places in Egypt. Against the awesome backdrop of eroded hills and a sea of sand dunes, Siwa appears like the proverbial mirage – a wealth of green date palms shading mud-brick villages which are connected by streams and springs and irrigated gardens.

Siwa lies on the old date caravan route via Qara, Qattara and Kerdassa (near Cairo) which ended at Memphis. However, for centuries, apart from these desert caravans of ancient times or the occasional pilgrim who journeyed there to visit the famed Temple of Amun, few outsiders ventured to Siwa. Although Islam and Arabic did eventually reach this far into the desert, Siwa's solitary location had until recently allowed the predominantly Berber-speaking inhabitants to preserve many of their ancient traditions and customs, including their own language.

That is all changing now, and some observers feel the onslaught of the modern age and tourists will all but wipe out this unique place. The road linking the oasis to Marsa Matruh has now been joined by another to Bahariyya Oasis, to the south-east. What started as a trickle of travellers venturing down the new road from Marsa Matruh is really flowing. Even tour buses get down there now.

The least visitors can do to help preserve Siwa's culture is to respect local sensibilities and act accordingly – do not bring

SIWA OASIS

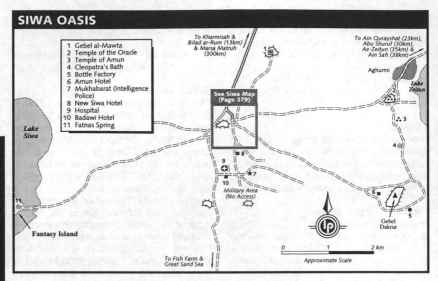

1 Gebel al-Mawta
2 Temple of the Oracle
3 Temple of Amun
4 Cleopatra's Bath
5 Bottle Factory
6 Amun Hotel
7 Mukhabarat (Intelligence Police)
8 New Siwa Hotel
9 Hospital
10 Badawi Hotel
11 Fatnas Spring

To Kharmisah &
Bilad ar-Rum (13km)
& Marsa Matruh
(300km)

To Ain Qurayshat (23km),
Abu Shuruf (30km),
Az-Zeitun (35km) &
Ain Safi (38km)

Aghurmi

Lake
Zeitun

See Siwa Map
(Page 379)

Lake
Siwa

Military Area
(No Access)

Gebel
Dakrur

Fantasy Island

To Fish Farm &
Great Sand Sea

0   1   2 km

Approximate Scale

WESTERN OASES

alcohol to the oasis or, as the tourist office puts it, show 'displays of affection' in public. Modest dress is also required. Women travellers should cover their upper arms and their legs and should avoid wearing bathing suits to dip in the numerous springs. Apart from respecting local customs, they will find themselves feeling very out of place wandering around in revealing clothes in light of the fact that life for Siwan women is very secluded. Girls are often married by the time they're 17 after which they may speak to male members of their immediate family only. In public, women must wear a demure blue/grey shawl, known as a *tarfodit*, which totally covers their face and upper body.

History

Siwa's original Berber settlers were attracted to this island of green in a desolate sea of sand many centuries ago, when they discovered several freshwater springs in the area.

The most illustrious of Siwa's early visitors was the young conqueror Alexander, who led a small party on an eight day trek through the desert in 331 BC to seek out the oracle of the Temple of Amun. Alexander's goal, which he apparently attained, was to seek confirmation that he was the son of Zeus, and also to uphold the traditional belief that, as the new pharaoh of Egypt, he was also the son of Amun.

Apart from a Greek traveller who visited in 160 AD, the people of Siwa did not see another European until 1792. Several Europeans narrowly escaped with their lives after trying to visit Siwa and the Siwans gained a reputation of being fiercely independent and hostile to non-Muslim outsiders. Throughout the 19th century the Egyptian government also had problems trying to gain the loyalty of the oasis. Then in WWII, the British and Italian forces chased each other in and out of Siwa and Jaghbub, 120km west in Libya, until Rommel decided not to bother with it any more. By then the Siwans were fully incorporated into Egypt, but the oasis remained isolated until the asphalt road connected it to Marsa Matruh in the 1980s. As a result Siwans

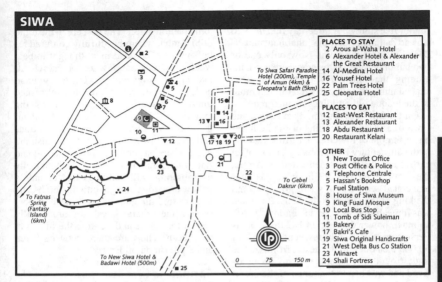

SIWA

To Siwa Safari Paradise
Hotel (200m), Temple
of Amun (4km) &
Cleopatra's Bath (5km)

To Fatnas
Spring
(Fantasy
Island)
(6km)

To Gebel
Dakrur (6km)

To New Siwa Hotel &
Badawi Hotel (500m)

0   75   150 m

PLACES TO STAY
2 Arous al-Waha Hotel
6 Alexander Hotel & Alexander
   the Great Restaurant
14 Al-Medina Hotel
16 Yousef Hotel
22 Palm Trees Hotel
25 Cleopatra Hotel

PLACES TO EAT
12 East-West Restaurant
13 Alexander Restaurant
18 Abdu Restaurant
20 Restaurant Kelani

OTHER
1 New Tourist Office
3 Post Office & Police
4 Telephone Centrale
5 Hassan's Bookshop
7 Fuel Station
8 House of Siwa Museum
9 King Fuad Mosque
10 Local Bus Stop
11 Tomb of Sidi Suleiman
15 Bakery
17 Bakri's Cafe
19 Siwa Original Handicrafts
21 West Delta Bus Co Station
23 Minaret
24 Shali Fortress

WESTERN OASES

still speak their own distinct Berber dialect and have a local culture separate from that of the rest of Egypt.

Information

The tourist office (☎ 460 2883) is across from the Arous al-Waha Hotel. The very helpful and knowledgeable Mahdi Hweiti can help arrange trips to some surrounding villages. The office is generally open daily except Friday from 8 am to 2 pm. Mahdi can also be reached at home (☎ 460 2130).

There is no bank in Siwa, so bring enough money to cover your needs, but there is a post office – it's in the same building as the police opposite the Arous al-Waha Hotel; it's open daily except Friday from 8 am to 2 pm. There's also a 24 hour telephone centrale nearby.

Permits If you're thinking of adventuring too far off the beaten track from Siwa, you will need to get a permit. Mahdi Hweiti at the Siwa tourist office can advise you. Most permits are issued fairly quickly from the local security and intelligence office. You'll

need one photo and your passport (plus a photocopy).

Things to See

Siwa's greatest attraction is the oasis itself, which boasts more than 300,000 palm trees, 70,000 olive trees and a great many fruit orchards. The vegetation is sustained by more than 300 freshwater springs and streams and the area attracts an amazing variety of bird life, including quails and falcons.

Around the corner from the local council offices is the small **House of Siwa Museum** which contains a modest display of traditional clothing, implements and the like. It was inspired by a Canadian diplomat who feared the disappearance of Siwan culture and its mud-brick houses in a flood of concrete and modernity. The museum is loosely open from 10 am to noon (closed Friday), but you can also arrange to see it through the tourist office. Entrance is E£1.50.

The centre of the town is dominated by the mud-brick remains of the 13th century fortress enclave of **Shali**. Built of large chunks of salt mixed with rock and plastered in local clay, the buildings originally rose up four or five storeys. A three-day rain in 1926 was so damaging that the inhabitants abandoned most of the town. Now only one or two buildings around the edges are used, including the mosque with the chimney-shaped minaret, and with each rainfall more of the unique old buildings disintegrate.

On the hill of Aghurmi, 4km east of the town of Siwa, are the ruins of the 26th dynasty **Temple of the Oracle**. Built sometime in the 6th century BC, probably on top of an earlier temple, it was dedicated to Amun, the ram-headed god of life, who was later associated with Egypt's sun-god, Ra, and the king of the Greek gods, Zeus. Its oracle was immediately famous and endowed with so much power that in 524 BC the famous Persian warrior, Cambyses, sent an army of 50,000 men out into the desert from Thebes to destroy it. The legendary army never arrived and was lost to the sands of the desert somewhere between Kharga and Siwa. A couple of centuries later Alexander the Great made his perilous desert journey specifically to consult with the oracle.

Today the Temple of the Oracle sits in the north-west corner of the ruins of Aghurmi village (look for the signs). It is in bad shape but worth a clamber through. The view of the surrounding oasis is also good.

A couple of hundred metres further along the track is the almost totally ruined **Temple of Amun** (also known as the Temple of Umm Ubaydah). Built in the 30th dynasty, all that's left standing is part of a wall covered with inscriptions.

Gebel al-Mawta (Mountain of the Dead) is a hill honeycombed with rock tombs, most dating back to Ptolemaic and Roman times. Only 1km from the centre of town, during WWII the tombs were used by the Siwans as shelters when the Italians bombed the oasis. Many new tombs were discovered at this time but were not properly excavated and, in his book on Siwa, Ahmed Fakhry recalls British soldiers paying families a few piastres to cut away large chunks of tomb paintings as souvenirs.

Despite the damage there are still some tomb paintings left. The best are in the tomb of Si Amun, where beautifully coloured reliefs portray the dead man, thought to be a wealthy Greek landowner or merchant, making offerings and praying to Egyptian gods. Also interesting are: the unfinished tomb of Miso-Isis, which contains the mummified skull of its original inhabitant; the tomb of Niperpathot, with inscriptions and crude drawings in the same reddish ink you can see on modern Siwan pottery; and finally the tomb of the crocodile, with badly deteriorating wall paintings that include a yellow crocodile. To get into the tombs you need to find the guardians. As well as possessing the crucial keys they are usually very informative and deserve the hinted-at baksheesh. They are there between 7 am and 2 pm (noon on Fridays).

Springs

Following the track that leads to the Temple of Amun through the palm groves, you will come across **Cleopatra's Bath**, also known as the Spring of Juba. The natural spring water pours into a stone pool, which is a popular bathing spot for the locals, but the scum floating on the surface doesn't make it very appealing. Women should think twice about swimming here, and if they decide to risk the stares should only bathe with clothes on. At the time of writing Abdu's restaurant was building changing rooms and a sitting area beside the pool and they've promised to clean the water.

There's a similar, but more pleasant and secluded pool at **Fatnas Spring** (sometimes annoyingly called Fantasy Island), an oasis ringed by the salt Lake Siwa, which is accessible across a narrow causeway. The pool, about 6km from Siwa, is in an idyllic setting amid palm trees and lush greenery. Although a safer place for a swim than Cleopatra's Bath, women going alone should be wary and, again, should leave their bikinis for the beach. There's a small cafe among the palms and sitting and puffing on a sheesha or sipping tea and watching the sun set over the lake is one of Siwa's magical experiences. To get there go past the council building and take the road to the left at the first fork. Follow it around the base of Shali – at the next intersection-of-possible-confusion a sign points the way.

Gebel Dakrur, about 4km from town, is a popular place with rheumatism sufferers. From July to September people flock here to be plopped into a bath of very hot sand for 20 minutes at a time, and then extracted and given a hot tea. Three days of this, they say, and no more rheumatism. The mountain also supplies the oasis with the reddish-brown pigment used to decorate Siwan pottery.

Around Siwa

There are a few interesting villages to the west of the main town of Siwa. **Kharmisah** and **Bilad ar-Rum** (City of the Romans) are 15km from the town and can be reached by local bus. They are Berber villages, and the latter has about 100 tombs cut into the rock of the nearby hills. A few kilometres from here is Maraki, where a Greek archaeologist claimed in 1995 to have found the tomb of Alexander the Great. She was proven wrong and the site remains off limits.

To the east of Siwa are some more springs. **Ain Qurayshat** is 27km out and **Abu Shuruf**, said by locals to be the biggest and cleanest in the oasis, is 7km further east at the next palm thicket. The clear water here is about 3m deep and spills into Lake Zeitun, another huge salt lake. Another 5km brings you to **Az-Zeitun**, an abandoned mud-brick village, beaten by the sand and wind, which sits alone on the sandy plain. Hundreds of Roman-era tombs have been discovered about 2km beyond Az-Zeitun and are currently under excavation, though little of interest has been found. From Az-Zeitun, another 3km brings you to **Ain Safi**, the last human vestige before the overwhelming wall of desert dunes which stretch for hundreds of kilometres, all the way south to Kharga Oasis. Some 30 Bedouin families live at Ain Safi.

To visit the sights east of Siwa you'll need your own sturdy vehicle. Mahdi from the tourist office, and every restaurant and hotel in town, organises trips (see the following Organised Tours section).

About 120km east of Siwa, near the Qattara Depression, is another oasis, **Qara**. The oasis is home to 300 Berbers who, like the Siwans, built their fortress-like town on top of a mountain. Unlike Shali, the town is still inhabited but increasingly the people are building new concrete houses down below. To get there, take the narrow asphalt road that branches off the Siwa-Marsa Matruh road at the rest house, 150km from Siwa. You can either rent a pick-up truck to take you there for about E£250 or talk to the many people in town offering desert safaris.

About 13km south of Siwa town you can visit a **fish farm**. This odd place is located among sand dunes in an area where oil exploration companies found only hot water and one chap decided to raise fish there.

Beyond lies the **Great Sand Sea**, the world's largest dune field. Straddling Egypt and Libya and stretching over 800km south to the Gilf Kebir, its beautiful but dangerous dunes can reach heights of 150m. Although a number of expeditions have travelled through this vast expanse it remains one of the least explored areas on earth.

Organised Tours

Every restaurant and hotel in Siwa offers tours ranging from half a day in the desert around Siwa, to a full five or six day safari. The tourist office can be a great help in organising trips around the oasis. Abdallah at the Siwa Original Handicrafts shop is also very helpful. Almost all desert trips require permits, which cost E£10.50 and are usually obtained by whoever you choose to take you. Prices and itineraries vary, but one of the most common day trips takes you to the desert hot spring at Bir Wahid at the edge of the Great Sand Sea, where you can have a simple meal or tea, then on to the nearby spring-fed lake (where you can take a dip in the summer). Usually you will do a spot of dune driving, stop at fossil sites and see some fantastic desert vistas before returning to Siwa. This costs about E£50.

There are no camels in Siwa so all trips are done by 4WD. As with any desert trip, ensure you have enough water and that the vehicle is roadworthy before you set out.

Special Events
Gebel Dakrur is the scene of an annual Siyaha festival. For three days around the October full moon, thousands of Siwan men gather to celebrate friendship and togetherness, presumably burying all the hatchets they may have taken up in the previous year. Siwan women do not attend the festivities, though girls up to about the age of 12 are present until sunset. Each year hundreds of non-Siwans, Egyptians and foreigners, attend the festival

Once a year the small shrine of Sidi Suleiman, behind the main mosque in the centre of town, is the scene of a moulid. On occasional Thursday nights, after the evening prayer, local sufis of the Arusiya order gather here for a *zikr* and don't mind the odd foreigner watching.

Places to Stay
Siwa's march into modernity has manifested itself in the unfortunate form of hotel touts, who now meet incoming buses in a bid to snaffle all new arrivals.

Camping As with most places in Egypt since the Luxor massacre, the police here are jittery about people camping out. However, you can go to the Amun Hotel on Gebel Dakrur and ask them if you can pitch your tent. You can also check with the tourist office to see if things have loosened up.

Hotels *Palm Trees Hotel* (☎ *460 2204*), just off the main square, is a popular place to stay. It has clean rooms with fans, screened windows and small balconies and charges E£5/6 per person in a double room without/with private bath. There's constant hot water and the bathrooms are clean. Best of all it has a shady tranquil garden with date-palm furniture where you can relax, and there are a also quite a few good bicycles to rent.

In close competition with the Palm Trees Hotel, is *Yousef Hotel* (☎ *460 162*) in the town centre. Some of the rooms here are tiny, but everything is clean, the beds are comfortable, and the showers steaming with hot water. The owner, Salama, is very helpful and, like everyone else, rents bikes. It's E£5 per night, without breakfast.

Next door is the oasis' long-time hotel *Al-Medina*. It's E£5 a night here too, but considerably more grotty. Both places are close to mosques.

If you head directly south of the main square you'll find *Cleopatra Hotel* (☎ *460 2148*). Rooms in its original building cost E£10/14 for singles without/with bathrooms, and E£13/18 for doubles. Far better are the more expensive chalets where rooms with ceiling fan and simple wooden furniture go for E£25/34. Prices don't include breakfast.

Next up is the cheapest and scummiest place in Siwa, *New Siwa Hotel*. It's E£2.50 a bed. A walk down the main road and off to the right is *Badawi Hotel*, run by a young gent of the same name. For E£5 you get a comfortable bed and maybe a fan; however, mixed couples wanting to stay here must be able to show their marriage certificate.

Just in from the telephone centrale is the brand new *Alexander Hotel* (☎ *460 2081*). With nine rooms and eight more planned, it has an inside staircase down to Alexander the Great restaurant below. The spotless singles/doubles are E£12/25 with bath, not including breakfast.

Opposite the tourist office is the 20 room *Arous al-Waha Hotel* (☎ *460 2100*). Although it resembles a modern government building rather than a hotel the management is friendly and helpful. Rooms have bathrooms with constant hot water and fans. Singles/doubles with breakfast cost E£54/72. An extra bed is E£15. There are also two suites for E£60 without breakfast. Prices include service and taxes.

Siwa Safari Paradise Hotel (☎ *460 2289/90, fax 460 2286*) is a three star place set in palm groves a couple of hundred metres down the road to the Temple of Amun. The architecture does not live up to its picturesque garden setting, however, and the prices are high. A double room with air-con, TV and fridge will set you back E£295/467 a single/double, on half-board basis. Bungalows without air-con cost E£242/354 for singles/doubles. There are tiny reed huts in another part of the hotel but at E£30 per person, without fans, they are way overpriced.

Out at Gebel Dakrur is *Amun Hotel*. This is generally only used by people seeking rheumatism cures at the height of summer. A bed costs E£5. There's not much in the way of food out here.

About 17km from the centre of Siwa, at the flat-topped White Mountain on the way to Bilad ar-Rum, is Egypt's first ecolodge, *Adrerere Amellal* (which means 'white mountain' in Siwa). Constructed using almost-forgotten traditional Siwan building techniques it has stunning views over the lake to the oasis and the edge of the Great Sand Sea and beyond. The owner, environmentalist Mounir Naematalla, claims that the site is mystical and after spending time there you begin to think that he may be right. With its simple but beautiful rooms and suites, a natural spring tucked in among date palms and innovative food that uses local produce from its own organically farmed garden, it is destined to become one of the best places to stay in the country. For information about the prices, call the office in Cairo (☎ 340 0052, fax 341 3331).

Places to Eat
There's a handful of restaurants/cafes in Siwa catering to tourists and, less so, to locals. They all offer a fairly similar menu, so trial and error is probably the only way of searching out any differences in quality.

The longest standing of them is the ever popular *Abdu Restaurant*, across the road from Yousef Hotel. It serves a wide range of traditional dishes, vegetable stews, couscous and roasted chickens. It also serves a very tasty pizza for E£5, though you might be waiting an hour or so for it.

Just as popular these days is *Alexander Restaurant* opposite Al-Medina Hotel.

The original chef at the Alexander Restaurant, Yousef, recently opened his own place around the corner. His *Alexander the Great Restaurant* offers much the same fare as the others, including the curries that appeared on all the town's menus after three Pakistanis spent a month in the oasis a couple of years back. It also has a lot of vegetarian dishes. Many people insist that Yousef is the reason that the Alexander became popular in the first place; you'll have to make up your own mind.

You could also try *East-West Restaurant*, facing the mosque across the square.

Down to the left of the Abdu Restaurant is *Restaurant Kelani* but nobody, locals included, ever seems to eat here. There are two cafes on the square where ta'amiyya are cooked early every morning. Hot bread can be bought from the little bakery just off the square; there's a market on the square each Friday morning.

Arous al-Waha Hotel has its own cafeteria and *Palm Trees Hotel* also serves food, though few people seem to patronise this place.

There are several places dotted around the square where you can have a sheesha or a cup of coffee and play some backgammon. *Bakri's Cafe* (also known as Sohag Rest House) next to Abdu Restaurant is one of the most popular.

Things to Buy
Several little craft shops around town compete for the tourist trade and sell replicas of old Siwan baskets, jewellery, the blue shawls worn by the local women, and pottery (see the special section 'Siwan Crafts' on pages 384-5 for more information). Compare prices and goods at the tiny shop at the back of Palm Trees Hotel, the shop just off the main square on the road towards Cleopatra Hotel, and at Hassan's Bookshop. Siwa Original Handicrafts, next to Abdu Restaurant, has set prices, which can make things easier. Owners Abdallah Baghi and his cousin Suleiman have also saved some old pieces in an effort to conserve at least part of Siwa's unique cultural heritage.

SIWAN CRAFTS

Siwa's rich culture is easily identified these days by the abundance of traditional crafts that are still made for local use as well as for tourists. Unfortunately, an estimated 98% of the older artefacts – such as jewellery, wooden chests and other family heirlooms – have become collectors' items and, over the years, have been sold to investors from around the world. With most of the original craftsmen now dead, these pieces of Siwan heritage are now lost to the Siwans themselves.

With the exception of the Nubians, Siwans adorn themselves with the biggest and most ornate jewellery to be found in Egypt. Although Siwan women only wear the heavy silver jewellery on special occasions these days, several interesting pieces are still made. The *aghrow* and the *adrim* are among the most impressive. The former is a heavy solid silver coil which is connected by a loop and hook. It used to be worn by young girls of marital age and announced their search for a husband. The *adrim*, a large silver disc with inscribed patterns, is attached to it; the whole ensemble was traditionally worn until the wedding night. To buy a new aghrow and adrim you'll be looking at several hundred pounds. If you find an old one, several thousand.

Perhaps the most distinctive piece of jewellery in the oasis is the *lugiyet*, a leather strap decorated with mother-of-pearl buttons with three silver rings dangling on each side. It is worn across the forehead, with the rings sitting against the temples. It is rare to find one for sale. Another dramatic head ornament is the *tiyalakan*, an enormous crescent shaped earing with dangling silver chains, some with bells or amulets attached. Too heavy to put through ears, they are attached to a hat-like leather harness.

Silver rings also abound in Siwa. Traditionally worn on all except the index finger, the rings have different shapes and are inscribed, usually geometric patterns. The *emhabis entad azoua* (thumb ring) is small and rectangular, while the *emhabis entad nammas* is a large disc worn on the middle finger after marriage. Large rectangular rings, called *emhabis entakoutout* are worn on the third finger, while the

Box: Siwan wedding ring (photo by Juliet Coombe/La Belle Aurore)

Left: Siwan torque (photo by Dennis Wisken/Sidewalk Gallery)

The Berber people, who originally settled in the west of Egypt around Siwa, have retained much of their own identity. Although many speak Arabic, they have preserved their own language.

Top: A Siwan Berber wedding ring. These rings are used to help the wearer navigate through the desert.

Bottom: Detail of a Siwan headdress, showing its tapestry-like beadwork.

Right: Siwan pendant (photo by Dennis Wisken/Sidewalk Gallery)

pointy-oval *emhabis entasart* goes on the little finger. Modern replicas of these traditional designs can be bought at craft shops for between E£50 and E£150.

Siwan wedding dresses are famous for their red, orange, green and black embroidery, which is often embelleshed with shells and beads. The black silk *asherah nazitaf* and the white cotton *ahserah namilal* dresses can both be found on the local market and can cost anywhere from E£250 to E£400. As with other handicrafts, old ones with finer workmenship will be more.

Siwa is also known for its baskets. Woven from date palm fronds by women and girls, they are traditionally utilitarian though these days they're often made simply as souvenirs for visitors. You can spot old baskets by their finer workmanship and the use of silk or leather instead of polyester and vinyl. The *tarkamt*, a woven plate that features a red leather centre, is traditionally used for serving sweets and sells for between E£5 and E£50, depending on the size. The largest basket is the *tghara*, which is used for storing bread. You can buy one for between E£100 and E£250. Smaller baskets include the *aqarush* and the red and green silk tasseled *nedibash*, which start at E£10 to E£15 and go up according to size.

Wood and clay are also crafted in Siwa. Local clays are mixed with straw and coloured with pigment from Gebel Dakrour to make pottery water jugs, drinking cups and incense burners. The *maklay* a round-bottomed cup, and the *adjra*, used for washing hands, are among the most popular buys, as are incense burners, or *timjamait*. They can be had for about E£5 upwards.

They will allow you to look through them but they're not for sale.

Siwa is also known for its dates and olives and they are available in shops around town. Usually someone will open a jar so you can try the olives to find the recipe you like. Everyone has their favourite brand of dates but Jawhara are particularly good.

Getting There & Away

The West Delta Bus Co station is on the main square. There is a daily bus at 7 am to Alexandria (E£15; eight hours), stopping at Marsa Matruh (E£8, four hours) on the way. There's a second bus to Alexandria, once again via Marsa Matruh, departing at 10 am, which has air-con and costs E£25 (E£10 to Matruh). You should book ahead for these services. There is an additional daily service to Marsa Matruh at 2 pm which costs E£9; no bookings are taken.

Although there is a road linking the oases of Siwa and Bahariyya, there is no public transport. Also, although asphalted, it is in bad shape and few people take it. Some entrepreneurial types in town will take you if you can manage the E£550 they're charging.

To/From Libya At the time of writing it was illegal to cross into Libya and go on to the town of Al-Jaghbub, about 120km away. Although the border is only 50km away it is reportedly mined, so things are unlikely to change soon. Should it become possible to cross, there is a paved road from Al-Jaghbub to the Libyan coast.

Getting Around

There is a local bus to Kharmisah and Bilad ar-Rum once or twice a day, usually at 7 am and 2 pm, from near the King Fuad Mosque. It costs E£1 and returns about 45 minutes after completing its route, so it's best to catch the morning bus and come back on the afternoon bus. Should anything happen to the afternoon bus, leaving you stranded overnight, you'll have to bunk with the locals as there's nothing in the way of accommodation or provisions in either of these places.

A better bet is one of the pick-up trucks plying the route between Siwa and Bilad ar-Rum. You'll be expected to pay between 50pt and E£1, depending on where you get off. Alternatively, you can get a group together and rent a pick-up truck. Mahdi at the tourist office or any of the restaurants will be able to help.

Bicycles are a terrific way to get around and can be rented from several sources, including Palm Trees Hotel, the small shop opposite Abdu Restaurant, and Arous al-Waha Hotel. The standard rate is about E£2.50/5 per half/full day.

Hiring a *careta*, a donkey-drawn cart, can be a more amusing, if less practical, way to get around. Expect to pay about E£10 for half a day.

Alexandria & the Mediterranean Coast

On the north coast of Egypt, west of where the Rosetta branch of the Nile leaves the Delta and where the desert meets the sparkling waters of the Mediterranean, is the charming – although somewhat jaded – city of Alexandria, once the shining gem of the Hellenistic world. Nearby is the famous town of El Alamein, where the tide of the African campaign during WWII was changed in favour of the Allies, and west beyond that are the Mediterranean resorts of Sidi Abdel Rahman and Marsa Matruh. The rest of this region is sparsely populated. The road westward beyond Matruh to the Libyan border runs along an almost deserted coast that greets the sea with craggy cliffs or smooth sandy beaches.

Alexandria

Alexandria (Iskendariyya) is often said to be the greatest historical city with the least to show: founded by Alexander the Great, yet it bears no trace of him; site of one of the wonders of the ancient world, but there's not a single notable monument remaining; ruled by Cleopatra and rival of Rome, now a provincial city overcrowded with people but short on prestige.

The reality of modern-day Alexandria is a grubby compress of apartment blocks jostling at the seafront. First time visitors can't help but be disappointed. But to judge Alexandria on first appearances is to sell the city short. It's a city of nuances and shades, with plenty to be discovered if you're prepared to invest the time.

HISTORY

Alexandria's history is the bridging link between the pharaohs and Islam. The city gave rise to the last great pharaonic dynasty and provided the entry into Egypt for the

HIGHLIGHTS

- **Seafood dining in Alexandria** The chance to eat excellent grilled fish at an open-air street restaurant is reason enough alone to visit Alex.

- **Strong coffee and cold Stellas** Alexandria has some wonderful period bars and cafes.

- **The Catacombs of Kom ash-Shuqqafa** A little visited but very odd series of subterranean tombs.

- **Montazah Palace** You can't actually go inside the palace but the grounds are lovely and the sea is clean.

- **The old Turkish houses in Rosetta** Rosetta could provide the dictionary defintion for 'backwater' but it has some stunning old domestic architecture.

- **The beaches at Marsa Matruh** You have to travel to get to them but the sand and sea way out west on the Mediterranean coast is the best in Egypt.

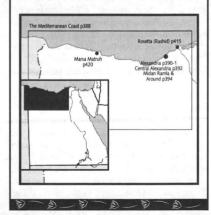

The Mediterranean Coast p388

Rosetta (Rashid) p415

Marsa Matruh p420

Alexandria p390-1
Central Alexandria p392
Midan Ramla &
Around p394

MEDITERRANEAN COAST

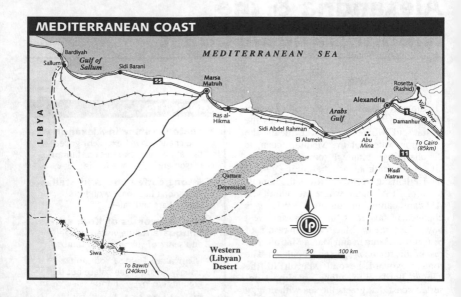

Romans and nurtured early Christianity before rapidly fading into near obscurity when Islam's invading armies passed it by to set up camp on the site that would later become Cairo.

The city began with the conquests of Alexander the Great. Having had his right to rule Egypt confirmed by the priests of Memphis, the Macedonian general followed the Nile up to the Mediterranean. There, on the shores of the sea very familiar to him, he chose a fishing village as the site on which he would found a new city. The foundations were laid in 331 BC.

It's recorded that Alexander devised the city's original street plan himself: a rectangular grid divided into regimented blocks. But he didn't stay around long enough to see his vision set in stone. Almost immediately Alexander departed for Siwa to consult the oracle there, before regathering his army and marching for Persia and then India where he was to die just two years later. His body was returned for burial to Alexandria, the city he had conceived as the cultural and political centre of his empire.

Instead, it was one of Alexander's generals, Ptolemy, who presided over the development of the city. Under Ptolemy's direction Alexandria was filled with architecture every bit as impressive as that of Rome or Athens. To create a sense of continuity between his rule and that of the pharaonic dynasties, Ptolemy made Alexandria look at least superficially Egyptian by adorning his city with sphinxes, obelisks and statues scavenged from the old sites of Memphis and Heliopolis. The city developed into a major port on the trade routes between Europe and Asia but, more notably, its economic wealth soon became matched by its intellectual standing. Alexandria became a renowned centre of scientific, philosophical and literary thought and learning, attracting some of the finest artists and scholars of the time. Its famed library contained 500,000 volumes, and its research institute, the Mouseion, produced some of the most scholarly works of the age.

A grand tower, the Pharos, built on an island just offshore, acted as both a beacon to guide ships entering the booming harbour

A marble head of Alexander the Great. Holes drilled around the head once supported a gilded sunburst.

and, at a deeper level, served as an ostentatious symbol of the city's greatness. Such were the massive dimensions of the Pharos that ancient scholars counted it as one of the Seven Wonders of the World.

During the reign of its most famous regent, Cleopatra, Alexandria rivalled Rome in everything but military power – a situation that Rome found intolerable and was eventually forced to act upon (see the History section in the Facts about Egypt chapter).

Under Roman control, Alexandria remained the capital of Egypt. Although the original great library was burned when the Romans first tried to conquer the city, Alexandria was still regarded as the most learned place on earth and with nearly a million inhabitants, was second only to Rome in size.

During the 4th century AD, however, insurrection, civil war, famine and disease ravaged Alexandria's populace, and although the city later became a centre of Christianity, it never regained its former glory. At the end of the century, the city's cultural importance was almost wiped out as Christianity became the official religion of the Roman empire. All pagan temples were razed and learned institutes (including the Mouseion), along with the theatre, were smothered.

Alexandria's decline was sealed when the conquering Muslim armies swept in to Egypt in the 7th century and ignored the Mediterranean city to establish their new capital (later to become Cairo) further south on the Nile.

All through the Middle Ages, Alexandria dwindled, superceded in importance as a seaport by the nearby town of Rosetta. Its monuments were destroyed by earthquakes and their ruins quarried for building materials; the former great classical city physically shrank to little more than a fishing village on the peninsula between the two harbours (now Anfushi) with a population of less than 10,000.

The turning point in Alexandria's fortunes came with Napoleon's invasion of 1798; recognising the city's strategic importance, he initiated its revival. During the subsequent reign of the Egyptian reformist Mohammed Ali, a new town was built square on the top of the old one, with a canal linking the city with the Nile. Alexandria once more became one of the Mediterranean's busiest ports and attracted an influx of wealthy Turkish-Egyptian traders, followed by Jews, Greeks, Italians and other Mediterranean races. French and British interests and investments increased with the advent of the Suez Canal. Multicultural, buoyant on the gains of commerce and built on the foundations of antiquity, Alexandria took on an almost mythical quality and served as the muse for a new string of poets, writers and intellectuals (see the boxed text 'Literary Alexandria' on page 402).

But it was a bright flame that burned briefly. The revolution that brought Gamal Abdel Nasser to power in 1952 also struck a death knell for Alexandria's cosmopolitan

MEDITERRANEAN COAST

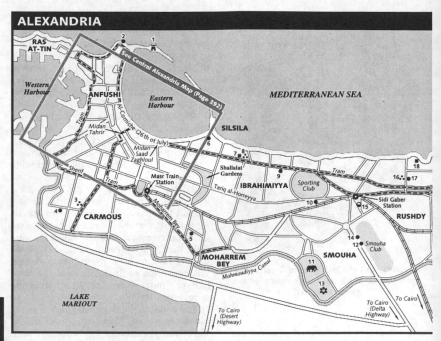

ALEXANDRIA

days. Foreigners flooded out of the country, many minus their properties and businesses which had all been hastily sold off before they could be nationalised by the new government.

Since that time, the character of the city has changed completely. From a population of 300,000 in the 1940s (of which around 40% were foreigners) Alexandria is now home to an almost exclusively Egyptian population of some five million, filled by a steady migration of rural dwellers to the city. The sophistication and glamour of the city may have gone but as an Egyptian character in Naguib Mahfouz's *Miramar* points out, 'Alexandria had to be claimed by its people'.

As well as being Egypt's largest port, Alexandria most notably serves as the country's unofficial summer retreat. Cooler by far than Cairo, anyone who can afford to

migrates from the capital to the Mediterranean. The richer part of society keeps summer houses in the exclusive, edge-of-town resorts like Mamoura and Agamy; those less well-off rent holiday apartments and throng the waterfront cafes and free public beaches in the eastern suburbs.

ORIENTATION

Alexandria is a true waterfront city, nearly 20km long from east to west and only about 3km wide. The city centre addresses the Eastern Harbour, which is almost closed by two spindly promontories.

The focal point of the city is Midan Ramla, also known as Mahattat Ramla (Ramla station) because this is the central terminus for all the city's tram lines. Immediately adjacent is Midan Saad Zaghloul, a large square running back from the seafront and joining Midan Ramla at the

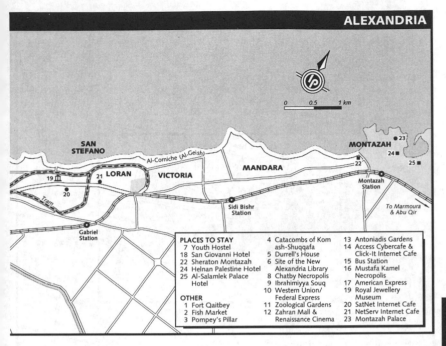

ALEXANDRIA

SAN STEFANO

Al-Corniche (Al-Geish)

MANDARA

MONTAZAH

23

24

22

25

LORAN VICTORIA

19

21

20

Tram

Montazah Station

Gabriel Station

Sidi Bishr Station

To Marmoura & Abu Qir

0   0.5   1 km

PLACES TO STAY		
7 Youth Hostel	4 Catacombs of Kom ash-Shuqqafa	13 Antoniadis Gardens
18 San Giovanni Hotel	5 Durrell's House	14 Access Cybercafe & Click-It Internet Cafe
22 Sheraton Montazah	6 Site of the New Alexandria Library	15 Bus Station
24 Helnan Palestine Hotel	8 Chatby Necropolis	16 Mustafa Kamel Necropolis
25 Al-Salamlek Palace Hotel	9 Ibrahimiyya Souq	17 American Express
	10 Western Union/ Federal Express	19 Royal Jewellery Museum
OTHER	11 Zoological Gardens	20 SatNet Internet Cafe
1 Fort Qaitbey	12 Zahran Mall & Renaissance Cinema	21 NetServ Internet Cafe
2 Fish Market		23 Montazah Palace
3 Pompey's Pillar		

MEDITERRANEAN COAST

corner. Around these two midans, and in the streets to the south and west, are the central shopping area, the tourist office, airline offices, restaurants and most of the cheaper hotels.

To the west of this central area are the older quarters of the city, like Anfushi, while east are a succession of newer districts such as Ibrahimiyya, with a good small *souq* (market); Chatby, which has some old catacombs; and Rushdy, a popular diplomatic and expat address. The eastern suburbs finally end with Montazah, site of a presidential palace and gardens.

The whole strip, from Anfushi to Montazah is tied together by the seafront Corniche (also known in parts as Sharia 26th of July and Sharia al-Geish) and by Tariq al-Horreyya ('tariq' means 'avenue'), which runs parallel to the seafront about 1km inland.

Note that whereas in Cairo 'sharia' is translated as 'street', in Alexandria French still rules and it's 'rue'.

INFORMATION
Visa Extensions
The passport office is at 28 Talaat Harb. You'll need one photo and a photocopy of the relevant pages of your passport (available from the machines out front) as well as the passport itself. The office is open from 8 am to 1.30 pm daily except Friday.

Tourist Office
The main tourist office (☎ 807 9885) is on the south-west corner of Midan Saad Zaghloul. It's open from 8 am to 6 pm. There is also a tourist office at Masr station on platform one. The central Alexandria branch of the tourist police (☎ 483 3378) is upstairs from the main tourist office.

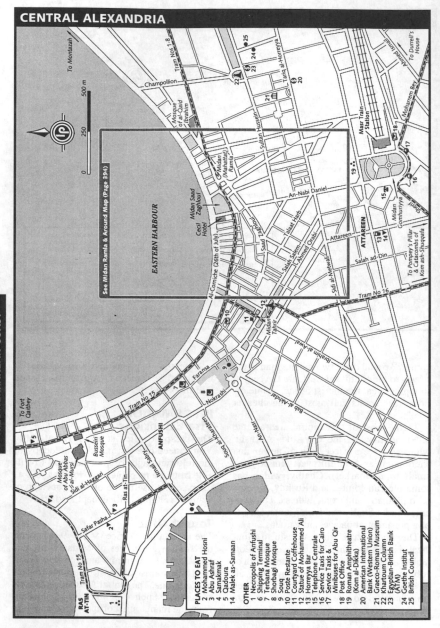

CENTRAL ALEXANDRIA

To Montazah

Tram Nos 1-8

Champollion

Mosque of al-Qaid Ibrahim

EASTERN HARBOUR

See Midan Ramla & Around Map (Page 394)

Cecil Hotel

Midan Saad Zaghloul

Al-Corniche (26th of July)

Midan (Mahattaz) Ramla

Sultan Hussein

Saad Zaghloul

An-Nabi Daniel

Salah Salem

Ahmed Orabi

Talaat Harb

Tariq al-Horreyya

Masr Train Station

ATTAREEN

Attareen

Sidi al-Metwall

Salah ad-Din

Midan Gomhuriyya

To Pompey's Pillar & Catacombs of Kom ash-Shuqqafa

Tram No 16

Ibrahim al-Awal

Midan Tahrir

Faransa

Nokrashi

Bab al-Akhdar

An-Nasri

ANFUSHI

Busseini Mosque

Ismail Sabry

Ras at-Tin

Soug al-Khurunful

Tram No 15

To Fort Qaitbey

Mosque of Abu Abbas Sidi al-Mursi al-Haggari

Safar Pasha

RAS AT-TIN

Tram No 15

MEDITERRANEAN COAST

PLACES TO EAT
1 Necropolis of Anfushi
2 Mohammed Hosni
3 Abu Ashraf
4 Samakmak
5 Qadoura
14 Malek as-Samaan

OTHER
1 Necropolis of Anfushi
6 Shipping Terminal
7 Terbana Mosque
8 Shorbagi Mosque
9 Souq
10 Poste Restante
11 Courtyard Coffeehouse
12 Statue of Mohammed Ali
13 Telephone Centrale
15 Service Taxis for Cairo
16 Service Taxis &
   Minibuses for Abu Qir
17 Service Taxis &
18 Post Office
19 Roman Amphitheatre
   (Kom al-Dikka)
20 American International
   Bank (Western Union)
21 Graeco-Roman Museum
22 Khartoum Column
23 Egyptian-British Bank
   (ATM)
24 Goethe Institut
25 British Council

Foreign Consulates

For details of foreign consulates in Alexandria refer to the Embassies section of the Facts for the Visitor chapter.

Money

For changing cash or cashing travellers cheques, the simplest option is to use one of the many exchange bureaus on the side streets between Midan Ramla and the Corniche. There are also dozens of currency exchange offices along Talaat Harb.

The Egyptian-British Bank (☎ 483 2839) at 47 Sultan Hussein, a five minute walk east of the centre, has an ATM where you can get cash advances on your Visa card.

American Express (Amex) (☎ 541 0177, fax 545 7363) is at 34 Al-Moaskar ar-Romani, some distance from the centre, in Rushdy. Hours are 8.30 am to 5 pm daily except Friday. This office is also a travel agency, and you can have mail forwarded here. The main Thomas Cook office (☎ 482 7830, fax 483 4073) is much more conveniently located at 15 Midan Saad Zaghloul, and it's open from 8 am to 5 pm.

If you need to have money wired to you, Western Union has two offices in town – see International Transfers in the Money section in the Facts for the Visitor chapter.

Post & Communications

The GPO is a small office just east of Midan Orabi. There's an EMS office round the side. Several other branches are dotted around the city including one adjacent to Masr train station (to the left as you exit the station) and another branch at Mahattat Ramla (open until 6 pm). Most offices are open daily (except Friday) from 8 am to 3 pm.

To pick up poste restante you must go to the mail sorting centre one block west of Midan Orabi and a block north of Midan Tahrir. It's a decrepit little stone building opposite a new 15 storey high-rise; enter around the back on Sharia Sahafa. It's open from about 6.30 am to 6 pm daily except Friday.

The telephone offices at Mahattat Ramla and on Midan al-Gomhuriyya opposite

Masr train station are open 24 hours. Ramla also has a fax section (fax 483 3136) where you can receive faxes for a fee of E£6.

Email & Internet Access

At the time of writing Alex has no less than four Internet cafes, although all of them, unfortunately, are some distance out of the centre.

Access Cybercafe
(☎ 425 5766, Web site www.cyberaccess .com.eg) 1st floor of the shopping mall beside the new Zahran Mall, Smouha. Open from 9 am to midnight daily; one hour for E£10.

Click-It Internet Cafe
(☎ 311 7520) ground floor of the shopping mall beside the new Zahran Mall, Smouha. Open from 10.30 to 1 am daily; one hour for E£12, 30 minutes for E£7.

NetServ Internet Cafe
(☎ 587 2269, email webmaster@netserv. com.eg) 678 Tariq al-Horreyya, Loran. Open from 9 am to 1 am daily; one hour for E£8 from 10 am to 3 pm or E£12 from 3 pm to midnight.

SatNet Internet Cafe
(☎ 312 9985) 603 Tariq al-Horreyya, Zizinia. Open from 10 am to midnight daily; one hour for E£12, minimum charge E£6.

To get to the two Smouha Internet cafes, catch a minibus from in front of the Cecil Hotel to Sidi Gaber bus station, head south, away from the train station, until you hit the main road, where you take a right. After 200m you'll reach a roundabout at which you take the second left. The shopping mall with the Internet cafes is between the mosque and the new pink multi-storey Zahran Mall. It's a 10 minute walk in all.

The other two places are further out still. Take tram Nos 2 or 5 from Mahattat Ramla and get off at San Stefano (take a seat on the right side of the tram and look out for the Landmark Hotel; San Stefano is the stop immediately after). From the tram halt, walk back past the Landmark and take the first left. This will take you up to busy Tariq al-Horreyya; from this point NetServ is 400m east (to your left), while SatNat is 200m back in the direction of town.

MIDAN RAMLA & AROUND

PLACES TO STAY
4 Windsor Palace Hotel
5 Hotel Crillon
6 Hotel Union
7 New Hotel Welcome House, Hotel al-Gamil and Hotel Normandie
8 Hotel Triomphe
9 Hotel Acropole
12 Semiramis Hotel
15 Philip House Hotel
17 Hotel Ailema & Hyde Park Hotel
18 Hotel Seastar
23 Metropole Hotel

PLACES TO EAT
19 KFC
22 Trianon
24 McDonald's
25 Mohammed Ahmed
32 Hassan Bleik

37 KFC
39 Restaurant Gad
42 Au Privé
46 Elite
47 Santa Lucia

OTHER
1 Tomb of the Unknown Soldier
2 National Grand
3 Post Office
10 West Delta Bus Co Booking Office
11 No 1 Minibus to Sidi Gaber
13 Pharmacie Suisse
14 Athineos
16 Thomas Cook
20 Post Office & Centrale
21 Newsstand
26 Synagogue
27 Brazillian Coffee Shop
28 Tourist Office

29 Spitfire Bar
30 Telephone Centrale
31 Cap d'Or
33 Sofianopoulo Coffee Shop
34 Baudrot
35 Passport Office
36 Brazillian Coffee Store
38 Banque Masr Building
40 Havana
41 Al-Ahram Bookshop
43 Said Darwish Theatre
44 Cavafy Museum
45 Sultan Hussein Coffee-house
48 Cinema Metro
49 Al-Mustaqbal Bookshop
50 Amir Cinema & Secondhand Bookstall
51 Pastroudi's
52 French Cultural Centre
53 Bookstalls
54 An-Nabi Daniel Mosque
55 Attareen Antique Market

EASTERN HARBOUR

To Fort Qaitbey

Al-Corniche (26th of July)

Midan Orabi

Midan Saad Zaghloul

Cecil Hotel

Midan (Mahattat) Ramla

Saad Zaghloul

Amin Fikry

Safiyya Zaghloul

An-Nabi Daniel

Shakor Pasha

Sultan Hussein

Salah Istanbul

Falaki

Sciottis

Talaat Harb

Mohammed Army

Salah Salem

Attareen

Ahmed Orabi

Tariq al-Horreyya

Sidi al-Metwali

An-Nabi Daniel

To the Train Station

0   100   200 m

Bookshops

Alexandria has no good bookshops and you'll be hard pressed to find even a copy of Laurence Durrell's *Alexandria Quartet* here. The small selection of English-language titles carried by Al-Ahram on the corner of Tariq al-Horreyya and Sharia an-Nabi Daniel is about the best there is. It's open from 9 am to 4 pm from Saturday to Thursday (until 1 pm on Sunday). Alternatively, the Al-Mustaqbal bookshop opposite the Cinema Metro at 32 Sharia Safiyya Zaghloul has a good selection of AUC publications as well as other locally produced Alexandria guides.

For second-hand books, you could trawl the stalls lining the top end of An-Nabi Daniel, but the pickings are usually slim, or visit the stand outside the Amir Cinema on Tariq al-Horreyya.

The situation with foreign-language newspapers and magazines is much better – the newsstand at Mahattat Ramla gets everything from *Elle* (English, French and Italian) to *The Economist*, *Der Spiegel* and *Le Monde*.

Cultural Centres

Most of the city's cultural centres run libraries and organise occasional films, lectures, exhibitions and performances – see *Egypt Today* or its harder-to-find sister publication *Alex Today* for notices of what's on. Take along your passport as you may have to show it before entering.

American Cultural Center
(☎ 482 1009) 3 Sharia al-Pharana (behind the consulate). The library is open from 10 am to 4 pm Sunday to Thursday (8 pm on Monday and Wednesday) and anyone temporarily visiting Alexandria is free to browse around.

British Council
(☎ 482 0199) 9 Sharia Batalsa, Bab Sharqi. Runs language courses, occasionally shows films and has an extensive library which is open from 10 am to 3 pm on Saturday and 10 am to 7.30 pm Sunday to Thursday. Temporary visitors can take out one-day membership for E£1.

French Cultural Centre
(☎ 492 0804) 30 An-Nabi Daniel. Open from 9 am to noon and 5 to 7.30 pm Sunday to Thursday. Films and/or videos are shown daily.

Goethe Institut
(☎ 483 9870) 10 Sharia Batalsa, Bab Sharqi. Has a busy program of films, lectures and concerts and also conducts German and Arabic language courses.

Medical Services

There's no shortage of pharmacies in Alexandria, especially along Sharia Saad Zaghloul. The one opposite Mahattat Ramla, next to the Baskin Robbins ice-cream shop, is open until midnight.

ANCIENT ALEXANDRIA

Ancient Alexandria is almost as intangible to us as Atlantis. It's a place of legendary status connected in the mind to half-remembered tales of Cleopatra, the Seven Wonders of the World and the great library. It borders on the mythological. Only an odd column or two or a gateway hints that it might once all have been real. But thanks to ongoing archaeological research, more and more evidence is continually being unearthed to give physical shape to the ancient city. Much remains inaccessible – the Alexandria of Cleopatra's time lies buried 6m down – but every now and then the city gives up some of its secrets, like the honeycomb of Graeco-Roman tombs accidentally exposed in 1997 by a road-building crew. In recent years the sea has also thrown up some dramatic finds – see the boxed text 'The Royal Palace & Other Underwater Discoveries' on page 397.

For the most part, it's still necessary to employ a little imagination. If you stand at the intersection of Sharia an-Nabi Daniel and Tariq al-Horreyya, for instance, with the Al-Ahram bookshop on one side and a patisserie on the other, you are at the crossroads of the ancient city. What's now Al-Horreyya was then the Canopic Way, extending from the city's Gate of the Sun in the east to the Gate of the Moon in the west with, according to a 5th century account, 'a range of columns ... from one end of it to the other'.

A little way south of this intersection, along **Sharia an-Nabi Daniel**, the Ptolemaic-era

Street of the Soma, is what's believed to be the site of the renowned Mouseion and library, where the greatest philosophers, writers and scientists gathered. It's thought these great institutions were on the west side of the road – the right as you head away from Al-Horreyya. But it's what may have lain – what may still lie, claim some – beneath the modern and fairly unnoteworthy **Mosque of an-Nabi Daniel** on the east side of the street that causes hearts to quicken. Certain scholars, amateur archaeologists and romantics believe, hope, and dream, that in crypts deep below the mosque lies the tomb of Alexander the Great. Trial excavations have revealed that the mosque does indeed rest on the site of a 4th century Roman temple but religious authorities have placed a halt on any further digging.

Pending further discoveries, the best of Alexandria's treasures are on display at the city's Graeco-Roman Museum.

Graeco-Roman Museum

The 24 rooms of this excellent museum contain about 40,000 valuable relics dating from as early as the 3rd century BC. Unfortunately, as is the case with so many of Egypt's museums, labelling is next to non-existent. Things to look out for include, in the very first room (Room 6), three carved heads of Alexander, the city's founder. These are overpowered by two impressive wall-hung mosaics, discovered in the Delta region and dating from about 100 years after Alexander, both portraying Queen Berenice, wife of Ptolemy III.

At the other end of the room, past the giant Apis bull found at the Serapeum, are two carvings of the god Serapis, one in wood, the other in marble. Serapis is a wholly Alexandrian creation, a divinity part Egyptian (the husband of Isis) and part Greek, with echoes of Zeus and Poseidon. King Ptolemy I invented him as a way of bringing together his Egyptian and Greek subjects in shared worship. It worked, and the museum is full of Serapises (the Apis bull is Serapis in another guise).

Room 9 contains a mummified crocodile, which would have been carried in processions devoted to Sobek the crocodile god. Beside the mummy is a carved wooden door that belongs to a temple discovered in Al-Fayoum, now rebuilt and exhibited in the museum's garden.

Room 12 has more examples of the melding of Greek and Egyptian; in this case pink granite statues of Egypt's Greek-Ptolemaic kings depicted wearing pharaonic dress and crowns in an attempt to legitimise them as heirs to the rule of the pharaohs. The fine statue at the centre of the room is of the Roman emperor Marcus Aurelius who visited Alexandria in 175 AD. It was found during the digging of the foundations for the Said Darwish theatre, just off Tariq al-Horreyya.

Room 18, fourth cabinet on the left, contains just about the only historical depictions of the Pharos in Alexandria; these come in the shape of several small terracotta lanterns dating back to the 3rd century BC showing the three stages of the tower (see the boxed text 'The Pharos of Alexandria' on page 404).

In the coin room (Room 24) there are several examples from Alexander's time, displaying a portrait of the Macedonian (panels 36-43) and several bearing profiles of Cleopatra VII (panel 88) – the Cleopatra of Shakespearian and Hollywood fame, though it has to be said, she looks more Virginia Woolf than Elizabeth Taylor.

The last few rooms contain objects from Egypt's Coptic period. The most striking is a huge, 4th century marble capital carved with a basketwork design (Room 2). It was discovered near Mahattat Ramla in central Alex and is believed to have come from one of the city's earliest churches.

For anyone with more than just a passing interest we strongly recommend that you pick up the well illustrated and well written *A Short Guide to the Graeco-Roman Museum* by Jean-Yves Empereur. It should be available at the museum bookshop.

The museum (☎ 483 6434) is at 5 Al-Mathaf ar-Romani, just north-west of Tariq

The Royal Palace & Other Underwater Discoveries

Just recently Alexandria has been giving up more of her hidden treasures. Underwater excavations have been going on for years in the Eastern Harbour and in 1998 the work finally started to pay off with some high profile discoveries that placed the Mediterranean city back in the international spotlight.

There are two separate dive sites currently under exploration: one is the area around the fortress of Qaitbey, the other is in the south-east part of the Eastern Harbour, which is where archaeologists had long suspected lay a submerged Ptolemaic-era royal quarter.

The Qaitbey dive has recorded hundreds of objects including sphinx bodies (their heads tugged off by the motion of the sea), columns and capitals, and fragments of obelisks. The divers have also discovered giant granite blocks, some of them broken as if by a fall from a great height – it's surmised that these blocks are likely the remains of the towering Pharos that was once regarded as one of the Seven Wonders of the World.

Finds in the royal quarter area are even more spectacular. The joint French-Egyptian diving team has discovered platforms, pavements and red granite columns that were part of the former palace, as well as remains of a 5th century wooden pier and a remarkably complete shipwreck that has been carbon dated to between 90 BC and 130 AD. But what has really captured the interest of the media and public at large are the statues. In October 1998, in front of a crowd of international journalists and cameramen, the archaeologists raised from the water a beautiful black granite statue of the goddess Isis holding a canopic jar, followed by a diorite sphinx adorned with the face of what's though to be Ptolemy XII, father of Cleopatra.

Following the viewing and photo-op the pieces were returned to the seabed. Rather than remove the antiquities from their aquatic site, the Egyptian authorities have the idea to establish an underwater museum (the world's first) with a Plexiglass tunnel through which visitors could walk 5m below the sea's surface and view the palace complex *in situ*. Given that technology and Egypt parted ways around the time the royal palace was originally built, this seems a little ambitious but if they pull it off then Alexandria may well be able to once more lay claim to possessing one of the wonders of the world.

al-Horreyya and a short walk from the junction with Sharia Safiyya Zaghloul. It's open from 9 am to 4 pm daily, with a prayer break on Friday for two hours from 11.30 am. Admission costs E£16/8 with an additional fee of E£10/150 if you use a camera or video.

Roman Amphitheatre (Kom al-Dikka)

The 13 white marble terraces of the only Roman theatre in Egypt were discovered in 1964, when the foundations for a new apartment building were being dug. Although the scale of the thing is unprepossessing, the terraces, arranged in a semicircle around the arena, are excellently preserved. The area under excavation has now shifted to the north of the theatre, where a team is still working on exposing the remains of Roman-era baths.

The theatre is on Sharia Yousef, at the north end of Midan Gomhuriyya (the square with the train station). It's open from 9 am to 4 pm daily and admission costs E£6/3. There's also the standard ridiculous video fee.

Pompey's Pillar & the Serapeum

This massive yet unimpressive 30m-high pink granite column, which the Crusaders mistakenly credited to Pompey, rises out of the disappointing remains of the acropolis known as the Serapeum. In Ptolemaic times this was a rocky outcrop with 100 steps which led up to a great temple devoted to Serapis, the man-made god of Alexandria (see the Graeco-Roman Museum section). One of the city's major sites of worship, it was surrounded by subsidiary shrines and included a library founded by Cleopatra. It's now a great lumpen earthen mound pocked by trenches and holes with a few sphinxes (originally from Heliopolis), a Nilometer and the pillar.

The pillar, which has a circumference of nine metres, was erected in 293 AD amidst the Serapeum complex for Diocletian, not Pompey. During the final assault on the pagan intellectuals of Alexandria in about 391 AD, the Christians destroyed the Serapeum and library, leaving only the pillar. (The pillar is, in fact, the only ancient monument remaining whole and standing in Alexandria.)

In the 19th century it was the done thing for visitors to climb the column and picnic up on top but, needless to say, that doesn't happen any more. There's very little to see aside from the pillar, which can be viewed quite well from a large break in the wall at the south end of the site. However, if you do want to get closer, the site is open from 9 am to 4 pm. Admission costs E£6/3, and there's no fee for using your camera.

To get there, take yellow tram No 16 from Mahattat Ramla for 15pt. It's about a 30 minute ride and it stops right by the entrance. Alternatively, from the square in front of the train station (Midan al-Gomhuriyya) follow the tram tracks west along Sharia Sherif and turn left where they do; this should bring you onto a busy market street and the entrance to the Serapeum is 300m ahead on the right. It's a walk of about 1.5km.

Catacombs of Kom ash-Shuqqafa

These catacombs, the largest known Roman burial site in Egypt, were discovered accidentally in 1900 when a donkey disappeared through the ground. They consist of three tiers of tombs and chambers cut out of the rock to a depth of about 35m. The bottom level is flooded and inaccessible but the areas that can be visited are impressive enough.

Enter by descending the spiral staircase cut into a circular shaft; the bodies of the dead would have been lowered on ropes down the centre of the shaft. The staircase gives off to a **rotunda** with a central well piercing down into the gloom of the flooded lower level. When the catacombs were originally constructed in the 2nd century AD, probably as a family crypt, the rotunda would have led to the triclinium (to your left) and principal tomb chamber (straight ahead) only, but over time more chambers were hacked out until the complex had expanded to accommodate more than 300 corpses.

The **triclinium** is a banqueting hall where grieving relatives paid their last respects with a funeral feast. Diners would have reclined on the raised benches at the centre of the room around a low table. When the first archaeologists entered this chamber they found tableware and wine jars.

Back in the rotunda, head down the stairs to the **principal tomb**, the centrepiece of the catacombs – and prototype for a Hammer horror film set. A miniature funerary temple complete with an antechamber with columns and pediment leading through to an inner sanctum, it's decorated with a weird synthesis of ancient Egyptian, Greek and Roman death iconography. For instance, as you enter the inner chamber, either side of the doorway are carved figures representing Anubis, the Egyptian god of the dead, but dressed as a Roman legionary and with a serpent's tail representative of Agathodaemon, a Greek divinity.

It's not known who is buried here but one theory is that it's the man and woman standing in the niches in the antechamber, who may have been Roman nobles.

From the antechamber a couple of short passages lead to a large, basically U-shaped chamber lined with the pigeonholes – or to give them their proper name, *loculi* – in

CATACOMBS OF KOM ASH-SHUQQAFA

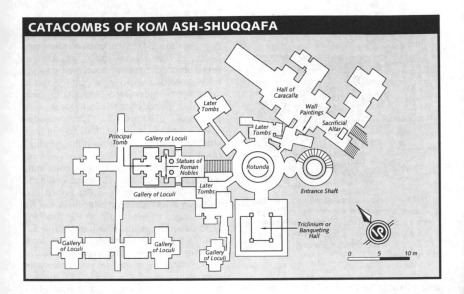

which the bodies were placed. After the body (or bodies, as many of the loculi held more than one) had been placed inside, the small chamber was then sealed with a plaster slab.

Back up in the rotunda there are four other passageways leading off to later, small clusters of tombs. One of these gives access to an entirely different complex, known as the **Hall of Caracalla**. This had its own staircase access (long-since caved in) and has been joined to Kom ash-Shuqqafa, which it predates, by the efforts of tomb robbers who hacked a new passageway. As you pass through this hole-in-the-wall entrance look to your right for some barely discernible wall paintings.

Jean-Yves Empereur's *A Short Guide to the Catacombs of Kom el Shoqafa* has some great photos and a very readable text but, unfortunately, it's not on sale at the Catacombs and you'll have to look for it in town – try the Al-Mustaqbal bookshop on Safiyya Zaghloul.

Kom ash-Shuqqafa (☎ 482 5800) is about five minutes walk south of Pompey's Pillar.

Follow the wall around to the right after you leave the Serapeum and keep straight on. The entrance to the catacombs is on the left about 150m beyond the small midan. It's open from 9 am to 4 pm and admission costs E£12, or E£6 for students, plus E£10 for taking photographs and E£150 for videos.

CENTRAL ALEXANDRIA
Midan Ramla & the Corniche

'Like Cannes with acne,' was Michael Palin's verdict on Alexandria's looping Corniche (in his book of the TV series *Around the World in 80 Days*). But among the many blemishes are some real beauty spots, foremost of which is the **Cecil Hotel**, overlooking Midan Saad Zaghloul. Built in 1930, it's an Alexandrian institution and a memorial to the city's belle époque when guests included Somerset Maugham and Winston Churchill, and the British Secret Service operated out of a suite on the first floor.

The area around Midan Ramla is full of snapshots of the city's cosmopolitan past –

Not the obvious refreshment on a roasting summer's day, but nonetheless sellers of termis – Smartie-sized yellow beans served in a paper cone – do a roaring trade along Alexandria's Corniche.

take a look in the **Pharmacie Suisse with** its beautiful dark wood and glass cabinets painted with skull and crossbones and the warning 'substances toxique'; and next door, **Athenios,** a once grand tea room frequented by Greek girls and besuited Egyptian pashas. Athenios has faded but, diagonally across the midan, the **Trianon** still pulls a select crowd. It's a great place to breakfast on black coffee and croissants.

Incidentally, Midan Ramla is located roughly on the site of the Caesareum, a large sanctuary and temple built by the first Roman ruler of Egypt, Octavian. To mark the entrance to the complex he had two great obelisks brought up from Heliopolis. They stood where the Trianon stands today. Long after the Caesareum disappeared they remained standing – at least one of them did, the other toppled – and were frequently sketched by visitors who nicknamed them 'Cleopatra's Needles'. Then, after more than 1800 years in Alexandria, in 1877 one of the obelisks was removed to Britain, to stand beside the River Thames in London, whilst the other was carted off to New York just two years later to be re-erected in Central Park.

A short walk away from the midan, west along Sharia Saad Zaghloul and then left opposite the Brazilian coffee store into Sharia an-Nabi Daniel you'll find Alexandria's chief **synagogue** (down the first alley on your left). Built over a century ago to serve a thriving Jewish community of about 15,000, it now serves (since the wars with Israel)only a handful of elderly people, mainly women. It's a fabulous Italian-built structure with pink marble pillars, though it's not often open.

Just south of the synagogue, off Sharia an-Nabi Daniel, is the side street leading to the Cavafy Museum (see the boxed text 'Literary Alexandria' on page 404), but for more grandeur bear right at the fork and head down to the junction with Sharia Talaat Harb and the wonderful **Banque Masr Building**. It's a working bank so you can stick your nose in and take a look at the church-like interior with its high-backed benches, Gothic arches and stained glass. It's absolutely beautiful. From here you can then take a right and head down Talaat Harb to Midan Tahrir and Anfushi.

Midan Tahrir & Anfushi

Midan Tahrir Midan Tahrir, which is more popularly known as Midan Mansheiyya, was laid out in 1830 as the centrepiece of Mohammed Ali's new Alexandria. It's Mohammed Ali who's depicted in the equestrian statue standing high on a plinth at the centre of the midan. There's some fine architecture around the big open space but it's hard to recognise it as such after the decades of neglect.

Souqs At the north end of the midan the battered, grand architecture switches scale to something more intimate as you enter the city's souq district. Two main streets head into the market: to the left, Sharia Nokrashi, to the right, Sharia Faransa. Nokrashi runs for about a kilometre and it's one long, heaving bustle of fruit, vegetables, fish and meat stalls, bakeries, cafes and sundry shops selling every imaginable household item. Sharia Faransa begins with cloth, clothes and all things connected with dressmaking. The tight weave of covered alleys running off to the west are collectively known as Zinqat as-Sittat, or 'the women's squeeze' and here you'll find buttons, braid, baubles, bangles, beads and much more, from junk jewellery to those enormous padded bras. Beyond the haberdashery is gold and silver, and then herbalists and spice vendors.

Anfushi At the junction of Faransa and Souq al-Kharateen is the interesting little **Terbana Mosque**. Built in the late 17th century, it incorporates bits of ancient Alexandria in its structure – look round the side for the two classical columns that support the minaret. The red and black painted brickwork on the facade is a common Delta style. (**Shorbagi Mosque**, nearby on Sharia Nokrashi, is another similar style mosque, also built with salvaged remnants of antiquity.)

At this point, you're deep into Anfushi, the old Turkish part of town. While Ramla and the Midan Tahrir area were developed along the lines of a European model in the 19th century, Anfushi remained an untouched, indigenous quarter standing in counterpoint to the new cosmopolitan city and was considered a bit beyond the pale. Today it remains one of the poorest parts of the city, with a high population density squeezed into old, decaying buildings, many of which seem on the verge of collapsing. **Sharia Ras at-Tin**, in particular, has a few formerly grand places in shocking states of decay.

If you continue on Sharia Faransa north of Ras at-Tin, the street becomes much narrower, opening suddenly into a midan dominated by the large white **Mosque of Abu Abbas al-Mursi**. Raised up in 1943 on the site of an earlier mosque built over the tomb of a 13th century Muslim saint, this is a modern but impressive example of Islamic architecture. On feast days and during Ramadan, this is the place to come as thousands converge here to enjoy the night-time festivities.

From the mosque the fortress of Qaitbey is just over 1km along the Corniche. Alternatively, if you're keen on tombs there's the **Necropolis of Anfushi**, five tombs dating back to around 250 BC, 1km to the west. The two main ones contain some much faded wall decoration, supposedly imitating marble, but they're not nearly as interesting as the catacombs of Kom ash-Shuqqafa. The necropolis is open from 9 am to 4 pm and entry costs E£12/6.

Fort Qaitbey

Fort Qaitbey is unfortunate in that it looks like a piece of Toytown architecture, and its greatest point of interest is that it occupies the site of the much more famous Pharos lighthouse (see the boxed text 'The Pharos of Alexandria' on page 402).

The lighthouse had been gone for a century when, in about 1480, the Mamluk sultan Qaitbey ordered the fortification of the city's harbour peninsulas and the construction of a fort and mosque. Naturally, debris from the Pharos was used. Mohammed Ali modernised the fort in the 19th century, for which we can blame its twee appearance, but if you get up close to the outer walls you can pick out some great pillars of red granite which in all likelihood come from the ancient lighthouse.

These days the three floors of the fort house a small naval museum (☎ 480 9144) with various displays including Ottoman weaponry and bits and pieces recovered from Napoleon's unhappy fleet, savaged by Nelson in 1798. The fort is open from 9 am to 4 pm and admission is E£6/3, plus an extra E£10 to get into the naval museum, but it really isn't worth it. Do make the walk to the fort though, if just to look for evidence of the Pharos – plus there's an interesting boat-building yard just before it. It's at this end of the Corniche that all the small fishing boats are harboured, which makes for a great photo with the fort in the background. There's also a pungent fish market nearby.

Getting There & Away To walk to the fort from the Ramla area along the Corniche takes about 30 to 45 minutes. It's a really

MEDITERRANEAN COAST

Literary Alexandria

Just a couple of years ago there was a nationwide survey conducted through the press and bookshops in the UK to find the country's 100 most popular books. The *Alexandria Quartet* by Lawrence Durrell came in somewhere in the 40s. It's probably safe to say then that more people have visited Alexandria through that book than have by physically stepping foot in the city. Alexandria – which somebody once called the 'city of the literary cross reference' – is better known through its literature and writers then through any stone-built monuments or other tourist sites.

It's somewhat ironic then that outside of serious poetry fans and Alexandriophiles the city's finest writer, Constantine Cavafy, is these days so little known. Born of Greek parents, Cavafy (1863-1933) lived all but a few of his 70 years in Alexandria, spending most of his working life as a clerk for the Ministry of Public Works, occupying an office above the still-existent Trianon patisserie. Never collected in his lifetime but since widely translated and published, his poems resurrect events and figures from the era of the Ptolemies, while others are fragments of the city and its routines or recalled encounters:

He must be barely twenty-two years old –,
yet I'm certain almost that many years ago,
I enjoyed the very same body.

The last 25 years of his life, Cavafy lived in a 2nd floor apartment at 4 rue Lepsius (now Sharia Sharm el-Sheikh) above a ground floor brothel. (With a Greek church around the corner and a hospital opposite, Cavafy thought this the ideal place to live, catering for the flesh, the forgiveness of sins and providing a place in which to die.) The flat is now preserved as the **Cavafy Museum** with two of the six rooms arranged as Cavafy kept them, while in the others, spread out on tables, are editions of the poet's publications and photocopies of his manuscripts, notebooks and correspondence. It's open from 10 am to 3 pm daily except Monday and admission is E£8. There's also a small exhibit devoted to fellow Alexandrian-Greek writer Stratis Tsirkas, author of poems and short stories and of the monumental *Drifting Cities*, a weighty trilogy centred around Greek underground politics in wartime Jerusalem, Cairo and Alexandria. It has resonances of Durrell's quartet and is available in English, though it's hard to find.

Cavafy was first introduced to the English-speaking world by EM Forster, the celebrated English novelist who'd already published *A Room With A View* and *Howards End* when he

---

nice walk but if you don't feel up to it take yellow tram No 15 from Mahattat Ramla for 15pt or flag down any of the microbuses barrelling along the Corniche. A taxi should cost E£2.

EASTERN SUBURBS
The Necropolis at Chatby

If you haven't had enough of tombs, there are two more sets of them. The necropolis at Chatby (next to the youth hostel) is considered to be the oldest found in Alexandria. Discovered in 1904, the burials here date from the 4th century BC, soon after the city's founding, and belong to the first generations of Alexandrians. Further east, on Sharia al-Moaskar ar-Romani opposite Amex, is the **Mustafa Kamal** necropolis. Two of the four tombs are interesting for the Doric columns at their centre. Both places are open from 9 am to 4 pm. Entry is E£6 for the former and E£12 for the latter;

Literary Alexandria

arrived in Alexandria in 1916. Working for the Red Cross, Forster spent three years in the city and although it failed to find a place in his subsequent novels (he instead was struggling with *A Passage To India* at the time) he did write for the local English-language press and compiled what he referred to as an 'anti-guide'. His *Alexandria: A History & Guide* (sadly, now out of print) was intended as a guidebook to things not there, based on the premise that 'the sights of Alexandria are in themselves not interesting, but they fascinate when we approach them from the past'.

The guide provided an introduction to the city to Lawrence Durrell, arriving in Egypt 22 years after Forster's departure. Durrell had been evacuated from Greece and resented both Cairo, where he first settled, and then Alex which he regarded as 'a broken-down version of Naples' (so says Gordon Bowker in his *Through the Dark Labyrinth: A Biography of Lawrence Durrell*). But this was 1942-5 and Durrell found great distraction in the slightly unreal air of decadence and promiscuity engendered by the uncertainties and transiency caused by the on-going desert war. He worked as a press attaché and lived in the tower room of a great house in Moharrem Bey at 19 Sharia Maamoun, which is where he entertained and wrote poetry and his short novel *The Dark Labyrinth*. On our last visit in late 1998, the house and its corner tower (illustrated on the cover of the Faber & Faber edition of the collected *Quartet*) still stood but the developers – who had recently demolished the adjacent villa – were just itching to haul it down. It may well be gone by now but if you want to seek out the house then starting at the train station walk south-east down Sharia Moharrem Bey, turn left onto Ahmed Ismail then right at the end beside the Art Museum. After 300m you come to a small roundabout at which you turn right and Maamoun is about the second or third side street on the left.

In truth, those Egyptians that are aware of Durrell's *Quartet* are not particularly fond of the book. It deals with a city they don't recognise. Durrell felt little affinity with the locals and instead his opus is peopled by Greeks and Jews and expatriates; the odd Copt aside, Egyptians don't figure much at all. The heavy eroticism and sensual nature that underlies the work has also always had far more to do with Durrell himself than it did with most people's reality of Alexandria.

Certainly, anyone who comes to Alexandria today with visions of the city gleaned from the *Quartet* will gain as much satisfaction as they would looking for the world of Mary Poppins in London.

half-price for students. The guardians of these places may want some baksheesh for their efforts.

Getting There & Away Bus No 218 from Mahattat Ramla will drop you near the Chatby necropolis. To get to the Mustafa Kamal necropolis, take tram No 1 or No 2 to Mustafa Kamal as-Sughayyer and walk east a couple of blocks to Al-Moaskar ar-Romani. Turn left here (towards the sea)

and walk a couple more blocks. The necropolis is on the left.

Royal Jewellery Museum

This brings together an impressive collection of jewels and kitsch that was formerly part of the royal dressing room from the time of Mohammed Ali's early 19th century rule until the dissolution of the monarchy in 1952. Aside from the standard stuff, it includes diamond-encrusted garden tools, jewelled

Pharos of Alexandria

According to classical accounts, the Egyptian coast was notoriously treacherous with hidden rocks and sand banks and a flat featureless shoreline offering little in the way of navigation aids. So it was that Ptolemy I ordered a great tower to be built, one that took 12 years to complete and was finally inaugurated in 283 BC. The finished structure was of such massive proportions and of such a unique nature that ancient scholars regarded it as one of the Seven Wonders of the World.

In its original form the Pharos was a simple marker, probably topped with a statue, as was common at the time. The tower became a lighthouse, so historians believe, in the 1st century AD, when the Romans added a beacon, probably in the form of an oil-fed flame that was reflected by sheets of polished bronze. Some excellent descriptions of the Pharos exist from as late as the 12th century. It had a square base, an octagonal central section and a round top (which is the form seen in early minarets, leading some historians to speculate that the Pharos was the original inspiration for this Islamic structure). Contemporary images of the Pharos still exist, most notably in a mosaic in St Mark's cathedral in Venice and in two little terracotta representations displayed in Alexandria's Graeco-Roman museum.

In all, the Pharos withstood winds, floods and the occasional tidal wave for a total of 17 centuries. However, in the year 1303 a violent earthquake rattled the entire eastern Mediterranean, from Egypt to Greece and the Pharos was totally destroyed. A century later the sultan Qaitbey quarried the ruins for the fortress that he built on the same site.

Now, some 700 years after it's collapse, a sort of Pharos may rise again. In 1998 famous French fashion designer Pierre Cardin announced his intention to grace Alexandria with a new 133m-high lighthouse near the site of the old. The plans are for a concrete tower covered in mirrored glass with computer operated lights that will cast coloured beams over 50km out to sea. It's proposed that the whole thing should be completed by the year 2000 but at the time of writing, there's no sign of it – thank God.

watches with hand-painted miniature portraits and a diamond-studded chess set. The collection is housed in one of Farouk's old palaces, which is garishly fascinating in its own right – take a peek at the sumptuous tiled bathrooms. Tasteful they are not.

The museum (☎ 586 8348) is open from 9 am to 4 pm (closed for two hours on Friday from 11.30 am). Admission is E£10/5. It's located at 27 Sharia Ahmed Yehia Pasha, Glym. To get there take tram No 2 from Mahattat Ramla and get off at the Qasr as-Safa stop.

Montazah Palace

The Montazah Palace is the vaguely Florentine, vaguely Moorish, former summer residence of the royal family – since the Revolution it's become the summer residence of the president. South-east of the palace is a smaller, no-less-fanciful structure known as the Salamlek, also built by Abbas II, and designed in the style of a chalet to please his Austrian mistress – this has recently been refurbished and opened as a luxury hotel.

While the palace itself is closed to the public, the lush gardens and groves and the semiprivate beach (E£5 to use it) make this an ideal place to spend a relaxing day.

Admission to the grounds costs E£2 (E£3 on public holidays).

Getting There & Away The simplest way is to stand on the Corniche or on Tariq al-Horreyya and flag down a service (microbus); when it slows, shout 'Montazah' and if it's going that way (and most of them are) it'll stop and you can jump in. Most of these services originate at Midan al-Gomhuriyya, the square in front of the train station, so you could also catch one from there. You can also reach Montazah on the local train from Masr or Sidi Gaber stations on the way to Abu Qir but services are infrequent and slow.

BEACHES

There are a few public or semipublic beaches along Alexandria's waterfront, but most of the ones between the Eastern Harbour and Montazah are usually crowded and grubby. **Mamoura Beach**, about 1km east of Montazah Palace, is better – it even has a few small waves rolling in and is the only beach where women are likely to feel comfortable stripping down to a one-piece swimsuit. The local authorities are trying to keep this beach suburb exclusive by charging everyone who enters the Mamoura area a fee of E£3, payable at the toll booth as you drive in off Sharia Abu Qir. To get here jump in an Abu Qir microbus at Midan al-Gomhuriyya.

PLACES TO STAY

The summer months of June to September are the high season in Alexandria, when half of Cairo seems to decamp here in a bid to escape the heat in the capital. They mainly occupy the masses of holiday apartments out along the Corniche in the eastern suburbs but at the peak of the season, in August, you may have difficulty finding a hotel room even at some of the budget places.

For general information on places to stay see the Accommodation section in the Facts for the Visitor section.

PLACES TO STAY – BUDGET

Unless stated otherwise, the prices below include taxes and breakfast.

Hostels

Youth Hostel (☎ 597 4559, 13 Sharia Port Said, Chatby) is acceptable but not particularly pleasant. It suffers from a poor loca-

tion well out of the centre and its rooms don't have sea views. Rates are E£8 for members in dorms (eight beds) or E£14 to E£20 in one of the new double rooms. Nonmembers pay E£4 extra and breakfast is an additional E£2. To get there, take any blue tram from Ramla station and get off at the Chatby Casino, in front of the College of St Mark. Cross to the waterfront side of the college and walk back west a short way along Sharia Port Said.

Hotels

Almost all Alexandria's budget hotels are located in the side streets off the Corniche in the Ramla area, particularly in the streets just behind the Cecil. Most of these hotels at least partly front on to the Corniche so don't settle for a room that doesn't have a sea view – one of the best things about staying in Alex is pushing open the shutters in a morning to get a face full of the Mediterranean.

The hotels below are listed starting with the cheapest.

New Hotel Welcome House (☎ 480 6402, 8 Sharia Gamal ad-Din Yassin), on the street behind the Cecil, is one of three hostels occupying the top two floors of this building. It's easily the best of the bunch. The rooms are variable in quality but an attempt has been made to look after them. Try to get one of the three doubles that overlook the harbour; these have their own shower and toilet units and are a bit of a bargain at E£16. There's not much to choose between the other two hostels: *Hotel al-Gamil (☎ 481 5458)* has dirty rooms, smelly bathrooms, no sea views and charges E£17 a double, while *Hotel Normandie (☎ 480 6830)* does have rooms with sea views but they're filthy and no way do we recommend coming into contact with one of their mattresses – unless you have a good contact at a rare-diseases clinic.

Philip House Hotel (☎ 483 5513), located on the 2nd floor of one of the magnificent Italianate-Moorish mansion blocks on the north side of Midan Ramla, is really a pension, not a hotel, and not a great pension at that. But it's kept relatively clean and of the handful of rooms there's a double with an excellent harbour view and shared bath-room for E£30, and a double with a partial harbour view and shared bathroom for E£25. Avoid the Bahrain and New Bahrain hotels – they're real dives; both are in the same building as the Philip House.

Hotel Acropole (☎ 480 5980, 4th floor, 1 Gamal ad-Din Yassin) has rooms with great views over Midan Saad Zaghloul but none overlooking the harbour. Some of the rooms are also very shabby, the beds are not all that comfortable, and bathrooms (with erratic hot water) are all shared. Still, the place has a pleasant rambling, chaotic appeal. Rates are between E£15 and E£20 for a single, and E£25 to E£35 for a double, depending on the location of the room.

Hotel Triomphe (☎ 480 7585, 5th floor, 2 Gamal ad-Din Yassin) has no rooms with sea views either. It's a similar sort of place to the Acropole but considerably more scruffy. Room rates are roughly the same.

Hotel Ailema (☎ 484 7011, 7th floor, 21 Amin Fikry) is on the wrong side of Midan Ramla for sea views. But it does have an endearing, shuffling, sepia-toned quality. If you've read Mahfouz, then the Ailema is as close as you'll get to the pension Miramar in the book of the same name. Singles/doubles are E£40/60 with bathroom, or E£30/40 without; breakfast is included.

Hyde Park Hotel (☎ 483 5666, 6th floor, 21 Amin Fikry) is also south of Midan Ramla so, again, no sea views. It's not a bad place, similar in character to the Ailema on the floor above, but it's not as well kept or clean. Singles/doubles are E£30/40 with bathroom, or E£25/30 without; breakfast is included but it's not compulsory and the rooms are E£10 cheaper without it.

Hotel Seastar (☎ 480 5343, fax 483 2388, 24 Amin Fikry) is a large, modern place which looks like it should be mid-range. But its rooms are characterless and gloomy with no views. Worse still, they are not well looked after, with broken fittings and grubby sheets and carpets. This maybe explains the low rates – singles/doubles with bath for E£45/55, or E£35/40 without. They'll go even cheaper if you say you don't want breakfast.

Hotel Union (☎ 480 7312, fax 480 7350, 5th floor, 164 Sharia 26th), one block back from the Cecil, offers great value with three star-type accommodation at more or less budget rates. The rooms are some of the cleanest in Alex with sparkling tiled bathrooms. Most also have balconies and fantastic harbour views. Singles/doubles without bath cost E£30/38, or E£45/60 with bath. Breakfast is E£8 extra. Reservations are recommended.

Hotel Crillon (☎ 480 0330, 4th floor, 5 Sharia Adib Ishaq), two blocks back from the Cecil, runs a close second to the Union in the cleanliness stakes – although a few of the rooms are notably not as good than the rest. There's a lovely pre-Revolutionary reception/lounge area, and most rooms have polished wooden floors and French windows that give on to balconies with that great harbour view. Doubles with shower are E£53, while those with a bathroom are E£67. Reservations are a must.

PLACES TO STAY – MID-RANGE

Hotel Union and *Hotel Crillon* (listed in the budget section), though lacking facilities like international phones, bars and restaurants, are otherwise up to the standard of many mid-range hotels. Plus, they have the advantage of a good location, which is where almost all Alex's other mid-range options fall down – they're nearly all strung out in the eastern suburbs, mostly along the Corniche. They generally have good sea views but they're in no-mans land as far as sights, shops and other conveniences go. There are just a handful of exceptions.

Metropole Hotel (☎ 482 1465, fax 482 2040, 52 Sharia Saad Zaghloul) has a good, central location just off Midan Ramla, with most rooms overlooking Midan Saad Zaghloul and the harbour. It's a classy old joint that has been recently renovated, earning itself a four star rating. The lobby is horribly overdone but some of the rooms are beautiful. Singles go for E£160 to E£180, while doubles are E£180 to E£190. Breakfast is obligatory (E£14), plus there's 19% in taxes to be added.

San Giovanni Hotel (☎ 546 7775, fax 546 4480, 205 Sharia al-Geish) has a superb setting, jutting out over the sea at Stanley Bay, and you can hear the waves crashing as you fall asleep. It is a way from the centre but it's close to Rushdy, which is a busy district with plenty going on, and it's within walking distance of Sidi Gaber train and bus station. The restaurant is said to be one of the best in Alexandria and there's also a 24 hour coffee shop. Singles/doubles/triples are US$62/81/97 including breakfast and tax.

Semiramis Hotel (☎ 482 6837) on the Corniche beside the Italian consulate we mention only because it's so well located. Shame that it's such a lousy place, totally undeserving of the three stars it claims. The rooms are dirty with no fan or air-con, while the common areas are grim and very grubby. It charges E£120 for a double.

PLACES TO STAY – TOP END

Alexandria has its complement of the international five star chain hotels including *Helnan Palestine* (☎ 547 4033, fax 547 3378), *Mercure Alexandria-Romance* (☎ 588 0911, fax 587 0526), *Ramada Renaissance* (☎ 548 3977) and *Sheraton Montazah* (☎ 548 0550, fax 540 1331), all of which offer the standard fare and all of which are way out of the centre.

If you plan to stay in a top end hotel in Alex, make it *Cecil Hotel* (☎ 483 7173, fax 483 6401, Midan Saad Zaghloul, Ramla). It's now part of the Sofitel chain and as a result of refits over the years, some of the common areas like the lobby and bar have been stripped of all the elegance and charm they once had, but the rooms are excellent and the views unbeatable. There's also a very good Chinese restaurant on the roof. Singles range from US$84 to US$110, doubles from US$96 to US$125 (the higher prices are for the rooms with sea views). The buffet breakfast (price not included in the room rates) is obligatory as are the 22% taxes.

Al-Salamlek Palace Hotel (☎ 547 7999, fax 547 3585) is a recent conversion of an Italianate chateau in the grounds of the Montazah Palace built by Khedive Abbas II for his Austrian mistress. We haven't stayed there but reports are that the rooms are sumptuous. We can vouch for the fact that the setting is magnificent.

Windsor Palace Hotel (☎ 480 8439, fax 480 9090, 17 Sharia ash-Shohada) occupies a whole block on the Corniche just west of its more famous rival the Cecil. It's an elegant old thing, built in 1907, retaining plenty of its original fittings (the elevator is splendid). Unfortunately it's badly run and lacking in many of the facilities you'd expect of a top-end hotel. A standard double is US$95.

PLACES TO EAT

One of the great pleasures of visiting Alexandria is in sitting around in its various cafes and gorging yourself on the abundant fresh seafood.

Fast Food

Most of the fast food joints are out in the more fashionable suburbs like Rushdy, Smouha and Mamoura, but *McDonald's* has a city centre branch on Sharia Safiyya Zaghloul, just south of Midan Ramla, while *KFC* is around the corner on the midan itself. There's another KFC on Sharia al-Kineesa al-Kobtiyya, just off An-Nabi Daniel.

Budget Dining

The place for cheap eating is around the area where Sharia Safiyya Zaghloul meets Midan Ramla, and along Sharia Shakor Pasha, one street over to the west. There are plenty of little *fuul* and *ta'amiyya* places here as well as sandwich shops and the odd *kushari* joint.

Mohammed Ahmed (317 Sharia Shakor Pasha) is reckoned by all to be the best of the lot. It specialises in fuul, but also does ta'amiyya, omelettes, fried cheese, plus all the usual salad and dip accompaniments. The food's a bit greasy but Alexandrians swear by it and the place is always packed. A full meal will come to no more than E£4 to E£6 per person. There's also a takeaway section.

Eating Fish in Alex

While Alexandria has no shortage of good sit-down seafood restaurants, it's also a fun thing to go along and buy some take-away baked or grilled fish. You can do this at some of the Safar Pasha places but there are also many other fish shops scattered about town at which you can choose from the catch and then have it cooked while you wait and wrapped for you to take and eat *al fresco*.

The most popular fish with the locals are *balti*, which is about 15cm long, flattish and grey with a light belly, and the larger, tastier *bouri*, which is about 30cm, thin and silver, darkening toward the top. You tell the seller how many fish you want and they weigh it and you pay – balti is about E£12 per kilogram, bouri is E£18. Your fish is then cleaned and descaled, floured and spiced, and you have the choice of having it barbequed on a hotplate or baked in an oven. It takes about 15 to 20 minutes to cook. Eat with bread and humous. It's *very* messy but good.

Two highly recommended places at which to buy – and these recommendations come from a Red Sea captain who's lived his life in Alex eating little but fish – are *Salim al-Fouly* in the Ibrahimiyya souq (see Self-Catering in the Alexandria Places to Eat section), a tile fronted place on the first sidestreet to the right as you walk down the souq from the tram line, and an unnamed fish shop at the south end of Sharia al-Moaskar ar-Romani in Rushdy. In both instances, after you've bought your fish you can wander down to the seafront and dine on the rocks.

Hassan Bleik (18 Sharia Saad Zaghloul), next to the Sofianopoulo Coffee Store, is a venerable Lebanese restaurant nestled behind a patisserie. Never mind the grubby table-cloths, it has an excellent menu of traditional Levantine dishes like kibbeh in yoghurt sauce, fatta with chickpeas and lamb, and

chicken livers. Prices for dishes are from E£6 to E£14. It's open from noon to 6 pm only.

Havana (☎ *483 0661*) at the junction of Sharia Orabi and Tariq al-Horreyya, Atta-reen, is primarily a bar (see the Entertainment section) but it also does great food. The fried calamari is superb and heaped up with fries and salad it's a bargain at E£10. The pizzas are also highly recommended (E£9 to E£18), while other dishes available include omelettes (E£5 to E£8), chicken livers E£9.50 and – the owner is Coptic Christian – roast pork (E£13.50).

Restaurant Gad (Sharia Mohammed Azmy) is a branch of the Cairo restaurant of the same name serving cheap basic lunches to the area's office workers.

Restaurants

City Centre Most of the better places to eat are either on or just off Tariq al-Horreyya, especially around the junction with Safiyya Zaghloul.

Au Privé (☎ *484 1881*), tucked away down the little alley just east of the junction of Sharia an-Nabi Daniel and Tariq al-Horreyya, is currently Alexandria's sole hip night spot. It has a bar menu and a sit-down menu. The former includes lots of dips, salads and burgers, plus a wide variety of seafood – my grilled calamari, ungarnished but good, was E£16, but prices range from E£6 to E£40. The other, heavy-hitting menu has a strong French slant with dishes of duck and rabbit, plus seafood and steaks, all in rich sauces. Dishes start at E£30. Local Stella is E£8. A E£3 cover charge and 17% tax tops up your bill.

Elite (☎ *482 3592, 43 Sharia Safiyya Zaghloul)*, near the Cinema Metro, is another of those Alexandrian time warp affairs. Faintly resembling an old US diner, it seems sealed in a 1950s bubble, under the spell of the elderly but formidable Madame Christina, the ever-present proprietress. The menu is displayed outside, beside the door, and runs from spaghetti bolognese at E£4.50 to grilled meats in the E£25 to E£30 range. Beer is served (E£5.25). The place is open from 11 am until late.

Malek as-Samaan on Sharia Attareen, just south of the junction with Sharia Yousef, is by day a small courtyard clothes market; by night it's an open-air restaurant serving pigeon and quail. It's one of Egypt's most unusual dining out venues and is well worth a try. Beer's served too. It's open from about 8 pm onwards.

Santa Lucia (☎ 482 4240, 40 Sharia Safiyya Zaghloul) has long been acclaimed as one of Alexandria's best restaurants, although reports in recent years suggest that standards have declined. The Francophone menu leans heavily toward tarted up seafood dishes such *spaghetti aux fruits de la mer* or *crevettes á l'indienne* and a full meal with starter will cost you about E£40.

Anfushi Some of Alexandria's best restaurants for straightforward good value, streetside dining can be found in Anfushi's *baladi* district. Head for Sharia Safar Pasha, lined with maybe a dozen places all crackling and flaming with grills barbecuing meat and fish. You could chance a table at any of them and probably come away satisfied but those mentioned below are the ones we've tried and liked.

Abu Ashraf (☎ 481 6597, 28 Safar Pasha) is one of the street's fish specialists. Make your selection from the day's catch then take a seat under the green awning and watch it being cooked. Price is determined by weight and what you choose ie grey mullet at E£30 per kilogram or jumbo prawns at E£120. It's open almost round the clock, as are most places on this wonderful street.

Mohammed Hosni (48 Sharia Safar Pasha) is unlike most of the other restaurants on this street in that it does both meat and fish. Jumbo prawns, fish and quail were all on the grill when we visited but we opted for 500g of mixed kebab and kofta, a beautiful baked rice served on lamb, *tahina*, *babaghanoug* and bread; it was more than two of us could eat and came to just E£30.

Qadoura (☎ 480 0405, 33 Bairam al-Tonsi) has long been regarded as Alex's premier fish restaurant. Tables are out on the street beside the tram tracks, but first, as

is standard in this kind of place, pick your fish from the ice-packed selection which usually includes, at the least, sea bass, red and grey mullet, bluefish, sole, squid and shrimp. A selection of mezze comes with all orders (there's no menu). Most of the fish is about E£35 per kilogram, with prawns at E£80 per kilogram. The place is open 24 hours.

Samakmak (☎ 480 9523, 42 Qasr Ras as-Tin) is owned by the retired queen of the Alexandrian belly-dancing scene, Zizi Salem. Her restaurant places itself up-market of Abu Ashraf and Qadoura, and although you can have grilled or fried fish, the place is better known for seafood specials like crayfish, an excellent crab tajine and a delicious spaghetti with clams. Seating is indoors only. Expect to spend around E£50 per person.

Cafes
Alex has at least five 'must-visit' cafes. The best known is *Pastroudi's*, founded in 1923 by Greeks and immortalised in Durrell's *Alexandria Quartet*. It's no longer the haunt of any sort of smart or literary set and is in fact a bit fusty, but the pavement tables on its south side are a great late afternoon spot for some reading over lemon tea and pastries (which will easily take you over the E£5 minimum charge). It's at 39 Tariq al-Horreyya, beside the Amir Cinema.

Trianon, which faces Midan Ramla, was a favourite of the poet Cavafy, who worked in offices above. It's still immensely popular and a good place for a continental-style breakfast (although the coffee is lousy).

Much better coffee can be had at *Brazilian Coffee Store*, just 100m down Sharia Saad Zaghloul, or *Sofianopoulo Coffee Store*, down at the western end of the same street. Both of these places are dominated by huge silver coffee grinders and boxes, cases and sacks of the shiny dark aromatic beans. The drawback is that neither has any seating so you have to drink your coffee standing (there's a second branch of the Brazilian Coffee Store on Sharia Salah Salem which does have some chairs).

Almost next door to Sofianopoulo's, is **Baudrot**, which is completely dead in the winter but a must in the summer for its garden with vine hung trellises and wicker chairs and tables.

Self-Catering

For fruit and vegetables, either head for Souq Nokrashi on the street of the same name just west off Midan Tahrir, or the Ibrahimiyya souq, which is a couple of stops east of Mahattat Ramla on any tram – get off at the Al-Moaskar stop. These two areas are also the best for ba'als (grocers) where you can get cheese, olives, yoghurt, bread and the like. Takeaway beer is available in the centre at a dedicated Stella shop just off Midan Saad Zaghloul, a couple of doors along from the West Delta Bus Co ticket office.

ENTERTAINMENT

Alexandria's cultural life has never really recovered from the exodus of the Europeans and Jews in the 1940s and 50s. Since that time, Cairo has been the selfish proprietor of the arts, resulting in Alexandria playing host to just one theatre, one concert hall, no galleries, no opera house and, up until 1998, it had had no new cinema screens since the Revolution. It does have at least two of the best bars in the country, though.

Ahwas

During the summer the whole 20km length of the Corniche from Ras at-Tin to Montazah becomes one great strung out *ahwa*, or coffeehouse. Generally speaking though, these are not good places – they're catering for a passing holiday trade and so they tend to overcharge. A good, no nonsense friendly ahwa with excellent *sheesha* is the **Sultan Hussein**, which is the one with yellow awnings on the corner of sharias Sultan Hussein and Safiyya Zaghloul. For an odd, atmospheric place – which is admittedly a bit scruffy – take a look at the ahwa in the central courtyard of the big, battered old building on the corner where Midan Orabi meets Midan Tahrir; you have to squeeze

through a passageway almost closed by clothes stalls to find it.

Bars

Our vote for best bar in Egypt goes to the **Havana**. It's run by Nagy whose father bought the place from a departing Greek in the 1950s. Since that time some of the details may have changed but a cosmopolitan, *laissez-faire* air still prevails at its six tables. Nagy is also a great cook – see the Places to Eat section. The Havana is on Tariq al-Horreyya near the corner with Sharia Orabi; it's open from noon until around 2 am. There's no sign and the door is often kept locked but just knock and you'll be made welcome – that is, as long as you obey the posted notice: 'No entry with pyjamas and no spitting on the floor'.

Almost as good as the Havana is **Cap d'Or** at 4 Sharia Adib, just south of Sharia Saad Zaghloul. With stained glass windows, a big high bar and plenty of old bits and pieces hanging on the walls, it has the feel of an Andalusian tapas bar. Plenty of people come here to eat calamari, shrimp or fish, all of which are excellent, but it's an equally fine place just to pull up a stool and settle in for a Stella. It closes around 3 am. The nearby **Spitfire**, just north of Saad Zaghloul, has a totally different character and feels almost like a Bangkok bar – but without the women, of course. It has a reputation as a sailors' bar and the walls are plastered with stickers for shipping lines and photos of drunk regulars. Closing time is midnight.

Other bars worth investigating are **Horreyya** on Sharia Attareen, just south of the junction with Sharia Yousef, and the sadly dilapidated **National Grand**, diagonally opposite the GPO, just back from the Corniche. You can also drink without having to eat at **Elite**, which has the appeal of large windows so you can street-watch over your Stella.

Cinemas

The following cinemas regularly screen English-language films:

Amir Cinema (☎ 491 7972) 42 Tariq al-Horreyya, central Alexandria. Two screens, both of which are usually showing movies a year or two old. Nice cinema though.

Cinema Metro (☎ 483 0432) 26 Safiyya Zaghloul, central Alexandria. An absolutely beautiful old place, and very well looked after – pity the movies it screens are always so bad.

Renaissance Zahran Mall, Smouha. Alexandria's newest cinema with six screens all showing first run Hollywood films. For how to get there see how to get to the Smouha Internet cafes in the Internet & Email Access section earlier in this chapter. Alternatively, a taxi from the centre will cost about E£3.

Music, Theatre & Dance

There is virtually nothing going on in the way of theatre or music. What little there is, is usually staged at the Said Darwish Theatre (☎ 482 5602, 22 Tariq al-Horreyya). The Elite restaurant usually sticks notices up advertising anything that's happening or see *Egypt Today*. Also, check the French Cultural Centre (see Cultural Centres earlier in this chapter) as it is behind most of the few performances that do go on.

SHOPPING

There's the souq just west of Midan Tahrir and sharias Safiyya Zaghloul and Saad Zaghloul are lined with an assortment of pokey, old stores, but overall Alexandria is not a great place to shop. Not, that is, unless you like shopping for antiques and other miscellaneous historical debris. The confusion of backstreets and alleys of the Attareen district make up an antique market of world renown. When Alexandria's European high society was forced en masse to make a hasty departure from Egypt following the Revolution in 1952, they largely went without their personal belongings – much of what they left has over the years found its way into the shops of Attareen. But while there are some wonderful finds, there are few bargains. Dealers here know their stuff. Some of these guys have branches in Paris. The regular clientele is largely rich Egyptians and collectors from the Gulf, the US and Europe. Still, there are good buys around and there's no charge for just looking.

GETTING THERE & AWAY

Air

There are direct international flights from Alexandria to Athens (Olympic Airways) and Frankfurt (Lufthansa), and to Saudi Arabia and Dubai (EgyptAir). Airline offices in Alexandria include:

Air France
   (☎ 483 8901) 22 Salah Salem
British Airways
   (☎ 483 6668) 15 Midan Saad Zaghloul
EgyptAir
   (☎ 483 3357) 19 Midan Saad Zaghloul
Gulf Air
   (☎ 482 1711) 33 Safiyya Zaghloul
KLM
   (☎ 482 8547) 6 Tariq al-Horreyya
Lufthansa
   (☎ 483 7031) 6 Talaat Harb
Olympic Airways
   (☎ 482 1014) 19 Midan Saad Zaghloul
SAS
   (☎ 483 3973) Tariq al-Horreyya, opposite the
   Amir Cinema
TWA
   (☎ 483 4682) 2 Tariq al-Horreyya

Air travel to Alexandria from within Egypt is expensive; the one-way fare for the 40 minute flight from Cairo is E£248. Unless you are in a tremendous hurry, it is best to get to and from Alexandria by bus, taxi or train. And in fact, by the time you take getting to and from airports into account, you're not likely to save any time whatsoever – especially as there plans to move the airport further out of town (see the Getting Around section later in this chapter).

Bus

Long-distance buses all go from one garage behind Sidi Gaber train station; the No 1 minibus from outside the Cecil Hotel connects it with the city centre. (If you get dropped off at the front of the train station you need to take the underpass to the platform on the far side of the tracks, then down another flight of steps to get out.)

The main companies operating from here are Superjet (☎ 422 8566), whose ticket office and bays are almost immediately out

MEDITERRANEAN COAST

back of the train station, and West Delta (☎ 420 0916), who are about 100m to the east. Between these two are several little cabins beside the road which house the East Delta and Upper Egypt bus ticket offices.

West Delta also has a city centre booking office on Midan Saad Zaghloul, close by the main tourist office.

Cairo Superjet has buses to Cairo (also stopping at Cairo airport) every 30 minutes from 5.30 am to 10 pm. The trip takes 2½ hours and costs E£20 to E£25 until 6.30 pm after which it goes up to E£22 to E£31. There's also a 1 am service to the airport only (E£31). West Delta also has buses to Cairo every hour between 5 am and 1.30 am and charges E£16 to E£20. The Superjet buses are a bit bigger and more modern, but all the Cairo services are air-con with a toilet on board. ·

The North Coast & Siwa Superjet has a bus for Marsa Matruh (E£24; four hours) at 7.15 am on Thursday, Friday, Saturday and Sunday only. West Delta has 12 buses a day to Marsa Matruh (E£15 to E£23, depending on the bus), of which the 6 pm service goes on to Sallum (E£20; nine hours), while the 11 am service goes via Marsa Matruh to Siwa (E£25; nine hours).

Most of these buses stop in El Alamein, and will stop at Sidi Abdel Rahman if you want to get off there (which will cost about E£6).

Sinai Superjet has a daily 6.30 pm service to Sharm el-Sheikh (E£77; seven hours).

The Suez Canal & Red Sea Coast Superjet has one bus daily to Port Said (E£22, four hours) at 6.45 am, and one to Hurghada (E£75; nine hours) at 8 pm. West Delta has four services a day to Port Said (E£17 to E£20), two to Ismailia (E£17) at 7 am and 2.30 pm, and two to Suez (E£20) at 6.30 am and 2.30 pm. The Upper Egypt Bus Company also has a Hurghada (E£55) bus departing at 6.30 pm daily which continues on down to Port Safaga (E£60).

International Buses Superjet and West Delta both run buses to Benghazi and Tripoli in Libya. Superjet's bus leaves at 8.30 am daily and costs US$60 to Benghazi and US$123 for the 32 hour trip to Tripoli. The West Delta bus leaves at 1 pm, costs E£75 and terminates 17 hours later in Benghazi from where you can get another bus on to Tripoli.

Train

Alexandria's main train terminal is Masr station (Mahattat Masr), although Sidi Gaber, which serves the populous eastern suburbs is almost as busy. At Mahattat Masr, 1st and 2nd class air-con tickets must be bought from the ticket office next to the tourist information booth; 3rd class and 2nd class ordinary tickets are purchased from the front hall.

Cairo-bound trains leave from here at least hourly, from about 5 am to 10 pm (there's also one at 3.25 am), stopping five minutes later at Sidi Gaber station. The best trains, the Turbini (also known as the Spanish trains) don't stop again until 2½ hours later when they arrive in Cairo. They depart Mahattat Masr at 8 am and 2 and 7 pm and tickets for 1st/2nd class air-con cost E£22/17.

The next best trains, the Faransawi, the 'French-line' services, stop at Damanhur, Tanta and Benha arriving in Cairo after 2¾ hours. They depart at 7 am and 3 and 7.30 pm and cost E£20/12 in 1st/2nd class.

Two trains a day leave Alexandria for Marsa Matruh (about six hours) at 6.45 am and 1 pm, but they are not a good option; there's no 1st class, only 2nd and 3rd with the better seats costing E£8.10. The bus service on this route is faster and more comfortable.

Service Taxi

The service taxi depot is across the midan from the Masr train station. The fares are between E£8 and E£10 to Cairo or Marsa Matruh, depending on whom you talk to. To more local destinations, some sample fares are: Zagazig E£8; Tanta E£5; Mansura E£8; Abu Qir 50pt. There's also a second, bigger service taxi station at Moharrem Bay.

Boat

At the time of writing, there are absolutely no passenger boats operating out of Alexandria. They used to sail regularly up the coast to Beirut, Lattakia in Syria, and on up to Istanbul and even Odessa. There was also a regular ferry between Alex and Athens. But cheap airfares have taken away the trade and the last boats quit in 1997. This situation is not expected to change.

GETTING AROUND
To/From the Airport

The airport (☎ 420 1036) is south-west of the city centre. To get there, you can take bus No 203 from Mahattat Ramla or No 703 from Midan Orabi. A taxi should cost no more than E£10. Note, that at the time of writing there were plans to move the airport to the site of an old military airfield at Burg al-Arab, some 60km west of the city.

Bus & Minibus

As a visitor to Alex, you won't use the buses at all – the trams and microbuses are a much better way of getting around.

Train

About the only conceivable service you might use in Alexandria is the slow 3rd class train from Mahattat Masr to Abu Qir which stops, among other places, at Sidi Gaber, Montazah and Mamoura. The fare is 40pt.

Tram

Tram is the best way to travel in Alex. Mahattat Ramla is the main tram station and from here lime-yellow coloured trams go west:

No 14 goes to Masr station and Moharrem Bey
No 15 goes past the Mosque of Abu al-Abbas Mursi and Fort Qaitbey to Ras at-Tin
No 16 goes past Pompey's Pillar to the Carmous terminal.

And blue coloured trams travel east:

No 1 goes about two-thirds of the way to Montazah via
No 2 goes about two-thirds of the way to Montazah via Zizinia

Nos 3 and 7 go to Sidi Gaber North
Nos 4 and 6 go to Sidi Gaber South
Nos 5 and 8 go to San Stefano

Some trams have two or three carriages, in which case one of them is reserved for women. It causes considerable amusement when an unsuspecting foreigner gets in the wrong carriage. The standard fare is 15pt.

Taxi

You can expect to pay for taxis in Alexandria what you would pay in Cairo. A short trip, say from Midan Ramla to Masr train station will cost E£2, while between E£3 and E£4 is reasonable for a trip to the eastern beaches.

Around Alexandria

ABU QIR

This coastal town, 24km east of central Alexandria, is historically important for two major 18th century battles between the French and English. During the Battle of the Nile in 1798, Admiral Nelson surprised and destroyed the French fleet in the bay at Abu Qir. Although Napoleon still controlled Egypt, his contact with France by sea was effectively severed. The British landed 15,000 Turkish soldiers at Abu Qir in 1799, but the French force of 10,000 men, mostly cavalry led personally by Napoleon, forced the Turks back into the sea, drowning at least 5000 of them.

It is best to go to Abu Qir during the week to avoid the crowds of Alexandrians who flock there on the weekends. If you're into seafood, this is definitely a good place to go.

There are plenty of buses from central Alexandria to Abu Qir every day (for example bus Nos 260 and 261 or minibus No 729 from Midan Orabi), but it's probably easier to take a microbus for 60pt from in front of the train station. Remember Abu Qir is pronounced Abu 'Ir, ie Abu EAR.

ABU MINA

St Mina is said to have fallen victim to anti-Christian feeling in the Roman Empire of the early 4th century. Born in West Africa, he did a stint in the Roman army before deserting and finally being tortured and beheaded for his faith. He was buried at a place near the present site of Abu Mina, which eventually became a place of pilgrimage. Churches and even a basilica were built, all subsequently destroyed. In the 14th century, a Mamluk army supposedly rediscovered the site and the bones of St Mina, which could not be burned (proving to the Mamluks that they belonged to a saint).

A German team has been working on Abu Mina since 1969 (excavations have uncovered the early medieval Church of the Martyr, where St Mina's remains are believed to be buried), and there are grand plans for a museum and archaeological park. At present the site is not open to visitors.

ROSETTA (RASHID)

Rosetta, also known by its newer name of Rashid, is 65km east of Alexandria, where the western branch of the Nile empties into the Mediterranean, some 6680km from its source at Lake Victoria.

Founded in the 9th century, the town is most famous as the place of discovery of the stone stele that provided the key to deciphering hieroglyphics (see the boxed text 'Rosetta Stone' on page 416) but, during the 17th and 18th centuries, it was also Egypt's most vital port. Then, as Alexandria staged its comeback in the 19th century, Rosetta fell into decline, to the point where today it's a sleepy little provincial town sustained by fishing and dates. There are more donkey carts and horse and traps on the streets than there are cars.

The Nile here is particularly beautiful, wide and full, with boat builders along the Rosetta Corniche and little palms across on the far bank.

Warning Do not visit Rosetta if it has rained any time during the last few days – the town's streets are unsurfaced and after a downpour the whole place becomes one big mud bath.

Things to See & Do

Rosetta's main attraction is its fine old Ottoman-era merchants' houses. These are built in a distinctive Delta-style of small flat bricks painted alternately red and black. They tend to be three storeys high with each of the upper floors sticking out slightly from the one below it, and there's a lot of use of jutting *mashrabiyyas* – the intricately assembled wooden screens that serve for windows. The houses are beautiful things and there are at least 22 of them, all within a square 500m. Most have either been restored or are presently undergoing restoration work, and about eight are currently open to the public. Theoretically, there's a small admission fee but on our last visit the ticket office (which is in the small park in front of the museum – see Museum later in this section) was closed and we didn't have to pay anything.

Ramadan House Most impressive of all Rosetta's fine architecture is the Ramadan House, which is part of the grouping immediately west of the midan where the service taxis and minibuses pull up. Although it's devoid of furniture and totally bare – as are all the buildings – it's still possible to get a very clear idea of how the house worked. A series of rough stone chambers make up the ground floor, and these would have been used for storage. The 1st floor is for the men; one of the rooms here is a reception room, overlooked by a screened wooden gallery, which is where any women present would have sat, obscured from view. The stair to the gallery is hidden behind a false cupboard. As you go up the main staircase to the 2nd floor, notice at foot level there is a little revolving turntable; this was so the women could serve tea and coffee while remaining invisible.

Upstairs is the area for women and the first thing you encounter, off to the left, is the kitchen, identifiable as such by the huge flue. Notice how light it is up here and how airy, thanks to the mashrabiyya screens which allow cooling breezes to circulate around the house.

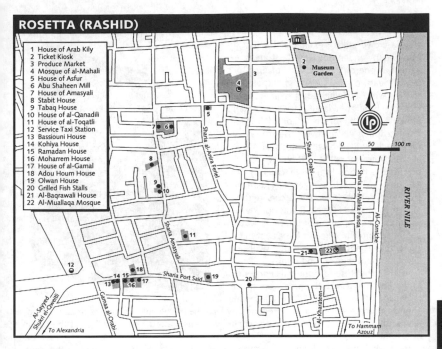

ROSETTA (RASHID)

1 House of Arab Kily
2 Ticket Kiosk
3 Produce Market
4 Mosque of al-Mahali
5 House of Asfur
6 Abu Shaheen Mill
7 House of Amasyali
8 Stabit House
9 Tabaq House
10 House of al-Qanadili
11 House of al-Toqatli
12 Service Taxi Station
13 Bassiouni House
14 Kohiya House
15 Ramadan House
16 Moharrem House
17 House of al-Gamal
18 Adou Houm House
19 Olwan House
20 Grilled Fish Stalls
21 Al-Baqrawali House
22 Al-Muallaqa Mosque

On the uppermost floor there's a tiny *hammam* (public bath) with a domed ceiling into which would have been set pieces of coloured glass.

Other Houses On leaving the Ramadan House head downhill and take the second left into Sharia Amasyali; there are a whole bunch of fine houses along this street and in the alleyways off to either side. The **House of al-Toqatli** (second street on the right), though closed to the public, has an interesting facade.

Back on Sharia Amasyali there are three more houses, all closed to the public, before you reach the splendid **House of Amasyali**, which has possibly the best facade of all, with beautiful small lantern lights and vast expanses of mashrabiyya. This one is open to visitors and has a painted ceiling with an Islamic motif in one of the ground floor

rooms, and some fine woodwork inlaid with mother-of-pearl on the upper floors.

Next door to the Amasyali house is the **House of Abu Shaheen**, which incorporates a reconstructed mill on the ground floor. Out back in the courtyard, the roof of the stables is supported by granite columns with Graeco-Roman capitols.

Mosque of al-Mahali There are more recycled ancient columns at this mosque, about 100m east of the Abu Shaheen house. An absolute forest of them fills the interior, nearly all of them different –fluted, carved, Doric, Corinthian. What were the buildings that they originally supported? We can only wonder. But chances are the columns were scavenged from Alexandria in the Middle Ages when that city was a ghost of its former Ptolemaic self and Rosetta was booming. The mosque's doorways are executed

The Rosetta Stone

Now a crowd-pulling exhibit at the British Museum in London, the Rosetta stone is regarded as one of the key finds of Egyptology. Unearthed in 1799 by Napoleon's soldiers while building a fort near Rosetta, the stone is part of a large black stele dating from the reign of Ptolemy V (about 196 BC). The inscription which covers the stone was supposedly written by the priests of Memphis in commemoration of Ptolemy's accession to the throne but, more crucially, it's executed in three languages: Egyptian hieroglyphs, demotic Egyptian (a cursive form of hieroglyphs) and Greek. It was quickly realised that a comparison of the texts would potentially provide a key to the as yet indecipherable script found on the walls of Egypt's ancient temples and tombs.

In 1801 the Rosetta stone was conceded to the British and first attempts were made to decode the hieroglyphs. An Englishman, Thomas Young, established the direction in which the hieroglyphs should be read, and deciphered that the hieroglyphs enclosed within oval rings (cartouches) were in fact the names of royalty.

However, it was Jean François Champollion who, in 1821, began to formulate the translation of Egyptian hieroglyphs based on the study of the Rosetta stone. By 1823 he had achieved a breakthrough and established a complete list of signs with their Greek equivalents. Champollion was the first Egyptologist to perceive that signs could be alphabetic, syllabic or determinative, and also established that the hieroglyphs inscribed on the Rosetta stone were actually a translation from the Greek, and not the other way around. His obsessive work not only solved the mystery of pharaonic script but also contributed significantly to a modern understanding of ancient Egypt.

in the Delta style and are beautiful, as is the central tomb chamber inside the prayer hall.

Museum The museum was closed for renovation at the time of our last visit but it occupies the **House of Arab Kily**, the former residence of the governor during Rosetta's heyday. In the gardens in front of the museum is the ticket kiosk (again, closed when we visited) from where tickets are bought to enter the houses.

From the museum head directly south, parallel to the river. This will take you past the back of the interesting **Al-Muallaqa Mosque**, which is raised up on ancient Graeco-Roman columns with the ground floor underneath used for storage and stalls. Continue on the same street and after about 200m you'll come to the Hammam Azouz.

Hammam Azouz The hammam, or public bath, is the two storey, beige-yellow build-

The 30m-high Pompey's Pillar in Alexandria.

Taking a break in an Alexandria *ahwa*.

Alexandria – 20km long and only 3km wide – is truly a waterfront city.

PATRICK SYDER

Mosque of Abu Abbas al-Mursi, Alexandria

PATRICK SYDER

WWII Commonwealth Memorial, El Alamein

MARK ECCLESTON

Alexandria's Fort Qaitbey was built in 1480 and modernised by Mohammed Ali in the 19th century.

ing with a broken column lying beside the doorway. It should be open to the public but if the door is locked and nobody answers your knocking, just hang around and somebody will run off and find the custodian. It's worth persevering because although the hammam hasn't yet been restored in any way, it can have only fallen out of use in recent history because it's in a remarkably complete state.

You enter into a chamber with a central fountain and raised platforms around the periphery; this is where bathers would first disrobe and where they'd later return, after scrubbing and steaming, to lie around, sip tea and chat. Notice, again, more recycled bits of antiquity – in this case the pink granite column. If you then go through the little doorway on the right, you pass through a warren of steam rooms with black and white marble floors, and these lead into a beautiful domed chamber, the ceiling of which is inset with coloured glass. The four small rooms at the corners are for washing in and some still have their stone basins.

Bathhouses like this were in common use until very recently but now that most houses in Egypt have some form of plumbing they've nearly all closed down. For more on hammams in Egypt see the Islamic Cairo section in the Cairo chapter.

Getting There & Away

Although buses and trains operate between Alexandria and Rosetta, the easiest way to do the trip is by minibus. From in front of Alexandria's train station jump in one for Abu Qir (60pt). After leaving Alex behind, you travel a long open road with the train track to the left and fields to the right; you need to get out at the point where the minibus swings a sharp left, crossing the tracks. On the north side of the tracks there's a little lot which is where the Rosetta minibuses stand (E£1.50; 45 minutes). Coming back, it's possible to get a minibus (E£2.50)from Rosetta straight in to central Alexandria (they travel the length of the Corniche, passing Midan Saad Zaghloul).

Mediterranean Coast

The stretch of coastline between El Alamein and Alexandria has largely disappeared under a spew of ugly concrete 'tourist villages' – the places that the moneyed classes of Cairo flock to through the wickedly hot summer months.

EL ALAMEIN

The small coastal village of El Alamein, 105km west of Alexandria, is most famous as the scene of a decisive Allied victory over the Axis powers during WWII – see the boxed text 'The Battle of El Alamein' on page 418. Today, it's a busy construction area intended to provide port facilities for shipping oil.

The town's two hotels, museum, Commonwealth cemetery, and so on, are actually along a side road that leaves the main highway at the Greek War Memorial and rejoins it again after passing right through the town. Should you need to make a phone call there's a centrale a little way beyond the museum.

Though it's possible to stay overnight, El Alamein is best visited as a day trip from Alexandria; there really isn't much here that would detain any but the most enthusiastic of military historians.

The War Museum

This contains a good collection of uniforms, memorabilia and pictorial material relating to the Battle of El Alamein and the North African campaigns in general. Maps and explanations of various phases in the campaign in Arabic, English, German and Italian complement the exhibits, and there's a 30 minute Italian-made documentary that you can watch. Outside the museum is a collection of tanks, artillery and hardware from the fields of battle.

It's open from 8 am to 6 pm and admission is E£5/2.50. Photography inside costs an extra E£5.

The Battle of El Alamein

The massive battle of El Alamein, between the Allied tank divisions under the command of Field Marshal Montgomery and the German-Italian armoured force of Field Marshal Rommel's Afrika Korps, altered the course of the war in North Africa.

In June 1942, Rommel, nicknamed the Desert Fox, launched an offensive from Tobruk, Libya in an attempt to push his troops and 500 tanks all the way through the Allied lines to Alexandria and the Suez Canal. It was not the first attempt in what had been two years of seesaw battles, but this time the Axis forces were confident of a breakthrough. However, the Allies stopped their advance with a line of defence stretching southward from El Alamein to the Qattara Depression. On 23 October 1942, Montgomery's 8th army swooped down from Alexandria with a thousand tanks, and within two weeks routed the German and Italian forces, driving Rommel and what was left of his Afrika Korps back to Tunis.

More than 80,000 soldiers were killed or wounded at El Alamein and the subsequent battles for control of North Africa. The thousands of graves in the three massive war cemeteries in the vicinity of the town, the area's main tourist attractions, are a bleak and moving reminder of the war.

Commonwealth War Cemetery

The cemetery, on the eastern side of town, is a haunting place where more than 7000 tombstones cover a slope overlooking the desert battlefield of El Alamein. Soldiers from the UK, Australia, New Zealand, France, Greece, South Africa, east and west Africa, Malaysia and India who fought for the Allied cause lie here. The cemetery is maintained by the War Graves Commission, and admission is free. Outside is a small separate memorial to the Australian contingent, and a little further east is a Greek war memorial.

German & Italian War Memorials

About 7km west of El Alamein, on a bluff overlooking the sea, is what looks like a hermetically sealed sandstone fortress. Inside this silent but unmistakable reminder of war lie the tombs of German servicemen and, in the centre, a memorial obelisk.

About 4km further on is the Italian memorial with, as its focal point, a tall, slender tower. Before reaching the German memorial, you may notice on the left side of the road what seems a little like a glorified milestone. On it is inscribed the Italian *Mancò la fortuna, non il valore* – 'We were short on luck, not on bravery'.

Places to Stay & Eat

Al-Amana Hotel, almost opposite the museum, has simple double rooms that are nothing special – but a damn sight better than rooms in the rest house down the road. E£20 gets a room without bath, E£30 gets one with. It also has a small cafeteria where you can get chicken and rice meals, omelettes and fuul as well as drinks and biscuits.

El Alamein Rest House (☎ 430 2785) was once *the* place to stay but it's now extremely dilapidated and not recommended.

Hotel Atic (☎ 03-492 1340), 15km east of El Alamein, is the nearest of the many beach resorts that blight this stretch of coastline. It charges E£120 for a double room.

It may be possible to camp on the beaches, but you'll have to hunt around for the police and attempt to get a *tasreeh* (permit).

Getting There & Away

Bus Catch any of the Marsa Matruh buses from Sidi Gaber in Alexandria (see the Alexandria Getting There & Away section). You'll be dropped on the main road about 200m down the hill from the museum.

Service Taxi Service taxis leave from the lot in front of Alexandria's train station and cost about E£6. More often than not they are of the microbus variety. It's easy to pick up one of these from El Alamein to get back to Alexandria or to head further west to Sidi Abdel Rahman. Otherwise traffic is regular, but remember to bring water with you, as the heat can be sweltering.

SIDI ABDEL RAHMAN

The fine, white sandy beach and the sparkling turquoise of the Mediterranean make this stunning place, 23km west of El Alamein, a real, as yet unspoilt, coastal beauty spot – though the developers can't be far away.

Bedouins occasionally congregate in a small village about 3km in from the beach. They belong to the Awlad Ali tribe, who came into the region several hundred years ago from Libyan Cyrenaica and subdued the smaller local tribes of the Morabiteen. There are now five main tribes subdivided into clans, each of which has several thousand members. The Egyptian government has been attempting to settle these nomads, so nowadays most of the Bedouins have forsaken their tents and herd their sheep and goats from the immobility of government-built stone and concrete houses.

The beach, the Bedouins, and an expensive hotel are about all there is to Sidi Abdel Rahman.

Places to Stay & Eat

El Alamein Hotel (☎ 492 1228, fax 492 1232) is ridiculously overpriced at E£440 for a rather unimpressive, three star standard double. About 3km further west there is a turn-off for Hanna Beach (Shaat al-Hanna), where during summer you might find a few tents set up here for passers-by, but don't count on it. You may well be able to camp further along the beach, but again, technically at least, you will need to have a permit.

Getting There & Away

The same buses that can drop you at El Alamein en route to or from Marsa Matruh can also drop you here. They generally stop for a break just after the Hanna Beach turn-off. There are service taxis operating between El Alamein and Sidi Abdel Rahman and to places further west, but nothing much happens after early afternoon.

RAS AL-HIKMA

About 48km short of Marsa Matruh, this is little more than another small Bedouin village with some attractive beaches. There is supposedly an official camping site here. Ordinary buses between Alexandria and Marsa Matruh can let you off here, or you can pick up the occasional service taxi to Marsa Matruh.

MARSA MATRUH

The large waterfront town of Marsa Matruh, built around a charming bay of clear Mediterranean waters and clean white sandy beaches, is a popular summer destination with Egyptians. This is a problem in that the place is packed in summer and the beaches – at least those close to town – are pandemonium. Away from the sand, the town itself, with a population of about 80,000, is dull and very unattractive. Outside of the summer season, it's also completely dead, with most of the hotels and restaurants closing down over winter.

Orientation & Information

There are really only two streets in Marsa Matruh that you need to know: the Corniche, which runs all the way around the waterfront, and Sharia Iskendariyya, which runs perpendicular to the Corniche, towards the hill behind the town.

The more expensive hotels are along the Corniche. Others are dotted around the town, mostly not too far from Sharia Iskendariyya. The bulk of the restaurants and shops are on or around Sharia Iskendariyya.

The passport office is just off Sharia Iskendariyya, a couple of blocks north of the train station. It's open daily from 8.30 am to 2 pm and 6 to 9 am in summer; 5 to 8 pm in winter. The tourist office (☎ 493 1841) is on the ground floor of the governorate building one block west of Sharia Iskendariyya on the corner of the Corniche. It's open daily from 8.30 am to 6 pm (until 9 pm in summer). The tourist police are next door.

There are two banks in Marsa Matruh. You can change cash and cheques at the National Bank of Egypt, a few blocks west

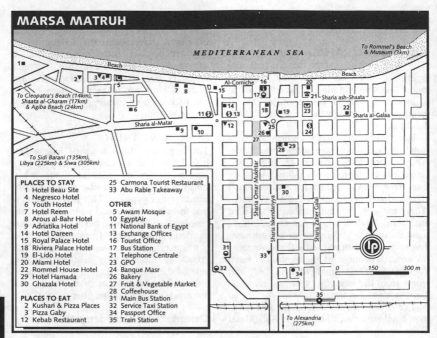

MARSA MATRUH

MEDITERRANEAN SEA

To Rommel's Beach
& Museum (3km)

Beach

Al-Corniche

Beach

To Cleopatra's Beach (14km),
Shaata al-Gharam (17km)
& Agiba Beach (24km)

Sharia ash-Shaata

Sharia al-Galaa

Sharia al-Matar

To Sidi Barani (135km),
Libya (225km) & Siwa (305km)

Sharia Omar Mukhtar

Sharia Iskendariyya

Sharia Zaher Galaa

0   150   300 m

To Alexandria
(275km)

PLACES TO STAY	25 Carmona Tourist Restaurant
1 Hotel Beau Site	33 Abu Rabie Takeaway
4 Negresco Hotel	
6 Youth Hostel	**OTHER**
7 Hotel Reem	5 Awam Mosque
8 Arous al-Bahr Hotel	10 EgyptAir
9 Adriatika Hotel	11 National Bank of Egypt
14 Hotel Dareen	13 Exchange Offices
15 Royal Palace Hotel	16 Tourist Office
18 Riviera Palace Hotel	17 Bus Station
19 El-Lido Hotel	21 Telephone Centrale
20 Miami Hotel	23 GPO
22 Rommel House Hotel	24 Banque Masr
29 Hotel Hamada	26 Bakery
30 Ghazala Hotel	27 Fruit & Vegetable Market
	28 Coffeehouse
PLACES TO EAT	31 Main Bus Station
2 Kushari & Pizza Places	32 Service Taxi Station
3 Pizza Gaby	34 Passport Office
12 Kebab Restaurant	35 Train Station

of Sharia Iskendariyya and south of the Corniche. You *might* be able to convince the Banque Masr branch on Sharia al-Galaa to accept Visa or MasterCard for a cash advance. There are also several exchange bureaus on Sharia al-Galaa.

The GPO is on Sharia ash-Shaata, a block south of the Corniche and two blocks east of Sharia Iskendariyya. Hours are from 8.30 am to 3 pm (closed Friday and Saturday). The 24 hour telephone centrale is across the street.

Rommel's Museum & Beach

Set in the caves Rommel used as his headquarters during part of the El Alamein campaign, this rather poor excuse for a museum contains a few photos, a bust of the Desert Fox, some ageing German, Italian and British military maps and what is purported to be Rommel's greatcoat. The museum is about 3km east of the town centre, out by the beach of the same name. The turn-off to the museum and beach is signposted. The museum is open from 9.30 am to 4 pm in summer only and costs 50pt. You can arrange to see it in winter through the tourist office or the staff at the governorate building.

Rommel's beach, a little east of the museum, is supposedly where the field-marshall took time off from tanks and troops to have his daily swim. It's popular with holidaying Egyptians in summer, and women will feel uncomfortable bathing here. To get here you can walk around the little bay (or hire a bike or *careta*, the donkey-drawn carts that serve as taxis in Marsa Matruh), or get a boat from the landing about 300m east of Sharia Iskendariyya.

Other Beaches

The stunning azure water of the Mediterranean would be even better if the town and its hotels were not here. But further away the water is just as nice and human infringement is minimal. Offshore lies the wreck of a German submarine, and sunken Roman galleys reputedly rest in deeper waters off to the east.

The **Lido**, the main beach in town, is no longer an attractive swimming spot, and although Rommel's Beach is OK, it is often too crowded for comfort.

The next choice is either **Cleopatra's Beach** or **Shaata al-Gharam** (Lovers' Beach), which are about 14km and 17km respectively west of town. The rock formations here are certainly worth a look and nearby is Cleopatra's Bath, where the great queen and Marc Antony are supposed to have bathed. A boat from near the Beau Site Hotel goes across the bay to Cleopatra's Beach and Shaat al-Gharam. Like most things in Marsa Matruh, the boats only run in summer.

Agiba means 'miracle' and **Agiba Beach**, about 24km west of Marsa Matruh, is just that. It is a small but spectacular beach, accessible only by a path leading down from the clifftop. There is a cafe (open in summer only) nearby where you can get light refreshments, and the hassle potential for women who want to strip down to a swimsuit is considerably lower than elsewhere.

Places to Stay

The accommodation situation in Matruh is bad. The hotels are all generally crummy and way over-priced but demand for rooms over summer is such that hoteliers really don't need to try very hard. There are a huge number of places, especially if you head out of town, but we just give a few of the better central options.

Prices vary greatly from winter to summer, and substantial discounts are sometimes available until early June.

Places to Stay – Budget

Although there are no official camp sites, it may be possible to pitch a tent along the beach or at Rommel's Beach – check with the tourist office.

Youth Hostel (☎ 493 2331), a couple of blocks south of the Awam Mosque, is just about OK. Members pay E£8 for a comfortable enough bunk bed in a cramped room of six or eight. There seems to be no problem if nonmembers stay. The toilets are fairly clean.

Ghazala Hotel (☎ 493 3519) just off Sharia Iskendariyya is the most popular backpackers' stop; the entry is sandwiched between some shops and is easily overlooked. The charge is E£10 per person for a basic but clean bed. Most rooms have balconies (but no view to speak of) and the shared toilet/shower combinations are clean, if lacking in hot water.

Hotel Hamada (☎ 493 3300) has a great central location just off Sharia Iskendariyya and, while basic, is at least clean. It charges E£15/20 for singles/doubles with shared bathrooms and toilets.

There are a few cheap and nasty places around town, some near the main bus station.

Places to Stay – Mid-Range & Top End

Town Centre The advantage of staying in the town centre is that you are close to what few shops and restaurants there are, but you've a way to go to find a decent beach.

Hotel Dareen (☎ 493 5607) has OK rooms that are not very well kept but at least the sheets are clean and there's hot water in the ensuite bathrooms. Singles/doubles are E£30/45 (E£10 more in summer) with breakfast, or E£5 cheaper if you want to skip the stale bread and jam.

El Lido Hotel (☎ 493 2249, fax 493 2248), on the corner of Sharia Iskendariyya and Sharia al-Galaa, has singles/doubles for E£35/44 with breakfast, or E£30/35 without. In summer, prices are about 50 percent more expensive. For that you'll get a poky room with TV, phone and bath.

Adriatika Hotel (☎ 493 5195) on Sharia al-Matar, a little way down the road from the EgyptAir office, was an acceptable lower mid-range option (singles/doubles for E£28/40) but at our last visit it was closed for renovations and nobody could say how much the room rates would be when it reopened.

Rommel House Hotel (☎ 493 5466, fax 347 1496) on Sharia al-Galaa, east of Sharia Iskendariyya, has rooms with bath, TV, refrigerator and breakfast for E£83/111 in summer or E£43/63 in winter.

Riviera Palace Hotel (☎ 493 3045, fax 493 0004) is one of the better places for the money. It has decent, large rooms with partial views of the bay, which in winter go for E£100 a double. In summer you must take the room plus half-board which comes to E£125/185.

Miami Hotel (☎ 493 1400) is a large, very gloomy three star place that does at least benefit from a Corniche setting. It's way over-priced though at E£162/200 in summer and E£120/144 in winter.

Along the Corniche There is a string of places along the waterfront heading west of Sharia Iskendariyya with little to choose between them; they all have good sea views but little else in the way of nearby amenities.

The first of them, the 10 storey, 126 room *Royal Palace Hotel* used to have very reasonably priced rooms (less than E£50 in summer) that came with bath, balcony and breakfast, but it was under going renovation when we last visited which may mean a hike in prices when it reopens.

Arous al-Bahr Hotel (☎ 493 4420) always had slightly grubbier rooms than the Royal Palace but, again, this place was undergoing a refit so who knows what the outcome will be. Singles/doubles in summer are E£70/115 half-board, while in winter they go for E£24.50/36.50 or E£35/53 plus breakfast.

Hotel Reem (☎ 493 3605) has clean rooms with balcony for E£86/140 half board in summer, or singles/doubles for E£30/50 with breakfast or E£25/40 without in winter.

Negresco Hotel (☎ 493 4491, fax 493 3960) has spotless rooms, but at E£145/240 in the high season, is a bit on the expensive side. In winter it's reasonable at E£45/75.

Hotel Beau Site (☎ 493 8555, fax 493 3319) is easily Matruh's most attractive option – if you have the money. The 'luxury' rooms on the beach cost E£390/577 in summer, or about half that in winter. The rooms come with breakfast and all mod cons. There are some tiny rooms available above the disco with great balconies but little else for substantially cheaper rates. The Beau Site also boasts the only private beach in Matruh.

Places to Eat
The dining situation in Matruh is also significantly less than impressive. When we last visited, which admittedly was in winter, we had a hard time getting anything to eat at all. The two main options were *Camona Tourist Restaurant* on the corner of sharias Al-Galaa and Iskendariyya, and another corner *kebab restaurant* about 200m west of that. Both the places had kebab, kofta and chicken. With the latter also serving *fiteer*, the Egyptian pancake/pizza. There's also a good takeaway in *Abu Rabie* at the train station end of Sharia Iskendariyya; it does fuul, ta'amiyya, salads and good *gamboury* (shrimp) or calamari sandwiches for about E£1.25 each.

For excellent pizza (summer only), head down to the Corniche. Just after the Negresco Hotel you'll find *Pizza Gaby*, where most of the pizzas cost around E£10. Just around the corner from Gaby's are a couple of other inferior pizza places plus a kushari joint.

Beau Site Restaurant in the hotel of the same name is fairly good, but beware of the prices.

Getting There & Away
Air EgyptAir flies between Cairo and Marsa Matruh for E£344 one way. The EgyptAir office is on the roundabout by the road to Siwa and Sallum.

Bus For details on buses from Cairo or Alexandria to Marsa Matruh, see the Getting There & Away sections in those cities.

Matruh has two bus stations: the main station is up near the railway line and there's a second, small station consisting of just a kiosk and lay-by near the tourist office.

Superjet has two services a day, one to Alexandria (E£24; four hours) at 2.30 pm and one to Cairo (E£37; five hours) at 3 pm. These go from the tourist office station.

West Delta has at least seven buses a day to Alex (E£11 to E£15) going from the main bus station, plus another three from the tourist office station – these latter three are luxury buses and cost E£20 or E£23. It has four services to Cairo daily, one from the main bus station at 7.30 am (E£25 but no air-con) and three later air-con services from the tourist office station all at E£35. Buses to Sallum (four hours) all depart from the main bus station and there are nine services a day, starting at 7 am. The buses are rough but then the fare starts at E£6.25, rising to all of E£10 for the better services that go later in the day. Siwa buses are also rough and non-air-con and go at 7.30 am, 1.30 pm and 4 pm. The fare is E£7 on the first two buses and E£10 on the third. The journey takes about five hours depending on breakdowns (and there always has to be at least one).

Train Don't do it. Even the station master at Matruh says that the trains are 'horrible'. Should you choose to ignore his advice, there are two per day to Alexandria, departing at 7 am and 3.40 pm with 2nd/3rd class tickets costing E£6.40/2.80. The journey takes anywhere from six to seven hours. There is nothing heading west to Sallum.

Service Taxi The service taxi lot in Marsa Matruh is across from the bus station. Service taxis to Siwa cost E£10, if there are enough people going. Other fares include: to Sidi Barani (E£6), Sallum (E£10) and Alexandria (E£8).

Getting Around
Caretas, or donkey carts, are the most common form of transport around the streets of Marsa Matruh. Some are like little covered wagons with colourful canvas awnings. A ride across town should cost no more than E£2. From the centre to Rommel's Museum is E£3.

Private taxis or pick-ups can be hired for the day, but you must negotiate and bargain aggressively, especially in the summer.

In summer there are supposedly regular buses to Cleopatra's and Agiba beaches from Sharia Iskendariyya.

SIDI BARANI
About 135km west of Marsa Matruh on the way to Libya is this small but busy Bedouin town. It serves as a bit of a food and petrol way-station for traffic coming in from Libya. But that's about it. There's a small hotel and a few unsanitary places to eat.

SALLUM
Nestled at the foot of Gebel as-Sallum on the gulf of the same name, Sallum (pronounced saLOOM) is in the proverbial middle of nowhere. The dearth of western travellers coming through here means there is little sign of the hassling so common elsewhere in the country. There is a post office here and a branch of the National Bank of Egypt.

As usual, the water is crystal clear, but in town the rubbish on the beach detracts from it. Head east for a while and you can pick yourself out some secluded stretch of sand, but ask first if the spot you've chosen is OK. Some parts of the beach are government property. And remember that being on the beach without a permit after about 5 pm can get you into strife.

On the eastern entrance to the town is a WWII Commonwealth War Cemetery, a somewhat more modest version of the El Alamein cemetery.

You really don't want to stay here but *Hotel al-Ahram* (☎ 480 0148) is probably the best of a bad bunch. It costs E£6/12 for basic rooms. When there is water, it's cold. There are a couple of *lokandas* (another name for a basic, cheap place to doss) with their names in Arabic only.

At the border, 12km further on, is *Hotel at-Ta'un* (name in Arabic only). There are one or two modest fuul stands around, but ask first how much the food costs.

Getting There & Away
There are buses and the odd service taxi from Alexandria and Marsa Matruh; see the relevant Getting There & Away sections.

From Sallum, buses for Marsa Matruh (E£7 and E£8; four hours) depart three times a day; some of these go on to Alexandria (E£20; eight hours). A service taxi to Marsa Matruh will cost about E£10.

Libya The border crossing point of Amsaad, just north of the Halfaya Pass, is 12km west of Sallum. Service taxis run up the mountain between the town and the Egyptian side of the crossing for E£2 to E£3. Once through passport control and customs on both sides (you walk through), you can get a Libyan service taxi on to Al-Burdi for about LD1. From there you can get buses on to Tobruk and Benghazi.

Note, it is not possible to get a Libyan visa at the border.

Suez Canal

The Suez Canal – one of the greatest feats of modern engineering – represents the culmination of centuries of effort to enhance trade and expand the empires of Egypt by connecting the Red Sea with the Mediterranean Sea. Although the modern canal was by no means the first project of its kind, it was the only one to bypass the Nile, excavating instead across the Isthmus of Suez to provide a major shipping route between Europe and Asia.

Construction of the first recorded canal was begun by Pharaoh Necho between 610 and 595 BC, and the canal stretched from the Nile Delta town of Bubastis, near present-day Zagazig, to the Red Sea via the Bitter Lakes. After reputedly causing the death of more than 100,000 workers, the project was abandoned. It was picked up again and completed about a century later under Darius, one of Egypt's Persian rulers. The canal was improved by the Romans under Trajan, but over the next several centuries it was either neglected and left to silt up, or dredged by various rulers for limited use, depending on the available resources.

It was again briefly restored in 649 AD for a period of 20 years by Amr ibn al-As, the Arab conqueror of Egypt.

Following the French invasion in 1798, the importance of some sort of sea route south to Asia was again recognised. For the first time the digging of a canal directly from the Mediterranean to the Red Sea, across the comparatively narrow Isthmus of Suez, was considered. The idea was abandoned, however, when Napoleon's engineers mistakenly calculated that there was a 10m difference between the two sea levels.

British reports corrected that mistake several years later, but it was the French consul to Egypt, Ferdinand de Lesseps, who pursued the Suez Canal idea through to its conclusion. In 1854 de Lesseps presented his proposal to the Egyptian khedive Said Pasha, who authorised him to excavate the canal; work began in 1859.

HIGHLIGHTS

- **The Canal** Watch supertankers appear to glide through the desert as they make their way through one of the world's most famous canals.

- **Ismailia** Walk through Egypt's colonial past in Ismailia's old European quarter.

- **Port Said** Hang out with sailors in Port Said's backstreets.

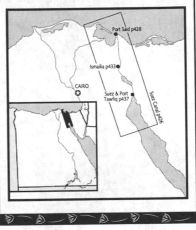

Port Said p428
Ismailia p433
CAIRO
Suez & Port Tawfiq p437
Suez Canal p426

A decade later the canal was completed amid much fanfare and celebration. When two small fleets, one originating in Port Said and the other in Suez, met at the new town of Ismailia on 16 November 1869, the Suez Canal was declared open and Africa was officially severed from Asia.

PORT SAID

The main attraction of Port Said, and the reason for its establishment on the Mediterranean, is the Suez Canal. The spectacle of the huge ships and tankers lining up to pass through the northern entrance of the canal is

SUEZ CANAL

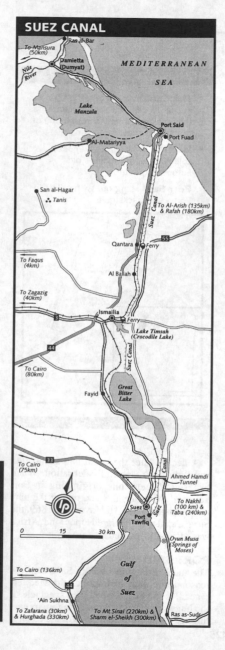

SUEZ CANAL

something to be seen. Port Said's status as a duty-free port means that of all the canal cities it is the most flourishing.

The city was founded in 1859 by its namesake, the khedive Said Pasha, when excavation for the Suez Canal began. Much of the city is an island, created by filling in part of Lake Manzala, to the west, with sand from the canal site. The city continued to grow until 1956, when much of it was bombed during the Suez Crisis. It suffered again during the 1967 and 1973 wars with Israel. Damage can still be seen but most of the city, which these days is home to about 400,000 people, has been rebuilt.

Along some of Port Said's original city streets are some fine old buildings with wooden balconies. The turn-of-the-century architecture, some in a sad state, seems to contain all of the convoluted history of this international port town in its very fibre, and its streets are well worth a wander around.

Egyptians think of Port Said as a summer resort, and hundreds of beach bungalows line the coast along the city's northern edge.

Orientation

Port Said is connected to the mainland by a bridge to the south and a causeway to the west. There is also a ferry across Lake Manzala to Al-Matariyya, and another between Port Said and its sister town Port Fuad on the other side of the canal.

Most of the banks and important services are on Sharia Palestine, which runs along the canal, or two blocks inland on Sharia al-Gomhuriyya.

Information

Visa Extensions If you need to get a visa extension, the passport office is in the Governorate building (left wing, 4th floor, window seven) and is open from 8 am to 2 pm (closed Friday).

Customs Port Said was declared a duty-free port in 1976, so everyone must pass through customs when entering and leaving the city. Be sure to have your passport with you, and if you are given the choice of declaring cameras and electronic goods on entering, do so. If you do want to buy anything, check in the shop whether or not duty must be paid on a particular item – some, including a few electrical items, can be taken out without problems; varying rates of tax apply.

Tourist Offices The tourist office (☎ 235 289) at 43 Sharia Palestine has maps and information about the Suez Canal and the port. The office is open from 9 am to 1.30 pm and 3 to 8 pm from Saturday to Thursday, closed on Friday. There's also a branch office at the train station.

Money There are a number of banks on Sharia al-Gomhuriyya. The National Bank of Egypt seems to be the least complicated at which to change travellers cheques.

Thomas Cook (☎ 227 559) at 43 Sharia al-Gomhuriyya is open daily from 9 am to 6 pm. Nearby, in the MenaTours office, is an American Express (Amex) (☎ 230 939) agent. It's open daily from 10 am to 3 pm but does not have foreign exchange facilities.

Post & Communications The GPO is opposite the Ferial Gardens, one block north of Sharia al-Gomhuriyya and is open from 9 am to 5 pm (closed Friday).

There are two telephone centrales: one is on Sharia Palestine two blocks north-west of the tourist office; the other is behind the Governorate building. Both are open 24 hours.

Suez Canal House

If you've ever seen a picture of Port Said, it was probably of the striking green domes of Suez Canal House. One of the best views of the Suez Canal used to be from this white-columned building south-west of the ferry terminal and tourist office, which was built in time for the inauguration of the canal in 1869. It is off-limits to visitors, although you could try to talk your way past the guards and go up to the central dome.

Town Centre

For many, Port Said is a boring stop on their trip through Egypt, and few bother with it at

Liberty on the Canal

A little-known fact about New York's Statue of Liberty is that it was originally to have stood at the entrance to the Suez Canal in Port Said. Inspired by the colossal statues at Abu Simbel, French sculptor Frederic Auguste Bartholdi drew up the idea of a huge statue of a woman bearing a torch. She was to represent progress – 'Egypt carrying the light of Asia', in Bartholdi's own words. He presented his idea to khedive Ismail who loved the idea of the grand gesture and was thrilled with the concept.

However, after two years of sketching and making models, Bartholdi was told that Ismail had decided (somewhat uncharacteristically) that the project was too expensive. The 'Light of Asia' was then sent to New York, where she became Lady Liberty. In her place a less idealistic statue of Ferdinand de Lesseps was erected at the head of the canal. It was ripped off its pedestal when Colonel Nasser, leader of the revolutionary Free Officers, announced the nationalisation of the canal in 1956. Although the statue was restored at French government expense in the early 90s it has yet to be re-erected.

all. The five-storey buildings with their wooden balconies and high verandahs in grand turn-of-the-century style are, however, one of those little surprises that should be fascinating for anyone with an interest in architecture and/or the life of late 19th century colonial centres.

You can see some odd colonial remnants as you wander around: the old Postes Françaises; a sign for the ship chandlers of the pre-Soviet 'volunteer Russian fleet' and another for the Bible Society. Perhaps the oddest sight is the Italian Consulate building, erected in the 1930s and adorned with a piece of engraved propaganda to the Fascist dictator Benito Mussolini: 'Rome – once again at the heart of an Empire'. On

SUEZ CANAL

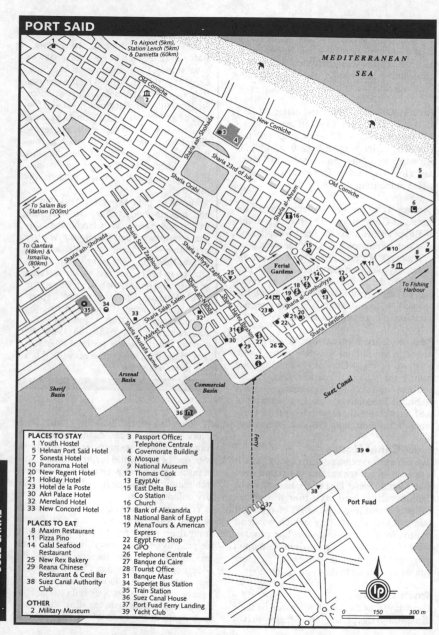

PORT SAID

MEDITERRANEAN SEA

To Airport (5km),
Station Lench (5km)
& Damietta (60km)

Old Corniche

New Corniche

Old Corniche

Sharia ash-Shohada

Sharia 23rd of July

Sharia Orabi

Sharia al-Ahram

To Salam Bus
Station (200m)

To Qantara
(48km) &
Ismailia
(80km)

Sharia ash-Shohada

Sharia Saad Zaghloul

Sharia Safiyya Zaghloul

Sharia am Gh...

Sharia Hafez Ibrahim

Ferial
Gardens

Sharia al-Gomhurriya

Sharia Salah Salem

Market St

Sharia Mustafa Kamel

Sharia Palestine

To Fishing
Harbour

Sherif
Basin

Arsenal
Basin

Commercial
Basin

Suez Canal

Ferry

Port Fuad

PLACES TO STAY
1   Youth Hostel
5   Helnan Port Said Hotel
7   Sonesta Hotel
10 Panorama Hotel
20 New Regent Hotel
21 Holiday Hotel
23 Hotel de la Poste
30 Akri Palace Hotel
32 Mereland Hotel
33 New Concord Hotel

PLACES TO EAT
8   Maxim Restaurant
11 Pizza Pino
14 Galal Seafood
    Restaurant
25 New Rex Bakery
29 Reana Chinese
    Restaurant & Cecil Bar
38 Suez Canal Authority
    Club

OTHER
2   Military Museum

3   Passport Office;
    Telephone Centrale
4   Governorate Building
6   Mosque
9   National Museum
12 Thomas Cook
13 EgyptAir
15 East Delta Bus
    Co Station
16 Church
17 Bank of Alexandria
18 National Bank of Egypt
19 MenaTours & American
    Express
22 Egypt Free Shop
24 GPO
26 Telephone Centrale
27 Banque du Caire
28 Tourist Office
31 Banque Masr
34 Superjet Bus Station
35 Train Station
36 Suez Canal House
37 Port Fuad Ferry Landing
39 Yacht Club

39 Yacht Club

38

Port Fuad

37

0   150   300 m

SUEZ CANAL

the canal near the new Sonesta Hotel is a huge stone block that held a statue of de Lesseps until it was torn down in 1956.

National Museum

Opened in 1987 at the top end of Sharia Palestine, this museum houses a varied collection representative of most periods in Egyptian history. The ground floor is dedicated to prehistory and the pharaonic period. You can see statuary, utensils, pottery and a couple of mummies and colourful sarcophagi. The 1st floor contains a modest display of Islamic and Coptic exhibits, including textiles, manuscripts and coins. There is also a room full of memorabilia of the Khedival family, which oversaw through the construction of the canal.

The museum is open daily from 9 am to 4 pm (but closed between 11 am and 1 pm on Friday), admission costs E£6 (E£3 for students).

Military Museum

This small museum on Sharia 23rd of July has some interesting relics from the 1956 Anglo-French War and the 1967 and 1973 wars with Israel. There are captured US tanks with the Star of David painted on them, a couple of unexploded bombs and various other unpleasant reminders of recent wars, as well as a small display of ancient pharaonic and Islamic conflicts. The museum is open daily from 9 am (8 am between June and August) to 2 pm; 10 am to 1.30 pm on Friday.

Al-Matariyya Ferry

For E£2, you can chug west across shallow lakes and lagoons to the Delta town of Al-Matariyya, and perhaps watch as becalmed feluccas are taken in tow on the way. There's nothing to do at Al-Matariyya but wait for the return boat. To get to the ferry, you must first go to Station Lench, about 15 minutes by taxi towards Damietta (Dumyat) north-west of the quay.

Port Fuad

Across the canal from Port Said, this is really a suburb of civil servants which was founded in 1925. The yacht club in Port Fuad is the place to go to find a passage or work on a vessel plying the canal, as the captains are sometimes looking for crew members. Free ferries from Port Said to Port Fuad offer a great view of the canal, and leave about every 10 minutes from a terminal near the tourist office.

Although not as interesting as canal-side central Port Said, a short visit and stroll around the streets near the quay is worth the effort. Sprawling residences with lush gardens and sloping tiled roofs are a refreshing sight after seeing nothing but standard Middle Eastern poured-concrete boxes – and a reminder of the west's one-time presence here.

Places to Stay – Budget

Youth Hostel (☎ 228 702) on Sharia 23rd of July, near the stadium, is the cheapest place to stay in Port Said. It costs E£3.25 with membership card and E£1 more without. It has basic bunk beds, with 20 beds per room. It's not bad, but it's in a highly inconvenient location.

The area around the canal used to be crawling with little dives, but most seem to be losing out in the gradual gentrification of Sharia al-Gomhuriyya. Two hotels offer better deals in town. The Greek-owned *Akri Palace Hotel* (☎ 221 013, 24 Sharia al-Gomhuriyya)* has reasonably clean singles/doubles for about E£13/25 or doubles with bath for E£37; breakfast is extra. The rooms have balconies, a bit of charm and are nicely furnished.

Two blocks north-west from the Akri is *Mereland Hotel* (☎ 227 020) in a lane between Sharia Saad Zaghloul and Sharia an-Nahda. It offers big clean rooms with decent communal bathrooms for E£15/20 or E£24/35 with private bath; breakfast is extra.

Places to Stay – Mid-Range & Top End

Hotel de la Poste (☎ 224 048, 42 Sharia al-Gomhuriyya)* has a fading elegance which the management has attempted to salvage through careful renovation. Singles/doubles on the street side with bath and balcony cost E£35/44 without breakfast. Other rooms cost E£28/38; some have TV and a fridge. There's a restaurant, bar and patisserie downstairs.

The three star *New Concord Hotel* (☎ *235 342, fax 235 930)* near the Superjet bus station has totally characterless rooms with wall-to-wall carpet, bath, fan and TV. Some of the rooms on the higher floors have reasonable views of the canal. At E£63/84 with breakfast, it's not a bad deal.

New Regent Hotel (☎ *235 000, fax 224 891)* in a lane just off Sharia al-Gomhuriyya is a smart three star hotel with decent, modern rooms for E£86/117, including breakfast; it also has a restaurant.

Edging into the top bracket is *Holiday Hotel* (☎ *220 711, fax 220 710, 23 Sharia al-Gomhuriyya)* diagonally opposite Hotel de la Poste. It has rooms for E£136/168, including tax and breakfast.

The modern three star *Panorama Hotel* (☎ *325 101, fax 325 103)* at the north-eastern end of Sharia al-Gomhuriyya has single/double rooms with air-con, private bath and TV for E£129/169. Its position directly opposite a mosque may be a drawback for some.

Helnan Port Said Hotel (☎ *320 890, fax 323 762)* on the beach front gets a five star rating from the tourist office, mostly because of the views. Rooms are E£520/700, including tax and breakfast. There's a restaurant, bar and several shops.

In direct competition to the Helnan is the newer *Sonesta Hotel* (☎ *325 511, fax 324 825)* at the northern end of the canal. Rooms facing the city are US$120/150, or US$150/185 overlooking the canal (including tax).

Places to Eat

Not surprisingly, there are plenty of seafood restaurants in Port Said. One of the cheapest is *Galal* on the corner of sharias al-Gomhuriyya and Gaberti. A plate of calamari will set you back E£12; fish dishes start at around E£14. There are a few tables outside and a takeaway stand selling shwarma and a range of Greek mezzes such as dolmades

(stuffed vine leaves). You can enjoy a beer with your meal only if you dine inside.

At the front of *Hotel de la Poste* there's a bar, cafe and restaurant. The latter has cheap hamburgers, sandwiches, salads and what is called pizza. The terrace here is a popular retreat for those wanting coffee and cake or a refreshing lime juice.

If you want real pizza, you could try the flashy *Pizza Pino* (☎ *239 949)* on Sharia al-Gomhuriyya, or the new branch of *Pizza Inn* inside the nearby Panorama Hotel.

For Chinese or Korean food and atmosphere there's *Reana*, also on Sharia al-Gomhuriyya. It's above the Cecil bar and has a wide range of dishes including seafood mains from E£15 to E£35 as well as a few vegetarian offerings. *Cecil* (☎ *223 911)* is one of the few bars in town where you come close to sitting on the pavement terrace; it's open until quite late.

For something a bit more upmarket try *Maxim* (☎ *234 335)* on the 1st floor of the shopping centre next to Sonesta Hotel, where a full fish dinner will set you back around E£30. Dishes such as fried squid or pasta are considerably cheaper.

If it's an unobstructed view of ships entering the canal that you're after, head over to *Suez Canal Authority Club* on the waterfront in Port Fuad. Serving lunch only, you can dine on chicken or meat with rice and salad for E£7 (plus a E£3 entry ticket) on the club's breezy terrace. The club is immediately to your left once you get off the ferry; the entrance is opposite the tennis courts.

Three blocks north of Sharia al-Gomhuriyya there's a lively fruit and vegetable market on Market St, as well as the popular *New Rex Bakery* at the interesction of Market St and Sharia Safiyya Zaghloul.

Shopping

Almost anything can be bought in Port Said, although since the government began liberalising the economy in the mid-1990s the merchandise is geared more to sailors passing through – cheap electronics and designer jeans seem to be the biggest selling items. The best deals can be found along

Sharia al-Gomhuriyya; try the Egypt Free Shop on this street.

Getting There & Away
You must go through a customs check before leaving Port Said, so leave enough time to do this. The train and bus stations all have customs halls.

Air EgyptAir (☎ 222 870) has an office at 39 Sharia al-Gomhuriyya, but it does not fly to Port Said.

Bus There are three bus terminals. The Superjet buses to Cairo (E£15, three hours) leave 11 times a day from in front of the train station. They also have a bus to Alexandria (E£22, four hours) at 4.30 pm. Bookings are advisable at the Superjet bus station, just east of the train station.

The East Delta Bus Co goes to destinations outside the Delta (and Tanta in the Delta for some reason) from its terminal near the Ferial Gardens (also known as the 'Lux terminal'). Buses to Cairo depart hourly between 6 am and 6 pm; fares range from E£13 to E£15. The most expensive buses don't make stops, usually shaving about 30 minutes off the three to 3½ hour ride. There are four buses to Alexandria (via Damietta) (E£17 to E£22) at 7 and 9 am and 2.30 and 4.30 pm. Buses south to Ismailia (E£5) depart hourly between 6 am and 6 pm. Buses to Suez (E£7.50, 2¼ hours) depart at 6 and 10 am and 1 and 4 pm. For Al-Arish on the Sinai peninsula, you must first go to Ismailia or Qantara and take a bus or service taxi from there. For more details see Getting There & Away in the following Ismailia section.

The other terminal, known as Salam station, is on Sharia an-Nasr, north-west of the train station. Buses to destinations within the Delta (except Tanta) depart from here. Every hour on the half hour, a bus also goes south to Qantara (E£2.50).

Train There are four trains daily to Cairo. These take four hours and are the slowest, but can also be the cheapest, way to get there. There are no 1st class services. Fares are E£14/5.50/3 for 2nd class air-con/2nd class ordinary/3rd class. The train stops in Ismailia.

There are an additional five trains daily to Ismailia only (E£6/2.30/1). Two trains make the long loop via Ismailia and Zagazig to Alexandria (E£28/8.50/4).

Service Taxi Service taxis leave from a mucky lot behind the Salam bus station, but there doesn't appear to be a lot happening in the afternoon. The Cairo fare (E£8) is cheaper than taking the bus. Other fares include: Qantara (E£2.50), Ismailia (E£3.50), Suez (E£6) and Zagazig (E£6).

Boat A number of ships ply the waters between Port Said and Limassol (Cyprus), although most are five-star cruisers offering package tours to Egypt and Israel. They sail between April and October. For more information on prices and schedules, call Mena-Tours (☎ 225 742) on Sharia al-Gomhuriyya.

In Cyprus can contact Paradis Island Tours (☎ 357-237 4699) or Louis Tours (☎ 357-237 4699). From Limassol you can connect with vessels heading on to Haifa (Israel) or to several Greek islands, but that's an expensive way to get around.

Getting Around
The best and most enjoyable way to tour Port Said, especially around sunset, is by *hantour* (horse-drawn carriage). A carriage and driver can be hired for about E£10 per hour. Otherwise there are plenty of blue-and-white taxis.

QANTARA
The only reason to visit the town of Qantara, 50km south of Port Said, is to cross to the east side of the canal and leave again as quickly as possible (see the boxed text 'Cruising the Canal' on page 432). Service taxis leave from the east bank – you'll be looking at about E£7 to Al-Arish (150km). A bridge across the canal is being built here.

Most of Qantara was destroyed during the 1973 war with Israel and the town's buildings are still sprayed with bullet holes.

SUEZ CANAL

Cruising the Canal

Although hundreds of ships cruise the Suez Canal each week, canal enthusiasts who want to do the same will find that it's not that easy. The port authorities do not appreciate you just hopping on a freighter for the ride and organised trips do not exist. However, there are one or two ways of seeing this famous waterway from a deck.

If you're in Suez you can rent a private boat for a cruise up to Port Said. Mohammed Moseilhy of Damanhur Shipping (☎ 062-572 177) can arrange this for you but he needs a few days notice. Expect to pay at least E£500 for a boat that holds a maximum of 12 people.

A cheaper option is the passenger ferry at Qantara, 35km north of Ismailia. Two ferries cross the canal throughout the day and can go even when a convoy is passing through, so if you're lucky you'll get a close-up view of a supertanker. The passenger ferry is free and is virtually opposite the town while the vehicle ferry crosses further to the south. Be prepared to join a stampede of people, chickens, donkeys and bicycles for a space on this ferry.

Noras I boat restaurant (☎ 326 804) docked at the top of the canal in Port Said, offers a 1¼ hour tour of the canal for E£10, including a soft drink. It departs daily at 3 and 8.30 pm. You can also have a decent seafood meal on board for between E£36 and E£60.

If you do manage to get on some sort of vessel, remember that photographs may not be appreciated – there is a strong military presence all along the canal; some travellers have had their film confiscated after inadvertently snapping a sensitive site.

ISMAILIA

Ismailia was founded by and named after Pasha Ismail, the khedive of Egypt during the time of the construction of the Suez Canal in the 1860s. Ferdinand de Lesseps, the director of the Suez Canal Company, lived in the city until the canal was completed.

As in Port Said, a stroll around the elegant colonial streets of Ismailia can be an unexpected pleasure. Obviously we're not talking about great monuments, but there are some beautiful old villas laid out in a shady, western-style grid. Apart from the architectural interest, it's interesting to see how this canal city grew in the image of the British and French masters who were pulling the strings in Egypt in the 19th and first half of the 20th century.

Orientation

Ismailia is perhaps the most picturesque of the new canal towns, yet it has been quickly developing, or rather devolving, into an urban mess. This city of about 300,000 people is divided in two by the train line, which marks a boundary between well-tended streets on one side and a veritable disaster area on the other.

Ismailia can be said to have a main street, it's probably Sharia Sultan Hussein, which runs between the train line and the Sweetwater Canal. The central square, Midan al-Gomhuriyya, is a quiet affair, and in fact the entire eastern side of town is rather exceptional in that it is all comparatively peaceful. The thoroughfare beside the Sweetwater Canal is known by three names: Mohammed Ali Quay, the Promenade and Sharia Salah Salem.

On the western side of the tracks you'll find the main bus and service taxi stations – these are a microcosm of the surrounding neighbourhood, which features muddy, potholed streets, horn-honking maniacs and smoking piles of garbage.

Information

Visa Extensions Should you need to get a visa extension, the passport office is on Midan al-Gomhuriyya and is open daily from 8 am to 2 pm (except Friday).

Tourist Offices The tourist office (☎ 321 074 ext 284) is in the Governorate building on Mohammed Ali Quay. It is open daily

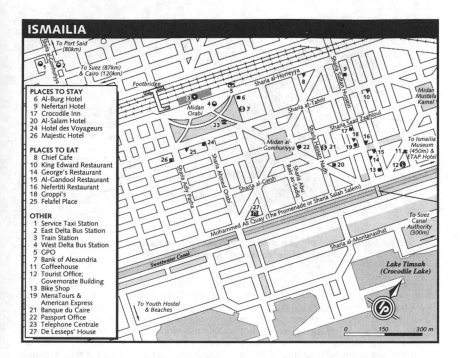

ISMAILIA

To Port Said (80km)

To Suez (87km) & Cairo (120km)

Footbridge

Sharia al-Horreyya

Midan Orabi

Sharia at-Tahrir

Midan Mustafa Kamel

Sharia Saad Zaghloul

Midan al-Gomhuriyya

Sharia Abu Bakr as-Sadiq

To Ismailia Museum (450m) & ETAP Hotel

Sharia al-Geish

Sharia Hassan Nadh

Sharia Adly Pasha

Sharia Ahmed Orabi

To Suez Canal Authority (300m)

Mohammed Ali Quay (The Promenade or Sharia Salah Salem)

Sharia al-Montanasihat

Sweetwater Canal

To Youth Hostel & Beaches

Lake Timsah (Crocodile Lake)

0   150   300 m

PLACES TO STAY
6 Al-Burg Hotel
9 Nefertari Hotel
17 Crocodile Inn
20 Al-Salam Hotel
24 Hotel des Voyageurs
26 Majestic Hotel

PLACES TO EAT
8 Chief Cafe
10 King Edward Restaurant
14 George's Restaurant
15 Al-Gandool Restaurant
16 Nefertiti Restaurant
18 Groppi's
25 Felafel Place

OTHER
1 Service Taxi Station
2 East Delta Bus Station
3 Train Station
4 West Delta Bus Station
5 GPO
7 Bank of Alexandria
11 Coffeehouse
12 Tourist Office;
     Governorate Building
13 Bike Shop
19 MenaTours &
     American Express
21 Banque du Caire
22 Passport Office
23 Telephone Centrale
27 De Lesseps' House

from 8 am to 2 pm (except Friday) but has little besides the standard glossy brochures.

Money There's a Bank of Alexandria across the square from the train station and a Banque du Caire on Sharia Hassan Nadh. Amex (☎ 324 361) has a branch in the Mena-Tours office at 12 Sharia Sultan Hussein.

Post & Communications The GPO is just up the tracks from the train station. The 24 hour telephone centrale is across the square from the station, virtually opposite the Bank of Alexandria.

Ismailia Museum

This small but interesting museum on Mohammed Ali Quay, several blocks north-east of the Governorate building, has more than 4000 objects from pharaonic and Graeco-Roman times. There are statues,

scarabs, stelae, and records of the first canal, built between the Bitter Lakes and Bubastis by the Persian ruler Darius. The highlight of the collection is a 4th century AD mosaic depicting classic characters from Greek mythology. At the top, Phaedra is sending a love letter to her stepson, Hippolytus (who ended up in a bad way after his father set Poseidon on to him). Below, Dionysus, the god of wine, tags along on a chariot driven by Eros. The bottom section recounts the virtues of Hercules, demi-god and son of Jupiter. The museum is open daily from 9 am to 4 pm, entry costs E£6 (E£3 for students).

Garden of the Stelae

Just south-west of the museum is a garden containing a poor little sphinx from the time of Ramses II. You need permission from the museum to visit the garden, but you can

SUEZ CANAL

The most fun you can have with your clothes on? Egyptians from Cairo flock to Ismailia to frolic in the lakes there, but all bathing is done fully clothed.

see the unremarkable statue from the street. Don't try to get into the pretty grounds of the majestic residence between the garden and the museum – it belongs to the head of the Suez Canal Authority, and the security chaps get rather on edge at the sight of unauthorised persons strolling in.

De Lesseps' House
The residence of the one-time French consul to Egypt used to be open to the public, but now you can only see the interior if you're a VIP of some sort, as it now serves as a kind of private guest house for important guests of the Suez Canal Authority. Inside the grounds is de Lesseps' private carriage encased in glass. His bedroom looks as if it has hardly been touched; old photos, books and various utensils are scattered around the desk by his bed and on the floor. The house is on Mohammed Ali Quay near the corner of Sharia Ahmed Orabi. If you want to look inside you may be able to get permission from the Suez Canal Authority.

Beaches
There are several good beaches around Lake Timsah, 12km south-east of town, but

as these have become highly popular among middle-class Cairenes, using them involves paying to get into one of the clubs and hotels that dot the shore. Entrance fees vary but on average they are E£20, and some include a buffet lunch as part of the admission price. All include access to a private swimming beach.

Places to Stay – Budget
The high-rise **Youth Hostel** (☎ 322 850), on a beach around Lake Timsah, has rooms with two/four/six beds for E£18/15/8 including breakfast. The rooms are clean and comfortable with lockers and views over the lake. The white-tiled toilets and showers blind you with their cleanliness. They don't seem too concerned about whether or not you have a membership card.

Hotel des Voyageurs on the corner of Sharia at-Tahrir and Sharia Ahmed Orabi, a short walk from the train station, is a big, derelict place that offers basic but acceptable singles/doubles for E£10/16; bathrooms are outside. **Atlanta**, across the road, is grotty and not recommended. **Majestic** (☎ 223 607), a block south-west, charges E£6/12/15 for singles/doubles/triples.

Al-Burg Hotel (*☎ 326 327*) on the northern side of the square, has rooms with bath, air-con and TV for E£30/50/75; breakfast is E£5 extra. It's OK, but the colourful exterior is simply a facade for drab, overpriced rooms.

Nefertari Hotel (*☎ 322 822, 41 Sharia Sultan Hussein*) has clean, comfortable singles/doubles with bath and air-con for E£36/54, including breakfast. They also have a small bar with dim red lights.

Places to Stay – Mid-Range & Top End

Al-Salam Hotel (*☎ 324 401*) on Sharia al-Geish has clean double rooms with bath and breakfast for E£60 (E£75 with air-con). You pay the same price for a single; some rooms have TV.

The five storey *Crocodile Inn* (*☎ 331 555, fax 331 666*) on the corner of sharias Saad Zaghloul and Sultan Hussein has a lounge and restaurant as well as a 24 hour coffeehouse and bar. The old, somewhat musty singles/doubles cost E£55/75 with breakfast. There are also newly renovated rooms for E£90/130 but they're hardly worth the extra money.

ETAP (*☎ 338 040, fax 338 043*) at the lake shore at Gezirat al-Fursan, has all the amenities of an expensive hotel; rooms start at US$97/150. For around E£20 per day nonguests can use their swimming pool and beach, but on Friday you have to pay for the buffet as well – E£47 all up.

Places to Eat

There are some cheap eateries in the mall near George's and Nefertiti restaurants. *Al-Gandool*, which is in among them, would like to sell you 1kg of mixed meats for E£35, but you can settle for a plate of spaghetti for a couple of pounds instead.

George's and *Nefertiti* (*☎ 220 494*), both on Sharia Sultan Hussein, serve fish and meat dishes. The fish at the Greek-run George's is an institution; the place has an intimate atmosphere and a lovely old bar that has been enticing drinkers for more than 40 years. Nefertiti is cheaper, with

meals ranging from E£12 to E£25, but the decor is bland. Both are open until 10 pm.

King Edward (*☎ 325 451, 171 Sharia at-Tahrir*) is more expensive. They have meat and fish dishes for around E£15 to E£30, as well as pizza from E£6.50. The chicken curry is quite good and makes a nice change from the usual fare; beer is not available.

Close to the train station on Sharia at-Tahrir is an excellent little *ta'amiyya* (felafel) place where you can dine in or takeaway.

The tiny *Chief Cafe* on Sharia al-Horreyya specialises in an unusual combination of kushari, cakes and chocolates. All are very good and the kushari is cheap. There are tables on the pavement only.

Groppi's is across the street from Nefertiti. It's a smaller version of Groppi's in Cairo, but with the same selection of pastries and ice cream.

A block from the bakery near the end of the pedestrian mall is an old *coffeehouse* with a great atmosphere. There are juice stalls at the bus station.

Getting There & Away

Bus There are two bus stations in Ismailia. On Medan Orabi, the West Delta Bus Co has frequent departures to Cairo (2½ hours, E£6). At 7 am and 2.30 pm buses leave for Alexandria (E£17). The East Delta Bus Co station is on Sharia al-Gomhurriya, on the other side of the railway line. It also has frequent buses to Cairo for E£6.

East Delta Buses to Port Said leave every 30 to 45 minutes and cost E£4, and to Suez every 15 to 20 minutes for E£3.50. Buses to Sinai also leave from here. There are buses every hour or so to Al-Arish (three hours) from 8 am to 5 pm. They usually cost E£7, but prices may fluctuate for through buses from Cairo. There are buses to Sharm el-Sheikh (E£25) at 6.30 am, noon and 2.30, 3.30, 9, 10 and 11 pm and midnight.

Train About 10 trains arrive in Ismailia every day from Cairo (via Zagazig). Tickets cost E£8/4.40/1.80 for 2nd class air-con/ 2nd class ordinary/3rd class; the trip can easily take more than three hours.

To Port Said, there are 10 trains per day (E£6/2.30/1, 1½ hours). There are also frequent trains to Suez (E£2.40/1.10 for 2nd/3rd class). It's a painfully slow way to go, and the station in Suez is a long way out of town.

Trains to Alexandria (E£15/6.70/3, five hours) leave at 8.30 am and 7.50 pm.

Service Taxi Service taxis depart from the lot across the road from the East Delta Bus Co station. Destinations include Suez (E£3), Port Said (E£3.50), Zagazig (E£3), Mansura (E£5.50), Cairo (E£5) and Al-Arish (E£7).

Getting Around
Ismailia's parks and tree-lined streets are good cycling territory. There is a bike shop behind the Al-Gandool Restaurant that rents bicycles for E£5 per day.

SUEZ
Suez is a city going through a metamorphosis. It was all but destroyed during the 1967 and 1973 wars with Israel, although there is little obvious evidence of the devastation today. The revamped main streets, however, are mostly a facade hiding a sordid mess of backstreet slums. A memorial on Sharia al-Galaa commemorates the wars.

Suez sprawls around the shores of the gulf where the Red Sea meets the southern entrance of the Suez Canal. The town itself is divided between Suez proper and Port Tawfiq. The latter is at the mouth of the canal and is a good place for watching the ships go by. It also has a few streets with gracious old colonial buildings that escaped the bombing. It is joined to the town itself by Sharia al-Geish, a wide highway that cuts through an industrial area before cutting through the heart of Suez. Here too there are one or two old buildings left, but they are fast being lost to the usual shoddily-built highrises.

Although the centre of Suez is marginally less laid back than Port Tawfiq there is nothing much to do in either except take in what could be the best view of ships passing in or out of the canal, and there's little in the way of tourist facilities. Suez is basically just a transit point, not only for the great tankers, cargo vessels and private yachts en route to or from the Mediterranean, but for travellers and the Muslim faithful as well. Suez is one of the departure points for the *haj* (pilgrimage to Mecca); most other people just pass through on their way to Sinai or the Red Sea beaches.

Information
Visa Extensions If you want to extend your visa, the passport office is in Suez just off Sharia Saad Zaghloul on Sharia al-Horreyya.

Tourist Offices The staff at the tourist office (☎ 223 589) in Port Tawfiq are keen to provide information about the city, canal and surrounding sites. The office is open daily from 8 am to 6 pm (Friday until 2 pm).

Foreign Consulates The Saudi Arabian consulate (☎ 222 461) in Port Tawfiq (around the corner from the tourist office) is open from 9 am to 3 pm; closed Friday. There are separate sections for work and haj visas; transit or tourist visas seems to fall between the two stools. Getting any sort of visa here can take up to one month – at a minimum you'll need to show an air ticket plus a letter from your embassy. If you're stopping over in Jeddah, you will also be asked to get a letter from the company issuing the ongoing ticket. Given the hoops you have to jump through, you're best off going through MenaTours (☎ 336 888) which will simplify the lengthy process and make sure you have the correct documents in advance.

Money Most of Egypt's main banks have branches in Suez. The MenaTours office houses a branch of Amex (☎ 220 269) at 3 Sharia al-Marwa next to the tourist office.

Post & Communications The GPO is on Sharia Hoda Shaarawi. There is another small post office in Port Tawfiq, next to the tourist office. The telephone centrale is on

SUEZ & PORT TAWFIQ

To Upper Egypt Bus
Station (1.3km), Train
Station (1.5km), Ahmed
Hamdi Tunnel (10km)
& Ismailia (87km)

Sharia al-Taatz

Sharia al-Taatz

Sharia Bangu

Sharia Rashed

Sharia at-Salaam (al-Geish)

Sharia Talaat Harb

Masr

Sharia Port Said

Sharia al-Galaa

Saad Zaghloul

20

See
Enlargement

SUEZ

21

To Youth Hostel (300m),
Ain Sukhna (45km),
Hurghada (445km)
& Cairo (135km)

El-Corniche

22

Sharia al-Geish

To Suez Canal
(1.3km)

PLACES TO STAY
5 Haramein Hotel
6 Hotel Chahen
7 Hotel al-Medina
8 Hotel at-Tahrir
11 Hotel d'Orient
12 White House Hotel
13 Star Hotel
15 Masr Palace Hotel
16 Sina Hotel
22 Green House Hotel
25 Red Sea Hotel
26 Summer Palace
27 Arafat Hotel

PLACES TO EAT
14 Fish Restaurant
19 Seaside Restaurant

OTHER
1 Service Taxi Station
2 Arba'een Bus Station
3 Bank of Alexandria
4 Banque Masr
9 Shipping Office
10 GPO
17 Banque du Caire
18 Telephone Centrale
20 Passport Office
21 War Memorial
23 Bank of Alexandria
24 Yacht Club
28 Telestar
29 Passenger Ferry Terminal
30 Tourist Office, MenaTours,
American Express & Post
Office
31 Saudi Arabian Consulate

Sharia Abdel as-Sarawat

Sharia as-Salaam (al-Geish)

Sharia al-Hareem

5

Sharia al-Tahrir

8

Sharia Mohammed Abdu

0   75   150 m

Sharia Ahmed Shawqi

Sharia Salah ad-Din al-Ayyubi

Sharia Shohada

Sharia Saad Zaghloul

15

16

14

9

7

6

Sharia Talaat Harb

Sharia Adly Yakan

11

10

13

12

Sharia Banque Masr

Sharia Hoda Shaarawi

Sharia Khedr

18

17

19

SUEZ BAY

0   250   500 m

29

PORT TAWFIQ

27

Sharia Arafat

28

23

25

24

26

Sharia al-Marwa

30

31

Ferry to Jeddah &
Port Sudan

SLEZ CANAL

the corner of sharias Shohada and Saad Zaghloul.

Places to Stay – Budget

During the month of the haj, budget places tend to fill up with passengers travelling to and from Saudi Arabia by sea.

Youth Hostel (☎ 221 945) is on the main road heading west out of Suez. It's cheap (E£5 with membership card, E£6 without), grungy and a long way from anything.

In the centre of Suez, there's a handful of cheapies clustered around Sharia at-Tahrir (known locally as Sharia an-Nimsa) and Sharia Talaat Harb. One of the cheapest is *Haramein Hotel* (☎ 320 051) near the end of Sharia at-Tahrir. The outside of the hotel looks much better than the dingy rooms inside, but at E£6/10 for a room without a fan it's quite popular with the impecunious. The communal facilities are passable.

In much the same league is the overpriced *Hotel at-Tahrir*, just down the road and signposted in Arabic only, and *Hotel Chahen*, on Sharia Talaat Harb, where rooms cost E£9/16 and they don't appreciate foreigners.

Marginally better is *Hotel al-Medina* (☎ 224 056), also on Sharia Talaat Harb, which charges E£10 per person. Up another rung on the ladder is *Hotel d'Orient* on Sharia Hoda Shaarawi, which has basic rooms for E£10/12.

Across Sharia as-Salaam *Star Hotel* (☎ 228 737) on Sharia Banque Masr, has double rooms with fans for E£20/25. The bathrooms here can be dirty and travellers have complained about the staff.

You'll do a bit better further along the street at *Sina Hotel* (☎ 334 181), which has singles/doubles/triples for E£17/26/34. Add E£5 for air-con and E£3 for breakfast.

If you have a hankering to stay in Port Tawfiq, the cheapest place there seems to be *Arafat Hotel* (☎ 338 355) in the street of the same name. Rooms cost E£15/22/33 without bath or E£24/30/37 with. The hotel has recently been renovated and is well run and spotlessly clean. There are even snacks and toiletries on sale in the lobby.

Places to Stay – Mid-Range & Top End

Masr Palace Hotel (☎ 223 031, 2 Sharia Saad Zaghloul) has 101 beds in rooms of varying price, standard and degree of cleanliness. Singles/doubles with bath, air-con and breakfast start at E£23.50/31 plus tax. It's good value without being spectacular.

White House Hotel (☎ 227 599, fax 223 330, 322 Sharia as-Salaam) is a clean, respectable and popular place, although a bit worn around the edges. Rooms with showers are E£32/40 including breakfast.

For views of the canal try *Green House Hotel* (☎ 331 553, fax 331 554) on the road out of Suez to Port Tawfiq, on the corner of sharias Port Said and Al Geish. The lobby area is a really sickly green colour. The hotel has a 24 hour restaurant, pool (E£3 for nonguests), bar and branch of the Banque du Caire. Comfortable rooms with bath, air-con, TV, fridge and balcony with a view of the canal cost US$38/48, not including breakfast and tax.

One thing *Summer Palace* (☎ 224 475, fax 321 944) is not, is a palace. Ordinary motel-style rooms, at US$34/44, not including tax and breakfast, are ridiculously expensive. You're paying for the Gulf views and the seawater pools, which you can use for E£10 if you're not a hotel guest. It has an ordinary restaurant (open 24 hours) and a tranquil waterfront bar where you can get a reasonably priced Stella.

Red Sea Hotel (☎ 334 302, fax 334 301, 13 Sharia Riad) in Port Tawfiq is Suez's premier establishment. Its 81 rooms have TV, bath, phone and air-con and are comfortable and clean. Rooms cost US$43/50, not including breakfast and tax. It has a 6th floor restaurant with a great panoramic view of the canal; meals cost between E£12 and E£33.

Places to Eat

For the cheap old favourites like ta'amiyya and shwarma, a wander around the streets bounded by Sharia Talaat Harb, Sharia Abdel as-Sarawat, Sharia Banque Masr and Sharia Khedr will soon reveal what you're after. There are also a few juice stands and plenty of cafes and coffeehouses around here. There's another clump of small restaurants in the streets west of the Arba'een bus station.

Fish Restaurant, just up from the White House Hotel on Sharia as-Salaam, is exactly what it calls itself. They sell the day's catch by weight and grill it, but sometimes they overcook it a bit. A big meal will cost around E£25; it's open until 2 am.

The restaurant at *White House Hotel* offers a wide range of meat and fish dishes for about E£21, soups and salad go for E£2 to E£4 and beers are available for E£8.

On Sharia Saad Zaghloul, not far from the telephone centrale, is the 24 hour *Seaside*. Half a chicken costs E£20, and it's not as good as it used to be; beer is not served. Attached to it is a popular kebab bar.

For a late afternoon soft drink, you could join the locals at the string of little drink kiosks, all with outdoor chairs and tables and loud music, along Sharia al-Galaa near the war memorial.

There is a series of cafes down in Port Tawfiq, if you happen to stumble off a boat and want to sit down for a breather.

Getting There & Away

Bus Buses to Cairo, Alexandria and the other canal cities leave from the East Delta Bus Co's Arba'een bus station on Sharia al-Faarz, not far from the centre of town. Buses to Cairo (E£6/7, 1½ hours) leave every 30 minutes from 6 am to 8 pm. Buses to Ismailia (E£3) depart every 15 to 20 minutes. There are three buses directly to Port Said (E£7.50) at 7 and 9 am and 3.30 pm, and two to Alexandria (E£20) at 7 am and 2.30 pm.

Buses to the Sinai peninsula also leave from the East Delta Bus Co station. If you want to go to Al-Arish, it's best to go to Ismailia and catch another bus from there. Alternatively, you can catch the bus for Nakhl (pronounced Nekhl) (E£8) at 3 pm and try to make a connection from there. However, very few vehicles use the road between Nakhl and Al-Arish, so there's a good

chance you'll be waiting a long time for a ride. The same bus goes on to Taba (E£30, five hours) and Nuweiba (E£25, six hours).

Five buses go nonstop to Sharm el-Sheikh (E£20, 5½ hours) along the direct route down the Gulf of Suez. They go on to Dahab (E£23, 6½ hours) and Nuweiba (E£25). A bus leaves for St Katherine's Monastery (E£17, five hours) via Wadi Feran at 11 am.

Buses to nearby Oyun Musa (one hour), Ras as-Sudr (E£7/8, 1¼ hours), Hammam Fara'un (1¾ hours) and El-Tor (four hours) leave at odd intervals throughout the day. The 11 am and 3 pm services to Sharm el-Sheikh, and the 11 am bus to St Katherine's Monastery can let you off at these places along the way.

Minibuses sometimes run to destinations in Sinai too – you'll be looking at about E£15 per person to St Katherine's Monastery, E£20 to Sharm el-Sheikh or Nuweiba and E£35 to Dahab. Ask around at the bus station for more details.

For buses to the Red Sea coast and Luxor and Aswan, you must go to the Upper Egypt Bus Co's station at about 3km north of town, just before the train station. There are buses heading to Hurghada (E£25 to E£35) almost every hour. You can ask to be let off at either Ain Sukhna or Zafarana (both E£8). Most of these go on to Qena (E£26/30, nine to 10 hours) via Port Safaga.

There are six buses a day to Luxor (E£35 to E£37, 10 hours), three of which continue to Aswan (E£40 to E£45, 14 hours). You can also catch an Upper Egypt Bus Co service en route to Cairo (E£10) from Red Sea destinations at around noon and 2.30 and 3 am; book ahead.

Departure times are always subject to change, so remember to check them in advance with the staff at the bus station.

Train Only a masochist would want to travel to or from Suez by train. The train station is 2km west of the Arba'een bus station; a microbus shuttles between them for 25pt. Six Cairo-bound trains depart daily (E£2.60/1.05 for 2nd/3rd class, 2¼ hours) and only make it as far as Ain Shams, 10km north-east of central Cairo.

There are nine very slow trains to Ismailia (E£2.40/1.10 for 2nd/3rd class, 2½ hours).

Service Taxi Service taxis depart from near the bus station to many of the destinations serviced by buses and trains.

No structured service taxi system exists in Sinai, which partly explains why getting a taxi there is so outrageously expensive. Destinations include Cairo (E£5), Ismailia (E£3), Port Said (E£6) and Hurghada (E£20, 3½ to four hours). The only place in Sinai served by service taxi is El-Tor (E£10).

With a group of seven people you can hire a 'special' taxi to get you to St Katherine's Monastery on the Sinai peninsula (E£175 to E£200), Ain Sukhna hot springs 45km south of Suez (E£100/150 one way/return) or to the Red Sea monasteries (E£350 return).

Boat While it used to be possible to travel by boat between Suez and Port Sudan (Sudan), the service is no longer running. However, if you're desperate to take this laborious journey, there are services from Jeddah to Port Sudan.

Should you find a boat, the Suez-Jeddah leg of the trip takes about two days. There are boats departing daily from Jeddah at 1 pm (you are supposed to be there a full five hours before departure time). Fares are E£270 in 1st class; E£230 in 2nd class; E£175 in Pullman and E£125 in deck class.

You can book tickets to Jeddah through Telestar in Suez (☎ 326 251) or MenaTours (☎ 228 821) in Tawfiq. Or call Mohammed Moseilhy at Damanhur Shipping Agency (☎ 572 177).

Apparently it's impossible to get a ticket during the haj and you won't be sold a ticket if you don't already have the necessary visas, which, considering the difficulty of getting them, is quite sensible.

Sometimes you can find private yachts which will take you with them to points south. Occasionally travellers have found passage on yachts to India, South Africa and even Australia. Mohammed Moseilhy can help with this.

Getting Around
There are regular microbus services along Sharia as-Salaam from the Arba'een bus station to Port Tawfiq. They stop to pick you up or drop you off wherever you want along the route and cost 25pt.

Red Sea Coast

Egypt's Red Sea coast stretches for more than 800km from Suez in the north to the village of Bir Shalatein near the disputed border with Sudan in the south. Famed for its brilliant turquoise waters, splendid coral and exotic creatures of the deep, the Red Sea attracts more than 200,000 tourists annually. It's Egypt's most rapidly developing area, with more hotels and resorts constructed here in the last few years than anywhere else in the country.

Unfortunately, much of the development during the freewheeling boom of the last decade has gone unchecked, resulting in massive environmental damage. An estimated 60% to 80% of the coral reefs around the coast's premier resort town, Hurghada, have been damaged due to illegal landfilling operations by developers and irresponsible use of the reef by tourist operators. In places the coast has simply eroded away due to developers building solid concrete jetties which have altered the natural shoreline. Though recently enacted laws have made many of these practices illegal, there appears to be little to contain the speculative boom on the area's future as a major source of tourist growth. Even towns south of Hurghada, including Port Safaga and picturesque Al-Quseir, are showing signs of going the same way.

AIN SUKHNA

Ain Sukhna, which simply means 'hot spring', is the site of springs originating from within Gebel Ataka, the northernmost mountain in the Eastern Desert. There's not much to the place, but it is quite an attractive bit of coast. The road squeezes along between the water and the hills that slope almost down to the relatively clean beach. Unfortunately, developers are currently carving it up and the entire coastline between here and Zafarana to the south will soon be a series of concrete resorts. To make matters worse, the government is also

HIGHLIGHTS

- **The Red Sea** Plunge into the turquoise waters off the coast and see the famed coral and marine life.

- **Monasteries of St Anthony & St Paul** See where Christian monasticism got its start.

- **Hurghada** Laze on a beach at one of Hurghada's huge seaside resorts.

- **Al-Quseir** Imagine yourself as a spice trader in the narrow lanes of historic Quseir, site of the last remaining Ottoman fortress on the Red Sea coast.

- **The Eastern Desert** Watch the sun set over the craggy mountains of the Eastern Desert.

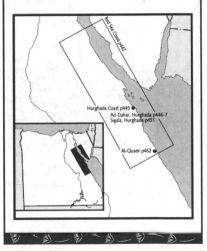

planning a massive industrial port just to the north.

It's possible to visit Ain Sukhna on a day trip from Cairo (via Suez) but as all the beaches are being taken over by tourist

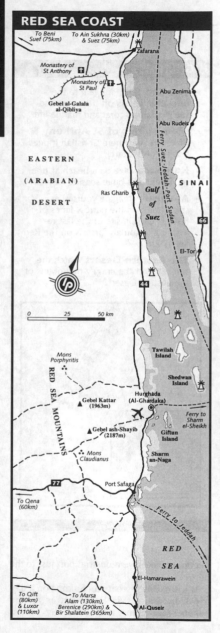

RED SEA COAST

To Beni Suef (75km)
To Ain Sukhna (30km) & Suez (75km)
Zafarana
Monastery of St Anthony
Monastery of St Paul
Abu Zenima
Gebel al-Galala al-Qibliya
Abu Rudeis
EASTERN
(ARABIAN)
DESERT
Ras Gharib
Gulf of Suez
SINAI
66
El-Tor
0   25   50 km
44
Mons Porphyritis
RED SEA MOUNTAINS
Tawilah Island
Shedwan Island
Gebel Kattar (1963m)
Hurghada (Al-Ghardaka)
Ferry to Sharm el-Sheikh
Gebel ash-Shayib (2187m)
Giftun Island
Mons Claudianus
Sharm an-Naga
77
Port Safaga
Ferry to Jeddah
To Qena (60km)
RED
SEA
El-Hamarawein
To Qift (80km) & Luxor (110km)
To Marsa Alam (130km), Berenice (290km) & Bir Shalatein (365km)
Al-Quseir

villages, you'll probably have to pay for the pleasure of stretching out on the sand.

There are three buses a day from Suez (E£5). However, there's little in the way of refreshments, so, unless you bring some food with you, you'll have to dine at the hotels.

If you want to stay longer there is a choice of resorts, all pretty much the same. A couple of these include the somewhat shabby *Ain Sukhna Hotel* (☎ 772 367, fax 378 3642) built just beside the hot spring, with a choice of 80 rooms for US$40/60 including breakfast, or *Al-Sukhna Portrait Hotel* (☎ 325 560, fax 322 003), a glitzy hotel/time-share resort where a double room costs E£308, half board.

ZAFARANA

This town, 62km south of Ain Sukhna and 150km east of Beni Suef on the Nile, is little more than a way-station for visits to the isolated Coptic monasteries of St Anthony and St Paul in the mountains overlooking the Gulf of Suez, although this may change since a huge number of resorts are under construction here. Should you want to stay overnight, there is the choice of *Sahara Inn Motel* or the five star *Windsor Zafarana* resort. Given the choice, we'd recommend that you keep going to Hurghada.

Buses running between Suez and Hurghada will drop you at Zafarana. There's also one bus a day from Beni Suef.

MONASTERIES

The Coptic Christian monasteries of St Anthony and St Paul are Egypt's oldest monasteries. As the crow flies, they are only about 35km apart, but thanks to the cliffs and plateau of Gebel al-Galala al-Qibliya (which lies between 900m and 1300m above sea level) they're around 82km apart by road.

It is possible to hike between the two monasteries along a so-called trail across the top of the plateau. However, this area is commonly known as 'devil's country' and hiking this uncharitable land is only for the fit and experienced and should be done with a guide. A wrong turn could see you over a cliff or lost without water. Those who have made the hike recommend starting from St Paul's; ideally, you should reach St Anthony's in two days.

Information

The monasteries are open to visitors between 9 am and 5 pm. It's possible to stay overnight at St Paul's but you'll need permission from its residence in Cairo. The monks at St Anthony's are reluctant to accept tourists overnight. Both St Paul's monastery residence (☎ 590 0218) and St Anthony's (☎ 590 6025) are around St Mark's Cathedral off Sharia al-Galaa in central Cairo. The monks won't accept visitors during Lent (February to the beginning of Easter in April) although if you show up they will sometimes let you in.

Monastery of St Anthony

Hidden away in the barren cliffs of the Eastern Desert, the establishing of the fortified religious community of St Anthony's represented the beginning of the Christian monastic tradition. Built in the 4th century AD by the disciples of St Anthony, the walled village at the foot of Gebel al-Galala al-Qibliya is the largest of the Coptic monasteries.

This founding monastic order sprang up around the son of a merchant who had given up his worldly possessions to devote his life to God. Anthony actually retreated into the desert, in about 294 AD, to escape the disciples he had attracted to his hermit's cave by the Nile. While his followers adopted an austere communal life at the foot of the mountain, Anthony took himself off to a cave, high above the developing monastery village, where he lived to the ripe old age of 105.

Despite its isolation, the monastery suffered Bedouin raids in the 8th and 9th centuries, attacks from irate Muslims in the 11th century and a 15th century revolt by bloodthirsty servants that resulted in the massacre of the monks.

Following the example set by St Anthony, St Paul and their followers 16 centuries ago, the 60 monks and five novices who live at St Anthony's today have dedi-

Warning

There is a heavy military presence along much of the coast and some areas are mined. Although some of these are clearly marked with signs and barbed wire, others are not, particularly in the south. If you decide to check out that secluded beach, always look for tyre tracks or footprints – better still, check with local authorities to be sure. Because of the military installations along the Red Sea coast, be prudent about where you aim your cameras, too.

cated their lives to poverty, chastity, obedience and prayer – when they're not showing tourists around.

St Anthony's has several churches, chapels and dormitories, a guesthouse, bakery, vegetable garden and spring. The oldest part of the monastery is the **Church of St Anthony**, built over the saint's tomb. It contains the largest array of Coptic wall paintings in Egypt and at the time of writing they were being restored to their former glory. Painted in *secco* (where paint is applied on dry plaster) they date back to the early 13th century. Stripped of the dirt and grime of centuries, the colours are clear and bright and, experts say, demonstrate how medieval Coptic art was connected to the wider Byzantine and Islamic Eastern Mediterranean.

The monks here are in the process of building a museum that will contain, among other things, part of the monastery's extensive collection of old manuscripts and crosses.

If you're hiking in from the main road make sure you're properly equipped, especially with water, as it's a long, hot and dry walk. If you do get this far you should also hike up to the **Cave of St Anthony**, which is north-east of the monastery, some 300m – or 1158 wooden steps – up a cliff. It takes about an hour to get there. Inside there is a small chapel with an altar. The medieval graffiti on the walls is fascinating and there is a breathtaking view of the hills and valley below.

Beach or building site? The great natural beauty of the Red Sea coast is rapidly being submerged under a tidal wave of concrete development.

Monastery of St Paul

The most fascinating part of this large complex, in the cliffs of Gebel al-Galala al-Qibliya, is the **Church of St Paul**, cluttered with altars, candles, ostrich eggs (the symbol of the Resurrection) and colourful murals. It was built in and around the cave where Paul lived for nearly 90 years, during the 4th century, after founding the monastery as a show of devotion to St Anthony. Legend has it that the latter outlived his follower and at the age of 90 made the difficult trek through the mountains to bury him. The **fortress**, above the church, was where the monks retreated during Bedouin raids.

Visitors are more than welcome and a couple of the monks, who speak excellent English, give guided tours. St Paul's has two guesthouses, one inside the monastery for men and one outside for women. Food and lodging are provided free of charge, so don't abuse the monks' hospitality.

Getting There & Away

Buses running between Suez and Hurghada will take you to Zafarana but direct access to the monasteries is limited to private vehicles and tour buses from Cairo or Hurghada. The easiest way is to join one of the tours from Hurghada.

St Anthony's is 45km inland from the Red Sea. To get there follow the road which runs between Zafarana and Beni Suef. The turn-off to the monastery is about 30km from Zafarana and from there it's a 13km walk south through the desert to St Anthony's.

To get to St Paul's you can take one of the buses that run between Suez and Hurghada and get off after Zafarana at the turn-off to the monastery, which is south of the Zafarana lighthouse. Buses between Suez and Qena go along the Red Sea coast road and can also drop you at the turn-off. It's then a 13km hike along the badly surfaced road through the desert.

Another alternative is to hire a taxi from Suez or Hurghada to the monasteries. Otherwise you'd be better off with your own transport to make this journey.

AL-GOUNA

A brand new resort town built by one of Egypt's biggest tycoons, Al-Gouna, about 20km north of Hurghada, boasts, among other things, six hotels, an airport, a hospital, an open-air amphitheatre, a golf course and a shopping mall. The playground for Egypt's rich and famous, it often hosts concerts and sporting events. Despite being a resort it is far more tastefully designed than anywhere else in Hurghada and if you only want to laze on a beach staying here avoids the hassle of the town. The three star *Al-Khan Hotel* (☎ 549 712) (singles/doubles US$26/32 including breakfast) and the four star *Dawar al-Umda* (☎ 545 060) (US$30/40 including breakfast) are both in the style of the work of Egypt's most famous architect, Hassan Fathy, complete with domes and arches. At the top end, is the five star *Sheraton Miramar* (☎ 545 606), a pastel-coloured, postmodern desert fantasy, designed by world-famous architect Michael Graves. Double rooms here start at US$135 in the off-peak season.

HURGHADA (AL-GHARDAKA)

Little more than a decade and a half ago Hurghada had two hotels separated by nothing more than virgin beach. A one-time isolated and modest fishing village, it's now home to more than 35,000 people and packed with more than 100 resorts and hotels catering to sun-seekers and diving enthusiasts on package tours from the world over. But while the crystal-clear waters and fascinating reefs have made Hurghada, or Al-Ghardaka as the Egyptians call it, Egypt's most popular resort town, if you're not into beaches, diving or snorkelling then this ever-developing resort town has little to offer.

Much of the town is marred by chunks of concrete, iron rods and empty oil drums – the results of the ongoing construction boom. Every spare bit of dirt or sand in the town is being turned into a building site. For more than 20km to the south, a dense band of concrete in the form of four and five-star resorts has created the kind of disaster that you can also see on the southern shores of Europe. Even worse is that developers, not content with having all but destroyed this part of the Red Sea coast, are repeating their mistakes further and further south.

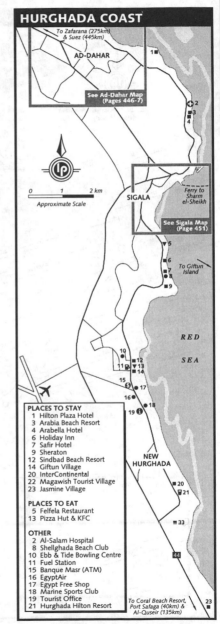

HURGHADA COAST

To Zafarana (275km) & Suez (445km)

AD-DAHAR

See Ad-Dahar Map (Pages 446-7)

Ferry to Sharm el-Sheikh

SIGALA

See Sigala Map (Page 451)

0   1   2 km
Approximate Scale

To Giftun Island

RED SEA

NEW HURGHADA

PLACES TO STAY
1 Hilton Plaza Hotel
3 Arabia Beach Resort
4 Arabella Hotel
6 Holiday Inn
7 Safir Hotel
9 Sheraton
12 Sindbad Beach Resort
14 Giftun Village
20 InterContinental
22 Magawish Tourist Village
23 Jasmine Village

PLACES TO EAT
5 Felfela Restaurant
13 Pizza Hut & KFC

OTHER
2 Al-Salam Hospital
8 Shellghada Beach Club
10 Ebb & Tide Bowling Centre
11 Fuel Station
15 Banque Masr (ATM)
16 EgyptAir
17 Egypt Free Shop
18 Marine Sports Club
19 Tourist Office
21 Hurghada Hilton Resort

To Coral Beach Resort, Port Safaga (40km) & Al-Quseir (135km)

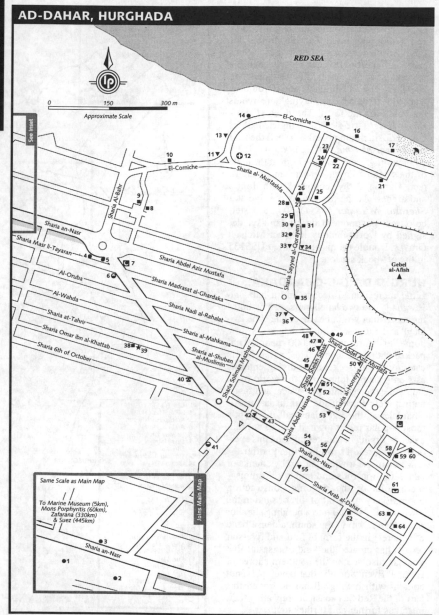

AD-DAHAR, HURGHADA

RED SEA

0   150   300 m
Approximate Scale

El-Corniche

Sharia al-Mustashfa

El-Corniche

Sharia Al-Bahr

Sharia an-Nasr

Sharia Masr li-Tayaran

Sharia Abdel Aziz Mustafa

Sharia Madrasat al-Ghardaka

Al-Oruba

Al-Wahda

Sharia at-Tahrir

Sharia Nadi al-Rahalat

Sharia Omar ibn al-Khattab

Sharia al-Mahkama

Sharia 6th of October

Sharia al-Shuban al-Muslimin

Sharia Soliman Mazhar

Sharia Abdel Hasan

Sharia Shukri Sabah

Sharia Abdel Aziz Mustafa

Sharia al-Horreya

Sharia Sayyed al-Qorayen

Gebel al-Afish ▲

Gebel al-Afish

Sharia an-Nasr

Sharia Arab al-Dahar

Same Scale as Main Map

To Marine Museum (5km),
Mons Porphyritis (60km),
Zafarana (330km)
& Suez (445km)

Sharia an-Nasr

Joins Main Map

See Inset

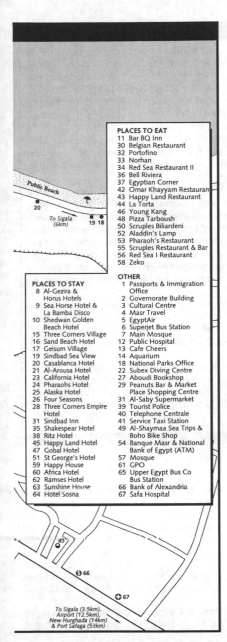

PLACES TO EAT
11 Bar BQ Inn
30 Belgian Restaurant
32 Portofino
33 Norhan
34 Red Sea Restaurant II
36 Bell Riviera
37 Egyptian Corner
42 Omar Khayyam Restaurant
43 Happy Land Restaurant
44 La Torta
46 Young Kang
48 Pizza Tarboush
50 Scruples Biliardeni
52 Aladdin's Lamp
53 Pharaoh's Restaurant
55 Scruples Restaurant & Bar
56 Red Sea I Restaurant
58 Zeko

PLACES TO STAY
8 Al-Gezira & Horus Hotels
9 Sea Horse Hotel & La Bamba Disco
10 Shedwan Golden Beach Hotel
15 Three Corners Village
16 Sand Beach Hotel
17 Geisum Village
19 Sindbad Sea View
20 Casablanca Hotel
21 Al-Arousa Hotel
23 California Hotel
24 Pharaohs Hotel
25 Alaska Hotel
26 Four Seasons
28 Three Corners Empire Hotel
31 Sindbad Inn
35 Shakespear Hotel
38 Ritz Hotel
45 Happy Land Hotel
47 Gobal Hotel
51 St George's Hotel
59 Happy House
60 Africa Hotel
62 Ramses Hotel
63 Sunshine House
64 Hotel Sosna

OTHER
1 Passports & Immigration Office
2 Governorate Building
3 Cultural Centre
4 Masr Travel
5 EgyptAir
6 Superjet Bus Station
7 Main Mosque
12 Public Hospital
13 Cafe Cheers
14 Aquarium
18 National Parks Office
22 Subex Diving Centre
27 Aboudi Bookshop
29 Peanuts Bar & Market Place Shopping Centre
31 Al-Saby Supermarket
39 Tourist Police
40 Telephone Centrale
41 Service Taxi Station
49 Al-Shaymaa Sea Trips & Boho Bike Shop
54 Banque Masr & National Bank of Egypt (ATM)
57 Mosque
61 GPO
65 Upper Egypt Bus Co Bus Station
66 Bank of Alexandria
67 Safa Hospital

One of the few positive observations that can be made about all this is that the destruction of the environment has been so alarming that action is finally being taken to try and control future construction. The Egyptian National Parks Office has belatedly established an office here and an NGO, the Hurghada Environmental Protection and Conservation Association (HEPCA), is also helping to address many of the local environmental problems.

Hurghada's peak tourist season is from November to February. At this time it feels as if half of Europe – well, all the Germans, Dutch, Belgians, Russians and Eastern Europeans at any rate – have flown in on all-inclusive package holidays.

Orientation

The main town area, where virtually all the budget accommodation is located and most of the locals live, is at the northern end of the stretch of resorts that makes up the whole area. It is called **Ad-Dahar** and sits at the base of Gebel al-Afish, which effectively blocks any breeze or views of the sea. The main road through Ad-Dahar is Sharia an-Nasr, which is the highway linking Hurghada to Port Safaga and Suez.

A few kilometres down the coast is **Sigala**, where new hotels, restaurants and resorts are springing up like mushrooms. This is also where you'll find the port for boats to Sharm el-Sheikh.

South of Sigala, a road winds down along the coast through the 'resort strip'. At the five star tourist village of Magawish, about 15km south of Ad-Dahar, the road meets another a few kilometres inland to head down past the newer resorts and the rapidly growing shells of future pleasure domes on the way to Port Safaga.

Information

Visa Extensions You can obtain visa extensions and re-entry visas at the passports section in the Passports & Immigration office (☎ 546 727) at the northern end of Ad-Dahar on Sharia an-Nasr. It's open daily (except Friday) from 8 am to 2 pm.

Rescuing the Red Sea

Conservationists estimate that more than 700 boats each week ply back and forth between Hurghada and the many reefs situated within an hour of the town. Up until recently, there was nothing to stop captains on these boats from anchoring to the coral, or snorkellers and divers breaking off a colourful chunk to take home. But thanks largely to the efforts of the Hurghada Environmental Protection and Conservation Association (HEPCA) and the belatedly established National Parks Office in Hurghada, the Red Sea's reefs are at last being protected.

Set up in 1992 by 15 of the town's larger and more reputable dive companies, HEPCA's program to conserve the Red Sea's reefs is manifold. Public awareness campaigns are underway, direct community action has been taken, and the Egyptian government has been lobbied to introduce appropriate laws. Now the whole coast south of Suez Governorate is known as the Red Sea Protected Area.

Environmental protection measures already undertaken include the installation of more than 350 mooring buoys at popular dive sites around Hurghada and further south, enabling boat captains to drop anchor on a buoy rather than on the coral itself. Marine rangers police the seas and captains found mooring to the reef rather than to the buoys are prosecuted.

A 'reef conservation tax' of E£1 has been introduced and is payable by anyone using the reefs for diving, snorkelling or any other boating activity. The tax is a symbolic gesture, designed to make the public aware that the reefs and offshore islands are now protected areas, rather than a fundraising measure. For details of the rules for marine protectorates see the Diving the Red Sea chapter.

Both HEPCA and the National Parks Office encourage visitors to take an active role in helping to protect Hurghada's beleaguered reefs. The National Parks Office is next to the Sindbad Seaview Hotel, opposite the public beach in al-Dahar. You can drop by the office and pick up a brochure or call ☎ 549 632 between 8.30 am and 2 pm for information on the office's slide shows of Hurghada's reefs.

HEPCA is just up from the old port and sells a guide to the main dive sites around Hurghada and Safaga for about E£70, which goes toward the cost of setting up and maintaining mooring buoys. If you have any questions about safe diving practices or about how you can help HEPCA in its efforts to protect the Red Sea's reefs, call ☎ 445 035 Saturdays through Thursdays, from 9 am to 6 pm.

Tourist Offices Hurghada's tourist office (☎ 446 513), on the main road at the beginning of the resort strip, is open daily (except Friday) from 8.30 am to 3 pm.

Money In Ad-Dahar, branches of Banque Masr, the National Bank of Egypt (with an ATM machine) and the Bank of Alexandria are dotted along Sharia an-Nasr. The first two give cash advances on Visa or Master-Card. They are generally open seven days a week for exchange purposes, from 9 am to 1 pm and 6 to 9 pm.

In Sigala, you'll find an office of Thomas Cook (☎ 443 338) on Sharia Sheraton, it is open daily from 9 am to 2 pm and 6 to 9 pm.

On the resort strip, the only bank is the branch of Banque Masr just south of the old youth hostel. It has an ATM, and will give you cash advances on your Visa or Master-Card if the ATM is broken. Most of the resorts have a branch of the National Bank of Egypt and there is an ATM at the InterContinental.

Post & Communications The GPO is on Sharia an-Nasr, towards the southern end of

St Katherine's Monastery at Mt Sinai.

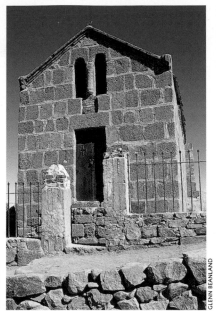

Greek Orthodox chapel on Mt Sinai.

Originally a Bedouin village in Sinai, Assalah is now a busy little seaside town.

The famous stream of Ain Umm Ahmed, Sinai.

Shark Observatory at Ras Mohammed Park.

The nomadic lifestyle of Egypt's 500,000 Bedouins is changing as age-old customs disappear.

Ad-Dahar. The 24 hour telephone centrale is further north-west along the same road. Opposite the telephone centrale is a fax booth (fax 544 581) open daily (except Friday) from 8 am to 2 pm and 8 to 10 pm.

Email & Internet Access Aboudi Bookshop in Ad-Dahar on Sharia al-Mustashfa has Hurghada's first Internet cafe, and it is currently charging E£20 for an hour's use between 10 am and 5 pm, or E£25 between 5 pm and midnight. The Ebb & Tide Bowling Centre, just north of the Sindbad Beach Resort, is also supposed to be opening an Internet cafe. You can call ☎ 442 944 to check if it's open.

Travel Agencies There are at least 45 travel agencies in Hurghada, so you've got lots of choice. Misr Travel (☎ 548 715) has an office in Ad-Dahar near the main mosque. For details on the trips they offer, see Organised Tours later in this section. The Thomas Cook office (☎ 443 388) in Sigala can organise general travel arrangements.

Bookshops Aboudi Bookshop, opposite the Market Place shopping centre in Ad-Dahar, is the only place in town with a small selection of foreign and Egyptian literature, maps, guidebooks, foreign newspapers and postcards. It has a few French and German books too, and is open daily from 10 am to midnight.

Newspapers & Magazines *Hurghada Bulletin* is a free magazine that you can find on stands around Hurghada (there's one beside Peanuts Bar in Ad-Dahar). It's free and has listings of what's happening around town. With the odd exception the articles are pretty useless but it's invaluable for finding out about special events, restaurants, clubs and the like.

Medical Services & Emergency There are three hospitals in Ad-Dahar: the private Safa Hospital is near the Upper Egypt Bus Co bus station. A new private hospital, Al-Salam Hospital (☎ 548 785/6/7) about halfway between Ad-Dahar and Sigala has

A Word of Caution

Despite being Egypt's premier resort, Hurghada is filled with young men from Upper Egypt and is thus a traditional town. Local sensibilities must be considered when you move away from the beach area. In recent years an alarming number of tourists have taken to wandering around the market quarter in Ad-Dahar in shorts and skimpy tops, and the trend seems to be growing. If you do this, don't be surprised when you are grabbed, pinched or otherwise harassed.

a 24 hour emergency department and is next to the Arabia Beach Resort. The public hospital (☎ 546 740) is at the other end of town near Shedwan Golden Beach Hotel.

Other emergency telephone numbers include: ambulance (☎ 546 490), police (☎ 546 303) and tourist police (☎ 546 765).

Aquarium
If you've ended up in Hurghada and don't want to put your head under the water, you can still get an idea of some of the life teeming in the waters of the Red Sea by paying a visit to the aquarium, just north of the public hospital in Ad-Dahar. They have quite a good selection of fish and various other odd-looking creatures. It's open from 9 am to 11 pm and costs E£5 (no student discount); permits to use cameras/videos cost E£2/10 extra.

Marine Museum
The marine biology station, about 5km north of town, has a decrepit museum and a mini-aquarium. It's open daily from 8 am to 8 pm and costs E£4. To get there you can pick up a microbus from near the big mosque heading out on the highway to Suez for 50pt.

Beaches & Pools
Hurghada's beaches are not the most stunning in the world; in fact, they're often quite bare and stark.

There are two public beaches, one in Ad-Dahar and a much smaller version in Sigala near the port. Though relatively clean, the sand resembles fine dirt and the rubbish bobbing around in the water is very off-putting. Also, the beach at Sigala is next to a mosque, which makes stripping down to anything more daring than long trousers and a T-shirt inappropriate. Women may also feel uncomfortable sunbathing or swimming in Ad-Dahar as men often congregate along the beach wall to sit and stare. Admission to either costs E£1.

Your only other option close to town is to pay to use one of the beaches at the resorts, or head to the small beach at Al-Sakia restaurant in Sigala, where there's a minimum charge of E£15 (including a drink). Unfortunately, being so close to the port, the water here is still pretty dirty.

You may be able to sneak onto one of the paying beaches at the resorts if you act confident enough, but many of them have caught on to this and are much stricter than before; otherwise you'll be looking at daily fees from E£10 to E£40.

Snorkelling

Although there is some easily accessible coral at the beach south of the Sheraton, the best reefs are offshore and the only way to see them is to take a boat and make a snorkelling or diving excursion for at least one day.

For years, **Giftun Island** has been one of the most popular sites. The average day trip to Giftun, including transport to and from the harbour, two stops on a reef, snorkelling gear and lunch on the boat or the island, starts at US$30. Overnight trips are also possible, however, you'll need to carefully choose the captain and crew. Groups of women alone may face unwanted advances or worse from their male 'guides'.

You will find no shortage of places offering these kinds of trips. The best advice is to shop around a little and see where you can get a deal that suits you. Simply relying on your hotel (and many of the smaller hotels work hard to get you to join the trips for

which they are getting commission) may not be the best way to do things. Several people have complained of not getting everything they thought they would. Eliminating at least one intermediary might reduce the risk of disappointment. Some of the more reputable dive clubs also take snorkellers out and, by going with one of them, you're almost assured of environmental reef protection practices being put into action.

Take your passport with you on any boat excursions, you may have to show it at the port.

Remember to use sun screen when swimming and snorkelling. It is probably a good idea to wear a T-shirt as the sun's rays easily penetrate the surface of the water. For more information about marine life and possible snorkelling sites, see the Diving the Red Sea chapter.

Diving

For detailed information about diving see the Diving the Red Sea chapter.

Other Water Sports

Plenty of the bigger resorts cater for most tastes in water sports. The best-known windsurfing places in the area are Three Corners Village Resort, Jasmin Village or Giftun Village. Keep in mind that the huge amount of construction along the coast has affected the wind here, so if you're a windsurfing buff, you're better off in Sinai or further south along the coast. If you decide to do it, you're looking at about E£120 for an hour's lesson, with equipment, or about E£660 to E£700 for a week's equipment rental. Paragliding and water-skiing are also available at some resorts.

Hot Air Ballooning

Cast Ballooning Egypt is a German-run company offering hot air balloon trips in the desert behind Hurghada. A five or six hour trip includes a one hour balloon ride, plus jeep safari and breakfast at a Bedouin camp for US$180 per person. Call for more information on ☏ 444 928 or 012-218 2355.

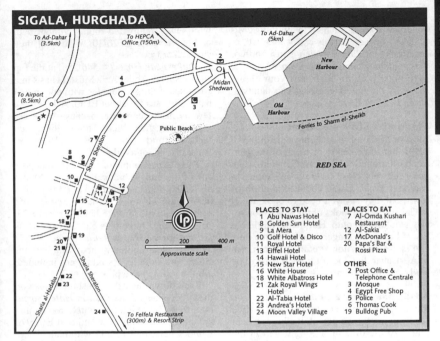

SIGALA, HURGHADA

To Ad-Dahar (3.5km)
To HEPCA Office (150m)
To Ad-Dahar (5km)
New Harbour
Midan Shedwan
To Airport (8.5km)
Old Harbour
Ferries to Sharm el-Sheikh
Public Beach
Sharia Sheraton
RED SEA
Sharia Sheraton
Sharia al-Hadaba
0   200   400 m
Approximate scale
To Felfela Restaurant (300m) & Resort Strip

PLACES TO STAY
1 Abu Nawas Hotel
8 Golden Sun Hotel
9 La Mera
10 Golf Hotel & Disco
11 Royal Hotel
13 Eiffel Hotel
14 Hawaii Hotel
15 New Star Hotel
16 White House
18 White Albatross Hotel
21 Zak Royal Wings Hotel
22 Al-Tabia Hotel
23 Andrea's Hotel
24 Moon Valley Village

PLACES TO EAT
7 Al-Omda Kushari Restaurant
12 Al-Sakia
17 McDonald's
20 Papa's Bar & Rossi Pizza

OTHER
2 Post Office & Telephone Centrale
3 Mosque
4 Egypt Free Shop
5 Police
6 Thomas Cook
19 Bulldog Pub

Organised Tours

The range of possible organised excursions from Hurghada is all-encompassing. Most of the bigger hotels and most travel agents organise some or all of the following, many of them aimed at people flying in directly on charters and not planning on travelling through the rest of the country. For those with a lot of stamina, the more ambitious tours include a whirlwind one day tour to Cairo for E£200 or a slightly more leisurely two day tour for E£450. A one day jaunt to Luxor costs around E£250.

More feasible are some of the desert jeep safaris, which tend to include visits to at least one of two Roman sites: Mons Porphyritis and Mons Claudianus. These trips cost about E£150. A full-day excursion to the monasteries of St Paul and St Anthony costs about E£150. A half-day desert safari including a one hour camel trek is US$30;

an evening excursion into the desert including a sunset drive, camel ride and BBQ dinner costs at least E£75.

A minimum number of people is needed for most of these trips, so it's best to inquire several days in advance.

Water Excursions A ride in the Sindbad Submarine is one way to plumb the depths and stay bone dry. This yellow submarine can carry 46 people to a depth of 22m. It costs US$50 a head for the 'two hour' trip; however, an hour of this is spent on a boat travelling between Sindbad Beach Resort and the site where the submarine is moored. For more information, contact Sindbad Beach Resort (☎ 443 261).

Alternatively there's the Aquascope, a new contraption that looks like it escaped from a 1970's science fiction movie. It floats and has a submerged bubble-shaped cabin from where a maximum of 10 people can view the underwater world. An hour in this thing costs US$40. For more details call ☎ 443 710, or inquire at Hor Palace, which is just north of the InterContinental on the resort strip.

If glass-bottom boats are your thing, many of the hotels can organise jaunts at about E£25 to E£35 an hour.

Places to Stay – Budget

Most of the hotels in this range are either in Ad-Dahar town centre or north of the centre, built around the base of Gebel al-Afish and relatively close to the sea. There is a National Youth Camp about 5km north of town, but they say you need to book ahead in Cairo – by the looks of the place, you really wouldn't want to. Hurghada's little old youth hostel no longer exists and the new one is a construction site about 5km north of Ad-Dahar that doesn't look like it will be ready any time soon.

Ad-Dahar Centre *Sunshine House* on Sharia an-Nasr opposite the post office seems to have gone downhill a bit in recent times. At the time of writing it was in the middle of a construction site. Many travellers have reported that the staff tend to be very pushy when it comes to snorkelling trips. There's a common room and a kitchen with a fridge available for guests. It is E£6 per person.

Happy House (☎ 549 611) on the main square by the mosque in the centre of Ad-Dahar, is a humble pension with five very clean double rooms with fans, as well as a kitchen and fridge. Rates are E£15 for a single room, or E£10 per person in a double, including breakfast. A room with its own bathroom goes for E£25.

Africa Hotel (☎ 548 124), on the edge of the souq, claims to be recommended by a number of guidebooks – but not by this one. Its dingy rooms appear to be used only by the junior staff of other hotels. Singles/doubles with bathrooms go for E£15/20, including breakfast.

St George's Hotel (☎ 548 246) just by Aladdin's Lamp Restaurant in the centre of

Ad-Dahar, is a pleasant family-run place with newly renovated rooms without bath or breakfast for E£20/30. With bath they cost E£25/35.

Shakespear Hotel (☎ 546 256) at the top end of Sharia Abdel Aziz Mustafa has some spacious, if dingy, doubles with communal baths and fans for about E£30. Ask to see a few rooms to compare, because some are much better than others. Those with private facilities and air-con cost E£15 more. Breakfast is not available.

There are a couple of places in the upper end of the budget bracket nearby on Sharia al-Sheikh Sebak. *Gobal Hotel* (☎ 546 623) has singles/doubles with breakfast, and sometimes with private bath, for E£15/25. All the rooms have fans but the bathrooms are not great. *Happy Land Hotel* (☎ 547 373) has clean rooms without/with bath for E£25/30 a double, breakfast not included. All the rooms have phones.

Back down near the Sunshine House on the other side of the road is *Hotel Sosna* (☎ 546 647), which has double rooms that are clean, relatively new and cost E£15/20 without bath, or E£25/35 with bath. There are also a couple of rooms with air-con for another E£10.

On the opposite side of the road from the Sosna is *Ramses Ghardaka* (☎ 548 941) which is more expensive than most of these other options but far better. It has very clean singles/doubles with air-con, telephone and fridge for E£45/55, including breakfast. Without air-con, rooms go for E£40/50.

Ad-Dahar Seaside There's quite a family of little hotels in the dirt lanes between the Market Place shopping centre and the sea. Though relatively close to the water, very few rooms in these places have sea views.

California Hotel (☎ 549 101) is one of the best for the price in this area. It sports exotic murals and has rooms with private bath and balcony on the new 2nd floor. The older rooms with shared bathrooms cost E£10/15 including breakfast, the new rooms are a bit more. By the time you read this four of the rooms should have air-con.

Four Seasons (☎ 549 260) is just down the road from Aboudi Bookshop and has 14 rooms with private bathrooms, six of which have air-con. Those without air-con (but with fan, balcony and breakfast) are good value at E£15/25. Air-con rooms cost a little more. For E£5 you can also use the beach at the Geisum Village Hotel.

Alaska Hotel (☎ 548 413) on the slope up behind the Aboudi bookshop, charges E£8.50 per person plus E£2 for breakfast and is a good, comfortable place to stay.

Close to the public beach is *Casablanca Hotel* (☎ 548 292), formerly known as the Sea Oasis. The name changed with the management and the rooms are clean, bright and spacious and go for E£15/25, including breakfast. Rooms with bath and air-con are E£25/40.

Pharaohs Hotel (☎ 547 577) has reduced its prices thanks to stiff competition and the drop in tourists that came after the 1997 Hatshepsut massacre. If you like big rooms, this may be your place. A single/double with a balcony and shared bathroom goes for E£15/25, including breakfast.

Sigala Should you want to be close to the port, try *Abu Nawas Hotel* (☎ 442 830) behind the post and telephone office. It has big, clean rooms with fan and communal bathrooms for E£15/25, but it's a tad overpriced and usually pretty empty. There's a pleasant street-front terrace where you can get a beer.

Places to Stay – Mid-Range
Ad-Dahar Centre *Ritz Hotel* (☎ 547 031) is a laid-back place, next to a tiny tourist police office, with air-con singles/doubles for E£30/60. There's a restaurant and bar, and you get access to the beach at Sand Beach Hotel for E£5.

There is a trio of places just off Sharia al-Bahr north of the main mosque. *Sea Horse Hotel* (☎/fax 547 016) is an old but quite OK three star place that, as with many of its ilk, caters mainly to German tour groups. Most rooms have air-con, TV, phone, wall-to-wall carpet and bath. Low season rates are E£75/95, with breakfast.

Adjacent to the Sea Horse and also one of the older establishments in this bracket is *Al-Gezira Hotel* (☎ 548 709, fax 548 708). If you don't mind taking half board (obligatory) it's quite a good deal, with singles/doubles/triples going for E£65/93/121. High season rates are about E£25 per person extra. All rooms have air-con, telephone and private bathroom, a few rooms also have TV. The same company owns the Sand Beach Hotel, so you can use their beach and pool for free.

Next door to the Al-Gezira is the six storey *Horus Hotel* (☎/fax 549 801), popular with Belgian tourists, which has tacky rooms with air-con, TV and fridge for E£60/100 including breakfast.

Ad-Dahar Seaside *Sindbad Inn* (☎ 544 404) on Sayyed al-Qorayem is a 32-room, clean, well-run place with singles/doubles for E£70/100, including breakfast. You also get free use of the beach at the Sindbad Beach Resort on the resort strip.

Just up from the sea is the enormous, 366-room *Three Corners Empire Hotel* (☎ 549 200, fax 549 213; email info@three corners.com). Looking more like a public housing block than a hotel it nevertheless has the advantage of a central location and is only two minutes from the beach at the Three Corners Village. Rooms cost US$24/28, including breakfast.

Up by the sea is *Al-Arousa Hotel* (☎ 548 434, fax 549 190), one of the best places in this price range. It has immaculate air-con rooms all with private bath, TV, phone and balconies with sea views for E£80/130 with obligatory half board. It has an indoor pool (E£10 fee for nonguests) and a poolside bar, and guests have free access to the beach at Geisum Village across the road. Bookings are recommended as it's popular with divers.

Geisum Village (☎ 548 048, fax 547 995) is the cheapest of the three places right on the beach. It charges E£80/140 for singles/doubles, half board.

On the other side of the road, facing the public beach is *Sindbad Sea View* (☎ 443 261). This latest addition to Hurghada's

Sindbad empire has 32 rooms with air-con and satellite TV for E£80/110, it also has a small indoor pool. There is a shuttle bus to Sindbad Beach Resort, where you can use the beach for free.

Sigala There's a bewildering array of mid-range places on and around Sharia Sheraton and more seem to be opening every month.

La Mera (☎ 442 075) is a small hotel on the main street with somewhat shabby air-con rooms for E£35/60. Just behind it is the friendly *Golden Sun Hotel (☎ 444 403, fax 443 862)*, where you can get spotless, air-con rooms for E£50/75, including breakfast and tax. The management makes an effort here: there are flowers on the towels and an Egyptian 'cafe' with sheeshas has been set up in the courtyard.

Back on the main street is *Golf Hotel (☎ 442 828)*, which has small rooms for E£45/80, including breakfast. It is very popular with Czech, Polish and Russian groups and has a disco (no minimum charge).

Across the road is *White House (☎ 443 688, fax 442 085)* which is losing out to the fierce competition in the area. It has air-con singles/doubles/triples at the back of the building for E£39/59/74, or street-front rooms for E£51/71/86. Breakfast is included. Guests get free access to the beach at Giftun Village on the resort strip.

Just down the road, *New Star Hotel (☎ 442 588)* has stuffy rooms with air-con for E£25/40/70, not including breakfast. The hotel has suffered with the recent downturn in tourism and is old and unappealing.

Across the street is *White Albatross Hotel (☎/fax 442 519, 162 Sheraton Rd)* a 40-room family-owned hotel with air-con singles/doubles for E£59/89, including breakfast. For E£10 you can use the beach at the Pasha Cataract Hotel across the road.

Back on the road by the Al-Sakia restaurant and close to the sea is another cluster of two and three star establishments, with little to choose between them.

Royal Hotel (☎ 447 728) is a five storey orange and blue concrete box with singles/doubles for US$13/24 including break-

fast. Just along the street is the 129 room *Eiffel Hotel (☎ 444 570)*, with air-con rooms for E£60/90, including breakfast. Just behind the Royal Hotel is the newest of the three, *Hawaii Hotel (☎ 445 101)*, which has spotless rooms for E£45/80 including breakfast.

There's yet another new group of medium range hotels on Sharia al-Hadaba just beyond where Sharia Sheraton branches off towards the resort strip. The oddly named *Zak Royal Wings Hotel (☎/fax 446 012)* has clean air-con rooms clustered around a pool for E£65/80, including breakfast.

Across the road is *Andrea's Hotel*, owned by an Italian-trained chef. Air-con rooms go for US$20/34, including breakfast. It is associated with the Sheraton Hotel's diving centre and there's a free shuttle bus between the two hotels.

Just beside Andrea's is the kitsch *Al-Tabia Hotel (☎ 442 350, fax 442 351)*, with castle-like crenellations on top of the building. Rooms are US$22/34 half board.

Moon Valley Village (☎ 442 811), Sharia Sheraton, at the start of the resort strip, has a nice garden and the best location of any of the mid-range places in Sigala. It has a choice of 44 rooms for E£60/95 and a good aspect over the Red Sea. They have a private chunk of beach directly across the road.

Places to Stay – Top End

With the exception of Cairo, Hurghada has the greatest concentration of four and five-star hotels and resorts in all of Egypt and the number is increasing as developers swallow the land further south. Most of these places are on the resort strip which starts just south of Sigala and stretches for 20-odd kilometres down the coast, but as land becomes ever more precious, hotels are also appearing along beach between Ad-Dahar and Sigala. In keeping with the character of the city, most of the resorts here are cheaply built and meant to appeal to the package tourist, so don't expect much in the way of pleasing aesthetics.

The following is a short list of some of the better ones on offer. Keep in mind that travel agencies in Europe and Cairo can offer reductions if you book in advance and that prices fluctuate according to the season and state of tourism. Prices include breakfast unless otherwise indicated.

Shedwan Golden Beach Hotel (☎ 547 007, fax 548 045) is conveniently located near the centre of Dahar on the Corniche. It's a huge 370-room resort which has dropped its prices somewhat in recent years. With a vast swimming pool, a decent beach and reportedly good food, it is popular with German and French tourists. Tiled, air-con singles/doubles are $US35/50.

Sheraton (☎ 442 000, fax 443 333) gives one of Hurghada's main streets its name and was the first resort to be built on the strip. It has a circular modernist design that is definitely out of fashion but may yet come back into style if it is not replaced with yet another concrete box. It may not be beautiful but it has far more character than most of its neighbours as well as two beaches and a marina. Rooms cost US$60/80 half board.

Giftun Village (☎ 442 665, fax 442 666), further south along the resort strip is another of Hurghada's older resorts. Its 380 whitewashed chalet rooms are newly renovated and comfortable. Friendly staff and well-prepared buffet food make the rooms good value at US$50/58 on a half-board basis. There's also a popular German-run diving and windsurfing centre.

Jasmine Village (☎ 446 442, fax 446 441) is another of Hurghada's older establishments. It has 434 bungalow-style air-con rooms and caters mostly to German groups. There is a full water-sports centre, which includes a reputable diving club and windsurfing facilities. There is also a playground and disabled access. Rooms start at US$32/48, half board.

Magawish Tourist Village (☎ 442 621, fax 442 759) may not be the most chic hotel in Hurghada but its spaceship architecture is priceless. This former Club Med also has a children's play area, a huge beach and decent sports facilities, as well as Hurghada's only decompression chamber. Rooms start at US$29/38, half board. It's operated by

Masr Travel, so you can get more information, and details of possible discounts, from their branches throughout the country.

Coral Beach (☎ 447 160) is the last resort on the strip – at least until the next one is finished. While it is far from town (a blessing if you want to look at your surroundings instead of other concrete resorts) it has well-appointed rooms, good sports facilities and a large beach with a reef. It's popular with Italians. Rooms cost US$55/80, half board.

Places to Eat

The beginning of April to mid-October is lobster spawning season and during this period it is illegal to catch lobsters. Even so, you may see some unscrupulous restaurants offering them at this time.

Places to Eat – Budget

Ad-Dahar Centre Many of the cheap eateries around the tourist souq have transformed into yet more souvenir shops but there are a few places opposite the Happy House Hotel, including one called **Zeko** which, like many others, specialises in grilled chicken. You'll also find a couple of coffeehouses around here.

La Torta on Sharia al-Sheikh Sabak is a pristine little cafe quite unlike anything else in Ad-Dahar that serves a small selection of pastries and cakes at six small tables.

Bell Riviera on Sharia Abdel Aziz Mustafa (not to be confused with its more expensive sister restaurant with the similar name across the road) has excellent lentil soup for E£3, spaghetti for E£3.50, pizzas for between E£7 and E£10 and calamari for E£9. You can also get breakfast for E£4. But avoid the toilets.

Egyptian Corner on Sharia Abdel Aziz Mustafa, next door to the Bell Riviera, is a tiny little place popular with travellers. It has a very limited menu that includes a E£5 breakfast, spaghetti bolognaise for E£4 and simple meals like chicken for E£8.

Ad-Dahar Seaside Sharia Sayyed al-Qorayem, the road running from the Shakespear

Hotel right around to the Shedwan Golden Beach Hotel (on the Corniche), is lined with shops and restaurants. For self-caterers, the Al-Saby supermarket is reasonably well stocked.

Norhan is an unpretentious little diner with a few terrace tables and a limited menu. Mains such as shepherds pie or chicken range from E£5 to E£9 and come with a complimentary soft drink (no beer is served). Pizza starts at E£6 and is cheap enough though a bit doughy.

Cafe Cheers is a small roadside restaurant on Sharia el-Corniche that purports to be open 24 hours and has beer in frosty mugs for E£7.50, as well as burgers, pizzas and a few kebab meals for reasonable prices.

Sigala Apart from several fairly nondescript cheapies at the beginning of Sharia Sheraton, there is *Al-Omda Restaurant*, where you can get a decent plate of kushari for around E£2.50. Most of the other budget places have been forced out of here along with rising land prices. If you're desperate for junk food, *McDonald's* has a branch on Sharia Sheraton.

Resort Strip A couple of kilometres along the road, past the Moon Valley Village, is the best located *Felfela Restaurant* (☎ 442 410) in the country. Sitting on a rise and gentle bend in the coastline and overlooking the turquoise sea, it is a splendid place for a modestly priced meal (see under Budget Dining in the Places to Eat section of the Cairo chapter for details on the original restaurant). Beers are a little more pricey than the food at E£10 for a local Stella.

Further along on the resort strip you'll find *Pizza Hut* and *KFC*.

Restaurants
Ad-Dahar Centre *Young Kang* on Sharia Sheikh Sabak does decent Far Eastern cuisine in slightly grubby surroundings. Fried rice is E£10 and sweet & sour chicken costs E£17.

Pizza Tarboush (☎ 548 456) on Sharia Abdel Aziz Mustafa is another popular option with pizzas covered in a variety of toppings for between E£9 and E£18.

Omar Khayyam on Sharia an-Nasr has fried fish for E£15 and Stella beers for E£7.

Scruples, on Sharia an-Nasr across from the National Bank, is a 'pub and steak house' which has a couple of other outlets around Ad-Dahar. It's a rather formal air-con place with a dark upstairs bar that tends to entice cuddling Egyptian couples only. A reasonable fillet of beef with rice and vegetables will set you back about E£25. The same management also runs a pool hall, *Scruples Biliardeni*, at the end of Sharia Abdel Aziz Mustafa, where you can get the same menu as at the original Scruples, and beer for E£7.

Red Sea I Restaurant (☎ 547 704) in a street off Sharia an-Nasr is popular with package tourists wanting a night away from their resorts, the rooftop terrace gets quite crowded in the evenings. With a wide selection of seafood, plus Egyptian dishes and pizza, you can tailor the menu to fit most budgets. Main courses go for between E£15 and E£40.

Pharaoh's Restaurant, just around the corner from the Red Sea I, has Egyptian food, including a decent *kebab hala* for E£13. Beer is available for E£7.

Ad-Dahar Seaside *Red Sea Restaurant II* (☎ 549 630) is another branch of the successful Red Sea I Restaurant in central Ad-Dahar. It has the same popular menu as the original.

Bar BQ Inn, next door to the Red Sea, does calamari for about E£25 and barbecued chicken for E£16. Stella is only E£6.50. The place is popular with Russians and groups of tourists from the nearby Shedwan Golden Beach Hotel.

Portofino (☎ 546 250) across the road from the Red Sea II on Sharia Sayyed el-Qorayem is a friendly Italian place with good, medium priced Italian (and some Egyptian) food. Its pasta dishes are about the best in town and prices start around E£15. Most evenings the gregarious owner wanders around talking to customers.

Belgian Restaurant (☎ *547 816*) next to the Three Corners Empire on Sharia Sayyed al-Qorayem serves relatively expensive food that sounds good but is usually disappointing when it arrives at the table. But the pizzas aren't bad, prices start at E£16.

Bierkeller Restaurant (☎ *545 086*) at Arabella Hotel on the way to Sigala is more a bar than a restaurant but it has a E£9.99 set menu special between 6 and 10 pm every night. No doubt the management is banking on you spending far more than that on the wide variety of beer available, but it's a good deal for a plate of hearty German food. The month's menu is usually published in *Hurghada Bulletin*.

Sigala As the number of hotels in Sigala mushrooms, so too does the number of restaurants.

Al-Sakia (☎ *442 497*) is right down on the water's edge and has a wonderful view of the fishing boats in the old port. The food, a mixture of seafood and Egyptian cuisine, is good, with mains averaging E£20. If nothing else, it's a pleasant place to sit outside and enjoy a beer (E£8).

Rossi Pizza (☎ *446 053*), located just at the point where Sharia Sheraton forks, is a popular hangout for divers and expat Hurghada residents. It serves a variety of toppings on crispy crusts for between E£9 and E£17 as well as other dishes. The service is laid-back and single women can relax without being hassled.

Resort Strip If you fancy lunch on an island, a company has opened a daytime resort/restaurant called *Mahmya* (which means 'protectorate') on Giftun island, despite the fact that it is a protected area. The owners swear that they are cleaning up the island and do not leave any garbage; all waste water is supposedly returned by a special tank. There are tents and showers provided for daytime use (no overnight stays are allowed). A half-day trip (9.30 am to 3 pm) with boat trip and lunch included will cost you US$30. For more information call ☎ 444 806.

Entertainment

Bars If it's just a beer or two you're after, apart from the licensed restaurants there's *Peanuts Bar* in the market place near the Three Corners Empire in Ad-Dahar. Open 24 hours, this place is the haunt of dive instructors and has Stellas for E£8.50 plus German beers on-tap for E£10 and up. Those with the munchies can stuff themselves on an unlimited supply of unshelled peanuts. On Tuesday nights there are specials for divers.

Papa's Bar, attached to Rossi Pizza in Sigala, is another popular hangout. As with the restaurant, this is a place single women can go without problems. *Bulldog Pub* across the street is another popular drinking spot with divers and Hurghada expats, and often offers free food. Check in *Hurghada Bulletin* for information. Every Thursday night *Hilton Pub* (at the Hurghada Hilton Resort) has a diver's special with limited free Stella. Once it's finished, they cost E£6.

Discos & Nightclubs Most of the bigger hotels offer some sort of spectacle – usually a Russian or African show – as well as belly-dancing performances in their clubs. *Cha Cha Disco* next to the Shedwan Golden Beach Hotel in Ad-Dahar has a happy hour between 10 and 11 pm. Admission is E£15 and you get a card on which your drinks are noted (if you lose this you shell out E£100). In the summer there are open-air discos at *Al-Sakia*, *Hilton Resort* and *Sheraton*. There's also *Shellghada Beach Club*, next to the Safir Hotel, a popular open-air club. The DJ works from a tree house and you dance on the sand.

Also popular are the *Kalaboush* at Arabella Hotel, which has specials almost every night, *Regina* at Sindbad Beach Resort and *The Dome*, at InterContinental. There are also events held at *The Arena* or *Zeituna Beach Bar* out at Al-Gouna, often with transport laid on. Check the listings in *Hurghada Bulletin* for more information.

Casinos There's a casino at the InterContinental Hotel on the resort strip. Admission is free but you might be asked to show your passport. Smart casual dress is required and only foreign currencies are accepted.

Shopping

With the influx of Russian and Eastern European tourists to Hurghada in the past few years, the trade in marine curios has taken off. There's an alarming number of stalls and shops in Ad-Dahar selling everything from stuffed sharks to lamps made out of triggerfish. At the time of writing, the police had started raiding these stalls and many had been shut down. However, if demand warrants it, they'll probably spring up again in the back alleys around the market area. Refusing to buy such hideous *objets d'art* will at least help to break this trade.

Tax-free goods are available at either the Egypt Free Shop opposite EgyptAir on the resort strip or at the new pyramid-shaped emporium at the roundabout in Sigala.

Getting There & Away

Air There are two EgyptAir offices in Hurghada: one (☎ 546 788) is beside the Superjet bus station in Ad-Dahar and the other (☎ 447 503) is on the resort strip almost opposite the Marine Sports Club. There are daily flights between Hurghada and Cairo (E£453 one way), plus three flights per week to Sharm el-Sheikh (E£330) and one each week to Luxor (E£190) and Aswan (E£324, via Luxor).

There are charter flights from various European cities to Hurghada throughout the winter. If you want to head directly to Europe, it is a good idea to check around to see what charters are available for the one-way flight.

Orascom Aviation flies a turbo-prop from Cairo to Al-Gouna airport every Thursday afternoon and returns to Cairo on Saturday evening. Flights cost approximately US$120 return, call ☎ 547 934 for more information.

Bus Two bus companies operate services from Hurghada.

Superjet has its office (☎ 546 768) and terminal near the main mosque in Ad-

Dahar. It has three buses a day to Cairo (six hours), departing at noon, 2.30 and 6 pm (E£47). There's also a daily 2.30 pm bus to Alexandria (E£75, nine hours).

The Upper Egypt Bus Co operates from the main bus station at the southern end of Ad-Dahar from where it runs buses every couple of hours to Cairo (six hours) from 7 am to 12.30 am. They cost E£35 to E£45, depending on the on-board services and the time of day. A couple of these set down in Suez as well, but some bypass it. There are other buses bound only for Suez (E£25 to E£35, five hours) leaving throughout the day.

About 10 Upper Egypt Bus Co buses go daily to Qena (E£8, three hours), starting at 6 am and finishing at 11 pm. Buses to Luxor (E£20 to E£22, five hours) leave at 10 am, 3.30, 10 and 11 pm, and they all go on to Aswan (E£35 to E£40). There are buses to Marsa Alam and Bir Shalatein via Al-Quseir (E£12) and Safaga (E£5) at 5 am, 3 pm and midnight.

There are also daily services to Beni Suef (E£25), Minya (E£30 to E£35), Sohag (E£16) and Asyut (E£20), and regular buses to Qift and Qus. However, the police may not allow you to complete your trip.

These details should be checked with the staff at the bus station, as changes are more than likely. It may be an idea to book ahead on long distance journeys such as Luxor and Cairo.

Service Taxi The service taxi station is near the telephone centrale in Ad-Dahar. Taxis go to Cairo for E£30 per person (six hours). Others go to Port Safaga (E£3), Al-Quseir (E£7), Qena (E£10), Marsa Alam (E£15) and Suez (E£20, 3½ to four hours). They don't go to Luxor or Aswan, although you could always talk one into going. If you bargain hard it'll cost about E£200 for a car that seats 7 people. Keep in mind that you'll have to go in one of the police convoys listed below.

Police Convoys Whether you're going by taxi or private car, if you're heading across to the Nile Valley you're likely to be forced to go in police convoy. They leave from

Hurghada's southernmost checkpoint at 6, 9 and 11 am and 5 pm, but you should check with the tourist office to make sure the times haven't changed.

Boat At the time of writing, two vessels were plying the waters from Hurghada to Sharm el-Sheikh, departing daily (except Wednesday and Friday) from Hurghada.

The old ferry takes five to seven hours to cover the 144km. As the boat is relatively small, it can be an uncomfortable ride if the Red Sea is heaving at all – lie down or look up, and try to ignore the people being sick around you. The service is cancelled when waves east of Shedwan island are above 3m, this usually only happens between November and January. On a more positive note, it's not uncommon to see flying fish or to have dolphins racing beside the boat as you near Ras Mohammed. Although it's possible to get a ticket at the port on the morning, it's safer to book ahead. Most hotels and all travel agents will do this for you. The cost is E£100 one way and the boat departs from the old port in Sigala sometime between 9 and 10 am; you should be there at least half an hour beforehand.

The second boat is a luxury high-speed ferry operated by Travco that departs Hurghada every Monday (5 am and 3.30 pm), Tuesday (6 am and 8 pm) and Saturday (6 am). It also leaves from the old port in Sigala and costs US$33 per person, US$75 per car. The boat is air-con and makes the trip to Sharm el-Sheikh in 1½ hours. For more information call Travco ☎ 446 024/5.

There is also a 'flying boat' from Hurghada to Duba, Saudi Arabia. At the time of writing there were departures four days a week and tickets cost E£160 per person, E£340 per car; the trip takes three hours. Call MenaTours in Cairo (☎ 348 2230) or the Telestar Lines office in Port Safaga (☎ 452 315) for more information.

Getting Around
To/From the Airport A taxi from the airport, which is close to the resort strip, to downtown Ad-Dahar should cost E£10.

Microbus In the mornings, microbuses full of labourers go from anywhere along Sharia an-Nasr almost anywhere along Sharia an-Nasr. Throughout the day, microbuses regularly run from central Ad-Dahar at least as far south as the InterContinental for E£1. This appears to be the terminus. Short rides around Ad-Dahar cost 25pt.

Taxi Taxis from central Ad-Dahar will take you as far south as the Sheraton for about E£10 (or more if there are plenty of tourists around).

Bicycle Bicycles can be rented in Ad-Dahar from Boho, next to Al-Shaymaa Sea Trips on Sharia Abdel Aziz Mustafa, for E£3/10 per hour/day. Be warned, though, strong headwinds can make cycling very hard going.

Hitching While it is possible to hitch around town or out to the beaches, the locals seem accustomed to receiving payment from travellers.

AROUND HURGHADA
Mons Porphyritis
About 40km into the desert, along a side track off the main coast road 20km north of Hurghada, lie ancient porphyry quarries worked by the Romans. The precious white and purple crystalline stone was mined for use in sarcophagi, columns and other decorative work. The quarries were under the direct control of the imperial family in Rome, which had encampments, workshops and even temples built for the workers and engineers here. Evidence, albeit not much of it standing, of this quarry town can still be seen. Tours out of Hurghada increasingly make the trip. Failing that you'll have to hire a taxi.

Sharm an-Naga
About halfway down to Port Safaga, this is a fairly low-key beach resort used mainly by divers, though those with their own tent can also camp. Day-trippers wanting to use the beach (there's some good snorkelling

here) must pay E£10. Masr Travel in Hurghada often runs snorkelling excursions to this spot.

PORT SAFAGA
Port Safaga (often referred to simply as Safaga) is 53km south of Hurghada and is first and foremost a port for the export of phosphates from local mines (and from the mines at Abu Tartur hundreds of kilometres away in the New Valley). During the *haj*, plenty of pilgrims embark here on their voyage to Mecca.

It is hardly an attractive place and there's not much in the way of accommodation for budget travellers, though there are some expensive resorts north of town where you can organise diving and windsurfing courses. The plague of construction around Hurghada is repeated on a smaller scale here.

Orientation & Information
Sharia al-Gomhuriyya, the main road on the waterfront, has most of the services you might need. The bus station is near the southern end of town. Heading north there is a motley collection of small, cheap eateries and tacky souvenir stalls, and beyond them the post office. About 2km north of the bus station is the service taxi station. Next to it is the main telephone centrale and next to this are branches of Banque Masr and Banque du Caire. Further north, next to Maka Hotel, is the Bank of Alexandria. You can catch a microbus up and down Sharia al-Gomhuriyya for 25pt, when heading south many of these vehicles will drop you about 400m north of the bus station. Microbuses also shuttle back and forth between the town and the northern resorts.

Windsurfing
Safaga is a famously windy place and a number of the resort hotels have windsurfing centres. The wind here comes along the coast from the north and the construction boom has not affected it as it has in Hurghada. Shams Safaga hotel (☎ 451 783) (see the following Places to Stay & Eat section) is probably the best known place for

windsurfing and has a German-run Mistral windsurfing centre.

Places to Stay & Eat
The budget options here all seem to be used by truckers waiting for their cargo to arrive at the port. These include the *Maka Hotel* (☎ 451 866) at the northern end of town near the turn-off to Qena, which is a rip-off at E£28 for a shabby double with fan and dirty bathroom, and the marginally better but also overpriced *Al-Ezz Hotel*, with singles/doubles for E£35/40 with private bath.

Cleopatra ASI Hotel (☎ 453 926), a few hundred metres further north of the Maka, is much better, but costs E£69/99 for rooms with bathroom.

Safaga Hotel & Marina (☎ 451 133, fax 452 670), about 200m up from the Cleopatra on the northern edge of town, is a new, ugly resort with air-con rooms starting at US$21/36, including breakfast.

Heading north out of town there are at least six resorts: *Menaville* and *Lotus Bay* are on the main road while *Sun Beach Camp*, *Shams Paradise*, *Holiday Inn* and *Shams Safaga* (see the previous windsurfing section) are all on a side road leading around a bay. *Lotus Bay* (☎ 451 040) is the cheapest of the lot, charging US$41/62 for rooms, half board. At the other end of the scale is *Holiday Inn* (☎ 452 821), charging US$90/100 for rooms, half board.

There is an entire string of cheap eats heading north from the bus station along Sharia al-Gomhuriyya, otherwise, you could try the small *pizzeria* attached to *Cleopatra Hotel* (which, incidentally, also has a bar) or the expensive resort restaurants.

Getting There & Away
Bus There are five buses a day passing through Port Safaga en route to Cairo (E£25 to E£50). These buses stop in Suez (E£40), or there are Suez services (E£22 to E£40) every hour or two, all of which stop in Hurghada (E£2.50 to E£5). Buses to Al-Quseir (E£5 to E£8) leave at 6 am and 1.30 and 4 pm. To Marsa Alam (E£10) there are buses at 1 and 6 am. Regular services to Qena cost

between E£7 and E£10. There are five buses to Luxor (E£15 to E£20) and four to Aswan (E£30 to E£40) each day at 11 am, 1.30 (Luxor only), 4.30 and 11.30 pm and 1 am.

Service Taxi The taxis basically do three routes. Hurghada takes about 40 minutes and costs E£5. The trip to Al-Quseir (try asking early in the morning) costs E£5, Qena E£10, Marsa Alam E£25 and to Suez E£25. Be prepared to haggle.

Boat The only passenger boats from Port Safaga are those going to Duba. There's a daily boat, *Al-Salam al-Seoudi*, which costs E£170 in 1st class, E£120 in 2nd class and E£85 in deck class. It takes about seven hours. Tickets can be bought at the Telestar Line office in Safaga (☎ 452 315/6). There is no longer a regular service to Jeddah, except during the haj. Ask at the Telestar office to see if it's resumed.

AROUND PORT SAFAGA
Mons Claudianus
About 40km along the Qena road, a track breaks off north towards a one-time Roman granite quarry/fortress complex. This stark and impossibly remote place was the end of the line for Roman prisoners brought to hack the granite out of the barren mountains, and was a hardship post for the soldiers sent to guard them. More a concentration camp than a quarry you can still see the remains of the tiny cells that these unfortunates inhabited. There is also an immense cracked pillar, left where it fell 2000 years ago, a small temple and some other remains. You really need a guide for this trip, but the bigger hotels organise excursions. If you have your own vehicle there's a turn-off of sorts to the right on the Qena road. Follow the old broken asphalt as it winds through the mountains and you'll eventually get there.

AL-QUSEIR
The port town of Al-Quseir is 85km south of Port Safaga and about 160km east of Qift on the Nile. Although its history stretches back to pharaonic times, when it was the

launching point for boats sailing to Punt, its ancient port is now silted up and lies some 8km north of town. Still, the 'modern' town is just as interesting. Until the 10th century it was one of the most important ports on the Red Sea and a major exit point for pilgrims travelling to Mecca. It was also a thriving centre of trade and export between the Nile Valley and the Red Sea and beyond. Even in decline it remained a vibrant port and was sufficiently important for the Ottomans to fortify the town in the 16th century. Later the British beat the French for control of it and at one point it was the point of importation for all spices going to Britain from India. However, the opening of the Suez Canal in 1869 put an end to all that and the town's decline sped up, with a brief burst of prosperity as a phosphate processing centre in the early decades of the 20th century.

With its long history and sleepy present, Al-Quseir has a charm absent from Egypt's other Red Sea towns. Dominated by an Ottoman fortress, old coral-block buildings with wooden balconies surround the waterfront in the centre of town and are interspersed by the domed tombs of a number of saints – mostly pious pilgrims who died en route to or from Mecca. Because tourist development has not quite reached this far south (although it's only a matter of time) local people tend to be friendlier and less aggressive than in Hurghada or Port Safaga, making the town well worth visiting.

Orientation & Information
A branch of the National Bank of Egypt is just north-west of the main roundabout on the way into town from Port Safaga. The 24 hour telephone centrale is right on the roundabout, while the post office is off to the east, down towards the waterfront.

Things to See
The 16th century **Ottoman fortress** is the town's most important remaining building. It was modified by the French and then rained on by some 6000 British cannonballs during a heated battle in the 19th century.

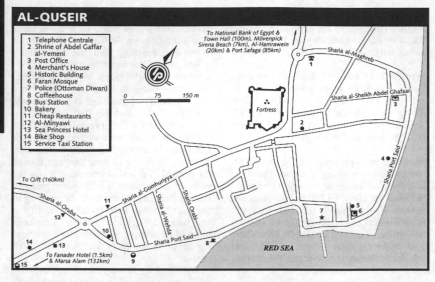

AL-QUSEIR

1 Telephone Centrale
2 Shrine of Abdel Gaffar al-Yemeni
3 Post Office
4 Merchant's House
5 Historic Building
6 Faran Mosque
7 Police (Ottoman Diwan)
8 Coffeehouse
9 Bus Station
10 Bakery
11 Cheap Restaurants
12 Al-Minyawi
13 Sea Princess Hotel
14 Bike Shop
15 Service Taxi Station

To National Bank of Egypt & Town Hall (100m), Mövenpick Sirena Beach (7km), Al-Hamrawein (20km) & Port Safaga (85km)

Sharia al-Maghreb

Sharia al-Sheikh Abdel Ghafaar

Fortress

0   75   150 m

Sharia Port Said

To Qift (160km)

Sharia al-Oruba

Sharia al-Gomhuriyya

Sharia al-Wehda

Sharia Orabi

Sharia Port Said

RED SEA

To Fanader Hotel (1.5km) & Marsa Alam (132km)

The British then added a fortified gate to make sure nobody else could take it away from them. At the time of writing the finishing touches were being put on a restoration of the building, which will house a visitors' centre with displays on local history, Red Sea mining, monasteries and trade and the history of the haj.

Just across from the fortress is the 19th century shrine of a Yemeni sheikh, with the old gravestone in a niche in the wall.

If you wander down to the waterfront you will see the picturesque **police station**, originally an Ottoman *diwan* and later the town hall. Because of its present function you cannot take pictures and you're unlikely to be allowed inside, but there is talk of moving the police to a new location and restoring the building.

If you continue your walk along the waterfront, you will see a newly restored **merchant's house** dating back to the 1920s. Back towards the police station and up a side street is another **historic building**, now a health centre, which dates back to the reign of the Ottoman sultan Selim II. Just

next to it is the **Faran Mosque**, which dates back to 1704.

Places to Stay

The only choice for those travelling on a tight budget is *Sea Princess Hotel* (☎ *431 880*), just south of the bus stop. Small cabin-like singles/doubles with fan cost E£15/20 plus tax. Breakfast is E£5 extra. They have a few masks and snorkels to rent. The toilet/shower combinations can be a bit smelly, but hot water is reliable.

About 1.5km south of the Sea Princess is the four star *Fanader Hotel* (☎ *430 861, fax 431 415*). Named after a rocky islet just to the south, it has 55 adjoining domed bungalows plus two large villas for US$35/60 a single/double, half board.

Top of the range in Al-Quseir is the five star *Mövenpick Sirena Beach* (☎ *432 100, fax 432 128*), 7km to the north of the town. This low-set, domed ensemble is one of the best resorts along the coast – if not the whole country – and is designed to harmoniously blend in with the desert environment. Although it boasts excellent food and the usual five-star amenities, it avoids the glitz so common in Egyptian hotels and evenings are accompanied by the lapping of the waves against the shore rather than a thumping disco beat. The management is famous for its environmentally conscious approach and will haul guests out of the sea if it finds them breaking off coral on the hotel's reef. With a Subex diving centre and wide range of sports on offer, this is the place to go if you want total comfort and relaxation in a beautiful setting. Standard rooms start at US$120/165, including breakfast.

Daly Dive Resort (☎ 432 039, fax 436 661) about 20km north of town at Al-Hamrawein has easy access to some great, unspoilt dive sites and is popular with diving groups from Europe. Independent travellers are welcome to stay if there's room – you'll be looking at US$38/56 a single/double, half board.

If you're heading south towards Marsa Alam there are a couple of other places to look out for. Roughly 20km from Al-Quseir is the unmistakable *Utopia Beach Club*, a green Nile cruiser that was brought here a few years ago and converted into a diving centre. *Mangrove Bay*, is another 30km south.

Places to Eat
Foodwise, the options are very limited. The people at *Sea Princess Hotel* can cook you up something. Otherwise, there are a few ta'amiyya and fish joints around it and the bus station. There is also a bakery close to the bus station. On the road to Qift is a cafe called *Al-Minyawi*, which has the best chicken in town, but you must order in advance. At *Fanader Hotel*, the buffet dinner costs E£60 and is open to nonguests. The best meals to be had around here are at *Mövenpick* but you're looking at least E£75 for the dinner buffet.

The nicest place to have a cup of coffee is at the *coffeehouse* on the waterfront.

Getting There & Away
Bus There are four buses that go all the way through to Cairo (E£55, 11 hours) via

Port Safaga (E£5 during the day, E£8 at night) and via Hurghada (E£10 and E£15), departure times are 5 and 5.30 am, 7.45 and 8.30 pm. The 5 am and 7.45 pm also go to Suez. There are two buses south to Marsa Alam (E£5) at 11.30 am and 1 pm. There are four buses daily to Qena (E£5 to E£10, four hours) via Qift; they leave at 3, 4.30 and 7.30 am and 12.30 pm. There's talk of moving the bus station to a new purpose-built place off the road to Port Safaga but nobody seems in a hurry to leave the town centre.

Service Taxi The service taxi station is at the southern end of town. The officially prescribed fares are: Cairo E£35, Suez E£25, Qena E£8, Hurghada E£7, Port Safaga E£5. As in Hurghada you have to hire the entire taxi for the trip to Luxor. Drivers ask for about E£250 but you may be able to bargain them down. Because of the security situation, you have to go via Port Safaga.

Getting Around
There is a no-name bike shop virtually opposite the service taxi station. The owner wants E£15 for a day's bike rental, but this can probably be bargained down.

AROUND AL-QUSEIR
Wadi Hammamat
About halfway along the road connecting Al-Quseir to the town of Qift, Wadi Hammamat contains a fascinating but rarely visited collection of **pharaonic graffiti**. The wayward chisellings of Wadi Hammamat were first extensively examined by the Russian Egyptologist Vladimir Golenischeff late in the 19th century. The high, smooth walls of the wadi have made it an ideal resting place for travellers through the ages, and indeed there is graffiti from post-pharaonic times as well, right down to Egypt's 20th century King Farouk. The road runs on an ancient trade route, and remains of old wells and other evidence of the trail's long history can also be seen. In Greco-Roman times watch towers were

built along the trail at short enough intervals for signals to be visible.

The police are very nervous about foreigners taking this road these days so you may not be able to go. But you could try to get the early bus from either Al-Quseir or Qena (one leaves each way at 7 am) to drop you at Wadi Hammamat, and try to get a lift on the next one either way about four or five hours later. Other than that you will have to bargain with a taxi driver.

MARSA ALAM

Marsa Alam is a fishing village 132km south of Al-Quseir. A road also connects the village with Edfu, 230km across the desert to the west. Phosphate mining is the big thing in this part of the country, although it is fast being overtaken by tourism. The village is basically a T-junction of the road from Edfu with the coast road. South of the junction is the bulk of the village with a small, incongruous-looking shopping arcade which has a pharmacy, a school and a telephone centrale, from where you can sometimes call overseas. An airport is being built halfway between here and Port Safaga.

The main thing to do here is snorkel or dive. As a military pass (issued from Cairo) is currently required for travel south of Marsa Alam, you may not be able to use what is apparently a particularly good snorkelling beach 7km south of the town. However, as two new resorts were about to open south of here at the time of writing, it is likely that the permit situation will change and, for better or for worse, the area south of here will soon be open for tourists.

About 145km south-west into the desert at Wadi Humaysara is the **Tomb of Sayyed ash-Shadhli**, a 13th century sheikh who is revered by many as one of the more important Sufi leaders. His tomb was restored under the orders of King Farouk in 1947 and there is an asphalt road leading to it, but you're unlikely to make it through the checkpoints. His *moulid*, on the 15th of the Muslim month of Shawal, is attended by thousands of Egyptians and, according to locals, a planeload of Germans, each year.

Places to Stay

Pharaoh's Gold Mining company's rest house (istiraha) is the only place to stay in town but is often fully occupied by employees. If you want to try your luck just look for the cluster of three houses on the northern edge of town about 700m from the Edfu turn-off.

There are three diving camps dotted along the coast heading north from Marsa Alam.

Coral Cove Beach Safari (☎ 364 7970) is about 7km north of the town. Draped around two azure bays, the camp has 10 semipermanent 'tents' and a communal shower block with very limited water. At E£55 per night half board or E£70 full board it's not cheap, but if you've got your own tent you can pitch it here for about E£15. If you do stay here, don't walk along the beach north of the main headland – it's definitely mined. To get there (and to the other camps) you can either bargain for a taxi (E£10 to E£15) from Marsa Alam or you can get the bus or hitch.

Red Sea Diving Safari (☎ 339 9942, fax 349 4219) at Marsa Shaqara, 20km north of Marsa Alam is owned by Hossam Helmi, a lawyer and a committed environmentalist as well as a diving enthusiast. He has 10 tents, 10 huts and 10 stone chalets, at US$30/40/50 full board, respectively. All are spotlessly clean and more comfortable than anything else available on this stretch of coast. Nondivers in search of beautiful vistas and tranquillity are welcome too.

Al-Nabaa, about 20km further north again, is another camp catering mainly to divers. At the moment there are 30 tents and 10 wooden bungalows but a 100 room hotel is planned. Single/double rates are US$20/30, full board.

Places to Eat

In town there are a couple of *cafes* at the junction where you can occasionally get some dubious looking ta'amiyya, and there is a pair of grocery shops with scant supplies. The only other option is the *cafeteria* next to the service station. The young owner is very friendly but the choice of food is limited to stale sandwiches, packet soups and frozen hamburgers. There's a *bakery* next door.

Getting There & Away

The bus across the desert to Marsa Alam departs from Aswan at 6.15 am, passes through Edfu between 8 and 8.30 am and arrives in Marsa Alam about three hours later. It goes on to Bir Shalatein but, at the time of writing, it was unlikely you'd get past the military checkpoint south of Marsa Alam. The bus going back to Aswan (E£10.50) via Edfu (E£9) leaves from the cafes at the T-junction of the Edfu and coast roads at about 7 am.

There are three buses to Al-Quseir (E£5, 1½ hours), departing at 2 and 4 am and 5 pm from where there are more frequent connections to destinations north.

BERENICE

The military centre and small port of Berenice, 150km south of Marsa Alam, was founded in 275 BC by Ptolemy II Euergetes I and was an important trading post until the 5th century AD. Near the town, the ruins of the **Temple of Seramis** can be seen. The US Navy occasionally brings its aircraft carriers here. Apparently, this is one of the staging areas for the US Rapid Deployment Forces. As a military permit is required for land travel south of Marsa Alam, it may not be possible to get this far south down the coast.

BIR SHALATEIN

This tiny village 90km south of Berenice marks the administrative boundary between Egypt and Sudan, although Egypt at least considers the political boundary to be another 175km south-east, beyond the town of Halaib, once an important Red Sea port but long fallen into obscurity.

Some of the best dive sites in the Red Sea are located in this area and dive companies from further north are increasingly organising boat safaris to the region. Divers and the odd desert trekker are about the only civilians who make it this far south these days as all the necessary permits are either arranged well in advance, or hastily put together thanks to a bit of baksheesh by the various dive clubs.

Diving the Red Sea

From mountains of coral that rise from the sea bed, to shallow reefs swarming with fish; from sheer drop-offs that descend to unknown depths, to coral-encrusted ship-wrecks – the Red Sea is a diver's paradise. In 1989 an international panel of scientists and conservationists selected the northern portion of this 1800km-long body of water as one of the Seven Underwater Wonders of the World. Since then its popularity as a diving destination has taken off and thousands of visitors come here each year.

Surrounded by desert on three sides, the Red Sea was formed some 40 million years ago when the Arabian Peninsula split from Africa, allowing the waters of the Indian Ocean to rush in. Bordered at its southern end by the 25km-long straits of Bab al-Mandab, the Red Sea is the only tropical sea that is almost entirely closed. No river flows into it and the influx of water from the Indian Ocean is slight. These unique geographical features combined with the arid desert climate and extremely high temperatures make the sea extremely salty. It is also windy; on average the sea is flat for only 50 days a year.

Diving tends to be concentrated at the northern end of the Egyptian Red Sea. The most popular destinations are around the southern tip of the Sinai Peninsula, most famously the thin strip of land that juts out into the sea and forms **Ras Mohammed National Park** – often called the jewel in the crown of the Red Sea. Another major diving area is the **Straits of Tiran**, which form the narrow entrance to the Gulf of Aqaba. The currents sweeping through the deep narrow channel here allow coral to grow prolifically and attract all manner of marine life. The reefs further north along the Egyptian shores of the Gulf of Aqaba are also popular. On the western side of the Sinai Peninsula lie the **Straits of Gubal** a series of coral pinnacles that lie just beneath the surface of the sea and are famous for snagging ships trying to navigate their way

HIGHLIGHTS

- **Ras Mohammed** Teeming with coral and fish, this world-renowned national park has 20 dive sites to choose from.

- **The Thistlegorm** Bombed in WWII and discovered on the seabed by Jacques Cousteau, this is one of the most sought after wreck dives in the world.

- **The Straits of Tiran** Abundant marine life, a huge variety of dives and a dramatic landscape above.

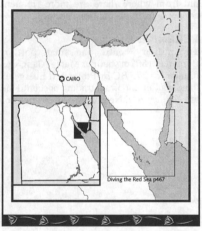

CAIRO

Diving the Red Sea p467

north to the Suez Canal. This is where you will find the majority of Egypt's wrecks, including the famous World War II freighter, the **Thistlegorm**.

Heading south along the Red Sea coast, the best reefs are found around the proliferation of offshore islands and reefs. Although most shore reefs near Hurghada have been damaged by uncontrolled tourist development, further south pristine dive sites can still be reached from the shore.

DIVING THE RED SEA

DIVE SITES
1 Blue Hole, The Bridge
2 The Canyon
3 Oasis
4 Ras Nasrany (The Light)
5 Small & Large Lagoons
6 Jackson Reef
7 Ras Nasrany (The Point)
8 Shark's Bay
9 Gordon Reef
10 The Tower
11 Amphoras
12 Ras Um Sid, Temple
13 Ras Mohammed
14 The Thistlegorm
15 Sha'abal-Erg
16 Fanadir, Fenous
17 Umm Qamar, Careless
18 Sha'ab Torfa
19 Sha'ab Abu Ramada

MARINE LIFE

The Red Sea is teeming with more than 1000 species of marine life and is an amazing spectacle of colour and form. Reef sharks, stingrays, turtles, dolphins, colourful corals, sponges, sea cucumbers and a multitude of molluscs all thrive in these waters.

Coral is what makes a reef and, though thought for many centuries to be some form of flowering plant, it is in fact an animal. Both hard and soft corals exist, their common denominator being that they are made up of polyps – tiny cylinders ringed by waving tentacles that sting their prey and draw it into their stomach. During the day corals retract into their tube and only at night do they display their real colours.

Most of the bewildering variety of fish species in the Red Sea, of which many are endemic, are closely associated with the coral reef, and live and breed in the reefs or nearby seagrass beds. These include grouper, wrasse, parrotfish and snapper. Others, such as shark and barracuda, live in open waters and usually only venture into the reefs to feed or breed.

Code of Ethics for Reef Protection

- Do not collect, remove or damage any material, living or dead (including, for example, coral, shells, fish, plants or fossils).
- Do not touch, kneel on or kick coral. Coral are delicate creatures that are damaged when touched.
- Do not stir up sand as coral uses a lot of energy to remove sand particles, this depletion of energy interferes with their feeding and reduces their growth.
- Do not disturb any part of the reef community by, for example, picking up and playing with sea creatures.
- Do not litter.
- Do not walk or anchor on any reef area. Try to time snorkelling with the high tide, so that you can swim, rather than walk, over the living reef to get to a good drop-off.
- Do not feed fish. This disturbs the reef's ecological balance and can upset the digestive system and natural behaviour of marine creatures.
- Do not fish or spearfish, but do report spearfishing.

When snorkelling or diving, the sharks you're most likely to encounter include white or black-tipped reef sharks. Tiger sharks, and the huge, plankton-eating whale sharks, are generally found in deeper waters only. Shark attacks in the Red Sea are extremely rare, and there are no sea snakes here.

The most common type of turtle in these waters is the green turtle, although the leatherback and hawksbill are occasionally sighted. Turtles are protected in Egypt and, although they're not deliberately hunted, they are sometimes caught in nets and end up on menus in restaurants in Cairo and along the coasts.

As intriguing as they may seem, there are some creatures that should be avoided, especially sea urchins, blowfish, fire coral, feathery lionfish, moray eels, turkeyfish, stonefish, triggerfish and, needless to say, sharks. Familiarise yourself with pictures of these creatures before snorkelling or diving. Single-page colour guides to the Red Sea's most common marine hazards can often be bought in hotel bookshops around diving areas. Providing you don't touch things, or stand on the reef or attempt to feed a moray eel, you shouldn't have too many worries with these creatures.

REEF PROTECTION

The natural wonders of the Red Sea parallel (many would say surpass) the splendours of Egypt's pharaonic heritage, but care is needed if the delicate world of coral reefs and fish is not to be permanently damaged. Almost the entire Egyptian coastline in the Gulf of Aqaba is now a protectorate, as is the Red Sea coast from Hurghada south to Sudan. This means you could be liable to penalties if you violate any of the rules listed in the Code of Ethics below. Divers and snorkellers should heed the requests of instructors *not* to touch or tread on coral. If you kill the coral, you'll eventually kill or chase off the fish too.

The same principle applies with paying baksheesh to do something you shouldn't be doing, such as breaking off a bit of coral or collecting shells to take home as souvenirs. Doing so is illegal and you can be prosecuted. Don't be tempted to flaunt these rules just because you can bribe someone to get around them. As Egypt's National Parks Office gets more clout it is cracking down on offenders and checking bags at the country's exit points. You can be fined and in some cases forbidden from diving here again.

The boxed text 'Code of Ethics for Reef Protection' is something that everybody needs to have in mind before leaving land but if there's one single guideline paramount above all, it's that you should *take nothing with you, leave nothing behind.*

In addition to the code of ethics for reef protection, there are a few other things to keep in mind when diving that will help preserve the ecology and beauty of reefs:

- Do not wear gloves. As you're not touching marine life you won't need them anyway. The wearing of gloves is banned in Ras Mohammed National Park and around the southern islands, but some dive clubs are lax in enforcing this rule.
- Be conscious of your fins. Even without contact the surge from heavy fin strokes near the reef can damage delicate organisms. When treading water in shallow reef areas, take care not to kick up clouds of sand. Settling sand can easily smother the delicate organisms of the reef.
- Practice and maintain proper buoyancy control. Major damage can be done by divers descending too fast and colliding with the reef. Because the Red Sea is so salty you'll need to add extra weight to overcome the increased buoyancy. Make sure you are correctly weighted and that your weight belt is positioned so that you stay horizontal. If you have not dived for a while, have a practice dive in a pool before taking to the reef. Be aware that buoyancy can change over the period of an extended trip: initially you may breathe harder and need more weight; a few days later you may breathe more easily and need less weight.
- Take great care in underwater caves. Spend as little time within them as possible as your air bubbles may be caught within the roof and thereby leave previously submerged organisms high and dry. Taking turns to inspect the interior of a small cave will lessen the chances of damaging contact.
- Resist the temptation to collect or buy corals or shells. Aside from the ecological damage, taking home marine souvenirs depletes the beauty of a site and spoils the enjoyment of others. The same goes for marine archaeological sites (mainly shipwrecks). These sites are protected by Egyptian law and the authorities are cracking down on violators.
- Ensure that you take home all your rubbish and any litter you may find as well. Plastics in particular are a serious threat to marine life. Turtles can mistake plastic for jellyfish and eat it.

A Change of Heart

After much public pressure, the Egyptian government has decided to reopen 15 Red Sea islands to divers and snorkellers. The islands were originally placed off limits due to the destructive impact of tourism on the coral reefs, known to feature some of the best diving and snorkelling in the world. Dive sites off Zabargad, Rocky, Brothers and Abul Kizan islands are now limited to two diving tours a week, with a maximum of six boats per tour containing no more than 15 divers.

DIVE SITES

The following list of dive sites is not exhaustive but does include the most popular destinations.

Dahab Area

Bells A cliff dive that is only for the relatively experienced.

The Blue Hole An 80m-deep pool in the reef, only a few metres out from shore. This infamous deep dive has claimed the lives of many divers in recent years due to nitrogen narcosis or improper use of equipment (which isn't difficult at such a depth). It can't be stressed enough that it is only for very experienced divers, and even then they should be wary – many of those who've lost their lives here have been instructors or divemasters. There is nothing to see down there and, according to some dive club managers, it's way overrated.

The Bridge This dip in the reef close to the Blue Hole attracts much more marine life than the hole itself, and is close enough to the surface to be viewed by snorkellers.

The Canyon A popular shore dive but, to an inexperienced diver, it will seem somewhat harrowing at first. From the shore, you snorkel along the reef before diving, past a wall of coral, to the edge of the Canyon. It is dark, narrow and seems capable of swallowing you. Other sights in the vicinity include Canyon's Table, Abu Talha and Abu Helal.

Eel Garden About 15 minutes walk north of the lighthouse area in Assalah, this is a popular snorkelling spot which is also good for learner divers. The maximum depth is 17m and there's a sandy bottom.

DIVING THE RED SEA

The Islands A collection of coral pinnacles about 18km south of Dahab.

Oasis A secluded spot excellent for a variety of marine life, 8km south of Dahab City. Nearby are the Three Pools.

Sharm el-Sheikh & Na'ama Bay Area

Note that Sanafir Island is off limits to divers and landing on Tiran Island is strictly prohibited – it is mined.

Small & Large Lagoons Off the north-west tip of Tiran Island, featuring a shallow reef and the wreck of the *Sangria*. The currents are strong here, and there is a mooring so that boats don't have to drop anchor onto the reef. The Large Lagoon, just below it, has reef and sand fish.

Jackson Reef Midway between Tiran Island and the mainland, home to sharks and large pelagic fish. There is a 70m drop-off, but be warned: this is not for beginners. The currents are dangerous.

Gordon Reef Close to Ras Nasrany and a popular site with experienced divers. There are sharks and open-water fish here and a wreck on the reef. Thomas and Woodhouse reefs also have some good diving.

Ras Nasrany There are two sites worth noting here: The Light and The Point. There are 40m drop-offs and heaps of reef and pelagic fish.

Shark's Bay A good shore entry dive for beginners but with plenty for more advanced divers, with a sloping reef and deep canyon right offshore. Famous for manta rays.

The Tower South of Na'ama Bay, this is a remarkable wall dropping 60m into the depths just offshore and is frequented by (among other amazing fish) sea horses and ghost-pipe fish. Its deep colours are very good for photography.

Amphoras Also known as Mercury. A Turkish galleon lies at the bottom of the sea here. Evidence of its cargo of mercury can still be seen in among the coral. Other dives between here and Ras Um Sid include Turtle Bay, Paradise and Fiasco.

Ras Um Sid A prime diving site to a deep, sloping wall, easily accessible near the lighthouse. The beautiful coral garden has lots of colourful fan coral and a great variety of fish. Because the small beach here is divided between a number of hotels, nonguest divers and snorkellers must use the access path to the left of the lighthouse.

Temple Three large pinnacles rising to the surface from a depth of about 20m, just around the point.

Ras Mohammed Without doubt, one of the best diving sites in the world. In an attempt to protect the national marine park, the number of boats that can bring in divers is subject to limits and water access is restricted to designated areas. You'll have to organise dives here through the dive clubs. There are 20 dive sites within the park, including Shark Observatory, Sting Ray Alley and Eel Garden – descriptive names! There's a shipwreck (at 10m to 15m) which scattered hundreds of toilet bowls on the ocean floor, and off to the south-west is the wreck of the *Dunraven*, a British vessel which went down (and turned over) in 1876 on a voyage from Bombay to Newcastle in England. Many dive clubs combine diving this wreck with that of the *Thistlegorm*. When you're diving here remember that there are designated access points to reduce damage to reefs.

The Thistlegorm Sinai's most prized wreck, which was discovered by Jacques Cousteau in the 1950s. It was a British war ship that sank with a full consignment of war supplies, including tanks, jeeps and guns, after being bombed during WWII. Rediscovered in 1993, lying at a depth of 17m to 35m to the north-west of Ras Mohammed, it is currently *the* wreck to explore in the Red Sea (though it has already been stripped of much of its wartime memorabilia). It's best dived on an overnight trip, as it takes 3½ hours each way from Sharm el-Sheikh by boat. It is often too rough to dive here.

Sha'ab Abu Nahas A group of small submerged islands at the southern entrance to the Straits of Gubal that have snagged more ships than any other reefs since the opening of the Suez Canal in 1869. One of the most famous in this marine graveyard is the *Carnatic*, which went down in 1879 and, with its rotting wooden beams, is now almost a reef in itself. It's a popular site among divers, along with the nearby wrecks of two Greek cargo ships, the *Giannus D* and the *Chrisoula K*, which both sank in the early 1980s. The three are about 45 minutes by boat from the point of Ras Mohammed but can also be visited from Hurghada, about two hours away.

Hurghada & Safaga

The reefs close to Hurghada have been all but trashed by the unfettered touristic development of the past few years and experienced divers these days look for sites further afield, often sailing at least two hours from Hurghada. Some simply opt for dive clubs further down the coast. With conservation efforts finally being put into place, there is a chance the situation around Hurghada will improve. Some of the best sites near Hurghada and Safaga include:

Shedwan Island 25km-long island with long sheer walls that attract sharks and other pelagic fish. At its northern end is Blind Reef, another deep wall. Accessible by boat from Hurghada.

Sha'ab al-Erg Horseshoe-shaped reef with a shallow lagoon about 1½ hours north of Hurghada. Famous for dolphins and manta rays. Among the many other species around here you can sometimes find whitetips.

Umm Qamar Long, thin reef about 1½ hours north of Hurghada, with a vertical wall plunging down on the east side. Three coral towers just off the wall are swathed in beautiful purple soft coral and surrounded by glassfish.

Carless A mid-sea reef 5km north of Giftun Island and often off-limits because of strong, unpredictable currents. Famous for its two ergs on a plateau leading to a spectacular drop-off. The ergs are surrounded by a forest of coral around which swim swarms of fish, including a group of moray eels.

Fanadir Popular reef close to Hurghada. Coral gardens lead above a ledge that drops off into the depths. Teeming with many different species of fish, but known for stonefish and scorpionfish. Also frequented by dolphins.

Fanous Made up of two reefs, Fanous East and Fanous West, about 45 minutes from Hurghada. Known for dolphins and occasional rare fish sightings, as well as beautiful coral pinnacles.

Giftun Islands A short boat ride from Hurghada and very popular dive destinations, the islands of Giftun Kebir and Giftun Sughayer (Big Giftun and Little Giftun) are surrounded by a number of spectacular reefs teeming with marine life. They include Hamda, Banana Reef, Sha'ab Sabrina and Erg Somaya.

Sha'ab Torfa Long crescent reef in strait between the Giftun Islands, with several types of coral teeming with fish, including clownfish.

Sha'ab Abu Ramada About 11km south-east of Hurghada and nicknamed the aquarium because of its enormous schools of fish.

Tobia Arbaa Just south of Ras Abu Soma, a group of seven 12m-high ergs with stunning coral and fish life.

Gamul Sughayar Only 15 minutes from Port Safaga and the second in a chain of reefs stretching north from Safaga Island. Diveable in any weather and famous for a hollow pillar of coral with gorgonian inside – and, of course, its abundant marine life.

Panorama Surrounds a small island with a beacon just over an hour outside Safaga. A plateau at 15m to 25m leads down to a dramatic drop-off. Large fish abound here and you can see turtles, schools of barracuda, and various species of sharks, rays and dolphins.

Southern (Far) Islands

As Egypt's dive sites become increasingly popular, divers are looking further afield for new underwater vistas. Four islands down in Egypt's southernmost waters, **The Brothers** (Big Brother and Little Brother), **Zabargad**, **Rocky** and **Abu Kizan**, are said to offer some of the best diving in the Red Sea and are coveted destinations for divers. However, they have only recently been re-opened after a three year hiatus, during which a conservation and management plan was drawn up and mooring buoys installed. Access here is strictly regulated and in the first six months after opening only one boat, *Orchid I*, was given permission to go, although recently another, *Oyster*, has also been licensed. Divers going here must have completed a minimum of 50 dives. Night diving or landing on the islands is prohibited and national park rules apply, so fishing, spear-fishing and the use of gloves are banned. Permission must be given for each trip and a park ranger will accompany boats to ensure that the rules are being enforced and to monitor the site.

If you've been offered a trip to these remote areas, you might want to call the National Park office in Hurghada or Sharm el-Sheikh to check that the boat is licensed; if you are caught on an unlicensed boat you could have your own equipment or belongings confiscated and find yourself in custody. Even if you do make it to the islands, the strong currents and choppy seas often mean you can't even get in the water. But if you do, you'll be rewarded by spectacular and rarely visited reefs and amazing marine life. As veterans of these islands will tell you, once you've dived there nothing else will compare.

DIVE CLUBS

As Egypt's Red Sea and Sinai coasts continue to develop at a break-neck speed, the number of dive clubs is mushrooming. Almost all of the large resorts in Sinai and along the Red Sea have a dive centre. There are also smaller places, some of which have been around for years and some of which are fly-by-night outfits set up by someone out to cash in on the popularity of the area for divers. Given the huge choice, there is something to suit everyone. Some clubs are laid-back and informal, others are slick and structured, but two considerations should be uppermost in your mind when deciding on which one to use: the club's attention to safety and its sensitivity to the environmental issues already discussed.

Safety Concerns

There is no regulatory body responsible for overseeing dive clubs in Egypt and although most are well-equipped and staffed by professionals, some are not. Accidents do occasionally happen as a result of neglect so it is important to check a club carefully before diving with them. A few common sense safety measures include:

- Take your time when choosing clubs and dive sites – don't let yourself be pressured into accepting something, or someone, you're not comfortable with.
- Don't choose a club based solely on cost. Safety should be your paramount concern and if a dive outfit cuts corners to keep prices low, you could be in danger.
- If you haven't dived for more than three months, take a check-out dive. This is for your own safety and the cost is usually put towards your later dives.
- If you're taking lessons, ensure that the instructor speaks your language well. If you can't understand him/her, request another.
- Make sure all equipment is clean and stored away from the sun.
- Check all hoses, mouthpieces and valves for cuts and leakage.

- Make sure wet suits are in good condition. Some divers have reported getting hypothermia because of dry, cracked suits.
- Make sure that there is oxygen on the dive boat in case of accidents.
- If you're in Sinai, ask if the club donates US$1 per diver each day to the decompression chamber; this is often a reflection of safety consciousness.

Diving Courses

Dive clubs in Egypt offer a variety of certifications. PADI, NAUII, SSI and CMAS are all taught here, although PADI is the most popular. Prices vary but not greatly. PADI open-water dive courses, which usually take five (intensive) days, cost between US$250 and US$330. When comparing prices, check to see whether the certification fee is included. If not, it is an extra US$30.

Beginner courses are designed to drum into you things that have to become second nature when you're under water. They usually consist of classroom work, where you learn the principles and basic knowledge needed to dive, followed by training in a confined body of water, such as a pool, before heading out to the open sea. If you've never dived before and want to give it a try before you commit yourself, all dive clubs offer introductory dives for between US$35 and US$50, including equipment.

Most of the well-established clubs on the Red Sea also offer a variety of more advanced courses. An Advanced open-water course will cost in the region of US$220, while you're looking at about US$80 to US$100 for a one-day Medic First Aid course. Some of the clubs offer professional level courses or training in technical diving. Again, prices vary but most are in the region of about US$500 for a divemaster course.

Equipment

Operators all rent scuba and snorkelling equipment, usually at competitive prices. Some divers prefer to bring their own masks, snorkels and fins, and some like to have their own regulator, but all these are

The inviting blue waters of the Red Sea have long been a favourite destination for divers, but Sharm el-Sheikh's sheltered lagoons are also the perfect place for snorkelling.

The Red Sea swarms with more than 1000 species of marine life. Many of these species are endemic, in particular the vast array of fish which live within the thriving coral reef.

Red Sea divers should familiarise themselves with pictures of the poisonous lionfish.

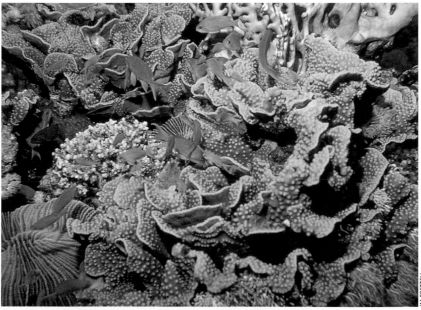

Divers must resist the temptation to touch the beautiful but delicate coral.

A goby keeps an eye out for predators from its home within the coral reef.

A baby clown anenome fish.

The bizarre and colourful spotted nudibranch.

A mushroom coral growing at the base of red Gorgonia fans.

available for rent. Masks and snorkels usually go for US$4 and US$1 per day respectively. Full scuba equipment is in the region of US$20 to US$35 per day.

Despite the intense desert heat of the Egyptian coast the waters of the Red Sea are surprisingly cool and you'll need some sort of wetsuit for diving, even in the summer. In winter you may even need a dry suit. Again, although many people like to bring their own, these are all available for between US$6 and US$20 per day, depending on the type and size.

Trips

When you agree to dive with a club, make sure you know where they are going to take you. Apart from seeing the best coral, it is important to ensure that you are experienced enough for the site. Sometimes dive centres will put a novice on a boat going to reefs that demand a high level of expertise. A reputable dive club should not do this but if you feel unsure of yourself, ask to go somewhere else.

If you're going to Ras Mohammed or Nabq Protected Area remember that you may have to pay the US$5 park fees in addition to the cost of the dive. Make sure you bring your passport with you too. There are often supplementary charges for going to the wrecks in the Straits of Gobal. Usually you're looking at US$15 to US$20 extra for a dive at the *Dunraven*. Day trips from Sharm el-Sheikh to the *Thistlegorm* go for between US$75 to US$100, depending on whether food is included.

Many clubs organise dive safaris to remote sites ranging from one night to two weeks. When it comes to 'liveaboard' dive safaris, the cost varies according to the boat. The choice, especially around Hurghada, is wide and although you can negotiate directly with captains, arrangements are usually made through the dive clubs, many of which have at least one or two boats of their own. Make sure you see the boat before agreeing to sail on it. Also, if a trip is very cheap, check whether or not the cost of diving and food are included.

Clubs

Sharm el-Sheikh & Na'ama Bay There are dozens of dive clubs around this area, which is not surprising considering its popularity for divers. The following are just a few of the more respectable ones:

African Divers (☎/fax 660 307, email african@ sinainet.com.eg) PADI, NAUII, CMAS, SSI. Run by Claude and Liza Antoine and with its own liveaboard, this is a reputable and long-standing club that is known for catering to individuals.

Anemone (☎ 600 995, email anemone@sinainet .com.eg) PADI, NAUI, SSI. Laid-back centre based at the Pigeon House Hotel.

Aquamarine Diving Centre (☎ 600 276, fax 600 176) PADI. Based at the Novotel, this is a popular, reputable club offering a wide variety of diving possibilities. It runs courses through the Red Sea Diving College.

Aquanaute (☎ 600 187, fax 600 619) PADI. A Belgian outfit with a good reputation, near the New Tiran Village.

Camel Dive Club (☎ 600 700, fax 600 601, email reservations1@cameldive.com) PADI, CMAS, NAUII, SSI. Just up from the Sanafir, a highly respected club owned by long-time Sinai diver Hisham Gabr. It also has facilities for disabled divers.

Oonas Diving Centre (☎ 600 581) PADI. At the northern end of the bay. This is a popular cheery centre and, for those following a course, it offers reasonably cheap (by Sharm el-Sheikh standards) accommodation: air-con rooms cost US$40/60 including breakfast. See also Organised Tours in the Getting There & Away chapter.

Red Sea Diving College (☎ 600 313, fax 600 312, email college@sinainet.com.eg) PADI. Operates in conjunction with Scuba Pro International, which provides one of the world's best diving curricula. It runs courses only and also has reasonably cheap accommodation for course members: B&B in an air-con dorm (eight beds) for U$10.

Sinai Divers (☎ 600 150, email sinai_divers@ sinainet.com.eg) PADI, CMAS, SSI. At the Ghazala Hotel, offering 20% discounts to members of the Cairo Divers Group.

Subex (☎ 600 100) CMAS. Swiss-based dive club at the Mövenpick Hotel with years of experience in the Red Sea.

Dahab Apart from the very good local reefs, the advantage to diving here is the camel/dive safaris on offer. Most involve a day trip by jeep and camel along the desert shore to a remote offshore dive site. You can spend the night or return the same day. It's a great way of combining desert travel with underwater adventure. There are currently 22 dive clubs in Dahab, although not all of them have reputable safety records. The following dive clubs come with the best reputations:

Club Red (☎ 640 380, email clubred@intouch .com) PADI. Offers technical diving certificates as well as regular diving packages. There's a new-age element with the massage and yoga on offer, but they swear it helps with the diving.

Fantasea Dive Centre (☎/fax 640 043, email fdc@intouch.com) PADI, SSI. Owned by Chris Harding and Mohammed Rafaie, an Australian/Egyptian couple who recently set up on the northern end of Assalah. At the time of writing, the club was building accommodation for its divers. They do one day camel/diving safaris for US$85.

Inmo (☎ 640 370, fax 640 372, Web site www .inmodivers.com) PADI. Run by Mohammed and Ingrid al-Kabany. One of the first dive clubs to start operating in Dahab, it has an attractive domed complex, with hotel accommodation and restaurant, and offers the full range of diving services. Its three day camel/diving safari goes to virgin dive sites south of Dahab and costs US$115 a day. You can contact them through their Web site.

Nesima Dive Centre (☎ 640 320, fax 640 321, email nesima@intouch.com) PADI. A well-managed and highly reputable club owned by local environmental activist and veteran diver Sherif Ebeid. Also has a very pleasant hotel attached (see Places to Stay in the Dahab section in the Red Sea Coast chapter). One-day camel/diving safaris cost US$85.

Sphinx Dive Centre (☎ 640 458, fax 640 032, email sphinx_d@intouch.com) PADI, NAUI. Managed by the energetic Arman Gazeryan, this centre has a good reputation and is one of the few in Dahab that is not exclusively PADI certified.

Nuweiba Nuweiba doesn't have as much diving on offer as the resorts further south, but there are three centres to choose from, if you happen to find yourself there.

Aquasport (☎ 520 321, fax 520 327) PADI. In the Nuweiba Hilton Coral Resort. Offers the usual pen-water courses for US$275 plus US$80 for all the extras.

Diving Camp Nuweiba (☎ 500 402) PADI, CMAS. Run by Hartmut Janssen and Sylvia May in the Helnan Nuweiba Hotel, it offers the usual courses but is considerably more expensive than dive clubs in Dahab or Na'ama Bay. CMAS certificate courses for beginners cost US$330; the manual, log books and certificate are US$25 extra. The club's boat has been heavily criticised for anchoring on coral, so check this situation out carefully before agreeing to dive here.

Scuba Divers La Siréne (☎ 500 701, fax 500 702, email SCUBA@gega.net) SSI. German-run centre that does shore diving as well as two to seven-day dive safaris for a minimum of two people for about US$115 per day.

Hurghada & Red Sea Coast Because the offshore reefs of Hurghada are not as rich as they once were, this is the place for 'live-aboards': dive safaris, usually of several days to a week, which take in distant sites ranging from the relatively close Shedwan Island to the distant shores south of Marsa Alam. With more than 122 dive centres to choose from, the following is only a small sample.

Aquanaut Red Sea (☎ 549 891, fax 547 045, email peterd@hurghada.ie-eg.com) PADI. Founder member of the Hurghada Quality Dive Club, a group of clubs who try to maintain basic standards of safety and service. This club has multilingual staff and two custom-built liveaboards.

Daly Dive (Cairo ☎ 383 0447, fax 388 3470, email dalytv1@intouch.com). Well-established dive centre in Al-Hamrawein, 65km south of Safaga, with its own liveaboard. Popular with European dive groups.

Jasmin Diving Center (☎/fax 446 455, email jasmindc@intouch.com) PADI, SSI. In the Jasmin Hotel, Hurghada, this is another member of the Hurghada Quality Dive Club. Runs dive safaris from its own liveaboards.

Red Sea Diving Center (☎ 442 960, fax 442 234, email wrkneip@intouch.com) PADI, SSI, CMAS. Highly reputable long-standing diving centre in Hurghada, formerly known as Rudi Kneip. Another founder of the Hurghada Quality Dive Club. Has six liveaboards and gives instruction in English and German.

Red Sea Diving Safari (☎ 337 1833, fax 349 4219, email redseasaf@hotmail.com). In Marsa Shagara, near Marsa Alam. Run by environmentalist Hossam Hassan on a quiet unspoiled bay. Has two liveaboards for offshore diving.

Red Sea Scuba Schools (☎ 444 854, email info hurghada@emerordivers.com) PADI. At Hilton Resort in Hurghada. Has a branch in Sharm el-Sheikh. Also known as Emperor Divers.

Shams Safaga Diving Center (☎ 451 781, fax 451 780) PADI. Reputable diving centre in Shams Safaga Resort that is about to open a new divers lodge some 40km south of Marsa Alam.

Sharm al-Naga Dive Center (☎ 444 109, email willys@red-sea.com) PADI, CMAS, NAUI. Dutch-managed diving centre, on a secluded bay between Hurghada and Safaga at Sharm al-Naga on Safaga road, gives instruction in six languages. There is tented accommodation on the beach for divers; also offers safaris.

Sub Aqua (☎ 442 473, email subaqua@red-sea.com) PADI, NAUI, CMAS. Branch of Diveteam Sub Aqua at Sofitel Hotel, Hurghada, which specialises in diving around the world.

Subex
This well-known Swiss outfit has three branches on the coast: Subex Hurghada (☎ 547 593, fax 547 471) is in Ad-Dahar, Subex Paradiso (☎ 547 934, fax 547 933) is out at Al-Gouna, while Subex Quseir is at the Mövenpick in Quseir (☎ 432 100, fax 432 124).

TIPS FOR SAFE DIVING IN THE RED SEA

You've chosen your club, you've got your gear, and you've memorised reef protection measures, so there's just one more thing to remember – use your head.

There were more than 22 diving fatalities around Sinai in 1997 and most were due to divers forgetting some of the basic rules of diving. In Dahab, where the majority of accidents occurred, drink and drugs often played a starring role in these tragic and largely avoidable deaths. Many of those who lost their lives were experienced divers who should have known better than to go beyond safety limits or dive under the influence. Others were divers who were not experienced enough for the situations they found themselves in – next time you complain about having to take a check-out dive, remember that dive clubs have a reason to be cautious.

The following are a few common-sense tips for safe diving.

• Don't drink and dive. Of 160 serious cases seen by the folks at the decompression chamber in Sharm el-Sheikh in 1997, 46% involved people who'd been drinking the night before. Alcohol dehydrates, especially in a dry climate like Egypt's, and increases your susceptibility to decompression sickness.

• If you are taking any prescription drugs, inform your medical examiner that you intend to be diving. Sometimes drugs can affect your metabolism and your dosage might need to be changed.

• Dive within your scope of experience. The Red Sea's clear waters and high visibility often lull divers into going too deep. The depth limit for sports divers is 30m. Stick to it.

• Do not fly within 24 hours of diving. You should not climb above 300m either, so don't take that trip to St Katherine's Monastery or into the Eastern Desert mountains the day after a dive.

• Make sure you can recognise your boat from in the water. Some dive sites get crowded and boats can look similar from underneath. It's not unknown for divers to get left behind because they didn't realise that their boat had left without them.

• Get insured. The most reputable clubs will make insurance a condition for diving with them. If something happens to you, treatment in the decompression chamber can cost as much as US$6000. If you hadn't planned to dive before arriving in Egypt, many of the better clubs can provide insurance. The recompression chamber in Sharm el-Sheikh can help too.

Emergency Information

Note, the VHF emergency channel is 16.

Sharm el-Sheikh
(☎ 660 922/3) Hyberbaric Medical Center. Recompression chamber run by Dr Adel Taher (mobile ☎ 012-212 4292).

Hurghada
(☎ 442 625, fax 442 255) Recompression centre at Megawish Village is run by Dr Hossam Nasef (☎ 442 625, mobile 012-218 7550).

The following people are hyperbaric specialists: Dr Wael Nasef (☎ 442 350), Dr Ehab (☎ 442 519), Willy Schmidhamer (hyperbaric paramedic) (☎ 444 109).

FURTHER INFORMATION

There's no shortage of glossy coffee table books with beautiful photos of Red Sea flora and fauna on sale at hotel bookshops around Egypt's Red Sea resorts. More useful for divers are guides to the area's dive sites. One of the best is *The Red Sea Diver's Guide: Volume 2, From Sharm el-Sheikh to Hurghada* by Shlomo & Roni Cohen. It gives detailed descriptions of dive sites around Sharm el-Sheikh and Hurghada, including photographs, information on currents, and what type of fish you're likely to see.

Useful, though not nearly as extensive, is John Ratterree's *Diving and Snorkelling Guide to the Red Sea*. A slim volume, it has some beautiful photographs and information on 32 dive sites covering the Red Sea from Eilat as far south as Eritrea.

Hurghada's first (and so far only) environmental NGO, HEPCA, has published its own guide to the sites around Hurghada and Safaga: *The Official HEPCA Dive Guide*. Available at HEPCA's office in Hurghada (see the Hurghada section for more information) it costs E£70 and the proceeds go towards maintaining the mooring buoys they have installed throughout the area. The guide details 46 sites with artists' drawings and diagrams; it also has a small fish index.

The Egyptian government's Virtual Dive Center on the Web has excellent, detailed descriptions of more than 73 dive sites, along with ratings of the level of expertise needed to dive there (although they tend to underestimate slightly). Go to www.tour egypt.net and click on the 'Red Sea Virtual Diving Center'. Less informative but sometimes helpful is www.red-sea.com which has an index of dive centres and liveaboards as well as some other information on the Red Sea.

Sinai

Sinai, a region of awesome and incredible beauty, has been a place of refuge, conflict and curiosity for thousands of years. Wedged between Africa and Asia, its northern coast is bordered by the Mediterranean Sea, and its southern peninsula by the Red Sea gulfs of Aqaba (east side) and Suez (west side). Row upon row of barren, jagged, red-brown mountains fill the southern interior, surrounded by relentlessly dry, yet colourful, desert plains. From the palm-lined coast, dunes and swamps of the north to the white-sand beaches and superb coral reefs of the Red Sea, Sinai is full of contrasts.

In pharaonic times, the quarries of Sinai provided enormous quantities of turquoise, gold and copper. The great strategic importance of the 'Land of Turquoise' also made it the goal of empire builders and the setting for countless wars.

Sinai is the 'great and terrible wilderness' of the Bible, across which the Israelites journeyed in search of the Promised Land and were delivered from the Egyptian army with the celebrated parting of the Red Sea. It was here that God is said to have first spoken to Moses from a burning bush and it was from the summit of Mt Sinai that God delivered his Ten Commandments to Moses:

Tell the children of Israel; Ye have seen what I did unto the Egyptians ... If ye will obey my voice and keep my covenant, then ye shall be a peculiar treasure unto me above all people: for all the earth is mine. And ye shall be unto me a kingdom of priests, and a holy nation.

And Mount Sinai was altogether in smoke, because the Lord descended upon it in fire; and the whole mount quaked greatly ... And the Lord came down upon Mount Sinai ... and called Moses up to the top of the mount ... And God spoke all these words, saying, I am the Lord thy God, which have brought thee out of the land of Egypt, out of the house of bondage. Thou shalt have no other gods before me ...

(Exodus 19:4-6;19:18-20:3)

HIGHLIGHTS

- **The Red Sea** Lose yourself in another world diving among the underwater wonders at Ras Mohammed National Park.

- **Embark on a camel/dive safari** Combine desert and underwater adventure with the help of the Bedouin of Dahab.

- **Trekking** Discover hidden oases and mountain springs on a trek through the rugged Sinai desert.

- **Sunrise from Mt Sinai** Get inspired on the slopes where Moses received the Ten Commandments and spend the night up there to see the first light creep across the mountains.

- **The Coloured Canyon** Listen to the eerie silence and see the subtle desert palette of one of Sinai's most famous rock formations.

- **Serabit al-Khadim** See how far the pharaohs would go for turquoise at this remote temple and ancient mine.

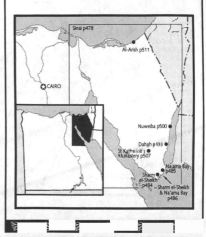

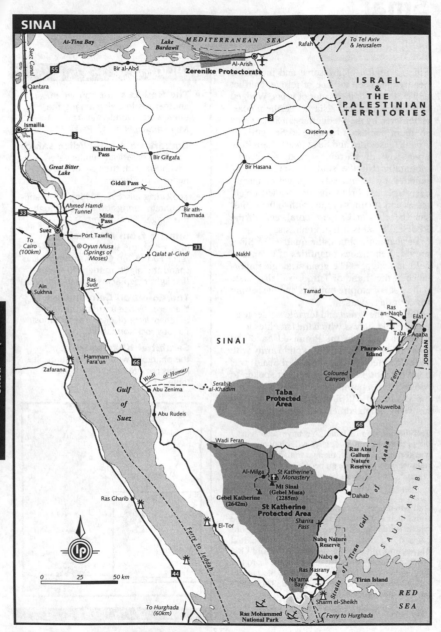

SINAI

MEDITERRANEAN SEA

At-Tina Bay

Lake Bardawil

Rafah

To Tel Aviv & Jerusalem

Suez Canal

55

Bir al-Abd

Al-Arish

Zerenike Protectorate

Qantara

3

ISRAEL & THE PALESTINIAN TERRITORIES

Ismailia

3

Khatmia Pass

Bir Gifgafa

Bir Hasana

Quseima

Great Bitter Lake

Giddi Pass

Ahmed Hamdi Tunnel

Mitla Pass

Bir ath-Thamada

33

Suez

Port Tawfiq

To Cairo (100km)

Oyun Musa (Springs of Moses)

Qalat al-Gindi

33

Nakhl

Ain Sukhna

Ras Sudr

Tamad

Ras an-Naqb

Eilat

Taba

Aqaba

SINAI

JORDAN

Hammam Fara'un

66

Wadi al-Homur

Serabit al-Khadim

Taba Protected Area

Pharaoh's Island

Coloured Canyon

Zafarana

Abu Zenima

Gulf of Suez

Abu Rudeis

Nuweiba

66

Ras Abu Gallum Nature Reserve

Wadi Feran

Al-Milga

St Katherine's Monastery

Mt Sinai (Gebel Musa) (2285m)

Gulf of Aqaba

Ras Gharib

Gebel Katherine (2642m)

St Katherine Protected Area

Dahab

SAUDI ARABIA

El-Tor

Sharira Pass

Ferry to Jeddah

Nabq Nature Reserve

Nabq

Ras Nasrany

Na'ama Bay

Strait of Tiran

Tiran Island

0   25   50 km

44

RED SEA

To Hurghada (60km)

Sharm el-Sheikh

Ferry to Hurghada

Ras Mohammed National Park

SINAI

In recent years Sinai has become the focus of development and 'reconstruction' in much the same way as the New Valley in the Western Desert was during the 1970s and 1980s, when landless *fellaheen* (peasant farmers) from an overcrowded Nile Valley were encouraged to move to the oases. The government has built a new pipeline, called the Al-Salam Canal, to bring freshwater from the Suez Canal to various areas of North Sinai targeted for resettlement. Roads are being paved and desalination plants are being installed in coastal towns. Tourism, too, has made great inroads in the last 15 or so years, especially around the south-east. Surveys estimate that the southern tourist town of Sharm el-Sheikh has seen its population increase eight times during the past decade. The Bedouin, the traditional inhabitants of Sinai, are now a minority in their native land and have little means to resist all this change.

Geology
Some of Egypt's most striking geological features appear in Sinai. Sandstone and granitic mountains are cut by deep wadis and coral reefs embrace the peninsula. Here, some 40 million years ago, the African and Arabian continental plates began to move apart, creating the rather shallow (95m deep) Gulf of Suez and the much deeper (1800m) Gulf of Aqaba. The Gulf of Aqaba, which varies from 14km to 25km in width, is actually part of a rift (a crack in the earth's top layer) which extends for some 6000km from the Dead Sea in Israel through the Red Sea, Ethiopia and Kenya down to Mozambique in southern Africa.

Climate
It gets hot in Sinai, so remember to carry water always, use copious amounts of sun screen, wear sensible clothes to avoid sunburn (wearing a T-shirt while snorkelling is advisable) and use a hat or scarf. While summer temperatures can climb to 50°C (120°F), it gets very cold at night and the mountains can be freezing even during the day; come prepared with warm clothing.

Warning – Land Mines

Despite what local tour operators may tell you, some areas of Sinai still contain land mines left over from the wars with Israel. Don't rely on tourist operators, signs or barbed wire to alert you to a potentially dangerous area and be very wary about going off the beaten track as there are no warnings. Two American tourists were killed in mid-1995 after going off-track with a guide in the area around the well travelled Nabq protectorate. Flash floods sometimes carry mines away from their original location so that even Bedouin who know the area occasionally fall victim. Wherever you go, stick to tracks and don't explore that pristine beach until you've checked that it's safe with locals.

Camping out in winter definitely requires a sleeping bag – it has been known to snow on Mt Sinai.

Information
Visas If you're entering Egypt by way of Sinai from Israel, you will need an Egyptian visa. This can only be obtained before you get to the border.

If you intend only to visit the eastern Sinai coast from Taba down to Sharm el-Sheikh, you can get a 14 day pass at the border. See the Getting There & Away chapter and the Taba section later in this chapter for more information on crossing from Israel into Egypt.

In Sinai visa extensions are available only from the office in El-Tor.

Money Changing money in Sinai is not a problem. The banks and hotels in Sharm el-Sheikh, Na'ama Bay, Dahab, Nuweiba, Taba, St Katherine's Monastery and Al-Arish will change cash, travellers cheques and occasionally accept credit cards.

Water Sports
Although Sinai's waters are most famous for diving, they are becoming increasingly

SINAI

Balancing Sinai's Ecosystem

Although much of Sinai is hot dry desert, it is not devoid of life. A very delicate ecosystem is in place; however, it's under direct threat from the onslaught of tourism.

Sinai is a unique land of craggy mountains sliced by dry gravel wadis in which the odd acacia tree or clump of gnarled tamarisk manages to survive. On the edge of all this are the coastal dunes where a variety of plants tenuously hold onto life in loose, sandy soil. Once every few decades, when storm clouds gather over the mountains and dump colossal amounts of water on this parched landscape, the entire scene is transformed into a sea of greenery. Seeds that have lain dormant in the soil for years suddenly burst into life. For Sinai's wildlife, such as the gazelle and rock hyrax (as well as for the goats herded by local Bedouin), these rare occasions are times of plenty.

Up until relatively recently, the only people to wander through this region were Bedouin on camel; nowadays, groups of tourists looking for outback adventure and pristine spots are ploughing their way through in 4WD vehicles and quads (four wheeled motorcycles) which churn up the soil, uproot plants and create erosion. Aware of the danger this poses to Sinai's ecosystem, the authorities have banned vehicles from going off-road in certain areas, such as Ras Mohammed National Park and in the protected areas of Nabq and Ras Abu Gallum. Soon these rules will also apply to the new Taba National Monument, site of the Coloured Canyon and other popular off-road trips. But banning something and actually enforcing it in areas as vast as these are two different things. Rangers do patrol protectorates but it's largely up to tourists themselves to follow the rules. So try not to be persuaded by over-eager guides wanting to show you something that's off the beaten track. If you really want to explore the region in depth, do it in the age-old fashion – go by foot or hire a camel.

A much more obvious impact of tourism is rubbish. Each year, volunteer clean-ups of beaches and reefs yield several tons of garbage. In 1997, a month-long cooperative effort by local dive centres and nongovernmental organisations to clear Dahab of garbage yielded a colossal 5000 cubic tons of debris. In late 1998, Lonely Planet helped fund a clean-up in the Abu Gallum protectorate. A total of 640kg of garbage was found on the reef alone. Even more was found on land. Why ruin a beautiful place by leaving garbage in the water, on the beach or in the mountains? Carry out all rubbish with you, and dispose of it thoughtfully.

On the bright side, isolated efforts are being made to resist the tide of junk. Apart from the clean-ups, the establishment of new protectorates in St Katherine and around Taba, and the increasingly strict enforcement of national park rules in other protected areas is helping these vulnerable sites resist the onslaught of tourism. It's still far from perfect, but any sign of improvement is welcome. Treat Sinai, above and below the sea, with care and do what you can to preserve the natural beauty of this very special place.

well known for other water sports. For those wary of donning oxygen tanks and descending into the depths, many of the area's spectacular reefs can be seen by snorkellers. All the major tourist centres also offer glass-bottomed boats for those who don't want to get wet. Most of the resort towns also offer jet skis, despite them being illegal. Banana boats and parasailing are also on offer.

With the steady winds that blow down both sides of the peninsula, the parts of Sinai's coast that have not been over-developed offer excellent windsurfing. One of the most famous places for those in the know is Moon Beach Resort at Ras as-Sudr, where the British magazine *Boards* tests equipment each year. Dahab is also famous for its offshore winds. See the relevant sections for hotels offering windsurfing.

Getting Around
The few paved roads through the desert and hills link only the permanent settlements, and transport is not as regular as elsewhere in Egypt. You can get to most places by bus, but in many cases there are only a couple of connections a day, sometimes only one. Service taxis, in the organised sense of the word, do not exist. As drivers in Suez will tell you, beyond the coast route to El-Tor, you can only get hold of a service taxi by bargaining and paying far more than would be the case over similar distances elsewhere in Egypt. The reason is simple: there are not enough locals around in need of a fully built up transport system.

If you are driving yourself, you will see occasional signs forbidding foreigners to leave the roads. This is rarely enforced these days but you should still exercise care. When at the wheel in winter, remember that it rains in Sinai more than you might think and that flash floods often wash out paved roads, particularly around Wadi Feran. Taxi drivers will often know of any trouble spots.

OYUN MUSA
Oyun Musa, or the 'springs of Moses', is said to be the place where Moses, on discovering that the water there was too bitter to drink, took the advice of God and threw a special tree into the springs, miraculously sweetening the water.

Seven of the 12 original springs still exist and, around them, a small settlement has grown up. The palm trees are a bit unusual, as most have had their crowns blown off in various Sinai wars and still haven't quite returned to their previous state.

Oyun Musa is about 25km south of the Ahmed Hamdi Tunnel, which goes under the Suez Canal near Suez. Completed in 1982, the 1.6km-long tunnel is named after a martyr of the 1973 war and is now open

24 hours. Camping at Oyun Musa is possible but, as the spring water is too brackish, there is no drinkable water – and there's no sign of the special tree that Moses used.

Getting There & Away
The buses from Cairo (six per day) and from Suez (leaving at 11 am and 3 pm) to Sharm el-Sheikh and St Katherine's Monastery pass through Oyun Musa.

RAS AS-SUDR
Ras as-Sudr, or Sudr, is about 60km south of the Ahmed Hamdi Tunnel. The town developed around one of the country's biggest oil refineries, yet because of its proximity to it has also become a resort area. At the time of writing, a large number of new tourist villages were under construction starting from about 35km south of the tunnel and stretching south of Sudr, most geared to weekenders from Cairo.

Places to Stay & Eat
About 10km north of Sudr, there's a cluster of decidedly shabby resorts, including *Al-Mahrosa* and *Mesalla Beach*. *Banana Beach Village* (☎/fax 247 5258) has been renovated and has single/double rooms for E£100/140, on a half-board basis.

Helnan Royal Beach Hotel (☎ 400 101), just south of Sudr, has the usual resort amenities, including muzak piped throughout the hotel. Rooms cost US$70/90, not including breakfast or taxes. It advertises itself as a windsurfing destination but the winds are choppy and unreliable because of the enormous amount of construction going on here.

Further south still, about 38km from Ras as-Sudr, is the three star *Moon Beach Resort* (☎/fax 336 5103) which offers beachfront bungalows with balconies, air-con and fridges for E£145/230, half-board. A famous windsurfing destination (see the Water Sports section earlier), it offers lessons for E£70 per hour, including equipment, and the price goes down with the number of hours reserved. Deals are available to windsurfers who book from outside

SINAI

Egypt. In the UK you can book on ☎ 01580-753 824.

Getting There & Away

All buses from Cairo and Suez to Sharm el-Sheikh and St Katherine's Monastery pass through Sudr. The journey from Suez takes about 1½ hours.

QALAAT AL-GINDI & NAKHL

About 80km south-east of the Ahmed Hamdi Tunnel is Qalaat al-Gindi, which features the 800 year old Fortress of Salah ad-Din. In the 12th century AD, Muslims from Africa and the Mediterranean streamed across Sinai on their way to Mecca. As the three caravan routes they followed all converged at Qalaat al-Gindi, Salah ad-Din built a fortress here to protect the pilgrims making their haj. He also planned to use the fort, which is still largely intact, as a base from which to launch attacks on the Crusaders, who had advanced as far as Jerusalem. As it turned out, Salah ad-Din managed to evict the Crusaders from the Holy City even before the completion of his fortress.

Qalaat al-Gindi is definitely off the beaten track and it is rarely visited. From the coast, you must turn off at Ras as-Sudr. There is no public transport, so you must either have your own vehicle or hire a taxi.

Continuing north from Qalaat al-Gindi for about 20km you'll get to the turn-off for Nakhl, another 60km east. This little community sits almost smack in the centre of the Sinai peninsula and is surrounded by a vast wilderness. It boasts a population of about 60 people, and has a hotel (of sorts) for the odd traveller who passes this way, a petrol station, supermarket and bakery.

HAMMAM FARA'UN

Hammam Fara'un, or 'the pharaoh's bath', is about 50km south of Ras as-Sudr. The hot springs are said to have curative powers and a big sign at the entrance to the area proclaims that a huge five star spa is to be built here. In the meantime, the garbage-strewn beach is used by day-tripping locals, and women visitors should avoid swimming in anything more daring than leggings and a baggy T-shirt.

Sinai buses from Cairo and Suez or going the other way can drop you off at the turn-off to Hammam Fara'un and the beach is not too far from the main road. It's about 1¾ hours to Suez.

SERABIT AL-KHADIM

Several of Egypt's development schemes in Sinai are being implemented along this 90km stretch of coastline beside the Gulf of Suez. Most of the projects relate to the off-shore oil fields; consequently, the area is marred by jumbled masses of pipes, derricks and machinery.

The community of **Abu Zenima** has a manganese processing plant and a rest house on the highway where buses stop.

Just past Abu Zenima is a turn-off of sorts which leads to the old turquoise mines and dramatic pharaonic temple remains at **Serabit al-Khadim**. Despite its remote location, turquoise was mined here as far back as the Old Kingdom. The temple dates back to the 12th dynasty and is dedicated to the goddess Hathor; next to it is a New Kingdom shrine to Sopdu, god of the Eastern Desert. Throughout the temple's many courts, inscriptions list the temple's benefactors, who included Hatshepsut and Tuthmosis III. It is thought to have been abandoned during the reign of Ramses VII.

In the nearby **Wadi Maragha** and **Wadi Mukattab** (Valley of Inscriptions), more stelae and rock inscriptions, some dating back to the 3rd Dynasty, give further evidence of turquoise mining that was carried out here. Unfortunately, many of the workings and stelae were damaged when the British tried – and failed – to revive the mines in 1901.

Serabit al-Khadim and its environs have become a popular desert safari destination and most of the outfits in Na'ama Bay will offer to take you there. If you're driving, you'll be better off in a 4WD. Follow the road/track that leads off into the desert, just south of Abu Zenima, for about 39km.

When you see a white dome on your right, take the track to your left. After about 3km you'll come to the village of Sheikh Barakat. There you can find a guide to take you the remaining 7km to the trail leading up to the temple. From here it is a 40 to 45 minute climb. Another track connects the village to Wadi Feiran, 40 to 45km away. Make sure you stick to the trails and have a guide – some of the areas near here are mined.

EL-TOR

El-Tor, also known as **Tur Sinai**, is the administrative capital of the South Sinai Governorate. It's something of a boom town, with a broad, clean central avenue bordered by new apartment buildings. If you do decide to stay here, there are a couple of hotels in town, such as *Tur Sinai Hotel* (☎ 770 059) at the bus station, which has singles/doubles for E£48/69, or *Lido Hotel* (☎ 771 780) down on the waterfront, with rooms for E£20/30, without breakfast. There are also several banks, and this is the nearest place for visa extensions to the resorts of Sharm el-Sheikh and beyond – go to the town's Mogamma, the main administrative building on the main road in the centre of town.

RAS MOHAMMED NATIONAL PARK

Ras Mohammed is Egypt's first national park. It occupies Sinai's most southern point and was declared a National Marine Park in 1988, though its boundaries were pushed up close to the town of Sharm el-Sheikh the following year. It now occupies a total of 829 sq km of land and sea, including Tiran Island. The actual headland of Ras Mohammed is about 30km short of Sharm el-Sheikh, on the road from El-Tor.

At the time of its declaration, the park was the subject of much controversy, but the project has been very successful in preventing the area's fragile environment from being destroyed by the sort of development that has transformed the Sharm el-Sheikh coast. Hotels cannot develop the area, and

only 12% of the park is accessible to visitors. In addition, a ceiling has been applied to the number of boats allowed into the area with divers. However, despite these limitations, Ras Mohammed is the catch cry of nearly every tourist operator in Sharm el-Sheikh and nearby Na'ama Bay, and the park is inundated with more than 50,000 visitors each year.

There are two entries to the park – one to the north-west and the other in the north-east corner closer to Sharm el-Sheikh. The park's salmon-toned, fish-shaped visitors centre and restaurant are also in the northeast in an area known as Marsa Ghoslane. Videos are shown here, and you may be able to pick up an interesting booklet highlighting the park's fauna. Camping permits (E£5 per person per night) are also available from the centre but camping is allowed only in designated areas. Vehicles are permitted to enter (US$5 per person), but access is restricted to certain parts of the park and, for conservation reasons, it's forbidden to leave the official tracks.

If you are going to camp, respect the environment you're in and clean up after yourselves. Camp rules are enforced by rangers and if you're caught violating them you can be prosecuted, so don't enter areas you know to be off-limits. To get around you really need your own vehicle, or you can join one of the many day tours by jeep or bus from Sharm el-Sheikh and Na'ama Bay. Divers are often brought in by boat instead.

Take your passport with you to Ras Mohammed. Visitors to Sinai who are on Sinai-only permits cannot go to Ras Mohammed because it is beyond the Sharm el-Sheikh boundary of the permit, but should not have any problem on boat dive trips. Check with the dive clubs if you have any doubts. See the Diving the Red Sea chapter for details on underwater activities within Ras Mohammed itself.

SHARM EL-SHEIKH & NA'AMA BAY

The southern coast of the Gulf of Aqaba, between Tiran Island in the straits and Ras

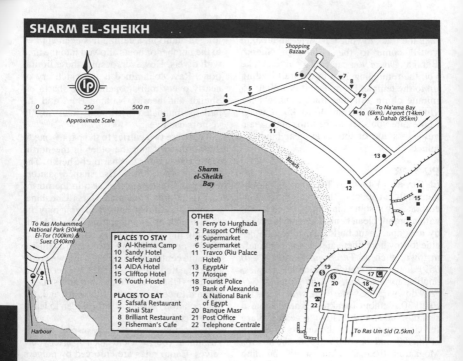

SHARM EL-SHEIKH

Shopping Bazaar

0   250   500 m
Approximate Scale

To Na'ama Bay (6km), Airport (14km) & Dahab (85km)

Sharm el-Sheikh Bay

Beach

To Ras Mohammed National Park (30km), El-Tor (100km) & Suez (340km)

Harbour

To Ras Um Sid (2.5km)

PLACES TO STAY
3   Al-Kheima Camp
10 Sandy Hotel
12 Safety Land
14 AIDA Hotel
15 Clifftop Hotel
16 Youth Hostel

PLACES TO EAT
5   Safsafa Restaurant
7   Sinai Star
8   Brilliant Restaurant
9   Fisherman's Cafe

OTHER
1   Ferry to Hurghada
2   Passport Office
4   Supermarket
6   Supermarket
11 Travco (Riu Palace Hotel)
13 EgyptAir
17 Mosque
18 Tourist Police
19 Bank of Alexandria & National Bank of Egypt
20 Banque Masr
21 Post Office
22 Telephone Centrale

Mohammed National Park at the tip of Sinai, features some of the world's most brilliant and amazing underwater scenery. The crystal-clear water, the rare and lovely reefs and the incredible variety of exotic fish darting in and out of the colourful coral have made this a snorkelling and scuba diving paradise, attracting people from all over the globe.

Na'ama Bay is a resort that has grown from virtually nothing since the early 1980s, while Sharm el-Sheikh (or Sharm), initially developed by the Israelis during their occupation of the peninsula (1967-82), is a relatively long-standing settlement. Both are heading in the direction of Hurghada – becoming unending building sites, spreading the blight of hotels up and down a once untouched coastline. Although the two are 6km apart, they are rapidly joining together into one long development strip. Almost all the construction is of four and five star resorts and the place is geared to package tourists flown in direct from Europe. Budget travellers, or those in search of something small and unique, will have little luck here.

Information
Passport Office The passport office in Sharm el-Sheikh is open every day from 9.30 am to 2 pm except Friday but visa extensions are available only at the office in El-Tor.

Tourist Police There is no tourist office. The tourist police office is up on the hill in Sharm el-Sheikh. They also have a booth next to the Marina Sharm Hotel in Na'ama Bay.

Money Banque Masr, the Bank of Alexandria and the National Bank of Egypt all have

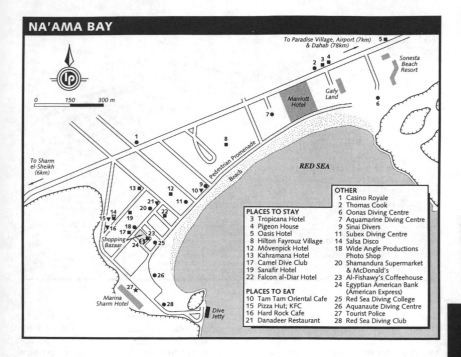

NA'AMA BAY

To Paradise Village, Airport (7km) & Dahab (78km)

Sonesta Beach Resort

Gafy Land

Marriott Hotel

To Sharm el-Sheikh (6km)

Pedestrian Promenade

Beach

RED SEA

To Sharm el-Sheikh (6km)

Shopping Bazaar

Marina Sharm Hotel

Dive Jetty

PLACES TO STAY
3 Tropicana Hotel
4 Pigeon House
5 Oasis Hotel
8 Hilton Fayrouz Village
12 Mövenpick Hotel
13 Kahramana Hotel
17 Camel Dive Club
19 Sanafir Hotel
22 Falcon al-Diar Hotel

PLACES TO EAT
10 Tam Tam Oriental Cafe
15 Pizza Hut; KFC
16 Hard Rock Cafe
21 Danadeer Restaurant

OTHER
1 Casino Royale
2 Thomas Cook
6 Oonas Diving Centre
7 Aquamarine Diving Centre
9 Sinai Divers
11 Subex Diving Centre
14 Salsa Disco
18 Wide Angle Productions Photo Shop
20 Shamandura Supermarket & McDonald's
23 Al-Fishawy's Coffeehouse
24 Egyptian American Bank (American Express)
25 Red Sea Diving College
26 Aquanaute Diving Centre
27 Tourist Police
28 Red Sea Diving Club

0   150   300 m

SINAI

branches in Sharm el-Sheikh (on the hill) and in Na'ama Bay. Banque Masr handles MasterCard and the Bank of Alexandria handles Visa. American Express (Amex) operates through the Egyptian American Bank in the shopping bazaar just off the mall at Na'ama Bay. It's open from 8.30 am to 2 pm and 6 to 9 pm Sunday to Thursday, and from 10 am to 1 pm and 6 to 9 pm Friday and Saturday.

At the time of writing there were three ATMs in Na'ama Bay: in the lobby of the Mövenpick Hotel, at the entrance to the Sanafir Hotel and outside the Banque Masr (under Best Tours) in the shopping bazaar. A machine at the Sharm el-Sheikh branch of Banque Masr (beside the telephone centrale) should also be working by the time this book is published.

Thomas Cook (☎ 601 808) has a new office on the main road in Na'ama Bay. It handles cash advances and is open daily from 9 am to 9 pm.

Post & Communications The post office is in Sharm el-Sheikh on the hill. It is open daily from 8 am to 3 pm, except Friday. The nearby telephone centrale is open 24 hours. There are a number of card phones in Na'ama Bay – one at the Shamandura supermarket and at least two on the beachfront promenade (one in front of the Red Sea Diving College). But be warned, shops in the vicinity have been known to charge E£30 for a E£15 card.

Email & Internet Access There is a cybercafe/bar just off the boardwalk at the Hilton Fayrouz in Na'ama Bay. As there is a local server, the cost is more in line with Cairo than cybercafes in Upper Egypt, at E£15 per hour. The Sanafir Hotel was also planning to start Internet services.

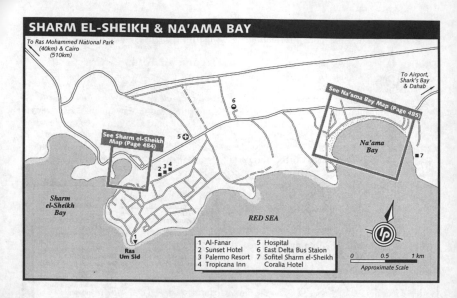

SHARM EL-SHEIKH & NA'AMA BAY

To Ras Mohammed National Park
(40km) & Cairo
(510km)

To Airport,
Shark's Bay
& Dahab

See Na'ama Bay Map (Page 485)

See Sharm el-Sheikh
Map (Page 484)

Na'ama
Bay

Sharm
el-Sheikh
Bay

RED SEA

Ras
Um Sid

1 Al-Fanar	5 Hospital
2 Sunset Hotel	6 East Delta Bus Staion
3 Palermo Resort	7 Sofitel Sharm el-Sheikh
4 Tropicana Inn	Coralia Hotel

0   0.5   1 km
Approximate Scale

Bookshops There are bookshops in the Hilton Fayrouz Village and Mövenpick hotels stocked with the usual tourist books and glossy guides to diving in the Red Sea.

Underwater Photography Underwater cameras are easy to come by in Na'ama Bay. Most of the dive clubs rent out cameras to snap some underwater memories. Wide Angle productions has branches next to Camel Dive Club and on the promenade in front of the Red Sea Diving College and rents specialist underwater cameras starting at US$20 per day and video cameras starting at US$60.

Snorkelling
Na'ama Bay itself has reefs, but far better are the stunning Near and Middle gardens and the even more incredible Far Garden. The Near Garden is near the point at the northern end of the bay just below the Sofitel Hotel, and the Far Garden is another hour's trek along the coast. You can try walking to the reefs but because large hotels have now been built on the shore, you may

find access blocked and you may have to take a boat organised by one of the diving centres. No matter how you get there, remember to take plenty of water and sun screen with you.

Another excellent spot for snorkelling is Ras Um Sid near the lighthouse at Sharm el-Sheikh. The small beach here is now parcelled up between a number of resorts and gets quite crowded, but the area near the lighthouse is open to the public and is free, although there's no beach as such.

It's possible to get to some of the more distant sites by joining a dive boat – inquire at some of the dive clubs in town. You'll be looking at anywhere between US$20 to US$50 for a day trip. Many of the clubs also do snorkelling trips to Ras Mohammed National Park for at least US$50; however, the deep drop-offs there are not ideal for snorkelling, and the cross currents (formed by the collision of the two gulfs) can be very strong.

Most of the dive clubs rent masks, snorkels and fins. Remember that if you do snorkel, the same reef protection rules apply to you as they do to divers. See the Diving the Red Sea chapter for more information.

Diving

Sharm el-Sheikh is one of the world's premier diving destinations and with a huge number of dive clubs here, you are sure to find something that suits you. See the Diving the Red Sea chapter.

Other Water Sports

Most of the big hotels also offer above-water sports, including sailing lessons (E£35 per hour), windsurfing (E£40 per hour), parasailing (E£120 per hour), pedalos (E£20 per hour), glass-bottomed boats (E£30 per hour), banana boats (E£25 for 15 minutes) and the like.

The use of a hotel swimming pool costs about E£45 per person, per day. All of the beach space at Na'ama Bay has been taken up by hotels. Not all the hotels take much notice of nonguests using their beach, but many do, so if you're unable to blend in with the crowd you'll have to pay. It's illegal to swim off Na'ama Bay after 11 pm. Remember also that despite all the development the beaches and waters of Na'ama Bay are part of the Ras Mohammed protectorate and its regulations apply here – see the earlier Diving the Red Sea chapter for more details.

Camel Rides

Camel rides to 'traditional Bedouin villages' for 'traditional Bedouin meals' are offered for about US$35 to US$60. However, you often end up in the midst of a large group of package tourists. If you want to experience the desert from the back of a camel and in the company of the Bedouin, it's better negotiating treks directly with the Bedouin at one of the tourist spots further north, such as Dahab.

Horse Riding

There are a couple of hotels that offer horse rides in the desert. However, you're looking at a minimum of US$10 per hour – far more than anywhere else in Egypt. If the price

doesn't dissuade you, try the Oasis or Sanafir hotels in Na'ama Bay.

Organised Tours

Most bigger hotels and travel agencies are organising a growing range of things to do out of the water. Jeep or bus trips to St Katherine's Monastery or such desert sights as the Coloured Canyon (see the Nuweiba section, later in this chapter) are available for about US$45 or more. If you're heading up to Dahab or Nuweiba, better deals can be had there.

For those only visiting Sinai, quick excursions are also organised to Cairo.

Places to Stay – Budget

Sharm el-Sheikh The cheapest, but by no means the best, place to stay in an area geared to tourists with comparatively fat wallets is the *Youth Hostel* (☎ 660 317) which is up on the hill. A bed in a fairly standard eight-bed dorm costs E£18.60 (E£19.60 for nonmembers) with breakfast. It's open from 6.30 to 9 am and 2 to 10 pm, and doesn't seem overly fussed about membership cards.

Safety Land (☎ 660 359, fax 660 458) was undergoing extensive renovation at the time of writing. The management claims that singles/doubles in its newly renovated bungalows will cost E£37/54, not including breakfast. Air-con rooms will be E£70/90/120 for singles/doubles/triples. They have a bit of beach to themselves, although this used to be Sharm's main marina and the water is none too clean.

Al-Kheima Camp (☎ 660 167, fax 660 166), the first place you pass on your way from the port, has bamboo-covered huts at E£36/45 and air-con rooms for E£92/115. Breakfast is E£8. However, it's inconveniently located and the desert behind is strewn with garbage.

Na'ama Bay *Pigeon House* (☎ 600 996, fax 600 965) on the northern edge of town is only a budget option because everything else around here is so expensive. It has three types of rooms. Bottom rung are the basic

Jts with fans which go for E£38/56/76 a single/double/triple. Then there are small rooms, which though clean and comfortable are way overpriced at E£65/85/105. Both options involve shared communal facilities. Superior rooms with air-con and private bathrooms go for E£120/170/205. These are summer rates and they may increase during winter. Also, as one of the area's cheaper hotels it is often fully booked, so reserve ahead.

Red Sea Diving College and *Camel Divers* offer cheap(ish) accommodation but only for people taking their diving courses with the college.

Places to Stay – Mid-Range

Sharm el-Sheikh A new strip of hotels is emerging from the construction sites in the Ras Um Sid area above Sharm el-Sheikh. Although most are, like everything else here, fairly pricey, a few are not so bad.

Clifftop Hotel (☎ 660 251), part of the Helnan group of hotels, is one of the originals and has reasonable singles/doubles/triples with TV, air-con, fridge, phone and bathroom for US$50/65/78 including breakfast. You also get the use of the beach at Marina Sharm Hotel.

Sunset Hotel (☎/fax 661 673/4) is a brand new three star and one of the better deals in town with singles/doubles for E£100/120 including breakfast. You get to use the beach at Ras Um Sid.

Palermo Resort (☎ 661 561) is another three star hotel with singles/doubles for US$31/40 including breakfast. They have a large pool and a section of beach at nearby Ras Um Sid.

Tropicana Inn (☎ 661 384) has 70 rooms and 16 villas and singles/doubles with air-con go for US$52/65. It runs hourly buses to Na'ama Bay.

Sandy Hotel (☎ 661 177, fax 660 377) is down in Sharm el-Sheikh itself. It has a pool and the air-con singles/doubles go for US$30/50 including breakfast.

Na'ama Bay *Sanafir Hotel (☎ 600 197, fax 600 196)* is one of the best places in this range (although it's rapidly spiralling out of mid-range). It has two classes of rooms and seasonal rates. You'll be looking at US$64/78/99 for a 'superior' air-con single/double/triple in the low season, and US$82/98/126 in the high season. The prices include breakfast but not tax. With a pool and the addition of new rooms, it's no longer the intimate place that it used to be but the older rooms, with their whitewashed walls, domed ceilings, and beds raised two or three steps above the floor are the nicest in town. Guests receive a free pass to use the beach at Aquanaute dive club.

Not as nice to look at but slightly cheaper is *Kahramana Hotel (☎ 601 071, fax 601 076)*, which sits one block away from the beach and has singles/doubles for US$50/60, including breakfast.

Tropicana Hotel (☎ 600 652, fax 600 649), a new place on the western side of the highway, can best be described as a cheap imitation of the Sanafir (though its rooms are more expensive). Rooms with air-con, TV, phone and breakfast cost US$70/90/110. The hotel does not have direct access to a beach but there is a small pool from where you get good views of the mountains.

Virtually across the road and with its own patch of beach is *Gafy Land (☎ 600 211, fax 600 210)*, which offers modern rooms with low ceilings, TV, air-con, phone, minibar and a big bath for US$60/70, including breakfast but not taxes.

On the other side of the road at the north end of Na'ama Bay is *Oasis Hotel (☎ 602 624)*. It has rooms with air-con but shared baths for US$32/39, including breakfast (but not taxes). Rooms with baths go for US$37/44. There are also concrete and reed huts available for E£40/60.

Not far away is *Paradise Village (☎ 601 280/8, fax 601 289)* at the northern end of the main road. Guests have the use of the Sonesta's beach facilities and singles/doubles/triples go for a relatively reasonable E£130/200/270.

Places to Stay – Top End

The entire coast from north of Na'ama Bay has been subject to an incredible construction boom over the past couple of years. There is now a golf course and a line of resorts, some of them enormous, terracing the cliffs down to the sea. Now the developers have turned their attention to the area near Ras Um Sid. Most of these places are geared to package tourists and, as in Hurghada, are considerably cheaper if booked from outside Egypt. Unless stated otherwise, prices for the following places include breakfast but not taxes.

AIDA Beach Hotel (☎ 660 719, fax 660 722) in Sharm el-Sheikh is one of the better hotels in Sharm el-Sheikh (not that the choice is exactly great). Double-storey rooms, all with air-con and satellite TV, are built around a large swimming pool. One of the unique facilities of this place is the 10 lane bowling alley. Prices start at US$85 for a double.

Your options are far better down in Na'ama Bay. *Camel Dive Club* (☎ 600 700, 600 601) just up from the promenade is a small, pleasant hotel with well decorated rooms attached to its diving centre. An antidote to most of the big resorts on offer around here, it is very well run and has five rooms specially equipped for guests with disabilities. There is also a specially designed swimming pool. Singles/doubles cost US$75/94, including taxes. There is a discount if you dive with the centre.

Falcon al-Diar (☎ 600 827) down on the promenade is another of the smaller places. Like its bigger neighbours it has the usual pool, beach and restaurant facilities but the setting is far more intimate. Guests recommend its buffet meals. Standard singles/doubles cost US$88/110, which doesn't include breakfast, but prices are negotiable out of season.

Included here simply because it dominates Na'ama Bay's promenade is the five star *Mövenpick Hotel* (☎ 600 100/5, fax 600 111). If you like sprawling resorts, you'll be happy at this place, the biggest and perhaps most awful addition to the waterfront. The hotel has three zones – Villa Area (facing the promenade), Front Area (between the Villa Area and the road) and

the so-called Sports Area (spilling into the desert across the highway). Singles/doubles in the 'cheap' sports area start at US$90/130 (summer) and US$160/190 (winter), including taxes. Rooms in the other sections are even more expensive. And in case all this isn't enough, 5km east of Na'ama Bay there is now the 270 room *Golf Hotel Sharm Mövenpick* (☎ 603 200) with an 18 hole golf course and a conference centre.

Also large but less of a monstrosity than the Mövenpick is *Hilton Fayrouz Village* (☎ 600 137, fax 601 040), a sprawl of deluxe air-con bungalows along the promenade. Although it has less than beautiful architecture, it is well located and somehow feels a little more intimate than some of its giant neighbours. As you'd expect of a Hilton, it has the usual pools, restaurants and beach facilities. Singles/doubles start at US$65/80.

Dominating Na'ama Bay's northern cliffs is *Sofitel Sharm el-Sheikh Coralia Hotel* (☎/fax 626 000), one of the newest and most luxurious hotels to open in the area. The vaguely Moorish-looking whitewashed rooms have tasteful wooden furniture and have stunning views over the bay, as do some of the bars and restaurants. Food here is reported to be among the best in Na'ama Bay. Singles/doubles will set you back US$180/208.

Places to Eat

Sharm el-Sheikh There are a couple of small restaurants/cafes in the shopping bazaar behind the bus station. *Sinai Star* serves some excellent fish meals for about E£12 per person.

Brilliant Restaurant offers a range of traditional Egyptian food at reasonable prices. A plate of chicken with salad should cost about E£15. It also has dessert.

Fisherman's Cafe serves chicken or fish with generous portions of rice, salad, tahina and bread for E£1. Beers are E£10.

Safsafa Restaurant in the old Sharm 'mall' is one of the best places in this area. It's a small, eight-table, family-run affair and local residents say the fish here is the

SINAI

freshest in Sharm. The clientele is a mixture of families and divers. A plate of calamari and rice, with tahina and babaghanoug, will cost you E£18. Whole fish is priced at E£45 per kilogram. There is no beer.

Al-Fanar at Ras Um Sid beach at the base of the lighthouse is an open-air Bedouin-style restaurant with sunken alcoves and not-so-cheap prices (a substantial lunch will cost upwards of E£30), but the view of the sea is marvellous, the food is good and you can get a cold Stella (E£10).

If you're into dining under the stars while the waves wash gently up onto the beach, try *Safety Land*. There's no formal restaurant here, but meals (fish or calamari for E£25) and snacks (omelettes and salad) can be arranged, and you can dine within metres of the water. Beers are a reasonable E£7.50.

Self-caterers will find a well stocked supermarket in the bazaar, as well as a wholesale beer shop – talking the manager into selling a bottle or two (rather than the customary crate) is not too difficult.

Na'ama Bay There are a lot of places to eat here, but don't expect to dine cheaply (by the standards of the rest of the country anyway). The hotels have a wide range of restaurants, offering everything from seafood to Thai dishes, although none of these places suits a budget traveller's pocket – but what does around here?

Tam Tam Oriental Cafe is one of the cheapest restaurants in Na'ama Bay and is deservedly popular. Jutting out onto the beach, it's a laid-back place where you can delve into a range of Egyptian fare including mezzes for E£3.75 a bowl, kushari for E£7.50, and roast pigeon for E£17. Wash it all down with a Stella (E£7.50). There are *sheeshas* (waterpipes) too for E£3.50.

Chef Jurgen's Restaurant over at the Pigeon House is deservedly popular. Pasta dishes here start at E£10.50 and there's a good selection of vegetarian food, plus fruit and pancakes for dessert. Beers are E£9.50.

Another popular choice is *Danadeer Restaurant (☎ 600 321)* just along from the Sanafir on a corner opposite the Falcon al-

Diar. There is a selection of seafood and Egyptian dishes on offer and you can get a fish meal for about E£35.

Next door at the Kahramana Hotel, *Which Way Cafe* has some of the most reasonably priced food around Na'ama Bay, with pizzas starting at E£8.

If you want something a little different there is a branch of the Cairo Chinese chain *Peking* in the Sanafir Hotel, while the new Sofitel has a highly recommended, but expensive, Indian restaurant, *Rangoli Restaurant*. Reservations are recommended here during high season.

Fishta Cafe at the Sanafir Hotel offers Mövenpick ice cream for E£5 and sheeshas for E£6. If you're looking for tea and sheesha you can also head into the mall and sit at *Al-Fishawy's*, a poor imitation of its Cairo namesake.

The usual fast food outlets are also represented here: *McDonald's*, *KFC* and *Pizza Hut* are all on or close to the street that runs in front of the Sanafir. There is even a newly opened *Hard Rock Cafe (☎ 602 665)* which is very popular with the young middle class Cairenes who flock here on weekends and national holidays.

Entertainment

With so many tourists milling around in the evenings, Sharm el-Sheikh has a growing number of bars and dance establishments. The club of the moment is *Bus Stop* at the Sanafir Hotel, which has an entrance charge of E£20 and rocks on until 4 or 6 am. *Salsa* at the Cataract Hotel is another popular place. Most of the big hotels also have discos.

If you're just after a drink, the *rooftop bar* at Sanafir Hotel in Na'ama Bay is also popular and has a minimum charge of E£10 (beers here cost E£8).

Divers tend to congregate at the Hilton Fayrouz Village's *Pirates Bar* where there is a happy hour between 5.30 and 7.30 pm and all drinks are discounted by 30%. There is sometimes food on offer too.

Harry's Pub at the Marriott Hotel is another, more expensive hang-out, with a large selection of beers on tap. Occasionally it has special nights with unlimited draft beer for only E£20.

Somehow the **Hard Rock Cafe** pulls in huge numbers in the evening and occasionally has special events to spice up the chain's usual fare.

The Mövenpick's **Casino Royale** is the only place in town where visitors (no Egyptians allowed) can gamble away their foreign bucks (no Egyptian pounds, thank you very much).

Getting There & Away

Air EgyptAir (☎ 661 056) has a new office in Sharm el-Sheikh near the start of the road to Na'ama Bay. It flies daily to Cairo (E£477) and three times a week to Hurghada (E£330). On Saturdays and Thursdays there are also flights to Luxor (E£415).

Air Sinai currently flies from Cairo to Sharm el-Sheikh every Monday in the winter only. The one-way fare is E£477, and these flights proceed to Tel Aviv.

Charter flights from various European cities run virtually all year round.

Bus & Minibus The bus station is in Sharm el-Sheikh; buses heading on to Dahab and beyond occasionally stop on the highway in Na'ama Bay but don't count on it. Likewise, if you're catching a bus in the direction of Suez or Cairo, it's advisable to go to the East Delta Co bus station, which is behind the Mobil Station halfway between Na'ama Bay and Sharm el-Sheikh. Seats to Cairo can and should be booked ahead.

From Sharm el-Sheikh, the cheapest East Delta Co direct services to Cairo (seven hours) run at 7.30, 10.30 and 11.30 am and 12.30, 1.30, 3 and 4.30 pm and cost between E£40 and E£50 (the 11.30 am bus is E£40). There are four buses between 10 pm and midnight and a seat on one of those costs E£65.

Superjet has a bus to Cairo (E£55) leaving at 11 pm from its terminus next to East Delta Co.

It is cheaper, but more time-consuming, to get a bus to Suez and then another bus or service taxi from there to Cairo (the same is

also true in reverse). Buses to Suez (E£25 or E£30, 5½ hours) depart almost every hour throughout the day, starting at 7 am and finishing at 11 pm.

Seven buses go to Dahab (1½ hours), at 6.30, 7.30 and 9 am, 3, 5 and 9 pm and at midnight. Tickets cost E£10. The same 9 am and 5 pm buses go on to Nuweiba (E£25) and the 9 am bus then continues all the way to Taba (E£35). The 7.30 am bus goes on to St Katherine's Monastery (E£25).

Minibuses also cover the route between Sharm el-Sheikh and Suez and Cairo, as well as north to Dahab, but they're not all that common or frequent – ask around at the bus station.

Boat Barring breakdowns and other problems, there's a ferry between Sharm el-Sheikh and Hurghada leaving on Monday, Wednesday and Friday, departing the harbour at 9 or 10 am. You can book tickets through most hotels or at Thomas Cook in Na'ama Bay. For details see the Hurghada Getting There & Away section in the Red Sea Coast chapter.

Travco (☎ 661 111) operates a high-speed air-con ferry that travels between Sharm and Hurghada in 1½ hours (although some travellers have said that it can take much longer). The boat departs on Monday at 7.30 am and 6 pm, Tuesday at 8.30 am and 10.30 pm, and Saturday at 6 pm. A ticket costs US$33 (vehicles US$75). For more information contact the Travco office at the Riu Palace Hotel.

Getting Around

To/From the Airport The airport is about 8km north of Na'ama Bay at Ras Nasrany. A taxi will cost about E£20 from Na'ama Bay.

Bus You can also get Toyota pick-ups for between 50pt and E£1, although they are less rigid about extracting the tourist rate. Other than that, it is quite possible to hitch, as there is a fair amount of traffic on the roads. The usual warnings about hitching apply.

Many of the hotels up by Ras Um Sid have their own shuttles to Na'ama Bay.

Car Many of the big name car rental companies have offices in Na'ama Bay, usually in one of the bigger hotels. Avis (☎ 600 979) is in the Sonesta Beach Resort, Hertz (☎ 600 459) is at the Mövenpick and Sanafir hotels and Max Europcar (☎ 600 686) is at the Hilton Fayrouz Village. Sanafir Hotel rents 4WD jeeps for US$85 per day while Fox Safari (☎ 601 074 ext 510), also in Na'ama Bay, has them for US$120 including a driver.

Bicycle Normal and cross-country bicycles are for hire from stands along the promenade in Na'ama Bay for E£10 or more per day.

Boat Sharm el-Sheikh's marina has been moved to a new location just west of Sharm el-Sheikh. Some dive clubs operating out of Na'ama Bay bring their boats around to the jetty on Na'ama Bay early each morning; others ferry passengers to the marina. It's possible to hitch a ride either way on one of these vessels – ask around at the marina or on the jetty in Na'ama Bay about 6.30 am. You can also check with one of the dive clubs.

SHARK'S BAY

Shark's Bay, or Beit al-Irsh, used to be a quiet, low-key resort camp about 6km north of Na'ama Bay (look for the unmarked asphalt turn-off), but unfortunately the giant Pyramisa Hotel has colonised half of the beach and Italians doing aerobics to loud music interrupt the solitary bliss of the place. Still, from its pebbly beach you can walk in to some quite good snorkelling and diving. The place is particularly popular with Germans and Israelis, most of whom dive in a nearby 15m to 20m-deep canyon with the Embarak dive club there.

The only way in and out is to hitch or bargain with taxi drivers. Trying to get there in the dead of night may well entail walking the whole way.

Places to Stay & Eat

The two star *Shark's Bay Camp* (☎ 600 947, fax 600 943) has clean and comfortable huts on the beach for E£50/65 a single/double and huts higher up on the hillside with fans for E£60/75. The camp has clean toilets and showers with hot water. There is also a mini-market and a Bedouin-style *restaurant* with meals starting at E£21.

DAHAB

A village beach resort 85km north of Sharm el-Sheikh, Dahab is the wannabe Koh Samui of the Middle East. Banana fritters and Bob Marley, stoned travellers in tie-dyes and shops with names like 'Laughing Buddha' offering tarot card readings – it's all here. Accommodation virtually on the beach can cost as little as E£5 per night and common is the backpacker who pitches up here for a night or two and ends up saying on for weeks, if not months.

But despite the town's somewhat unfair reputation as a drug-infested hippie hangout, there is more to it. A short walk away you can find tranquil beach-side hotels and restaurants without the hippie hype. And while Dahab is not immune to the construction that plagues much of Sinai's coastline, it is still a place where individual travellers are the rule rather than the exception, making it an antidote to the big groups and plastic resorts of Sharm el-Sheikh and Hurghada.

Orientation

There are two parts to Dahab – in the new part, referred to by the locals rather euphemistically as Dahab City, are some of the more expensive hotels, the bus station, post and phone offices and a bank. Along the beach to the north is the other part, **Assalah**, which was originally a Bedouin village but now has more Egyptian entrepreneurs and low-budget travellers than Bedouin in residence. The village proper has moved further north. Assalah is divided into **Masbat** and **Mashraba**. Masbat starts roughly at the lighthouse at the northern end of Assalah

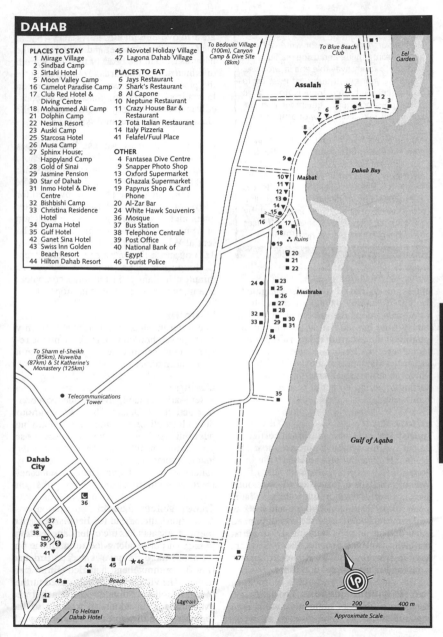

DAHAB

PLACES TO STAY
1 Mirage Village
2 Sindbad Camp
3 Sirtaki Hotel
5 Moon Valley Camp
16 Camelot Paradise Camp
17 Club Red Hotel & Diving Centre
18 Mohammed Ali Camp
21 Dolphin Camp
22 Nesima Resort
23 Auski Camp
25 Starcosa Hotel
26 Musa Camp
27 Sphinx House; Happyland Camp
28 Gold of Sinai
29 Jasmine Pension
30 Star of Dahab
31 Inmo Hotel & Dive Centre
32 Bishbishi Camp
33 Christina Residence Hotel
34 Dyarna Hotel
35 Gulf Hotel
42 Ganet Sina Hotel
43 Swiss Inn Golden Beach Resort
44 Hilton Dahab Resort

45 Novotel Holiday Village
47 Lagona Dahab Village

PLACES TO EAT
6 Jays Restaurant
7 Shark's Restaurant
8 Al Capone
10 Neptune Restaurant
11 Crazy House Bar & Restaurant
12 Tota Italian Restaurant
14 Italy Pizzeria
41 Felafel/Fuul Place

OTHER
4 Fantasea Dive Centre
9 Snapper Photo Shop
13 Oxford Supermarket
15 Ghazala Supermarket
19 Papyrus Shop & Card Phone
20 Al-Zar Bar
24 White Hawk Souvenirs
36 Mosque
37 Bus Station
38 Telephone Centrale
39 Post Office
40 National Bank of Egypt
46 Tourist Police

To Bedouin Village (100m), Canyon Camp & Dive Site (8km)

To Blue Beach Club

Eel Garden

Assalah

Dahab Bay

Masbat

Ruins

Masbraba

To Sharm el-Sheikh (85km), Nuweiba (87km) & St Katherine's Monastery (125km)

Telecommunications Tower

Dahab City

Gulf of Aqaba

Beach

Lagoon

To Helnan Dahab Hotel

0   200   400 m
Approximate Scale

SINAI

Drugs & Dahab

Nothing anyone can say or write will stop people from buying and using marijuana in Dahab. It's freely available and in wide use. If you are going to indulge, at least try to be discreet. Although there is not a huge police presence here, remember that the authorities take a dim view of drug use, especially as the business has escalated to harder drugs like heroin. You'll certainly gain no exemption from police attention just because you're a tourist – westerners have been arrested in Dahab for possession and jailed. Penalties for drug offences are high in Egypt; dealing and smuggling attract sentences of 25 years or death by hanging. Executions for such offences have been taking place since 1989.

and is made up of a higgledy-piggledy stretch of 'camps', hotels and laid-back restaurants among the palm trees, as well as a busy little bazaar. To the south, starting roughly at the excavation site, is Mashraba, named after the freshwater springs that apparently exist around the beach. This is where the newest small hotels and camps are starting to spring up and it is much quieter than Masbat.

Information

Tourist Police There's no tourist office in Dahab but the tourist police are near the Novotel Holiday Village in Dahab City.

Money There is a branch of the National Bank of Egypt at the Novotel Holiday Village (open from 9.30 am to 12.30 pm and 6.30 to 8.30 pm) and another near the bus station. A rather dubious looking Banque 'de' Caire is just along from the Snapper Photo Shop in Assalah. It's open daily from 9 am to 2 pm (9 to 11 am on Fridays) and 6 to 9 pm.

Post & Communications The post and telephone offices are opposite the bus station in Dahab City. The latter is open 24

hours every day and has a card phone. There are also two card phones in Assalah – one at the Oxford supermarket and the other at the papyrus shop in the heart of the bazaar, both of which sell phonecards. To save going to the post office, you can also drop stamped letters into the air mail postal box (supposedly emptied every day at 10 am) outside the Ghazala supermarket in Assalah.

Email & Internet Access Dahab boasts two Internet cafes. At the Snapper Photo Shop on the bay, you can send emails for 50pt per minute, with a minimum charge of E£3. You can also send photos by email for E£10 for the first, and E£5 for all subsequent pictures. Opening hours are 10.30 am to 2 pm and 4 to 10 pm. Emails can also be sent at White Hawk Souvenir Shop (☎ 640 377) opposite the entrance to Auski camp. It charges E£25 per hour, E£7.50 for 15 minutes. It plans to install more computers and phone lines so prices can drop.

Warning

Tap water in Dahab is not drinkable (plenty of shops sell bottled water). Also, please respect local sensitivities and refrain from sunbathing topless.

Diving

After loafing around, diving is the most popular activity in Dahab. The town's various dive clubs all offer a full range of diving possibilities; however, you should choose your club carefully as some places have lousy reputations when it comes to safety standards. See the Diving the Red Sea chapter for more information.

Other Water Sports

Many snorkellers head for Eel Garden, just north of Assalah. You can hire snorkelling gear from places along the restaurant strip for about E£20 per day, as well as pedalos (E£20 per hour) and kayaks (E£10 per hour). There's a windsurfing school at the Novotel Holiday Village – the bay there is excellent for it. Windsurfers can also be rented at the northern end of Dahab Bay.

SINAI

Although they are supposedly banned, jet skis can be hired for E£50/60 for one/two people for 15 minutes. The drone from these noisy beasts is in flagrant opposition to the tranquillity of Dahab.

There's no 'beach' to speak of in Assalah itself; instead the rocky coastline leads straight out onto the reef. For the golden sands, after which Dahab ('gold') was named, you must go down to the lagoon area where the resorts are clustered.

Camel Treks

Many of the local Bedouin organise camel trips to the interior of Sinai. In the morning, camel drivers and their camels congregate along the waterfront in the village. Register with the police before beginning the trek, and don't pay the camel driver until you return to the village. Prices for a one day trip start at E£70. As all drivers seem to have agreed among themselves on this price, bargaining will probably get you nowhere. The price includes food.

Jeep Treks

All the hotels and dive centres arrange jeep trips to the Coloured Canyon (see the Nuweiba section later in this chapter for details) and Ras Abu Gallum. Itineraries are pretty much custom-designed but, as an example of prices, you'll be looking at E£15 per person (with a minimum of four people) for a morning of snorkelling at the Blue Hole or E£35 and up for an evening jeep into the mountains with dinner at a Bedouin camp.

Horse Riding

If you want to ride a horse just wait on the beach in Mashraba and wait for one of the Bedouin who walk up and down the beach with horses for hire. Expect to pay about E£15 per hour. You can also ask around the camps. From the Novotel Holiday Village you can ride around the lagoon on horseback for E£45.

Places to Stay – Budget

Most, if not all, low-budget travellers head straight for Assalah. There's a plethora of so-called camps there, which are basically compounds with spartan stone, cement or reed huts, usually with two or three mattresses tossed on the floor, and communal bathroom facilities. The camps south of Nesima Resort tend to be the best as they are sheltered from the wind, have more space and some even have attractive waterfront areas shaded by groves of palms.

Many of the camps are starting to introduce proper rooms with private bathrooms. These are considerably more expensive than the huts, but the good news is prices are negotiable.

There are a few things to keep in mind when hunting for a good place. Remember that concrete huts with iron roofs are hotter than those made of reeds, but the latter may be less secure; ask for a padlock. Check that there's electricity and running water – some places have hot water – as well as decent mattresses, fly screens and fans. The following (not exhaustive) options are listed from north to south. Keep in mind that prices can often be negotiated in low season.

Auski Camp, next to Starcosa Hotel, is a popular camp run by the amiable Nasser, who charges E£10 for an ordinary room, E£15 with fans. Big rooms with private baths go for E£25 and newly built rooms with air-con are either E£40 or E£60. There's hot water but unfortunately no beach.

Bishbishi Camp is probably the cleanest camp in Dahab. Although set back on the other side of the road from the beach, it has become deservedly popular among travellers. It has 18 rooms, ranging from huts with mattresses on the floor for E£12 (E£10 single) to rooms with fans and private bathrooms for E£30/40. All the rooms have screened windows and the shared facilities, with plenty of hot water, are spotless.

Camelot Paradise Camp (☎ 640 136) is a small camp/hotel that can be reached by an alley running beside the Ghazala supermarket. It has huts for E£10 double, E£7 for singles, but you can bargain. There is also a building with clean, good-sized rooms with their own bathrooms and fans for E£20/30. If the camp is full you can sleep on the roof of its hotel building for E£3. There is a kitchen that you can use as well as a laundry area. Breakfast starts at E£3.

SINAI

olphin Camp (☎ 640 018), next to Nesima Resort, has huts for E£10/15 without fans, or E£20 with fans. There are also clean rooms with bathrooms for E£30. Although the facilities are clean some travellers have reported theft here, so make sure you lock up all your valuables.

Gold of Sinai is yet another camp/hotel set back slightly from the beachfront; there are 20 concrete rooms here. Singles/doubles with shared facilities cost E£7/14, while those with private bathrooms and fans cost E£20/30. Air-con rooms cost E£20 more.

Happyland Camp, next to Sphinx House, has been recommended by some travellers, although the bathrooms are not very clean. Doubles are E£20 per person with bathrooms and fans. Rooms with air-con go for E£40. It also has huts without bathrooms for E£5 per person. There is a nice beach restaurant which has umbrellas.

Jasmine Pension (☎ 640 110) is a small, well run hotel in a building on the seafront just down from Gold of Sinai. It has singles/doubles with private bathrooms and fans for E£15/30. Rooms with seafront balconies go for E£15. There is also a small beachfront restaurant where owner Rabi'a Arabi and his English wife Claire Ward serve home-cooked meals.

Mirage Village (☎ 640 341), on the waterfront just north of the lighthouse area, is run by the very helpful Salama and is very friendly and secure but, like many camps, is transforming itself to a hotel and has gone up in price. The few basic rooms left cost E£25 to E£30, although they are unlikely to be around much longer. Singles/doubles cost E£50/82 without shower, E£68/100 with facilities. Triples/quads without shower cost E£61/68. All the rooms have fly screens, a fan and a cupboard. Meals and beers are available.

Mohammed Ali Camp, in the centre of Assalah, is the largest and longest running of the camps. However, it has expanded greatly in recent years and now boasts 128 rooms with private bathrooms and fans, which go for between E£30 and E£40. Double rooms with air-con cost E£60. There are one or two old rooms for E£5 but they are pretty filthy. Although it is clean, the place is often noisy and the staff is known to be overly friendly towards single women.

Moon Valley Camp (☎ 640 338) is in the thick of things along the restaurant strip. This camp costs E£10 per person in a hot box or in one of the huts, both of which have fans. Without fans it'll cost you E£5. The place is in the process

of upgrading to a hotel and is planning to add air-con rooms.

Musa Camp has double rooms with shower, toilet and mosquito nets for E£40 as well as cheaper huts. A lush palm grove provides considerable shade for the gravel-coated beach and makes it particularly inviting.

Sindbad Camp, just north of the point on Dahab Bay, has semi-clean huts, starting at E£6 per person. There are also rooms with bathrooms for E£15. The owner is a helpful Bedouin chap named Nabil.

Star of Dahab, next to Inmo, charges E£15/20 for single/double occupancy in one of the small, apricot-toned rooms or in a beehive-shaped reed hut (which have candles only) near the water. The communal bathrooms are reasonably clean and there's hot water. There is also a small laundry. If you have a tent you can sometimes camp on the gravel-coated waterfront area for E£5 per person, although there's room for two small tents only and there's no shade.

Places to Stay – Mid-Range

There's an increasing number of mid-range hotels available in Dahab. If diving is your passion and you don't mind being away from the action, there's **Canyon Dive Resort** (☎/fax 640 197) located at the site of the same name, about 8km north of Dahab. There are 17 fairly basic rooms with fans and shared bathrooms for US$15 per person, including breakfast. Rooms with air-con and baths will set you back US$25 per person.

Back in town, north of Masbat is the new **Blue Beach Club** (☎/fax 640 413). Very clean rooms with fans will set you back US$35/40, including breakfast. This place is filled mainly with Swiss and German groups.

Sirtaki Hotel (☎ 640 417) is a new four star with attached diving centre that sticks out on the point near the lighthouse, spoiling the view on the north end of Dahab Bay. Still, the views looking out over the sea are nice and rooms with air-con, TV and a balcony go for US$43/66 for singles/doubles, including breakfast.

Club Red Hotel (☎/fax 640 380) is attached to the Club Red Diving Centre in

Masbat and has reasonable rooms with baths and fans for US$15/25/32/36, including breakfast. There is a 15% discount if you dive with them.

A bit further south, **Starcosa Hotel** (☎/fax 640 388) is a comfortable place to stay offering singles/doubles with fans, private bathroom and hot water for E£37/60, not including breakfast.

The nearby **Sphinx House** (☎ 640 032) charges E£30/40 for a reasonable room with fan, fly screens, breakfast and communal bath, or E£100/120 with private bath and air-con. Rooms in the better new building are more expensive at E£130/150. The rooms are big, there's a pool, a restaurant and billiard room, and beers are available.

About 100m south of here on the other side of the road is the Swiss-run **Christina Residence Hotel** (☎ 640 390, fax 640 406) with two triples and eight doubles including fans and private bathrooms. Very clean doubles cost US$15 to US$22 and triples are US$22 to US$30. Breakfast costs about E£3 to E£10.

The nearby **Inmo Hotel** (☎ 640 370, fax 640 372) caters mainly to people on diving packages from Europe, especially Germany, although it does take in stray travellers if there's room. It has two types of rooms and different rates for divers and nondivers. Singles/doubles/triples with private bathrooms are E£138/176/208 for divers, or about E£15 more for nondivers. The smaller 'backpacker' rooms go for E£61/84 a single/double for divers, or E£59/81 for nondivers. The colourful rooms have fans, domed ceilings and attractive furnishings. There are a few mountain bikes for guests to use.

The 42 room **Dyarna Hotel** (☎ 640 120, fax 640 122) has a variety of rooms on offer. Its name means 'our home' in Arabic but, unfortunately, it's nothing special though the staff are very friendly. There's a pool, two restaurants, a roof bar and a disco. Rooms with fans are E£40/60/80 or E£80 for a double with air-con.

Gulf Hotel (☎ 640 147, fax 640 460) south of Assalah is an old and pretty bleak place with double rooms with air-con for E£120,

including breakfast. There's no concession for single occupancy. Beers are available.

Lagona Dahab Village (☎ 640 352, fax 640 351) is in the middle of nowhere on the beach between Dahab City and Assalah. The domed-shaped rooms cost E£50/80 for a single/double with fans, including breakfast and taxes. Rooms with air-con are about E£20 per person more. It is a comfortable enough place but it has the air of a structured resort. There's a restaurant where alcohol is not served.

Places to Stay – Top End

Overlooking the beach in Mashraba is the highly recommended **Nesima Resort** (☎ 640 320, fax 640 321) which has simple but very comfortable domed rooms with or without air-con for US$41/52, including breakfast. Calm yet central, it also has a fantastic pool with a juice bar overlooking the beach. Child care is also available.

Most of Dahab's higher priced accommodation is grouped around the beach near Dahab City. Moving from north to south, there is the old **Novotel Holiday Village** (☎/fax 640 301) which, despite its prime location, is an unattractive place. Rooms in various categories range from US$50 to US$90 (singles) and US$68 to US$116 (doubles). It also has two-bed bamboo huts for US$20 per person, including breakfast – relatively expensive considering how cheaply you can get the same thing in Assalah. Outsiders can use the beach for E£40. There is also a dive club.

Next to the Novotel is the brand new **Hilton Dahab Resort** (☎ 640 310). Rooms in whitewashed domed rooms cost US$110/130, including breakfast and taxes. There are two pools and the usual five-star amenities.

Slotted in next to the Hilton is the four star **Swiss Inn Golden Beach Resort** (☎ 640 471/2, fax 640 470). Another five star with a gigantic marble lobby, it has doubles for US$80, including breakfast. You can use the beach for E£25.

Furthest south (until the next resort is built) is **Ganet Sina Hotel** (☎ 640 440, fax 640 441) on the bay in Dahab City. Popular with groups from Cairo, it has singles/doubles without breakfast for US$45/60/75 plus taxes. The small, chalet-style rooms are comfortable, but really overpriced and the grounds have sparse vegetation. All in all it's pretty unenticing. However, it does have a very good, German-run windsurfing club, where you can have three hours of lessons for E£205. It is one of the few places in Egypt where children can windsurf.

On its own, away from the other hotels, is the isolated **Helnan Dahab Hotel** (☎ *640 427, fax 640 428*) which has a swimming pool, bars, restaurants and single/double rooms for US$60/80, on a half-board basis. It also has a Club Mistral windsurfing centre.

Places to Eat

There is a string of places to eat at along the waterfront in Assalah. They serve breakfast, lunch and dinner and most seem to have identical menus hanging up out the front. A meal will generally cost between E£6 and E£25. It's best not to turn up with a raging hunger as service can be slow. Generally, people hang out in these places, occasionally summoning the strength of mind and soul to flop into the sparkling waters of the Gulf of Aqaba for a while and then emerge to collapse back into a state of idyllic inertia and order a tea or cola.

Jays Restaurant on the strip in Masbat is a favourite of local residents and serves the usual mixture of Egyptian and western fare. Just next door is the very popular **Shark's Restaurant** which has an extensive choice of main courses for E£10 and more and serves a vegetarian special most days. Both serve beer and are only open for dinner.

If you want a change from the usual traveller fare, at **Neptune Restaurant** you can get Chinese food. Dishes start at about E£8.

Tota, a ship-shaped place in the heart of Assalah, has the best Italian kitchen on the strip. It serves excellent soup complete with garlic bread for E£4.50, large doughy pizzas (which are a bit light on toppings) for E£9, as well as a range of other meals for less than E£20, and chocolate cake for E£3.50. It also has beer for E£7.50.

Two doors along, next to the Oxford Supermarket, the two storey *Italy Pizzeria* does arguably better pizzas for E£8 and more. If you prefer a thin crust, this is your place.

Few people seem to stay at **Dolphin Camp** but the food here is good, the servings generous and it's one of the few camps where you can drink a beer with your meal.

A few of the restaurants, including *Al Capone* and *Crazy House*, serve fish meals, displaying their catch out the front and selling by weight.

If eating in front of the parade of people on the strip doesn't appeal to you, the restaurant at **Nesima Resort** is more intimate. It also serves very good food. The steaks here are famous around Sinai and cost about E£25.

For lunch you could also wander down to the beachfront restaurant at **Jasmine Pension**, where reasonably priced food is cooked by the London-trained owner.

The big hotels down by the lagoon also have restaurants, but you'll pay considerably more to eat here and the food will not necessarily be any better.

Entertainment

If it's beer, wine or billiard tables you're after, try *Crazy House*. *Al-Zar Bar*, next to the Dolphin Camp, has cold Stellas at E£6 and generally loud rock music, although it's rarely full.

Shipwreck Bar at Nesima Resort is very popular with divers and others; in summer you can drink on the rooftop terrace and it has a happy hour from 8 to 10 pm, when Stella is available for E£5. It also has a couple of other beers on tap.

Otherwise your only options are **Black Prince** disco (E£5 entry) in the Gulf Hotel or the Dyarna Hotel's rustic *Savana Disco* which gets going from 9 pm and is free.

Away from Assalah there are also bars at the big resort hotels.

Getting There & Away

Bus The bus station is in Dahab City. The most regular connection is to Sharm el-Sheikh (E£10, 1½ hours) with buses at 8.30

and 10 am and 1, 2.30, 9 and 10 pm. Buses to Nuweiba (E£8) leave at 10.30 am and 6.30 pm. The 10.30 am service goes on to Taba (E£20). The 9.30 am bus to St Katherine's (E£15) takes two to three hours. Buses to Cairo (nine hours) leave at 8.30 am and 1 and 2.30 pm (all E£55) and at 10 pm (E£70). Buses for Suez (E£28, 6½ hours) depart at 8.15 and 10 am and 9 pm. At the time of writing, the departure times posted at the bus station were not correct, so you should check the times with the ticket office (if you find it open).

Service Taxi As a rule, service taxis are much more expensive than buses – they know you're only using them because the bus doesn't suit and hitching possibilities are limited. They have a captive market. Although a trip to, say, St Katherine's can cost as little as E£10 per person, it will often cost closer to E£20. An entire taxi (with a maximum of seven passengers) to Nuweiba or Sharm el-Sheikh costs about E£50 to E£60, and to Taba it's about E£15 per person.

Getting Around
Pick-ups usually meet incoming buses and will shuttle you to Assalah for about E£1.

NUWEIBA
Nuweiba is certainly not the most attractive of Sinai's beach resorts. It is strung out over a long distance and the area has become something of a major port, with a continual flow of people and vehicle traffic on and off the ferry between Nuweiba and Aqaba. However, the mountain scenery is beautiful and the offshore reefs, for which Nuweiba is renowned, are spectacular. During the Israeli occupation, it was also the site of a major *moshav* (farming settlement), which has now been converted into a residence for Egyptian government officials.

Orientation
Nuweiba is divided into three parts. To the south is the port with a large bus station, banks, a couple of fairly awful hotels and the new Hilton Coral Resort. About 8km

further north is 'Nuweiba City', a small but spread-out settlement with a variety of accommodation options, a bazaar with tourist shops and several cheap places to eat. As more and more hotels are being built the south of the 'city' is gradually linking up with the port. Further north still, a 15 minute walk along the beach, is Tarabin. Draped along the northern end of Nuweiba's calm bay, this once tranquil beachside oasis is rapidly turning into a party and pick-up place, especially during Israeli holidays. While it offers a wide beach, tepid waters and cheap beachfront accommodation, it is less popular among international travellers than Dahab and has a distinctly artificial air.

Information
The post office and the telephone centrale (open 24 hours) are near the hospital in Nuweiba City. There's another post office at the port, as well as branches of the National Bank of Egypt and Banque Masr (neither will handle Jordanian dinars), a Masr Travel office and an Egypt Free (duty-free) shop. The tourist police are located near the Helnan Nuweiba Hotel in Nuweiba City, and a branch of the National Bank of Egypt is inside the Helnan. The latter is open from Saturday to Thursday from 9 am to 1 pm and 7 to 9 pm and Friday from 9 to 11 am.

Warning Topless sunbathing is gaining ground among visitors to Nuweiba, especially Israelis staying in Tarabin. You should think twice before taking part in what is little more than a strip show for the local men.

Coloured Canyon
The Coloured Canyon, which lies between St Katherine's and Nuweiba, derives its name from the layers of bright, multi-coloured stones that resemble paintings on the canyon's very steep, narrow walls. Total silence (the canyon is sheltered from the wind) adds to the eeriness. However, this is a popular day trip from Sinai's resorts and it's often difficult to appreciate the quiet

NUWEIBA

PLACES TO STAY
1 Sababa Camp
3 Betra Camp
4 Jamal
6 Palm Beach
7 El Salam
8 Camp David
9 Elsebaey Village Hotel
10 Blue Bus Camp & Restaurant
11 Soft Beach
12 City Beach Village
19 Helnan Nuweiba Hotel
23 Al-Waha Tourism Village

24 Duna Camp
25 Habiba Camp
28 Motel Marina
29 Al-Haramein Hotel
30 Zahraa Nwabia Hotel

PLACES TO EAT
2 White Palace Restaurant
5 Aid Abu Goma Fish Restaurant
14 Sendbad
15 Pizzina
16 Dr Shishkebab
22 Morgana Restaurant

To Al-Salam Village Hotel (700m)

Tarabin

Beach

Dune

Nuweiba City

To Taba (70km)

Main East Coast Highway

Gulf of Aqaba

0   100   200 m

To Nuweiba Port (8km, See Inset), Dahab (87km) & St Katherine's Monastery (120km)

To Nuweiba, Hilton Coral Resort & Nuweiba City (8km, See Main Map)

Nuweiba Port

Same Scale as Main Map

To Mizena Village (1km)

Port

To Sultana Village, La Sirène & Nuweiba Hilton Coral Resort

OTHER
13 Police
17 Hospital
18 Post Office & Telephone Centrale
20 Diving Camp Nuweiba
21 Tourist Police
26 Post Office & Telephone Centrale
27 Bus Station
31 Egypt Free Shop
32 Ferry Ticket Booth
33 Bank of Alexandria & Banque du Caire
34 National Bank of Egypt
35 Banque Masr
36 Service Taxi Station

SINAI

with the groups that crowd in here every day. Fortunately, the Coloured Canyon falls inside the boundaries of the new Taba National Monument and the Egyptian National Parks office will soon start managing the site, hopefully controlling some of the increasing numbers who visit here. In a year or two you will probably have to pay a fee to enter the area. The canyon is about 5km from the main road; vehicles can drive to within 100m of it.

Water Sports

Once again, underwater delights are the feature attraction and scuba diving and snorkelling are the prime activities. For further information see the Diving the Red Sea chapter.

Those into kayaks should ask at the Al-Waha Tourism Village or the Hilton Coral Resort, where they cost US$6 per hour. The latter also has jet skis for US$15 for 10 minutes.

Camel & Jeep Treks

Nuweiba is probably the best place in Sinai to arrange camel and jeep trips into the dramatic mountains that line the coast here. The trip to the **Coloured Canyon** can be done in a day, but there are some beautiful wadis and oases that can be visited on two or three-day trips – or longer if you prefer. Popular destinations include **Ain al-Furtega**, an oasis easily accessible from Nuweiba by regular car; **Ain Hudra**, the place where Miriam was supposed to have been struck by leprosy for criticising Moses; **Wadi Ghazala**, named for the gazelles that can sometimes be spotted in its dunes; and **Ain Umm Ahmed**, which has a famous stream that becomes an icy river in the winter months.

Almost every camp and supermarket in Tarabin offers these trips, but take care that whoever you pick is a local Bedouin – there have been some nasty tales of travellers lost without water in the desert because their so-called guides didn't know where they were going. Travellers have recommended Usama at the White Palace Camp in Tarabin

for day trips to the Coloured Canyon. For longer excursions, ask around Tarabin for Aynaz, a local Bedouin. You might want to head up to Basata or Ras Shaitan (see Nuweiba to Taba section later) where reliable Bedouin will take you by camel for about E£80 per day, including food.

If you want to go by jeep, you can find highly recommended guides at Abanoub Travel (☎ 520 201, fax 520 206). Jeep treks usually cost about US$35 per day, including food, while camel treks are US$45. For more information on jeep/safari options, see the boxed text 'Desert Safaris' on pages 358-9.

Places to Stay

Nuweiba Port There are only three hotels close to the port, all of which are fairly unimpressive. *Zahraa Nwaiba* is the worst and it has the cheek to ask for E£25/37 for a single/double. Avoid. *Al-Haramein* is slightly cheaper and marginally better; however, it's very reluctant to take in solo women.

Motel Marina is the best of the trio, which isn't saying much. Small doubles with shower and air-con are E£75, while tiny rooms without baths or air-con go for E£30.

The only other option in the vicinity is the tacky four star *Nuweiba Hilton Coral Resort* (☎ 520 320, fax 520 327) on the beachfront just north of the port. Singles/doubles start from US$115/149, including taxes and breakfast.

Nuweiba City There are a couple of simple camps with a few huts along the beach south of the Al-Waha Tourism Village, including *Habiba* and the relaxing *Duna*.

Morgana Restaurant looks like a construction site but they may let you pitch a tent there for E£3. However, there's precious little shade and the bathrooms are vile.

Helnan Nuweiba Hotel (☎ 500 401, fax 500 407) caters mainly to package tourists or middle class Cairenes. It has singles/doubles with breakfast from US$45/60 plus taxes. Next door, in its *Holiday Camp*,

The Dolphin of Nuweiba

A few years back, a young, mute Bedouin named Abdullah from Mizena, the tiny village about 1km south of Nuweiba port, noticed a lone dolphin frequenting the bay over which his village looks. He started to befriend her, swimming out into the turquoise water and diving to her depths. Although he was unable to talk to humans, Abdullah was somehow able to communicate with the dolphin, which he named Holeen, and she began to turn up regularly and take Abdullah for a swim. In the months and years that have followed, the two have become 'an item'.

This incredible bonding between a human and a wild marine mammal has, of course, attracted plenty of onlookers and eager participants, and visitors are now swamping Abdullah's village in the hope of swimming with Holeen. To ensure her return to the bay each day the villagers now feed her. They also charge visitors E£10 to go for a swim and E£10 to rent a mask and snorkel.

If you do take the plunge, remember to take off any jewellery or sharp items before entering the water and try to be content with viewing rather than chasing and grabbing at Holeen. One flick of her tail is enough to propel her away from unwanted suitors, but if the attention becomes too much this graceful creature of the deep is just as likely to go back from where she came.

there are cheaper cabins for E£46/62 singles/doubles, including breakfast. Camping costs E£10 and is a bit of a rip-off; but simply using its beach for the day would cost the same anyway.

Further down the road is *Al-Waha Tourism Village* (☎/fax 500 420/1) which has 16 large tents at E£12.50 per person. Stuffy, pastel-toned wooden huts cost E£55 a double. It also has slightly better air-con rooms with bathrooms at E£80/100. Break-

fast and taxes are not included in these prices. The restaurant here is ordinary but there's an attractive beach-side bar (E£9 for a Stella).

Youth Camp next door is for Egyptians only.

Habiba Camp (☎/fax 500 770) has 10 huts at E£15/25 for single/doubles, as well as dormitory tents where you can sleep for E£10. The huts are fairly large and they have a beachfront restaurant where Bedouin bread is made. The only disadvantage is that groups on day trips from Sharm stop here for lunch. Still, the beach is beautiful and it's a calm place to hang out.

Heading towards the Hilton there are two more hotels. *Sultana Village* (☎ 500 490, fax 500 491) has small stone huts on the beach, each with electricity and couch-style beds. There is also a restaurant. However, at E£80/120 for doubles/triples without air-con or bathrooms (E£110/165 with air-con) it's a little overpriced.

Further down the beach is *La Siréne Resort* (☎ 500 701) with 40 tasteful, whitewashed rooms with air-con, telephone, bathrooms and TV. Singles/doubles/triples cost US$36/48/65. There is also a beach restaurant and bar and a German-run diving centre.

City Beach Village, halfway between Nuweiba City and Tarabin, is not a bad option if you just want to sit all day on a tranquil beach. You can pitch a tent for E£5, camp out in one of its reed huts for E£10 per person or go for a clean, comfortable single/double room for E£45/55, in which case breakfast is included. The restaurant has a limited range of food, including breakfast (from E£5 to E£8) and fish and steak meals (about E£20); beers are E£8.

Tarabin As Tarabin develops along Dahab lines, the choice of accommodation is becoming wider. You can get a mattress in a bamboo or concrete hut at one of the camps for E£5, and there are a couple of hotels.

Camps Judge for yourself which camps have the more solid huts – the differences are not too great. Most of these places have cafes selling food and drinks. Sudanese run a few of them, inducing their own special laid-back touch. From north to south, the camps include:

Sababa Camp (☎ 500 855) is the northernmost camp at the moment, although no doubt someone will build next to it soon. Small, clean huts with shared facilities go for E£10.

Betra Camp, also at the northern end of the beach, has 35 bungalows with fans and shared bathrooms at E£10 per person. Although it's generally tidy, the bathrooms are not as great as they could be.

Jamal is a large place popular with young Israelis; all the signs are in Hebrew. It has recently been renovated and has 40 rooms and 40 bungalows jammed into a small area. Double rooms with bath and air-con cost E£60. Huts for two people are E£20; some rooms are located on the roof. There is a 24 hour restaurant on the ground floor.

Palm Beach is a tidy place that boasts a large relaxation area, draped with vines and shaded by palms. Singles/doubles in huts with fans will set you back E£10/15 in summer. In winter they go down to E£5 per person. Breakfast costs E£8 and there are plans to open a fuul and ta'amiyya restaurant.

El Salam has sterile surroundings, loud music and aggressive people.

Camp David now has 20 rooms with air-con and their own bathrooms for E£50. Huts with fans and shared bathrooms go for E£20.

Blue Bus is one of Tarabin's original establishments. This is more like a place to eat than a camp. However, it does have a few huts with fans (E£10 per person) with rickety old reed recliners.

Soft Beach is a 30-hut camp just south of the sand dune and run by Sudanese. They charge E£15 for two, or E£10 for one in small huts. The outdoor showers have cold water only, although they swear that there is hot water available in the winter. There are horses for rent next door at E£30 to E£40 per hour.

Hotels **Elsebaey Village Hotel (☎ 500 373)** is a small, clean hotel in the heart of Tarabin with 15 tiled rooms with fan, cupboard, and a double bed, plus communal bathroom facilities, for E£40 per room. Rooms with bathroom and air-con cost E£80. There is also a rooftop bar, a ground floor restaurant and a supermarket.

Al-Salam Village (☎ 500 440) is a spacious 100 room place occupying the point at the northern end of Nuweiba bay. However, the setting is austere and inconvenient for anything but the sea. Many Israelis stay here but, at US$35/45 for air-con singles/doubles (with breakfast, TV and refrigerator), it's overpriced for the slightly shabby prefab rooms.

Places to Eat

If you're staying at either the port or Tarabin, dining options are limited mainly to the hotels and camps. At the port, you'll also find a gang of cheap eateries about 150m off to your left (with your back to the port entrance). In Tarabin there's a supermarket in front of Elsebaey Village Hotel selling junk food and basic groceries. Across the street **Blue Bus Camp** is a popular eating spot and has pizzas starting at E£12 and meals for about E£20. **Supermarket Aiwa** between Palm Beach camp and El Salam camp also sells food supplies and has an international card phone outside. Further along on the seafront is the small but popular **Aid Abu Goma** fish restaurant. This place serves fresh fish dishes beginning at E£25 but remember that it gets extremely crowded during Israeli holidays.

The choice of eateries in Nuweiba City is significantly better; in fact, the open-air bazaar here has some of the best budget diners found in all of Sinai. The immensely popular **Dr Shishkebab** offers a generous spread of ta'amiyya, salad, fried eggplant and humous with all meals. All this with a big serving of very good *daoud pasha* (meatballs in a rich tomato sauce) and rice costs E£17. The unmistakable 'doctor' is a white-turbaned, big, cheerful man wandering from table to table, attentively waiting on all those who eat here. Sometimes he and his friends will bring out their *tablas* and hold an impromptu concert.

Another superb place in the bazaar is **Sendbad**. Its portions are even bigger and cheaper than at Dr Shishkebab, and the owner is just as genial.

Around the corner is the tiny *Pizzina* restaurant which has excellent pizzas with fresh toppings for E£12 and more.

At the Helnan Holiday Camp's *beach-side bar* you can get chicken/fish meals for E£18/25, as well as cheaper snacks and Stella.

Getting There & Away

Bus Getting a bus out of Nuweiba can be a bit confusing, especially if you're staying in nearby Tarabin. Buses going to or from Taba pass down the highway and turn at the hospital to do a circuit past the Helnan Holiday Camp and Dr Shishkebab, before heading out again and proceeding on their way. They usually also call in at the port, stopping at either the bus station or in front of the Motel Marina just opposite. You can presumably pick the buses up at any of these places (you can certainly get off). However, if it's possible, make sure you check the routing for your specific bus with the locals as the pick-up points have been known to change and not all the buses call into the port.

Buses to Cairo and other destinations generally meet incoming ferries. The bus from Taba to Cairo (E£50) via St Katherine's (E£10) stops at the police station by the Helnan at 10 to 10.30 am and arrives at the port at around 11 am (sometimes earlier). There's another bus to Cairo at 3 pm which costs E£55. Buses to Sharm el-Sheikh (E£20) via Dahab (E£10) leave at 6.30 am and 4 pm; to Taba at 6 am (E£10) and at noon (E£19); and to Suez at 6 am (E£25, six hours via Nakhl).

Service Taxi There is a big service-taxi station by the port, and for once in Sinai there are flat rates more in line with what Egyptians might be prepared to pay. The fare to Suez is E£40 and E£50 to Midan Ulali in Cairo.

As Tarabin's popularity has escalated, service taxis here take people directly out on the road north to Israel or south to Dahab, St Katherine's Monastery or Sharm el-Sheikh.

Car Rental vehicles are available from Europcar at the Hilton Coral Resort.

Boat For detailed information about ferries and speedboats to Aqaba in Jordan, see the Sea section in the Getting There & Away chapter.

Getting Around

A *tof-tof* (open-sided bus) supposedly shuttles between the port, Nuweiba City and Tarabin from about 6 am to 6 pm but it seems to be constantly broken down. If it starts working again it should cost E£1 and will stop anywhere.

In Tarabin, service taxis ask an outrageous E£5 to E£10 for the few kilometres between Tarabin and Nuweiba City, and E£15 to the port. The only other option here for getting to one of the bus stops in Nuweiba City is to walk the 2km.

NUWEIBA TO TABA

Along the stunning coastline north of Nuweiba, especially near Taba, are many large, expensive 'tourist villages', in various stages of completion. Although most of them have been designed with at least some modesty (no skyscrapers here), they mar the wild beauty of this desert coast, as indeed will the plane and bus loads of package tourists they are hoping to attract.

Beaches

There are still some desolate beaches backed by stunning blue waters and pockets of fringing reefs to be found along this stretch of road. The only way to get to them is by service taxi, hitching or bus (but you'll probably have to pay the full Nuweiba to Taba fare).

About 8km north of Nuweiba is *Maagana Beach* where a row of huts, in honeycomb formation, is stretched out along a lovely bay.

On the road a little further north from Maagana Beach is a place for snacks and drinks.

About 2 to 3km further on lies **Ras Shaitan** ('Satan's Head'), a rocky point jutting out into the water and harbouring on its northern side a small cluster of simple Bedouin-run camps with names like *Mazag* (which roughly translates as 'mood') that cost between E£15 to E£20 per person. The New Age types that frequent this place can be a little over the top but there is excellent snorkelling and a peaceful atmosphere.

Another 7km on is *Barracuda Village* which has a series of waterfront stone huts (and a big ugly resort nearby). About 3km further is the quite isolated three star *Bawaki Beach Hotel (☎ 500 470)* where you can walk virtually from your beachfront hut straight into some great snorkelling sites.

Basata (☎ 500 481 or Cairo ☎ 350 1829) is one of the most famous hotels/camps in Sinai and is about 23km north of Nuweiba. Basata means 'simplicity' in Arabic, and this simple, clean, ecologically minded travellers' settlement reflects its name. Owner Sherif Ghamrawy is an environmentalist who recently started Nuweiba's first recycling program and his concern for the environment is reflected in the philosophy of the hotel, where the produce is organically grown and guests separate their garbage into marked bins for recycling. There is a common kitchen hut, a bakery and a camping ground. Its 18 bamboo huts cost E£25 per person and if you want to sleep on the beach it costs E£15 per person. You can come and use the beach here if the hotel is not crowded, but there is a E£10 day entrance charge. There is great snorkelling in the bay but scuba diving is not allowed. It's advisable to book ahead as it gets very crowded on Egyptian and Israeli holidays.

About 5km north of Basata is the 90 room *Club Aqua Sun (☎ 530 391, fax 530 390)* which has rooms for US$24/35/40, including breakfast. Like most of these beach hotels/camps it has a great beach and wonderful reef.

Beyond this is the two star *Sally Land Holiday Village (☎ 530 380, fax 530 381)*. Singles/doubles here cost US$42/50 including breakfast. Despite its somewhat unlikely name, Sally Land is frequented by New Age tourists from Europe and they do not look kindly on kids or adults who make noise on the beach and disturb their meditation sessions.

The Fjord

This small, protected bay is a popular sunbathing spot only about 15km short of Taba. Up on the rise to the north is the small, clean *Salima Motel (☎ 530 130/1)* run by the amiable Mohammed Magdi. It has six basic rooms where you can stay for E£40/60 for singles/doubles; meals cost E£10/20/25 for breakfast/lunch/dinner. Book ahead if you want to stay overnight as it's very popular with Israelis.

Pharaoh's Island

Only 7km short of Taba, Pharaoh's Island (Gezirat Fara'un) lies about 250m off the Egyptian coast. The islet is dominated by the much restored Castle of Salah ad-Din, a fortress actually built by the Crusaders in 1115, but captured and expanded by Salah ad-Din in 1170 as a bulwark against feared Crusader penetration south from Palestine. At the height of Crusader successes, it was feared they might attempt to head for the holy cities of Mecca and Medina. Some of the modern restoration is painfully obvious (concrete was not a prime building material in Salah ad-Din's time), but the island is a pleasant place for a half-day trip. The limpid aqua waters are extremely inviting, and a lot of Israeli pleasure boats carrying divers cruise down here from nearby Eilat. From the island you can see the Taba Hilton and the port city of Aqaba in Jordan.

Pharaoh's Island is open from 9 am to 5 pm and entry costs US$6 (US$3 for students), but the boat ride there and back is an outlandish US$4. Tickets for the boat are available in the cafeteria next to the Salah ad-Din Hotel and those for the island on landing.

Salah ad-Din Hotel (☎ 530 340/2, fax 530 343), opposite Pharaoh's Island, has 120 low-key rooms, where singles/doubles are overpriced at US$72/93. All rooms have air-con and bathrooms and there's a

SINAI

restaurant, with dinner for US$13. There is also a fairly pricey *cafe* on the island.

TABA

Until 1989, a few hundred metres of beach, a luxury hotel and a coffee shop at Taba, a place on the Israel-Egypt border, was a minor point of contention between the two countries. After several years of squabbling and formal arbitration, the land was returned to Egypt. Since 1982, when the rest of Sinai was returned by Israel, Taba has served as a busy border crossing. The border is open 24 hours a day, except from Friday to Saturday night, the Jewish Sabbath.

There is a small post and telephone office in the 'town', along with a hospital, bakery and an EgyptAir office (often closed). You can change money at booths of Banque du Caire (unreliable opening hours) and Banque Masr (open 24 hours), both 100m before the border, or at the Taba Hilton Hotel. Their rates vary only slightly.

Places to Stay & Eat

The 11 storey *Taba Hilton* (☎ 530 300) has rooms for US$160/208 a single/double, including taxes, and a diving centre. At its new addition, *Nelson Village* (☎ 530 140), rooms are even pricier at US$185/233.

Sometime in 1999, the first hotels in a gigantic new touristic development called Taba Heights are due to open near here and you will have the choice of yet more big, overpriced resorts.

Panorama Restaurant, opposite the bus station, seems to have been abandoned by all and sundry, probably because it charges E£5 for a cola. Slightly cheaper but pretty unwelcoming is the *cafeteria* at the bus station where you'll need to bargain for a meal of fish, rice and salad (E£15) as well as for a coffee or water.

Getting There & Away

Air EgyptAir has flights to Ras an-Naqb airport, 38km away from Taba, each Monday for E£497. Once the gigantic Taba Heights development gets going in late 1999, Orascom Air will also have flights here.

Bus East Delta Bus Co runs several buses from Taba. The 10 am bus goes to Nuweiba (E£10), St Katherine's Monastery (E£25) and on to Cairo (E£60). Another bus to Cairo (E£65) leaves at 2 pm but goes via Nakhl. Other buses leave at 9 am and 3 pm for Sharm el-Sheikh (E£35), stopping at Nuweiba (E£10) and Dahab (E£15). To Nuweiba only there's another bus at 2 pm. To Suez (E£40, five hours via Nakhl) there's one at 7 am.

Getting Around

Service Taxi A taxi (up to seven people) to Nuweiba costs E£30 per person or E£210, and E£300 to Sharm el-Sheikh. To Cairo you're looking at E£50 to E£60 per person. You may also find a minibus or two which will take you to Dahab for about E£15 per person. Your bargaining power increases if the bus is not too far off.

Car The only rental car option here is Europcar (☎ 379 222, fax 379 660) at the Taba Hilton Hotel.

ST KATHERINE'S MONASTERY

There are 22 Greek Orthodox monks living in this ancient monastery at the foot of Mt Sinai. The monastic order was founded in the 4th century AD by the Byzantine empress Helena, who had a small chapel built beside what was believed to be the burning bush from which God spoke to Moses.

The chapel is dedicated to St Katherine, the legendary martyr of Alexandria, who was tortured on a spiked wheel and then beheaded for her Christianity. Her body was supposedly transported by angels away from the torture device (which spun out of control and killed the pagan onlookers) and onto the slopes of Gebel Katarina, the highest mountain in Egypt, which is about 6km south of Mt Sinai. The body was 'found' about 300 years later by monks from the monastery.

In the 6th century, Emperor Justinian ordered the building of a fortress, with a basilica and a monastery, as well as the original chapel, to serve as a secure home for the

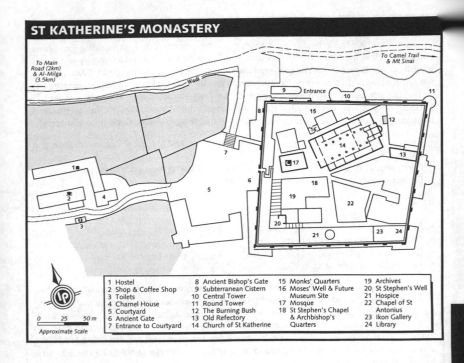

ST KATHERINE'S MONASTERY

To Main
Road (2km)
& Al-Milga
(3.5km)

To Camel Trail
& Mt Sinai

Wadi

9 Entrance
10
11
8
15
12
16
14
13
7
17
1
6
18
2
4
5
19
22
3
20
21
23 24

0   25   50 m
Approximate Scale

1 Hostel	8 Ancient Bishop's Gate	15 Monks' Quarters	19 Archives
2 Shop & Coffee Shop	9 Subterranean Cistern	16 Moses' Well & Future	20 St Stephen's Well
3 Toilets	10 Central Tower	Museum Site	21 Hospice
4 Charnel House	11 Round Tower	17 Mosque	22 Chapel of St
5 Courtyard	12 The Burning Bush	18 St Stephen's Chapel	Antonius
6 Ancient Gate	13 Old Refectory	& Archbishop's	23 Ikon Gallery
7 Entrance to Courtyard	14 Church of St Katherine	Quarters	24 Library

monks of St Katherine's and as a refuge for the Christians of southern Sinai. Since then it has been visited by Christian pilgrims from throughout the world, many of whom braved extremely difficult and dangerous journeys in order to get to this isolated place.

Nowadays the hazards accompanying a trip here have disappeared and the monastery and Mt Sinai can be choked with tour buses and people, especially in the morning. When you visit, remember that this is still a functioning monastery, not a museum piece. The only parts of the monastery to which members of the public are admitted are the chapel and a rather macabre room full of the bones of deceased monks; you are also permitted to view part of a splendid collection of icons and jewelled crosses. St Katherine's monastery is open to visitors daily except on Friday, Sunday and holidays from 9 am to noon.

Orientation & Information

The monastery is about 3.5km from the village of Katreen, called Al-Milga or the 'meeting place' by local Jabaliya Bedouin, or 2km from the large roundabout on the road between the two. At Al-Milga there is a bank, telephone centrale (open 24 hours), police station, tourist police office (next to the mosque), several hotels and a variety of shops and cafes. The Banque Masr will change cash or travellers cheques and may accept Visa and MasterCard for a cash advance. It's open from 9 am to 2 pm and 6 to 9 pm.

Mt Sinai

Although some archaeologists and historians dispute Mt Sinai's biblical claim to fame, it is revered by Christians, Muslims and Jews, all of whom believe that God delivered his Ten Commandments to Moses from its summit.

SINAI

St Katherine Protectorate

By the early 1990s the impact of mass tourism on the monastery and surrounding mountains was being felt in the form of huge amounts of garbage on Mt Sinai and seemingly unfettered touristic development in Al-Milga, where hotels were multiplying alarmingly. In 1996, authorities finally acted and a prime ministerial decree created the 4350 sq km St Katherine Protectorate.

This large, mountainous area contains a unique high-altitude desert ecosystem as well as a wealth of historical sites sacred to the world's three monotheistic religions. In order to limit the impact of tourists upon this special place, the following **Trekkers Code** is now in force:

- Respect the area's religious and historical importance and the local Bedouin culture and traditions.
- Carry your litter out with you, bury your bodily waste and burn your toilet paper.
- Do not contaminate or overuse water sources.

It is illegal to:

- Remove any object, including rocks, plants and animals.
- Disturb or harm animals or birds.
- Cut or uproot plants.
- Write, paint or carve graffiti.

The protectorate has also published informative guides to four 'interpretive trails' established in the area, including Mt Sinai. The well produced booklets take you through each trail, explaining flora and fauna as well as sites of historical and religious significance, and are available from the Visitors Centre at the monastery for E£5 each. The money is used to maintain the trails. To allow the local population to benefit from tourism, you are also requested to hire a local Bedouin guide. They can be found in Al-Milga and charge about E£20 to E£25 for a half-day's walk.

At a height of 2285m, Mt Sinai (Gebel Musa is the local name) towers over St Katherine's Monastery. It is easy to climb and there are two well defined routes to the summit – the camel trail and the Steps of Repentance. Mt Sinai is not, however, the mountain directly up the valley behind the monastery; that one is far lower! From the top you can look across to the even higher summit of Gebel Katarina.

The camel trail is the easier route and this climb takes about two hours. Usually, there are at least four or five tea and Coca-Cola stands on the trail, catering to those in need of a caffeine fix. At the stand where the camel trail meets the steps, a full breakfast is sometimes available.

The alternative path to the summit, the taxing 3000 Steps of Repentance, was laid by one monk as a form of penance. If you want to try both routes, it's best to take the path on the way up and the steps on the way back down, particularly if you want a great view of the monastery.

During the summer, you should avoid the heat by beginning your hike at 2 or 3 am. This way, you'll also see the sunrise. Although stone signs have been placed on the trail to guide you, it can be a bit difficult in parts, so a torch (flashlight) is essential.

Because of the sanctity of the mountains and the tremendous pressure that large groups place on the desert environment, the National Parks office has instituted a few much-needed rules to staying here. Apart from the basic trekkers code (see the boxed text 'St Katherine Protectorate' opposite), if you spend the night on the mountain, you are asked to sleep just below the summit at the small plateau known as Elijah's Basin. It is dominated by a 500 year old cypress tree, marking the spot where the prophet Elijah heard the voice of God. Five composting toilets have been placed here to prevent pollution of the site. You can climb to the summit to watch the sunrise.

If do you plan to spend the night on the summit, make sure you have plenty of food and water. As it gets cold and windy there, even in summer, you will also need warm clothes and a sleeping bag (there is no space to pitch a tent). Sometimes you can rent a blanket for a pound or two. As late as mid-May, be prepared to share the summit with hordes of tourists, some bearing ghetto-blasters, others carrying Bibles and hymn books. With the music and singing, and people nudging each other for a space on the holy mountain, don't expect to get much sleep, especially in the wee small hours before sunrise.

On the summit itself is a Greek Orthodox chapel containing beautiful paintings and ornaments, and a small mosque. However, these were so desecrated by tourists in the 1980s that they're usually kept locked. The summit also offers spectacular views of the surrounding bare, jagged mountains and plunging valleys where, throughout the day, the rocks and cliffs change colour as if they were stone chameleons.

Places to Stay

St Katherine's Monastery runs a *hostel*. Although the reception is open all day, check-in is only between 8 am and 1 pm, and 4 and 10 pm. The hostel offers single-sex dormitories (seven beds) which cost E£35 per person, and rooms with three beds and private bathroom for E£40 per person. The facilities are basic and many travellers have complained that the bathrooms are less than clean. Breakfast costs E£4, lunch or dinner is E£8. You can leave your baggage in one of the rooms

while you hike up Mt Sinai. This service will cost you about E£2 in baksheesh.

Blending in with the surrounding landscape, right by the roundabout 2km west of the monastery, is the pricey *St Katherine's Tourist Village* (☎ 470 333, fax 470 323) where singles/doubles/triples cost US$130/156/197 including breakfast and dinner. The air-con rooms, all with TV and bathroom, have views of the distant monastery.

Off to your right about 400m before you reach the mosque in Al-Milga, on the hill opposite the Al-Fairoz hotel, is a cluster of three hotels. The three star *Daniela Village* (☎ 470 225) has 52 stone bungalows with comfortable enough rooms for US$49/65/79, including breakfast. Inexplicably they're planning on doubling their capacity, although they're usually only half full.

Next door, *Al-Wadi al-Mouqudus* (☎ 470 225), a 58 room, two star place with rooms for E£130/180/230, including breakfast. Beside this is the totally incongruous *Catherine Plaza Hotel* (☎ 470 289, fax 470 292), a flashy 128 room, five star hotel with a pool and several restaurants and bars. Rooms here cost US$75/100/115 which includes breakfast.

About 6km on the Nuweiba road is *Morgenland Village* (☎ 470 331) where singles/doubles cost US$80/102. Breakfast is extra. About 4km further on, at the turn-off to Dahab, is the very basic *Green Lodge Camping* (☎ 470 314) with restaurant. Another 10km on, 5km down the Dahab turn-off and next to the airport, is *Al-Salam Hotel* (☎ 470 409) where you can get a double room with breakfast for US$16.

Places to Eat

In Al-Milga there's a *bakery* opposite the mosque and a couple of well stocked *supermarkets* in the shopping arcade. Just behind the bakery are a few small restaurants, the most reasonable of which is *Kafeteria Ikhlas*; try its chicken meal with soup for E£12. Just by the bus stop *Katrien Rest House* (no accommodation) is open for lunch only and also serves a filling chicken, rice and vegetable meal.

Across the square, near the bank, is the popular *Restaurant for Friends* where meals go for about E£8.

The modern *Al-Monaga* cafeteria by the roundabout principally caters to tour bus groups. A chicken meal, with soup and salad, will cost you E£17.

Getting There & Away

Bus You can ask the driver to drop you off at the roundabout, which is closer to the monastery. Buses leave from the square in front of the mosque in Al-Milga. Sometime between noon and 1 pm, a bus leaves for Sharm el-Sheikh (E£20) via Dahab (E£15). The bus for Suez (E£20, five hours) leaves at 6 am, which is much better value than the direct Cairo bus, as you can get a bus or service taxi from Suez to Cairo for about E£8. At 10 am there's a bus to Cairo (E£40) en route from Taba. A bus to Taba (E£20) via Nuweiba (E£15) departs at 3.30 pm, but it sometimes goes to Nuweiba only.

Service Taxi Service taxis travel in and out of the village irregularly and infrequently. If you're lucky, you might be able to find a taxi driver who is willing to take you all the way to Cairo for about E£300 for the taxi (up to seven people). A similar taxi to Suez will cost about E£200, after intense bargaining. At the monastery taxis often wait for people coming down from Mt Sinai in the early afternoon. Count on between E£10 and E£20 per person to Dahab or Nuweiba.

WADI FEIRAN

This lush date-palm oasis, a Bedouin outpost between the west coast of Sinai and St Katherine's Monastery, lies amid rough, barren desert and harsh, rocky hills. There is a convent on the western edge of Wadi Feiran, but you need permission from St Katherine's Monastery if you want to visit it.

AL-ARISH

Much of the north coast of Sinai, from Port Fuad most of the way to Al-Arish, is dominated by the swampy lagoon of Lake Bardawil, separated from the Mediterranean by a limestone ridge and making the area hardly attractive for swimming. The road follows what must be one of the oldest march routes throughout history, used by the pharaohs to penetrate into what is now Israel, Jordan and on to Syria, and by the Persians, Greeks, Crusaders, Arab Muslims and many others coming the other way.

Al-Arish, beyond Lake Bardawil, is the capital of North Sinai Governorate and has a population of about 40,000. Its greatest asset, a palm-fringed beach, is becoming increasingly fragmented by expanding construction along the coast. The place, at present, is not heavily visited by either Egyptians or foreign tourists, except in the height of summer, when middle class Cairo moves in *en masse*.

Orientation & Information

The main coastal road, Sharia Fuad Zikry, forms a T-junction with Sharia 23rd of July, which runs a couple of kilometres south (changing name to Sharia Tahrir on the way) to the bus and service-taxi stations.

The tourist office is on Sharia Fuad Zikry, just down from Sinai Beach Hotel. Opening hours are unclear – it never seems to be open.

The National Bank of Egypt, on Sharia Tahrir, is open Sunday to Thursday from 9 am to 2.30 pm. Nearby, a street back from Sharia Tahrir, is Banque Masr. The Bank of Alexandria and Banque du Caire both have branches on Sharia 23rd of July.

The post office, open from 8.30 am to 2.30 pm except on Friday, is a block east of Banque Masr. The 24 hour telephone centrale is around the corner from the post office.

Things to See & Do

The **Zerenike Protectorate** is a haven for migrating birds that was established by Egypt's National Parks office in 1985. It covers a 220 sq km area running along the coast from the eastern part of Lake Bardawil until about 25km east of Al-Arish. The entrance to the protectorate is about 35km east of Al-Arish and there is a US$5 entrance fee. Inside the gates there is a Visi-

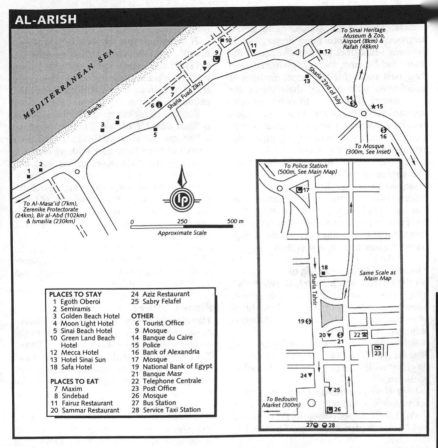

AL-ARISH

MEDITERRANEAN SEA

Beach

To Sinai Heritage
Museum & Zoo,
Airport (8km) &
Rafah (48km)

Sharia Fuad Zikry

Sharia 23rd of July

To Mosque
(300m, See Inset)

To Al-Masa'id (7km),
Zerenike Protectorate
(24km), Bir al-Abd (102km)
& Ismailia (230km)

0   250   500 m
Approximate Scale

To Police Station
(500m, See Main Map)

Sharia Tahrir

Same Scale as
Main Map

To Bedouin
Market (300m)

PLACES TO STAY	24 Aziz Restaurant
1 Egoth Oberoi	25 Sabry Felafel
2 Semiramis	
3 Golden Beach Hotel	OTHER
4 Moon Light Hotel	6 Tourist Office
5 Sinai Beach Hotel	9 Mosque
10 Green Land Beach	14 Banque du Caire
Hotel	15 Police
12 Mecca Hotel	16 Bank of Alexandria
13 Hotel Sinai Sun	17 Mosque
18 Safa Hotel	19 National Bank of Egypt
	21 Banque Masr
PLACES TO EAT	22 Telephone Centrale
7 Maxim	23 Post Office
8 Sindebad	26 Mosque
11 Fairuz Restaurant	27 Bus Station
20 Sammar Restaurant	28 Service Taxi Station

SINAI

tors Centre with a cafeteria and information about the protectorate and some of the many species of birds that stop here on their journey between Europe and Africa. It is open every day between sunrise and sunset.

The **Sinai Heritage Museum**, on the coastal road to Rafah on the outskirts of town, was established several years ago to inform people about life in Sinai. The museum's displays include Bedouin handicrafts, tools, clothing and traditional medicines, supplemented by the odd English explanation. It's

open Saturday to Thursday from 9.30 am to 2 pm. Entry is E£1 plus E£5/25 for a camera/video.

Next door is a miserable **zoo** and among its unhappy inmates is a range of nocturnal desert creatures that are kept in barred cages, unprotected from the blazing sun. There's not even a darkened antechamber where they can secrete themselves. This is a disgrace to animal lovers.

Every Thursday, when the **souq** is held in the oldest part of town, Bedouin come in om the desert in pick-up trucks or on camels. The veiled women trade silver, beadwork and embroidered dresses, while the men sell camel saddles. Although the crafts can be fine, the savvy women save their best items for the large numbers of middlemen who buy up their wares for Cairo shops. They tend to palm off substandard stuff to tourists. Still, it is a sight to see the women arrive and bargain. Sometimes you can see them buying gold after having sold their handiwork.

The other main attraction is the **beach**. The parade of palms, fine white sand and clean water (even the odd small wave) make this one of the nicer Mediterranean spots in Egypt. As is unfortunately so often the case, women may feel somewhat uncomfortable swimming here. There is supposedly a beach curfew after dark.

Places to Stay – Budget
On the beach *Golden Beach Hotel* (☎ 342 270) has a conglomeration of drab cement bungalows with up to three beds at E£15 per bungalow. It also has cold showers; breakfast is not included.

Just up the road and marginally better is *Moon Light Hotel* (☎ 341 362) which has singles/doubles costing E£15/30 including breakfast.

Safa Hotel, on Sharia Tahrir, is a noisy place and has doubles with private bath (cold) for E£10 per person or E£5 without bath. Solo women would be ill-advised to stay here.

Behind the New Golden Beach is *Mecca Hotel* (☎/fax 344 909), a friendly, good, clean place that has singles/doubles with fan and hot water for E£30/40.

One of the better deals is the *Green Land Beach Hotel* (☎ 340 601), virtually on the beach. Clean and comfortable double/triple rooms with bathroom cost E£25/30. Breakfast is extra and most rooms have terraces.

Places to Stay – Mid-Range & Top End
The popular beachfront restaurant *Maxim* (☎ 340 850) has expanded to now offer rooms and chalets as well. They are only open in summer.

Hotel Sinai Sun (☎ 341 855) is a reasonable place with single/double rooms at US$14/18 (winter) and US$21/25 (summer). The price does not include breakfast (E£6), but rooms come with bath, TV, phone and air-con.

Slightly better but quite a bit more pricey is *Sinai Beach Hotel* (☎ 341 713). Some of the rooms, which cost E£115/130 without breakfast, have balconies looking across to the sea. There's also a restaurant and a coffee shop.

Further to the south-west are Al-Arish's two luxury places. *Semiramis* (☎ 344 167, fax 344 168) has rooms away from the beach for US$37/64. The pool costs E£10 for nonguests.

Rooms at *Egoth Oberoi* (☎ 351 321, fax 352 352) cost US$102/116 not including breakfast. Those not staying at the hotel can use the pool for E£25.

Places to Eat
There's not a huge range of places in Al-Arish. About as good as you'll find in the budget range is *Aziz Restaurant* on Sharia Tahrir. It has good meals of fuul and ta'amiyya as well as grilled chicken, kofta, rice and spaghetti, and is also open for breakfast.

Sabry, opposite Aziz in the back corner of a little square, makes the best felafel. At *Sammar Restaurant* (signposted in Arabic) on Sharia Tahrir you can get kebab and kofta.

At the junction of Sharia Fuad Zikry and Sharia 23rd of July is *Fairuz Restaurant* (☎ 343 307). It serves kofta, kebab, fish and chicken in reasonably generous portions, although the main drawback is it's closed in winter.

Further west along Sharia Fuad Zikry is *Sindebad*, a fuul and ta'amiyya place.

On the beach, among the palms, is the classier *Maxim*, specialising in fish dishes which will set you back about E£25 to E£40. It serves good food, but is open in summer only.

Getting There & Away
Bus Buses for Cairo (five hours) leave Al-Arish at 7 am (E£25) and 4 pm (E£35). There is a bus via Qantara (E£5) to Ismailia (E£7, three hours) every hour until 3 pm. The 7 am and 3 pm Ismailia buses go on to Mansura (E£11), and the 7, 7.45 and 9 am and 3 pm buses go to Zagazig (E£9). For Suez, you have to go to Ismailia and take another bus from there. At 7.15 and 10.30 am there's a bus to Rafah (E£1.50). The bus bypasses Rafah town and takes you directly to the Egyptian border post at which point you disembark with your bags and go through passport control. After this you are forced to take a shuttle bus to the Israeli border post (you're prohibited from walking). You have to pay a tax of about E£20 before continuing on to Rafah.

Service Taxi A cheaper alternative to the expensive Sinai buses to Cairo is a service taxi, which costs about E£12 per person. Service taxis to Qantara cost E£5, E£6 to Ismailia, and to the border (or vice versa) they like to charge anything from E£5 to E£7.

Getting Around
There is a regular stream of buses, microbuses and service taxis (huge US limousines dating back to the 1960s at least) running between the bus station and the satellite residential area of Al-Masa'id to the south-west. It'll cost you between E£3 and E£5 to take a taxi. Microbuses shuttle between the bus station and the beach for 25pt.

RAFAH
This coastal town, 48km north of Al-Arish, marks the border with the Gaza Strip and Israel. Although town fathers apparently feel the warm Mediterranean location could make it an ideal resort, it has no hotels (there are some *chalets*). The nearest cheap hotel is in Sheikh Zuweid, 17km short of Rafah.

The border crossing is actually 4km from the town.

Getting There & Away
A couple of local buses run between Rafah town and Al-Arish for E£1. For border crossing details see the Getting There & Away chapter.

SINAI

Language

Arabic is the official language of Egypt. However, the Arabic spoken on the streets differs greatly from the standard Arabic written in newspapers, spoken on the radio or recited in prayers at the mosque.

Egyptian Colloquial Arabic (ECA) is fun, but difficult to learn. It is basically a dialect of the standard language, but so different in many respects as to be virtually like another language. As with most dialects, it is the everyday language that differs the most from that of Egypt's other Arabic-speaking neighbours. More specialised or educated language tends to be pretty much the same across the Arab world, although pronunciation may vary considerably. An Arab from, say, Jordan or Iraq, will have no problem having a chat about politics or literature with an Egyptian, but might have more trouble making himself understood in the bakery.

There is no official written form of the Egyptian Arabic dialect, although there is no practical reason for this – Nobel Prize-winning author Naguib Mahfouz has no trouble writing out whole passages using predominantly Egyptian (or Cairene) slang.

For some reason though, foreigners specifically wanting to learn the Egyptian dialect (instead of Modern Standard Arabic, or MSA, the written and spoken lingua franca understood by most, and in fact not so far removed from the daily language of the Arab countries of the Levant) are told that it can't be written, and then presented with one system or other of transliteration as a poor substitute – none of them totally satisfactory. For the student of MSA, such systems can be a hindrance rather than a help. An esoteric argument flows back and forward between those who say you should learn MSA first and then a dialect (which could mean waiting a very long time before you can converse adequately with people on the streets), and those who argue the opposite. If you're getting a headache now, that will give you some idea of why few

non-Arabs and non-Muslims embark on the study of the language.

Nevertheless, if you take the time to learn even a few words and phrases, you'll discover and experience much more while travelling through the country. For a more comprehensive guide to the language, get hold of Lonely Planet's *Egyptian Arabic phrasebook*.

Pronunciation

Pronunciation of Arabic can be somewhat tongue-tying for someone unfamiliar with the intonation and combination of sounds. Pronounce the transliterated words and phrases slowly and clearly.

The following guide should help, but it isn't complete because the myriad rules governing pronunciation and vowel use are too extensive to be covered here.

Short Vowels

a	as in 'had' (sometimes very short)
e	as in 'bet' (sometimes very short)
i	as in 'hit'
o	as in 'hot'
u	as in 'book'

Long Vowels

Long vowels are indicated by a macron (stroke above the letter).

ā	as the 'a' in 'father'
ē	as the 'e' in 'ten', but lengthened
ī	as the 'e' in 'ear', only softer
ō	as the 'o' in 'four'
ū	as the 'oo' in 'food'

You may also see long vowels transliterated as double vowels, eg 'aa' (ā), 'ee' (ī) and 'oo' (ū).

Diphthongs (vowel combinations)

aw	as the 'ow' in 'how'
ay	as 'y' in 'why'
ei	as the 'a' in 'cake'

The Arabic Alphabet

Final	Medial	Initial	Alone	Transliteration	Pronunciation
ا			ا	ā	as the 'a' in 'father'
ب	ج	ب	ب	b	as in 'bet'
ت	ت	ت	ت	t	as in 'ten'
ث	ث	ث	ث	th	as in 'thin'
ج	ج	ج	ج	g	as in 'go'
ح	ح	ح	ح	H	a strongly whispered 'h', almost like a sigh of relief
خ	خ	خ	خ	kh	as the 'ch' in Scottish *loch*
د	د		د	d	as in 'dim'
ذ	ذ		ذ	dh	as the 'th' in 'this'
ر			ر	r	a rolled 'r', as in the Spanish word *caro*
ز			ز	z	as in 'zip'
س	س	س	س	s	as in 'so', never as in 'wisdom'
ش	ش	ش	ش	sh	as in 'ship'
ص	ص	ص	ص	ş	emphatic 's'
ض	ض	ض	ض	ḍ	emphatic 'd'
ط	ط	ط	ط	ṭ	emphatic 't'
ظ	ظ	ظ	ظ	ẕ	emphatic 'z'
ع	ع	ع	ع	'	the Arabic letter 'ayn; pronounce as a glottal stop – like the closing of the throat before saying 'Oh oh!' (see Other Sounds on p. 516)
غ	غ	غ	غ	gh	a guttural sound like Parisian 'r'
ف	ف	ف	ف	f	as in 'far'
ق	ق	ق	ق	q	a strongly guttural 'k' sound; in Egyptian Arabic often pronounced as a glottal stop
ك	ك	ك	ك	k	as in 'king'
ل	ل	ل	ل	l	as in 'lamb'
م	م	م	م	m	as in 'me'
ن	ن	ن	ن	n	as in 'name'
ه	ه	ه	ه	h	as in 'ham'
و			و	w	as in 'wet'; or
				ū	long, as the 'oo' on 'fool'; or
				aw	as the 'ow' in 'how'
ي	ي	ي	ي	y	as in 'yes'; or
				ī	as the 'e' in 'here'; or
				ay	as the 'y' in 'by' or as the 'ay' in 'way'

Vowels Not all Arabic vowel sounds are represented in the alphabet. See the pronunciation guide on p. 514

Emphatic Consonants To simplify the transliterations in this book, emphatic consonants have not been included

These last two are tricky, as one can slide into the other in certain words, depending on who is pronouncing them. Remember that these rules are an outline, and far from exhaustive.

Consonants

Pronunciation for all Arabic consonants is covered in the alphabet table on the preceding page. Note that when double consonants occur in transliterations, both are pronounced. For example, *el-hammam* (toilet), is pronounced 'el-ham-mam'.

Other sounds

Arabic has two sounds that are very tricky for non-Arabs to produce, the 'ayn and the glottal stop. The letter 'ayn represents a sound with no English equivalent that comes even close. It is similar to the glottal stop (which is not actually represented in the alphabet) but the muscles at the back of the throat are gagged more forcefully – it has been described as the sound of someone being strangled! In many transliteration systems 'ayn is represented by an opening quotation mark, and the glottal stop by a closing quotation mark. To make the transliterations in this language guide (and throughout the rest of the book) easier to use, we have not distinguished between the glottal stop and the 'ayn, using the closing quotation mark to represent both sounds. You'll find that Arab speakers will still understand you.

Transliteration

Converting what for most outsiders is just a bunch of squiggles into meaningful words (ie, those written using the roman alphabet) is a tricky business – in fact no really satisfactory system of transliteration has been established, and probably never will be. For this edition, an attempt has been made to standardise some spellings of place names and the like. There is only one word for 'the' in Arabic: 'al'. (Before certain consonants, it modifies: in Arabic, Saladin's name is Salah ad-Din, meaning 'righteousness of the faith'; here, 'al' has been modified to 'ad' before the 'd' of 'Din'.) Nevertheless, 'el' is often used. This has been left only in

a few circumstances such as well-known place names (El Alamein, Sharm el-Sheikh) or where locals have used it in, say, restaurant and hotel names. Riverside boulevards in Nile cities are often called Corniche el-Nil (pronounced Corniche an-Nil). Whichever way you see these little blighters spelt, either in the book or in the signs you come up against, remember that they are all the same word.

The whole business is fraught with pitfalls, and in a way there are no truly 'correct' answers. The locals themselves can only guess at how to make the conversion – and the result is often amusing. The fact that French and English have had a big influence (though the latter has all but 'conquered' the former in modern Egypt) has led to all sorts of interesting ideas on transliteration. Egypt's high rate of illiteracy doesn't help either. Don't be taken aback if you start noticing half a dozen different spellings for the same thing.

For some reason, the letters 'q' and 'k' have caused enormous problems, and have been interchanged willy-nilly in transliteration. For a long time, Iraq (which in Arabic is spelled with what can only be described as its nearest equivalent to the English 'q') was written, even by scholars, as 'Irak'. Other examples of an Arabic 'q' receiving such treatment are *souq* (market), often written 'souk'; *qasr* (castle), sometimes written 'kasr'; and the Cairo suburb of Doqqi, which is often written Dokki, although the

---

The Transliteration Dilemma

TE Lawrence, when asked by his publishers to clarify 'inconsistencies in the spelling of proper names' in *Seven Pillars of Wisdom* – his account of the Arab Revolt in WWI – wrote back:

'Arabic names won't go into English. There are some 'scientific systems' of transliteration, helpful to people who know enough Arabic not to need helping, but a washout for the world. I spell my names anyhow, to show what rot the systems are.'

Egyptian habit of swallowing 'q' and pronouncing the place 'Do'i' is a dead giveaway. It's a bit like spelling English 'as she is spoke' – imagine the results if Australians, Americans, Scots and Londoners were given free rein to write as they pronounce!

Greetings & Civilities

Arabic is more formal than English, especially with greetings; thus even the simplest greetings, such as 'hello', vary according to when and how they are used. In addition, each greeting requires a certain response that varies according to whether it is being said to a male, female or group of people.

Hello.
  salām 'alēkum
  (lit: peace upon you)
  (response)
  wa 'alēkum es salām
  (lit: and peace upon you)
Hello/Welcome.
  ahlan wa sahlan
  (response)
  ahlan bīk (to m)
  ahlan bīkī (to f)
  ahlan bīkum (to group)
Pleased to meet you. (when first meeting)
  tasharrafna (polite)
  fursa sa'īda (informal)
Good morning.
  sabāH al-khēr
  (response)
  sabāH an-nūr
Good evening.
  misa' al-khēr
  (response)
  misa' an-nūr
Good night.
  tisbaH 'ala khēr (to m)
  tisbaHī 'ala khēr (to f)
  tisbaHu 'ala khēr (to group)
  (response; also used as 'Good afternoon' in the late afternoon)
  wenta bikhēr (to m)
  wentī bikhēr (to f)
  wentū bikhēr (to group)
Goodbye.
  ma'as salāma (lit: go in safety)

Basics

There are three ways to say 'Please' in Egyptian Arabic, each of which is used somewhat differently:

When asking for something in a shop, say: *min fadlak* (to m) *min fadlik* (to f) *min fadlukum* (to group)

Under similar, but more formal, circumstances (eg when trying to get a waiter's attention), say: *law samaHt* (to m), *law samaHtī* (to f), *law samaHtu* (to group)

When offering something to someone, for example a chair or bus seat, or when inviting someone into your home or to join in a meal, say: *tfaddal* (to m), *tfaddalī* (to f), *tfaddalū* (to group)

The same words beginning with 'i' (eg *itfaddal*) can be used to mean much the same thing or 'Please, go ahead' (and do something)

Excuse me.
  'an iznak, esmaHlī (to m)
  'an iznik, esmaHīlī (to f)
  'an iznukum, esmaHūlī (to group)
Thank you.
  shukran
Thank you very much.
  shukran gazīlan
No thank you.
  la' shukran
You're welcome.
  'afwan, al-'affu
Yes.
  aywa
  na'am (more formal)
No.
  la'
Sorry.
  'assif

Small Talk

How are you?
  izzayyak? (to m)
  izzayyik? (to f)
  izzayyukum? (to group)

I'm fine.
kwayyis ilHamdu lillah (to m, lit: fine, thanks be to God)
kwaysa ilHamdu lillah (to f)
kwaysīn ilHamdu lillah (to group)

(On their own, *kwayyis*, *kwaysa* and *kwaysīn* literally mean 'good' or 'fine', but they are rarely heard alone in response to 'How are you?')

What's your name?	*ismak ēh?* (to m)
	ismīk ēh? (to f)
My name is ...	*ismī ...*

America	*amrīka*
Australia	*ustralya*
Canada	*kanada*
England	*inglaterra*
France	*fransa*
Germany	*almanya*
Italy	*itāliyya*
Japan	*al-yaban*
Netherlands	*holanda*
Spain	*isbanya*
Sweden	*as-swīd*
Switzerland	*swīsra*

One of the most useful words to know is *imshī*, which means 'Go away'. Use this at the pyramids or at other tourist sites when you are being besieged by children. Do not use it on adults; instead, just say, *la' shukran* ('No thank you').

Language Difficulties

I understand.	*ana fāhem*
I don't understand.	*ana mish fāhem*
Do you speak English?	*enta bititkallim inglīzī?* (to m)
	entī bititkallimī inglīzī? (to f)

Getting Around

How far is ...?	*kam kilo li ...?*
I want to go to ...	*ana 'ayiz arūH ...*
How many buses per day go to ...?	*kam otobīs fil yōm yerūH...?*
Does this bus go to ...?	*al-otobīs da yerūH ...?*
Which bus goes to...?	*otobīs nimra kam yerūH...?*

What is the fare to ...?	*bikam at-tazkara li ...?*
Please tell me when we arrive in ...	*min fadlak, ullī emta Hanūsel ...*
Stop here, please.	*wa'if/hassib hena, min fadlak*
Please wait for me.	*mumkin tantazarnī*
May I/we sit here?	*mumkin eglis/neglis hena?*
Wait!	*istanna!*

When does the ... leave/arrive?	*emta qiyam/wusuul...?*
bus	*al-otobīs*
train	*al-'atr*
boat	*al-markib*
ferry	*ma'atiya*

Where is the ...?	*fein ..?*
airport	*matār*
bus station	*maHattat al-otobīs*
railway station	*maHattat al-'atr*
ticket office	*maktab at-tazāker*
street	*ash-shāri'*
city	*al-medīna*
village	*al-qarya*
bus stop	*maw'if al-otobīs*
station	*al-maHatta*

Where can I rent a ...?	*fein e'aggar ...?*
bicycle	*'agala*
boat	*markib*
car	*sayyāra/'arabiyya*
camel	*gamal*
donkey	*Humār*
horse	*Husān*

Directions

Where is the hotel ...?	*fein al-funduq ...?*
Can you show me the way to the hotel ...?	*mumkin tewarrīnī at-tarīqlil-funduq ...?*
Where?	*fein?*
here	*hena*
there	*henek*
this address	*al-'anwān da*

north	*shimāl*
south	*ganūb*
east	*shark*
west	*gharb*

Around Town

Where is the ...?	*fein ...?*
bank	*al-bank*
barber	*al-Hallē'*
beach	*al-plā/ash-shaata*
citadel	*al-'ala*
embassy	*as-sifāra*
female toilet	*twalēt al-Harīmī*
market	*as-sūq*
male toilet	*twalēt ar-ragel*
monastery	*dēr*
mosque	*al-gāme'*
museum	*al-matHaf*
old city	*al-medīna/ al-'adīma*
palace	*al-'asr*
police station	*al-bolīs*
post office	*al-bōsta/ maktab al-barīd*
restaurant	*al-mat'am*
synagogue	*al-ma'bad al-yehūdī/ al-kinees*
university	*al-gam'a*
zoo	*Hadīqat al-Haywān*

Money

The Egyptians have a collection of names for their own money, used in most everyday transactions.

pound	*guinay*
½ pound (50 pt)	*nuss guinay*
¼ pound (25 pt)	*ruba' guinay*
20 pt	*riyal*
10 pt	*barisa*
5 pt	*shilling*

I want to change ...	*ana 'ayiz usarraf ...*
money	*fulūs*
travellers cheques	*shīkāt siyaHiyya*

US$	*dolār amrikānī*
UK£	*guinay sterlīnī*
A$	*dolār ustrālī*
DM	*mārk almānī*

Accommodation

I'd like to see the rooms.	*awiz ashūf al-owad*
May I see other rooms?	*mumkin ashūf owad tānī?*
How much is the room per night?	*kam ugrat al-odda bil-laila?*
Do you have any cheaper rooms?	*fī owad arkhas?*
It's too expensive.	*da ghālī 'awī*
This is fine.	*da kwayyis*
air-conditioning	*takyīf hawa*

Shopping

Where can I buy ...?	*fein mumkin ashtirī ...?*
How much is this/that ...?	*bikam da ...?*
It costs too much.	*da ghālī 'awī*
Do you have ...?	*fī 'andak ...?*

Time & Dates

What time is it?	*sā'ah kam?*
When?	*emta?*
day	*yom*
month	*shaher*
today	*el nharda*
tomorrow	*bokra*
week	*esbuwa*
year	*sana*
yesterday	*mberrah*
early	*badrī*
late	*mut'akhar*
daily	*kull yōm*

Sunday	*(yōm) al-aHadd*
Monday	*(yōm) al-itnīn*
Tuesday	*(yōm) at-talāt*
Wednesday	*(yōm) al-arba'a*
Thursday	*(yōm) al-khamīs*
Friday	*(yōm) al-gum'a*
Saturday	*(yōm) as-sabt*

East of Egypt, in addition to the Hjira calendar, there is also another set of names for the Gregorian calendar. In Egypt the names of the months are virtually the same as their European counterparts and easily recognisable.

Numbers

Don't let the visual similarity of some Western and Arabic number symbols confuse you. Pay attention to the order of the words in numbers from 21 to 99.

0	.	sifr, zero
1	١	wāHid
2	٢	itnein
3	٣	talāta
4	٤	arba'a
5	٥	khamsa
6	٦	sitta
7	٧	sab'a
8	٨	tamanya
9	٩	tis'a
10	١.	'ashara
11	١١	Hidāshar
12	١٢	itnāshar
13	١٣	talattāshar
14	١٤	arba'tāshar
15	١٥	khamastāshar
16	١٦	sittāshar
17	١٧	saba'tāshar
18	١٨	tamantāshar
19	١٩	tisa'tāshar
20	٢.	'ishrīn
21	٢١	wāHid wi 'ishrīn
22	٢٢	itnein wi 'ishrīn
30	٣.	talatīn
40	٤.	arba'īn
50	٥.	khamsīn
60	٦.	sittīn
70	٧.	sab'īn
80	٨.	tamanīn
90	٩.	tis'īn
100	١..	miyya
101	١.١	miyya wi wāHid
110	١١.	miyya wi 'ashara
1000	١...	'alf
2000	٢...	'alfein
3000	٣...	talattalāf
4000	٤...	arba'talāf
5000	٥...	khamastalāf

Ordinal Numbers

first	'awwal
second	tānī
third	tālit
fourth	rābi'
fifth	khāmis

January	yanāyir
February	fibrāyir
March	māris
April	abrīl
May	māyu
June	yunyu
July	yulyu
August	aghustus
September	sibtimbir
October	'uktoobir
November	nufimbir
December	disimbir

For a list of Hjira calendar months, see the Public Holidays & Special Events section in the Facts for the Visitor chapter.

Health & Emergencies

I need a doctor.	'awiz doktōr
Where is the hospital?	fein el mustashfa?
My friend is ill.	sadīqi 'ayan
I feel dizzy.	ana dayikh
I'm allergic to ...	'andī Hasasiyya dodd ...
antibiotics	el entībiyotik
penicillin	el binisilīn
I'm ...	'andī ...
asthmatic	hasāsiyya fi sadri
diabetic	marad es sukkar
epileptic	marad es sar'
accident	Hadsa
antiseptic	mutahhir
aspirin	asbirin
Band-Aids	blāstir
condoms	kabābīt
diarrhoea	is-hāl
fever	sukhūna
headache	sudā'
hospital	mustashfa
pharmacy	agzakhana
pregnant	Hāmel
prescription	roshetta
sanitary napkins	
stomachache	waga' fil batn
tampons	hifāz al-'āda al-shahriyya

Glossary

abd – servant of
abeyya – women's gown
abu – father, saint
ahwa – coffee or coffeehouse
ain – well, spring

bab – gate or door
bahr – river
baksheesh – tip
baladi – local, rural
bawwab – doorman
beit – house
bey – term of respect
bir – spring, well
birket – lake
Book of the Dead – ancient theological compositions, or hymns, that were the subject of most of the colourful paintings and reliefs on tomb walls
burg – tower

caliph – Islamic ruler; also spelt khalif
Canopic jars – pottery jars which held the embalmed internal organs and viscera (liver, stomach, lungs, intestines) of the mummified pharaoh
capital – top, decorated part of a column
caravanserai – merchants' inn
cartouche – oblong figure enclosing the *hieroglyphs* of royal or divine names
cenotaph – symbolic tomb, temple or place of cult worship that was additional to the pharaoh's actual burial place

dahabiyya – houseboat
darb – track, street
deir – monastery, convent

eid – feast
emir – Islamic ruler, military commander or governor

false door – fake, seemingly half-open *ka* door in a tomb wall which enabled the pharaoh's spirit, or life force, to come and go at will

fellaheen – the peasant farmers or agricultural workers who make up the majority of Egypt's population. Fellahin literally means 'ploughman' or 'tiller of the soil'.
filoos – money
finial – the top part of a minaret
fiteer – a kind of pizza made with a flaky pastry base
fuul – mashed fava beans usually ladled into a piece of bread

galabiyya – full-length robe worn by men
gebel – mountain or mountain range
gezira – island
guinay – pound

haj – pilgrimage to Mecca. All Muslims should make the journey at least once in their lifetime.
hamman – bathhouse
hantour – horse-drawn carriage
hara – small lane, alley
haramlik – women's quarters
Heb-Sed Festival – five day celebration of royal rejuvenation, held after 30 years of a pharaoh's reign and then every three years after that
Heb-Sed Race – traditional re-enactment, during the Heb-Sed Festival, of a pharaoh's coronation. The king sat first on the throne of Upper Egypt and then on the throne of Lower Egypt to symbolise the unification of the country and the renewal of his reign.
hieroglyphs – ancient Egyptian form of writing, which used pictures and symbols to represent objects, words or sounds
hypostyle hall – hall in which the roof is supported by columns

iconostasis – screen with doors and icons set in tiers, used in eastern Christian churches
imam – a man schooled in Islam and who often doubles as the *muezzin*
ithyphallic – denoting the erect phallus of a pharaoh or god (usually used in reference to the god Min); a sign of fertility

iwan – vaulted hall, opening into a central court, in the *madrassa* of a mosque

ka – spirit, or 'double', of a living person which gained its own identity with the death of that person. The survival of the ka, however, required the continued existence of the body, hence mummification. The ka was also the vital force emanating from a god and transferred through the pharaoh to his people.
khamseen – hot wind from the Western Desert
khan – another name for a *caravanserai*
khanqah – *Sufi* monastery
khedive – Egyptian viceroy under Ottoman suzerainty (1867-1914)
khwaga – foreigner
kineesa – church
kubri – bridge
kuttab – Quranic school

lotus – white waterlily regarded as sacred by the ancient Egyptians

madrassa – a school where Islamic law is taught
mahatta – station
makwagee – laundry man
mammisi – birth house. In these small chapels or temples, erected in the vicinity of a main temple, the rituals of the divine birth of the living king were performed. All pharaohs were believed to be incarnations of the falcon-god Horus.
mashrabiyya – ornate carved wooden panel or screen; feature of Islamic architecture
Masr – Egypt (also means Cairo)
mastaba – Arabic word for 'bench'; a mud-brick structure above tombs from which the pyramids were developed
matar – airport
midan – town or city square
mihrab – niche in the wall of a mosque that indicates the direction of Mecca
minbar – pulpit in a mosque
mortuary complex – a pharaoh's last resting place. It usually comprised: a pyramid which was the king's tomb and the repository for all his household goods, the clothes and

treasure; a funerary temple on the east side of the pyramid which served as a cult temple for worship of the dead pharaoh; pits for the *solar barques*; a valley temple on the banks of the Nile, where the mummification process was carried out; and a massive causeway from the river to the pyramid.
moulid – festival celebrating the birthday of a local saint or holy person
muezzin – mosque official who calls the faithful to prayer five times a day from the minaret
mugzzabin – *Sufi* followers who participate in *zikrs* in order to achieve unity with Allah

natron – whitish mineral of hydrated sodium carbonate that occurs in saline deposits and salt lakes and acts as a natural preservative. It was used in ancient Egypt to pack and dry the body during mummification.
Nilometer – pit descending into the Nile containing a central column marked with graduations. The marks were used to measure and record the level of the river, especially during the inundation.
nome – administrative division or province of ancient Egypt, introduced during the Old Kingdom era. There were 22 nomes in Upper Egypt and 20 in Lower Egypt.

obelisk – monolithic stone pillar, with square sides tapering to a pyramidal, often gilded, top; used as a monument in ancient Egypt. Obelisks were usually carved from pink granite and set up in pairs at the entrance to a tomb or temple. A single obelisk was sometimes the object of cult worship.
Opet Festival – celebration held in Luxor (Thebes) during the Nile inundation season, when statues of the Theban triad – Amun, Mut and Khons – would be transported by river from Karnak Temple to Luxor Temple to join in the festivities
oud – a kind of lute

papyrus – plant identified with Lower Egypt; writing material made from the pith of this plant; a document written on such paper
pasha – lord, but also a term used more generally to denote someone of standing

porphyry – from Greek *porphyros* (purple); a reddish-purple rock highly resistant to erosion. Many sarcophagi were made from this rock.

pylon – monumental gateway at the entrance to a temple

pyramid texts – paintings and reliefs on the walls of the internal rooms and burial chamber of pyramids and often on the *sarcophagus* itself. The texts recorded the pharaoh's burial ceremonies, associated temple rituals, the hymns vital to his passage into the afterlife and, sometimes, major events in his life.

qa'a – reception room
qala'a – fortress
qasr – palace

Ramadan – ninth month of the lunar Islamic calendar during which Muslims fast from sunrise to sunset
ras – headland

sabil – public drinking fountain
sarcophagus – huge stone or marble coffin used to encase other wooden coffins and the mummy of the pharaoh or queen
scarab – dung beetle regarded as sacred in ancient Egypt and represented on amulets or in hieroglyphs as a symbol of the sun-god Ra
serapeum – network of subterranean galleries which were constructed as tombs for the mummified sacred Apis bulls; the most important temple of the Graeco-Egyptian god Serapis
serdab – hidden cellar in a tomb, or a stone room in front of some pyramids, containing a coffin with a lifesize, lifelike, painted statue of the dead king. Serdabs were designed so that the pharaoh's *ka* could communicate with the outside world.
shadouf – waterwheels used for irrigation purposes
shai – tea
sharia – Arabic for road or way

Shari'a – Islamic law, the body of doctrine that regulates the lives of Muslims
sharm – bay
sheesha – waterpipe
solar barque – wooden boat placed in or around the pharaoh's tomb. It was the symbolic vessel of transport for his journey over the sea of death to the Kingdom of the Dead to be judged before Osiris, and for his final passage to the eternal afterlife.
souq – market
speos – rock-cut tomb or chapel
stele (pl: stelae) – stone or wooden commemorative slab or column decorated with inscriptions or figures
Sufi – follower of any of the Islamic mystical orders which emphasise dancing, chanting and trances in order to attain unity with God

ta'amiyya – mashed chickpeas and spices fried in a patty and stuffed into a piece of shammy with salad and tahina
tabla – small hand-held drum
tarboosh – the hat known elsewhere as a fez
towla – backgammon

ulema – group of Muslim scholars or religious leaders; a member of this group
umm – mother of
uraeus – rearing cobra with inflated hood, associated with the goddess Renenutet. This was the most characteristic symbol of Egyptian royalty and was worn on the pharaoh's forehead or crown. The sacred fire-spitting serpent was an agent of destruction and protector of the king.

wadi – desert watercourse, dry except in the rainy season
waha – oasis
wikala – another name for a *caravanserai*

zikr – long sessions of dancing, chanting and swaying usually carried out by Sufi *mugzzabin* to achieve oneness with God

cknowledgments

THANKS

Many thanks to the travellers who used the last edition and wrote to us with helpful hints, useful advice and interesting anecdotes:

Vistor Abrash, Sabah Akbar, Colin Allin, Tim Allratt, Dan Andrews, Bob Applebaum, Maggie Armstrong, Ian Ashbridge, Fares Abdel Aziz, Carminia Banares, Melinda Banki, Danielle Baron, Stephen Bateson, Anita Batistic, AJ Beekman, Sue Bellamy, Connie J Bennett, Patricia Bernard, A Biery, Jan Blazek, Eric Blyboon, Jacqui Boardman, Harry Boehme, Gwen Boelems, Bonki & Andi Bonin, Eric Boudin, Oliver Bradley, Kim Brattinga, Sonja Bregman, BJ Gidon Bromberg, Michelle Bromley, Daniel Brons, Andeas Bruckmeier, Todd Bryan, Geoff Budd, Luc Buseyne, Jonathon Butchard, Paola Buzi, Tina Calov, Mark Cameron, Rees Cameron, M Caroe, Deborah Carr, Michael Carroll, Tom Cauchon, Ken Chamberlain, Patrick & Beryl Chambers, Jon Chion, Kwok Chorying, G Chow, Stephen Chubb, Ann Clark, Rodney & Rosemary Clark, Sylvia Clark, Amy Clifton, Alice Coelho, Basil Condos, Eric Cooper, Colin Cotterill, Jeff Crandall, Amanda Cranmer, A Cressaty, Vanessa Cross, Anne Croxford, Megan Curtis, Warren Da Costa, Lee D'Alterio, Isobel Dams, Susan Daniels, RAH Davies, Simon Davies, Melanie Delieu, Peter Denby, Patrick Dennis, Spencer Denyer, Mieke Denys, Kari Dolezal, Mike Dolota, M Donahue, Shirley Doss, Sheri Stanford Driver, AL Duffy, Audrey Duffy, Yvonne Duncan, Laura Dunham, David Dunkley, Rosemary Dunning, Phil Dunnington, Greg Eastwood, Amro Elio, Erwin van Engelen, Andreas Engelmayer, Coenoden Engelsman, Michael Esinger, Tim Eyre, Marc Fabien, Tammy Fellin, Robyn Ferguson, Scott Fincham, Jonah Fisher, Marilyn Flax, Sulveigh Ford, John Fowler, Ellen Frankel, Ines Freuz, P Wayne Frey, Per-Axel Frielingsdorf, Simon Froehling, Adam Fry, Dave Fuller, Michelle Gallagher, Belinda Gaskell, EPG Gearon, Stefan Gerke, Helen Gibbs, Mark Giddens, Maria Gil, Richard Gillingham, Angela Godfrey, David Goldberg, Leigh Goldstein, Wolf Gotthilf, Louise Goulding, Nadia Graham, John Grainger, Alexander Groenewege, Xavier Gros, Jana Hamplova, Marisa Handler, David Hannam, Amanda Harvey, Mike Hayes, Andrew Hecht, Eric & Patricia M Hicks, Karsten Hilbert, Lana Hinton, Andrew Hirsch, Cynthia Holmes, Melainie Holten, David Hooper, Vita Hribar, Petr Hruska, Andrew Hubbard, A Hurley, Candi Hutchison, PJ Hyland, Ameer Ibrahi, Jan Iversen, Keith G Jackson, Thomas Jacobs, Barbara & Pete Jeene, Meg Jolliffe, Margie Jones, Malene Jorgensen, Julie Anne Justus, Catherine Kean, Kate Keen, AA Kelly, Dave Kento, Prof Hanan J Kisch, Willem Klaassen, Heidi Klaschka, Alexander Klupp, John Knight, Andrea Koeninger, Kostya & Sasha, Mike Krosin, Arthur van der Laak, Nadya Labib, Alexandra Lang, Tony Lattari, Paul Lau, Luc Lauwers, Brenda Lee, Darren Lee, Joanne Lee, Gina Lennox, Veerle Libberecht, Simon Lim, Jenny Linde, Eric Linder, Daniel Lindhagen, Fabrizio Loschi, T Lout, Hans Lubbinje, Jamie Maler, Yasser Mamdouh, M Marchini, Cheinan Marks, Jean-Denis Martin, Neil Masey, Richard Maurice, Jason McGrath, Maureen McGuire, James McKechne, Jane McKenzie, Chelsea McKinny, Kuwakubo Megumi, Stefan Meier, Mari Mellum, S & M Merz-Kubesch, Sarah Michael, Michael Middleton, Sharon Midge, Fizh Mike, Ian Millard, Gilbert Moase, Mario Moeller, Amanda Mohabir, Toni Mooy, Steffi Morjan, Robert Morris, Mohamed Moseilhy, Dietrich Mulder, Samuel Mullerstraat, Franklin Murillo, Carol & Sean Murphy, Phil Murphy, Randy Nelson, Ben Nicholls, Stuart Norgrove, Pat O'Brien, Caren Ogland, Amanda O'Neill, Valentina Othmacic, Jennifer Parkes, Wendy Parnell, James Parsons, Alesandro Pascale, Bostjan Payntan, Pieter Peeters, Jimmy Pegg, Stepan Peichl, Daniel Pfund, Nick Picton, Anna Plandiura Riba, Shirley Porsche, Matthew Price, Tony Pringle, Leon Punt, Marie-Lise Quaradeghini, Ambrogio Radaelli, Zeena Rasheed, Melissa Reid, Victoria Relf, Dr Mark Rembrandt, David Roberts, Jacob Rode, Brittany Rogers, Graham Rogers, Renatus Rohde, Pilar Rojo, David Rowe, Antony Sachs, Tarek Sadek, Sara & Massimiliano, Barbara Sawyer, Sam Schaeffer, Erica Sefton, Victor Sheahan, Thomas Siffer, Janna Silverstein, Amelia Simpson, Helen Simpson, BJ Skane, Richard Skilton, Bob Skinner, Alex Sky, Stuart Slater, Fiona Slaw, Judith Slot, Doris Smith, Rebecca Smith, Stephen Smith, Annette Snow, Andrea Solotar, Ricardo Sosa, Steve Sosa, Damien Spry, Carla Stacey, Rana J Standal, Niels Stougaard, Ida Strasser, Thorsten Strufe, Paul Stuart, Craig Summers, Mari Swanston, J Swinden, John Sylvester, Grant Tarliang, John M Taylor, Ruth Thompson, Alfred J Tinao, Gerhard Topfer, Monique Tortrat, Darin Triplett, Ramses Valvekens, Arlette Vanderheijden, Johan Verheyden, Vincent Vermeire, Sonan Janzan Vertregt, Hugo Vet, Sonya Virtu, Radim Vovesny, Carl Wahlen, Louise Walker, Kevin Wall, Ron & Olga Wallace, Ayesha Walmsley, Chris Ward, Michael Ward, Lisa Warren, Phil Watmough, Marjan Weeda, Sheila Weinberg, Kathryn Weir, Izak Wessels, Kate Whittington, Kirsten Willoughby, Toni Wills, Diana Wilson, Jennifer P Wilson, Dan Wolf, Daniel Worsley, Faisal Yafai, Fran Yniguez, Paola Zancanaro, Jane Z Zhang, Carolien van Zoest, Erik Zoonleif, Aleksandra Ztobinska, Daan Zuyderland, Jum Zwijnenburg.

LONELY PLANET

FREE Lonely Planet Newsletters

We love hearing from you and think you'd like to hear from us.

Planet Talk

Our FREE quarterly printed newsletter is full of tips from travellers and anecdotes from Lonely Planet guidebook authors. Every issue is packed with up-to-date travel news and advice, and includes:

- a postcard from Lonely Planet co-founder Tony Wheeler
- a swag of mail from travellers
- a look at life on the road through the eyes of a Lonely Planet author
- topical health advice
- prizes for the best travel yarn
- news about forthcoming Lonely Planet events
- a complete list of Lonely Planet books and other titles

To join our mailing list, residents of the UK, Europe and Africa can email us at go@lonelyplanet.co.uk; residents of North and South America can email us at info@lonelyplanet.com; the rest of the world can email us at talk2us@lonelyplanet.com.au, or contact any Lonely Planet office.

Comet

Our FREE monthly email newsletter brings you all the latest travel news, features, interviews, competitions, destination ideas, travellers' tips & tales, Q&As, raging debates and related links. Find out what's new on the Lonely Planet Web site and which books are about to hit the shelves.

Subscribe from your desktop: www.lonelyplanet.com/comet

Lonely Planet On-line

Whether you've just begun planning your next trip, or you're chasing down specific info on currency regulations or visa requirements, check out Lonely Planet On-line for up-to-the minute travel information.

As well as mini guides to more than 250 destinations, you'll find maps, photos, travel news, health and visa updates, travel advisories, and discussion of the ecological and political issues you need to be aware of as you travel. You'll also find timely upgrades to popular guidebooks which you can print out and stick in the back of your book.

There's also an on-line travellers' forum where you can share your experience of life on the road, meet travel companions and ask other travellers for their recommendations and advice.

And of course we have a complete and up-to-date list of all Lonely Planet travel products including travel guides, diving and snorkeling guides, phrasebooks, atlases, travel literature and videos, and a simple on-line ordering facility if you can't find the book you want elsewhere.

Lonely Planet Diving & Snorkeling Guides

Known for indispensible guidebooks to destinations all over the world, Lonely Planet's Pisces Books are the most popular series of diving and snorkeling titles available.

There are three series: **Diving & Snorkeling Guides**, **Shipwreck Diving** series and **Dive Into History**. Full colour throughout, the **Diving & Snorkeling Guides** combine quality photographs with detailed descriptions of the best dive sites for each location, giving divers a glimpse of what they can expect both on land and in water. The **Dive Into History** series is perfect for the adventure diver or armchair traveller. The **Shipwreck Diving** series provides all the details for exploring the most interesting wrecks in the Atlantic and Pacific oceans. The list also includes underwater nature and technical guides.

LONELY PLANET

Lonely Planet Travel Atlases

Lonely Planet has long been famous for the number and quality of its guidebook maps. Now we've gone one step further and produced a handy companion series: Lonely Planet travel atlases – maps of a country produced in book form.

Unlike other maps, which look good but lead travellers astray, our travel atlases have been researched on the road by Lonely Planet's experienced team of writers. All details are carefully checked to ensure the atlas corresponds with the equivalent Lonely Planet guidebook.

- full-colour throughout
- maps researched and checked by Lonely Planet authors
- place names correspond with Lonely Planet guidebooks
- no confusing spelling differences
- legend and travelling information in English, French, German, Japanese and Spanish
- size: 230 x 160 mm

Available now: Chile & Easter Island • Egypt • India & Bangladesh • Israel & the Palestinian Territories • Jordan, Syria & Lebanon • Kenya • Laos • Portugal • South Africa, Lesotho & Swaziland • Thailand • Turkey • Vietnam • Zimbabwe, Botswana & Namibia

Lonely Planet TV Series & Videos

Lonely Planet travel guides have been brought to life on television screens around the world. Like our guides, the programs are based on the joy of independent travel, and look honestly at some of the most exciting, picturesque and frustrating places in the world. Each show is presented by one of three travellers from Australia, England or the USA and combines an innovative mixture of video, Super-8 film, atmospheric soundscapes and original music.

Videos of each episode – containing additional footage not shown on television – are available from good book and video shops, but the availability of individual videos varies with regional screening schedules.

Video destinations include: Alaska • American Rockies • Australia – The South-East • Baja California & the Copper Canyon • Brazil • Central Asia • Chile & Easter Island • Corsica, Sicily & Sardinia – The Mediterranean Islands • East Africa (Tanzania & Zanzibar) • Ecuador & the Galapagos Islands • Greenland & Iceland • Indonesia • Israel & the Sinai Desert • Jamaica • Japan • La Ruta Maya • Morocco • New York • North India • Pacific Islands (Fiji, Solomon Islands & Vanuatu) • South India • South West China • Turkey • Vietnam • West Africa • Zimbabwe, Botswana & Namibia

The Lonely Planet TV series is produced by: Pilot Productions
The Old Studio
18 Middle Row
London W10 5AT, UK

NELY PLANET

Guides by Region

L onely Planet is known worldwide for publishing practical, reliable and no-nonsense travel information in our guides and on our Web site. The Lonely Planet list covers just about every accessible part of the world. Currently there are thirteen series: travel guides, shoestring guides, walking guides, city guides, phrasebooks, audio packs, city maps, travel atlases, diving & snorkeling guides, restaurant guides, first-time travel guides, healthy travel and travel literature.

AFRICA Africa on a shoestring • Africa – the South • Arabic (Egyptian) phrasebook • Arabic (Moroccan) phrasebook • Cairo • Cape Town • Cape Town city map • Central Africa • East Africa • Egypt • Egypt travel atlas • Ethiopian (Amharic) phrasebook • The Gambia & Senegal • Healthy Travel Africa • Kenya • Kenya travel atlas • Malawi, Mozambique & Zambia • Morocco • North Africa • Read This First Africa • South Africa, Lesotho & Swaziland • South Africa, Lesotho & Swaziland travel atlas • Swahili phrasebook • Tanzania, Zanzibar & Pemba • Trekking in East Africa • Tunisia • West Africa • Zimbabwe, Botswana & Namibia • Zimbabwe, Botswana & Nambia Travel Atlas • World Food Morocco

Travel Literature: The Rainbird: A Central African Journey • Songs to an African Sunset: A Zimbabwean Story • Mali Blues: Traveling to an African Beat

AUSTRALIA & THE PACIFIC Auckland • Australia • Australian phrasebook • Bushwalking in Australia • Bushwalking in Papua New Guinea • Fiji • Fijian phrasebook • Healthy Travel Australia, NZ and the Pacific • Islands of Australia's Great Barrier Reef • Melbourne • Melbourne city map • Micronesia • New Caledonia • New South Wales & the ACT • New Zealand • Northern Territory • Outback Australia • Out To Eat – Melbourne • Out to Eat – Sydney • Papua New Guinea • Pidgin phrasebook • Queensland • Rarotonga & the Cook Islands • Samoa • Solomon Islands • South Australia • South Pacific • South Pacific Languages phrasebook • Sydney • Sydney city map • Sydney Condensed • Tahiti & French Polynesia • Tasmania • Tonga • Tramping in New Zealand • Vanuatu • Victoria • Western Australia

Travel Literature: Islands in the Clouds • Kiwi Tracks: A New Zealand Journey • Sean & David's Long Drive

CENTRAL AMERICA & THE CARIBBEAN Bahamas, Turks & Caicos • Bermuda • Central America on a shoestring • Costa Rica • Cuba • Dominican Republic & Haiti • Eastern Caribbean • Guatemala, Belize & Yucatán: La Ruta Maya • Jamaica • Mexico • Mexico City • Panama • Puerto Rico • Read This First Central & South America • World Food Mexico

Travel Literature: Green Dreams: Travels in Central America

EUROPE Amsterdam • Amsterdam city map • Andalucía • Austria • Baltic States phrasebook • Barcelona • Berlin • Berlin city map • Britain • British phrasebook • Brussels, Bruges & Antwerp • Budapest city map • Canary Islands • Central Europe • Central Europe phrasebook • Corfu & Ionians • Corsica • Crete • Crete Condensed • Croatia • Cyprus • Czech & Slovak Republics • Denmark • Dublin • Eastern Europe • Eastern Europe phrasebook • Edinburgh • Estonia, Latvia & Lithuania • Europe on a shoestring • Finland • Florence • France • French phrasebook • Germany • German phrasebook • Greece • Greek Islands • Greek phrasebook • Hungary • Iceland, Greenland & the Faroe Islands • Istanbul City Map • Ireland • Italian phrasebook • Italy • Krakow •Lisbon • London • London city map • London Condensed • Mediterranean Europe • Mediterranean Europe phrasebook • Munich • Norway • Paris • Paris city map • Paris Condensed • Poland • Portugal • Portugese phrasebook • Portugal travel atlas • Prague • Prague city map • Provence & the Côte d'Azur • Romania & Moldova • Rome • Russia, Ukraine & Belarus • Russian phrasebook • Scandinavian & Baltic Europe • Scandinavian Europe phrasebook • Scotland • Slovenia • Spain • Spanish phrasebook • St Petersburg • Switzerland • Trekking in Spain • Ukrainian phrasebook • Venice • Vienna • Walking in Britain • Walking in Ireland • Walking in Italy • Walking in Spain • Walking in Switzerland • Western Europe • Western Europe phrasebook • World Food Italy • World Food Spain

Travel Literature: The Olive Grove: Travels in Greece

INDIAN SUBCONTINENT Bangladesh • Bengali phrasebook • Bhutan • Delhi • Goa • Hindi & Urdu phrasebook • India • India & Bangladesh travel atlas • Indian Himalaya • Karakoram Highway • Kerala • Mumbai (Bombay) • Nepal • Nepali phrasebook • Pakistan • Rajasthan • Read This First: Asia & India • South India • Sri Lanka • Sri Lanka phrasebook • Trekking in the Indian Himalaya • Trekking in the Karakoram & Hindukush • Trekking in the Nepal Himalaya

Travel Literature: In Rajasthan • Shopping for Buddhas • The Age Of Kali

LONELY PLANET

Mail Order

onely Planet products are distributed worldwide. They are also available by mail order from Lonely Planet, so if you have difficulty finding a title please write to us. North and South American residents should write to 150 Linden St, Oakland, CA 94607, USA; European and African residents should write to 10a Spring Place, London NW5 3BH, UK; and residents of other countries to PO Box 617, Hawthorn, Victoria 3122, Australia.

ISLANDS OF THE INDIAN OCEAN Madagascar & Comoros • Maldives • Mauritius, Réunion & Seychelles

MIDDLE EAST & CENTRAL ASIA Arab Gulf States • Central Asia • Central Asia phrasebook • Dubai • Hebrew phrasebook • Iran • Israel & the Palestinian Territories • Israel & the Palestinian Territories travel atlas • Istanbul • Istanbul to Cairo • Jerusalem • Jerusalem City Map • Jordan & Syria • Jordan, Syria & Lebanon travel atlas • Lebanon • Middle East on a shoestring • Syria • Turkey • Turkey travel atlas • Turkish phrasebook • Yemen
Travel Literature: The Gates of Damascus • Kingdom of the Film Stars: Journey into Jordan • Black on Black: Iran Revisited

NORTH AMERICA Alaska • Backpacking in Alaska • Baja California • California & Nevada • California Condensed • Canada • Chicago • Chicago city map • Deep South • Florida • Hawaii • Honolulu • Las Vegas • Los Angeles • Miami • New England • New Orleans • New York City • New York city map • New York Condensed • New York, New Jersey & Pennsylvania • Oahu • Pacific Northwest USA • Puerto Rico • Rocky Mountain • San Francisco • San Francisco city map • Seattle • Southwest USA • Texas • USA • USA phrasebook • Vancouver • Washington, DC & the Capital Region • Washington DC city map
Travel Literature: Drive Thru America

NORTH-EAST ASIA Beijing • Cantonese phrasebook • China • Hong Kong • Hong Kong city map • Hong Kong, Macau & Guangzhou • Japan • Japanese phrasebook • Japanese audio pack • Korea • Korean phrasebook • Kyoto • Mandarin phrasebook • Mongolia • Mongolian phrasebook • North-East Asia on a shoestring • Seoul • South-West China • Taiwan • Tibet • Tibetan phrasebook • Tokyo
Travel Literature: Lost Japan • In Xanadu

SOUTH AMERICA Argentina, Uruguay & Paraguay • Bolivia • Brazil • Brazilian phrasebook • Buenos Aires • Chile & Easter Island • Chile & Easter Island travel atlas • Colombia • Ecuador & the Galapagos Islands • Healthy Travel Central & South America • Latin American Spanish phrasebook • Peru •Quechua phrasebook • Rio de Janeiro • Rio de Janeiro city map • South America on a shoestring • Trekking in the Patagonian Andes • Venezuela
Travel Literature: Full Circle: A South American Journey

SOUTH-EAST ASIA Bali & Lombok • Bangkok • Bangkok city map • Burmese phrasebook • Cambodia • Hanoi • Healthy Travel Asia & India • Hill Tribes phrasebook • Ho Chi Minh City • Indonesia • Indonesia's Eastern Islands • Indonesian phrasebook • Indonesian audio pack • Jakarta • Java • Laos • Lao phrasebook • Laos travel atlas • Malay phrasebook • Malaysia, Singapore & Brunei • Myanmar (Burma) • Philippines • Pilipino (Tagalog) phrasebook • Read This First Asia & India • Singapore • South-East Asia on a shoestring • South-East Asia phrasebook • Thailand • Thailand's Islands & Beaches • Thailand travel atlas • Thai phrasebook • Thai audio pack • Vietnam • Vietnamese phrasebook • Vietnam travel atlas • World Food Thailand • World Food Vietnam

ALSO AVAILABLE: Antarctica • The Arctic • Brief Encounters: Stories of Love, Sex & Travel • Chasing Rickshaws • Lonely Planet Unpacked • Not the Only Planet: Travel Stories from Science Fiction • Sacred India • Travel with Children • Traveller's Tales

Lonely Planet Journeys

Journeys is a unique collection of travel writing – published by the company that understands travel better than anyone else. It is a series for anyone who has ever experienced – or dreamed of – the magical moment when they encountered a strange culture or saw a place for the first time. They are tales to read while you're planning a trip, while you're on the road or while you're in an armchair in front of a fire.

These outstanding titles explore our planet through the eyes of a diverse group of international writers. JOURNEYS books catch the spirit of a place, illuminate a culture, recount a crazy adventure or introduce a fascinating way of life. They always entertain, and always enrich the experience of travel.

MALI BLUES
Traveling to an African Beat
Lieve Joris (translated by Sam Garrett)

Drought, rebel uprisings, ethnic conflict: these are the predominant images of West Africa. But as Lieve Joris travels in Senegal, Mauritania and Mali, she meets survivors, fascinating individuals charting new ways of living between tradition and modernity. With her remarkable gift for drawing out people's stories, Joris brilliantly captures the rhythms of a world that refuses to give in.

THE GATES OF DAMASCUS
Lieve Joris (translated by Sam Garrett)

This best-selling book is a beautifully drawn portrait of day-to-day life in modern Syria. Through her intimate contact with local people, Lieve Joris draws us into the fascinating world that lies behind the gates of Damascus. Hala's husband is a political prisoner, jailed for his opposition to the Assad regime; through the author's friendship with Hala we see how Syrian politics impacts on the lives of ordinary people.

THE OLIVE GROVE
Travels in Greece
Katherine Kizilos

Katherine Kizilos travels to fabled islands, troubled border zones and her family's village deep in the mountains. She vividly evokes breathtaking landscapes, generous people and passionate politics, capturing the complexities of a country she loves.

'beautifully captures the real tensions of Greece' – *Sunday Times*

KINGDOM OF THE FILM STARS
Journey into Jordan
Annie Caulfield

Kingdom of the Film Stars is a travel book and a love story. With honesty and humour, Annie Caulfield writes of travelling in Jordan and falling in love with a Bedouin with film-star looks.

She offers fascinating insights into the country – from the tent life of traditional women to the hustle of downtown Amman – and unpicks tight-woven western myths about the Arab world.

LONELY PLANET

Phrasebooks

Lonely Planet phrasebooks are packed with essential words and phrases to help travellers communicate with the locals. With colour tabs for quick reference, an extensive vocabulary and use of script, these handy pocket-sized language guides cover day-to-day travel situations.

- handy pocket-sized books
- easy to understand Pronunciation chapter
- clear & comprehensive Grammar chapter
- romanisation alongside script to allow ease of pronunciation
- script throughout so users can point to phrases for every situation
- full of cultural information and tips for the traveller

'... vital for a real DIY spirit and attitude in language learning'
— *Backpacker*

'the phrasebooks have good cultural backgrounders and offer solid advice for challenging situations in remote locations'
— *San Francisco Examiner*

Arabic (Egyptian) • Arabic (Moroccan) • Australian *(Australian English, Aboriginal and Torres Strait languages)* • Baltic States *(Estonian, Latvian, Lithuanian)* • Bengali • Brazilian • British • Burmese • Cantonese • Central Asia (Uyghur, Uzbek, Kyrghiz, Kazak, Pashto, Tadjik • Central Europe *(Czech, French, German, Hungarian, Italian, Slovak)* • Eastern Europe *(Bulgarian, Czech, Hungarian, Polish, Romanian, Slovak)* • Ethiopian (Amharic) • Fijian • French • German • Greek • Hebrew • Hill Tribes • Hindi & Urdu • Indonesian • Italian • Japanese • Korean • Lao • Latin American Spanish • Malay • Mandarin • Mediterranean Europe *(Albanian, Croatian, Greek, Italian, Macedonian, Maltese, Serbian, Slovene)* • Mongolian • Nepali • Pidgin • Pilipino (Tagalog) • Portugese • Quechua • Russian • Scandinavian Europe *(Danish, Finnish, Icelandic, Norwegian, Swedish)* • South-East Asia *(Burmese, Indonesian, Khmer, Lao, Malay, Tagalog Pilipino, Thai, Vietnamese)* • South Pacific Languages • Spanish (Castilian) *(also includes Catalan, Galician and Basque)* • Sri Lanka • Swahili • Thai • Tibetan • Turkish • Ukrainian • USA *(US English, Vernacular, Native American languages, Hawaiian)* • Vietnamese • Western Europe *(Basque, Catalan, Dutch, French, German, Greek, Irish, Italian, Portuguese, Scottish Gaelic, Spanish (Castilian), Welsh)*

Notes

ndex

Text

A

Abdeen Palace 148
Abdel Katkhuda, Sabil-Kuttab of 169-70
Abu Mina 413-14
Abu Qir 413
Abu Shuruf 381
Abu Simbel, Temple of 352-4, **353**
Abu Sir 226-7, **226**
Abydos 263-6, **264**
accommodation 104-6
activities, see individual entries
Agouza 188-90, **186**
ahwas 108-9, 212-13, 410
Ain al-Furtega 501
Ain as-Siliyiin 239
Ain Bishoi 372
Ain Hudra 501
Ain Qurayshat 381
Ain Safi 381
Ain Sukhna 441-2
Ain Umm Ahmed 501
air travel
    to/from Egypt 116-22
    within Egypt 129
Akhenaten 153, 256
Akhmin 262-3
Al-Arish 510-13, **511**
Al-Azhar 164-6
    Mosque 164-5
Al-Balyana 263-6
Alexander the Great 14, 155, 388
Alexandria 387-413, **390-1**, **392**, **394**
    entertainment 410-11
    getting around 413
    getting there & away 411-13
    places to eat 407-10
    places to stay 405-7
Al-Fayoum Oasis 234-40
Al-Ghouri Complex 171
Al-Ghouri, Wikala of 171
Al-Gouna 444-5
Al-Kab 320-1
Al-Kharga 358-64, **361**
Almasy, Ladislaus 'Laszlo' 362

Al-Milga 508
Al-Qasr 367-8
Al-Quseir 461-3, **462**
Al-Qusiya 258-9
Amada 351-2
Amenophis II 18
Amenophis III 18
Amenophis IV 18
American University in Cairo 145
Amunherkhepshep, Tomb of 302, **302**
Amun, Temple of 277, 380, **278**
antiques 111-12
Aqaba, Gulf of 479
aquariums 449
Arabic 514-20
architecture 40-1, 44-5, 48-62
    mastabas 51-2
art galleries 199-200
arts 25, 35-41, 237, 384
Aswan 326-42, **327**, **329**
Aswan Dam 342, 350, **342**
Asyut 259-61, **260**
Augustus 343
Ay, Tomb of 257, 290
Az-Zeitun 381

B

Bab Zuweila 172
Bahariyya Oasis 373-7, **374**
baksheesh, see money
Balat 368
ballooning 304, 450-1
Banana Island 259
bargaining, see money
Baris 364
Baron's Palace 198-9
bars 213-14, 215
Barquq, Madrassa & Mausoleum of 170
Bawiti 374-7, **375**
beaches 405, 420-1, 434, 449, 504-5, 512
Bedouins 34
Bein al-Qasreen 170
Beit as-Suhaymi 169
belly-dancing 215
Ben Ezra Synagogue 183
Beni Hasan 253-4
Beni Suef 249-50, **250**

Bent Pyramid 234
Berbers 34
Berenice 465
bicycle, see cycling
Bilad ar-Rum 381
Birqash Camel Market 241-2
Bir al-Gebel 369
Bir al-Ghaba 374-5
Bir al-Mattar 375
Bir ar-Ramla 374
Bir Shalatein 465
Bir Sitta 372
birdwatching 101
Birket Qaran 239
Black Desert 375
Black Saturday 26
Blue Mosque 173
boat travel
    felucca 133, 200, 304, 331, 340-1
    Nile cruises 132-3
    to/from Egypt 124-5
    within Egypt 132-3, 432
    yacht 133
books
    culture 79
    Egyptian Museum 151
    general history 79
    guidebooks 77-8
    health guides 79
    literature 35-6, 79-80
    Lonely Planet 77
    pharaonic Egypt 78-9
    travel 78
Brooke Hospital for Animals 282
Bubastis 244
bus travel
    to/from Egypt 123-4
    within Egypt 129-30, 133-4
business hours 98
Buto 245

C

Cairo 136-223, **138-9**, **146-7**, **163**, **165**, **167**, **171**, **178**, **181**, **186**, **189**
    Egyptian Museum 149-60, **150**
    entertainment 212-15
    getting around 221-3
    getting there & away 216-21

Bold indicates maps.

Great Pyramids of Giza
191-7, **192**
history 137-40
places to eat 206-12
places to stay 201-6
Sphinx, The 195-6
Cairo Tower 185
Cairo Zoo 190
camel market 325, see also
Birqash Camel Market
camel riding 487
treks 495, 501
carpets 112
car travel
driving licence 67
rental 132
road rules 131-2
to/from Egypt 122-3
within Egypt 131-2
Carter's House 286
casinos 214
Catacombs of Kom ash-
Shuqqafa 398-9, **399**
Cave of St Anthony 443
Cave of the Swimmers 362
Cheops 14
Chephren 14, 152, 195
children, travel with 95-6
churches 183
Hanging 182
St Anthony 443
St Barbara 183
St Paul 444
St Sergius 183
cinemas 214
Citadel 174-7, **175**
Cleopatra VII 19
Cleopatra's Bath 380
climate 28-9
clothing 114
Colossi of Memnon 18, 285-6
Coloured Canyon 499-501
Commonwealth War
Cemetery 418
Complex of Sultan Ashraf
Barsbey 180
conduct, see cultural
considerations
conservation, see environmental
considerations
Convent of St George 182-3
Convent of the Holy Virgin 261
Coptic Museum 182
Copts 43-4
costs, see money
courses 101-2
crafts 112-14, 384-5

credit cards, see money
cultural considerations 41-2, 73
currency, see money
customs 70-1
cycling 101, 132

D
Dahab 492-9, **493**
Dahshur 233-4
Dairut 258
Dakhla Oasis 365-71, **366**
Damietta 245-6
dance 38-9
Daraw 325-6
Deir Abu Makar 242-3
Deir al-Adhra 250
Deir al-Bahri 294-5
Deir al-Baramus 243
Deir al-Kashef 361-3
Deir al-Medina 300
Deir al-Muharraq 258
Deir as-Suriani 242
de Lesseps, Ferdinand 425, 434
Dendara 266-8, **268**
desert explorers 362
desert safaris 101, 358-9
diarrhoea 88-9
disabled travellers 95
discos, see bars
diving 101, 127-8, 466-76, **467**
Alexandria 397
clubs 473-5
courses 472
equipment 472-3
safety 472, 475-6
sites 469-72
Doqqi 188-90, **189**
drinks 107-8
driving, see car travel
duty free 70-1

E
ecology 480, see also
environmental considerations
economy 33
Edfu 321-3, **321**
education 34-5
Egyptian Museum 149-60, **150**
Egyptian National Railways
Museum 162
El Alamein 417-19
electricity 83
Elephantine Island 331-2
El-Tor 483
email 77
embassies 68-70

entertainment 108-11
bars 110
belly-dancing 110
casinos 110
cinema 81, 110
theatre 111
environmental considerations
29-31, 448, 468-9, 480, 508
Esna 318-20, **320**
etiquette, see cultural
considerations

F
Farafra Oasis 371, **371**
Fatimid Cemetery 330
Fatnas Spring 380-1
fauna 31-2, 34-6,
see also marine life
fax 76
felucca rides, see boat travel
festivals 100
film 39-40
fishing 355
Fjord, The 505
flora 31
food 106-7
Fort Qaitbey 401-2
Fustat 183, **181**

G
Garden City 162-4, **189**
Gayer Anderson Museum 178-9
gay travellers 95
Gebel al-Ingleez 375
Gebel al-Mawta 380
Gebel at-Teir 250-1
Gebel Dakrur 381
Gebel Uwaynat 362
geography 28
German & Italian War
Memorials 418
Gezira 185, **189**
Giftun Island 450
Gilf Kebir 362
Giza 190-1, **189**
Pyramids of 191-7, **192**
government 32-3
Great Sand Sea 381
Gubal, Straits of 466
Gulf of Aqaba 479
Gulf of Suez 479

H
Hammam Azouz 416-17
Hammam Fara'un 482

_hurch 182
_n, Ahmed 362
_psut 18
_nple of 294-6, **294**
_h 83-93
diarrhoea 88-9
food 86
hepatitis 84, 89
HIV/AIDS 89-90
immunisations 84
insurance 84
nutrition 86
water 86
women's health 92-3
Heliopolis 197-9, **198**
Hermopolis 255, **255**
High Dam 344-5
history 14-28
  Alexander & the Ptolemies 19-20
  Arab Conquest, The 20-1
  British Occupation 24-6
  Egypt Today 28
  Independent Egypt 26-8
  Middle Kingdom 15-19
  New Kingdom 18-19
  Old Kingdom, The 14-19
  Pharaonic Egypt 14
  Roman Rule 20
  Turkish Rule 21-4
hitching 132
holidays 98-100
Holy Virgin, Convent of the 261
Horemheb, Tomb of 291-2, **292**
horse riding 101, 200, 304, 487, 495
Horus, Temple of 321-2, **322**
hot springs 366, 372, 374-5, 380-1, 482
Hurghada 445-59, **446**, **451**

I
Ibn Barquq, Khanqah-Mausoleum of 180
Ibn Tulun, Mosque of 177-8
immunisations 84
Internet 77
Isadora, Mummy of 256
Islam 42-3
Islamic Art, Museum of 173-4, **174**
Ismailia 432-6

J
jewellery 114-15

K
Karanis 237-8
Karnak Temple 277-82, **278**
Kerdassa 191
Khaemhet, Tomb of 297-8, **298**
Khan al-Khalili 166-7, **165**
Khanqah-Mausoleum of ibn Barquq 180
Kharga Oasis 357-64, **360**
Kharmisah 381
Kitchener's Island 332
Kolthum, Umm 37
Kom al-Dikka 397
Kom al-Ahmar 321
Kom ash-Shuqqafa, Catacombs of 398-9, **399**
Kom Ombo 323-5, 340, **324**
KV5 (tomb) 293

L
Lake Bardawil 510
Lake Nasser 349-55, **346**
language 45-6
  Arabic 514-20
laundry 83
lesbian travellers, see gay travellers
literature, see books
Lower Nubia 345-55, **346**
Luxor 270-317, 340, **272-3**
  West Bank 282-304, **283**
Luxor Temple 275-7, **276**

M
Madrassa & Mausoleum of Barquq 170
Madrassa & Mausoleum of Qalaun 170
Mahfouz, Naguib 35, 168
Mahmoud Khalil Museum 190
Mahmoud Mokhtar Museum 185
Mallawi 254
Mamluks 21, 176
Manial 162-4, **189**
Mansura 245
maps 63-4
marine life 467-8, 502
Marsa Alam 464-5
Marsa Matruh 419-23, **420**
mastabas 51-2
Mastabat al-Faraun 232

Mausoleum of the Aga Khan 332-3
media 80-2
medical treatment, see health
Medinat al-Fayoum 235-7, **236**
Medinat Habu 302-4, **303**
Mediterranean Coast 417-24, **388**
Meidum, Pyramid of 240-1
Memnon, Colossi of 18, 285-6
Memphis 14, 224-6
Menkaura 152
Mentuhotep I 18
Mentuhotep II 15, 153
Metro 134, **222**
Minya 251-3, **252**
Modern Art, Museum of 185
Mohammed Ali 23-4
Mohandiseen 188-90, **186**
monastries
  Deir Abu Makar 242-3
  Deir al-Adhra 250
  Deir al-Baramus 243
  Deir al-Kashef 361-3
  Deir al-Medina 300
  Deir al-Muharraq 258
  Deir as-Suriani 242
  Red 261-2
  St Anthony 443
  St George 182
  St Jeremiah 230
  St Katherine's 506-10, **507**
  St Paul 444
  St Simeon 333
  White 261-2
money
  ATMs 72
  baksheesh 73
  bargaining 74, 112
  costs 73-4
  credit cards 72
  exchange rates 71
  travellers cheques 71-2
Mons Claudianus 461
Mons Porphyritis 459
Montazah Palace 404-5
mosques
  Abu Abbas al-Mursi 401
  Abu al-Haggag 277
  Al-Aqmar 169
  Al-Azhar 164-5
  Al-Fath 162
  Al-Hakim 168-9
  Al-Mahali 415-16
  Al-Maridani 173
  Al-Mu'ayyad 172
  Amir Qurqumas 180

Bold indicates maps.

Amr ibn al-As 183-4
An-Nabi Daniel 396
An-Nasir Mohammed 176
Ar-Rifai 177
Blue 173
Faran 462
Ibn Tulun 177-8
Mohammed Ali 175-6
Qaitbey 180
Qijmas al-Ishaqi 173
Sayyidna al-Hussein 166
Shorbagi 401
Suleiman Pasha 177
Suleiman Silahdar 169
Sultan Hassan 177
Terbana 401
motorcycle travel, see car travel
moulids 99, 305
Mt Sinai 507-9
Mubarak, Hosni 27
Mummification Museum 275
museums
  Agricultural 190
  Aswan 332
  Badr's 372
  Carriage 176
  Cavafy 402
  Coptic 182
  Egyptian 149-60, 150
  Egyptian National
    Railways 162
  Ethnographic 366
  Gayer-Anderson 178-9
  Graeco-Roman 396-7
  House of Siwa 379
  Islamic Art 173-4, 174
  Ismailia 433-6
  Luxor 275
  Mahmoud Khalil 190
  Mahmoud Mokhtar 185
  Marine 449
  Military 429
  Modern Art 185
  Mummification 275
  National 429
  National Military 176
  Nubian 328-30
  Oasis Heritage 374
  Palace 162-3
  Police 176
  Rommel's 420
  Royal Jewellery 403-4
  Seized Antiquities 176
  Sinai Heritage 511
  Solar Barque 195
  Umm Kolthum 184
  War 417

music 36-8, 115, 215
  Nubian 348
  Saidi 315
Mustafa Kamal, Tomb of 402-3
Mut 365-71, 367

N
Na'ama Bay 483-92, 485, 486
Nakhl 482
Napoleon 23
Nasser, Colonel Gamal Abdel
  26, 389-90
National Museum 429
National Military Museum 176
Naucratis 245
Necropolis at Chatby 402-3
Necropolis of al-Bagawat 361
Necropolis of Anfushi 401
Nefertari, Tomb of 300-2, 301
Nefertiti 18
Nekhen 321
New Gurna 304
newspapers, see media
nightclubs, see bars
Nile Barrages 243-4
Nile Delta 243-6
Nile Valley 247-355, 248
Nilometer 184, 332
Northern Cemetery 179-80
Nubians 34
Nuweiba 499-504, 500

O
obelisks 330-1
October War Panorama 199
Osiris 265
Oyun Musa 481

P
painting 36
papyrus 115
perfume 115
Pharaoh's Island 505-6
Pharos of Alexandria 404
Philae 342-4
  Temple 342, 343
Philosophers' Circle 231
photography 82
Pompey's Pillar 397-8
population 33-4
Port Fuad 429
Port Safaga 460-1
Port Said 425-31, 428
post 74-5
Ptolemy XIII 19

pyramids 52-3
  Al-Lahun 238-9
  Bent 234
  Chephren 195
  Giza 191-7, 192
  Hawara 238
  Meidum 240-1
  Mycerinus 195
  Neferirkare 227
  Nyuserre 227
  Pepi II 232
  Raneferef 227
  Red 234
  Sahure 226-7
  Sekhemket 230-1
  Unas 230
  Zoser's Step 53, 228-30

Q
Qaitbey 21
Qalaat al-Gindi 482
Qalaun, Madrassa & Mausoleum
  of 170
Qantara 431
Qara Oasis 381
Qarat al-Firakhi 376
Qasr ad-Dush 364
Qasr al-Farafra 371-3, 372
Qasr al-Ghueita 364
Qasr az-Zayyan 364
Qasr Ibrim 352
Qasr Qarun 239-40
Qena 266-9, 267
Qift 269
Queen Tawsert/Sethnakt
  289, 289
Qus 269

R
radio, see media
Rafah 513
Ramadan 99-100
Ramesseum, The 298-300, 299
Ramose, Tomb of 297-8, 298
Ramses II, Temple of 266
Ramses VI, Tomb of 288-9
Ras al-Hikma 419
Ras as-Sudr 481-2
Rashid, see Rosetta
Ras Mohammed National Park
  31, 466, 483
Red Monastery 261-2
Red Pyramid 234
Red Sea 466-76
Red Sea Coast 441-65
rental, see car travel

17, **415**
 ne 416

uttab of Abdel
 tkhuda 169-70
 at 27
 ety 94, 96-8, 249, 319, 449,
 479
Saidis 315
sailing 355
Sais 245
Sallum 423-4
Saqqara 227-33, **226, 228**
scams 220
Sehel Island 342
senior travellers 95
Serapeum 231-2, 397-8
Shali 379-80
Shark's Bay 492
Sharm an-Naga 459-60
Sharm el-Sheikh 483-92, **484,
 486**
shopping 111-15
Sidi Abdel Rahman 419
Sidi Barani 423
Silsila 323
Sinai 477-513, **478**
Siwa 379-86, **379**
Siwa Oasis 377-8, **378**
Sneferu 14
snorkelling 101, 450, 486-7, 494
Sohag 261-3, **262**
souqs 145, 161, 171, 400-1,
 511-12
Sphinx, The 195-6
spices 115
sport 111
St Anthony
 Cave of 443
 Church of 443
 Monastery of 443
St Barbara, Church of 183
St George
 Convent of 182-3
 Monastery of 182
St Jeremiah, Monastery of 230
St Katherine Protectorate 508
St Katherine's Monastery
 506-10, **507**
St Paul, Church of 444
Straits of Gubal 466
Straits of Tiran 466

Bold indicates maps.

St Sergius, Church of 183
St Simeon, Monastery of 333
Suez 436-40
Suez Canal 425-40, **426**
Suez Canal House 427
Suez, Gulf of 479
Sultan Ashraf Barsbey,
 Complex of 180
Sultan Hassan, Mosque of 177
swimming 200, 304-5, 334

T

Taba 506
taboos, see cultural considerations
Tanis 244-5
Tanta 245
taxi 130-1, 134-5
telephone 75-6
Tell al-Amarna 18, 256-8, **255**
temples
 Abu Simbel 352, **353**
 Amada 351
 Amun 277, 380, **278**
 An-Nadura 360-1
 Beit al-Wali 350
 Dakka 351
 Deir al-Medina 300
 Derr 352
 Hathor 353-4
 Hatshepsut 294-6, **294**
 Hibis 360
 Horus 321-2, **322**
 Kalabsha 349, 351
 Karnak 277-82, **278**
 Kertassi 351
 Khnum 319-20
 Kom Ombo 323-4, **324**
 Luxor 275-7, **276**
 Maharaqa 351
 Oracle, The 380
 Philae 342, **343**
 Ramses II 266
 Ramses-Mery-Amun 351
 Seramis 465
 Seti I 264-6, 286
 Theban Triad 277
 Wadi as-Subua 351
Teneida 368
terrorism 97-8
theatre 215
Thistlegorm, The 466
time 83
tipping, see money
Tiran, Straits of 466
toilets 83
tomb robbing 297

tombs
 Ahmose 257
 Akhti-Hotep 231
 Al-Muzawaka 369
 Amenemhet 254
 Amenhotep II 291
 Amunherkhepshep 302, **302**
 Aneuka 300
 Ankhma-Hor 232
 Assasif 296
 Ay 257, 290
 Baqet 254
 Benia 296
 Dhutmosi 298
 Frazer 250-1
 Heqaib 334
 Horemheb 291-2, **292**
 Huya 257
 Khaemhet 297-8, **298**
 Khenthawes 196
 Kheti 253-4
 Khnumhotep 254
 Khonsu 296
 Kubbet al-Hawa 334
 KV5 293
 Mahu 257
 Mastaba of Ti 232
 Mekhu 333
 Menna 296-7
 Mereruka 232
 Merirye 257
 Merneptah 288
 Mery-Re II 257
 Mir 258
 Monthu-Hir-Khopshef 290
 Mustafa Kamal 402-3
 Nakht 296-7
 Nefer-Ronpet 298
 Nefer-Sekheru 298
 Nefertari 300-2, **301**
 Nobles 333
 Panehse 257
 Pennut 352
 Persian 230
 Peshedu 300
 Petosiris 256
 Prince Sarenput I 333-4
 Prince Sarenput II 333
 Ptah-Hotep 231
 Queen Tawsert/Sethnakt
  289, **289**
 Ramose 297-8, **298**
 Ramses I 289-90
 Ramses II 288
 Ramses III 289
 Ramses IV 288
 Ramses IX 288

Ramses VI 288-9
Rekhmire 298
Sabni 333
Saptah 291
Sayyed ash-Shadhli 464
Sennedjem 300
Sennofer 298
Seti I 290
Seti II 289
Tutankhamun 292-4,
    292
Tuthmosis III 290, **290**
Tuthmosis IV 291
Userhet 296, 297-8
tourist offices 64
tours 125-8,
    see also desert safaris
train travel 130
travel insurance 67
Tuna al-Gebel 255-6, **255**
Tur Sinai, see El-Tor
Tutankhamun 19, 156-8,
    292-4, **292**
Tuthmosis I 18

Tuthmosis III 18
    tomb 290, **290**
Tuthmosis IV 18
TV, see media

U
Umm Kolthum Museum 184
Userhet, Tomb of 296, 297-8

V
Valley of the Kings 18, 287-94,
    287
Valley of the Queens 300-2
video 82
visas 64-7
    permits 66, 67

W
Wadi Feiran 510
Wadi Ghazala 501
Wadi Hammamat 463-4
Wadi Maragha 482
Wadi Mukattab 482

Wadi Natrun 242-3
Wadi Rayan 240
War Museum 417
West Bank (Luxor) 282-304,
    283
Western Oases 356-86, **357**
White Desert 372-3, 375
White Monastery 261-2
Wikala of al-Ghouri 171
wildlife, see fauna
windsurfing 101, 460
Wissa Wassef Art Centre 191
women travellers 93-5
work 102-3

Z
Zafarana 442
Zagazig 244
Zamalek 185-8
Zawiyyet al-Mayyiteen 251
Zerenike Protectorate 510-11
Zoser 14, 152
    Step Pyramid 53, 228-30

Boxed Text

Air Travel Glossary 118-19
Art of Bargaining, The 112
Backhand Economy – the Art
    of Baksheesh 73
Balancing Sinai's Ecosystem 480
Battle of El Alamein, The 418
Bed, Board & Legends 104-5
Beginners Guide to Egyptian
    Pop, A 38
Bilharzia 88
Change of Heart, A 469
Chronology of the Islamic
    Period 22
Chronology of the Pharaohs
    16-17
Code of Ethics for Reef
    Protection 468
Cruising the Canal 432
Cult of Osiris, The 265
Desert Safaris 358-9
Dialling Codes 75
Discovery of the Orient & its
    Subsequent Plunder, The 25
Dolphin of Nuweiba, The 502
Drugs & Dahab 494
Eating Fish in Alex 408
Egypt at the Cinema 81
Everyday Health 90

Felucca Trips 340-1
Greatest Find Since
    Tutankhamun, The 293
Guardians or Thieves? 297
Highlights & Suggested
    Itineraries 65
Islamic Holidays 100
Lesson to Salman Rushdie,
    A 35
Liberty on the Canal 427
Literary Alexandria 402-3
Long Dry Walk, The 368
Mahfouz's Cairo 168
Massacre of the Mamluks 176
Medical Kit Check List 85
Mosque & How it Functions,
    The 44-5
Moulids Around Luxor 305
Moulid, The 99
Mummy Find 295
Neighbouring Countries 116
Nubian Music 348
Nutrition 86
Pharos of Alexandria 404
Phonophobia 76
Portraits of the Past 237
Preserving Egypt's Finest
    Tomb 301

Real English Patient (& Other
    Desert Explorers), The 362
Rescuing the Red Sea 448
Responsible Shopping 114
Responsible Tourism 30
Rosetta Stone, The 416
Royal Palace & Other Under-
    water Discoveries, The 397
Safety Tips for Women
    Travellers 94
Saidi Music 315
Saqqara Itinerary 229
Saving Nubia's Monuments 350
Scams & Hustles 97
Shi'ia Head, Sunni Body 166
St Katherine Protectorate 508
Taking Camels to Market 325
Taxi! 135
That Special Something 113
Ticket Scams 220
Travelling in the South 319
Travelling Salesmen 134
Troubles in the Nile Valley 249
Warning – Land Mines 479
What They Said About the
    Pyramids 193
Where First? 286
Word of Caution, A 449

MAP LEGEND

BOUNDARIES

─■─■─■─■─ ....International
─ ─ ─ ─ ─ ....Disputed

HYDROGRAPHY

.....................Coastline
.................River, Creek
............................Lake
.........Intermittent Lake
..................Salt Lake
..........................Canal
⊚ ⇥ ....Spring, Rapids
─⫫─ ....Waterfalls
⸲⸲ ⸲⸲ ⸲⸲ ....Swamp

○ **CAPITAL** ....National Capital
◎ **CAPITAL** ....State Capital
● **CITY** ....City
● **Town** ....Town
• **Village** ....Village
○ ....Point of Interest

■ ....Place to Stay
Å ....Camping Ground
⊕ ....Caravan Park
▼ ....Place to Eat
■ ....Pub or Bar
≡ ....Coffeehouse
✈ ....Airport

ROUTES & TRANSPORT

.....................Freeway
.....................Highway
.....................Major Road
.....................Minor Road
══════ ....Unsealed Road
.......................City Freeway
.......................City Highway
........................City Road
......................City Street, Lane

AREA FEATURES

...............................Building
✿ ....Park, Gardens
⁺ ⁺ ⁺ ˣ ....Cemetery

MAP SYMBOLS

⌒⌒ ....Ancient or City Wall
∴ ....Archaeological Site
⋔ ....Beach
Ä ....Castle or Fort
⌒ ....Cave
⊞ ⛪ ......Church, Monastery
⌒⌒⌒ ......Cliff or Escarpment
◩ ....Dive Site
◐ ....Embassy
⊕ ....Hospital
◑ ....Mosque, Islamic
◪ ....Mosque, Working
▲ ....Mountain or Hill
🏛 ....Museum

─────.............Pedestrian Mall
⇒════ ....Tunnel
├─┼─●─┼─ ....Train Route & Station
─●─Ⓜ─ ....Metro & Station
....Tramway
⊩─⊩─⊩─ ....Cable Car or Chairlift
─ ─ ─ ─ ─ ....Walking Track
· · · · · · · · · ....Walking Tour
─ ─ ─ ─ ─ ....Ferry Route

...........................Market
☀ ....Beach, Oasis
..................Urban Area

← ....One Way Street
Ⓟ .... Parking
)(............................. Pass
★ ....Police Station
✉ .... Post Office
⊠ ....Pyramid
❖ ....Shopping Centre
☎ ....Telephone
🏛 ....Temple, Classical
◔ .... Toilet
⊡ ....Tomb
ⓘ .... Tourist Information
⊖ .... Transport
🐘 ....Zoo

Note: not all symbols displayed above appear in this book

LONELY PLANET OFFICES

Australia
PO Box 617, Hawthorn, Victoria 3122
☎ 03 9819 1877 fax 03 9819 6459
email: talk2us@lonelyplanet.com.au

USA
150 Linden St, Oakland, CA 94607
☎ 510 893 8555 TOLL FREE: 800 275 8555
510 893 8572
info@lonelyplanet.com

UK
10a Spring Place, London NW5 3BH
☎ 020 7428 4800 fax 020 7428 4828
email: go@lonelyplanet.co.uk

France
1 rue du Dahomey, 75011 Paris
☎ 01 55 25 33 00 fax 01 55 25 33 01
email: bip@lonelyplanet.fr

World Wide Web: www.lonelyplanet.com *or* **AOL keyword: lp**
Lonely Planet Images: lpi@lonelyplanet.com.au